W9-BPK-893

McGraw Hill Education create™

Course First Year Writing:
Common Reader

Suffolk University

First Edition

create™

http://create.mcgraw-hill.com

Copyright 2014 by McGraw-Hill Education. All rights
reserved. Printed in the United States of America. Except as
permitted under the United States Copyright Act of 1976, no part
of this publication may be reproduced or distributed in any form
or by any means, or stored in a database or retrieval system,
without prior written permission of the publisher.

This McGraw-Hill Create text may include materials submitted to
McGraw-Hill for publication by the instructor of this course.
The instructor is solely responsible for the editorial content of such
materials. Instructors retain copyright of these additional materials.

ISBN-10: 1308169051   ISBN-13: 9781308169057

Contents

Preface   xxxvii

4. Education and Society   180
5. Family Life and Gender Roles   228
8. Business and Economics   372
9. Media and Popular Culture   426
10. Literature and the Arts   486
12. Health and Medicine   592
13. Nature and the Environment   644
14. Science and Technology   702
    Glossary   G-1
    Credits   C-1
    Index   I-1
    Endsheets   463

Credits

Preface: *Chapter from The McGraw-Hill Reader: Issues Across the Disciplines, 12th Edition by Muller, 2014*   xxxvii

4. Education and Society: *Chapter 4 from The McGraw-Hill Reader: Issues Across the Disciplines, 12th Edition by Muller, 2014*   180

5. Family Life and Gender Roles: *Chapter 5 from The McGraw-Hill Reader: Issues Across the Disciplines, 12th Edition by Muller, 2014*   228

8. Business and Economics: *Chapter 8 from The McGraw-Hill Reader: Issues Across the Disciplines, 12th Edition by Muller, 2014*   372

9. Media and Popular Culture: *Chapter 9 from The McGraw-Hill Reader: Issues Across the Disciplines, 12th Edition by Muller, 2014*   426

10. Literature and the Arts: *Chapter 10 from The McGraw-Hill Reader: Issues Across the Disciplines, 12th Edition by Muller, 2014*   486

12. Health and Medicine: *Chapter 12 from The McGraw-Hill Reader: Issues Across the Disciplines, 12th Edition by Muller, 2014*   592

13. Nature and the Environment: *Chapter 13 from The McGraw-Hill Reader: Issues Across the Disciplines, 12th Edition by Muller, 2014*   644

14. Science and Technology: *Chapter 14 from The McGraw-Hill Reader: Issues Across the Disciplines, 12th Edition by Muller, 2014*   702

Glossary: *Chapter from The McGraw-Hill Reader: Issues Across the Disciplines, 12th Edition by Muller, 2014*   G-1

Credits: *Chapter from The McGraw-Hill Reader: Issues Across the Disciplines, 12th Edition by Muller, 2014*   C-1

Index: *Chapter from The McGraw-Hill Reader: Issues Across the Disciplines, 12th Edition by Muller, 2014*   I-1

Endsheets: *Chapter from The McGraw-Hill Reader: Issues Across the Disciplines, 12th Edition by Muller, 2014*   463

Preface

ISSUES ACROSS DISCIPLINES, LITERACIES ACROSS MEDIA

Like its previous bestselling editions, the twelfth edition of *The McGraw-Hill Reader* continues to engage students with the finest classic and contemporary essays—works that span myriad ages, cultures, and disciplines—and prompts students to read, watch, research, listen to, interact with, and compose in multiple media.

Eudora Welty (whose work appears in this collection) speaks of reading as "a sweet devouring," and *The McGraw-Hill Reader* invites students to participate in—and enjoy—the vast and varied pleasures of responding to texts in any form; additionally, this book's approach affords opportunities to experiment with numerous contexts for academic discourse. Addressing the abiding national interest in core liberal arts programs, interdisciplinary issues, and multicultural perspectives, this edition offers students and instructors a full range of quality prose models important to writing courses, reading sequences, and key undergraduate disciplines. With the high quality of its essays, its consistent humanistic emphases, its clear organization, and its focus on the importance of digital and multimedia literacies, *The McGraw-Hill Reader* offers instructors a lively, sophisticated, and eminently flexible text for college composition programs.

Organization

Composed of three parts and 16 chapters, *The McGraw-Hill Reader* covers the major modes of writing and many of the disciplines that college students will encounter as undergraduates. In Part 1, Chapter 1 presents an overview of the ways we read and respond to texts today. Chapter 2 focuses on strategies for critical thinking, reading, and writing. Chapter 3 provides extensive coverage of argument and persuasion. In Part 2, Chapters 4 to 14 explore core liberal arts disciplines, including education, the social sciences, business and economics, the humanities, and the sciences. Each chapter asks a key question, drawn from the disciplines it represents, designed to elicit constructive class discussion and sound critical writing. Prose models encourage students to practice skills they will need throughout college—including analysis, criticism, argumentation, as well as facility with digital texts. In Part 3, Chapter 15 provides an updated tour of research, research writing, and MLA documentation. Chapter 16 uses student work to walk through the process of writing a research essay.

Highlights of the Twelfth Edition

- **Twenty-one new selections.** Fresh essays appear on topics of current and enduring interest. Topics like class and the Occupy movement, marriage equality, racism, global climate change, social networking, online dating, and the power of comics should elicit lively student response and effective writing.
- **Expanded research section now divided into two chapters:** Chapter 15: Writing a Research Project and Chapter 16: A Research Project Casebook: Working with Sources across Media.
- **Updated and new "Networking: Applying Digital and Multimedia Literacies" assignments.** Designed to foster a range of real-world literacy skills, these assignments send students online; to video, audio, or interactive sources; or away from their desks to create visual texts or conduct primary research.
- **New case study for synthesis on class and culture and three new readings for the case study on social networking.**

Proven Features

Throughout many editions, instructors and students have found the following features of *The McGraw-Hill Reader* useful:

- **A rich selection of readings.** The essays in this book have been selected carefully to embrace a rich assortment of authors, to achieve balance among constituencies, to cover major historical periods, and to provide prose models and styles for class analysis, discussion, and imitation.
- **A text that works with a wide variety of levels and approaches.** With more than one hundred selections that range from very simple essays to more abstract and complex modes of discourse, teachers and students will be able to use *The McGraw-Hill Reader* at virtually all levels of a program. This reader can be used as a writing-across-the-curricula text, as the basis for a rhetorically focused course, as a thematic reader, as a multicultural anthology, or as an in-depth reader.
- **Chapter introductions that encourage students to reflect on major issues in the discipline.** The introduction to each disciplinary chapter gives students a broad perspective on the field at hand by putting major issues and concerns in context. Each introduction ends with a previewing section that alerts students to strategies for reading, discussion, and writing.
- **Integrated and focused treatment of argument, plagiarism, summary and précis, and research.** The chapters in Parts 1 and 3 provide integrated guidelines on these topics. Additionally, argumentation is stressed throughout the text, with a writing assignment following all selections.
- **Uniform apparatus that reinforces critical reading and writing accompanies every essay.** Each selection is preceded by a brief introduction that offers biographical information about the author. The questions that follow each essay are arranged in four categories—Comprehension, Rhetoric, Writing, and Networking: Applying Digital and Multimedia Literacies—to move students from audience analysis to various modes, processes, and media of composition. The integrated design of these questions makes each essay—simple or complex, short or long, old or new—accessible to college students who possess varied reading and writing abilities.

- **Chapter 16's Research Project Casebook.** A walk through of one student's process in finding, evaluating, and working with sources to craft a research essay. The casebook examines how to choose, research, synthesize, and document sources in five widely used media: a print book, a scholarly journal article accessed through a library database, a popular magazine article accessed online, a Web site, and an image.
- **"Synthesis: Connections for Critical Thinking" sections.** The topics listed at the end of each chapter help students to gain practice in synthesis and critique, and make comparative assessments of various groups of essays.
- **Classic and Contemporary Images.** Opening each chapter, these paired images along with the accompanying "Using a Critical Perspective" questions, serve to interest students in the chapter's central topics and get them thinking and writing.

USEFUL SUPPLEMENTS

The following supplements are designed to help instructors and students derive the full benefit from *The McGraw-Hill Reader:*

- *A Guide to the McGraw-Hill Reader.* This supplement—revised by Jim Iddings, Karen Laing-Urbina, and Christian Clark (all of the College of Southern Nevada)—offers well-considered strategies for teaching individual essays, sample rhetorical analyses, answers to questions, additional thought-provoking questions, comparative essay discussion formats, and tips for prewriting and guided writing activities. There is also a bibliography of criticism and research on the teaching of composition. This guide is available for instructors at http://www.mhhe.com/mhreader12e.

ACKNOWLEDGMENTS

It is a pleasure to acknowledge the support, assistance, and guidance of numerous individuals who helped create *The McGraw-Hill Reader.* I want to thank the excellent McGraw-Hill family of assistants, editors, and executives who participated enthusiastically in the project from the outset and who encouraged me at every step. My editor, Nancy Huebner has been a loyal, enthusiastic supporter of *The McGraw-Hill Reader* for many years. Thanks, too, to others on the McGraw-Hill editorial team who have made valuable contributions to this edition: Dawn Groundwater, Zachary Norton, Katie Fuller, Arpana Kumari, Chris Greene and Leonard Behnke. Thanks to Jim Iddings, Karen Laing-Urbina, and Christian Clark (all from the College of Southern Nevada) for their excellent revisions of the *Guide to The McGraw-Hill Reader.* I also want to thank Sheryl Rose, my astute copyeditor, and Jolynn Kilburg, my superlative production editor. Above all, I offer sincere thanks to Anne Stameshkin, my development editor, who in countless ways helped make this revision fresh and exciting.

The final content and design of *The McGraw-Hill Reader,* Twelfth Edition, reflects the expertise and advice offered by college instructors across the country who gave generously of their time when asked to review the text:

Adam Cleary, Southern Illinois University-Edwardsville
Anushiya Ramaswamy, Southern Illinois University-Edwardsville

April Van Camp, Indian River State College Central
Cleatta Morris, Louisiana State University-Shreveport
Dennis Lynch, Elgin Community College
Deron Walker, California Baptist University
Dorie Larue, Louisiana State University-Shreveport
Helen Becker, Shepherd University
Heidi Hanrahan, Shepherd University
John Freeman, University of Detroit Mercy
John Hodgson, Cameron University
Patrick Quinn, College of Southern Nv
Rebecca Babcock, University of Texas Permian Basin
Rosemary Weatherston, University of Detroit Mercy
Susan Trudeau, University of Detroit Mercy
Tammy Powley, Indian River State College Central
William Carney, Cameron University

I am pleased to acknowledge support from the Mellon Foundation, the Graduate Center of The City University of New York, and the United States Department of Education (Title III and Title IV) that enabled me to develop this text.

Gilbert H. Muller

chapter *4*

Education and Society
How, What, and Why Do We Learn?

In "Learning to Read and Write," a chapter from his autobiography, Frederick Douglass offers a spirited affirmation of the rights we all should have to pursue an education. For Douglass, who was born into slavery, knowledge began not only with experience but also with the need to articulate that experience through literacy. The ability to read and write should be the possession of all human beings, and Douglass was willing to risk punishment—even death—to gain that ability. Today, all over the globe, as ethnic and political conflicts arise, men and women face the same challenge of expressing themselves. For even with a tool like the Internet, if one does not have the tools to express oneself or if the expression of thought is suppressed, the vehicle for conveying ideas, no matter how powerful, is rendered useless.

Perhaps the struggle for an education always involves a certain amount of effort and risk, but the struggle also conveys excitement and the deep, abiding satisfaction that derives from achieving knowledge of oneself and of the world. Time and again in the essays in this chapter, we discover that there is always a price to be paid for acquiring knowledge, developing intellectual skills, and attaining wisdom. However, numerous task forces and national commissions tell us that students today are not willing to pay this price and that, as a consequence, we have become academically mediocre. Is it true that we no longer delight in educating ourselves through reading, as Richard Rodriguez recounts in "The Lonely, Good Company of Books"? Is it true that we take libraries for granted—we expect them to be available but never visit them? A democratic society requires an educated citizenry, people who refuse to commit intellectual suicide or self-neglect. The writers in this chapter, who take many pathways to understanding, remind us that we cannot afford to be passive or compliant when our right to an education is challenged.

Today we are in an era of dynamic change in attitudes toward education. Such issues as sex education, multiculturalism, racism, sexism, and immigration suggest the liveliness of the educational debate on campus. Any debate over contemporary education touches on the themes of politics, economics, religion, or the social agenda, forcing us to recognize that configurations of power are at the heart of virtually all educational issues in society today.

Without education, many of our ideas and opinions can be stereotyped or prejudiced, bearing no relationship to the truth. It is easy to understand how such views can arise if we are merely passive vessels for others' uninformed opinions rather than active learners who seek true knowledge. If we judge the tenor of the essayists in this section, we discover that many of them are subversives, waging war against both ignorance *and* received dogma.

These writers treat education as the key to upsetting the status quo and effecting change. Operating from diverse backgrounds, they challenge many assumptions about our educational system and invite us to think critically about its purpose.

PREVIEWING THE CHAPTER

As you read the essays in this chapter and respond to them in discussion and writing, consider the following questions:

- What is the main educational issue that the author deals with?
- What tone does the author establish in treating the subject? Does the author take a positive or a negative position?
- Does the author define *education?* If so, how? If not, does the author suggest what he or she means by it?
- What is the impact of society at large on how education is perceived?
- What forms of evidence do the authors use to support their views on education?
- How do the rhetorical features of the essays that focus on personal experience differ from those of the essays that examine education from a more global perspective?
- What have you learned about the value of education from reading these selections?
- Which essays persuaded you the most? Which the least? Why?

Classic and Contemporary Images
DOES EDUCATION CHANGE OVER TIME?

Using a Critical Perspective   Consider these two photographs of students in science laboratories, the first from the 19th century and the second from the present. What is the setting of each laboratory like? Who are the people? What does each photographer frame and leave out of the scene? Which educational setting seems more conducive to scientific or educational inquiry? Why?

Founded in 1833, Oberlin College in Ohio was the first U.S. college
to grant undergraduate degrees to women. The photograph reprinted
here shows both male and female students in a zoology lab
at Oberlin sometime during the 1890s.

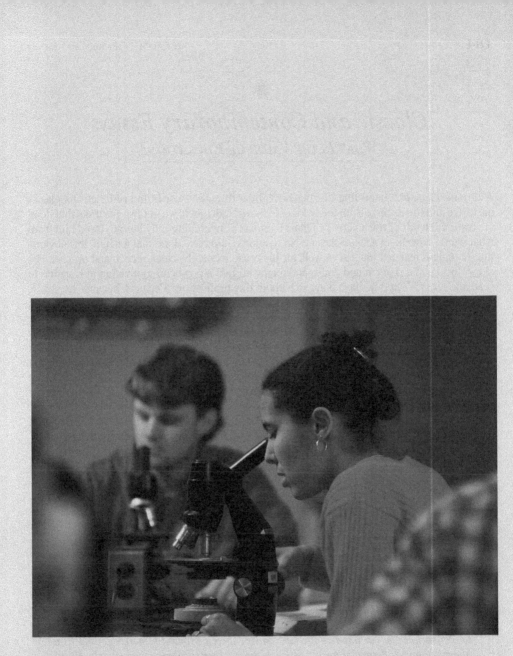

At the beginning of the 21st century, most colleges and universities in the United States are coeducational, and it is no longer unusual to see both male and female students in a laboratory setting, as shown in this contemporary photo of a biology lab at the University of Maine.

❋

Classic and Contemporary Essays
WHAT IS THE VALUE OF EDUCATION?

A famous adage proclaims that "the pen is mightier than the sword." In Frederick Douglass's narrative and the excerpt from the work of Richard Rodriguez, we get two portraits that demonstrate the truth of the adage. Douglass's efforts at becoming fully literate freed him from what would have been a life of slavery. No weapon could have done that for him. It is obvious that Douglass learned his lesson well, for his prose is stately, clear, direct, and precise. His story speaks of a determined youth and man who had a powerful motivation in learning to read and write. Would he have done so without this motivation? Perhaps, because he seems to be a very self-directed individual, as is evident from the anecdotes he relates. Rodriguez, too, has a strong motivation to master, and even to excel at, reading and writing. Writing nearly 150 years after Douglass, and at a time when he needn't fear slavery looming over him, Rodriguez nevertheless perceived that by emulating his teachers, who promoted book reading, his own reading would make him a better person. He, like Douglass, sensed that there was something about acquiring knowledge and about expanding one's view of the world by learning how others viewed it that would provide him with a certain amount of independence. As you read the following two essays, you may wish to consider whether the quiet, modest tone each author projects may have something to do with the subject matter. For reading, although active and mind-opening, is still a private and "lonely" activity.

✺

Learning to Read and Write

Frederick Douglass

Frederick Douglass (1817–1895) was an American abolitionist, orator, and journalist. Born of the union between a slave and a white man, Douglass later escaped to Massachusetts. An impassioned antislavery speech brought him recognition as a powerful orator; thereafter he was much in demand for speaking engagements. He described his experience as a black man in America in Narrative of the Life of Frederick Douglass *(1845). After managing to buy his freedom, Douglass founded the* North Star, *a newspaper he published for the next 17 years. In the following excerpt from his stirring autobiography, Douglass recounts the tremendous obstacles he overcame in his efforts to become literate.*

1   I lived in Master Hugh's family about seven years. During this time, I succeeded in learning to read and write. In accomplishing this, I was compelled to resort to various stratagems. I had no regular teacher. My mistress, who had kindly commenced

to instruct me, had, in compliance with the advice and direction of her husband, not only ceased to instruct, but had set her face against my being instructed by any one else. It is due, however, to my mistress to say of her, that she did not adopt this course of treatment immediately. She at first lacked the depravity indispensable to shutting me up in mental darkness. It was at least necessary for her to have some training in the exercise of irresponsible power, to make her equal to the task of treating me as though I were a brute.

My mistress was, as I have said, a kind and tender-hearted woman; and in the simplicity of her soul she commenced, when I first went to live with her, to treat me as she supposed one human being ought to treat another. In entering upon the duties of a slaveholder, she did not seem to perceive that I sustained to her the relation of a mere chattel, and that for her to treat me as a human being was not only wrong, but dangerously so. Slavery proved as injurious to her as it did to me. When I went there, she was a pious, warm, and tender-hearted woman. There was no sorrow or suffering for which she had not a tear. She had bread for the hungry, clothes for the naked, and comfort for every mourner that came within her reach. Slavery soon proved its ability to divest her of these heavenly qualities. Under its influence, the tender heart became stone, and the lamb-like disposition gave way to one of tiger-like fierceness. The first step in her downward course was in her ceasing to instruct me. She now commenced to practise her husband's precepts. She finally became even more violent in her opposition than her husband himself. She was not satisfied with simply doing as well as he had commanded; she seemed anxious to do better. Nothing seemed to make her more angry than to see me with a newspaper. She seemed to think that here lay the danger. I have had her rush at me with a face made all up of fury, and snatch from me a newspaper, in a manner that fully revealed her apprehension. She was an apt woman; and a little experience soon demonstrated, to her satisfaction, that education and slavery were incompatible with each other.

From this time I was most narrowly watched. If I was in a separate room any considerable length of time, I was sure to be suspected of having a book, and was at once called to give an account of myself. All this, however, was too late. The first step had been taken. Mistress, in teaching me the alphabet, had given me the *inch,* and no precaution could prevent me from taking the *ell.*

The plan which I adopted, and the one by which I was most successful, was that of making friends of all the little white boys whom I met in the street. As many of these as I could, I converted into teachers. With their kindly aid, obtained at different times and in different places, I finally succeeded in learning to read. When I was sent on errands, I always took my book with me, and by doing one part of my errand quickly, I found time to get a lesson before my return. I used also to carry bread with me, enough of which was always in the house, and to which I was always welcome; for I was much better off in this regard than many of the poor white children in our neighborhood. This bread I used to bestow upon the hungry little urchins, who, in return, would give me that more valuable bread of knowledge. I am strongly tempted to give the names of two or three of those little boys, a testimonial of the gratitude and affection I bear them; but prudence forbids—not that it would injure me, but it might embarrass them; for it is almost an unpardonable offence to teach slaves to read in this Christian country. It is enough to say of the dear little fellows, that they lived on Philpot Street, very near Durgin and Bailey's ship-yard. I used to talk this matter of slavery over with them. I would sometimes say to them, I wished I could be as free as they would be when they got to be men. "You will be free as soon as you are twenty-one, *but I am a slave for life!* Have not I as good a right to be free as you have?" These words used to trouble them; they would express for me the liveliest sympathy, and console me with the hope that something would occur by which I might be free.

5   I was now about twelve years old, and the thought of being a *slave for life* began to bear heavily upon my heart. Just about this time, I got hold of a book entitled "The Colombian Orator." Every opportunity I got, I used to read this book. Among much of other interesting matter, I found in it a dialogue between a master and his slave. The slave was represented as having run away from his master three times. The dialogue represented the conversation which took place between them, when the slave was retaken the third time. In this dialogue, the whole argument in behalf of slavery was brought forward by the master, all of which was disposed of by the slave. The slave was made to say some very smart as well as impressive things in reply to his master—things which had the desired though unexpected effect; for the conversation resulted in the voluntary emancipation of the slave on the part of the master.

6   In the same book, I met with one of Sheridan's mighty speeches on and in behalf of Catholic emancipation. These were choice documents to me. I read them over and over again with unabated interest. They gave tongue to interesting thoughts of my own soul, which had frequently flashed through my mind, and died away for want of utterance. The moral which I gained from the dialogue was the power of truth over the conscience of even a slaveholder. What I got from Sheridan was a bold denunciation of slavery, and a powerful vindication of human rights. The reading of these documents enabled me to utter my thoughts, and to meet the arguments brought forward to sustain slavery; but while they relieved me of one difficulty, they brought on another even more painful than the one of which I was relieved. The more I read, the more I was led to abhor and detest my enslavers. I could regard them in no other light than a band of successful robbers, who had left their homes, and gone to Africa, and stolen us from our homes, and in a strange land reduced us to slavery. I loathed them as being the meanest as well as the most wicked of men. As I read and contemplated the subject, behold! that very discontentment which Master Hugh had predicted would follow my learning to read had already come, to torment and sting my soul to unutterable anguish. As I writhed under it, I would at times feel that learning to read had been a curse rather than a blessing. It had given me a view of my wretched condition, without the remedy. It opened my eyes to the horrible pit, but to no ladder upon which to get out. In moments of agony, I envied my fellow-slaves for their stupidity. I have often wished myself a beast. I preferred the condition of the meanest reptile to my own. Any thing, no matter what, to get rid of thinking! It was this everlasting thinking of my condition that tormented me. There was no getting rid of it. It was pressed upon me by every object within sight or hearing, animate or

freedom

inanimate. The silver trump of freedom had roused my soul to eternal wakeful-ness. Freedom now appeared, to disappear no more forever. It was heard in every sound, and seen in every thing. It was ever present to torment me with a sense of my wretched condition. I saw nothing without seeing it, I heard nothing without hearing it, and felt nothing without feeling it. It looked from every star, it smiled in every calm, breathed in every wind, and moved in every storm.

I often found myself regretting my own existence, and wishing myself dead; 7 and but for the hope of being free, I have no doubt but that I should have killed my-self, or done something for which I should have been killed. While in this state of mind, I was eager to hear anyone speak of slavery. I was a ready listener. Every little while, I could hear something about the abolitionists. It was some time before I found what the word meant. It was always used in such connections as to make it an interesting word to me. If a slave ran away and succeeded in getting clear, or if a slave killed his master, set fire to a barn, or did any thing very wrong in the mind of a slaveholder, it was spoken of as the fruit of *abolition.* Hearing the word in this con-nection very often, I set about learning what it meant. The dictionary afforded me little or no help. I found it was "the act of abolishing"; but then I did not know what was to be abolished. Here I was perplexed. I did not dare to ask any one about its meaning, for I was satisfied that it was something they wanted me to know very lit-tle about. After a patient waiting, I got one of our city papers, containing an account of the number of petitions from the north, praying for the abolition of slavery in the District of Columbia, and of the slave trade between the States. From this time I understood the words *abolition* and *abolitionist,* and always drew near when that word was spoken, expecting to hear something of importance to myself and fellow-slaves. The light broke in upon me by degrees. I went one day down on the wharf of Mr. Waters; and seeing two Irishmen unloading a scow of stone, I went, unasked, and helped them. When we had finished, one of them came to me and asked me if I were a slave. I told him I was. He asked, "Are ye a slave for life?" I told him that I was. The good Irishman seemed to be deeply affected by the statement. He said to the other that it was a pity so fine a little fellow as myself should be a slave for life. He said it was a shame to hold me. They both advised me to run away to the north; that I should find friends there, and that I should be free. I pretended not to be inter-ested in what they said, and treated them as if I did not understand them; for I feared they might be treacherous. White men have been known to encourage slaves to escape, and then, to get the reward, catch them and return them to their masters. I was afraid that these seemingly good men might use me so; but I nevertheless remembered their advice, and from that time I resolved to run away. I looked for-ward to a time at which it would be safe for me to escape. I was too young to think of doing so immediately; besides, I wished to learn how to write, as I might have occasion to write my own pass. I consoled myself with the hope that I should one day find a good chance. Meanwhile, I would learn to write.

The idea as to how I might learn to write was suggested to me by being in 8 Durgin and Bailey's ship-yard, and frequently seeing the ship carpenters, after hew-ing, and getting a piece of timber ready for use, write on the timber the name of that part of the ship for which it was intended. When a piece of timber was intended for the larboard side, it would be marked thus—"L." When a piece was for the starboard side, it would be marked thus—"S." A piece for the larboard side forward, would be marked thus—"L. F." When a piece was for starboard side forward, it would be marked thus—"S. F." For larboard aft, it would be marked thus—"L. A." For starboard aft, it would be marked thus—"S. A." I soon learned the names of these letters, and for what they were intended when placed upon a piece of timber in the ship-yard. I immediately commenced copying them, and in a short time was able to make the four letters named. After that, when I met with any boy who I knew could write, I would tell him I could write as well as he. The next word would be, "I don't believe you. Let me see you try it." I would then make the letters which I had been so fortunate as to learn, and ask him to beat that. In this way I got a good many lessons in writing, which it is quite possible I should never have gotten in any other way. During this time, my copy-book was the board fence, brick wall, and pavement; my pen and ink was a lump of chalk. With these, I learned mainly how to write. I then commenced and continued copying the Italics in Webster's Spelling Book, until I could make them all without looking on the book. By this time, my little Master Thomas had gone to school, and learned how to write, and had written over a number of copy-books. These had been brought home, and shown to some of our near neighbors, and then laid aside. My mistress used to go to class meeting at the Wilk Street meetinghouse every Monday afternoon, and leave me to take care of the house. When left thus, I used to spend the time in writing in the spaces left in Master Thomas's copy-book, copying what he had written. I continued to do this until I could write a hand very similar to that of Master Thomas. Thus, after a long, tedious effort for years, I finally succeeded in learning how to write.

COMPREHENSION

1. What strategies does Douglass use to continue his education after his mistress's abandonment?
2. Why did the author's mistress find his reading newspapers particularly threatening?
3. Why does Douglass call learning to read "a curse rather than a blessing" (paragraph 6)?

RHETORIC

1. What is the thesis of Douglass's narration? How well is it supported and developed by the body paragraphs? Explain.
2. The first couple of sentences in the story, though simple, are very powerful. How do they serve to set up the mood of the piece and the reader's expectations?
3. Cite examples of Douglass's use of metaphors, and discuss why they work in those paragraphs.
4. How would you describe Douglass's writing style and level of language? Does it reveal anything about his character? Justify your response.
5. Explain the way in which the author uses comparison and contrast.
6. What is Douglass's definition of *abolition*, and how does he help the reader define it? How does this method contribute to the reader's understanding of the learning process?

WRITING

1. What does Douglass mean when he writes that "education and slavery were incompatible with each other" (paragraph 2)? Write an essay in which you consider the relationship between the two.
2. Both Douglass and his mistress were in inferior positions to Master Hugh. Write an essay in which you compare and contrast their positions in society at the time.
3. Illiteracy is still a major problem in the United States. Write an account of what your day-to-day life would be like if you couldn't write or read. What impact would this deficiency have on your life? Use concrete examples to illustrate your narrative.
4. **Writing an Argument:** Write an essay in which you argue for or against the proposition that American education continues to discriminate against minority groups.

NETWORKING
Applying Digital and Multimedia Literacies

Analyzing a News Report on 21st-Century Illiteracy: Go to *http://www.cbsnews. com/video/watch/?id=4711567n* and watch this 2009 CBS report on adult illiteracy in the United States. What challenges has John Jones faced because of his illiteracy? Why do you think the report chose to focus not only on larger statistics, such as results from the Board of Education's report, but also on illiteracy's effects on an individual? How does John Jones's story contribute to the report's purpose and argument? How does the report make use of its medium (television) to convey its message?

The Lonely, Good Company of Books

Richard Rodriguez

Richard Rodriguez (b. 1944) was born in San Francisco and received degrees from Stanford University and Columbia University. He also did graduate study at the University of California, Berkeley, and at the Warburg Institute, London. Rodriguez became a nationally known writer with the publication of his autobiography, Hunger of Memory: The Education of Richard Rodriguez *(1982). In it, he describes the struggles of growing up biculturally—feeling alienated from his Spanish-speaking parents yet not wholly comfortable in the dominant culture of the United States. He opposes bilingualism and affirmative action as they are now practiced in the United States, and his stance has caused much controversy in educational and intellectual circles. Rodriguez continues to write about social issues such as acculturation, education, and language in* Days of Obligation: An Argument with My Mexican Father *(1992) and* Brown: The Last Discovery of America *(2002). In the following essay, Rodriguez records his childhood passion for reading.*

1   From an early age I knew that my mother and father could read and write both Spanish and English. I had observed my father making his way through what, I now suppose, must have been income tax forms. On other occasions I waited apprehensively while my mother read onion-paper letters air-mailed from Mexico with news of a relative's illness or death. For both my parents, however, reading was something done out of necessity and as quickly as possible. Never did I see either of them read an entire book. Nor did I see them read for pleasure. Their reading consisted of work manuals, prayer books, newspapers, recipes. . . .

2   In our house each school year would begin with my mother's careful instruction: "Don't write in your books so we can sell them at the end of the year." The remark was echoed in public by my teachers, but only in part: "Boys and girls, don't write in your books. You must learn to treat them with great care and respect."

3   OPEN THE DOORS OF YOUR MIND WITH BOOKS, read the red and white poster over the nun's desk in early September. It soon was apparent to me that reading was the classroom's central activity. Each course had its own book. And the information gathered from a book was unquestioned. READ TO LEARN, the sign on the wall advised in December. I privately wondered: What was the connection between reading and learning? Did one learn something only by reading it? Was an idea only an idea if it could be written down? In June, CONSIDER BOOKS YOUR BEST FRIENDS. Friends? Reading was, at best, only a chore. I needed to look up whole paragraphs of words in a dictionary. Lines of type were dizzying, the eye having to move slowly across the page, then down, and across. . . . The sentences of the first books I read were coolly impersonal. Toned hard. What most bothered me, however, was the isolation reading required. To console myself for the loneliness I'd feel when I read, I tried reading in a very soft voice. Until: "Who is doing all that talking to his neighbor?" Shortly after, remedial reading classes were arranged for me with a very old nun.

4   At the end of each school day, for nearly six months, I would meet with her in the tiny room that served as the school's library but was actually only a storeroom for used textbooks and a vast collection of *National Geographics*. Everything about our sessions pleased me: the smallness of the room; the noise of the janitor's broom hitting the edge of the long hallway outside the door; the green of the sun, lighting the wall; and the old woman's face blurred white with a beard. Most of the time we took turns. I began with my elementary text. Sentences of astonishing simplicity seemed to me lifeless and drab: "The boys ran from the rain. . . . She wanted to sing. . . . The kite rose in the blue." Then the old nun would read from her favorite books, usually biographies of early American presidents. Playfully she ran through complex sentences, calling the words alive with her voice, making it seem that the author somehow was speaking directly to me. I smiled just to listen to her. I sat there and sensed for the very first time some possibility of fellowship between a reader and a writer, a communication, never *intimate* like that I heard spoken words at home convey, but one nonetheless *personal*.

5   One day the nun concluded a session by asking me why I was so reluctant to read by myself. I tried to explain; said something about the way written words made me feel all alone—almost, I wanted to add but didn't, as when I spoke to

myself in a room just emptied of furniture. She studied my face as I spoke; she seemed to be watching more than listening. In an uneventful voice she replied that I had nothing to fear. Didn't I realize that reading would open up whole new worlds? A book could open doors for me. It could introduce me to people and show me places I never imagined existed. She gestured toward the bookshelves. (Bare-breasted African women danced, and the shiny hubcaps of automobiles on the back covers of the *Geographic* gleamed in my mind.) I listened with respect. But her words were not very influential. I was thinking then of another consequence of literacy, one I was too shy to admit but nonetheless trusted. Books were going to make me "educated." *That* confidence enabled me, several months later, to overcome my fear of the silence.

In fourth grade I embarked upon a grandiose reading program. "Give me the names of important books," I would say to startled teachers. They soon found out that I had in mind "adult books." I ignored their suggestion of anything I suspected was written for children. (Not until I was in college, as a result, did I read *Huckleberry Finn* or *Alice's Adventures in Wonderland.*) Instead, I read *The Scarlet Letter* and Franklin's *Autobiography.* And whatever I read I read for extra credit. Each time I finished a book, I reported the achievement to a teacher and basked in the praise my effort earned. Despite my best efforts, however, there seemed to be more and more books I needed to read. At the library I would literally tremble as I came upon whole shelves of books I hadn't read. So I read and I read and I read: *Great Expectations;* all the short stories of Kipling; *The Babe Ruth Story;* the entire first volume of the *Encyclopaedia Britannica* (A–ANSTEY); the *Iliad; Moby Dick; Gone with the Wind; The Good Earth; Ramona; Forever Amber; The Lives of the Saints; Crime and Punishment; The Pearl.* . . . Librarians who initially frowned when I checked out the maximum ten books at a time started saving books they thought I might like. Teachers would say to the rest of the class, "I only wish the rest of you took reading as seriously as Richard obviously does."

But at home I would hear my mother wondering, "What do you see in your books?" (Was reading a hobby like her knitting? Was so much reading even healthy for a boy? Was it the sign of "brains"? Or was it just a convenient excuse for not helping around the house on Saturday mornings?) Always, "What do you see . . . ?"

What *did* I see in my books? I had the idea that they were crucial for my academic success, though I couldn't have said exactly how or why. In the sixth grade I simply concluded that what gave a book its value was some major idea or theme it contained. If that core essence could be mined and memorized, I would become learned like my teachers. I decided to record in a notebook the themes of the books that I read. After reading *Robinson Crusoe,* I wrote that its theme was "the value of learning to live by oneself." When I completed *Wuthering Heights,* I noted the danger of "letting emotions get out of control." Rereading these brief moralistic appraisals usually left me disheartened. I couldn't believe that they were really the source of reading's value. But for many years, they constituted the only means I had of describing to myself the educational value of books.

9   In spite of my earnestness, I found reading a pleasurable activity. I came to enjoy the lonely, good company of books. Early on weekday mornings, I'd read in my bed. I'd feel a mysterious comfort then, reading in the dawn quiet—the blue-gray silence interrupted by the occasional churning of the refrigerator motor a few rooms away or the more distant sounds of a city bus beginning its run. On weekends I'd go to the public library to read, surrounded by old men and women. Or, if the weather was fine, I would take my books to the park and read in the shade of a tree. Neighbors would leave for vacation and I would water their lawns. I would sit through the twilight on the front porches or in backyards, reading to the cool, whirling sounds of the sprinklers.

10   I also had favorite writers. But often those writers I enjoyed most I was least able to value. When I read William Saroyan's *The Human Comedy,* I was immediately pleased by the narrator's warmth and the charm of his story. But as quickly I became suspicious. A book so enjoyable to read couldn't be very "important." Another summer I determined to read all the novels of Dickens. Reading his fat novels, I loved the feeling I got—after the first hundred pages—of being at home in a fictional world where I knew the names of the characters and cared about what was going to happen to them. And it bothered me that I was forced away at the conclusion, when the fiction closed tight, like a fortune-teller's fist—the futures of all the major characters neatly resolved. I never knew how to take such feelings seriously, however. Nor did I suspect that these experiences could be part of a novel's meaning. Still, there were pleasures to sustain me after I'd finish my books. Carrying a volume back to the library, I would be pleased by its weight. I'd run my fingers along the edge of the pages and marvel at the breadth of my achievement. Around my room, growing stacks of paperback books reinforced my assurance.

11   I entered high school having read hundreds of books. My habit of reading made me a confident speaker and writer of English. Reading also enabled me to sense something of the shape, the major concerns, of Western thought. (I was able to say something about Dante and Descartes and Engels and James Baldwin in my high school term papers.) In these various ways, books brought me academic success as I hoped that they would. But I was not a good reader. Merely bookish, I lacked a point of view when I read. Rather, I read in order to acquire a point of view. I vacuumed books for epigrams, scraps of information, ideas, themes—anything to fill the hollow within me and make me feel educated. When one of my teachers suggested to his drowsy tenth-grade English class that a person could not have a "complicated idea" until he had read at least two thousand books, I heard the remark without detecting either its irony or its very complicated truth. I merely determined to compile a list of all the books I had ever read. Harsh with myself, I included only once a title I might have read several times. (How, after all, could one read a book more than once?) And I included only those books over a hundred pages in length. (Could anything shorter be a book?)

12   There was yet another high school list I compiled. One day I came across a newspaper article about the retirement of an English professor at a nearby state college. The article was accompanied by a list of the "hundred most important books of Western Civilization." "More than anything else in my life," the professor

told the reporter with finality, "these books have made me all that I am." That was the kind of remark I couldn't ignore. I clipped out the list and kept it for the several months it took me to read all of the titles. Most books, of course, I barely understood. While reading Plato's *Republic,* for instance, I needed to keep looking at the book jacket comments to remind myself what the text was about. Nevertheless, with the special patience and superstition of a scholarship boy, I looked at every word of the text. And by the time I reached the last word, relieved, I convinced myself that I had read *The Republic.* In a ceremony of great pride, I solemnly crossed Plato off my list.

COMPREHENSION

1. What was Rodriguez's parents' attitude toward reading? Did it influence his attitude? Cite examples from the essay that support your opinion.
2. What does Rodriguez mean by the "fellowship between a reader and a writer" (paragraph 4)? Why does he differentiate between "intimate" and "personal" forms of communication?
3. Rodriguez hoped that reading would fill "the hollow" inside him. What was the cause of his emptiness? Did he succeed in filling the void? Why did he find reading a lonely experience? Did reading fulfill any of his expectations?

RHETORIC

1. What is the thesis of Rodriguez's essay? Is it stated or implied? Explain.
2. How does the author's use of narrative advance his views on reading and education?
3. What is the writer's tone? How effective is it in conveying his point of view?
4. Rodriguez uses uppercase letters (small capitals) when referring to signs advocating reading. Why does he use this device? How does it support his point of view?
5. The essay ends with an ironic anecdote. Why did Rodriguez choose to conclude this way? Does it satisfactorily illustrate his attitude?
6. What words or phrases imply that there is an ethnic component in Rodriguez's conflict? Is the subtlety effective? Justify your response.

WRITING

1. Rodriguez's parents had a pragmatic attitude toward reading. What was the attitude in your home as you were growing up? Did your parents encourage your interest in reading? Did they read themselves? What is the first book you remember reading by yourself? Write an essay in which you describe your reading history.
2. Is reading still a significant source of information and entertainment, or has it been usurped by television? Is it important (or necessary) to be a reader today?
3. **Writing an Argument:** Rodriguez believed reading would make him "educated." Do you agree or disagree? Is reading vital to a person's education? How do you define *education?* Can it be acquired only through reading, or are there other contributing factors? Write an argumentative essay on this topic.

NETWORKING
Applying Digital and Multimedia Literacies

Considering the Impact of e-Books: Locate online and read "How the e-Book Will Change the Way We Read and Write" from the *Wall Street Journal*. If Richard Rodriguez had embarked on reading in a world like the one Johnson describes, how might his experience with books have been different? In what ways do you think it would have been less, or more, rewarding? What do you see as some advantages of reading offline, alone, and what are some advantages of reading online, in a network?

Synthesis: Classic and Contemporary Questions for Comparison

1. Both Rodriguez and Douglass were motivated to educate themselves in a society in-imical to this achievement. Compare and contrast their struggles and attitudes in their quests for knowledge.
2. Pretend you are Rodriguez, and write a letter to Douglass addressing the issues of minorities and education in present-day America. What would Rodriguez say about the progress of minorities in our society?
3. Although Rodriguez and Douglass treat a similar theme, they communicate their messages differently. Which narration do you consider more powerful, and why?
4. Rodriguez explores the theme of isolation in his story. Is there any evidence that this feeling was shared by Douglass in his efforts to learn how to read? Use proof from both narratives to support your view.
5. Slavery was an obvious obstacle to Douglass's attempt to educate himself. What impeded Rodriguez's progress? Were similar forces at work? Cite examples from Rodriguez's narrative to prove your point.

What College Can Mean to the Other America

Mike Rose

Mike Rose (b. 1944) is a nationally recognized writer, educator, and specialist in composition. He was born in Altoona, Pennsylvania to Italian immigrants, and moved with his parents to a working-class neighborhood in south Los Angeles when he was seven years old. Rose recounts his early years and education in a bestselling book, Lives on the Boundary (1989). Based on his own experience of having been tracked into a vocational slot in high school, Rose advocates a reevaluation of remedial *writers in such books as* Writer's Block *(1984),* When a Writer Can't Write *(1985),* *and other texts. He also is a prominent spokesperson for the value of public education* *in a democracy, a position articulated in his collection of essays,* Why School? Reclaiming Education for All of Us *(2009), and elsewhere. Rose received a PhD in* *education from UCLA, and he has taught there for nearly forty years. In this essay* *that he wrote for* The Chronicle of Higher Education *in 2011, Rose argues for* *educational policy initiatives that will benefit the poor.*

The stakes go beyond the economic to the basic civic question: What kind of society 1 do we want to become?

It has been nearly 50 years since Michael Harrington wrote *The Other America,* 2 pulling the curtain back on invisible poverty within the United States. If he were writing today, Harrington would find the same populations he described then: young, marginally educated people who drift in and out of low-pay, dead-end jobs, and older displaced workers, unable to find work as industries transform and shops close. But he would find more of them, especially the young, their situation worsened by further economic restructuring and globalization. And while the poor he wrote about were invisible in a time of abundance, ours are visible in a terrible recession, although invisible in most public policy. In fact, the poor are drifting further into the dark underbelly of American capitalism.

One of the Obama administration's mantras is that we need to "out-innovate, 3 out-educate, and out-build" our competition in order to achieve fuller prosperity. The solution to our social and economic woes lies in new technologies, in the cutting edge. This is our "Sputnik moment," a very American way to frame our problems. However, the editors of *The Economist* wrote a few months back that this explanation of our economic situation is "mostly nonsense."

Instead, the business-friendly, neoliberal magazine offered a sobering—at 4 times almost neo-Marxist—assessment of what it considers the real danger in our economy, something at the core of Harrington's analysis: chronic, ingrained joblessness that is related to our social and economic structure. We are looking toward the horizon of innovation when we should be looking straight in front of us at the tens of millions of chronically unemployed Americans and providing comprehensive occupational, educational, and social services. Otherwise, to cite an earlier issue of *The Economist* that also dealt with American inequality, we risk "calcifying into a European-style class-based society." For people without school or work, we already have.

There are a few current policy initiatives that are aimed at helping the disadvan- 5 taged gain economic mobility, mostly through some form of postsecondary education. Sadly, the most ambitious of these—the federal American Graduation Initiative—was sacrificed during the health-care negotiations, although some smaller projects remained in the stimulus package and the Department of Education. Private foundations, notably Gates and Lumina, have been sponsoring such efforts as well. These efforts reach a small percentage of poor and low-income Americans and, on average, are aimed at the more academically skilled among them—although many still require remedial English and mathematics. A certificate or degree alone will not automatically lift them out of hard times—there is a bit of magic-bullet thinking in these college initiatives—but getting a decent basic education could make a significant difference in their lives. At the least, these efforts are among the few antipoverty measures that have some degree of bipartisan support.

6   For the last year and a half, I have been spending time at an inner-city community college that serves this population, and I have seen firsthand the effects of poverty and long-term joblessness. Although some students attend the college with the goal of transfer, the majority come for its well-regarded occupational programs. More than 90 percent must take one or more basic-skills courses; 60 percent are on financial aid. A fair number have been through the criminal-justice system.

7   As I have gotten to know these students, the numbers have come alive. Many had chaotic childhoods, went to underperforming schools, and never finished high school. With low-level skills, they have had an awful time in the labor market. Short-term jobs, long stretches of unemployment, no health care. Many, the young ones included, have health problems that are inadequately treated if treated at all. I remember during my first few days on the campus noticing the number of people who walked with a limp or irregular gait.

8   What really strikes me, though, is students' level of engagement, particularly in the occupational programs. There are a few people who seem to be marking time, but most listen intently as an instructor explains the air-supply system in a diesel engine or the way to sew supports into an evening dress. And they do and redo an assignment until they get it right. Hope and desire are brimming. Many of the students say this is the first time school has meant anything to them. More than a few talk about turning their lives around. It doesn't take long to imagine the kind of society we would have if more people had this opportunity.

9   But right at the point when opportunity is offered, it is being threatened by severe budget cuts in education and social services. For several years, the college—like so many in the United States—has been able to offer only a small number of summer classes, and classes are being cut during the year. Enrollment in existing classes is growing. Student-support services are scaled back. And all the while, more people are trying to enroll at the college; some will have to be turned away, and those who are admitted will tax an already burdened system.

10   Given the toll the recession has taken on state and local governments, policy makers face "unprecedented challenges" and say they "have no other choice" but to make cuts in education. Secretary of Education Arne Duncan, borrowing a now-ubiquitous phrase, has called the necessity to do more with less "the new normal."

11   I don't dispute the difficulty of budgeting in the recession, nor the fact that education spending includes waste that should be cut. But we need to resist the framing of our situation as inevitable and normal. This framing makes the recession a catastrophe without culpability, neutralizing the civic and moral dimensions of both the causes of the recession and the way policy makers respond to it.

12   The civic and moral dimensions also are diminished by the powerful market-based orientation to economic and social problems. Antigovernment, anti-welfare-state, antitax—this ideology undercuts broad-scale public responses to inequality.

13   If the editors of *The Economist* are right, the deep cuts in education—especially to programs and institutions that help poor people connect to school or work—will

have disastrous long-term economic consequences that far outweigh immediate budgetary gains. And rereading *The Other America* reminds us that the stakes go beyond the economic to the basic civic question: What kind of society do we want to become? Will there be another Michael Harrington 50 years from now writing about an America that has a higher rate of poverty and even wider social divides?

COMPREHENSION

1. Circle, underline, highlight, or flag all references that Rose makes to Michael Harrington and his book, *The Other America*. Explain the importance that Rose gives to Harrington's study and its relevance to his topic.
2. Summarize Rose's perception of the current state of educational policy for the poor in the United States.
3. Why does Rose venture to a community college to investigate his subject? What does he learn there?

RHETORIC

1. Examine Rose's introductory paragraph. How does he structure this opening unit? Where does he state his thesis or claim, and how effective do you find this placement?
2. Rose writes for an academic audience in this essay—and specifically for college administrators. How does he tailor his message for this audience? What secondary audiences would be interested in his argument and analysis?
3. Explain Rose's tone and voice in this essay. Where does he personalize his argument, and what is the effect?
4. How does Rose use a problem-solution pattern of organization in developing his argument? Point to specific passages where this pattern becomes apparent.
5. What is the relationship of Rose's concluding paragraph to his claim and to the evidence that he offers in the body of his essay?

WRITING

1. Compose a position paper in which you outline your own plan for addressing the educational needs of the poor in American society.
2. In a personal essay, explore your own place in American society—or in the nation where you were born and raised—and how this molded your educational experience.
3. **Writing an Argument:** Argue for or against the proposition that the two major political parties in the United States are not seriously interested in providing a solid education for the poor.

NETWORKING
Applying Digital and Multimedia Literacies

Collaborating in small groups, go online to find out more about Michael Harrington's seminal study, *The Other America*. Based on your findings and discussion, present your response to the work of both Harrington and Rose.

Sex Ed

Anna Quindlen

Anna Quindlen (b. 1953) was born in Philadelphia and educated at Barnard College (BA, 1974). A journalist and novelist, she began her writing career as a reporter for the New York Post *and later moved on to the* New York Times, *where she was a syndicated columnist. Quindlen has written a number of books, including* Living Out Loud *(1986),* Object Lessons *(1991),* One True Thing *(1994),* Blessings *(2002),* Being Perfect *(2005), and* Rise and Shine *(2006). Quindlen received the Pulitzer Prize for Commentary in 1992. In this essay, Quindlen focuses on the problem of teenage pregnancy and suggests that children be given more than textbook information to help them cope with their sexuality.*

1   Several years ago I spent the day at a family planning clinic in one of New York City's poorest neighborhoods. I sat around a Formica table with a half-dozen sixteen-year-old girls and listened with some amazement as they showed off their knowledge of human sexuality.

2   They knew how long sperm lived inside the body, how many women out of a hundred using a diaphragm were statistically likely to get pregnant and the medical term for the mouth of the cervix. One girl pointed out all the parts of the female reproductive system on a placard; another recited the stages of the ovulation cycle from day one to twenty-eight. There was just one problem with this performance: Although the results of their laboratory tests would not be available for fifteen more minutes, every last one of them was pregnant.

3   I always think of that day when someone suggests that sex education at school is a big part of the answer to the problem of teenage pregnancy. I happen to be a proponent of such programs; I think human sexuality is a subject for dispassionate study, like civics and ethics and dozens of other topics that have a moral component. I'd like my sons to know as much as possible about how someone gets pregnant, how pregnancy can be avoided, and what it means when avoidance techniques have failed.

4   I remember adolescence about as vividly as I remember anything, however, and I am not in the least convinced that that information alone will significantly alter the rate of teenage pregnancy. It seemed to me that day in the clinic, and on days I spent at schools and on street corners, that teenage pregnancy has a lot more to do with what it means to be a teenager than with how someone gets pregnant. When I was in high school, at the tail end of the sixties, there was a straightforward line on sex among my friends. Boys could have it; girls couldn't. A girl who was not a virgin pretended she was. A girl who was sleeping with her boyfriend, no matter how long-playing the relationship, pretended she was not.

5   It is the nature of adolescence that there is no past and no future, only the present, burning as fierce, bright, and merciless as a bare light bulb. Girls

had sex with boys because nothing seemed to matter except right now, not pregnancy, not parental disapprobation, nothing but those minutes, this dance, that face, those words. Most of them knew that pregnancy could result, but they assured themselves that they would be the lucky ones who would not get caught. Naturally, some of them were wrong, and in my experience they did one of three things: They went to Puerto Rico for a mysterious weekend trip; visited an aunt in some faraway state for three months and came back with empty eyes and a vague reputation; or got married, quickly, in Empire-waist dresses.

What seems to have changed most since then is that there is little philosophical 6 counterpoint, hypocritical or not, to the raging hormones of adolescence, and that so many of the once-hidden pregnancies are hidden no more.

Not long after the day at the family planning clinic, I went to a public high 7 school in the suburbs. In the girl's room was this graffito: Jennifer Is a Virgin. I asked the kids about it and they said it was shorthand for geek, nerd, weirdo, somebody who was so incredibly out of it that they were in high school and still hadn't had sex. If you were a virgin, they told me, you just lied about it so that no one would think you were that immature. The girls in the family planning clinic told me much the same thing—that everyone did it, that the boys wanted it, that not doing it made them seem out of it. The only difference, really, was that the girls in the clinic were poor and would have their babies, and the girls in the high school were well-to-do and would have abortions. Pleasure didn't seem to have very much to do with sex for either group. After she learned she was pregnant, one of the girls at the clinic said, without a trace of irony, that she hoped child-birth didn't hurt as much as sex had. Birth control was easily disposed of in both cases. The pill, the youngsters said, could give you a stroke; the IUD could make you sterile. A diaphragm was disgusting.

One girl told me the funniest thing her boyfriend—a real original thinker— 8 had told her: They couldn't use condoms because it was like taking a shower with a raincoat on. She was a smart girl and pretty, and I wanted to tell her that it sounded as if she was sleeping with a jerk who didn't deserve her. But that is the kind of basic fact of life that must be taught not in the classroom, not by a stranger, but at home by the family. It is this that, finally, I will try to teach my sons about sex, after I've explained fertile periods and birth control and all the other mechanics that are important to understand but never really go to the heart of the matter: I believe I will say that when you sleep with someone you take off a lot more than your clothes.

COMPREHENSION

1. Does Quindlen approve of sex education? Explain.
2. How does the writer characterize the attitude of adolescents regarding sex and pregnancy?
3. What advice or information about sex will the writer give her sons? Why?

RHETORIC

1. Why did Quindlen choose "Sex Ed" as a title? What is its significance in relation to the thesis?
2. What is Quindlen's thesis? Where is it contained in the essay? Is it directly stated or implied?
3. Is Quindlen's writing an argumentative essay? Support your position with citations from the text.
4. What point is the writer making through use of accumulated details in paragraph 2?
5. What does Quindlen mean by the term "moral component" in paragraph 3? Where else in the essay does she allude to it? How does she employ definition in this essay?
6. What does Quindlen mean by her final statement that "when you sleep with someone you take off a lot more than your clothes"? How does this ending serve to underscore the thesis of the essay?

WRITING

1. Write a paper analyzing the most common forms of birth control available and listing the advantages and disadvantages of each.
2. In an essay, consider possible solutions to the problem of teenage pregnancy. What role do you think sex education has in ameliorating the problem? Use support from the Quindlen essay if applicable.
3. **Writing an Argument:** Quindlen claims that sex education is like "civics" and "ethics" and should be taught in schools. Do you agree or disagree? Write an essay defending your position.

NETWORKING
Applying Digital and Multimedia Literacies

Interpreting Advocacy Group Web Sites: Explore each of the following Web sites, each of which is published by an advocacy group dedicated to preventing teen pregnancy. For each, sum up (in 1–2 sentences) its position on educating teens about sex. How does the site's various features, as well as its design; organization; and use of images, video, and links, contribute to its message?

- U.S. Department of Health and Human Services: http://www.policyalmanac.org/health/archive/hhs_teenage_pregnancy.shtml
- Stayteen.org: http://www.stayteen.org/teen-pregnancy
- The National Campaign to Prevent Teen and Unplanned Pregnancy: http://www.thenationalcampaign.org
- The Candie's Foundation, including videos featuring Bristol Palin: http://www.candiesfoundation.org/videos.html

The Next Kind of Integration

Emily Bazelon

Emily Bazelon *(b. 1971) is an American essayist and journalist as well as senior editor for the online magazine* Slate. *She was born in Philadelphia and graduated from Yale University in 1993 and Yale Law School in 2000. After law school, Bazelon served as a law clerk on the United States Court of Appeals for the First Circuit. Prior to joining the staff at* Slate, *she was a writer and senior editor at* Legal Affairs *magazine. Bazelon's writing focuses on law, family affairs, and women's issues, especially abortion rights; she is considered a prominent pro-choice advocate. Her writing has appeared in the* Atlantic, *the* Washington Post, *the* New Republic, *and elsewhere. This essay, which appeared in the* New York Times Magazine *in 2008, examines (as the title suggests) a fresh approach to affirmative action.*

In June of last year, a conservative majority of the Supreme Court, in a 5-to-4   1
decision, declared the racial-integration efforts of two school districts unconstitutional. Seattle and Louisville, Ky., could no longer assign students to schools based on their race, Chief Justice John Roberts wrote in his lead opinion in *Meredith v. Jefferson County School Board* (and its companion case, *Parents Involved in Community Schools v. Seattle School District No. 1*). Justice Stephen Breyer sounded a sad and grim note of dissent. Pointing out that the court was rejecting student-assignment plans that the districts had designed to stave off de facto resegregation, Breyer wrote that "to invalidate the plans under review is to threaten the promise of *Brown.*" By invoking *Brown v. Board of Education*, the court's landmark 1954 civil rights ruling, Breyer accused the majority of abandoning a touchstone in the country's efforts to overcome racial division. "This is a decision that the court and the nation will come to regret," he concluded.

Breyer's warning, along with even more dire predictions from civil rights   2
groups, helped place the court's ruling at the center of the liberal indictment of the Roberts court. In Louisville, too, the court's verdict met with resentment. Last fall, I asked Pat Todd, the assignment director for the school district of Jefferson County, which encompasses Louisville and its suburbs, whether any good could come of the ruling. She shook her head so hard that strands of blond hair loosened from her bun. "No," she said with uncharacteristic exasperation, "we're *already doing* what we should be."

Todd was referring to Louisville's success in distributing black and white stu-   3
dents, which it does more evenly than any district in the country with a comparable black student population; almost every school is between 15 and 50 percent African-American. The district's combination of school choice, busing and magnet programs has brought general, if not uniform, acceptance—rather than white

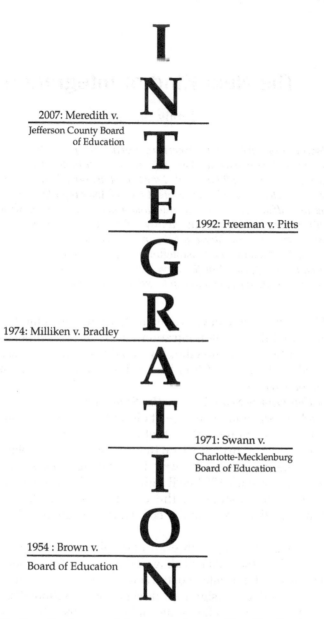

2007: Meredith v.
Jefferson County Board
of Education

1992: Freeman v. Pitts

1974: Milliken v. Bradley

1971: Swann v.
Charlotte-Mecklenburg
Board of Education

1954 : Brown v.
Board of Education

flight and disaffection, the legacy of desegregation in cities like Boston and Kansas City, Mo. The student population, which now numbers nearly 100,000, has held steady at about 35 percent black and 55 percent white, along with a small and growing number of Hispanics and Asians.

4   With its decision in *Meredith*, the court was forcing Louisville to rethink the way it would assign elementary-school students and, in the process, to confront some tricky questions. Is the purpose of integration simply to mix students of different colors for the sake of equity or to foster greater familiarity and comfort

among the races? Should integration necessarily translate into concrete gains like greater achievement for all students? If so, is mixing students by race the most effective mechanism for attaining it?

In Louisville, the achievement gap between whites and blacks is 20 percent- 5 age points at many grade levels. For Todd and her team, whatever their reservations about the decision in *Meredith,* coming up with an alternative assignment plan was an opportunity to think about a new kind of integration and what it might accomplish. In Louisville, integration would no longer focus solely on race but also on the barriers of class, of advantage and disadvantage. Other cities have been thinking along these lines. In the wake of the Supreme Court's decision, four other districts—Des Moines, Burlington, Vt., Omaha and Beaumont, Tex.— announced a switch to class-based integration. Seattle, too, is discussing setting aside 5 to 15 percent of the spots (a relatively small percentage) in desired high schools for low-income students. Some of the plans go into effect this fall; others, including Louisville's, begin a year from September.

The chief justice didn't address the idea of class-based integration in his opinion. 6 But Justice Anthony Kennedy did, in a separate concurrence. And because Kennedy cast the fifth vote for the majority, his view controls the law. Though he agreed with Roberts that public school districts should not make school assignments based on the race of individual students, he added that the court's ruling "should not prevent school districts from continuing the important work of bringing together students of different racial, ethnic and economic backgrounds."

How were schools to do this? Around the country, school-district lawyers 7 studied Kennedy's opinion and came to a rough consensus. In its amicus brief before the court, the Bush administration cited socioeconomic integration as a "race neutral" alternative to race-based assignment plans. Kennedy picked up on this, and no other justice wrote to contradict him. As a result, the school-district lawyers concluded that districts could assign an individual child to a school based on any kind of socioeconomic measure they chose—income, assets, parental education attainment. Districts could also be "race conscious," according to Kennedy, when they drew school boundaries, chose sites for new schools and directed money to particular programs. But in these situations, they would usually be limited to taking into account the racial composition of a neighborhood rather than the race of an individual student.

In terms of the court's jurisprudence, this is a major change. Race has been 8 the organizing principle of integration since *Brown v. Board of Education.* At the time of the court's ruling in *Meredith,* hundreds of districts were pursuing some sort of racial integration, with or without a court order, while only a few dozen at most were trying any form of socioeconomic integration. Over the years, racial integration has proved to have tangible benefits. Amy Stuart Wells, an education professor at Columbia Teachers College, has found that going to school with substantial numbers of white students helped black students to form cross-racial friendships and, by giving them access to white social networks, eventually to find work in jobs higher up the economic ladder.

9   However important these gains are, they are long-term and cannot be easily or quickly assessed. And increasingly, schools are held to a standard of immediately measurable outcomes. The No Child Left Behind Act, signed into law in 2002, demands student test scores that climb ever upward, with a mandate for all students to be proficient in reading and math by 2014. Test scores may not be the best way to assess the quality of a teacher or a school, but the pressure to improve scores, whatever its shortcomings, is itself on the rise. And if high test scores are the goal, it turns out, class-based integration may be the more effective tool.

10   Researchers have been demonstrating this result since 1966, when Congress asked James S. Coleman, a Johns Hopkins sociologist, to deliver a report on why the achievement of black students lagged far behind that of white ones. The expected answer was that more than a decade after *Brown,* black kids were still often going to inferior schools with small budgets. But Coleman found that the varying amount of money spent on schools didn't account for the achievement gap. Instead, the greater poverty of black families did. When high concentrations of poor kids went to school together, Coleman reported, all the students at the school tended to learn less.

11   How much less was later quantified. The Harvard sociologist Christopher Jencks reanalyzed Coleman's data in the 1970s and concluded that poor black sixth-graders in majority middle-class schools were 20 months ahead of poor black sixth-graders in majority low-income schools. The statistics for poor white students were similar. In the last 40 years, Coleman's findings, known informally as the Coleman Report, have been confirmed again and again. Most recently, in a 2006 study, Douglas Harris, an economist at the University of Wisconsin, found that when more than half the students were low-income, only 1.1 percent of schools consistently performed at a "high" level (defined as two years of scores in the top third of the U.S. Department of Education's national achievement database in two grades and in two subjects: English and math). By contrast, 24.2 percent of schools that are majority middle-class met Harris's standard.

12   There are, of course, determined urban educators who have proved that select schools filled with poor and minority students can thrive—in the right circumstances, with the right teachers and programs. But consistently good education at schools with such student bodies remains the rare exception. The powerful effect of the socioeconomic makeup of a student body on academic achievement has become "one of the most consistent findings in research on education," Gary Orfield, a U.C.L.A. education professor, and Susan Eaton, a research director at Harvard Law, wrote in their 1996 book, *Dismantling Desegregation.*

13   Most researchers think that this result is brought about by the advantages that middle-class students bring with them. Richard Kahlenberg of the Century Foundation lays them out in his 2001 book, *All Together Now*: more high-level classes, more parent volunteers and peers who on average have twice the vocabulary and half the behavioral problems of poor students. And, especially,

more good teachers. Harris, the economist, says that poor minority students still don't have comparable access to effective teachers, measured by preparation and experience. The question, then, is whether a plan that integrates a district by class as well as by race will help win for all its schools the kind of teaching that tends to be linked to achievement. "The evidence indicates that it would," Harris says.

Ronald Ferguson, an economist at the Kennedy School of Government at 14 Harvard, is less persuaded. His research highlights the nagging persistence of a racial achievement gap in well-off suburbs. "What happens with the achievement gap in a place like Louisville," he says, "will depend on how vigilant their leaders are to make sure high-quality instruction is delivered across the board." Such teaching is more likely in a school with a critical mass of middle-class parents, he concedes. But he stresses that to reap the benefits, poor kids have to be evenly distributed among classrooms and not just grouped together in the lowest tracks. "To the degree a district takes the kids who struggle the most academically and spreads them across different classrooms, they're making teachers' work more doable," he says. "And that may be the biggest effect."

Once they started looking for them, Todd and her colleagues saw the effects of class 15 division and poverty in the Jefferson County schools. Thorough racial desegregation had not, it seemed, led to thorough class desegregation. At 40 of 90 elementary schools in the district, 75 percent or more of the students came from low-income homes. And the effects of these high concentrations of poverty were striking: poor students in Louisville, black and white, fared worse when they attended schools filled with other poor kids. In elementary school, 61 percent of poor students at mostly low-income schools scored proficient in reading, compared with 71 percent of poor students at majority-middle-class schools. For math, the comparative proficiency rates were 52 percent to 63 percent. Because black students were disproportionately poor, they were more likely to attend high-poverty schools, and this was contributing to the district's pronounced black-white achievement gap.

Todd and her planners wanted to tackle the problem, she says, but they were 16 mindful of going too far in their efforts and losing the support of parents. In other districts—including Cincinnati, Evanston, Ill., Bibb County, Ga., and Madison, Wis.—the reaction to the Supreme Court's ruling had been to move to dismantle racial-integration programs. Todd and other school officials didn't want integration redefined to turn into no integration all. To get a handle on a new plan, Todd, turned to an heir of James Coleman: the researcher John Powell.

In the 1960s, Powell was one of the only African-American students in his ad- 17 vanced high-school classes in Detroit; when he became the class valedictorian, a teacher told him he wasn't the smartest student. He now directs the Kirwan Institute for the Study of Race and Ethnicity at Ohio State University, and he says he still thinks that race is a category with singular power. But he also appreciates the stark effects of segregating poor kids. "Ever since the Coleman Report, we've seen that there's a high correlation between good schools and schools that are integrated socioeconomically as well as racially," he says. "I think everyone agrees that what we need are more good schools."

18   In Louisville, Powell lent his expertise to Todd and her team. They came up with a computer-generated map that shows what Powell defines as the district's areas of "low opportunity." Todd, who is 61 and taught every grade in the Louisville schools before becoming an administrator, went over the map with me one day last December. The map used two different measures of class to identify Jefferson County's areas of disadvantage: income level and the educational attainment of adults. (To gauge disadvantage, districts embarking on class-based integration often use who among their students receives free or reduced lunch; Powell, however, contends that this is a relatively crude measure.) Using census data, Todd's team identified the zones in the district in which households fall below the average income and education levels, with fewer adults who have finished high school or gone to college or beyond. Finally, the team added one more factor: a higher-than-average number of minorities, almost all of them African-Americans or Hispanics.

19   The map's class-plus-race formula revealed a major partition. One region, which Todd's team called Geographic Area A, is a mermaid-shaped swath of blue, with its head in Louisville's West End, just south of the Ohio River, and its tail to the south. The region encompasses the parts of the district with a higher-than-average minority population, lower-than-average median income and lower-than-average adult educational attainment. In Geographic Area A live about 30 percent of Jefferson County's students. The rest of the county, colored yellow, included everyone else—the better off, better educated and whiter Geographic Area B.

20   What if the district were to use this map as a guide for school integration? Instead of maintaining each school as no less than 15 percent and no more than 50 percent black, Todd's team could propose that each school have no less than 15 percent and no more than 50 percent of students from Geographic Area A. By distributing students from the district's residential zones of disadvantage, the new plan would integrate the schools by class. There would no longer be 40 elementary schools with heavily poor-student populations. There could potentially be no such schools.

21   Given the presumed boost to test scores resulting from distributing poor students more widely, you might wonder why Todd's team retained race as an admissions factor at all. To answer this, it's worth considering the country's existing examples of purely class-based integration. The best known is in Wake County, N.C. With 134,000 students, the Wake County school district ranks 19 among the country's 20 largest, spanning 800 square miles that include bleak tracts in the city of Raleigh, mansion-filled suburban cul-de-sacs and rural roads ending in the fresh earth of a new subdivision. The student population is about half white, one-quarter African-American and one-quarter Hispanic, Asian and multiracial. The district voluntarily pursued race-based integration in the 1980s and '90s. In 2000, after the U.S. Court of Appeals for the Fourth Circuit began to frown on the use of race in student assignment—a harbinger of the Supreme Court's stance last year—the district began assigning kids to schools based on the income level of the geographic zone they lived in. The aim was to balance the schools so that no more than 40 percent of the students at each one come from a low-income area. (This year, the district added another goal: to have no more than 25 percent of students at any one school for whom English is a second language.)

Wake County adopted class-based integration with the hard-nosed goal of 22 raising test scores. The strategy was simple: no poor schools, no bad schools. And indeed, the district has posted striking improvements in the test scores of black and low-income students: in 1995, only 40 percent of the black students in Wake County in the third through eighth grades scored at grade level in state reading tests; by last year, the rate had almost doubled, to 82.5 percent. Statewide scores for black students also got better over the same time period, but not by as much. Wake County's numbers improve as students get older: 92 percent of all eighth graders read at or above grade level, including about 85 percent of black students and about 80 percent of low-income students. (Math scores are lower, following a statewide trend that reflects a change in the grading scale.) The district has achieved these results even as the share of low-income students over all has increased from about 30 percent a decade ago to about 40 percent today.

But the lessons of Wake County, Powell and Todd argue, don't apply every- 23 where. "In different districts, you have different geographic patterns," Powell says. "So you need different integration models to shop around." To begin with, Louisville is less affluent—more than 60 percent of its elementary school students receive free or reduced lunches, compared with Wake County's 40 percent. In Wake County, the vast majority of the poor students are black and Hispanic, and so mixing kids by class tightly correlates to mixing them by race. But in Jefferson County, more than a third of the kids who receive free or reduced lunches are white. As a result, redistributing students by class alone might still isolate them by race.

This is a limitation of class-based integration that holds true elsewhere. The city 24 of San Francisco, for instance, has undergone substantial racial resegregation since retooling its diversity plan to emphasize socioeconomic factors. Even in Wake County, the fraction of students in racially segregated schools has climbed a bit over the last decade, from 25 percent to 32 percent. A 2006 paper by the education researchers Sean Reardon, John T. Yun and Michal Kurlaender crunched census data across the country and concluded that "given the extent of residential racial segregation in the United States, it is unlikely that race-neutral income-integration policies will significantly reduce school racial segregation, although there is reason to believe that such policies are likely to have other beneficial effects on schooling."

Many big cities have a different problem. Simple demographics dictate that they 25 can't really integrate their schools at all, by either race or class. Consider the numbers for Detroit (74 percent low-income students; 91 percent black), Los Angeles (77 percent low-income; 85 percent black and Hispanic), New York City (74 percent; 63 percent), Washington (64 percent; 93 percent), Philadelphia (71 percent; 79 percent), Chicago (74 percent; 88 percent) and Boston (71 percent; 76 percent). In theory, big cities can diversify their schools by class and race by persuading many more middle-class and white parents to choose public school over private school or by combining forces with the well-heeled suburbs that surround them. But short of those developments, big cities are stuck. "The options have shrunk," says Tom Payzant, a former superintendent of schools in Boston.

Notably, there are a good many districts that have evaded this predicament. 26 They are particularly found in the South, in part because of a historical accident.

Because it was predominantly rural for longer, the South has more countywide school districts than the North. An unintended consequence was to ease the way to integration. Instead of city schools filled with poor black and Hispanic kids separated from a burgeoning ring of suburban districts stocked with affluent whites (and in some places, Asians), *one* district controls student assignment for the region.

27   Even in school districts with a mix of students of different races and income levels, however, there is no one-size-fits-all approach to socioeconomic integration, as underscored by the differences between Wake County and Jefferson County. Wake County's demographics entail that mixing kids by class, on its own, produces a fair degree of racial integration. Jefferson County's demographics don't necessarily work this way. And so civil rights lawyers suggest that districts configured like Jefferson County should continue to pursue racial diversity directly. They point to cities like Berkeley, Calif., which has an assignment plan that primarily relies on socioeconomics, but like Geography Area A also factors in the racial composition of a neighborhood to guard against resegregation along racial lines. "It's not either-or," says Anurima Bhargava, an education lawyer at the NAACP Legal Defense Fund.

28   In addition, there's a tacit liberal constitutional agenda at work in hybrid class-race approaches to integration: better to test Kennedy's opinion, with its support for the drawing of "race conscious" school boundaries, than to retreat further than is in fact required. "For Kennedy, there are ways of taking race into account," John Powell says. "It's just the method that's in question. How do you do it? We need to find out what's still permitted." He also points out that African-Americans are more likely than whites to be poor over generations—a bigger hurdle than a short stint in a low-income bracket.

29   The continuing attention to race aligns with the internal politics of Louisville and its suburbs. Many of today's parents grew up there and tend to remember and care about overcoming their county's Jim Crow legacy. In 1975, when a federal judge first ordered the city and its suburbs to desegregate, the Ku Klux Klan demonstrated, and the next day about 150 white protestors attacked eight school buses filled with black students. "We had tough times here when the buses burned," says Ann Elmore, a black member of the Jefferson County School Board. "We can still include race as a factor in our plan, and let me say I think it's important that we do."

30 Elsewhere in the United States, it is too soon to tell how the politics of class-based integration (Wake County) or class-plus-race (Jefferson County) will play out. Richard Kahlenberg makes the case for shifting integration policies primarily or solely to being class-based over the next decade or two. What's fair, he asks, about giving a spot in a coveted magnet program to the son of a South Asian college professor or an African-American politician over the daughter of a white waitress? Over time, such injustices threaten to sour white parents on the whole diversity enterprise, whereas giving poor kids a boost, whatever their color, is far less controversial. Polls at the time of the Supreme Court's 2003 decision in *Grutter v. Bollinger,* which concerned affirmative action at public universities, showed public support running 2 to 1 for giving poorer kids a leg up in going to college, as opposed to 2 to 1 against race-based preferences. In her majority opinion in the case, Justice Sandra Day

O'Connor famously said she thought that racial preferences would continue only for another 25 years. Barack Obama has said, looking ahead to his daughters' college applications, that they don't deserve an admissions break—an acknowledgment that the mix of race, affirmative action and privilege is a complicated one.

To catch on nationwide, however, class-based integration would have to gen- 31 erate momentum that it has so far lacked. In his State of the Union address in January, President Bush urged action "to help liberate poor children trapped in failing public schools." And yet a provision in the No Child Left Behind Act that theoretically allows students to transfer depends on the availability of open spaces elsewhere and has barely been utilized. The administration may have advocated class-based integration to the Supreme Court, but Bush officials haven't used their signature education law to make it happen.

If Congress were to revise No Child Left Behind to encourage more transfers 32 of poor students to middle-class schools, would poor students drag down their better-off peers? In the end, the prospects of class-based integration will probably rise or fall on the answer to this question. Socioeconomic integration may be good for the have-nots, but if the haves think their kids are paying too great a price, they will kill it off at the polls. Richard Kahlenberg argues that the key is to ensure there is a solidly middle-class majority at as many schools as possible. That majority will then set the tone, he argues. Kahlenberg says that more research is needed to pin down the percentage of middle-class kids that a school needs to have to serve all its students well. Maybe a school can go as high as 50 percent low-income without losing ground. Or maybe it's telling that in Wake County, a proposal to increase the ceiling for low-income students from 40 percent to 50 percent died a swift death last fall after concerted protest.

Whatever the exact answer, there is some support for the view that schools can 33 handle a substantial fraction of poor students without sacrificing performance. In Wake County, test scores of middle-class students have risen since instituting income-based integration. Additionally, Kahlenberg points out that middle-class students are generally less influenced by a school's environment because they tend to learn more at home, and that the achievement of white students has not declined in specific schools that experienced racial (and thus some class) desegregation.

Would schools need to track students by ability to protect middle-class stu- 34 dents, who are more often higher-achieving than their low-income peers? Perhaps not. In a 2006 longitudinal study of an accelerated middle-school math program in Nassau County, N.Y., which grouped students heterogeneously, the authors found that students at all achievement levels, as well as minority and low-income students, were more likely than the students in tracked classes to take advanced math in high school. In addition, the kids who came into the program as math whizzes performed as well as other top-achievers in homogenous classes.

This study underscores Ronald Ferguson's point about the value of seating stu- 35 dents of different backgrounds and abilities in class together, as opposed to tracking them. Still, it's worth noting that less than 15 percent of the students studied in Nassau County were low-income. So the math study doesn't tell us what happens to the high-achieving middle-class kids when close to half of their classmates aren't as well off.

36 At the end of February, Todd started showing the map of mermaid-shaped Geographic Area A, which she hoped to use to implement the new assignment system, to the parents of Jefferson County. Todd would start her presentation with quotes from Justice Kennedy and from Justice Breyer's dissent; she especially wanted to remind her audiences of the sentiment Breyer expressed by quoting former Justice Thurgood Marshall: "Unless our children begin to learn together, there is little hope that our people will ever learn to live together."

37   Todd's first stop was at a forum sponsored jointly by the Urban League and the NAACP groups associated with Louisville's black establishment. Most of their members supported the school district, but some clergy members who worked with the city's black youth spoke against it. The Rev. John Carter, associate minister at Green Street Baptist Church, pointed to the district's black-white achievement gap and called for a return to neighborhood schools and an earlier era of black self-reliance.

38   As more forums followed in high-school auditoriums across the county, white parents asked a different question: How would the new assignment plan affect their kids? Would they be forced to switch schools in second, third or fourth grade? "We like the diversity," a white parent named Niki Noe told me the next morning at her son's elementary school, St. Matthews. "But if we have to go to Chenoweth"—a school with lower test scores—"we'll pull out and go to private school."

39   That's a serious threat to the district's well-being, but one that Todd anticipated. She designed a grandfather clause for kids like Noe's, so that the new assignments would apply almost entirely to new students. Meanwhile, at every meeting, Todd polled parents on whether they cared about maintaining diverse schools. The University of Kentucky also conducted a telephone survey with 654 parents of elementary schoolers. In April, Todd called me, elated and relieved, with the results: 88 percent of parents supported enrollment guidelines "to ensure that students learn with students from different races and backgrounds." Todd said she had dropped Breyer's dissent in *Meredith* from her presentation; she was no longer feeling frustrated with the court. "It's been a personal emotional trek, but I think we've come out better for it," she said in May.

40   Carter, the proponent of black-self reliance, was feeling more at ease, too. He had come to see the virtue of mixing kids by income level. "Once I did the research, I was pretty impressed by the economic part of it," he said. Carter had taken note of the district's data showing that a switch to neighborhood schools, as he had first advocated, would mean that median household income would range from a high of more than $100,000 at the wealthiest school to about $8,300 at the poorest. A split between rich students and poor schools, he agreed, was the wrong path.

41   It is, of course, the path taken by most of the country. And yet at the end of May, the Jefferson County School Board voted unanimously to make Geographic Area A the basis for integrating elementary schools for the 2009 school year, a new chapter in the district's history. As the schools shift to the new class-plus-race formula, the district will closely watch the test scores of black students and poor students, hoping for an upsurge, and those of middle-class students, hoping

to see achievement hold steady. And if they do, maybe the court's decision in *Meredith* will come to seem less like a cause for regret and more like an unexpected opportunity.

COMPREHENSION

1. According to Bazelon, what are the positive and negative aspects of class-based integration?
2. Summarize the challenges confronting the Louisville, Kentucky school system in light of the Supreme Court decision in the case of *Meredith v. Jefferson County School Board.*
3. List the many school systems and districts mentioned by Bazelon. What do they share in common? How do they differ?

RHETORIC

1. What is the purpose of Bazelon's opening paragraph? Does she avoid a negative or critical tone? How does she avoid taking sides in the debate over affirmative action? Or do you think that she does reflect a bias? Explain.
2. Does Bazelon provide a thesis statement? Why or why not? How might her essay embody or imply a thesis?
3. Bazelon divides her essay into sections. How many are there? What is unique about each section? How do all sections relate to the writer's main subject?
4. Where do definition, comparison and contrast, and causal analysis appear as rhetorical strategies in this essay?
5. Consider the relationship of the introductory paragraph to the conclusion. Why do these beginning and end units provide an effective frame for the essay? Does Bazelon's voice or tone change? Explain.

WRITING

1. Compose a demographic case study of your high school or more generalized school district. Analyze your school experience based on the racial and socioeconomic composition of the school body. Draw conclusions about each group's academic performance.
2. Write your own response to the Supreme Court's decision in the Louisville school case. Conduct additional research if necessary.
3. **Writing an Argument:** Argue for or against the proposition that class-based integration is the solution to educational inequality in America.

NETWORKING
Applying Digital and Multimedia Literacies

Collaborating with one other class member, visit the blog that Bazelon maintains at *Slate* (*XXFactor* or *DoubleX*). Locate here and elsewhere Bazelon's writing on school bullying and cyber-bullying. Also find responses to Bazelon, especially to the writer's three-part series on the death of a fifteen-year-old girl in Hadley, Massachusetts who was the victim of bullying. Share your findings in a class discussion.

Unplugged: The Myth of Computers in the Classroom

David Gelernter

David Gelernter *(b. 1955) is a professor of computer science at Yale University. He is a leading figure in the field of human cognition and a seminal thinker in the field known as parallel computing. Gelernter, who was injured by a package sent by the Unabomber in 1993, is the author of* Mirror Worlds *(1991),* The Muse in the Machine *(1994),* 1939: The Lost World of the Fair *(1995), and* Machine Beauty *(1998). In the following essay, published in the* New Republic *in 1994, Gelernter offers a cogent analysis of the limits of technology in the classroom.*

1 Over the last decade an estimated $2 billion has been spent on more than 2 million computers for America's classrooms. That's not surprising. We constantly hear from Washington that the schools are in trouble and that computers are a godsend. Within the education establishment, in poor as well as rich schools, the machines are awaited with nearly religious awe. An inner-city principal bragged to a teacher friend of mine recently that his school "has a computer in every classroom . . . despite being in a bad neighborhood!"

2   Computers should be in the schools. They have the potential to accomplish great things. With the right software, they could help make science tangible or teach neglected topics like art and music. They help students form a concrete idea of society by displaying onscreen a version of the city in which they live—a picture that tracks real life moment by moment.

3   In practice, however, computers make our worst educational nightmares come true. While we bemoan the decline of literacy, computers discount words in favor of pictures and pictures in favor of video. While we fret about the decreasing cogency of public debate, computers dismiss linear argument and promote fast, shallow romps across the information landscape. While we worry about basic skills, we allow into the classroom software that will do a student's arithmetic or correct his spelling.

4 Take multimedia. The idea of multimedia is to combine text, sound and pictures in a single package that you browse on screen. You don't just *read* Shakespeare; you watch actors performing, listen to songs, view Elizabethan buildings. What's wrong with that? By offering children candy-coated books, multimedia is guaranteed to sour them on unsweetened reading. It makes the printed page look even more boring than it used to look. Sure, books will be available in the classroom, too—but they'll have all the appeal of a dusty piano to a teen who has a Walkman handy.

5   So what if the little nippers don't read? If they're watching Olivier instead, what do they lose? The text, the written word along with all of its attendant pleasures.

Besides, a book is more portable than a computer, has a higher-resolution display, can be written on and dog-eared and is comparatively dirt cheap.

Hypermedia, multimedia's comrade in the struggle for a brave new class- 6 room, is just as troubling. It's a way of presenting documents on screen without imposing a linear start-to-finish order. Disembodied paragraphs are linked by theme; after reading one about the First World War, for example, you might be able to choose another about the technology of battleships, or the life of Woodrow Wilson, or hemlines in the '20s. This is another cute idea that is good in minor ways and terrible in major ones. Teaching children to understand the orderly unfolding of a plot or a logical argument is a crucial part of education. Authors don't merely agglomerate paragraphs; they work hard to make the narrative read a certain way, prove a particular point. To turn a book or a document into hypertext is to invite readers to ignore exactly what counts—the story.

The real problem, again, is the accentuation of already bad habits. Dynamit- 7 ing documents into disjointed paragraphs is one more expression of the sorry fact that sustained argument is not our style. If you're a newspaper or magazine editor and your readership is dwindling, what's the solution? Shorter pieces. If you're a politician and you want to get elected, what do you need? Tasty sound bites. Logical presentation be damned.

Another software species, "allow me" programs, is not much better. These 8 programs correct spelling and, by applying canned grammatical and stylistic rules, fix prose. In terms of promoting basic skills, though, they have all the virtues of a pocket calculator.

In Kentucky, as *The Wall Street Journal* recently reported, students in grades 9 K–3 are mixed together regardless of age in a relaxed environment. It works great, the *Journal* says. Yes, scores on computation tests have dropped 10 percent at one school, but not to worry: "Drilling addition and subtraction in an age of calculators is a waste of time," the principal reassures us. Meanwhile, a Japanese educator informs University of Wisconsin mathematician Richard Akey that in his country, "calculators are not used in elementary or junior high school because the primary emphasis is on helping students develop their mental abilities." No wonder Japanese kids blow the pants off American kids in math. Do we really think "drilling addition and subtraction in an age of calculators is a waste of time"? If we do, then "drilling reading in an age of multimedia is a waste of time" can't be far behind.

Prose-correcting programs are also a little ghoulish, like asking a computer for 10 tips on improving your personality. On the other hand, I ran this article through a spell-checker, so how can I ban the use of such programs in schools? Because to misspell is human; to have no idea of correct spelling is to be semiliterate.

There's no denying that computers have the potential to perform inspiring feats in 11 the classroom. If we are ever to see that potential realized, however, we ought to agree on three conditions. First, there should be a completely new crop of children's software. Most of today's offerings show no imagination. There are hundreds of similar reading and geography and arithmetic programs, but almost nothing on electricity or physics or architecture. Also, they abuse the technical capacities of new media to glitz up old forms instead of creating new ones. Why not build a time-travel program that gives kids a feel for how history is structured by zooming you backward? A spectrum program that lets users twirl a frequency knob to see what happens?

12   Second, computers should be used only during recess or relaxation periods. Treat them as fillips, not as surrogate teachers. When I was in school in the '60s, we all loved educational films. When we saw a movie in class, everybody won: Teachers didn't have to teach, and pupils didn't have to learn. I suspect that classroom computers are popular today for the same reasons.

13   Most important, educators should learn what parents and most teachers already know: You cannot teach a child anything unless you look him in the face. We should not forget what computers are. Like books—better in some ways, worse in others—they are devices that help children mobilize their own resources and learn for themselves. The computer's potential to do good is modestly greater than a book's in some areas. Its potential to do harm is vastly greater, across the board.

COMPREHENSION

1. State Gelernter's thesis or claim in one sentence.
2. In the final paragraph, Gelernter defines what he believes to be the most important shortcoming of the computer as a teaching tool. Explain the reason why this weakness is so significant.
3. In your own words, explain the author's dislike of hypermedia as a pedagogic tool (as expressed in paragraph 6) and why the orderly arrangement of paragraphs in a book is superior to this newer technological capability.

RHETORIC

1. The introductory paragraph goes from a general fact to a specific quotation. What is the effect of this method of paragraph patterning?
2. Much of Gelernter's argument hinges on providing evidence that one medium is superior to another. Explain terms such as *linear argument* (paragraph 3), *agglomerate paragraphs* (paragraph 6), and *"allow me" programs* (paragraph 8). How do these terms help Gelernter prove his point?
3. The essay has a three-part structure, each section divided by space. How would you characterize the purpose of each section? How does the author use transitions to move from one section to the next?
4. Gelernter states that the overuse of computers in the classroom can hinder the development of clear thinking and reasoned argument. How clearly written is *his* essay? How reasoned is his argument? Gather evidence for your answer by reviewing the essay and determining whether each sentence seems to flow logically to the next and whether each paragraph seems to move reasonably to the next.
5. The author uses metaphors, similes, and other rhetorical devices. Explain the effectiveness of expressions such as "have all the appeal of a dusty piano to a teen who has a Walkman handy" (paragraph 4), "dynamiting documents" (paragraph 7), and "software species" (paragraph 8). Locate other unconventional descriptions.

6. Who is the intended audience for this essay? Educators? Parents? Students? Politicians? What evidence can you cite to back up your view?
7. What rhetorical device is Gelernter using in his title? What is the implicit meaning of the title?

WRITING

1. Visit the writing or reading computer lab in your school. As an objective observer, study the interaction of student and computer. Write a descriptive essay focusing on the demeanor and behavior of the student and the atmosphere of the classroom. If you wish, compare it to a traditional classroom.
2. Copy a paragraph from the essay, and enter it into a word-processing program that has a grammar-check function. Record any comments that the program makes in response to its evaluation of the writing. Do the computer's responses to the author's sentence structure make sense?

NETWORKING
Applying Digital and Multimedia Literacies

WRITING AN ARGUMENT   **Weighing the Potential of Smart Classrooms:** Select one of the teaching capabilities of modern computers—multimedia, hypertext, or spell- and grammar-check programs. Argue for the benefits of one of these features, noting how it could be used effectively in a smart classroom. Consider at least one counterargument to your position, and describe how you would rebut it.

When Bright Girls Decide That Math Is "a Waste of Time"

Susan Jacoby

Susan Jacoby (b. 1945) has worked as an educator and as a reporter for the Washington Post *and a columnist for the* New York Times. *As a freelance journalist in the former Soviet Union (from 1969 to 1971), she produced two books about her experiences. Jacoby now contributes to the* Nation *and* McCall's; *her books include* The Possible She *(1979), a collection of autobiographical essays;* Wild Justice: The Evolution of Revenge *(1983);* Half-Jew: A Daughter's Search for Her Buried Past *(2000); and* The Age of American Unreason *(2008). In this essay from the* New York Times, *Jacoby examines the reasons girls are often deficient in math and science.*

1   Susannah, a 16-year-old who has always been an A student in every subject from algebra to English, recently informed her parents that she intended to drop physics and calculus in her senior year of high school and replace them with a drama seminar and a work-study program. She expects a major in art or history in college, she explained, and "any more science or math will just be a waste of my time."

2   Her parents were neither concerned by nor opposed to her decision. "Fine, dear," they said. Their daughter is, after all, an outstanding student. What does it matter if, at age 16, she has taken a step that may limit her understanding of both machines and the natural world for the rest of her life?

3   This kind of decision, in which girls turn away from studies that would give them a sure footing in the world of science and technology, is a self-inflicted female disability that is, regrettably, almost as common today as it was when I was in high school. If Susannah had announced that she had decided to stop taking English in her senior year, her mother and father would have been horrified. I also think they would have been a good deal less sanguine about her decision if she were a boy.

4   In saying that scientific and mathematical ignorance is a self-inflicted female wound, I do not, obviously, mean that cultural expectations play no role in the process. But the world does not conspire to deprive modern women of access to science as it did in the 1930s, when Rosalyn S. Yalow, the Nobel Prize–winning physicist, graduated from Hunter College and was advised to go to work as a secretary because no graduate school would admit her to its physics department. The current generation of adolescent girls—and their parents, bred on old expectations about women's interests—are active conspirators in limiting their own intellectual development.

5   It is true that the proportion of young women in science-related graduate and professional schools, most notably medical schools, has increased significantly in the past decade. It is also true that so few women were studying advanced science and mathematics before the early 1970s that the percentage increase in female enrollment does not yet translate into large numbers of women actually working in science.

6   The real problem is that so many girls eliminate themselves from any serious possibility of studying science as a result of decisions made during the vulnerable period of midadolescence, when they are most likely to be influenced—on both conscious and subconscious levels—by the traditional belief that math and science are "masculine" subjects.

7   During the teen-age years the well-documented phenomenon of "math anxiety" strikes girls who never had any problem handling numbers during earlier schooling. Some men, too, experience this syndrome—a form of panic, akin to a phobia, at any task involving numbers—but women constitute the overwhelming majority of sufferers. The onset of acute math anxiety during the teen-age years is, as Stalin was fond of saying, "not by accident."

8   In adolescence girls begin to fear that they will be unattractive to boys if they are typed as "brains." Science and math epitomize unfeminine braininess in a way

that, say, foreign languages do not. High-school girls who pursue an advanced interest in science and math (unless they are students at special institutions like the Bronx High School of Science where everyone is a brain) usually find that they are greatly outnumbered by boys in their classes. They are, therefore, intruding on male turf at a time when their sexual confidence, as well as that of the boys, is most fragile.

A 1981 assessment of female achievement in mathematics, based on research conducted under a National Institute for Education grant, found significant differences in the mathematical achievements of 9th and 12th graders. At age 13 girls were equal to or slightly better than boys in tests involving algebra, problem solving and spatial ability; four years later the boys had outstripped the girls. 9

It is not mysterious that some very bright high-school girls suddenly decide that math is "too hard" and "a waste of time." In my experience, self-sabotage of mathematical and scientific ability is often a conscious process. I remember deliberately pretending to be puzzled by geometry problems in my sophomore year in high school. A male teacher called me in after class and said, in a baffled tone, "I don't see how you can be having so much trouble when you got straight A's last year in my algebra class." 10

The decision to avoid advanced biology, chemistry, physics and calculus in high school automatically restricts academic and professional choices that ought to be wide open to anyone beginning college. At all coeducational universities women are overwhelmingly concentrated in the fine arts, social sciences and traditionally female departments like education. Courses leading to degrees in science- and technology-related fields are filled mainly by men. 11

In my generation, the practical consequences of mathematical and scientific illiteracy are visible in the large number of special programs to help professional women overcome the anxiety they feel when they are promoted into jobs that require them to handle statistics. 12

The consequences of this syndrome should not, however, be viewed in narrowly professional terms. Competence in science and math does not mean one is going to become a scientist or mathematician any more than competence in writing English means one is going to become a professional writer. Scientific and mathematical illiteracy—which has been cited in several recent critiques by panels studying American education from kindergarten through college— produces an incalculably impoverished vision of human experience. 13

Scientific illiteracy is not, of course, the exclusive province of women. In certain intellectual circles it has become fashionable to proclaim a willed, aggressive ignorance about science and technology. Some female writers specialize in ominous, uninformed diatribes against genetic research as a plot to remove control of childbearing from women, while some well-known men of letters proudly announce that they understand absolutely nothing about computers, or, for that matter, about electricity. This lack of understanding is nothing in which women or men ought to take pride. 14

15   Failure to comprehend either computers or chromosomes leads to a terrible sense of helplessness, because the profound impact of science on everyday life is evident even to those who insist they don't, won't, can't understand why the changes are taking place. At this stage of history women are more prone to such feelings of helplessness than men because the culture judges their ignorance less harshly and because women themselves acquiesce in that indulgence.

16   Since there is ample evidence of such feelings in adolescence, it is up to parents to see that their daughters do not accede to the old stereotypes about "masculine" and "feminine" knowledge. Unless we want our daughters to share our intellectual handicaps, we had better tell them no, they can't stop taking mathematics and science at the ripe old age of 16.

COMPREHENSION

1. What reasons does Jacoby give for girls' deficiency in math and science?
2. Why does Jacoby call it a "self-inflicted female disability" (paragraph 3)?
3. What are the consequences of being math- and science-illiterate?

RHETORIC

1. Explain the main idea of Jacoby's essay in your own words.
2. Does the writer use abstract or concrete language in her essay? Cite examples to support your response.
3. What technique does Jacoby use in paragraphs 1 and 2? How does it aid in setting up her argument?
4. What rhetorical strategies does the writer use in her essay?
5. How does the use of dialogue aid in developing paragraph 10? What effect does the general use of dialogue have on Jacoby's point?
6. How is Jacoby's conclusion consistent in tone with the rest of the essay? Does it supply a sense of unity? Why or why not?

WRITING

1. Write an essay describing a school-related phobia you once had or continue to have (for example, in math, writing, physical education, or biology). Explain where you think that fear came from, how it affected your performance in school, and what you did (or are doing) to cope with the problem.
2. Write an essay about the need for math and science literacy in today's world. Use support from Jacoby's essay.
3. **Writing an Argument:** Write an argumentation essay proposing that math and science phobia is not "self-inflicted" but is caused primarily by the continued presence of sexism in society.

NETWORKING
Applying Digital and Multimedia Literacies

Analyzing How Design Informs a Web Site's Purpose: Find *BrainCake,* the Web site of the Girls' Math and Science Partnership. Watch the whole opening video, and then explore the site itself. How might an organization like this one address the issues Susan Jacoby raises in her essay? How does this Web site aim to make science and math (and the Carnegie Science Center's programs) seem appealing and important to girls ages 11–17—and to their parents? What questions might Jacoby have for its organizers?

Two Cheers for *Brown v. Board of Education*

Clayborne Carson

Clayborne Carson (b. 1944) is professor of history and director of the Martin Luther King Jr. Papers Project at Stanford University. He was born in Buffalo, New York, and educated at the University of California at Los Angeles, where he received his BA (1967), MA (1968), and PhD (1977). A specialist in African-American and civil rights history, Carson has written and edited numerous books, including In Struggle: SNCC and the Black Awakening of the 1960s *(1981, rev. ed. 1995), which received the Frederick Jackson Turner Award;* Eyes on the Prize: America's Civil Rights Years *(1987); and* The Malcolm X File *(1991). Asked by Coretta Scott King to handle her late husband's literary estate, Carson is the lead editor of* The Papers of Martin Luther King Jr. *(University of California Press). "It was a job you couldn't say no to," Carson said. In this essay, published in the* Journal of American History *in 2004, Carson offers an evaluation of the impact of a major Supreme Court decision on school segregation.*

My gratuitous opinion of *Brown v. Board of Education* (1954) is somewhat ambivalent and certainly arrives too late to alter the racial policies of the past fifty years. But for those of us who practice history, hindsight offers a far more reliable kind of wisdom than does foresight. We see clearly now that while the *Brown* decision informed the attitudes that have shaped contemporary American race relations, it did not resolve persistent disputes about the nation's civil rights policies. The Supreme Court's unanimous opinion in *Brown* broke decisively with the racist interpretations of traditional American values set forth in

Scott v. Sandford (1857) and *Plessy v. Ferguson* (1896), offering instead the optimistic "American Creed" that Gunnar Myrdal saw as the solution to "the Negro problem."[1] Like the two earlier landmark decisions, *Brown* overestimated the extent of ideological consensus among Americans and soon exacerbated racial and regional conflicts instead of resolving them. The Court's ruling against school segregation encouraged African Americans to believe that the entire structure of white supremacy was illegitimate and legally vulnerable. But the civil rights struggles *Brown* inspired sought broader goals than the decision could deliver, and that gap fostered frustration and resentment among many black Americans. In short, the decision's virtues and limitations reflect both the achievements and the failures of the efforts made in the last half century to solve America's racial dilemma and to realize the nation's egalitarian ideals.

2   That the *Brown* decision spurred subsequent civil rights progress seems apparent, but its impact and its significance as a source of inspiration are difficult to measure.[2] Although the Court's initial unwillingness to set firm timetables for school desegregation undercut *Brown*'s immediate impact, African Americans expanded the limited scope of the decision by individual and collective challenges to the Jim Crow system. Small-scale protests escalated during the decade after 1954, becoming a sustained mass movement against all facets of segregation and discrimination in the North as well as the South. Civil rights protests and litigation prompted Congress to pass the Civil Rights Act of 1964 and the Voting Rights Act of 1965, both of which extended the *Brown* decision's egalitarian principles well beyond education. The historic mass struggle that followed *Brown* ultimately destroyed the legal foundations of the Jim Crow system, and their destruction prepared the way for a still more far-reaching expansion of prevailing American conceptions of civil rights and of the role of government in protecting those rights. During the past forty years, women and many minority groups, including immigrants and people with disabilities, have gained new legal protections modeled on the civil rights gains of African Americans.[3]

---

[1] *Scott v. Sandford,* 19 How. 393 (1857); *Plessy v. Ferguson,* 163 U.S. 537 (1896); *Brown v. Board of Education,* 347 U.S. 483 (1954); Gunnar Myrdal, *An American Dilemma: The Negro Problem and Modern Democracy* (2 vols., New York, 1944).

[2] On *Brown*'s direct and indirect consequences, see, for example, Michael J. Klarman, "How *Brown* Changed Race Relations: The Backlash Thesis," *Journal of American History,* 81 (June 1994), 81–118. Klarman correctly points out that *Brown* had limited impact on school desegregation, especially in the Deep South, and stimulated southern white resistance to racial reform. He concludes that the contributions of *Brown* to the broader civil rights struggle were mostly indirect.

[3] Cf. Hugh Davis Graham, *The Civil Rights Era: Origins and Development of National Policy, 1960–1972* (New York, 1990); Hugh Davis Graham, *Collision Course: The Strange Convergence of Affirmative Action and Immigration Policy in America* (New York, 2002); and John D. Skrentny, *The Minority Rights Revolution* (Cambridge, Mass., 2002).

But the *Brown* decision also created racial aspirations that remain unreal- 3
ized. Although the decision may have been predicated on the notion of a shared
American creed, most white Americans were unwilling to risk their own racial
privileges to bring about racial equality. The decision was neither universally
accepted nor consistently enforced. "Instead, it provoked overwhelming resistance
in the South and only tepid interest in the North," the historian John Higham
insisted. "In the South the decision released a tidal wave of racial hysteria that
swept moderates out of office or turned them into demagogues. State and local
officials declined to obstruct a revival of the Ku Klux Klan. Instead, they
employed every conceivable device to maintain segregation, including harass-
ment and dissolution of NAACP chapters."[4] By the 1970s, resistance to school
desegregation had become national. Northern whites in Boston and elsewhere
demonstrated their unwillingness to send their children to predominantly black
schools or to allow large-scale desegregation that would drastically alter the
racial composition of "their" schools in "their" neighborhoods. Voters in the
states of Washington and California passed initiatives to restrict the right of
school boards (Washington) and state courts (California) to order busing to
achieve school desegregation (the Supreme Court later held the Washington
initiative unconstitutional). Nationwide, white racial resentments encouraged an
enduring shift of white voters from the Democratic to the Republican party. The
1964 election would be the last presidential contest in which the majority of
black voters and of white voters backed the same candidate. Since 1974, when
the Supreme Court's *Milliken v. Bradley* decision set limits on busing, the legal
meaning of desegregation has been scaled back to conform to American racial
and political realities.[5]

African Americans generally applauded the *Brown* decision when it was 4
announced, but the Court's failure to realize *Brown*'s bold affirmation of egalitarian ideals fueled subsequent black discontent and disillusionment. *Brown*
cited studies that demonstrated the harmful psychological impact of enforced
segregation on black students, reporting, "To separate them from others of
similar age and qualifications solely because of their race generates a feeling of
inferiority as to their status in the community that may affect their hearts and
minds in a way unlikely ever to be undone." Yet the Court did not offer an effective means to correct the problem it had identified. During the decades after

[4]John Higham, "Introduction: A Historical Perspective," in *Civil Rights and Civil Wrongs: Black-White Relations since World War II*, ed. John Higham (University Park, 1997), 4. See also Klarman, "How Brown Changed Race Relations"; Numan V. Bartley, *The Rise of Massive Resistance: Race and Politics in the South in the 1950s* (Baton Rouge, 1969); and Neil McMillen, *The Citizens' Council: Organized Resistance to the Second Reconstruction, 1954–1964* (Urbana, 1971).

[5]See Ronald P. Formisano, *Boston against Busing: Race, Class, and Ethnicity in the 1960s and 1970s* (Chapel Hill, 1991); and J. Anthony Lukas, *Common Ground: A Turbulent Decade in the Lives of Three American Families* (New York, 1985). *Washington v. Seattle School District*, 458 U.S. 457 (1982); *Crawford v. Los Angeles Board of Education*, 458 U.S. 527 (1982); *Milliken v. Bradley*, 418 U.S. 717 (1974). See Gary Orfield and Susan E. Eaton, *Dismantling Desegregation: The Quiet Reversal of* Brown v. Board of Education (New York, 1996).

Brown, most southern black children continued to suffer the psychological consequences of segregation, while a small minority assumed the often considerable psychological and physical risks of attending newly integrated public schools. Rather than bringing large numbers of black and white students together in public schools, the *Brown* decision—and the subsequent years of litigation and social conflict—enabled a minority of black students to attend predominantly white schools. Ten years after the *Brown* decision, according to data compiled by the U.S. Department of Education, almost 98 percent of southern black students still attended predominantly black schools. Now, at the beginning of the twenty-first century, the Court's ideal of educational opportunity as "a right which must be made available to all on equal terms" is still far from being realized. American schools, both public and private, are still highly segregated. According to a recent study, the typical Latino or black student in the United States still attends a school where members of minority groups are predominant.[6]

5   Certainly, the *Brown* decision's most significant deficiency is its failure to address the concerns of the majority of African American students who have been unable or unwilling to seek better educational opportunities by leaving predominantly black schools for predominantly white ones. While it opened the door for the Little Rock Nine, who desegregated Central High School in 1957, the *Brown* decision offered little solace to the hundreds of students who remained at Little Rock's all-black Horace Mann High School. When Arkansas officials reacted to desegregation by closing all of Little Rock's high schools, those students were denied even segregated educational opportunities.[7] With the encouragement of the lawyers for the National Association for the Advancement of Colored People's (NAACP) Legal Defense and Education Fund, the Supreme Court largely abandoned previous efforts to enforce the separate but equal mandate in order to adopt a narrowly conceived strategy for achieving equal educational opportunity through desegregation. The pre-*Brown* equalization effort had encouraged social scientists to develop increasingly sophisticated ways of measuring differences in the quality of schools. But during the 1950s, pro–civil rights scholars shifted their focus from the educational environment of black students in black schools to the psychological state of black students experiencing desegregation. The NAACP's initial strategy of forcing southern states to equalize facilities at all-black schools had resulted in tangible improvements, whereas the removal of racial barriers in public schools was advertised as offering intangible psychological gains.

---

[6]*Brown v. Board of Education,* 347 U.S. at 494, 493; Gary Orfield and Chungmei Lee, "*Brown* at Fifty: King's Dream or Plessy's Nightmare?" Jan. 17, 2004, *The Civil Rights Project, Harvard University.* <http://www.civilrightsproject.harvard.edu/research/reseg04/resegregation04.php> (April 4, 2004). In every region of the nation, at least 30% of black students still attend schools with less than 10% white enrollment. *Ibid.*

[7]Cf. Melba Beals, *Warriors Don't Cry: A Searing Memoir of the Battle to Integrate Little Rock's Central High* (New York, 1995); and Melba Beals, *White Is a State of Mind: A Memoir* (New York, 1995).

For Thurgood Marshall, who headed the NAACP legal staff, the equalization 6
effort had always been a means of achieving the ultimate goal of desegregation.
After the Supreme Court decided in *Sweatt v. Painter* (1950) that a makeshift segregated law school at a black college could not provide educational opportunities
equal to those offered by the University of Texas Law School, Marshall exulted,
"The complete destruction of *all* enforced segregation is now in sight." Despite
having attended predominantly black schools at every stage of his academic career, he saw segregation as a racial stigma that could not be removed by increased
state appropriations for Jim Crow schools. In the early 1950s he noted that social
scientists were "almost in universal agreement that segregated education produces inequality." He therefore concluded "that segregated schools, perhaps
more than any other single factor, are of major concern to the individual of public
school age and contribute greatly to the unwholesomeness and unhappy development of the personality of Negroes which the color caste system in the United
States has produced."[8]

Few African Americans would wish to return to the pre-*Brown* world of 7
legally enforced segregation, but in the half century since 1954, only a minority
of Americans has experienced the promised land of truly integrated public education. By the mid-1960s, with dual school systems still in place in many areas of
the Deep South, and with de facto segregation a recognized reality in urban areas,
the limitations of *Brown* had become evident to many of those who had spear-
headed previous civil rights struggles. The ideological gulf that appeared in
African American politics during the period was largely the result of efforts to
draw attention to the predominantly black institutions neglected in the drive for
racial integration. The black power movement arose in part as an effort by
African Americans to control and improve such institutions. Some black power
proponents exaggerated the benefits of racial separatism, but their extremism
can be best understood as a reaction against the unbalanced post-*Brown* strategy
of seeking racial advancement solely through integration. Although James S.
Coleman's landmark 1966 study of equality of educational opportunity found
that black children attending integrated schools did better than students attending predominantly black schools, it was by no means clear that the gap was the
result of interracial interactions rather than of differences in the socioeconomic
backgrounds of the students involved. By the late 1960s, growing numbers of
black leaders had concluded that improvement of black schools should take
priority over school desegregation. In 1967, shortly before the National
Advisory Commission on Civil Disorders warned that the United States was
"moving toward two societies, one white, one black—separate and unequal,"
Martin Luther King Jr. acknowledged the need to refocus attention, at least in
the short run, on "schools in ghetto areas." He also insisted that "the drive for

---

[8]*Sweatt v. Painter,* 339 U.S. 629 (1950); *Baltimore Afro-American,* June 17, 1950, quoted in Juan
Williams, *Thurgood Marshall: American Revolutionary* (New York, 1998), 195; Thurgood Marshall,
"An Evaluation of Recent Efforts to Achieve Racial Integration in Education through Resort to the
Courts," *Journal of Negro Education,* 21 (Summer 1952), 316–27, esp. 322.

immediate improvements in segregated schools should not retard progress toward integrated education later." Even veterans of the NAACP's legal campaign
had second thoughts. *"Brown* has little practical relevance to central city
blacks," Constance Baker Motley commented in 1974. "Its psychological and
legal relevance has already had its effect."[9]

8   Black power advocates sometimes sought to replace the narrow strategy of
achieving racial advancement through integration with the equally narrow strategy
of achieving it through racial separatism. In both instances, claims of psychological gains often substituted for measurable racial advancements, but the continued
popularity of Afrocentric educational experiments indicates that many African
Americans now see voluntary segregation as psychologically uplifting. Having
personally experienced the burden of desegregating numerous classrooms and
having watched my son move with great success from a predominantly black
college to a predominantly white law school, I am skeptical of sweeping claims
about the impact of racial environment on learning. While believing that debates
among African Americans during the last half century about their destiny have
been useful, I regret that those debates have often exacerbated ideological conflict
rather than encouraging us toward collective action. Rather than having to choose
between overcoming racial barriers and improving black community institutions,
we should be able to choose both.

9   In hindsight, the nation would have been better served if the *Brown* decision
had evinced a more realistic understanding of the deep historical roots of America's
racial problems—perhaps a little more familiarity with the writings of W. E. B.
DuBois and Carter C. Woodson as well as those of Myrdal and his colleagues.
Rather than blandly advising that desegregation of public schools be achieved with
"all deliberate speed," the Supreme Court—and the NAACP lawyers who argued
before it—should have launched a two-pronged attack, not only against racial segregation but also against inferior schools, whatever their racial composition. Such an
attack would have heeded the admonition that DuBois offered in 1935, soon after
his forced resignation as editor of the NAACP's journal, the *Crisis:*

> Theoretically, the Negro needs neither segregated schools nor mixed schools.
> What he needs is Education. . . . Other things being equal, the mixed school is the
> broader, more natural basis for the education of all youth. It gives wider contacts;
> it inspires great self-confidence; and suppresses the inferiority complex. But other
> things seldom are equal, and in that case, Sympathy, Knowledge, and the Truth,
> outweigh all that the mixed school can offer.[10]

[9]J. S. Coleman et al., *Equality of Educational Opportunity* (Washington, 1966), *passim; Report
of the National Advisory Commission on Civil Disorders* (New York, 1968), 1; Martin Luther
King Jr., *Where Do We Go from Here: Chaos or Community?* (New York, 1967), 228. For
Constance Baker Motley's statement (quoted from the *New York Times,* May 13, 1974), see
James T. Patterson, Brown v. Board of Education: *A Civil Rights Milestone and Its Troubled
Legacy* (New York, 2001), 168.

[10]*Brown v. Board of Education,* 349 U.S. 294 (1955); W. E. B. DuBois, "Does the Negro Need Separate
Schools?" *Journal of Negro Education,* 4 (July 1935), in *The Oxford W. E. B. DuBois Reader,* ed. Eric J.
Sundquist (New York, 1996), 431.

Because the *Brown* decision was a decisive departure from *Plessy*'s separate 10
but equal principle, it was an important turning point in African American history.
Nevertheless, fifty years later the Court's assumptions about the psychological
consequences of legally enforced segregation seem dated. The Jim Crow system
no longer exists, but most black American schoolchildren still attend predominantly black public schools that offer fewer opportunities for advancement than
typical predominantly white public schools. Moreover, there is no contemporary
civil rights movement able to alter that fact. Yet, if *Brown* represents a failed attempt to achieve comprehensive racial advancement, the opinion nonetheless
still challenges us by affirming egalitarian ideals that remain relevant: "In these
days, it is doubtful that any child may reasonably be expected to succeed in life if
he is denied the opportunity of an education. Such an opportunity, where the
state has undertaken to provide it, is a right which must be made available to all
on equal terms."[11]

COMPREHENSION

1. According to Carson, what are the benefits and shortcomings of the *Brown v. Board of Education* decision? Why does he give two cheers (instead of the traditional three cheers) for the Supreme Court's 1954 verdict?
2. What are the psychological effects of both segregation and desegregation on black students?
3. Why does Carson say that the impact of the *Brown* decision is difficult to measure? What evidence does he provide to support this assessment?

RHETORIC

1. Who is Carson's audience for this essay? How does he fit his style to the expectations he holds for this specific audience? Provide examples of vocabulary, syntax, and abstract language to support your response. Why would the article also be of interest to a more general audience?
2. Carson lays out a well-informed argument. What is his claim or major proposition? What are his warrants? What is his support? How does he deal with opposing viewpoints? What conclusions does he draw to convince the reader of his position?
3. Analyze the pattern of cause and effect that Carson presents in this essay.
4. Carson has very strong topic sentences at the start of virtually every paragraph. List these topic sentences, and then show how they control the flow of his thoughts within paragraphs while at the same time advancing his argument.
5. Examine the writer's footnotes. What are his sources? What range and variety of evidence do these notes suggest?

---

[11]"*Brown v. Board of Education of Topeka:* Opinion on Segregation Laws," in *Civil Rights and African Americans: A Documentary History,* ed. Albert P. Blaustein and Robert I. Zangrando (Evanston, 1991), 436.

WRITING

1. Using Carson's article as a reference point, write an essay describing the ethnic and racial composition of your former high school or the college you now attend. How does this demographic profile support some of Carson's key insights into *Brown v. Board of Education?*
2. Write an essay in which you offer your own analysis of the ways in which varieties of discrimination you encounter in education can have psychological consequences. Feel free to offer personal experience to support your analysis.
3. **Writing an Argument:** Unlike Carson, who argues both sides of the *Brown* decision in terms of the historical aftermath, write an argumentative essay in which you defend or criticize the results of *Brown* since 1954. Conduct research and collaborate with class members if you wish.

NETWORKING
Applying Digital and Multimedia Literacies

Supporting an Argument with Visuals: Enhance your response to the Writing an Argument assignment above by incorporating three images from the electronic exhibit *In Pursuit of Freedom & Equality: Kansas and the African American Public School Experience, 1855–1955* (find this by doing a Google search). Be sure to credit your sources and not to misuse the images; that said, you can certainly debate what they *mean* in this argument and either draw on or argue with the way they are portrayed in the exhibit.

Synthesis: Connections for Critical Thinking

1. Compare and contrast the rhetoric of the personal essay as it is represented in Rodriguez's "The Lonely, Good Company of Books" with the rhetoric of such expository and argumentative essays as Quindlen's "Sex Ed" or Carson's "Two Cheers for *Brown v. Board of Education.*"
2. Analyze an event in your education when you had a disagreement with a teacher or administrator. Explain and explore whether the differences in viewpoint were based on emotional perspective, intellectual perspective, or both.
3. Select the essay in this chapter you find most pertinent to your life as a student. Explain why you selected the essay, and explore your intellectual and emotional responses to it.
4. Does your college seem to support Jacoby's views regarding the educational lives of women? Explain why or why not.
5. Argue for or against the view that the publicized sexual activity of politicians and other celebrities makes the decision whether to keep sex education out of the schools entirely moot.
6. It is 2050. Write an essay in which you explore the demographics of a typical college classroom. Refer to the ideas contained in the Bazelon, Jacoby, and Carson essays.

7. Write an essay that classifies at least three educational issues that the authors in this chapter examine. Establish a clear thesis to unify the categories you establish.
8. Analyze the patterns and techniques used by Rose, Gelernter, and Jacoby to advance their claims about education today.

NETWORKING
Applying Digital and Multimedia Literacies

---

1. Do an online search for *sex education* and *France* (or another country of your choice). Write an essay describing the policies of your chosen country on the topic.
2. Argue for or against the proposition that despite Gelernter's warnings about the purported shortcomings of computers in the classroom, in the future many students will prefer to obtain a degree completely via computer and the Internet. To support your viewpoint, research and report on at least three online sites that offer college degrees.

chapter 5

Family Life and Gender Roles

How Do We Become Who We Are?

Every culture has its own ideas about what identity is, how it is formed, and where it comes from. What is the influence of family, of environment, of gender, and, as we saw in Chapter 4, of education on the creation of identity? Although it is challenging to reconcile these various cross-cultural ideas, the writers in this chapter attempt to make sense of identity from the perspectives of family and gender, and they invite readers to liberate themselves from the tyranny of stereotyping.

Families nourish us during childhood, and the values our families seek to maintain usually affect our identities in powerful ways, whether we adopt them wholly, modify them, or reject them outright. Writers have always been aware of the importance of the family in human development and behavior, and have written about it from various perspectives, using narration, sociological and psychological analysis, and cultural criticism, among other approaches. Tolstoy wrote that "happy families are all alike; every unhappy family is unhappy in its own way." But we shall discover that Tolstoy had a limited view of family life and its values—probably circumscribed by the mores of the time he lived in. Some of our finest essayists and observers of social life today demonstrate in this chapter that what constitutes the definition of a family is up for grabs as we begin the new millennium.

The family is one of the few institutions that we find in every society throughout the world, at least every thriving society. Anthropologists, sociologists, and psychologists tell us that family patterns are exceedingly diverse even in the same societies. In the past and even more so today, children grow up in many ways: in nuclear and in nontraditional households; in single-parent and in dual-parent arrangements; in extended families and in blended families; and in patriarchal and matriarchal, heterosexual and homosexual, monogamous and polygamous situations. And the dynamics of family life assume added dimension as we move across cultures, studying European families, African American families, Hispanic families, Asian families, and so forth. Even within these groups, we find variables that affect family life and values, such as economic class, social class, and educational levels.

Unlike in previous periods in our history, Americans today seem to be groping for a definition of what constitutes the happy family. With the influences of the media and of peer pressure on children, the rise in the number of latchkey children, and the fact that there is a growing diversity of cultures in America owing to the new wave of immigration, the family appears to be less of a traditional haven than it was even a generation ago. This chapter contains vivid accounts of the long-standing bonds within the family that have been treasured for their capacity to build values of love and sharing. It also contains essays that demonstrate how family life is filled with emotional complexities and conflicts that the child must negotiate as she or he finds meaning and attempts to construct an identity. Each writer, whether writing narration, exposition, or argumentation, shows how significant the family is for the development of our values, personalities, and lifestyles.

As much as our identities are shaped by powerful institutional forces like the family, what we are might be even more powerfully determined by the forces of sexuality and gender. Freud asserted that human behavior is rooted in sexuality, that gender (rather than family or school or any social institution) is destiny. Clearly, notions of what it means to be a man or a woman have an impact on the construction of our identities.

The identity issues discussed in this chapter might prove to be controversial, but they will encourage you to confront your sense of identity. These essays are like a mirror in which you can see and evaluate what you really are.

PREVIEWING THE CHAPTER

As you read the essays in this chapter and respond to them in discussion and writing, consider the following questions:

- What form of rhetoric is the author using: narration, exposition, or argumentation? Why is this form appropriate for the author's purpose?
- What perspective does the writer take on the subject of identity formation? Is the writer optimistic, pessimistic, or something else?
- What are the cultural, social, and economic issues addressed in the essay?
- How do you regard the authority of the author? Does she or he seem to be speaking from experience and knowledge? In essays that explain or argue, does the evidence appear substantial or questionable? Explain.
- What stylistic devices does the author employ to re-create a memory, explain a function, or argue a stance regarding an issue of identity?
- Which essays appear alike in purpose and method, and why?
- What have you learned or discovered about your own identity from reading these essays?
- Do you prefer one rhetorical form over another—for example, personal narration over argumentation? If so, why?

Classic and Contemporary Images

HOW DO WE RESPOND TO MARRIAGE?

Using a Critical Perspective   What was your first impression of Brueghel's *Rustic Wedding* and Elise Amendola's *Gay Marriage?* What details do you see? What senses do the artist and the photographer draw on to convey the atmosphere of the wedding? What does each want to say about the institution of marriage? How do you know?

The Flemish artist Pieter Brueghel the Elder (1525–1569) was one of the greatest painters of the 16th century and was renowned for his exuberant depictions of peasant life. His son Pieter Brueghel the Younger (1564–1638) copied many of his father's works and also painted religious subjects. He was responsible for *Rustic Wedding*, shown here.

Hillary, left, and Julie Goodridge, lead plaintiffs in the landmark Massachusetts gay marriage lawsuit, receive their wedding rings from their daughter, Annie, 8, as Unitarian Reverend William Sinkford presides over their marriage ceremony in Boston during the first day of state-sanctioned gay marriage in the United States on May 17, 2004.

✳

Classic and Contemporary Essays
HOW DOES CHILDHOOD SHAPE US?

E. B. White and Ann Hood represent two generations, but each writer was raised with enduring values regarding the function, structure, and role of the family. Both authors are
superb stylists. White writes in clear, elegiac prose that marches in a quiet, even rhythm.
Tradition is to be treasured; continuity is to be celebrated. For White, it seems, pleasure
derives from connectivity and permanence—in nature as well as family life. Like E. B. White,
the contemporary novelist and essayist Ann Hood recaptures a sense of the past and family
life through a style that is purposefully fast-paced. Hood's site of memory is not a lake in
Maine as it is in White's essay, but rather a road that she travels time and again. The route
that she takes is as familiar to her as the lake is to White. And both lake and road are
symbolic of the creative effort by these two writers to recapture the past—a tapestry of
childhood and family life that can be recreated through the very act of writing.

✴

Once More to the Lake

E. B. White

E(lwyn) B(rooks) White (1899–1985), perhaps the finest American essayist of the
20th century, was at his most distinctive in his treatments of people and nature.
A recipient of the National Medal for Literature, and associated for years with the New
Yorker, *White is the author of* One Man's Meat *(1942),* Here Is New York *(1949),*
and The Second Tree from the Corner *(1954), among numerous other works. He*
was also one of the most talented writers of literature for children, the author of
Stuart Little *(1945),* Charlotte's Web *(1952), and* The Trumpet of the Swan *(1970).*
In this essay, White combines narration and description to make a poignant and
vivid statement about past and present, youth and age, life and death.

1 One summer, along about 1904, my father rented a camp on a lake in Maine and
took us all there for the month of August. We all got ringworm from some kittens
and had to rub Pond's Extract on our arms and legs night and morning, and my
father rolled over in a canoe with all his clothes on; but outside of that the vacation
was a success and from then on none of us ever thought there was any place
in the world like that lake in Maine. We returned summer after summer—always on
August 1st for one month. I have since become a saltwater man, but sometimes
in summer there are days when the restlessness of the tides and the fearful cold
of the sea water and the incessant wind which blows across the afternoon and into

the evening make me wish for the placidity of a lake in the woods. A few weeks ago this feeling got so strong I bought myself a couple of bass hooks and a spinner and returned to the lake where we used to go, for a week's fishing and to revisit old haunts.

I took along my son, who had never had any fresh water up his nose and who 2 had seen lily pads only from train windows. On the journey over to the lake I began to wonder what it would be like. I wondered how time would have marred this unique, this holy spot—the coves and streams, the hills that the sun set behind, the camps and the paths behind the camps. I was sure the tarred road would have found it out and I wondered in what other ways it would be desolated. It is strange how much you can remember about places like that once you allow your mind to return into the grooves which lead back. You remember one thing, and that suddenly reminds you of another thing. I guess I remembered clearest of all the early mornings, when the lake was cool and motionless, remembered how the bedroom smelled of the lumber it was made of and of the wet woods whose scent entered through the screen. The partitions in the camp were thin and did not extend clear to the top of the rooms, and as I was always the first up I would dress softly so as not to wake the others, and sneak out into the sweet outdoors and start out in the canoe, keeping close along the shore in the long shadows of the pines. I remembered being very careful never to rub my paddle against the gunwale for fear of disturbing the stillness of the cathedral.

The lake had never been what you would call a wild lake. There were cottages 3 sprinkled around the shores, and it was in farming country although the shores of the lake were quite heavily wooded. Some of the cottages were owned by nearby farmers, and you would live at the shore and eat your meals at the farmhouse. That's what our family did. But although it wasn't wild, it was a fairly large and undisturbed lake and there were places in it which, to a child at least, seemed infinitely remote and primeval.

I was right about the tar: It led to within half a mile of the shore. But when I 4 got back there, with my boy, and we settled into a camp near a farmhouse and into the kind of summertime I had known, I could tell that it was going to be pretty much the same as it had been before—I knew it, lying in bed the first morning, smelling the bedroom, and hearing the boy sneak quietly out and go off along the shore in a boat. I began to sustain the illusion that he was I, and therefore, by simple transposition, that I was my father. This sensation persisted, kept cropping up all the time we were there. It was not an entirely new feeling, but in this setting it grew much stronger. I seemed to be living a dual existence. I would be in the middle of some simple act, I would be picking up a bait box or laying down a table fork, or I would be saying something, and suddenly it would be not I but my father who was saying the words or making the gesture. It gave me a creepy sensation.

We went fishing the first morning. I felt the same damp moss covering the 5 worms in the bait can, and saw the dragonfly alight on the tip of my rod as it hovered a few inches from the surface of the water. It was the arrival of this fly that convinced me beyond any doubt that everything was as it always had been, that the years were a mirage and there had been no years. The small waves were the same, chucking the rowboat under the chin as we fished at anchor, and the boat was the same boat, the same color green and the ribs broken in the same place, and under the floor boards the same fresh-water leavings and debris—the dead hellgrammite, the wisps of moss, the rusty discarded fishhook, the dried blood from yesterday's catch. We stared silently at the tips of our rods, at the dragonflies that came and went. I lowered the tip of mine into the water, tentatively, pensively dislodging the fly, which darted two feet away, poised, darted two feet back, and came to rest again a little farther up the rod. There had been no years between the ducking of this dragonfly and the other one—the one that was part of memory. I looked at the boy, who was silently watching his fly, and it was my hands that held his rod, my eyes watching. I felt dizzy and didn't know which rod I was at the end of.

6   We caught two bass, hauling them in briskly as though they were mackerel, pulling them over the side of the boat in a businesslike manner without any landing net, and stunning them with a blow on the back of the head. When we got back for a swim before lunch, the lake was exactly where we had left it, the same number of inches from the dock, and there was only the merest suggestion of a breeze. This seemed an utterly enchanted sea, this lake you could leave to its own devices for a few hours and come back to, and find that it had not stirred, this constant and trustworthy body of water. In the shallows, the dark, water-soaked sticks and twigs, smooth and old, were undulating in clusters on the bottom against the clean ribbed sand, and the track of the mussel was plain. A school of minnows swam by, each minnow with its small individual shadow, doubling the attendance, so clear and sharp in the sunlight. Some of the other campers were in swimming, along the shore, one of them with a cake of soap, and the water felt thin and clear and unsubstantial. Over the years there had been this person with the cake of soap, this cultist, and here he was. There had been no years.

7   Up to the farmhouse to dinner through the teeming, dusty field, the road under our sneakers was only a two-track road. The middle track was missing, the one with the marks of the hooves and the splotches of dried, flaky manure. There had always been three tracks to choose from in choosing which track to walk in; now the choice was narrowed down to two. For a moment I missed terribly the middle alternative. But the way led past the tennis court, and something about the way it lay there in the sun reassured me; the tape had loosened along the back-line, the alleys were green with plantains and other weeds, and the net (installed in June and removed in September) sagged in the dry noon, and the whole place steamed with midday heat and hunger and emptiness. There was a choice of pie for dessert, and one was blueberry and one was apple, and the waitresses were the same country girls, there having been no passage of time, only the illusion of it as in a dropped curtain—the waitresses were still fifteen; their hair had been washed, that was the only difference—they had been to the movies and seen the pretty girls with the clean hair.

8   Summertime, oh summertime, pattern of life indelible, the fade-proof lake, the woods unshatterable, the pasture with the sweetfern and the juniper forever and ever, summer without end; this was the background, and the life along the

shore was the design, the cottagers with their innocent and tranquil design, their tiny docks with the flagpole and the American flag floating against the white clouds in the blue sky, the little paths over the roots of the trees leading from camp to camp and the paths leading back to the outhouses and the can of lime for sprinkling, and at the souvenir counters at the store the miniature birch-bark canoes and the post cards that showed things looking a little better than they looked. This was the American family at play, escaping the city heat, wondering whether the newcomers in the camp at the head of the cove were "common" or "nice," wondering whether it was true that the people who drove up for Sunday dinner at the farmhouse were turned away because there wasn't enough chicken.

It seemed to me, as I kept remembering all this, that those times and those 9 summers had been infinitely precious and worth saving. There had been jollity and peace and goodness. The arriving (at the beginning of August) had been so big a business in itself, at the railway station the farm wagon drawn up, the first smell of the pine-laden air, the first glimpse of the smiling farmer, and the great importance of the trunks and your father's enormous authority in such matters, and the feel of the wagon under you for the long ten-mile haul, and at the top of the last long hill catching the first view of the lake after eleven months of not seeing this cherished body of water. The shouts and cries of the other campers when they saw you, and the trunks to be unpacked, to give up their rich burden. (Arriving was less exciting nowadays, when you sneaked up in your car and parked it under a tree near the camp and took out the bags and in five minutes it was all over, no fuss, no loud wonderful fuss about trunks.)

Peace and goodness and jollity. The only thing that was wrong now, really, 10 was the sound of the place, an unfamiliar nervous sound of the outboard motors. This was the note that jarred, the one thing that would sometimes break the illusion and set the years moving. In those other summertimes all motors were inboard; and when they were at a little distance, the noise they made was a sedative, an ingredient of summer sleep. They were one-cylinder and two-cylinder engines, and some were make-and-break and some were jump-spark, but they all made a sleepy sound across the lake. The one-lungers throbbed and fluttered, and the twin-cylinder ones purred and purred, and that was a quiet sound too. But now the campers all had outboards. In the daytime, in the hot mornings, these motors made a petulant, irritable sound; at night, in the still evening when the afterglow lit the water, they whined about one's ears like mosquitoes. My boy loved our rented outboard, and his great desire was to achieve singlehanded mastery over it, and authority, and he soon learned the trick of choking it a little (but not too much), and the adjustment of the needle valve. Watching him I would remember the things you could do with the old one-cylinder engine with the heavy flywheel, how you could have it eating out of your hand if you got really close to it spiritually. Motor boats in those days didn't have clutches, and you would make a landing by shutting off the motor at the proper time and coasting in with a dead rudder. But there was a way of reversing them, if you learned the trick, by cutting the switch and putting it on again exactly on the final dying revolution of the flywheel, so that it would kick back against compression and begin reversing.

Approaching a dock in a strong following breeze, it was difficult to slow up sufficiently by the ordinary coasting method, and if a boy felt he had complete mastery over his motor, he was tempted to keep it running beyond its time and then
reverse it a few feet from the dock. It took a cool nerve, because if you threw the
switch a twentieth of a second too soon you would catch the flywheel when it still
had speed enough to go up past center, and the boat would leap ahead, charging
bull-fashion at the dock.

11   We had a good week at the camp. The bass were biting well and the sun
shone endlessly, day after day. We would be tired at night and lie down in the
accumulated heat of the little bedrooms after the long hot day and the breeze
would stir almost imperceptibly outside and the smell of the swamp drift in
through the rusty screens. Sleep would come easily and in the morning the red
squirrel would be on the roof, tapping out his gay routine. I kept remembering
everything, lying in bed in the mornings—the small steamboat that had a long
rounded stern like the lip of a Ubangi, and how quietly she ran on the moonlight
sails, when the older boys played their mandolins and the girls sang and we ate
doughnuts dipped in sugar, and how sweet the music was on the water in the
shining night, and what it had felt like to think about girls then. After breakfast
we would go up to the store and the things were in the same place—minnows in
a bottle, the plugs and spinners disarranged and pawed over by the youngsters
from the boys' camp, the fig newtons and the Beeman's gum. Outside, the road
was tarred and cars stood in front of the store. Inside, all was just as it had always
been, except there was more Coca Cola and not so much Moxie and root beer
and birch beer and sarsaparilla. We would walk out with a bottle of pop apiece
and sometimes the pop would backfire up our noses and hurt. We explored the
streams, quietly, where the turtles slid off the sunny logs and dug their way into
the soft bottom, and we lay on the town wharf and fed worms to the tame bass.
Everywhere we went I had trouble making out which was I, the one walking at
my side, the one walking in my pants.

12   One afternoon while we were there at that lake a thunderstorm came up. It
was like the revival of an old melodrama that I had seen long ago with childish
awe. The second-act climax of the drama of the electrical disturbance over a lake
in America had not changed in any important respect. This was the big scene, still
the big scene. The whole thing was so familiar, the first feeling of oppression and
heat and a general air around camp of not wanting to go very far away. In midafter-
noon (it was all the same) a curious darkening of the sky, and a lull in everything that had made life tick; and then the way the boats suddenly swung the
other way at their moorings with the coming of a breeze out of the new quarter,
and the premonitory rumble. Then the kettle drum, then the snare, then the bass
drum and cymbals, then crackling light against the dark, and the gods grinning
and licking their chops in the hills. Afterward the calm, the rain steadily rustling
in the calm lake, the return of light and hope and spirits, and the campers running
out in joy and relief to go swimming in the rain, their bright cries perpetuating the
deathless joke about how they were getting simply drenched, and the children
screaming with delight at the new sensation of bathing in the rain, and the joke

about getting drenched linking the generations in a strong indestructible chain. And the comedian who waded in carrying an umbrella.

When the others went swimming my son said he was going in too. He pulled 13 his dripping trunks from the line where they had hung all through the shower, and wrung them out. Languidly, and with no thought of going in, I watched him, his hard little body, skinny and bare, saw him wince slightly as he pulled up around his vitals the small, soggy, icy garment. As he buckled the swollen belt suddenly my groin felt the chill of death.

COMPREHENSION

1. At what point in the essay do you begin to sense White's main purpose? What is his purpose? What type of reader might his purpose appeal to?
2. What motivates White to return to the lake in Maine? Explain the "simple transposition" that he mentions in paragraph 4. List the illustrations that he gives of this phenomenon. What change does he detect in the lake?
3. Explain the significance of White's last sentence. Where are there foreshadowings of this statement?

RHETORIC

1. Describe White's use of figurative language in paragraphs 2, 10, and 12.
2. Identify those words and phrases that White invokes to establish the sense of mystery about the lake. Why are these words and their connotations important to the nature of the illusion that he describes?
3. Explain the organization of the essay in terms of the following paragraph units: 1–4, 5–7, 8–10, and 11–13. Explain the function of paragraphs 8 and 12.
4. There are many vivid and unusual descriptive details in this essay—for example, the dragonfly in paragraph 5 and the two-track road in paragraph 7. How does White create symbolic overtones for these descriptive details and others? Why is the lake itself a complex symbol? Explain with reference to paragraph 6.
5. Describe the persona that White creates for himself in the essay. How does this persona function?
6. What is the relation between the introductory and concluding paragraphs, specifically in terms of irony of statement?

WRITING

1. Explore in an essay the theme of nostalgia in "Once More to the Lake." What are the beauties and the dangers of nostalgia? Can the past ever be recaptured or relived? Justify your answer.
2. Referring to revisiting a site on the lake that he had visited years before with his father, White remarks in paragraph 4, "I could tell that it was going to be pretty much the same as it had been before." How does this observation reflect the general sentiment White has about the role and function of the family? Respond to the question in an analytical essay.

3. **Writing an Argument:** Argue for or against the proposition that nostalgia can obscure the true nature of family relationships and even suppress painful memories that
should be confronted.

⊕	### NETWORKING *Applying Digital and Multimedia Literacies*

Alluding to Print on the Web: Do a Google Images search for *once more to the
lake*. Explore how various people around the world used this caption or description
with their own photographs, blog entries, or professional articles. Choose three or
four examples and discuss how they use this allusion to the E. B. White essay. Do
they mention the piece itself, or only its title? What power of nostalgia might this essay possess in and of itself, for readers who have known it for years? What books,
poems, stories, or songs make you nostalgic—for family, friends, a particular time in
your life? How does thinking about these specific examples influence your response
to question 3 under Writing?

❋

Street Scenes

Ann Hood

*Ann Hood (b. 1956) is a prize-winning novelist and essayist. She was born and raised
in West Warwick, Rhode Island, and received a BA from the University of Rhode Island
in 1978. Subsequently she was a flight attendant for Trans World Airlines until 1986.
"As a flight attendant," she recalls, "I carried a notebook with me and wrote on the
subway to the airport, on the plane, and in hotels on layovers. In fact that's where I
wrote* Somewhere Off the Coast of Maine" *(Hood's first novel, published in 1987).
Hood has published a dozen novels, most recently* Little Lion *(2011). She has also
written two memoirs and a short story collection,* An Ornithologist's Guide to Life
(2004). Her essays and fiction have appeared in such diverse publications as McCall's,
the Paris Review, *the* New York Times, *and* Cosmopolitan. *In this piece from the
Spring 2011 issue of* American Scholar, *Hood finds herself driving on a road that for
her links past, present, and future.*

1   Yesterday, I did it again. Driving from my house in Providence to my mother's house
in West Warwick, 12 miles down Route 95 South, I took Exit 12, the same exit I've
taken to go home since I got my driver's license in 1972. Off the exit, I come up by
the Toys R Us on my right and the junior college on my left. At the light sits Rhode
Island's first mall, built in October of 1967, when I was 10 years old. I got my first pair
of bell-bottoms there, and a Nehru jacket, and more 45s than I can remember. At
some point, while I lived out of state, they changed its name from Midland Mall to the

Rhode Island Mall. But I still call it Midland Mall. At the next light, I find myself looking at the Dunkin' Donuts where my mother would take me at three in the morning for coffee and a plain cruller when I was in high school and suffered insomnia.

That's when I realized I'd done it again. I'd followed the route that is as familiar 2 to me as my mother's Chloe perfume–cigarette smoke smell, as familiar as the pattern of freckles on my chest. Ahead of me sits River Street, the street that should lead me on a meandering series of curves and turns until I reach the hill on top of which my mother's house sits. But during the flooding here in Rhode Island last spring, the Pawtuxet River rose higher than it had in a hundred years. The shopping mall, Route 95, and River Street were under water. River Street is closed indefinitely. What I see from the driver's seat of my VW are orange cones keeping me out.

For most of my childhood, River Street connected me to the rest of the world. 3 It was not a broad or beautiful street. It had potholes. Lots of them. Tired mill houses painted off-shades of green and yellow lined half of it. The other half had some commercial buildings: a barber shop, an Italian deli, a gun store. The roller rink sat in a lot farther back, long-abandoned railroad tracks cut the street in half, and a small bridge on one end stretched over the Pawtuxet River, which was brown and frothy back in the '60s. But at the other end there was a Dunkin' Donuts, and beyond that pink square building was the world: two shopping malls, two fancy restaurants (The Golden Lantern and The Duncan Fyffe), and the on-ramp to Route 95. Route 95 could take me to Maine or all the way to Florida. When it first opened, I imagined that all I had to do was get on that highway and magically I would be under palm trees eating oranges.

Those railroad tracks led to a big empty lot that remained deserted except for 4 litter most of the year. But every August a carnival came to town and set up its flashy rides and impossible-to-win games there. I lost my first tooth at that carnival, biting into a candy apple. The highlight of the carnival was the Little Miss Natick Beauty Pageant, and the summer I was six, my mother entered me in it. My Auntie Julia, a seamstress, sewed me a leopard bikini. My Great Aunt Nuneen set my hair in rags to make perfect banana curls. Because I had no talent to speak of, my mother taught me a poem to recite for the talent competition:

> I have 10 little fingers and 10 little toes,
> Long blonde hair and a turned up nose,
> A great big smile and a cute little figure,
> Stay away boys! Till I get bigger!

She choreographed it, too, showing me when to hold up my fingers and how 5 to sashay my hips. For the last two lines, I marched right up to the judges' table and wagged my fingers at them. With that, I won Little Miss Natick 1963. I got a giant trophy, my picture in the paper, and a ride in a parade perched on top of my Uncle Eddie's white Cadillac convertible. The mother of one of the other contestants stole my leopard bikini, cut it into shreds, and threw it in a swimming pool because her daughter lost. It was that kind of town. And River Street, with its shabby beauty, epitomized it.

6   I pull into the Dunkin' Donuts parking lot. I have a choice. I can backtrack, head north again on Route 5 and take the shortcut, past the sewage treatment plant. Or I can continue south, down Route 2, which is now clogged with strip malls and big-box stores. Neither option feels right. For 38 years, River Street has taken me where I want to go. It took me to get those bell-bottoms. It took me to college, to the airport and train station. It took me to meet lovers and friends in far-flung places. It is the street I traveled on a hot summer day in 1982 when I learned that my brother Skip had died and I needed to get home. It is the street that led to the hospital where I was born and where my father died. For 38 years, River Street has taken me back home.

7   I get out of my car and the smell of doughnuts surrounds me like a hug. Growing up, I wanted nothing more than to go as far away as I could, way beyond that shiny Dunkin' Donuts. Now, a middle-aged woman, I want to drive down this street and feel the bumps of its untended road, let my body lean into the wide curve near where my cousin Anthony had a deli, see the little girl I once was, alone and friendless in my elementary school playground playing jacks, and the sassy teenager I became, storming out of Sacred Heart Church because I disagreed with the priest. Is it possible to love a street lined with years of disappointment and the echoes of carnival laughter? With a gun shop and a roller rink and mill houses? Standing there, yearning to travel it again, I realize I do love that street. River Street, which used to point to my future, now holds the connection to my past, to my long-ago childhood dreams and hopes, in its waterlogged arms. From that Dunkin' Donuts parking lot, I stand at its edge, to catch a glimpse of them.

COMPREHENSION

1. Hood speaks of a compulsive activity. What is it, and why is this compulsion revealing? What is her purpose in sharing this behavior with readers?
2. According to Hood, what was her childhood like? Who were the principal people in her life?
3. What ultimately is Hood's perception of childhood? How does childhood relate to her present circumstance and to future prospects?

RHETORIC

1. Hood is best known as a novelist. What elements of fiction do you detect in the essay? (For example, how does Hood create a certain mood or atmosphere?) Identify specific sentences and passages to support your response.
2. What is Hood's thesis? Where does this main idea appear or must we infer it? Explain.
3. Hood moves between present and past tenses in constructing her narrative. What is her purpose and what is the effect?
4. How might the repeated reference to Dunkin' Donuts function as a symbol in this essay?
5. How does Hood link her introductory and concluding paragraphs? In what ways do these two units frame her intended meaning?

WRITING

1. Write a narrative and descriptive essay about a place or route that is important to you and that you frequently return to.
2. Analyze three or more events in your childhood that are sources of influence for you today.
3. **Writing an Argument:** Hood implies that childhood shapes adult life and behavior. How do you feel about this idea? Are we inevitably molded by childhood or can we escape it if desired? Compose an argumentative essay in response to these questions.

NETWORKING
Applying Digital and Multimedia Literacies

Do a keyword search in your library's online databases for popular and scholarly articles about *family values*. Write an extended analysis about the result of this initial search. Which databases did you search? What kinds of sources did they (and these keywords) lead you to? If the term *family values* is defined in any of the abstracts you encountered, compile a few of these definitions and apply them to the essays by White and Hood.

Synthesis: Classic and Contemporary Questions for Comparison

1. Compare and contrast the tone of each writer. How does tone affect purpose? How does it affect mood? Select at least three passages from White and three from Hood that demonstrate how their tones differ. Do they offer any hints as to the "voice" or personality of the writers? Why or why not?
2. Consider that White was born in 1899 and Hood in 1956. What are their respective world views? What variables help us distinguish their concerns and outlooks—for example, gender, class, and environment?
3. What central values does each author have regarding the family? How are they similar? How do they differ? How do their values reflect their times?

※

An American Childhood

Annie Dillard

Annie Dillard (b. 1945 in Pittsburgh) received her BA and MA degrees from Hollins College. Her first book, Pilgrim at Tinker Creek *(1975), won the Pulitzer Prize for general nonfiction. Her other published works of nonfiction include* Teaching a Stone to Talk *(1982) and* An American Childhood *(1987). Dillard expanded her range of writing with the publication of her first novel,* The Living *(1992), and her latest novel,*

The Maytrees (2007). She has received awards from the National Endowment for the Arts and the Guggenheim Foundation as well as many other sources. As an essayist, poet, memoirist, and literary critic, she focuses her themes on the relationships among the self, nature, religion, and faith. Her writing is recognizable by its observations of the minutiae of life and its search for meaning in unlikely places, such as a stone or an insect. In this passage from An American Childhood, *the author gives us a portrait of her mother by focusing on her small idiosyncrasies of speech, gesture, and attitude.*

1   One Sunday afternoon Mother wandered through our kitchen, where Father was making a sandwich and listening to the ball game. The Pirates were playing the New York Giants at Forbes Field. In those days, the Giants had a utility infielder named Wayne Terwilliger. Just as Mother passed through, the radio announcer cried—with undue drama—"Terwilliger bunts one!"

2   "Terwilliger bunts one?" Mother cried back, stopped short. She turned. "Is that English?"

3   "The player's name is Terwilliger," Father said. "He bunted."

4   "That's marvelous," Mother said. "'Terwilliger bunts one.' No wonder you listen to baseball. 'Terwilliger bunts one.'"

5   For the next seven or eight years, Mother made this surprising string of syllables her own. Testing a microphone, she repeated, "Terwilliger bunts one"; testing a pen or a typewriter, she wrote it. If, as happened surprisingly often in the course of various improvised gags, she pretended to whisper something else in my ear, she actually whispered, "Terwilliger bunts one." Whenever someone used a French phrase, or a Latin one, she answered solemnly, "Terwilliger bunts one." If Mother had had, like Andrew Carnegie, the opportunity to cook up a motto for a coat of arms, hers would have read simply and tellingly, "Terwilliger bunts one." (Carnegie's was "Death to Privilege.")

6   She served us with other words and phrases. On a Florida trip, she repeated tremulously, "That . . . is a royal poinciana." I don't remember the tree; I remember the thrill in her voice. She pronounced it carefully, and spelled it. She also liked to say "portulaca."

7   The drama of the words "Tamiami Trail" stirred her, we learned on the same Florida trip. People built Tampa on one coast, and they built Miami on another. Then—the height of visionary ambition and folly—they piled a slow, tremendous road through the terrible Everglades to connect them. To build the road, men stood sunk in muck to their armpits. They fought off cottonmouth moccasins and six-foot alligators. They slept in boats, wet. They blasted muck with dynamite, cut jungle with machetes; they laid logs, dragged drilling machines, hauled dredges, heaped limestone. The road took fourteen years to build up by the shovelful, a Panama Canal in reverse, and cost hundreds of lives from tropical, mosquito-carried diseases. Then, capping it all, some genius thought of the word Tamiami: they called the road from Tampa to Miami, this very road under our spinning wheels, the Tamiami Trail. Some called it Alligator Alley. Anyone could drive over this road without a thought.

8   Hearing this, moved, I thought all the suffering of road building was worth it (it wasn't my suffering), now that we had this new thing to hang these new words on—Alligator Alley for those who liked things cute, and, for connoisseurs

like Mother, for lovers of the human drama in all its boldness and terror, the Tamiami Trail.

Back home, Mother cut clips from reels of talk, as it were, and played them back at leisure. She noticed that many Pittsburghers confuse "leave" and "let." One kind relative brightened our morning by mentioning why she'd brought her son to visit: "He wanted to come with me, so I left him." Mother filled in Amy and me on locutions we missed. "I can't do it on Friday," her pretty sister told a crowded dinner party, "because Friday's the day I lay in the stores." 9

(All unconsciously, though, we ourselves used some pure Pittsburghisms. We said "tele pole," pronounced "telly pole," for that splintery sidewalk post I loved to climb. We said "slippy"—the sidewalks are "slippy." We said, "That's all the farther I could go." And we said, as Pittsburghers do say, "This glass needs washed," or "The dog needs walked"—a usage our father eschewed; he knew it was not standard English, nor even comprehensible English, but he never let on.) 10

"Spell 'poinsettia,'" Mother would throw out at me, smiling with pleasure. "Spell 'sherbet.'" The idea was not to make us whizzes, but, quite the contrary, to remind us—and I, especially, needed reminding—that we didn't know it all just yet. 11

"There's a deer standing in the front hall," she told me one quiet evening in the country. 12

"Really?" 13

"No. I just wanted to tell you something once without your saying, 'I know.'" 14

Supermarkets in the middle 1950s began luring, or bothering, customers by giving out Top Value Stamps or Green Stamps. When, shopping with Mother, we got to the head of the checkout line, the checker, always a young man, asked, "Save stamps?" 15

"No," Mother replied genially, week after week, "I build model airplanes." I believe she originated this line. It took me years to determine where the joke lay. 16

Anyone who met her verbal challenges she adored. She had surgery on one of her eyes. On the operating table, just before she conked out, she appealed feelingly to the surgeon, saying, as she had been planning to say for weeks, "Will I be able to play the piano?" "Not on me," the surgeon said. "You won't pull that old one on me." 17

It was, indeed, an old one. The surgeon was supposed to answer, "Yes, my dear, brave woman, you will be able to play the piano after this operation," to which Mother intended to reply, "Oh, good, I've always wanted to play the piano." This pat scenario bored her; she loved having it interrupted. It must have galled her that usually her acquaintances were so predictably unalert; it must have galled her that, for the length of her life, she could surprise everyone so continually, so easily, when she had been the same all along. At any rate, she loved anyone who, as she put it, saw it coming, and called her on it. 18

She regarded the instructions on bureaucratic forms as straight lines. "Do you advocate the overthrow of the United States government by force or violence?" After some thought she wrote, "Force." She regarded children, even babies, as straight men. When Molly learned to crawl, Mother delighted in buying her gowns with drawstrings at the bottom, like Swee'pea's, because, as she explained energetically, you could easily step on the drawstring without the baby's noticing, so that she crawled and crawled and crawled and never got anywhere except into a small ball at the gown's top. 19

20 When we children were young, she mothered us tenderly and dependably; as we got older, she resumed her career of anarchism. She collared us into her gags. If she answered the phone on a wrong number, she told the caller, "Just a minute," and dragged the receiver to Amy or me, saying, "Here, take this, your name is Cecile," or, worse, just, "It's for you." You had to think on your feet. But did you want to perform well as Cecile, or did you want to take pity on the wretched caller?

21   During a family trip to the Highland Park Zoo, Mother and I were alone for a minute. She approached a young couple holding hands on a bench by the seals, and addressed the young man in dripping tones: "Where have you been? Still got those baby-blue eyes; always did slay me. And this"—a swift nod at the dumbstruck young woman, who had removed her hand from the man's—"must be the one you were telling me about. She's not so bad, really, as you used to make out. But listen, you know how I miss you, you know where to reach me, same old place. And there's Ann over there—see how she's grown? See the blue eyes?"

22   And off she sashayed, taking me firmly by the hand, and leading us around briskly past the monkey house and away. She cocked an ear back, and both of us heard the desperate man begin, in a high-pitched wail, "I swear, I never saw her before in my life . . ."

23 On a long, sloping beach by the ocean, she lay stretched out sunning with Father and friends, until the conversation gradually grew tedious, when without forethought she gave a little push with her heel and rolled away. People were stunned. She rolled deadpan and apparently effortlessly, arms and legs extended and tidy, down the beach to the distant water's edge, where she lay at once just as she had been, but half in the surf, and well out of earshot.

24   She dearly loved to fluster people by throwing out a game's rules at a whim—when she was getting bored, losing in a dull sort of way, and when everybody else was taking it too seriously. If you turned your back, she moved the checkers around on the board. When you got them all straightened out, she denied she'd touched them; the next time you turned your back, she lined them up on the rug or hid them under your chair. In a betting rummy game called Michigan, she routinely played out of turn, or called out a card she didn't hold, or counted backward, simply to amuse herself by causing an uproar and watching the rest of us do double-takes and have fits. (Much later, when serious suitors came to call, Mother subjected them to this fast card game as a trial by ordeal; she used it as an intelligence test and a measure of spirit. If the poor man could stay a round without breaking down or running out, he got to marry one of us, if he still wanted to.)

25   She excelled at bridge, playing fast and boldly, but when the stakes were low and the hands dull, she bid slams for the devilment of it, or raised her opponents' suit to bug them, or showed her hand, or tossed her cards in a handful behind her back in a characteristic swift motion accompanied by a vibrantly innocent look. It drove our stolid father crazy. The hand was over before it began, and the guests were appalled. How do you score it, who deals now, what do you do with a crazy person who is having so much fun? Or they were down seven, and the guests were appalled. "Pam!" "Dammit, Pam!" He groaned. What ails such people? What on earth possesses them? He rubbed his face.

She was an unstoppable force; she never let go. When we moved across town, 26 she persuaded the U.S. Post Office to let her keep her old address—forever— because she'd had stationery printed. I don't know how she did it. Every new post office worker, over decades, needed to learn that although the Doaks' mail is addressed to here, it is delivered to there.

Mother's energy and intelligence suited her for a greater role in a larger 27 arena—mayor of New York, say—than the one she had. She followed American politics closely; she had been known to vote for Democrats. She saw how things should be run, but she had nothing to run but our household. Even there, small minds bugged her; she was smarter than the people who designed the things she had to use all day for the length of her life.

"Look," she said. "Whoever designed this corkscrew never used one. Why 28 would anyone sell it without trying it out?" So she invented a better one. She showed me a drawing of it. The spirit of American enterprise never faded in Mother. If capitalizing and tooling up had been as interesting as theorizing and thinking up, she would have fired up a new factory every week, and chaired several hundred corporations.

"It grieves me," she would say, "it grieves my heart," that the company that made 29 one superior product packaged it poorly, or took the wrong tack in its advertising. She knew, as she held the thing mournfully in her two hands, that she'd never find another. She was right. We children wholly sympathized, and so did Father; what could she do, what could anyone do, about it? She was Samson in chains. She paced.

She didn't like the taste of stamps so she didn't lick stamps; she licked the 30 corner of the envelope instead. She glued sandpaper to the sides of kitchen drawers, and under kitchen cabinets, so she always had a handy place to strike a match. She designed, and hounded workmen to build against all norms, doubly wide kitchen counters and elevated bathroom sinks. To splint a finger, she stuck it in a lightweight cigar tube. Conversely, to protect a pack of cigarettes, she carried it in a Band-Aid box. She drew plans for an over-the-finger toothbrush for babies, an oven rack that slid up and down, and—the family favorite—Lendalarm. Lendalarm was a beeper you attached to books (or tools) you loaned friends. After ten days, the beeper sounded. Only the rightful owner could silence it.

She repeatedly reminded us of P. T. Barnum's dictum: You could sell anything 31 to anybody if you marketed it right. The adman who thought of making Americans believe they needed underarm deodorant was a visionary. So, too, was the hero who made a success of a new product, Ivory soap. The executives were horrified, Mother told me, that a cake of this stuff floated. Soap wasn't supposed to float. Anyone would be able to tell it was mostly whipped-up air. Then some inspired adman made a leap: Advertise that it floats. Flaunt it. The rest is history.

She respected the rare few who broke through to new ways. "Look," she'd 32 say, "here's an intelligent apron." She called upon us to admire intelligent control knobs and intelligent pan handles, intelligent andirons and picture frames and knife sharpeners. She questioned everything, every pair of scissors, every knitting needle, gardening glove, tape dispenser. Hers was a restless mental vigor that just about ignited the dumb household objects with its force.

33   Torpid conformity was a kind of sin; it was stupidity itself, the mighty stream against which Mother would never cease to struggle. If you held no minority opinions, or if you failed to risk total ostracism for them daily, the world would be a better place without you.

34   Always I heard Mother's emotional voice asking Amy and me the same few questions: "Is that your own idea? Or somebody else's?" "*Giant* is a good movie," I pronounced to the family at dinner. "Oh, really?" Mother warmed to these occasions. She all but rolled up her sleeves. She knew I hadn't seen it. "Is that your considered opinion?"

35   She herself held many unpopular, even fantastic, positions. She was scathingly sarcastic about the McCarthy hearings while they took place, right on our living-room television; she frantically opposed Father's wait-and-see calm. "We don't know enough about it," he said. "I do," she said. "I know all I need to know."

36   She asserted, against all opposition, that people who lived in trailer parks were not bad but simply poor, and had as much right to settle on beautiful land, such as rural Ligonier, Pennsylvania, as did the oldest of families in the finest of hidden houses. Therefore, the people who owned trailer parks, and sought zoning changes to permit trailer parks, needed our help. Her profound belief that the country-club pool sweeper was a person, and that the department-store saleslady, the bus driver, telephone operator, and house-painter were people, and even in groups the steelworkers who carried pickets and the Christmas shoppers who clogged intersections were people— this was a conviction common enough in democratic Pittsburgh, but not altogether common among our friends' parents, or even, perhaps, among our parents' friends.

37   Opposition emboldened Mother, and she would take on anybody on any issue— the chairman of the board, at a cocktail party, on the current strike; she would fly at him in a flurry of passion, as a songbird selflessly attacks a big hawk.

38   "Eisenhower's going to win," I announced after school. She lowered her magazine and looked me in the eyes: "How do you know?" I was doomed. It was fatal to say, "Everyone says so." We all knew well what happened. "Do you consult this Everyone before you make your decisions? What if Everyone decided to round up all the Jews?" Mother knew there was no danger of cowing me. She simply tried to keep us all awake. And in fact it was always clear to Amy and me, and to Molly when she grew old enough to listen, that if our classmates came to cruelty, just as much as if the neighborhood or the nation came to madness, we were expected to take, and would be each separately capable of taking, a stand.

COMPREHENSION

1. Dillard creates a picture of her mother's personality through a number of anecdotes and explanations. How would you sum up the mother's personality?
2. Dillard's mother appears to have a special appreciation for words and language. To what purpose does she apply this appreciation? What effect does it have on her family and acquaintances?
3. What values does the mother hold? What behaviors and attitudes does she abhor and discourage?

RHETORIC

1. In paragraph 7, Dillard explains that the highway from Tampa to Miami is referred to either as "Tamiami Trail" or "Alligator Alley." What is the connotation of each of these terms? Why does her mother prefer to call it "Tamiami Trail"?
2. The author herself seems to have inherited a special fascination for language. Study her use of dashes and semicolons in paragraphs 26 and 27. How do they help contribute to energetic writing?
3. What are the functions of the spaces between paragraphs 19 and 20, 22 and 23, and 32 and 33? How do these divisions contribute to the structure of the essay as a whole?
4. How does Dillard use her writing talents to create paragraph 8 out of one long sentence? What other examples can you provide of long sentences in the essay? How do they contribute to the overall style of the writing?
5. What is the overall emotional "tone" of the writer toward her subject—admiring, or loving, or cautionary? What adjectives does she use in describing her mother that provide the reader with clues to the tone?
6. Dillard quotes her mother directly on several occasions. Can we assume that she is quoting precisely, given that the essay was written years after the incidents described? Does it matter?
7. The final paragraph not only provides closure to the essay but transmits a lesson the mother wants her family to learn. How do the style and structure of this paragraph contribute to the ultimate message of the essay? In other words, how does the form help convey the meaning?

WRITING

1. Write a descriptive essay about someone you know very well, using at least five anecdotes from that person's life, so that by the end of the essay, we have a mental picture of your subject's personality, values, and attitudes. This could be someone in your biological family, or someone else you are or were very close to.
2. Describe an incident in your life when the unexpected taught you an important lesson.
3. **Writing an Argument:** Argue for or against the proposition that an effective parent should have—at least—a touch of unconventionality.

NETWORKING
Applying Digital and Multimedia Literacies

Creating a Playlist Narrative: Enhance your response to question 1 under Writing by creating a playlist of five songs that contribute to your description of that person you are or were close to. For each song, write a short paragraph about what it says about either this person or your relationship with him or her. The specific song might have a story behind it—if so, tell it—or it might describe (literally or figuratively) some aspect or quality of that person's character, appearance, beliefs, experiences, interests, location, talents, regrets, or hopes. What is the music capable of describing about this person that words couldn't?

In Sable and Dark Glasses

Joan Didion

Joan Didion (b. 1934) is a celebrated American essayist, nonfiction writer, novelist, and screenwriter. Born in Sacramento, California, Didion grew up as a self-described "shy, bookish child" who felt most at home in libraries as her family moved from place to place. Didion graduated from the University of California, Berkeley in 1956. In her senior year, she won first place in an essay contest sponsored by Vogue, *with the prize an entry-level position at the magazine. During her two years at* Vogue, *Didion rose to associate feature editor; wrote her first novel,* Run, River *(1963); and met her future husband, the writer John Gregory Dunne. In 1964, Didion and Dunne married and moved to Los Angeles, which would be their home until Dunne died in 2004. Among Didion's best known works are the novel* A Book of Common Prayer *(1977); the nonfiction books* Slouching Toward Bethlehem *(1968),* The White Album *(1979),* Miami *(1987), and* The Year of Magical Thinking *(2006); and the screenplay for the film* A Star is Born *(1974). In this essay, published in* Vogue *in 2011, Didion recounts vivid scenes from her childhood.*

1   I never had much interest in being a child. As a way of being it seemed flat, failed to engage. When I was in fact a child, six and seven and eight years old, I was utterly baffled by the enthusiasm with which my cousin Brenda, a year and a half younger, accepted her mother's definition of her as someone who needed to go to bed at six-thirty and finish every bite of three vegetables, one of them yellow, with every meal. Brenda was also encouraged to make a perfect white sauce, and to keep a chart showing a gold star for every time she brushed her teeth. I, meanwhile, was trying to improve the dinner hour by offering what I called "lettuce cocktails" (a single leaf of iceberg lettuce and crushed ice in a stemmed glass), and inventing elaborate scenarios featuring myself as an adult, specifically an adult 24 years old, an age on which I settled because my mother had assured me that 24 was the best, her favorite year. Over those years during which I was determined to bypass childhood, she and I discussed this question of age at a length she must have found tedious, but perhaps she did not: We are talking here about a woman, my mother, who tied what she construed to be her first gray hair in a bow and mailed it to her sister Gloria, she of the yellow-vegetable dictum. I once asked her what made 24 so memorable. It seemed that she had been married when she was 24. It seemed that I had been born when she was 24. It seemed that 24 was (I can hardly believe our discussions of age deteriorated to this, but possibly the lettuce cocktails had edged us both into a casino mode) her "lucky number."

2   My own fantasies of what life would be like at 24 tended to the more spectacular. In these dramas of my own devise I was sometimes wearing a sable coat, although I had never seen one. I was wearing this sable coat in an urban setting that looks in retrospect not unlike Shubert Alley. I was at other times walking on a moor, although

I had not yet read those English novels in which moors figured heavily. But here is how I most often preferred to visualize myself: not on a moor, not in Shubert Alley, but standing on the steps of a public building somewhere in South America (Argentina comes first to mind, although Argentina was like the sable coat, never actually seen, more concept than reality), wearing dark glasses and avoiding paparazzi. If you were to have asked me why I was standing on the steps of this public building in Argentina, I would have had a ready answer: I was standing on the steps of this public building in Argentina because I was getting a divorce. Hence the dark glasses, hence the paparazzi. I would let other six-year-olds (Brenda, say) imagine their wedding days, their princess dresses, their Juliet caps and seed pearls and clouds of white tulle: I had moved briskly on to the day of my (Buenos Aires) divorce, and the black silk mantilla the occasion would clearly require.

As a matter of fact I already had a black silk mantilla, dredged by me from one 3 of the many mysterious boxes in which my mother kept the clues to being 24. In another of those boxes I found the Jean Patou cape, red velvet with a white fur collar, that she reported having worn when she left her wedding reception. I also found the ankle-length red lace dress she wore when she "gave teas," a form of entertainment more popular than anyone might imagine it to have been in the part of rural California in which we then lived. My mother "gave teas" the way other mothers breathed. Her own mother "gave teas." All of their friends "gave teas," each involving butter cookies extruded from a metal press and pastel bonbons ordered from See's. "Giving a tea" was a process that entailed, as I had observed it, arranging translucent slices of lemon on white Wedgwood plates and spreading little pinwheel sandwiches with cream cheese and watercress, per the same Boston Cooking School Cookbook from which Brenda was being taught to make the perfect white sauce. And then, the most important step of all, the key to the eventual effect, the very point of giving a tea: taking that red lace dress from its box and dropping it over its own slip of ivory chiffon.

There were eventually other clues to adult life to be found in my mother's 4 boxes. There was the white silk shirt strewn with star-shaped silver sequins that she wore when my father was stationed at Peterson Field in Colorado Springs and she took me ice-skating at the Broadmoor Hotel. There was her petit-point evening bag. There was the plaid seersucker suit in which she crossed the country by train when, en route to meet my father in North Carolina in 1942, we traveled from Los Angeles to New Orleans on the Southern Pacific's Sunset Limited, a transcontinental train so crowded in those early days of World War II that my mother and small brother and I spent much of the trip standing in the couplings between the cars. I remember the rancid smell of the grease in the couplings. I remember a sailor on the train, a survivor of the USS *Wasp*, who once at a siding somewhere in the Southwest got off the train and came back with a Coca-Cola for my mother and a present for me, a silver-and-turquoise Navajo bracelet. I still today have the bracelet, too small now for my wrist. I also still today have snapshots taken on that trip. In these snapshots, which mainly show my mother and brother and me at moments when we have just missed or are just about to miss one or another key connection, for example looking forlorn between trains in Union Station in Los Angeles or for another example looking somewhat less forlorn between trains on the veranda of the St. Charles Hotel in New Orleans, my mother is wearing the plaid seersucker suit, spectator pumps, and, pinned at her temples, white silk gardenias.

5   From the snapshot evidence of the period, which shows me in pleated skirts and handknit cardigans and what appears to have been a Brownie uniform, she would have been less than entirely on board for the sable coat and the Buenos Aires divorce. The sable coat and the Buenos Aires divorce would have been more my grandmother's territory. It was my grandmother who knit the cardigans, yet it was also my grandmother who presented a more evolved idea of how I should appear to the world. She gave me Stroock vicuna coats, Lilly Daché hats, and flasks of Elizabeth Arden On Dit sealed with translucent paper and gold thread. The Lilly Daché hats were meant to encourage me to go to church. The Elizabeth Arden On Dit was meant to encourage me to get over the mumps. Brenda, as the next oldest granddaughter, was also the beneficiary of this method of child-rearing. When our grandmother took us for the day to San Francisco she ordered us Dungeness Crab Louis at El Prado and bought us dewy bunches of violets at the flower stand across Union Square. Both my mother and her sister Gloria seemed to feel a pro forma obligation to register disapproval of these tactics. "What will they have to look forward to?" I remember Gloria asking my grandmother.

6   "Let that be the greatest of your worries," I remember my grandmother answering.

7   Meanwhile I made up games to play with Brenda. In one game we were getting on an elevator at I. Magnin in San Francisco when we heard the operator speak. This is what the operator always said: "There is only room for one more." The operator had a spectral white face and spoke in an eerie voice. The spectral white face and eerie voice should (always) have warned us but we (always) missed the signals: This I. Magnin elevator was of course about to plunge, with Brenda and me on board, to the bottom of its shaft. I recognize this now as one more version of the hoary tale in which some stranger with a spectral face (an elevator operator, a nurse, a hotel clerk, a taxi driver, or, better still, a hearse driver) either does or does not save the life of the protagonist, by delivering the line about "only room for one more." The best version of this takes place not in an elevator but in a hospital, where the (inevitable) young woman discovers (too late) that the corridor she is about to enter—the corridor, of course, where there is "only room for one more"—leads to the hospital morgue.

8   This was Brenda's favorite game. I am ashamed to say that I could scare her witless with it, and often did. "Do only room for one more again," she would plead, and I would. My own favorite among our games, and this may or may not say something about the difference between growing up on yellow vegetables and growing up on lettuce cocktails, involved going page by page through an issue of *Vogue* and choosing what to "buy." Brenda could buy whatever she wanted from the left-hand pages; I was limited to the right. The point was to see which of us could assemble, given the options only as they turned up, the most desirable wardrobe. The rules, which I invented even as we turned the glossy pages, were quite strict. Either editorial or advertising pages qualified, but every page had to be considered. Dismissal of a page required a "reason," provided by me.

I am mortified to remember that I prevailed on Brenda to play this mindless 9
game for hours. I am also mortified to remember that 20 years later, when I was
no longer in danger of being mistaken for a child and Brenda herself was getting
married, I was still trying to run the game, make the rules, have it my way. There
would be at Brenda's wedding, I promised her, nothing banal, nothing ordinary.
She could forget the princess dress. She could forget the Juliet cap. She could
forget the seed pearls, the clouds of white tulle. I had decreed: There would instead be checked gingham and wreaths of daisies. I was the older cousin. We
would therefore do it my way. I myself would make the wreaths.

When the day of the wedding arrived I did make the wreaths, cutting tiny slits 10
in each stem and threading the daisies into one another. Cutting the slits and
threading the daisies took longer than I had planned. I was in fact still making the
wreaths as the guests were being seated. The bridesmaids waited in their checked
gingham dresses. Brenda waited in her own checked gingham dress. Her wedding, she later pointed out, turned out to be one more of my lettuce-cocktail
moments. That she might have preferred a yellow-vegetable moment never, not
ever, not once, not when I was pressing the gingham dresses and not when I was
threading the daisy wreaths, crossed my mind.

COMPREHENSION

1. In recalling her childhood, what does Didion reveal about her behavior, orientation, and beliefs?
2. Underline, highlight, or circle Didion's numerous references to clothing. What is her purpose here? How does the title capture this emphasis on dress, and from what perspective? According to Didion, what is the function of dress and other domestic rituals?
3. How does Didion distinguish herself from her cousin Brenda? What does Didion conclude about this relationship?

RHETORIC

1. Didion published this memoir in a magazine that is read largely by women. How does she tailor the piece for this specific audience? Might the essay appeal to a broader audience? Why or why not?
2. What tone or personal voice does Didion create to describe her childhood? What bearing does this self-description have on her thesis or claim?
3. Compare the introductory and concluding paragraphs. How do they serve to establish the boundaries of the essay?
4. What elements of style do you find especially effective in this essay? For example, what allusions can you detect? What is the rhetorical effect of Didion's repeated use of semicolons? Why are many of her sentences so complex in design?
5. Didion is a novelist who uses the techniques of fiction in her nonfiction. How do you see these strategies operating in this essay?

WRITING

1. Write a narrative essay in which you tell of a period in childhood when you wished you were older or played adult games.
2. Didion has been credited with popularizing the *new journalism*. Find out more about this literary movement, and then write an analytical essay applying the concept to Didion's article.
3. **Writing an Argument:** Do you agree or disagree with Didion's implicit suggestion that at some point in their lives, children or young people develop a distaste for childhood or yearn to be grown-ups? Respond to this issue in an argumentative essay.

NETWORKING
Applying Digital and Multimedia Literacies

In small groups, find at least three Web sites about Joan Didion's life and work. Focus on two events in her life: the death of her husband and that of her daughter. Examine how she has responded to these episodes in her writing, interviews, and work for the theater. Share your findings in a class discussion.

Why Gay Marriage Is Good for Straight America

Andrew Sullivan

Andrew Sullivan *(b. 1963) is a prolific and provocative writer, editor, and blogger. Born and raised in England, he was educated at Magdalen College, Oxford before moving to the United States to earn advanced degrees in public administration and politics at Harvard University. Identifying himself as Catholic, conservative, and gay, Sullivan was editor of the* New Republic *from 1991 to 1996. He began his influential blog,* The Daily Dish, *in 2000, taking it initially to the* Atlantic Monthly *magazine's Web site. Sullivan left* Atlantic Monthly *in 2011 to begin blogging at the* Daily Beast. *Among his notable books are* Virtually Normal: An Argument about Homosexuality *(1995) and* The Conservative Soul: How We Lost It, How to Get It Back *(2006). In this essay from the July 25, 2011, issue of* Newsweek, *Sullivan offers a highly personal defense of marriage equality.*

1 As a child, when I thought of the future, all I could see was black. I wasn't miserable or depressed. I was a cheerful boy, as happy playing with my posse of male friends in elementary school as I was when I would occasionally take a day by

myself in the woodlands that surrounded the small town I grew up in. But when I thought of the distant future, of what I would do and be as a grown-up, there was a blank. I simply didn't know how I would live, where I would live, who I could live with. I knew one thing only: I couldn't be like my dad. For some reason, I knew somewhere deep down that I couldn't have a marriage like my parents.

It's hard to convey what that feeling does to a child. In retrospect, it was a 2 sharp, displacing wound to the psyche. At the very moment you become aware of sex and emotion, you simultaneously know that for you, there is no future coupling, no future family, no future home. In the future, I would be suddenly exiled from what I knew: my family, my friends, every household on television, every end to every romantic movie I'd ever seen. My grandmother crystallized it in classic and slightly cruel English fashion: "You're not the marrying kind," she said. It was one of those things that struck a chord of such pain, my pride forced me to embrace it. "No, I'm not," I replied. "I like my freedom."

This wasn't a lie. But it was a dodge, and I knew it. And when puberty struck 3 and I realized I might be "one of them," I turned inward. It was a strange feeling— both the exhilaration of sexual desire and the simultaneous, soul-splintering panic that I was going to have to live alone my whole life, lying or euphemizing, concocting some public veneer to hide a private shame. It was like getting into an elevator you were expecting to go up, the doors closing, and then suddenly realizing you were headed down a few stories. And this was when the future went black for me, when suicide very occasionally entered my mind, when my only legitimate passion was getting A grades, because at that point it was all I knew how to do. I stayed away from parties; I didn't learn to drive; I lost contact with those friends whose interest suddenly became girls; and somewhere in me, something began to die.

They call it the happiest day of your life for a reason. Getting married is often the 4 hinge on which every family generation swings open. In my small-town life, it was far more important than money or a career or fame. And I could see my grandmother's point: the very lack of any dating or interest in it, the absence of any intimate relationships, or of any normal teenage behavior, did indeed make me seem just a classic loner. But I wasn't. Because nobody is. "In everyone there sleeps/A sense of life lived according to love," as the poet Philip Larkin put it, as well as the fear of never being loved. That, as Larkin added, nothing cures. And I felt, for a time, incurable.

You can have as many debates about gay marriage as you want, and over the last 5 22 years of campaigning for it, I've had my share. You can debate theology, and the divide between church and state, the issue of procreation, the red herring of polygamy, and on and on. But what it all really comes down to is the primary institution of love. The small percentage of people who are gay or lesbian were born, as all humans are, with the capacity to love and the need to be loved. These things, above everything, are what make life worth living. And unlike every other minority, almost all of us grew up among and part of the majority, in families where the highest form of that love was between our parents in marriage. To feel you will never know that, never feel that, is to experience a deep psychic wound that takes years to recover from. It is to become psychologically homeless. Which is why, I think, the concept of "coming out" is not quite right. It should really be called "coming home."

6   In the end, I had to abandon my home in order to find it again and know the place for the first time. I left England just after my 21st birthday for America and its simple foundational promise: the pursuit of happiness. And I gave myself permission to pursue it. I will never forget the moment I first kissed another man; it was as if a black-and-white movie suddenly turned into color. I will never forget the first time I slept next to another man—or rather tried to sleep. Never for a moment did I actually feel or truly believe any of this was wrong, let alone an "intrinsic evil," as my strict Catholicism told me that it was. It was so natural, so spontaneous, so joyous, it could no more be wrong than breathing. And as I experienced intimacy and love for the first time as an adult, all that brittleness of the gay adolescent, all that white-knuckled embarrassment, all those ruses and excuses and dark, deep depressions lifted. Yes, this was happiness. And America for me will always represent it.

7   And that is why marriage equality is, to my mind, the distillation of America. If you're a heterosexual reading this, have you ever considered for a millisecond that your right to pursue happiness did not include your right to marry the person you love? And that is why, over the centuries, the U.S. Supreme Court has upheld the right to marry for everyone, citizen or even traveler, as a core, inalienable right, bestowed by the Declaration of Independence itself. The court has ruled that the right to marry precedes the Bill of Rights; it has decided that prisoners on death row have a right to marry, even if they can never consummate it. It has ruled that no limitations may be put on it for anyone—deadbeat dads, multiple divorcees, felons, noncitizens. Hannah Arendt wrote in 1959 that "the right to marry whoever one wishes is an elementary human right. . . . Even political rights, like the right to vote, and nearly all other rights enumerated in the Constitution, are secondary to the inalienable human rights to 'life, liberty and the pursuit of happiness' proclaimed in the Declaration of Independence; and to this category the right to home and marriage unquestionably belongs." And, of course, after a long struggle, interracial marriage was finally declared a constitutional right, in perhaps the most sweeping ruling ever, with the court declaring that civil marriage was one of the "basic civil rights of man, fundamental to our very existence and survival." Barack Obama is a historic American figure not because he is black, but because he is the son of a black father and a white mother. He is the living embodiment of the pursuit of happiness that marriage represented.

8   I still didn't think it would ever happen to me. I thought I was too emotionally damaged, my emotions and sexuality severed by all those years of loneliness and arrested emotional development. I thought my heart had too much scar tissue, and I could live my life well enough with just friendship and occasional sexual encounters or dates. But when I first set eyes on my husband, I knew I had lucked out. Some things you simply know. And when we finally got married, a few years later, and our mothers walked us down the makeshift garden aisle, and my sister gave the reading through tears, and one of our beagles howled through the vows, and my father put his arms around me and hugged, I did not hear civilization crumble. I felt a wound being healed. It is a rare privilege to spend your adult life fighting for a right that was first dismissed as a joke, only finally to achieve it in six states and Washington, D.C. But how much rarer to actually stumble upon someone

who could make it a reality. And to have it happen to me in my own lifetime! This joy is compounded, deepened, solidified by the knowledge that somewhere, someone just like I was as a kid will be able to look to the future now and not see darkness—but the possibility of love and home. That, I realized, was really what I had been fighting for two decades: to heal the child I had once been—and the countless children in the present and future whose future deserved, needed, begged for a model of commitment and responsibility and love.

And that is why it has been such a tragedy that conservatives decided this   9 was a battle they were determined to fight against, an advance they were dedicated to reversing. It made no sense to me. Here was a minority asking for responsibility and commitment and integration. And conservatives were determined to keep them in isolation, stigmatized and kept on an embarrassing, unmentionable margin, where gays could be used to buttress the primacy of heterosexuality. We were for them merely a drop shadow for heterosexuality. What they could not see was that the conservative tradition of reform and inclusion, of social change through existing institutions, of the family and personal responsibility, all led inexorably toward civil marriage for gays.

Yes, the main stumbling block was religion. But we were not talking of reli-   10 gious marriage and were more than eager to insist, as in New York state, on the inviolable religious freedom of churches, mosques, and synagogues to retain their bans on gay marriage. We were talking about civil marriage—and in that respect, religious tradition had long since ceased to apply. Civil divorce changed marriage far more drastically for far more people than allowing the small percentage who were excluded to be included. And no one doubted an atheist's right to marry, outside of any church or any religion, just as no one doubted the marriages of childless couples, or infertile ones. In fact, every single argument against marriage equality for gays collapsed upon inspection. And when the data showed that in the era of gay marriage, straight marriage had actually strengthened somewhat, divorce rates had declined, and marriages lasted longer, even those who worried about unintended consequences conceded that the argument was essentially over. And that is why it remains so appropriate that George W. Bush's solicitor general, Ted Olson, would lead the legal fight against Proposition 8 in California; that a Reagan-appointed judge, Anthony Kennedy, would be the foremost Supreme Court justice affirming gay and lesbian equality; and that in Albany, in the end, the winning votes came from Republicans who voted their conscience.

Of course this is new and not so new. For a long time, gays and lesbians   11 braver than I was were effectively married and lived together, risking violence and opprobrium and isolation. For decades these bonds existed, and we knew of them even if we never spoke of them. I saw them up close as a young man in the darkest years of the AIDS plague. I saw spouses holding their dying husbands, cradling them at the hour of their death, inserting catheters, cleaning broken bodies, tending to terrified souls. This proved beyond any doubt for me that gay couples were as capable of as much love and tenacity and tenderness and fidelity as heterosexual couples. And when I heard their bonds denigrated or demonized, dismissed or belittled, the sadness became a kind of spur. For so long, so much pain. For so many, so much grief compounded by stigma. But we did not just survive the plague. We used it to forge a new future. And in the years of struggle, as more and more heterosexuals joined us, we all began finally to see that this was not really about being gay. It was about being human.

12   Just like being gay is no longer necessarily about being an outsider. It is about being an American.

COMPREHENSION

1. Briefly summarize Sullivan's childhood. How especially did he envision his future?
2. According to Sullivan, why did he immigrate to the United States after his 21st birthday? What did he find in America?
3. Explain what Sullivan means by his statement, "marriage equality is . . . the distillation of America" (paragraph 7).

RHETORIC

1. What voice does Sullivan create in this essay? What appeals to emotion, reason, and ethics does he make? How do these appeals contribute to his argument?
2. How does Sullivan use the rhetorical strategies of comparison and contrast, definition, and classification to organize this essay?
3. Sullivan employs analogy, allusion, and figurative language as stylistic elements in this essay. Identify these strategies and evaluate their contribution to Sullivan's argument.
4. Where does Sullivan acknowledge various forces of opposition to his argument? How does he refute those who oppose his position? In your mind, is his argument persuasive? Why or why not?
5. Sullivan's conclusion is very brief. Do you find it successful or not? Explain.

WRITING

1. Write a personal essay that explains your own sexual orientation, linking it to American values and the American experience.
2. Read Lisa Miller's "Our Mutual Joy: The Religious Case for Gay Marriage," which begins on page 569. Then write a comparative essay that analyzes the approaches of Sullivan and Miller to their subject.
3. **Writing an Argument:** Respond to Sullivan's claim that marriage equality is "the distillation of America."

NETWORKING
Applying Digital and Multimedia Literacies

Collaborating in small groups, conduct research on Sullivan's blog. Each member should read and summarize one or two of Sullivan's postings. Then discuss how Sullivan manages to be a Catholic, conservative, and homosexual. Share your insights with the class.

�֎

Family Values

Richard Rodriguez

Richard Rodriguez *(b. 1944) received degrees from Stanford University and Columbia University. He also did graduate study at the University of California, Berkeley, and at the Warburg Institute in London. He is a writer and editor for* Pacifica News Service *and a contributing editor and writer for many major American magazines and journals including* Harper's *and the* Los Angeles Times. *His books include* Hunger of Memory: The Education of Richard Rodriguez *(1982) and* Days of Obligation: An Argument with My Mexican Father *(1992). Both books have been profoundly influential in the public discussion on race, bilingualism, affirmative action, and biculturalism. He has also made many appearances as a commentator on the* PBS NewsHour. *In the following essay, originally published in the Sunday "Opinion" section of the* Los Angeles Times *in 1992, he addresses the concept of "family values" and focuses on the controversial thesis that homosexuality—rather than being a threat to family values—is actually a buttress against their dissolution.*

I am sitting alone in my car, in front of my parents' house—a middle-aged man 1 with a boy's secret to tell. What words will I use to tell them? I hate the word *gay,* find its little affirming sparkle more pathetic than assertive. I am happier with the less polite *queer.* But to my parents I would say *homosexual,* avoiding the Mexican slang *joto* (I had always heard it said in our house with hints of condescension), though *joto* is less mocking than the sissy-boy *maricon.*

The buzz on everyone's lips now: Family values. The other night on TV, the 2 vice president of the United States, his arm around his wife, smiled into the camera and described homosexuality as "mostly a choice." But how would he know? Homosexuality never felt like a choice to me.

A few minutes ago Rush Limbaugh, the radio guy with a voice that reminds 3 me, for some reason, of a butcher's arms, was banging his console and booming a near-reasonable polemic about family values. Limbaugh was not very clear about which values exactly he considers to be family values. A divorced man who lives alone in New York?

My parents live on a gray, treeless street in San Francisco not far from the 4 ocean. Probably more than half of the neighborhood is immigrant. India lives next door to Greece, who lives next door to Russia. I wonder what the Chinese lady next door to my parents makes of the politicians' phrase *family values.*

What immigrants know, what my parents certainly know, is that when you 5 come to this country, you risk losing your children. The assurance of family—continuity, inevitability—is precisely what America encourages its children to overturn. *Become your own man.* We who are native to this country know this too, of course, though we are likely to deny it. Only a society so guilty about its betrayal of family would tolerate the pieties of politicians regarding family values.

6   On the same summer day that Republicans were swarming in Houston (buzzing about family values), a friend of mine who escaped family values awhile back and who now wears earrings resembling intrauterine devices was complaining to me over coffee about the Chinese. The Chinese will never take over San Francisco, my friend said, because the Chinese do not want to take over San Francisco. The Chinese do not even see San Francisco! All they care about is their damn families. All they care about is double-parking smack in front of the restaurant on Clement Street and pulling granny out of the car—and damn anyone who happens to be in the car behind them or the next or the next.

7   Politicians would be horrified by such an American opinion, of course. But then, what do politicians, Republicans or Democrats, really know of our family life? Or what are they willing to admit? Even in that area where they could reasonably be expected to have something to say—regarding the relationship of family life to our economic system—the politicians say nothing. Republicans celebrate American economic freedom, but Republicans don't seem to connect that economic freedom to the social breakdown they find appalling. Democrats, on the other hand, if more tolerant of the drift from familial tradition, are suspicious of the very capitalism that creates social freedom.

8   How you become free in America: Consider the immigrant. He gets a job. Soon he is earning more money than his father ever made (his father's authority is thereby subtly undermined). The immigrant begins living a life his father never knew. The immigrant moves from one job to another, changes houses. His economic choices determine his home address—not the other way around. The immigrant is on his way to becoming his own man.

9   When I was broke a few years ago and trying to finish a book, I lived with my parents. What a thing to do! A major theme of America is leaving home. We trust the child who forsakes family connections to make it on his own. We call that the making of a man.

10   Let's talk about this man stuff for a minute. America's ethos is anti-domestic. We may be intrigued by blood that runs through wealth—the Kennedys or the Rockefellers—but they seem European to us. Which is to say, they are movies. They are Corleones. Our real pledge of allegiance: We say in America that nothing about your family—your class, your race, your pedigree—should be as important as what you yourself achieve. We end up in 1992 introducing ourselves by first names.

11   What authority can Papa have in a country that formed its identity in an act of Oedipal rebellion against a mad British king? Papa is a joke in America, a stock sitcom figure—Archie Bunker or Homer Simpson. But my Mexican father went to work every morning, and he stood in a white smock, making false teeth, oblivious of the shelves of grinning false teeth mocking his devotion.

12   The nuns in grammar school—my wonderful Irish nuns—used to push Mark Twain on me. I distrusted Huck Finn, he seemed like a gringo kid I would steer clear of in the schoolyard. (He was too confident.) I realize now, of course, that Huck is the closest we have to a national hero. We trust the story of a boy who has no home and is restless for the river. (Huck's Pap is drunk.) Americans are more forgiving of Huck's wildness than of the sweetness of the Chinese boy who walks

to school with his mama or grandma. (There is no worse thing in America than to be a mama's boy, nothing better than to be a real boy—all boy—like Huck, who eludes Aunt Sally, and is eager for the world of men.)

There's a bent old woman coming up the street. She glances nervously as she 13 passes my car. What would you tell us, old lady, of family values in America?

America is an immigrant country, we say. Motherhood—parenthood—is less 14 our point than adoption. If I had to assign gender to America, I would note the consensus of the rest of the world. When America is burned in effigy, a male is burned. Americans themselves speak of Uncle Sam.

Like the Goddess of Liberty, Uncle Sam has no children of his own. He steals 15 children to make men of them, mocks all reticence, all modesty, all memory. Uncle Sam is a hectoring Yankee, a skinflint uncle, gaunt, uncouth, unloved. He is the American Savonarola—hater of moonshine, destroyer of stills, burner of cocaine. Sam has no patience with mamas' boys.

You betray Uncle Sam by favoring private over public life, by seeking to ex- 16 empt yourself, by cheating on your income taxes, by avoiding jury duty, by trying to keep your boy on the farm.

Mothers are traditionally the guardians of the family against America— 17 though even Mom may side with America against queers and deserters, at least when the Old Man is around. Premature gray hair. Arthritis in her shoulders. Bowlegged with time, red hands. In their fiercely flowered housedresses, mothers are always smarter than fathers in America. But in reality they are betrayed by their children who leave. In a thousand ways. They end up alone.

We kind of like the daughter who was a tomboy. Remember her? It was always 18 easier to be a tomboy in America than a sissy. Americans admired Annie Oakley more than they admired Liberace (who, nevertheless, always remembered his mother). But today we do not admire Annie Oakley when we see Mom becoming Annie Oakley.

The American household now needs two incomes, everyone says. Meaning: 19 Mom is *forced* to leave home out of economic necessity. But lots of us know lots of moms who are sick and tired of being mom, or only mom. It's like the nuns getting fed up, teaching kids for all those years and having those kids grow up telling stories of how awful Catholic school was! Not every woman in America wants her life's work to be forgiveness. Today there are moms who don't want their husbands' names. And the most disturbing possibility: What happens when Mom doesn't want to be Mom at all? Refuses pregnancy?

Mom is only becoming an American like the rest of us. Certainly, people all 20 over the world are going to describe the influence of feminism on women (all over the world) as their "Americanization." And rightly so.

Nothing of this, of course, will the politician's wife tell you. The politician's wife 21 is careful to follow her husband's sentimental reassurances that nothing has changed about America except perhaps for the sinister influence of deviants. Like myself.

I contain within myself an anomaly at least as interesting as the Republican 22 Party's version of family values. I am a homosexual Catholic, a communicant in a tradition that rejects even as it upholds me.

23   I do not count myself among those Christians who proclaim themselves protec-
tors of family values. They regard me as no less an enemy of the family than the
"radical feminists." But the joke about families that all homosexuals know is that we
are the ones who stick around and make families possible. Call on us. I can think of
20 or 30 examples. A gay son or daughter is the only one who is "free" (married
brothers and sisters are too busy). And, indeed, because we have admitted the inad-
missible about ourselves (that we are queer)—we are adepts at imagination—we
can even imagine those who refuse to imagine us. We can imagine Mom's loneliness, for example. If Mom needs to be taken to church or to the doctor or ferried
between Christmas dinners, depend on the gay son or lesbian daughter.

24   I won't deny that the so-called gay liberation movement, along with feminism,
undermined the heterosexual household, if that's what politicians mean when they
say family values. Against churchly reminders that sex was for procreation, the gay
bar as much as the birth-control pill taught Americans not to fear sexual pleasure. In
the past two decades—and, not coincidentally, parallel to the feminist movement—
the gay liberation movement moved a generation of Americans toward the idea of a
childless adulthood. If the women's movement was ultimately more concerned about
getting out of the house and into the workplace, the gay movement was in its way
more subversive to puritan America because it stressed the importance of play.

25   Several months ago, the society editor of the morning paper in San Francisco
suggested (on a list of "must haves") that every society dame must have at least
one gay male friend. A ballet companion. A lunch date. The remark was glib and
incorrect enough to beg complaints from homosexual readers, but there was a
truth about it as well. Homosexual men have provided women with an alternate
model of masculinity. And the truth: The Old Man, God bless him, is a bore. Thus
are we seen as preserving marriages? Even Republican marriages?

26   For myself, homosexuality is a deep brotherhood but does not involve domestic
life. Which is why, my married sisters will tell you, I can afford the time to be a
writer. And why are so many homosexuals such wonderful teachers and priests
and favorite aunts, if not because we are freed from the house? On the other hand,
I know lots of homosexual couples (male and female) who model their lives on
the traditional heterosexual version of domesticity and marriage. Republican
politicians mock the notion of a homosexual marriage, but ironically such
marriages honor the heterosexual marriage by imitating it.

27   "The only loving couples I know," a friend of mine recently remarked, "are all
gay couples."

28   This woman was not saying that she does not love her children or that she is planning a divorce. But she was saying something about the sadness of American domestic
life: the fact that there is so little joy in family intimacy. Which is perhaps why gossip
(public intrusion into the private) has become a national industry. All day long, in forlorn houses, the television lights up a freakish parade of husbands and mothers-in-law
and children upon the stage of Sally or Oprah or Phil. They tell on each other. The
audience ooohhhs. Then a psychiatrist-shaman appears at the end to dispense
prescriptions—the importance of family members granting one another more "space."

29   The question I desperately need to ask you is whether we Americans have
ever truly valued the family. We are famous, or our immigrant ancestors were

famous, for the willingness to leave home. And it is ironic that a crusade under the banner of family values has been taken up by those who would otherwise pass themselves off as patriots. For they seem not to understand America, nor do I think they love the freedoms America grants. Do they understand why, in a country that prizes individuality and is suspicious of authority, children are disinclined to submit to their parents? You cannot celebrate American values in the public realm without expecting them to touch our private lives. As Barbara Bush remarked recently, family values are also neighborhood values. It may be harmless enough for Barbara Bush to recall a sweeter America—Midland, Texas, in the 1950s. But the question left begging is why we chose to leave Midland, Texas. Americans like to say that we can't go home again. The truth is that we don't want to go home again, don't want to be known, recognized. Don't want to respond in the same old ways. (And you know you will if you go back there.)

Little 10-year-old girls know that there are reasons for getting away from the family. They learn to keep their secrets—under lock and key—addressed to Dear Diary. Growing up queer, you learn to keep secrets as well. In no place are those secrets more firmly held than within the family house. You learn to live in closets. I know a Chinese man who arrived in America about 10 years ago. He got a job and made some money. And during that time he came to confront his homosexuality. And then his family arrived. I do not yet know the end of this story.

The genius of America is that it permits children to leave home, it permits us to become different from our parents. But the sadness, the loneliness of America, is clear too.

Listen to the way Americans talk about immigrants. If, on the one hand, there is impatience when today's immigrants do not seem to give up their family, there is also a fascination with this reluctance. In Los Angeles, Hispanics are considered people of family. Hispanic women are hired to be at the center of the American family—to babysit and diaper, to cook and to clean and to ease the dying. Hispanic attachment to family is seen by many Americans, I think, as the reason why Hispanics don't get ahead. But if Asians privately annoy us for being so family oriented, they are also stereotypically celebrated as the new "whiz kids" in school. Don't Asians go to college, after all, to honor their parents?

More important still is the technological and economic ascendancy of Asia, particularly Japan, on the American imagination. Americans are starting to wonder whether perhaps the family values of Asia put the United States at a disadvantage. The old platitude had it that ours is a vibrant, robust society for being a society of individuals. Now we look to Asia and see team effort paying off.

In this time of national homesickness, of nostalgia, for how we imagine America used to be, there are obvious dangers. We are going to start blaming each other for the loss. Since we are inclined, as Americans, to think of ourselves individually, we are disinclined to think of ourselves as creating one another or influencing one another.

But it is not the politician or any political debate about family values that has brought me here on a gray morning to my parents' house. It is some payment I owe to my youth and to my parents' youth. I imagine us sitting in the living room, amid my mother's sentimental doilies and the family photographs, trying to take the measure of the people we have turned out to be in America.

36   A San Francisco poet, when he was in the hospital and dying, called a priest to his bedside. The old poet wanted to make his peace with Mother Church. He wanted baptism. The priest asked why. "Because the Catholic Church has to accept me," said the poet. "Because I am a sinner."

37   Isn't willy-nilly inclusiveness the point, the only possible point to be derived from the concept of family? Curiously, both President Bush and Vice President Quayle got in trouble with their constituents recently for expressing a real family value. Both men said that they would try to dissuade a daughter or granddaughter from having an abortion. But, finally, they said they would support her decision, continue to love her, never abandon her.

38   There are families that do not accept. There are children who are forced to leave home because of abortions or homosexuality. There are family secrets that Papa never hears. Which is to say there are families that never learn the point of families.

39   But there she is at the window. My mother has seen me and she waves me in. Her face asks: Why am I sitting outside? (Have they, after all, known my secret for years and kept it, out of embarrassment, not knowing what to say?) Families accept, often by silence. My father opens the door to welcome me in.

COMPREHENSION

1. The title of this essay is "Family Values." What does Rodriguez mean by *family values?* According to the author, do Americans respect family values as they claim? Why or why not?
2. According to Rodriguez, do immigrants newly arrived to the United States possess a traditional allegiance to family values? Explain your answer.
3. In the conclusion, the author reflects—regarding his homosexuality—that "families accept, often in silence." Is this an aspect of traditional family values? Why or why not?
4. Why does Rodriguez think that gay men and women are often the primary upholders of family values within their families?
5. What is the thesis of the essay? Is it implicit or explicit? Explain.

RHETORIC

1. Although much of this essay is expository, Rodriguez begins and ends with an event— that is, visiting his family to announce his homosexuality. Why has he shaped his essay in this way? What is problematic about his relationship to the gay community? Why does he feel uncomfortable with the term *gay* to denote homosexual?
2. Rodriguez employs considerable irony in his essay. For example, in paragraph 15, he notes that two icons of American democracy, the Goddess of Liberty and Uncle Sam, are childless. Select two other ironic statements he makes in order to point out the contradiction between the idea of family values in America and the actual state of family values.
3. In paragraph 20, Rodriguez uses the term "Americanization." What does he mean by this term? How is it central to his thesis?
4. Does Rodriguez suggest that much of what is said in public regarding "family values" in America is hypocritical? If so, what group or groups does he focus on? How does he support his argument?

5. Explain the meaning of the following stylistic flourishes: "the word *gay* . . . [is a] little affirming sparkle more pathetic than assertive" (paragraph 1), "America's ethos is anti-domestic" (paragraph 10), "Oedipal rebellion" (paragraph 11), "American Savonarola" (paragraph 15), "psychiatrist-shaman" (paragraph 28), "national homesickness" (paragraph 34), and "willy-nilly inclusiveness" (paragraph 37).

6. In paragraph 10, Rodriguez states that the Kennedys and Rockefellers "are movies." What does he mean?

7. Describe the emotional tone of this essay, considering that it is written by a man who is openly gay and understands that he is considered suspect and outside the mainstream of the American "value" system. Is it angry? Thoughtful? Defiant? Sympathetic? Select three or four passages that led you to your conclusion regarding tone.

WRITING

1. Interview a member of your grandparents' generation, a member of your parents' generation, and a member of your own generation regarding their views on family values. Write an essay summarizing the similarities and differences among the three views.

2. Interview a counselor at your college or university. Ask the counselor to explain the various issues surrounding family conflict he or she comes across in the course of his or her job. Write an essay exploring your interview findings. Be sure to obtain permission from your interviewee and follow appropriate guidelines for protecting his or her anonymity.

3. **Writing an Argument:** Argue for or against the proposition that American society today is more tolerant of homosexuals than when Rodriguez published this essay in 1992.

NETWORKING
Applying Digital and Multimedia Literacies

Synthesizing Blog Entries: Locate and read some recent entries from author/blogger Andrew Sullivan's *The Daily Dish* and Sullivan's 1987 essay "Here Comes the Groom" (from the *New Republic* and available on Sullivan's blog). From these sources, what do you make of Sullivan's relationship with the gay community? With the right? With the left? How do these relationships influence his take on family values?

The Estrangement

Jamaica Kincaid

Jamaica Kincaid (b. 1949) was born Elaine Potter Richardson in St. John's, Antigua. She came to the United States at age 16 and attended the New School for Social Research and Franconia College. In time she became a staff writer for the New

Yorker *and started to publish her fiction in* Rolling Stone, *the* Paris Review, *and elsewhere. She has taught at several colleges, including Harvard University and currently Claremont-McKenna College, while compiling a distinguished body of fiction and nonfiction. Among her notable works are* Annie John *(1985),* A Small Place *(1988),* Lucy *(1991),* The Autobiography of My Mother *(1996), and* Among Flowers: A Walk in the Himalaya *(2005). In "The Estrangement," which appeared originally in a 2008 issue of* AARP Magazine, *Kincaid offers an account of the complicated relationship with her mother.*

1 Three years before my mother died, I decided not to speak to her again. And why? During a conversation over the telephone, she had once again let me know that my accomplishments—becoming a responsible and independent woman—did not amount to very much, that the life I lived was nothing more than a silly show, that she truly wished me dead. I didn't disagree. I didn't tell her that it would be just about the best thing in the world not to hear this from her.

2   And so, after that conversation, I never spoke to her, said a word to her of any kind, and then she died, and her death was a shock to me, not because I would miss her presence and long for it but because I could not believe that such a presence could ever be stilled.

3   For many years and many a time, her children, of which I was the only female, wondered what would happen to her, as we wondered what would happen to us; because she seemed to us not a mother at all but a God, not a Goddess but a God.

4   How to explain in this brief space what I mean? When we were children and in need of a mother's love and care, there was no better mother to provide such an ideal entity. When we were adolescents, and embracing with adolescent certainty our various incarnations, she could see through the thinness of our efforts, she could see through the emptiness of our aspirations; when we fell apart, there she was, bringing us dinner in jail or in a hospital ward, cold compresses for our temples, or just standing above us as we lay flat on our backs in bed. That sort of mother is God.

5   I am the oldest, by nine, eleven, and thirteen years, of four children. My three brothers and I share only our mother; they have the same father, I have a different one. I knew their father very well, better than they did, but I did not know my own. (When I was seven months in her womb, my mother quarreled with the man with whom she had conceived me and then ran away with the money he had been saving up to establish a little business for himself. He never forgave her.) I didn't mind not knowing my real father because in the place I am from, Antigua, when people love you, your blood relationship to them is not necessarily the most important component. My mother's husband, the father of my brothers, loved me, and his love took on the shape of a father's love: He told me about himself when he was a boy and the things he loved to do and the ways in which his life changed for better and worse, giving me some idea about how he came to be himself, my father, the father of my brothers, the person married to my mother.

6   She was a very nice person, apparently; that is what everybody said about her at her funeral. There were descriptions of her good and selfless deeds, kindnesses,

generosity, testaments of her love expressed in humor. We, her children, looked at one another in wonder then, for such a person as described was not at all known to us. The person we knew, our Mother, said horrible things to us more often than not.

The youngest of my three brothers died of AIDS when he was thirty-three years of age. In the years he spent actively dying, our mother tended to him with the greatest tenderness, a tenderness that was absent all the time before he was dying. Before he got sick, before he became afflicted with that disease, his mother, my mother too, quarreled with him and disparaged him. This was enabled by the fact that he did not know how to go off somewhere and make a home of any kind for himself. Yes, he had been unable to move out into the world, away from this woman, his mother, and become the sole possessor of his own destiny, with all the loss and gain that this implies. 7

The two remaining brothers and I buried her right next to him, and we were not sure we should have done that: For we didn't know then, and still don't know even now, if he wanted to spend eternity lying beside her, since we were sure we would rather be dead than spend eternity lying next to her. 8

Is this clear? It is to me right now as I write it: I would rather be dead than spend eternity with our mother! And do I really mean that when I say it? Yes, I really mean just that: After being my mother's daughter, I would rather be dead than spend eternity with her. 9

By the time my mother died, I was not only one of her four children, I had become the mother of two children: a girl and then a boy. This was bliss, my two children in love with me, and I with them. Nothing has gone wrong, as far as I can see, but tears have been shed over my not being completely enthusiastic about going to a final basketball game in a snowstorm, or my saying something I should have kept in my mind's mouth. A particularly unforgivable act in my children's eyes is a book's dedication I made to them; it read: "With blind, instinctive, and confused love to Annie and Harold, who from time to time are furiously certain that the only thing standing between them and a perfect union with their mother is the garden, and from time to time, they are correct." 10

I wrote this with a feeling of overbrimming love for them, my children. I was not thinking of my own mother directly, not thinking of her at all consciously at that exact time, but then again, I am always thinking of my mother; I believe every action of a certain kind that I make is completely influenced by her, completely infused with her realness, her existence in my life. 11

I am now middle-aged (fifty-nine years of age); I not only hope to live for a very long time after this, I will be angry in eternity if this turns out not to be the case. And so in eternity will my children want to be with me? And in eternity will I, their mother, want to be with them? 12

In regard to my children, eternity is right now, and I always want to be with them. In regard to my mother, my progenitor, eternity is beyond now, and is that not forever? I will not speak to her again in person, of that I am certain, but I am not sure that I will never speak to her again. For in eternity is she in me, and are even my children speaking to her? I do not know, I do not know. 13

COMPREHENSION

1. How does Kincaid describe her mother? Do you think she is fair-minded or biased in her perceptions? Explain.
2. In what ways does Kincaid resemble her mother? In what ways is she unlike this "God"? Is she aware of the complexities in this mother-daughter relationship? Why or why not? How does her mother's death alter her perception of this relationship?
3. Kincaid offers a brief, concentrated portrait of her family. Who are its members? Do you find this family to be traditional or atypical? Justify your response.

RHETORIC

1. What is the significance of Kincaid's title? What are its possible meanings? Does the title capture the complete meaning of the essay? Why or why not?
2. Does this essay have a thesis or claim? Justify your response by careful reference to the text.
3. Locate the details of her mother's life that Kincaid presents, and explain why the writer has selected these details. What tone emerges from these details?
4. This essay has three parts. What is the relationship among them?
5. Why does Kincaid pose a series of questions in the last two paragraphs? What is the final effect?

WRITING

1. Compose an honest and revealing appraisal of your relationship with your mother or another family member.
2. Write an essay in which you consider the roles that mothers play in various cultures. Base this essay on your own background and personal knowledge.
3. **Writing an Argument:** Can we ever escape or distance ourselves from the influence of our parents in our lives? Is such an escape even necessary or desirable? Write an argumentative essay in response to these questions.

NETWORKING
Applying Digital and Multimedia Literacies

Negotiating Parents, Privacy, and Technology: How do relatively recent innovations, like the wide use of personal cell phones and of social networking sites, influence your relationship with parents or guardians? Is your mother your Facebook friend? Is it harder to become independent and distance yourself from family when you can reach each other anywhere, anytime? In an essay, explore how parents or guardians and their adult children can create boundaries while staying connected in a 21st-century family.

Digital Scheherazades
in the Arab World

Fatema Mernissi

Fatema Mernissi (b. 1940), a contemporary sociologist, university professor, and feminist scholar, was born in Fez, Morocco. She received a degree in political science at Mohammad V University and a degree in sociology at the Sorbonne in Paris. In 1973, she earned a PhD in sociology at Brandeis University. At present, she is a research scholar at the University Institute for Scientific Research in Rabat. Mernissi's work focuses on the intersection of gender and religion in Muslim society. Among her numerous publications are The Veil and the Male Elite *(1975),* Islam and Democracy *(1992), and* Scheherazade Goes West *(2001). Two memoirs,* Dreams of Trespass *(1994) and* Harem Days *(1999), recount her life growing up as Muslim, Moroccan, and female. In this essay, published in* Current History *in 2006, Mernissi assesses the changing roles of women in the Arab Gulf as technology influences the thinking of a previously all-male elite.*

In May 2005, I listened attentively to the questions of the 30 journalists my Spanish 1 publisher had scheduled to meet with me in Madrid to promote the translation of my book, *Les Sindbads marocains: Voyage dans le Maroc civique (Moroccan Sinbads: Travels through Civic Morocco)*. From their questions, which all dealt with the veil and terrorism, it was clear that they had no clue about the strategic issue mobilizing the Arab world: *alfitna raqmiya* (digital chaos), the destruction of space frontiers by information technology.

The key problem that makes everyone anxious today in the Arab world—elites 2 and masses, heads of state and street vendors, men and women—is the digital chaos induced by information technologies such as the Internet. These new technologies have destroyed the *hudud,* the frontier that divided the universe into a sheltered private arena, where women and children were supposed to be protected, and a public one where adult males exercised their presumed problem-solving authority.

Now, according to a best-selling book, *The Internet and Love (Al Internet Wa* 3 *I-Hub),* by Imam Qaradawi, a star host on the Arab television network Al Jazeera, the satellite and the Internet have spawned apocalyptic chaos in Arab civilization by destroying that division of spheres. The imam's book, which is advertised on the popular IslamOnline website, is alerting crowds to the fact that Arab women and youth now navigate freely on the web and communicate intimately with strangers, escaping religious and parental censorship.

"Since the World Wide Web invaded our lives," explains Qaradawi, "we have 4 been going through nonstop transformations. . . . The faraway has become nearer with a simple push on the keyboard. This has deeply affected our societies, which

have suffered from a lack of communication and the lack of educational quality entertainment. . . . Suddenly, the new technologies have provided opportunities to communicate and entertain oneself, and this without the supervision of a censoring authority
or a controller to whom you are accountable. . . . This leaves individual responsibility
as the sole controlling agency. And unfortunately, we have never cared to develop an
educational system which focused on developing individual responsibility."

5   But what is also new is that even imams suggest we stop thinking about static
solutions like strengthening authority and reinforcing hudud and focus instead on
inventing strategies that nurture a civilization of ethical nomadism, where individual responsibility creates order. The Arab world is a besieged place, but in
many quarters the response to chaos is quietly shifting from crying to action.
This shift helps explain the emergence of what I call "digital Scheherazades,"
after the fictional storyteller of *1,001 Nights.* Her successors are Arab women
who take advantage of new communication strategies as the only initiatives likely
to liberate both themselves and their countries.

Digital Chaos

6 Imagine the anxiety of a parent reading "The Electronic Disfiguration of Our Children," an article by an Egyptian psychoanalyst, Dr. Khalil Fadel, that appeared in
the Kuwait-based *Al Arabi,* one of the most widely circulated cultural magazines
in the region. Fadel identifies the child as the most vulnerable victim of the West-
ern-made electronic war games that invade "our children's rooms and are available in the cyber-cafés which now exist on every street corner." According to Fadel,
these war games are responsible for inciting violent behavior among Arab youth
because they glorify "solitude, narcissism, and hatred of the other," all of which
reflect the cultural choices of the Westerners who produce these games.

7   But if electronic war games are bad enough, sex is worse, according to an
article—"Electronic Sex Attack on the Arab World"—by Ahmed Mohamed Ali in
the Saudi-based magazine *Al Majalla.* Ali, who believes this attack was first
launched in 1999, describes "the unimaginable profit made from selling virtual
prostitution or electronic sex on the Internet" to Arabs. Parents, he says, quoting
Al-Hami Abdelaziz, an Egyptian psychology professor, are totally at a loss about
what to do: "They know that the future of their children depends on their mastering
such technologies, but they are afraid they will slip into these pornographic web-
sites. The fact is that the parents are totally unarmed and ill-equipped to protect
their children from such dangers."

8   Add to this the booming Arab satellite industry of erotic video-clips targeting
youth. These clips constitute a terrifying challenge to the Islamic vision of the
world, where sex belongs exclusively to the private sphere (which explains why no
straightforward pornographic films are to be found on Arab satellite stations such
as Arabsat and Nilesat). The video-clip is a tricky phenomenon, since its official
objective is entertainment through music and songs. For Arabs, music and songs,
just like poetry, have been regarded, even before Islam and since, as important
sources of licit pleasure. Now they must confront the digital chaos induced by

music video-clips that slip into explicit sex between unmarried people surrounding the singer. As Patricia Kabala has written, the video-clip "has without doubt become a symbol of access via satellite television stations and the Internet to the previously inaccessible sexually explicit material that state-controlled television channels in the Middle East censored and continue to censor."

Yet what is interesting once again is that instead of wasting time in complaints   9
as Arabs usually do, a new attitude has appeared, the desire to invent solutions. Some ethically minded operators are trying to exploit that very video-clip technology to spread Islamic values among the youth. To counteract the sexual flood, investing in video-clips to promote young attractive religious singers as role models—such as Sami Yusuf Yusu, a British-born Muslim of Azeri origin—is one of the emerging positive responses to the previously frightening new information technologies. The lesson one gets from reading about the video-clip debate is that either you transform yourself into an agile digital surfer or you fade away.

It is this kind of immense civilizational shift in the Arab world, where men are   10
finally embarking on becoming skilled digital nomads instead of decrying the frontier's collapse and dreaming of harems for their wives, that I tried to share with the Spanish journalists obsessed by the veil and terrorism during my Madrid encounter in May 2005. Although the Spanish city of Gibraltar is just 13 kilometers from the Moroccan port of Tangiers, I realized that Spaniards had no idea about the revolution that information technologies have produced in our part of the world. And one reason for this is the fact that in Madrid's plush hotel, which advertised itself as satellite-connected, I could not connect to my favorite, Al Jazeera, or to any one of the two hundred pan-Arab satellite channels beaming now in the Mediterranean.

At one point, I tried to illustrate this change by sharing with them the extraor-   11
dinary emergence of women I saw in the Arab Gulf during a visit to Bahrain in March 2005. I tried to describe to them Mai al-Khalifa, a historian who in less than a decade has created modern spaces such as museums and cultural centers that encourage dialogue between the sexes and the generations. I tried to explain that this unexpected emergence of women in the oil-rich Arab Gulf is more significant than the question of the veil in the Muslim migrant community, but the Spanish journalists were trapped in their own veils and terror.

I left Madrid feeling guilty and helpless, an intellectual unable to carry out   12
her job of facilitating dialogue. The journalists continued to haunt me after my return to Morocco, and when I saw al-Khalifa on a pan-Arab satellite television one day, I caught myself wishing they could share that experience with me.

The Historian on TV

The café near University Mohamed V in Rabat was full of young students and teach-   13
ers when al-Khalifa appeared on Al Arabia, a new rival of Al Jazeera that is financed by the Saudis. The manager of the café automatically turned up the television's volume because he was a fan of Turki al-Dakhil, the show's anchor, an electrifying young man who appears on the screen dressed in the Gulf region's traditional white robes just to surprise you by his insolent remarks toward all kinds of authorities.

14   At this moment, I noticed a striking change in the café: Conversations came to a halt even though al-Khalifa was dressed like a professional woman in a white ouit and looked very much on guard, unlike belly dancers who blink their eyes and sway hands and buttocks. The dynamics of what occurred in my Rabat café were as important for me as what was happening on the television screen. (When I was a child, the only women one could see in my hometown, Fez, in movies or on television when it made its appearance in Morocco in the 1960s, were belly dancers and singers; intellectual women were not part of the fare.)

15   It was by chance that I was in the café, because I am a rather homebound creature. I was invited there by Kamal, one of my favorite colleagues, who is a *1,001 Nights* expert. He was intrigued by what I had told him about my March 2005 Bahrain trip because there is very little cultural exchange between North Africa and the Gulf. The gender ratio in the café was typical of Morocco: 10 women among 40 or so customers. Moroccan women, starting with myself, are so exhausted by their daily chores that they rarely think about going out in the evening.

16   One of al-Khalifa's best-known books deals with the Qarmatians, a controversial group of Shiites who rebelled in the tenth century against the Sunni Abbasid caliphs, described as terrorists by some historians and as the founders of the first republic in Islam by others. I thought this would be the topic al-Dakhil, the Al Arabia host, would start with. To my great surprise, he opted for a very personal angle instead: Why was al-Khalifa so controversial in her own country? One has to realize that the title of the show is *Idaat,* which literally means "Flashes." The host is supposed to help the viewer discover some secret corner of those he invites to his show.

17   Why, wondered al-Dakhil, was al-Khalifa generating so much debate in Bahrain concerning the projects she promoted as one of the first women to hold an official position? (Al-Khalifa was the first woman to be appointed in Bahrain as assistant undersecretary for culture and national heritage.) Was it because she was a woman, or because she was incompetent, coming from an academic background and being thus unfit for practical work? Some people at the Ministry of Information, al-Dakhil argued, were saying that academics are too isolated in their ivory towers to be effective cultural operators.

18   "That intellectuals are unable to invent effective cultural strategies is a totally wrong assumption," al-Khalifa responded brusquely, brushing her black hair away from her face. Such statements, she added, are typical of bureaucrats who are in fact totally unfit to design the dynamic cultural strategies the Arab world needs to face the challenges posed by new technologies, and this for the simple reason that they lack vision. "I am an intellectual who has both a clear vision (*ruya*) of the future and the capacity to go ahead and act by undertaking successful innovative projects." Only intellectuals, she stressed, have *ruya,* a precious gift amid today's global chaos.

19   The reaction to al-Khalifa's response in the café was amazing. The crowd laughed merrily. One of the students stood up to declaim the Palestinian Mahmoud Darwish's poem about his compatriot Edward Said, in which he celebrates a

strong vision rooted in one's reading of the past as the key allowing the Palestinian diaspora to survive and thrive: "If your past is a tough experience, make your future meaningful by developing a vision. . . . My dream directs my steps. And my vision places my dream in my lap like a friendly cat."

The Vision Thing

The absence of a clear vision of the future has been identified by Arab intellectuals [20] as a contributor to the dangerous political disengagement of Arab youth and their confusion, which makes them vulnerable to the violence spread on the Internet. The new voices of the Arab diaspora include the Palestinian Khaled Hroub, who lives in London but is extremely influential among young Arabs because he hosts a show on Al Jazeera. He argues in his recent book on Hamas that the generational gap is particularly explosive in Arab society.

Indeed, one of the causes of terrorism is the demographic split between the [21] aging minority of decision makers and the youthful majority they are supposed to represent. In a burlesque article published in the very academic journal of the Arab League, Hroub notices that being "decadently old" (*chaykhoukha*) does not help Arab leaders design pertinent strategies for the majority of the population, which is young. The tiny minority that monopolizes political decisions, he says, "operates on a set of concepts and reasoning frameworks that have very little relevancy to the youth's own problems." It is this politico-demographic divide, he concludes, that explains "the disastrous scorn of our younger generations for politics." And this brings us to the enigma of why the café youth reacted so strongly when the word *ruya* came up on the television show.

To stop terrorism, Arab leaders have to provide Arab youth with a vision of a fu- [22] ture in which they have a role to play as defenders of an ethical planet, explains Nabil Abdel-Fattah of the Al Ahram Center for Political and Strategic Studies in Egypt. The frustration of Arab youth results from the elite's failure to articulate a clear ethical view of a future in which every individual has a mission and a purpose. It is this emergence of the *ruya* as the antidote to terrorism that explains the café crowd's response to al-Khalifa's defiant answer to her television host. She was reminding him that her *ruya* is the likely reason why some Bahrain government bureaucrats were angered by her audacious cultural projects such as museums and cultural centers that teach children to understand that diversity is the root of their identity.

Because Arabs in general and youth in particular are fed up with fanaticism [23] and censorship, neighborhood cafés are turning, thanks to the new culture-focus satellite television outlets such as Al Jazeera and Al Arabia, to debates over *ruya*, visions of the future as the key to empowerment.

Many men in the café followed the rough exchange between al-Dakhil and his [24] guest with beaming smiles, including my colleague Kamal. I asked him why he was smiling and he said because al-Khalifa's quick response to al-Dakhil was so spontaneous: "I think Arab intellectuals should create a fund to support this lady," he said, "because she is creating fantastic publicity for us. If she continues appearing on television shows making such statements, we, the poor marginalized intellectuals, will soon be receiving well-paid job offers to replace our vision-blind bureaucrats in all the 22 Arab states!"

25   Kamal was right, because very few Arab male intellectuals would have dared to declare with so much self-confidence, as al-Khalifa did on television, that they are visionaries and that only far-sighted thinkers can invent futuristic strategies for an Arab world doubly assaulted by both new information technologies and the powerful American military. Yet one of the positive changes initiated by these assaults is that people have stopped complaining and are going one step further toward identifying concrete solutions: first defeat the bureaucrats who have monopolized power for decades.

26   It is a daring message that increasingly bold women, making use of the new information technologies, are proclaiming to fellow Arabs. In the Arab Gulf, the amazing thing about this new breed of women is that growing numbers of them, like al-Khalifa, do not limit themselves to writing but manage to jump into action as well. "She, like Sheikha Hussa Al-Sabah from Kuwait, builds museums and cultural centers like other women turn out couscous tagines!" remarked my colleague, who always condemned my decision not to get involved in politics. For Kamal, who, unlike me, became involved in politics and paid for it by having trouble with the Moroccan police, it is clear that now only intellectuals can help rulers to engineer power and engage the future.

27   The challenge for the intellectuals is to help rulers equip the youth to navigate responsibly on the Internet. In particular, these solutions must help young people navigate not only in space but also in time. In a globalized planet where meeting strangers daily is the only way to make a living, mastering time is the secret of graceful navigation. To travel in the past, that is, to navigate in time, is the best way to teach oneself tolerance and respect for diversity.

28   Mobility is the name of the game, be they men or women, local or exiled, Sunni or Shiite, upper-class or from modest backgrounds. We are seeing a sudden shift from complaining about the West and its technological superiority to deciding to begin using the new information technologies to protect ourselves by participating in building a more just and humanist planet. Oil wealth, which makes it easy for visionaries to step quickly from vision to realization, has helped fuel this shift in the Arab Gulf. But so has the emergence of women in a region supposedly condemned to archaic conservatism.

Women Can Play Too

29 Is it because the threats of destabilization and terrorism are so great in the oil-rich Arab Gulf that emirs and sheikhs are keen on promoting e-government and women as information technology and financial allies? Or is it because the new information technologies are perceived by them as a fantastic opportunity to get rid of American domination and empower themselves to become global cyber-surfers? What is certain is that electronic surfing has become a favorite sport of the Gulf rulers, and they are discovering a secret rule of this game: that it is essential for women to join in.

Al-Khalifa's emergence in Bahrain is impossible to understand if you do not 30 realize that Bahrain is one of the first Arab countries to invest in e-government. The first step was the creation of an electronic visa system—an e-visa service— that went into operation in mid-2004. The second was reported on the front page of the *Bahrain Tribune* on March 9, 2005: "King Stresses Larger Role for Women." The story explained that "His Majesty the King, Hamad bin Isa al-Khalifa, yesterday requested all government and civil administrations and organizations to help implement the National Strategy for the Advancement of Bahraini Women."

To make sure that his routine-inclined bureaucrats grasped what he meant, 31 the king provided a detailed description: "The implementation of the National Strategy, the first of its type in the country, will help us achieve our objective, which is to see women assume their roles fully as dependable partners to men and fully capable of contributing to building the family, the society, and the state, and eventually, to be involved in making decisions in modern Bahrain."

It is important to note, in this context, that the number of women employed in 32 Bahrain has risen from just over 5 percent in 1971 to more than 40 percent today. Now how can you explain this strange coincidence between the onset of e-government and women's invasion of the labor force and their promotion as public actors if not by a cataclysmic shift in the region's ideological references? Is there not a repudiation of fanatic conservatism to embark on new horizons where power implies feminization of decision making?

In a humorous 2004 article entitled "The 50 Most Powerful Arab Women," 33 which appeared in the Dubai-based Arabic version of *Forbes* magazine, the editor, Rasha Owais, and her team undertook a survey to answer that question. They came to the conclusion that, beyond the traditional profile of the wives and daughters of heads of state, a new breed of digitally literate and financially skilled women has emerged on the Arab scene.

Some of them do fit the profile of wives of leaders, but—unlike, say, Egypt's 34 Suzan Mubarak or Queen Rania of Jordan—the new Digital Scheherazades are themselves communication wizards. For example, Sheikha Muza, the wife of

A woman in charge: Sheikha Lubna al-Qasimi, minister of economy and planning for the UAE, speaks during a meeting in Abu Dhabi.

the emir of Qatar, the man who financed Al Jazeera, launched in September 2005 the first Arab children's channel. The ambitious objective, financed by a foundation she controls, is to snatch Arab kids from the foreign television influence by providing them with a new ethical content where education and entertainment mix.

35   Being from a royal family helps, of course, but not automatically: I know many wives of powerful, rich men who spend their time swallowing antidepression pills. Self-confidence and ability seem to be key characteristics of the new Digital Scheherazades.

36   When you start looking for them instead of focusing on the veiled women, as many Europeans do, you are amazed by their rapidly growing number. The minister of economy and planning for the United Arab Emirates, for example, is a woman: Lubna al-Qasimi. Before assuming this post, al-Qasimi, who has a computer science degree from the University of California, was a senior manager of the Information Systems department of the Dubai Port Authority and participated in the launch of her country as a planetary digital hub.

Investing in Female Brains

37 Did al-Qasimi owe her success to her being the niece of Sheikh Sultan bin Mohammed al-Qasimi, the ruler of Sharjah, one of the United Arab Emirate kingdoms? There are numerous nieces of powerful emirs and sheikhs in the Gulf who never manage to emerge as top players in the power game. One of her favorite slogans is "I have earned my desk."

38   Indeed, those who still identify the region with veiling women and traditional archaism miss the essential point: the Arab Gulf's previously all-male ruling elite is investing in female brains as the winning card for information-fueled power. "We have a system for our children whereby we encourage them to gain experience outside the group first," says Muhamed al-Sayer, the billionaire chairman of a Kuwait-based group of companies. "For example, my daughter Lulwa spent eight years with Gulf Bank and is its head of Treasury. Male and female family members are offered the same opportunities."

39   It is this fascinating paradox that explains the emergence of Digital Scheherazades. Because men in the Arab Gulf have chosen to invest in communication as a power base, we can understand why one of the most important modern museum initiatives in Kuwait was that of Hussa al-Sabah, who forced Saddam Hussein to give back the cultural heritage pieces stolen from Kuwait after Iraq's invasion, and whose main supporter was her husband. Kuwait is also home to the very young Maha al-Ghunaim, the vice chairwoman and managing director of Global Investment House, which had net profits of $73 million in 2004.

40   In Qatar, where the clever emir propelled his tiny capital of Doha into a global player by financing Al Jazeera, one would expect to find Digital Scheherazades taking advantage of the kingdom's new information technologies. Such is the case with Hanadi Nasser, a businesswoman who has become a key player as the managing director of Amwal, a well-funded Qatari investment company.

The Caliph's Partner

According to my friend Kamal, Caliph Harun al-Rashid, who took power in Baghdad   41
in 786 AD, is the key to elucidating the enigma of the Digital Scheherazades. The
caliph's wife, Zubaida, made herself famous by digging wells along the Baghdad-
Mecca road she had built to transform Muslims' yearly hajj into a comfortable and
engaging trip.

Both Harun and Zubaida were heroes of the *1,001 Nights,* invented by eighth-   42
and ninth-century Baghdad male street-storytellers who mirrored in their tales
the fascination of Muslim elites and crowds with strangers as a source of magic
diversity. And the primary fascinating strangers for men are indeed women. So,
although Scheherazade, the storyteller of the *1,001 Nights,* was supposed to be
Persian, it was Arab women like Princess Zubaida—who managed to seduce the
Caliph Harun while digging wells and building walls to provide creature comforts
during the hajj—who inspired our Baghdad storytellers.

These male storytellers forbade in their fiction the imaginary Scheherazade   43
to speak during the day and condemned her to limit her activity to the night only,
but modern historians are discovering that Zubaida exercised her power 24
hours a day.

Limiting women's power to the night while forbidding them from exercising   44
authority during daylight—the monopoly of males—is a deep-seated reflex that
goes back far into history. It is well condensed in the slogan-like sentence that
ends mechanically each of the 1,001 stories: "When dawn overtook Scheherazade,
she lapsed into silence." But limiting women's power to the private sphere has always been a male fiction. And the defensive fear of the feminine has always gone
together with the fear of strangers. When the leaders of a nation embark on communication as their way to glory, welcoming the different other as a partner is the
magic shift that explains their success.

To understand why modern Arab Gulf emirs are suddenly investing in in-   45
formation technology as their power base and promoting women as their partners, we must go back to Harun, who did the same when he decided to invest
in the paper industry to launch Islam as a communication-powered civilization
whose main weapon was the Arabic language. Just as today, Arabs were scientifically backward in the eighth century, but their switch to communication
enabled them to catch up with other nations by using language to navigate and
conduct dialogue. Arabic, the language of illiterate pagans, was transformed
into a medium of religion, the law, and sciences, promoting the Arabs to global
prominence.

Are we witnessing once again the emergence of women as brainy allies when   46
men opt for communication as their power base? Just to make sure you do not
take me to be blindly optimistic, let me tell you that Western television companies
such as the BBC and CBC are worried about competition in the United States
from Al Jazeera, which has decided to launch an English language channel. As a
woman, I will be more than thrilled if the competition between East and West
switches from bombs and armies to communication strategies.

COMPREHENSION

1. Who is Scheherazade? (If necessary, check Google or another site for information.) Where does she (or the connotations she evokes) appear in the essay?
2. What does Mernissi mean by "digital chaos"? What examples does she provide to illuminate this idea?
3. Explain the connections between digital chaos and the changing roles of women in Muslim society.

RHETORIC

1. Is Mernissi's purpose to inform or to argue—or perhaps both? Justify your response by citing specific sentences and passages.
2. Mernissi's essay appeared in the journal *Current History*. What assumptions does she make about her primary audience? How does she establish her authority for this audience? How might the article appeal to a broader audience?
3. What is the effect of Mernissi's dividing the essay into sections? How does she manage transitions?
4. Analyze the ways in which Scheherazade serves as both symbol and organizing strategy in the essay.
5. Mernissi uses several forms of evidence to support her key ideas. Identify these various strategies of exemplification, and cite specific passages reflecting them.
6. The author is a noted feminist scholar. How do her feminist assumptions affect the tone of the essay? Where does she inject personal opinion? Where, if anywhere, does she make ethical and emotional appeals?

WRITING

1. Although Mernissi writes about a part of the world that might not be familiar, she raises issues that have not just regional but global implications. Write an analytical essay in which you examine the ways in which "digital chaos" is changing gender relationships in the United States or elsewhere.
2. Write a comparative essay linking the articles by Andrew Sullivan and Fatema Mernissi appearing in this chapter.

NETWORKING
Applying Digital and Multimedia Literacies

WRITING AN ARGUMENT   Exploring the Effectiveness of New Communication Strategies: Do you believe that "new communication strategies," as Mernissi terms it, can actually liberate women and reform society? Argue for or against this proposition.

Synthesis: Connections for Critical Thinking

1. Annie Dillard's "An American Childhood" and E. B. White's "Once More to the Lake" explore the experience of childhood from a different perspective. Do they share a common voice or mood? What is distinctive about each essay? Which essay do you prefer, and why? Consider the style and emotional impact of the writing.
2. Both Andrew Sullivan's "Why Gay Marriage Is Good for America" and Richard Rodriguez's "Family Values" attempt to alter stereotypes commonly held about contemporary families. What type of family does each author address? How do the authors differ in their rhetorical strategies and their use of supporting points to buttress their arguments? Who is the implied audience for each of the essays? How did you reach your conclusion?
3. Argue for or against the claim that Kincaid's portrayal of her mother and Mernissi's analysis of Arab men are biased.
4. Argue for or against the idea that descriptions of the relatively new types of family relationships described by Mernissi's "Digital Scheherazades in the Arab World" or in Rodriguez's "Family Values" are presented in a biased, romanticized manner.
5. Argue for or against the view that changes in society and its norms—specifically, increased geographical mobility, an evolving workplace, ideas about economic class, individual liberties, and sexual preference—have resulted in new forms of identity. Use examples from the work of Hood, Mernissi, and Rodriguez.
6. Select the two more substantially argued essays in this chapter, Mernissi's "Digital Scheherazades in the Arab World" and Rodriguez's "Family Values." Compare and contrast their methods of argumentation.
7. Establish your own definition of what it means to be a male or a female. Refer to the essays of Didion, Kincaid, Mernissi, and Rodriguez.

NETWORKING
Applying Digital and Multimedia Literacies

1. Join several newsgroups or chat rooms that focus on online dating. Compare and contrast the ideological focus of the conversations among members.
2. Create your own blog, and post a selected quote regarding the family taken from one of your essays. Enable comments so fellow students can respond regarding the quotation. At the end of the semester, write a report and summary of the responses you received. You may ask students to include their country of origin or their ethnicity to help you find possible connections between these factors and the responses.

chapter 8

Business and Economics
How Do We Earn Our Keep?

Work is central to the human experience; in fact, it is work and its economic and social outcomes that provide us with the keys to an understanding of culture and civilization. Work tells us much about scarcity and abundance, poverty and affluence, the haves and have-nots in any society, as well as a nation's economic imperatives. Whether it is the rise and fall of cities, the conduct of business and corporations, or the economic policies of government, we see in the culture of work an attempt to impose order on nature. Work is our handprint on the world.

The work we perform and the careers we pursue also define us in very personal ways. "I'm a professor at Harvard" or "I work for Google" serve as identity badges. (Robert Reich, a contributor to this chapter, once worked at Harvard.) For what we do explains, at least in part, what and who we are. The very act of looking for work illuminates one's status in society, one's background, one's aspirations. Jonathan Swift, in his classic essay "A Modest Proposal," written in 1729, demonstrates how labor reveals economic and political configurations of power. Over 250 years later, Reich tells us the same thing in his analysis of the changing nature of work and the way these changes create an even broader gap between rich and poor.

Work is not merely an important human activity but an essential one for social and psychological health. You might like your work, or you might loathe it; be employed or unemployed; enjoy the reputation of a workaholic or a person who lives for leisure time; view work as a curse or as a duty. Regardless, it is work that occupies a central position in your relationship to society. In fact, Sigmund Freud spoke of work as the basis of one's social reality.

Regardless of your perspective on the issue, it is important to understand the multiple dimensions of work. In both traditional and modern societies, work prepares us for economic and social roles. It affects families, school curricula, and public policy. Ultimately, as many authors here suggest, it determines our self-esteem. Through work we come to terms with ourselves and our environment. The nature and purpose of the work we do provide us with a powerful measure of our worth.

PREVIEWING THE CHAPTER

As you read the essays in this chapter and respond to them in discussion and writing, consider the following questions:

- What are the significant forms of support the author uses in viewing the world of work: observation, statistics, personal experience, history, and so on?
- What assumptions does the author make about the value of work?
- Does the author discuss work in general or focus on one particular aspect of work?
- How does the writer define *work?* In what ways, if any, does she or he expand on the simple definition of work as "paid employment"?
- What issues of race, class, and gender does the author raise?
- What is the relationship of work to the changing social, political, and economic systems depicted in the author's essay?
- What tone does the writer take in his or her presentation of the work experience?
- What psychological insights does the author offer into the culture of work?
- What does the writer's style reveal about her or his attitude toward work?

Classic and Contemporary Images
WILL WORKERS BE DISPLACED BY MACHINES?

Using a Critical Perspective   Diego Rivera's mural and the photograph of an automobile assembly line present industrial scenes that reveal the impact of technology on workers. What details are emphasized in each illustration? How are these two images similar and dissimilar? What, for example, is the relation of human beings to the machines that are the centerpiece of each photograph? Are the artist and photographer objective or subjective in the presentation of each scene? Explain.

In the era known as the "Machine Age," 1918–1941, many artists, industrial designers, and architects in the United States and Europe evoked the mechanisms and images of industry in their works. During this time, the Mexican painter Diego Rivera (1886–1957) created a mural for the Detroit Institute of Arts (1932–33), a portion of which is reprinted here.

Today, computers are used to help
control assembly lines, as shown in
this photo of an automobile assembly line.

✳

Classic and Contemporary Essays
DOES EQUAL OPPORTUNITY EXIST?

Virginia Woolf's "Professions for Women" is ironic from the start as she readily admits she can speak expertly of only one profession, her own, which is writing. But her message is clear regarding the effect of living in a male-dominated society. Simply put, it is very difficult to break the shackles of conditioning that one acquires from being told over and over again by one's culture that gender is destiny, regardless of what one aspires to. The author—through personal experience—demonstrates how this discrimination has a profound effect on the ability to see with one's own eyes and to think with one's own mind. Henry Louis Gates Jr. presents an interesting variation on this theme. Although the outcome is the same, the premise is reversed. He demonstrates how correlating supposedly positive attributes to a group—that is, superior athletic performance and race—results in the same deadening of the sense of personal ambition and a limiting of the scope of what one can aspire to. The thoughtful reader should be able to learn valuable lessons from comparing and contrasting these essays—one of which is that misguided perception all too often can be a self-fulfilling prophecy.

✸

Professions for Women

Virginia Woolf

Virginia Woolf *(1882–1941), novelist and essayist, was the daughter of Sir Leslie Stephen, a famous critic and writer on economics. An experimental novelist, Woolf attempted to portray consciousness through a poetic, symbolic, and concrete style. Her novels include* Jacob's Room *(1922),* Mrs. Dalloway *(1925),* To the Lighthouse *(1927), and* The Waves *(1931). She was also a perceptive reader and critic; her criticism appears in* The Common Reader *(1925) and* The Second Common Reader *(1933). In the following essay, which was delivered originally as a speech to the Women's Service League in 1931, Woolf argues that women must overcome several "angels," or phantoms, in order to succeed in professional careers.*

1   When your secretary invited me to come here, she told me that your Society is concerned with the employment of women and she suggested that I might tell you something about my own professional experiences. It is true I am a woman; it is true I am employed; but what professional experiences have I had? It is difficult to say. My profession is literature; and in that profession there are fewer experiences

for women than in any other, with the exception of the stage—fewer, I mean, that are peculiar to women. For the road was cut many years ago—by Fanny Burney, by Aphra Behn, by Harriet Martineau, by Jane Austen, by George Eliot—many famous women, and many more unknown and forgotten, have been before me, making the path smooth, and regulating my steps. Thus, when I came to write, there were very few material obstacles in my way. Writing was a reputable and harmless occupation. The family peace was not broken by the scratching of a pen. No demand was made upon the family purse. For ten and sixpence one can buy paper enough to write all the plays of Shakespeare—if one has a mind that way. Pianos and models, Paris, Vienna and Berlin, masters and mistresses, are not needed by a writer. The cheapness of writing paper is, of course, the reason why women have succeeded as writers before they have succeeded in the other professions.

But to tell you my story—it is a simple one. You have only got to figure to 2 yourselves a girl in a bedroom with a pen in her hand. She had only to move that pen from left to right—from ten o'clock to one. Then it occurred to her to do what is simple and cheap enough after all—to slip a few of those pages into an envelope, fix a penny stamp in the corner, and drop the envelope into the red box at the corner. It was thus that I became a journalist; and my effort was rewarded on the first day of the following month—a very glorious day it was for me—by a letter from an editor containing a check for one pound ten shillings and sixpence. But to show you how little I deserve to be called a professional woman, how little I know of the struggles and difficulties of such lives, I have to admit that instead of spending that sum upon bread and butter, rent, shoes and stockings, or butcher's bills, I went out and bought a cat—a beautiful cat, a Persian cat, which very soon involved me in bitter disputes with my neighbors.

What could be easier than to write articles and to buy Persian cats with the 3 profits? But wait a moment. Articles have to be about something. Mine, I seem to remember, was about a novel by a famous man. And while I was writing this review, I discovered that if I were going to review books I should need to do battle with a certain phantom. And the phantom was a woman, and when I came to know her better I called her after the heroine of a famous poem, "The Angel in the House." It was she who used to come between me and my paper when I was writing reviews. It was she who bothered me and wasted my time and so tormented me that at last I killed her. You who come of a younger and happier generation may not have heard of her—you may not know what I mean by the Angel in the House. I will describe her as shortly as I can. She was intensely sympathetic. She was immensely charming. She was utterly unselfish. She excelled in the difficult arts of family life. She sacrificed herself daily. If there was a chicken, she took the leg; if there was a draught she sat in it—in short she was so constituted that she never had a mind or a wish of her own, but preferred to sympathize always with the minds and wishes of others. Above all—I need not say it—she was pure. Her purity was supposed to be her chief beauty—her blushes, her great grace. In those days—the last of Queen Victoria—every house had its Angel. And when I came to write I encountered her with the very first words. The shadow of her wings fell on my page; I heard the rustling of her skirts in the room.

Directly, that is to say, I took my pen in hand to review that novel by a famous man, she slipped behind me and whispered: "My dear, you are a young woman. You are writing about a book that has been written by a man. Be sympathetic; be tender; flatter; deceive; use all the arts and wiles of our sex. Never let anybody guess that you have a mind of your own. Above all, be pure." And she made as if to guide my pen. I now record the one act for which I take some credit to myself, though the credit rightly belongs to some excellent ancestors of mine who left me a certain sum of money—shall we say five hundred pounds a year—so that it was not necessary for me to depend solely on charm for my living. I turned upon her and caught her by the throat. I did my best to kill her. My excuse, if I were to be had up in a court of law, would be that I acted in self-defense. Had I not killed her she would have killed me. She would have plucked the heart out of my writing. For, as I found, directly I put pen to paper, you cannot review even a novel without having a mind of your own, without expressing what you think to be the truth about human relations, morality, sex. And all these questions, according to the Angel in the House, cannot be dealt with freely and openly by women; they must charm, they must conciliate, they must—to put it bluntly—tell lies if they are to succeed. Thus, whenever I felt the shadow of her wing or the radiance of her halo upon my page, I took up the inkpot and flung it at her. She died hard. Her fictitious nature was of great assistance to her. It is far harder to kill a phantom than a reality. She was always creeping back when I thought I had dispatched her. Though I flatter myself that I killed her in the end, the struggle was severe; it took much time that had better have been spent upon learning Greek grammar; or in roaming the world in search of adventures. But it was a real experience; it was an experience that was bound to befall all women writers at that time. Killing the Angel in the House was part of the occupation of a woman writer.

4   But to continue my story. The Angel was dead; what then remained? You may say that what remained was a simple and common object—a young woman in a bedroom with an inkpot. In other words, now that she had rid herself of falsehood, that young woman had only to be herself. Ah, but what is "herself"? I mean, what is a woman? I assure you, I do not know. I do not believe that you know. I do not believe that anybody can know until she has expressed herself in all the arts and professions open to human skill. That indeed is one of the reasons why I have come here—out of respect for you, who are in process of showing us by your experiments what a woman is, who are in process of providing us, by your failures and successes, with that extremely important piece of information.

5   But to continue the story of my professional experiences. I made one pound ten and six by my first review; and I bought a Persian cat with the proceeds. Then I grew ambitious. A Persian cat is all very well, I said; but a Persian cat is not enough. I must have a motor car. And it was thus that I became a novelist— for it is a very strange thing that people will give you a motor car if you will tell them a story. It is a still stranger thing that there is nothing so delightful in the world as telling stories. It is far pleasanter than writing reviews of famous novels. And yet, if I am to obey your secretary and tell you my professional experiences as a novelist, I must tell you about a very strange experience that befell me as a

novelist. And to understand it you must try first to imagine a novelist's state of mind. I hope I am not giving away professional secrets if I say that a novelist's chief desire is to be as unconscious as possible. He has to induce in himself a state of perpetual lethargy. He wants life to proceed with the utmost quiet and regularity. He wants to see the same faces, to read the same books, to do the same things day after day, month after month, while he is writing, so that nothing may break the illusion in which he is living—so that nothing may disturb or disquiet the mysterious nosings about, feelings round, darts, dashes and sudden discoveries of that very shy and illusive spirit, the imagination. I suspect that this state is the same both for men and women. Be that as it may, I want you to imagine me writing a novel in a state of trance. I want you to figure to yourselves a girl sitting with a pen in her hand, which for minutes, and indeed for hours, she never dips into the inkpot. The image that comes to my mind when I think of this girl is the image of a fisherman lying sunk in dreams on the verge of a deep lake with a rod held out over the water. She was letting her imagination sweep unchecked round every rock and cranny of the world that lies submerged in the depths of our unconscious being. Now came the experience, the experience that I believe to be far commoner with women writers than with men. The line raced through the girl's fingers. Her imagination had rushed away. It had sought the pools, the depths, the dark places where the largest fish slumber. And then there was a smash. There was an explosion. There was foam and confusion. The imagination had dashed itself against something hard. The girl was roused from her dream. She was indeed in a state of the most acute and difficult distress. To speak without figure she had thought of something, something about the body, about the passions which it was unfitting for her as a woman to say. Men, her reason told her, would be shocked. The consciousness of what men will say of a woman who speaks the truth about her passions had roused her from her artist's state of unconsciousness. She could write no more. The trance was over. Her imagination could work no longer. This I believe to be a very common experience with women writers—they are impeded by the extreme conventionality of the other sex. For though men sensibly allow themselves great freedom in these respects, I doubt that they realize or can control the extreme severity with which they condemn such freedom in women.

These then were two very genuine experiences of my own. These were two of 6 the adventures of my professional life. The first—killing the Angel in the House— I think I solved. She died. But the second, telling the truth about my own experiences as a body, I do not think I solved. I doubt that any woman has solved it yet. The obstacles against her are still immensely powerful—and yet they are very difficult to define. Outwardly, what is simpler than to write books? Outwardly, what obstacles are there for a woman rather than for a man? Inwardly, I think, the case is very different; she has still many ghosts to fight, many prejudices to overcome. Indeed it will be a long time still, I think, before a woman can sit down to write a book without finding a phantom to be slain, a rock to be dashed against. And if this is so in literature, the freest of all professions for women, how is it in the new professions which you are now for the first time entering?

7   Those are the questions that I should like, had I time, to ask you. And indeed, if I have laid stress upon these professional experiences of mine, it is because I believe that they are, though in different forms, yours also. Even when the path is nominally open—when there is nothing to prevent a woman from being a doctor, a lawyer, a civil servant—there are many phantoms and obstacles, as I believe, looming in her way. To discuss and define them is I think of great value and importance; for thus only can the labor be shared, the difficulties be solved. But besides this, it is necessary also to discuss the ends and the aims for which we are fighting, for which we are doing battle with these formidable obstacles. Those aims cannot be taken for granted; they must be perpetually questioned and examined. The whole position, as I see it—here in this hall surrounded by women practicing for the first time in history I know not how many different professions—is one of extraordinary interest and importance. You have won rooms of your own in the house hitherto exclusively owned by men. You are able, though not without great labor and effort, to pay the rent. You are earning your five hundred pounds a year. But this freedom is only a beginning; the room is your own, but it is still bare. It has to be furnished; it has to be decorated; it has to be shared. How are you going to furnish it, how are you going to decorate it? With whom are you going to share it, and upon what terms? These, I think, are questions of the utmost importance and interest. For the first time in history you are able to ask them; for the first time you are able to decide for yourselves what the answers should be. Willingly would I stay and discuss those questions and answers—but not tonight. My time is up; and I must cease.

COMPREHENSION

1. This essay was presented originally as a speech. What internal evidence indicates that it was intended as a talk? How do you respond to it today as a reader?
2. Who or what is the "angel" that Woolf describes in this essay? Why must she kill it? What other obstacles does a professional woman encounter?
3. Paraphrase the last two paragraphs of this essay. What is the essence of Woolf's argument?

RHETORIC

1. There is a significant amount of figurative language in the essay. Locate and explain examples. What does the figurative language contribute to the tone of the essay?
2. How do we know that Woolf is addressing an audience of women? Why does she pose so many questions, and what does this strategy contribute to the rapport she wants to establish? Explain the effect of the last two sentences.
3. How does Woolf use analogy to structure part of her argument?
4. Why does Woolf rely on personal narration? How does it affect the logic of her argument?
5. Evaluate Woolf's use of contrast to advance her argument.
6. Where does Woolf place her main proposition? How emphatic is it, and why?

WRITING

1. How effectively does Woolf use her own example as a professional writer to advance a broader proposition concerning all women entering professional life? Answer this question in a brief essay.
2. Discuss the problems and obstacles that you anticipate when you enter your chosen career.
3. **Writing an Argument:** Argue for or against the proposition that Woolf's essay has little relevance for women planning careers today.

NETWORKING
Applying Digital and Multimedia Literacies

Repurposing Text for a New Genre: Condense and rewrite Woolf's speech/essay as a blog entry. Preserve and do not distort her central message, but do not use more than 500 words. What else, besides length, will you modify to fit this new form?

❀

Delusions of Grandeur

Henry Louis Gates Jr.

Henry Louis Gates Jr. (b. 1950) is an educator, writer, and editor. He was born in West Virginia and educated at Yale and at Clare College in Cambridge. Gates has had a varied career, working as a general anesthetist in Tanzania and as a staff correspondent for Time *magazine in London. His essays have appeared in such diverse publications as* Black American Literature Forum, Yale Review, New York Times Book Review, *and* Sports Illustrated. *He is also the author of* Figures in Black: Words, Signs and the Racial Self *(1987) and* The Signifying Monkey: A Theory of Afro-American Literary Criticism *(1988) and is the editor, with Nellie Y. McKey, of* The Norton Anthology of African American Literature *(1996), and, with Hollis Robbins,* The Annotated Uncle Tom's Cabin *(2007). In this article from* Sports Illustrated, *Gates turns his attention to the limited career choices presented as viable to African American youth and to public misconceptions about blacks in sports.*

Standing at the bar of an all-black VFW post in my hometown of Piedmont, W.Va., I offered five dollars to anyone who could tell me how many African-American professional athletes were at work today. There are 35 million African-Americans, I said. [1]

"Ten million!" yelled one intrepid soul, too far into his cups. [2]

"No way . . . more like 500,000," said another. [3]

"You mean *all* professional sports," someone interjected, "including golf and tennis, but not counting the brothers from Puerto Rico?" Everyone laughed. [4]

5   "Fifty thousand, minimum," was another guess.

6   Here are the facts:

There are 1,200 black professional athletes in the U.S.

There are 12 times more black lawyers than black athletes.

There are 2½ times more black dentists than black athletes.

There are 15 times more black doctors than black athletes.

7   Nobody in my local VFW believed these statistics; in fact, few people would believe them if they weren't reading them in the pages of *Sports Illustrated*. In spite of these statistics, too many African-American youngsters still believe that they have a much better chance of becoming another Magic Johnson or Michael Jordan than they do of matching the achievements of Baltimore Mayor Kurt Schmoke or neurosurgeon Dr. Benjamin Carson, both of whom, like Johnson and Jordan, are black.

8   In reality, an African-American youngster has about as much chance of becoming a professional athlete as he or she does of winning the lottery. The tragedy for our people, however, is that few of us accept that truth.

9   Let me confess that I love sports. Like most black people of my generation—I'm 40—I was raised to revere the great black athletic heroes, and I never tired of listening to the stories of triumph and defeat that, for blacks, amount to a collective epic much like those of the ancient Greeks: Joe Louis's demolition of Max Schmeling; Satchel Paige's dazzling repertoire of pitches; Jesse Owens's in-your-face performance in Hitler's 1936 Olympics; Willie Mays's over-the-shoulder basket catch; Jackie Robinson's quiet strength when assaulted by racist taunts; and a thousand other grand tales.

10   Nevertheless, the blind pursuit of attainment in sports is having a devastating effect on our people. Imbued with a belief that our principal avenue to fame and profit is through sport, and seduced by a win-at-any-cost system that corrupts even elementary school students, far too many black kids treat basketball courts and football fields as if they were classrooms in an alternative school system. "O.K., I flunked English," a young athlete will say. "But I got an A plus in slamdunking."

11   The failure of our public schools to educate athletes is part and parcel of the schools' failure to educate almost everyone. A recent survey of the Philadelphia school system, for example, stated that "more than half of all students in the third, fifth and eighth grades cannot perform minimum math and language tasks." One in four middle school students in that city fails to pass to the next grade each year. It is a sad truth that such statistics are repeated in cities throughout the nation. Young athletes—particularly young black athletes—are especially ill-served. Many of them are functionally illiterate, yet they are passed along from year to year for the greater glory of good old Hometown High. We should not be surprised to learn, then, that only 26.6 percent of black athletes at the collegiate level earn their degrees. For every successful educated black professional athlete,

there are thousands of dead and wounded. Yet young blacks continue to aspire to careers as athletes, and it's no wonder why; when the University of North Carolina recently commissioned a sculptor to create archetypes of its student body, guess which ethnic group was selected to represent athletes?

Those relatively few black athletes who do make it in the professional ranks 12 must be prevailed upon to play a significant role in the education of all of our young people, athlete and nonathlete alike. While some have done so, many others have shirked their social obligations: to earmark small percentages of their incomes for the United Negro College Fund; to appear on television for educational purposes rather than merely to sell sneakers; to let children know the message that becoming a lawyer, a teacher or a doctor does more good for our people than winning the Super Bowl; and to form productive liaisons with educators to help forge solutions to the many ills that beset the black community. These are merely a few modest proposals.

A similar burden falls upon successful blacks in all walks of life. Each of us 13 must strive to make our young people understand the realities. Tell them to cheer Bo Jackson but to emulate novelist Toni Morrison or businessman Reginald Lewis or historian John Hope Franklin or Spelman College president Johnetta Cole— the list is long.

Of course, society as a whole bears responsibility as well. Until colleges 14 stop using young blacks as cannon fodder in the big-business wars of so-called nonprofessional sports, until training a young black's mind becomes as important as training his or her body, we will continue to perpetuate a system akin to that of the Roman gladiators, sacrificing a class of people for the entertainment of the mob.

COMPREHENSION

1. What does Gates suggest is the general assumption made about blacks in sports?
2. Why do American schools continue to perpetuate the myth that Gates is writing about?
3. According to Gates, what should successful black athletes do to help guide the career choices of young blacks?

RHETORIC

1. What is Gates's thesis? Where does it appear?
2. How does the introductory paragraph work to set up the writer's focus?
3. State Gates's purpose in using statistics in his essay.
4. What is the tone of Gates's essay? Cite specific sections where this tone seems strongest.
5. Examine the accumulation of facts in paragraph 11. How does this technique underscore Gates's point?
6. Explain Gates's allusion to Roman gladiators in his conclusion. How does it aid in emphasizing his main point?

WRITING

1. Write a brief essay in which you analyze your personal reaction to Gates's statistics. Were you surprised by them? What assumptions did you have about the number of black professional athletes? Why do you think most Americans share these assumptions?
2. Write a biographical research paper on the life and career of a black athlete.
3. **Writing an Argument:** Pretend you are addressing a group of young African Americans at an elementary school. Argue that sports and entertainment should (or should not) be their career choices.

NETWORKING
Applying Digital and Multimedia Literacies

Creating a Graphic from Data: Use selected statistics from this essay to create an effective graph, table, or chart.

Synthesis: Classic and Contemporary Questions for Comparison

1. Examine the argumentative styles of Woolf and Gates. What are their main propositions? Their minor propositions? What evidence do they provide?
2. Woolf first presented her paper as a speech before an audience of women. Gates wrote his essay as an opinion piece for *Sports Illustrated*. Write a comparative audience analysis of the two selections. Analyze the purpose, tone, style, and any other relevant aspects of these essays.
3. Argue for or against the proposition that white women and black men face the same barriers to employment in today's professions. Refer to the essays by Woolf and Gates to support your position.

The Money: Starting Out

Junot Diaz

Junot Diaz *(b. 1968) is an award-winning Dominican American writer and creative writing professor at Massachusetts Institute of Technology. He was born in Santo Domingo, the third child in a family of five. His family moved to New Jersey when Diaz was six. The family lived less than a mile from what Diaz recalls as "one of the largest landfills in New Jersey." Despite hardships that include his father's abandonment of the family, Diaz completed a BA at Rutgers University in*

*1992 and an MFA at Cornell University in 1995. While at Cornell, Diaz wrote
most of the stories that appear in his first collection,* Drown *(1966). In 2008, Diaz
received the Pulitzer Prize for his novel,* The Brief Wondrous Life of Oscar Wao
*(2007), an immigrant family saga drawing on the author's own experience. In
2010, Diaz was selected to sit on the Pulitzer Prize board of jurors, the first Latino
appointed to the twenty-member panel. The essay that follows, which reflects Diaz's
focus in his writing on the immigrant experience, appeared in the June 13–20,
2011 issue of the* New Yorker.

All the Dominicans I knew in those days sent money home. My mother didn't 1
have a regular job besides caring for us five kids, so she scrimped the loot together from whatever came her way. My father was always losing his forklift jobs,
so it wasn't like she ever had a steady flow. But my grandparents were alone in
Santo Domingo, and those remittances, beyond material support, were a way, I
suspect, for Mami to negotiate the absence, the distance, caused by our diaspora.
She chipped dollars off the cash Papi gave her for our daily expenses, forced our
already broke family to live even broker. That was how she built the nut—two,
maybe three hundred dollars—that she sent home every six months or so.

We kids knew where the money was hidden, but we also knew that to touch it 2
would have meant a violent punishment approaching death. I, who could take the
change out of my mother's purse without thinking, couldn't have brought myself
even to look at that forbidden stash.

So what happened? Exactly what you'd think. The summer I was twelve, my 3
family went away on a "vacation"—one of my father's half-baked get-to-know-our-
country-better-by-sleeping-in-the-van extravaganzas—and when we returned to
Jersey, exhausted, battered, we found our front door unlocked. My parents'
room, which was where the thieves had concentrated their search, looked as if it
had been tornado-tossed. The thieves had kept it simple; they'd snatched a portable radio, some of my *Dungeons & Dragons* hardcovers, and, of course, Mami's
remittances.

It's not as if the robbery came as a huge surprise. In our neighborhood, cars 4
and apartments were always getting jacked, and the kid stupid enough to leave a
bike unattended for more than a tenth of a second was the kid who was never
going to see that bike again. Everybody got hit; no matter who you were, eventually it would be your turn.

And that summer it was ours.   5

Still, we took the burglary pretty hard. When you're a recent immigrant, it's 6
easy to feel targeted. Like it wasn't just a couple of assholes that had it in for you
but the whole neighborhood—hell, maybe the whole country.

No one took the robbery as hard as my mom, though. She cursed the neigh- 7
borhood, she cursed the country, she cursed my father, and of course she cursed
us kids, swore that we had run our gums to our idiot friends and they had done it.

And this is where the tale should end, right? Wasn't as if there was going to be 8
any "C.S.I."-style investigation or anything. Except that a couple of days later I was
moaning about the robbery to these guys I was hanging with at that time and they

were cursing sympathetically, and out of nowhere it struck me. You know when you get one of those moments of mental clarity? When the nictitating membrane obscuring the world suddenly lifts? That's what happened. I realized that these two dopes I called my friends had done it. They were shaking their heads, mouthing all the right words, but I could see the way they looked at each other, the Raskolnikov glances. I knew.

9   Now, it wasn't like I could publicly denounce these dolts or go to the police. That would have been about as useless as crying. Here's what I did: I asked the main dope to let me use his bathroom (we were in front of his apartment) and while I pretended to piss I unlatched the window. Then we all headed to the park as usual, but I pretended that I'd forgotten something back home. Ran to the dope's apartment, slid open the bathroom window, and in broad daylight wriggled my skinny ass in.

10   Where the hell did I get these ideas? I have not a clue. I guess I was reading way too much *Encyclopedia Brown and the Three Investigators* in those days. And if mine had been a normal neighborhood this is when the cops would have been called and my ass would have been caught burglarizing.

11   The dolt and his family had been in the U.S. all their lives and they had a ton of stuff, a TV in every room, but I didn't have to do much searching. I popped up the dolt's mattress and underneath I found my D. & D. books and most of my mother's money. He had thoughtfully kept it in the same envelope.

12   And that was how I solved the Case of the Stupid Morons. My one and only case.

13   The next day at the park, the dolt announced that someone had broken into his apartment and stolen all his savings. This place is full of thieves, he complained bitterly, and I was, like, No kidding.

14   It took me two days to return the money to my mother. The truth was I was seriously considering keeping it. But in the end the guilt got to me. I guess I was expecting my mother to run around with joy, to crown me her favorite son, to cook me my favorite meal. Nada. I'd wanted a party or at least to see her happy, but there was nothing. Just two hundred and some dollars and fifteen hundred or so miles—that's all there was.

COMPREHENSION

1. What point is Diaz making about his childhood and family life?
2. According to Diaz, what is the role of money in Dominican immigrant life? What function does money serve for his mother?
3. How does Diaz's fascination with fiction and film influence his behavior?

RHETORIC

1. How does Diaz's title reflect the content of the essay?
2. How would you describe Diaz's audience for this essay? How successful is the writer in tailoring his style to this audience? Justify your response.

3. What is Diaz's thesis? Does he state or imply his main idea? Explain.
4. Trace the sequence of narrative events in this essay. What fictive techniques does Diaz rely on to advance the action?
5. Comment on Diaz's use of colloquial language. Point to specific examples. How does this language contribute to the tone of the essay?

WRITING

1. In a narrative essay, describe a time or episode in childhood when the notion of money became apparent to you.
2. Write an essay in which you consider the role of money in your family's life. What values and opinions concerning money did family members instill in you?
3. **Writing an Argument:** Argue for or against the proposition that children have an innate sense of right and wrong. Relate your argument to Diaz's essay.

NETWORKING
Applying Digital and Multimedia Literacies

Comparing Narrative, Argument, and Fiction: Working alone or with another class member, locate (online) the 1999 op-ed article that Diaz, with Edwidge Danticat (see her essay on page 94), published in the *New York Times* concerning the deportation of Haitians and Haitian Dominicans by the Dominican government. How does Diaz's writing—its content, form, structure, and voice—differ when he is telling a story (in "The Money") from when he is making a case (in "The Dominican Republic's War . . .")? How do these modes overlap? For instance, how do Diaz and Danticat use narrative to help drive their op-ed piece? Now locate a Junot Diaz short story either online (text, audio, or video) or at the library. What are some similarities and differences between his fiction and an essay like "The Money"? Share your insights in a brief essay.

The Death of Horatio Alger

Paul Krugman

Paul Krugman (b. 1953), who teaches at Princeton University, received the Nobel Prize for Economics in 2008 for his analysis of trade patterns and economic activity. Raised in the suburbs of New York City, Krugman attended Yale University for two years before transferring to Massachusetts Institute of Technology, where he received his PhD in economics in 1977. Krugman has published many highly specialized texts in economic theory, but also more popular works like Peddling Prosperity *(1994),* The Accidental Theorist: And Other Dispatches from the Dismal Science *(1998), and* The Return of Depression Economics and the Crisis of 2008 *(2008). A frequent contributor to such newspapers and magazines as the* New Republic, Financial Times, *and* Mother Jones, *Krugman currently is an op ed columnist for the* New York Times. *Known for his trenchant style and oppositional viewpoints, Krugman attempts to make complex economic trends comprehensible to a broad audience. In this essay from the* Nation, *published in 2004, Krugman looks into the causes of economic inequality.*

1   The other day I found myself reading a leftist rag that made outrageous claims about America. It said that we are becoming a society in which the poor tend to stay poor, no matter how hard they work; in which sons are much more likely to inherit the socioeconomic status of their father than they were a generation ago.

2   The name of the leftist rag? *BusinessWeek,* which published an article titled "Waking Up from the American Dream." The article summarizes recent research showing that social mobility in the United States (which was never as high as legend had it) has declined considerably over the past few decades. If you put that research together with other research that shows a drastic increase in income and wealth inequality, you reach an uncomfortable conclusion: America looks more and more like a class-ridden society.

3   And guess what? Our political leaders are doing everything they can to fortify class inequality, while denouncing anyone who complains—or even points out what is happening—as a practitioner of "class warfare."

4   Let's talk first about the facts on income distribution. Thirty years ago we were a relatively middle-class nation. It had not always been thus: Gilded Age America was a highly unequal society, and it stayed that way through the 1920s. During the 1930s and '40s, however, America experienced what the economic historians Claudia Goldin and Robert Margo have dubbed the Great Compression: a drastic narrowing of income gaps, probably as a result of New Deal policies. And the new economic order persisted for more than a generation: Strong unions; taxes on inherited wealth, corporate profits and high incomes; close public scrutiny of corporate management—all helped to keep income gaps relatively small. The economy was hardly egalitarian, but a generation ago the gross inequalities of the 1920s seemed very distant.

5   Now they're back. According to estimates by the economists Thomas Piketty and Emmanuel Saez—confirmed by data from the Congressional Budget Office— between 1973 and 2000 the average real income of the bottom 90 percent of American taxpayers actually fell by 7 percent. Meanwhile, the income of the top 1 percent rose by 148 percent, the income of the top 0.1 percent rose by 343 per cent and the income of the top 0.01 percent rose 599 percent. (Those numbers exclude capital gains, so they're not an artifact of the stock-market bubble.) The distribution of income in the United States has gone right back to Gilded Age levels of inequality.

6   Never mind, say the apologists, who churn out papers with titles like that of a 2001 Heritage Foundation piece, "Income Mobility and the Fallacy of Class-Warfare Arguments." America, they say, isn't a caste society—people with high

incomes this year may have low incomes next year and vice versa, and the route to wealth is open to all. That's where those commies at *BusinessWeek* come in: As they point out (and as economists and sociologists have been pointing out for some time), America actually is more of a caste society than we like to think. And the caste lines have lately become a lot more rigid.

The myth of income mobility has always exceeded the reality: As a general 7
rule, once they've reached their 30s, people don't move up and down the income ladder very much. Conservatives often cite studies like a 1992 report by Glenn Hubbard, a Treasury official under the elder Bush who later became chief economic adviser to the younger Bush, that purport to show large numbers of Americans moving from low-wage to high-wage jobs during their working lives. But what these studies measure, as the economist Kevin Murphy put it, is mainly "the guy who works in the college bookstore and has a real job by his early 30s." Serious studies that exclude this sort of pseudo-mobility show that inequality in average incomes over long periods isn't much smaller than inequality in annual incomes.

It is true, however, that America was once a place of substantial intergenera- 8
tional mobility: Sons often did much better than their fathers. A classic 1978 survey found that among adult men whose fathers were in the bottom 25 percent of the population as ranked by social and economic status, 23 percent had made it into the top 25 percent. In other words, during the first thirty years or so after World War II, the American dream of upward mobility was a real experience for many people.

Now for the shocker: The *BusinessWeek* piece cites a new survey of today's 9
adult men, which finds that this number has dropped to only 10 percent. That is, over the past generation upward mobility has fallen drastically. Very few children of the lower class are making their way to even moderate affluence. This goes along with other studies indicating that rags-to-riches stories have become vanishingly rare, and that the correlation between fathers' and sons' incomes has risen in recent decades. In modern America, it seems, you're quite likely to stay in the social and economic class into which you were born.

BusinessWeek attributes this to the "Wal-Martization" of the economy, the pro- 10
liferation of dead-end, low-wage jobs and the disappearance of jobs that provide entry to the middle class. That's surely part of the explanation. But public policy plays a role—and will, if present trends continue, play an even bigger role in the future.

Put it this way: Suppose that you actually liked a caste society, and you were 11
seeking ways to use your control of the government to further entrench the advantages of the haves against the have-nots. What would you do?

One thing you would definitely do is get rid of the estate tax, so that large 12
fortunes can be passed on to the next generation. More broadly, you would seek to reduce tax rates both on corporate profits and on unearned income such as dividends and capital gains, so that those with large accumulated or inherited wealth could more easily accumulate even more. You'd also try to create tax shelters mainly useful for the rich. And more broadly still, you'd try to reduce tax

rates on people with high incomes, shifting the burden to the payroll tax and other revenue sources that bear most heavily on people with lower incomes.

13   Meanwhile, on the spending side, you'd cut back on healthcare for the poor, on the quality of public education and on state aid for higher education. This would make it more difficult for people with low incomes to climb out of their difficulties and acquire the education essential to upward mobility in the modern economy.

14   And just to close off as many routes to upward mobility as possible, you'd do everything possible to break the power of unions, and you'd privatize government functions so that well-paid civil servants could be replaced with poorly paid private employees.

15   It all sounds sort of familiar, doesn't it?

16   Where is this taking us? Thomas Piketty, whose work with Saez has transformed our understanding of income distribution, warns that current policies will eventually create "a class of rentiers in the U.S., whereby a small group of wealthy but untalented children controls vast segments of the U.S. economy and penniless, talented children simply can't compete." If he's right—and I fear that he is—we will end up suffering not only from injustice, but from a vast waste of human potential.

17   Goodbye, Horatio Alger. And goodbye, American Dream.

COMPREHENSION

1. What reasons does Krugman give for the creation of a caste society in the United States?
2. Who is Horatio Alger? Why doesn't Krugman explain who he is in his essay?
3. Krugman alludes to the "leftist rag" *BusinessWeek*. What can you infer about the contents and political opinions of this publication?

RHETORIC

1. What is Krugman's claim, and where does he state it most clearly?
2. Comment on the types of evidence that Krugman uses to support his argument. Do you find this evidence to be sufficient and convincing? Why or why not?
3. Krugman's style is quite impersonal. Locate examples of this style, and explain the overall effect.
4. Much of this essay involves comparative analysis. What subjects and ideas does Krugman compare and contrast?
5. Krugman's conclusion is very brief. Do you find it effective? Explain.

WRITING

1. Do you think that your life will be better economically than that of your parents? Write a personal essay in response to this question.

2. Write your own analysis of class inequality in the United States or in another nation that you are familiar with.
3. **Writing an Argument:** Write a rebuttal to Krugman, arguing that the American Dream is still alive and well.

NETWORKING
Applying Digital and Multimedia Literacies

Making a Brochure: Create a brochure titled either "The American Dream Is Alive and Well" or "The Myth of Upward Mobility." Avoiding propaganda or other fallacious forms of argument, make a solid, convincing case. Consider creating or finding visuals to use in this project.

Globalization: The Super-Story

Thomas L. Friedman

Thomas L. Friedman *(b. 1953) was born in Minneapolis, Minnesota. He majored in Mediterranean studies at Brandeis University (BA 1975) and received an MA in modern Middle Eastern studies from Oxford University in 1978. As journalist, author, television commentator, and op-ed contributor to the* New York Times, *Friedman tries to provide unbiased viewpoints on cultural, political, and economic issues. From 1979 to 1984 he was the* Times *correspondent in Beirut, Lebanon, and subsequently until 1988 served as bureau chief in Jerusalem. His book recounting his 10 years in the Middle East,* From Beirut to Jerusalem *(1983), received the National Book Award for nonfiction. Friedman also has published* The Lexus and the Olive Tree: Understanding Globalization *(2000),* The World Is Flat: A Brief History of the Twenty-First Century *(2005),* Hot, Flat, and Crowded: Why We Need a Green Revolution—And How It Can Renew America *(2008), and a collection of essays,* Longitudes and Attitudes: Explaining the World after September 11 *(2002), which contains the following selection.*

I am a big believer in the idea of the super-story, the notion that we all carry 1
around with us a big lens, a big framework, through which we look at the world, order events, and decide what is important and what is not. The events of 9/11 did not happen in a vacuum. They happened in the context of a new international system—a system that cannot explain everything but *can* explain and connect more things in more places on more days than anything else. That new international system is called globalization. It came together in the late 1980s and replaced the previous international system, the cold war system, which had reigned since the end of World War II. This new system is the lens, the super-story, through which I viewed the events of 9/11.

2   I define globalization as the inexorable integration of markets, transportation systems, and communication systems to a degree never witnessed before—in a way that is enabling corporations, countries, and individuals to reach around the world farther, faster, deeper, and cheaper than ever before, and in a way that is enabling the world to reach into corporations, countries, and individuals farther, faster, deeper, and cheaper than ever before.

3   Several important features of this globalization system differ from those of the cold war system in ways that are quite relevant for understanding the events of 9/11. I examined them in detail in my previous book, *The Lexus and the Olive Tree,* and want to simply highlight them here.

4   The cold war system was characterized by one overarching feature—and that was *division.* That world was a divided-up, chopped-up place, and whether you were a country or a company, your threats and opportunities in the cold war system tended to grow out of who you were divided from. Appropriately, this cold war system was symbolized by a single word—*wall,* the Berlin Wall.

5   The globalization system is different. It also has one overarching feature—and that is *integration.* The world has become an increasingly interwoven place, and today, whether you are a company or a country, your threats and opportunities increasingly derive from who you are connected to. This globalization system is also characterized by a single word—*web,* the World Wide Web. So in the broadest sense we have gone from an international system built around division and walls to a system increasingly built around integration and webs. In the cold war we reached for the hotline, which was a symbol that we were divided but at least two people were in charge—the leaders of the United States and the Soviet Union. In the globalization system we reach for the Internet, which is a symbol that we are all connected and nobody is quite in charge.

6   Everyone in the world is directly or indirectly affected by this new system, but not everyone benefits from it, not by a long shot, which is why the more it becomes diffused, the more it also produces a backlash by people who feel overwhelmed by it, homogenized by it, or unable to keep pace with its demands.

7   The other key difference between the cold war system and the globalization system is how power is structured within them. The cold war system was built primarily around nation-states. You acted on the world in that system through your state. The cold war was a drama of states confronting states, balancing states, and aligning with states. And, as a system, the cold war was balanced at the center by two superstates, two superpowers: the United States and the Soviet Union.

8   The globalization system, by contrast, is built around three balances, which overlap and affect one another. The first is the traditional balance of power between nation-states. In the globalization system, the United States is now the sole and dominant superpower and all other nations are subordinate to it to one degree or another. The shifting balance of power between the United States and other states, or simply between other states, still very much matters for the stability of this system. And it can still explain a lot of the news you read on the front page of the paper, whether it is the news of China balancing Russia, Iran balancing Iraq, or India confronting Pakistan.

The second important power balance in the globalization system is between 9 nation-states and global markets. These global markets are made up of millions of investors moving money around the world with the click of a mouse. I call them the Electronic Herd, and this herd gathers in key global financial centers—such as Wall Street, Hong Kong, London, and Frankfurt—which I call the Supermarkets. The attitudes and actions of the Electronic Herd and the Supermarkets can have a huge impact on nation-states today, even to the point of triggering the downfall of governments. Who ousted Suharto in Indonesia in 1998? It wasn't another state, it was the Supermarkets, by withdrawing their support for, and confidence in, the Indonesian economy. You also will not understand the front page of the newspaper today unless you bring the Supermarkets into your analysis. Because the United States can destroy you by dropping bombs, but the Supermarkets can destroy you by downgrading your bonds. In other words, the United States is the dominant player in maintaining the globalization game board, but it is hardly alone in influencing the moves on that game board.

The third balance that you have to pay attention to—the one that is really the 10 newest of all and the most relevant to the events of 9/11—is the balance between individuals and nation-states. Because globalization has brought down many of the walls that limited the movement and reach of people, and because it has simultaneously wired the world into networks, it gives more power to *individuals* to influence both markets and nation-states than at any other time in history. Whether by enabling people to use the Internet to communicate instantly at almost no cost over vast distances, or by enabling them to use the Web to transfer money or obtain weapons designs that normally would have been controlled by states, or by enabling them to go into a hardware store now and buy a five-hundred-dollar global positioning device, connected to a satellite, that can direct a hijacked airplane—globalization can be an incredible force-multiplier for individuals. Individuals can increasingly act on the world stage directly, unmediated by a state.

So you have today not only a superpower, not only Supermarkets, but also 11 what I call "super-empowered individuals." Some of these super-empowered individuals are quite angry, some of them quite wonderful—but all of them are now able to act much more directly and much more powerfully on the world stage.

Osama bin Laden declared war on the United States in the late 1990s. After he 12 organized the bombing of two American embassies in Africa, the U.S. Air Force retaliated with a cruise missile attack on his bases in Afghanistan as though he were another nation-state. Think about that: on one day in 1998, the United States fired 75 cruise missiles at bin Laden. The United States fired 75 cruise missiles, at $1 million apiece, at a person! That was the first battle in history between a superpower and a super-empowered angry man. September 11 was just the second such battle.

Jody Williams won the Nobel Peace Prize in 1997 for helping to build an inter- 13 national coalition to bring about a treaty outlawing land mines. Although nearly 120 governments endorsed the treaty, it was opposed by Russia, China, and the United States. When Jody Williams was asked, "How did you do that? How did you organize one thousand different citizens' groups and nongovernmental organizations on five continents to forge a treaty that was opposed by the major powers?" she had a very brief answer: "E-mail." Jody Williams used e-mail and the networked world to super-empower herself.

14   Nation-states, and the American superpower in particular, are still hugely important today, but so too now are Supermarkets and super-empowered individuals. You will never understand the globalization system, or the front page of the morning paper—or 9/11—unless you see each as a complex interaction between all three of these actors: states bumping up against states, states bumping up against Supermarkets, and Supermarkets and states bumping up against super-empowered individuals—many of whom, unfortunately, are super-empowered angry men.

COMPREHENSION

1. What is Friedman's "super-story"? How does he define it?
2. What are the main features of globalization? How does globalization differ from the system characterized by the cold war? Explain the "three balances" (paragraphs 8–10) that Friedman writes about.
3. What does Friedman mean by "super-empowered" individuals (paragraph 11)?

RHETORIC

1. What is Friedman's thesis or claim in this essay? Where does it appear?
2. How and why does Friedman create a personal voice as well as a colloquial style in this selection? What is the effect?
3. What definitions does Friedman establish? Are the definitions too abstract, or does he provide sufficient explanations and evidence? Explain.
4. Locate instances of classification and of comparison and contrast. Why does Friedman use these rhetorical strategies? How do the two methods complement each other?
5. Friedman uses several metaphors in this essay. What are they, and how do they function to enhance meaning?
6. Why does the writer discuss 9/11 in the final three paragraphs? What is the effect on the overall message and purpose of the essay?

WRITING

1. In groups of three or four, use Friedman's essay to brainstorm about globalization. Construct a list of ideas and attributes. Using this list, write a definition essay exploring the subject of globalization. Include comparison and contrast or classification, or both, to help organize the essay.
2. Write a personal essay on how you think globalization is affecting your life.
3. **Writing an Argument:** Write a letter to Friedman, either agreeing or disagreeing with his opinions concerning globalization, supporting or refuting his ideas, or offering alternative views.

NETWORKING
Applying Digital and Multimedia Literacies

Crafting a Comment: Like letters to the editors of newspapers, comments on on-line articles and blog posts offer readers a chance to question or otherwise engage with published texts. Approach question 3 under Writing from a more concise angle: Imagine as you craft your response that it will be a comment posted after the article, a comment visible, potentially, to anyone from around the world. Include one or two link(s) to credible articles, data, or Web sites that support your response.

✳

Nickel and Dimed

Barbara Ehrenreich

Barbara Ehrenreich (b. 1941) was born in Butte, Montana. The daughter of working-class parents, she attended Reed College (BA 1963) and Rockefeller University, where she received a PhD in biology in 1968. After deciding not to pursue a career in science, Ehrenreich turned to political causes, using her scientific training to investigate a broad range of social issues. A prolific writer, Ehrenreich has contributed to Time, *the* New Republic, *the* Progressive, *and other magazines. She also has written several books, including* The American Health Empire *(1970),* Complaints and Disorders: The Sexual Politics of Sickness *(1978),* Nickel and Dimed: On (Not) Getting By in America *(2001),* Dancing in the Streets *(2007), and a collection of essays,* This Land Is Their Land: Reports from a Divided Nation *(2008). In the following excerpt from* Nickel and Dimed, *Ehrenreich recounts her experience working for a large cleaning agency.*

I am rested and ready for anything when I arrive at The Maids' office suite Mon- 1
day at 7:30 A.M. I know nothing about cleaning services like this one, which, ac-cording to the brochure I am given, has over three hundred franchises nationwide, and most of what I know about domestics in general comes from nineteenth-cen-tury British novels and *Upstairs, Downstairs.* Prophetically enough, I caught a re-run of that very show on PBS over the weekend and was struck by how terribly correct the servants looked in their black-and-white uniforms and how much wiser they were than their callow, egotistical masters. We too have uniforms, though they are more oafish than dignified—ill-fitting and in an overloud combi-nation of kelly-green pants and a blinding sunflower-yellow polo shirt. And, as is explained in writing and over the next day and a half of training, we too have a special code of decorum. No smoking anywhere, or at least not within fifteen min-utes of arrival at a house. No drinking, eating, or gum chewing in a house. No cursing in a house, even if the owner is not present, and—perhaps to keep us in

practice—no obscenities even in the office. So this is Downstairs, is my chirpy first thought. But I have no idea, of course, just how far down these stairs will take me.

2   Forty minutes go by before anyone acknowledges my presence with more than a harried nod. During this time the other employees arrive, about twenty of them, already glowing in their uniforms, and breakfast on the free coffee, bagels, and doughnuts The Maids kindly provides for us. All but one of the others are female, with an average age I would guess in the late twenties, though the range seems to go from prom-fresh to well into the Medicare years. There is a pleasant sort of bustle as people get their breakfasts and fill plastic buckets with rags and bottles of cleaning fluids, but surprisingly little conversation outside of a few references to what people ate (pizza) and drank (Jell-O shots are mentioned) over the weekend. Since the room in which we gather contains only two folding chairs, both of them occupied, the other new girl and I sit cross-legged on the floor, silent and alert, while the regulars get sorted into teams of three or four and dispatched to the day's list of houses. One of the women explains to me that teams do not necessarily return to the same houses week after week, nor do you have any guarantee of being on the same team from one day to the next. This, I suppose, is one of the advantages of a corporate cleaning service to its customers: There are no sticky and possibly guilt-ridden relationships involved, because the customers communicate almost entirely with Tammy, the office manager, or with Ted, the franchise owner and our boss. The advantage to the cleaning person is harder to determine, since the pay compares so poorly to what an independent cleaner is likely to earn—up to $15 an hour, I've heard. While I wait in the inner room, where the phone is and Tammy has her desk, to be issued a uniform, I hear her tell a potential customer on the phone that The Maids charges $25 per person-hour. The company gets $25 and we get $6.65 for each hour we work? I think I must have misheard, but a few minutes later I hear her say the same thing to another inquirer. So the only advantage of working here as opposed to freelancing is that you don't need a clientele or even a car. You can arrive straight from welfare or, in my case, the bus station—fresh off the boat.

3   At last, after all the other employees have sped off in the company's eye-catching green-and-yellow cars, I am led into a tiny closet-sized room off the inner office to learn my trade via videotape. The manager at another maid service where I'd applied had told me she didn't like to hire people who had done cleaning before because they were resistant to learning the company's system, so I prepare to empty my mind of all prior house-cleaning experience. There are four tapes—dusting, bathrooms, kitchen, and vacuuming—each starring an attractive, possibly Hispanic young woman who moves about serenely in obedience to the male voiceover: For vacuuming, begin in the master bedroom; when dusting, begin with the room directly off the kitchen. When you enter a room, mentally divide it into sections no wider than your reach. Begin in the section to your left and, within each section, move from left to right and top to bottom. This way nothing is ever overlooked.

4   I like *Dusting* best, for its undeniable logic and a certain kind of austere beauty. When you enter a house, you spray a white rag with Windex and place it

in the left pocket of your green apron. Another rag, sprayed with disinfectant, goes in the middle pocket, and a yellow rag bearing wood polish in the right-hand pocket. A dry rag, for buffing surfaces, occupies the right-hand pocket of your slacks. Shiny surfaces get Windexed, wood gets wood polish, and everything else is wiped dust-free with disinfectant. Every now and then Ted pops in to watch with me, pausing the video to underscore a particularly dramatic moment: "See how she's working around the vase? That's an accident waiting to happen." If Ted himself were in a video, it would have to be a cartoon, because the only features sketched onto his pudgy face are brown buttonlike eyes and a tiny pug nose; his belly, encased in a polo shirt, overhangs the waistline of his shorts. "You know, all this was figured out with a stopwatch," he tells me with something like pride. When the video warns against oversoaking our rags with cleaning fluids, he pauses it to tell me there's a danger in undersoaking too, especially if it's going to slow me down. "Cleaning fluids are less expensive than your time." It's good to know that *something* is cheaper than my time, or that in the hierarchy of the company's values I rank above Windex.

Vacuuming is the most disturbing video, actually a double feature beginning 5 with an introduction to the special backpack vacuum we are to use. Yes, the vacuum cleaner actually straps onto your back, a chubby fellow who introduces himself as its inventor explains. He suits up, pulling the straps tight across and under his chest and then says proudly into the camera: "See, I *am* the vacuum cleaner." It weighs only ten pounds, he claims, although, as I soon find out, with the attachments dangling from the strap around your waist, the total is probably more like fourteen. What about my petulant and much-pampered lower back? The inventor returns to the theme of human/machine merger: When properly strapped in, we too will be vacuum cleaners, constrained only by the cord that attaches us to an electrical outlet, and vacuum cleaners don't have backaches. Somehow all this information exhausts me, and I watch the second video, which explains the actual procedures for vacuuming, with the detached interest of a cineast. Could the model maid be an actual maid and the model home someone's actual dwelling? And who are these people whose idea of decorating is matched pictures of mallard ducks in flight and whose house is perfectly characterless and pristine even before the model maid sets to work?

At first I find the videos on kitchens and bathrooms baffling, and it takes me 6 several minutes to realize why: There is no *water,* or almost no water, involved. I was taught to clean by my mother, a compulsive housekeeper who employed water so hot you needed rubber gloves to get into it and in such Niagara-like quantities that most microbes were probably crushed by the force of it before the soap suds had a chance to rupture their cell walls. But germs are never mentioned in the videos provided by The Maids. Our antagonists exist entirely in the visible world—soap scum, dust, counter crud, dog hair, stains, and smears—and are to be attacked by damp rag or, in hard-core cases, by Dobie (the brand of plastic scouring pad we use). We scrub only to remove impurities that might be detectable to a customer by hand or by eye; otherwise our only job is to wipe. Nothing is said about the possibility of transporting bacteria, by rag or by hand, from bathroom to kitchen or even from one house to the next. It is the "cosmetic touches" that the videos emphasize and that Ted, when he wanders back into the room, continually directs my eye to. Fluff up all throw pillows and arrange them symmetrically. Brighten up stainless steel sinks with baby oil. Leave all spice jars, shampoos, etc., with their labels facing outward. Comb out the fringes of Persian carpets with a pick. Use the vacuum cleaner to create a special, fernlike pattern in the carpets. The loose ends of toilet paper and paper towel rolls have to be given a special fold (the same one you'll find in hotel bathrooms). "Messes" of loose paper, clothing, or toys are to be stacked into "neat messes." Finally, the house is to be sprayed with the cleaning service's signature floral-scented air freshener, which will signal to the owners, the moment they return home, that, yes, their house has been "cleaned."

7   After a day's training, I am judged fit to go out with a team, where I soon discover that life is nothing like the movies, at least not if the movie is *Dusting*. For one thing, compared with our actual pace, the training videos were all in slow motion. We do not walk to the cars with our buckets full of cleaning fluids and utensils in the morning, we run, and when we pull up to a house, we run with our buckets to the door. Liza, a good-natured woman in her thirties who is my first team leader, explains that we are given only so many minutes per house, ranging from under sixty for a 1½-bathroom apartment to two hundred or more for a multibathroom "first timer." I'd like to know why anybody worries about Ted's time limits if we're being paid by the hour but hesitate to display anything that might be interpreted as attitude. As we get to each house, Liza assigns our tasks, and I cross my fingers to ward off bathrooms and vacuuming. Even dusting, though, gets aerobic under pressure, and after about an hour of it—reaching to get door tops, crawling along floors to wipe baseboards, standing on my bucket to attack the higher shelves—I wouldn't mind sitting down with a tall glass of water. But as soon as you complete your assigned task, you report to the team leader to be assigned to help someone else. Once or twice, when the normal process of evaporation is deemed too slow, I am assigned to dry a scrubbed floor by putting rags under my feet and skating around on it. Usually, by the time I get out to the car and am dumping the dirty water used on floors and wringing out rags, the rest of the team is already in the car with the motor running. Liza assures me that they've never left anyone behind at a house, not even, presumably, a very new person whom nobody knows.

8   In my interview, I had been promised a thirty-minute lunch break, but this turns out to be a five-minute pit stop at a convenience store, if that. I bring my own sandwich—the same turkey breast and cheese every day—as do a couple of the others; the rest eat convenience store fare, a bagel or doughnut salvaged from our free breakfast, or nothing at all. The two older married women I'm teamed up with eat best—sandwiches and fruit. Among the younger women, lunch consists of a slice of pizza, a "pizza pocket" (a roll of dough surrounding some pizza sauce), or a small bag of chips. Bear in mind we are not office workers, sitting around idling at the basal metabolic rate. A poster on the wall in the office cheerily displays the number of calories burned per minute at our various tasks, ranging from

about 3.5 for dusting to 7 for vacuuming. If you assume an average of 5 calories per minute in a seven-hour day (eight hours minus time for travel between houses), you need to be taking in 2,100 calories in addition to the resting minimum of, say, 900 or so. I get pushy with Rosalie, who is new like me and fresh from high school in a rural northern part of the state, about the meagerness of her lunches, which consist solely of Doritos—a half-bag from the day before or a freshly purchased small-sized bag. She just didn't have anything in the house, she says (though she lives with her boyfriend and his mother), and she certainly doesn't have any money to buy lunch, as I find out when I offer to fetch her a soda from a Quik Mart and she has to admit she doesn't have eighty-nine cents. I treat her to the soda, wishing I could force her, mommylike, to take milk instead. So how does she hold up for an eight- or even nine-hour day? "Well," she concedes, "I get dizzy sometimes."

How poor are they, my coworkers? The fact that anyone is working this job at 9 all can be taken as prima facie evidence of some kind of desperation or at least a history of mistakes and disappointments, but it's not for me to ask. In the prison movies that provide me with a mental guide to comportment, the new guy doesn't go around shaking hands and asking, "Hi there, what are you in for?" So I listen, in the cars and when we're assembled in the office, and learn, first, that no one seems to be homeless. Almost everyone is embedded in extended families or families artificially extended with housemates. People talk about visiting grandparents in the hospital or sending birthday cards to a niece's husband; single mothers live with their own mothers or share apartments with a coworker or boyfriend. Pauline, the oldest of us, owns her own home, but she sleeps on the living room sofa, while her four grown children and three grandchildren fill up the bedrooms.

But although no one, apparently, is sleeping in a car, there are signs, even at 10 the beginning, of real difficulty if not actual misery. Half-smoked cigarettes are returned to the pack. There are discussions about who will come up with fifty cents for a toll and whether Ted can be counted on for prompt reimbursement. One of my teammates gets frantic about a painfully impacted wisdom tooth and keeps making calls from our houses to try to locate a source of free dental care. When my—or, I should say, Liza's—team discovers there is not a single Dobie in our buckets, I suggest that we stop at a convenience store and buy one rather than drive all the way back to the office. But it turns out I haven't brought any money with me and we cannot put together $2 between the four of us.

The Friday of my first week at The Maids is unnaturally hot for Maine in early 11 September—95 degrees, according to the digital time-and-temperature displays offered by banks that we pass. I'm teamed up with the sad-faced Rosalie and our leader, Maddy, whose sullenness, under the circumstances, is almost a relief after Liza's relentless good cheer. Liza, I've learned, is the highest-ranking cleaner, a sort of supervisor really, and said to be something of a snitch, but Maddy, a single mom of maybe twenty-seven or so, has worked for only three months and broods about her child care problems. Her boyfriend's sister, she tells me on the drive to our first house, watches her eighteen-month-old for $50 a week, which is a stretch on The Maids' pay, plus she doesn't entirely trust the sister, but a real day care center could be as much as $90 a week. After polishing off the first house, no problem, we grab "lunch"—Doritos for Rosalie and a bag of Pepperidge Farm Goldfish for Maddy—and head out into the exurbs for what our instruction sheet warns is a five-bathroom spread and a first-timer to boot. Still, the size of the place makes us pause for a moment, buckets in hand, before searching out an appropriately humble entrance. It sits there like a beached ocean liner, the prow cutting through swells of green turf, windows without number. "Well, well," Maddy says, reading the owner's name from our instruction sheet. "Mrs. W. and her big-ass house. I hope she's going to give us lunch."

12   Mrs. W. is not in fact happy to see us, grimacing with exasperation when the black nanny ushers us into the family room or sunroom or den or whatever kind of specialized space she is sitting in. After all, she already has the nanny, a cook-like person, and a crew of men doing some sort of finishing touches on the construction to supervise. No, she doesn't want to take us around the house, because she already explained everything to the office on the phone, but Maddy stands there, with Rosalie and me behind her, until she relents. We are to move everything on all surfaces, she instructs during the tour, and get underneath and be sure to do every bit of the several miles, I calculate, of baseboards. And be mindful of the baby, who's napping and can't have cleaning fluids of any kind near her.

13   Then I am let loose to dust. In a situation like this, where I don't even know how to name the various kinds of rooms, The Maids' special system turns out to be a lifesaver. All I have to do is keep moving from left to right, within rooms and between rooms, trying to identify landmarks so I don't accidentally do a room or a hallway twice. Dusters get the most complete biographical overview, due to the necessity of lifting each object and tchotchke individually, and I learn that Mrs. W. is an alumna of an important women's college, now occupying herself by monitoring her investments and the baby's bowel movements. I find special charts for this latter purpose, with spaces for time of day, most recent fluid intake, consistency, and color. In the master bedroom, I dust a whole shelf of books on pregnancy, breastfeeding, the first six months, the first year, the first two years—and I wonder what the child care–deprived Maddy makes of all this. Maybe there's been some secret division of the world's women into breeders and drones, and those at the maid level are no longer supposed to be reproducing at all. Maybe this is why our office manager, Tammy, who was once a maid herself, wears inch-long fake nails and tarty little outfits—to show she's advanced to the breeder caste and can't be sent out to clean anymore.

14   It is hotter inside than out, un-air-conditioned for the benefit of the baby, I suppose, but I do all right until I encounter the banks of glass doors that line the side and back of the ground floor. Each one has to be Windexed, wiped, and buffed—inside and out, top to bottom, left to right, until it's as streakless and invisible as a material substance can be. Outside, I can see the construction guys knocking back Gatorade, but the rule is that no fluid or food item can touch a maid's lips when she's inside a house. Now, sweat, even in unseemly quantities, is nothing new to me. I live in a subtropical area where even the inactive can expect to be

moist nine months out of the year. I work out, too, in my normal life and take a certain macho pride in the *V*s of sweat that form on my T-shirt after ten minutes or more on the StairMaster. But in normal life fluids lost are immediately re-placed. Everyone in yuppie-land—airports, for example—looks like a nursing baby these days, inseparable from their plastic bottles of water. Here, however, I sweat without replacement or pause, not in individual drops but in continuous sheets of fluid soaking through my polo shirt, pouring down the backs of my legs. The eyeliner I put on in the morning—vain twit that I am—has long since streaked down onto my cheeks, and I could wring my braid out if I wanted to. Working my way through the living room(s), I wonder if Mrs. W. will ever have occasion to realize that every single doodad and *objet* through which she expresses her unique, individual self is, from another vantage point, only an obstacle between some thirsty person and a glass of water.

When I can find no more surfaces to wipe and have finally exhausted the sup- 15 ply of rooms, Maddy assigns me to do the kitchen floor. OK, except that Mrs. W. is *in* the kitchen, so I have to go down on my hands and knees practically at her feet. No, we don't have sponge mops like the one I use in my own house; the hands-and-knees approach is a definite selling point for corporate cleaning ser-vices like The Maids. "We clean floors the old-fashioned way—*on our hands and knees*" (emphasis added), the brochure for a competing firm boasts. In fact, what-ever advantages there may be to the hands-and-knees approach—you're closer to your work, of course, and less likely to miss a grimy patch—are undermined by the artificial drought imposed by The Maids' cleaning system. We are instructed to use less than half a small bucket of lukewarm water for a kitchen and all adja-cent scrubbable floors (breakfast nooks and other dining areas), meaning that within a few minutes we are doing nothing more than redistributing the dirt evenly around the floor. There are occasional customer complaints about the cleanliness of our floors—for example, from a man who wiped up a spill on his freshly "cleaned" floor only to find the paper towel he employed for this purpose had turned gray. A mop and a full bucket of hot soapy water would not only get a floor cleaner but would be a lot more dignified for the person who does the clean-ing. But it is this primal posture of submission—and of what is ultimately anal accessibility—that seems to gratify the consumers of maid services.

I don't know, but Mrs. W.'s floor is hard—stone, I think, or at least a stonelike 16 substance—and we have no knee pads with us today. I had thought in my middle-class innocence that knee pads were one of Monica Lewinsky's prurient fantasies, but no, they actually exist, and they're usually a standard part of our equipment. So here I am on my knees, working my way around the room like some fanatical penitent crawling through the stations of the cross, when I realize that Mrs. W. is staring at me fixedly—so fixedly that I am gripped for a moment by the wild pos-sibility that I may have once given a lecture at her alma mater and she's trying to figure out where she's seen me before. If I were recognized, would I be fired? Would she at least be inspired to offer me a drink of water? Because I have de-cided that if water is actually offered, I'm taking it, rules or no rules, and if word of this infraction gets back to Ted, I'll just say I thought it would be rude to refuse.

Not to worry, though. She's just watching that I don't leave out some stray square inch, and when I rise painfully to my feet again, blinking through the sweat, she says, "Could you just scrub the floor in the entryway while you're at it?"

17   I rush home to the Blue Haven at the end of the day, pull down the blinds for privacy, strip off my uniform in the kitchen—the bathroom being too small for both a person and her discarded clothes—and stand in the shower for a good ten minutes, thinking all this water is *mine*. I have paid for it, in fact, I have earned it. I have gotten through a week at The Maids without mishap, injury, or insurrection. My back feels fine, meaning I'm not feeling it at all; even my wrists, damaged by carpal tunnel syndrome years ago, are issuing no complaints. Coworkers warned me that the first time they donned the backpack vacuum they felt faint, but not me. I am strong and I am, more than that, good. Did I toss my bucket of filthy water onto Mrs. W.'s casual white summer outfit? No. Did I take the wand of my vacuum cleaner and smash someone's Chinese porcelain statues or Hummel figurines? Not once. I was at all times cheerful, energetic, helpful, and as competent as a new hire can be expected to be. If I can do one week, I can do another, and might as well, since there's never been a moment for job-hunting. The 3:30 quitting time turns out to be a myth; often we don't return to the office until 4:30 or 5:00. And what did I think? That I was going to go out to interviews in my soaked and stinky postwork condition? I decide to reward myself with a sunset walk on Old Orchard Beach.

18   On account of the heat, there are still a few actual bathers on the beach, but I am content to sit in shorts and T-shirt and watch the ocean pummel the sand. When the sun goes down I walk back into the town to find my car and am amazed to hear a sound I associate with cities like New York and Berlin. There's a couple of Peruvian musicians playing in the little grassy island in the street near the pier, and maybe fifty people—locals and vacationers—have gathered around, offering their bland end-of-summer faces to the sound. I edge my way through the crowd and find a seat where I can see the musicians up close—the beautiful young guitarist and the taller man playing the flute. What are they doing in this rinky-dink blue-collar resort, and what does the audience make of this surprise visit from the dark-skinned South? The melody the flute lays out over the percussion is both utterly strange and completely familiar, as if it had been imprinted in the minds of my own peasant ancestors centuries ago and forgotten until this very moment. Everyone else seems to be as transfixed as I am. The musicians wink and smile at each other as they play, and I see then that they are the secret emissaries of a worldwide lower-class conspiracy to snatch joy out of degradation and filth. When the song ends, I give them a dollar, the equivalent of about ten minutes of sweat.

COMPREHENSION

1. Why do women work for The Maids when they could earn more money as independent cleaners? How does Ehrenreich distinguish her cleaning practices from her coworkers'? Why do the maids emphasize "cosmetic touches" (paragraph 6)?

2. Describe the plight of Ehrenreich's coworkers. What "signs . . . of real difficulty if not actual misery" (paragraph 10) does she detect? What, if anything, does she do to help them?
3. Who is Mrs. W.? What is her lifestyle like, and what does she expect of the maids? How does she treat Ehrenreich?

RHETORIC

1. How does Ehrenreich structure her narrative? How much time elapses? What elements of conflict develop? What transitional devices does she employ to unify the action?
2. Where does the writer employ description, and for what purpose? What descriptive details seem most striking to you? How, for example, does Ehrenreich bring her co-workers and Mrs. W. to life?
3. Identify those instances where the writer uses process analysis and comparison and contrast to organize her essay. Why does she select these strategies?
4. Explain the tone of this selection. What elements of irony and sarcasm do you detect?
5. Do you think this essay provides a straightforward account of Ehrenreich's experience working for The Maids, or does she have an argumentative point? Justify your response.
6. How does the writer conclude this selection? What elements in the last paragraph capture the main purpose behind her account?

WRITING

1. Write a narrative and descriptive essay of a job you have held that involved menial labor. Establish a time frame. Describe any colleagues who worked with you. Have a thesis or an argument that you either state explicitly or permit to emerge from the account.
2. Compare and contrast a bad job that you have held and a job that provided you with a degree of satisfaction.
3. **Writing an Argument:** In *Nickel and Dimed,* Ehrenreich set out to find minimum-wage jobs in several parts of the United States, including a Wal-Mart in Minnesota and a restaurant in Florida. However, she knew at the outset that these jobs were temporary and that she had the luxury of going back to her comfortable life and her career as a writer and activist. Argue for or against the proposition that Ehrenreich was being unethical and exploitative in her behavior. Refer to this selection to support your position.

NETWORKING
Applying Digital and Multimedia Literacies

Examining Comments on a Blog: Find Barbara Ehrenreich's blog and locate the 2009 entry "Rich Get Poorer, Poor Disappear." After reading the entry itself at least twice, go through the comments. How many, and which commenters, make valuable contributions to the conversation? How many, and which do not? Based on your findings, what makes a good blog comment? Do you think blog comments should be moderated by the blog's author? Why or why not?

Why the Rich Are Getting Richer and the Poor, Poorer

Robert Reich

Robert Reich *(b. 1946) is a professor of Public Policy at the University of California at Berkeley. He served as secretary of labor in the first Clinton administration and, before that, as a professor of economics at Harvard University. He has written numerous books on economics and has been a prominent lecturer for a dozen years. His books include* The Next American Frontier *(1983) and* The Work of Nations *(1991), which takes its title from Adam Smith's classic work on economics* The Wealth of Nations, *written in 1776. Reich is known for his ability to "think outside the box," in other words, to see things from a unique and original perspective. Here he warns of what exists—perhaps in front of our very noses—but that we are too caught up in the moment to consider.*

> *The division of labor is limited by the extent of the market.*
> —Adam Smith, An Inquiry into the Nature and Causes
> of the Wealth of Nations *(1776)*

1 Regardless of how your job is officially classified (manufacturing, service, manage-rial, technical, secretarial, and so on), or the industry in which you work (automo-tive, steel, computer, advertising, finance, food processing), your real competitive position in the world economy is coming to depend on the function you perform in it. Herein lies the basic reason why incomes are diverging. The fortunes of routine producers are declining. In-person servers are also becoming poorer, although their fates are less clear-cut. But symbolic analysts—who solve, identify, and bro-ker new problems—are, by and large, succeeding in the world economy.

2   All Americans used to be in roughly the same economic boat. Most rose or fell together as the corporations in which they were employed, the industries comprising such corporations, and the national economy as a whole became more productive—or languished. But national borders no longer define our economic fates. We are now in different boats, one sinking rapidly, one sinking more slowly, and the third rising steadily.

3 The boat containing routine producers is sinking rapidly. Recall that by mid-century routine production workers in the United States were paid relatively well. The giant pyramidlike organizations at the core of each major industry coordinated their prices and investments—avoiding the harsh winds of competition and thus main-taining healthy earnings. Some of these earnings, in turn, were reinvested in new plants and equipment (yielding ever-larger-scale economies); another portion went

to top managers and investors. But a large and increasing portion went to middle managers and production workers. Work stoppages posed such a threat to high-volume production that organized labor was able to exact an ever-larger premium for its cooperation. And the pattern of wages established within the core corporations influenced the pattern throughout the national economy. Thus the growth of a relatively affluent middle class, able to purchase all the wondrous things produced in high volume by the core corporations.

But, as has been observed, the core is rapidly breaking down into global webs 4 which earn their largest profits from clever problem-solving, -identifying, and brokering. As the costs of transporting standard things and of communicating information about them continue to drop, profit margins on high-volume, standardized production are thinning, because there are few barriers to entry. Modern factories and state-of-the-art machinery can be installed almost anywhere on the globe. Routine producers in the United States, then, are in direct competition with millions of routine producers in other nations. Twelve thousand people are added to the world's population every hour, most of whom, eventually, will happily work for a small fraction of the wages of routine producers in America.[1]

The consequence is clearest in older, heavy industries, where high-volume, 5 standardized production continues its ineluctable move to where labor is cheapest and most accessible around the world. Thus, for example, the Maquiladora factories clustered along the Mexican side of the U.S. border in the sprawling shanty towns of Tijuana, Mexicali, Nogales, Agua Prieta, and Ciudad Juárez—factories owned mostly by Americans, but increasingly by Japanese—in which more than a half million routine producers assemble parts into finished goods to be shipped into the United States.

The same story is unfolding worldwide. Until the late 1970s, AT&T had de- 6 pended on routine producers in Shreveport, Louisiana, to assemble standard telephones. It then discovered that routine producers in Singapore would perform the same tasks at a far lower cost. Facing intense competition from other global webs, AT&T's strategic brokers felt compelled to switch. So in the early 1980s they stopped hiring routine producers in Shreveport and began hiring cheaper routine producers in Singapore. But under this kind of pressure for ever lower high-volume production costs, today's Singaporean can easily end up as yesterday's Louisianan. By the late 1980s, AT&T's strategic brokers found that routine producers in Thailand were eager to assemble telephones for a small fraction of the wages of routine producers in Singapore. Thus, in 1989, AT&T stopped hiring Singaporeans to make telephones and began hiring even cheaper routine producers in Thailand.

---

[1]The reader should note, of course, that lower wages in other areas of the world are of no particular attraction to global capital unless workers there are sufficiently productive to make the labor cost of producing *each unit* lower there than in higher-wage regions. Productivity in many low-wage areas of the world has improved due to the ease with which state-of-the-art factories and equipment can be installed there.

7   The search for ever lower wages has not been confined to heavy industry. Routine data processing is equally footloose. Keypunch operators located anywhere around the world can enter data into computers, linked by satellite or transoceanic fiber-optic cable, and take it out again. As the rates charged by satellite networks continue to drop, and as more satellites and fiber-optic cables become available (reducing communication costs still further), routine data processors in the United States find themselves in ever more direct competition with their counterparts abroad, who are often eager to work for far less.

8   By 1990, keypunch operators in the United States were earning, at most, $6.50 per hour. But keypunch operators throughout the rest of the world were willing to work for a fraction of this. Thus, many potential American data-processing jobs were disappearing, and the wages and benefits of the remaining ones were in decline. Typical was Saztec International, a $20-million-a-year data-processing firm headquartered in Kansas City, whose American strategic brokers contracted with routine data processors in Manila and with American-owned firms that needed such data-processing services. Compared with the average Philippine income of $1,700 per year, data-entry operators working for Saztec earn the princely sum of $2,650. The remainder of Saztec's employees were American problem-solvers and -identifiers, searching for ways to improve the worldwide system and find new uses to which it could be put.[2]

9   By 1990, American Airlines was employing over 1,000 data processors in Barbados and the Dominican Republic to enter names and flight numbers from used airline tickets (flown daily to Barbados from airports around the United States) into a giant computer bank located in Dallas. Chicago publisher R. R. Donnelley was sending entire manuscripts to Barbados for entry into computers in preparation for printing. The New York Life Insurance Company was dispatching insurance claims to Castleisland, Ireland, where routine producers, guided by simple directions, entered the claims and determined the amounts due, then instantly transmitted the computations back to the United States. (When the firm advertised in Ireland for twenty-five data-processing jobs, it received six hundred applications.) And McGraw-Hill was processing subscription renewal and marketing information for its magazines in nearby Galway. Indeed, literally millions of routine workers around the world were receiving information, converting it into computer-readable form, and then sending it back—at the speed of electronic impulses—whence it came.

10   The simple coding of computer software has also entered into world commerce. India, with a large English-speaking population of technicians happy to do routine programming cheaply, is proving to be particularly attractive to global webs in need of this service. By 1990, Texas Instruments maintained a software development facility in Bangalore, linking fifty Indian programmers by satellite to TI's Dallas headquarters. Spurred by this and similar ventures, the

[2]John Maxwell Hamilton, "A Bit Player Buys into the Computer Age," *New York Times Business World,* December 3, 1989, p. 14.

Indian government was building a teleport in Poona, intended to make it easier and less expensive for many other firms to send their routine software design specifications for coding.[3]

This shift of routine production jobs from advanced to developing nations is a 11 great boon to many workers in such nations who otherwise would be jobless or working for much lower wages. These workers, in turn, now have more money with which to purchase symbolic-analytic services from advanced nations (often embedded within all sorts of complex products). The trend is also beneficial to everyone around the world who can now obtain high-volume, standardized products (including information and software) more cheaply than before.

But these benefits do not come without certain costs. In particular the burden 12 is borne by those who no longer have good-paying routine production jobs within advanced economies like the United States. Many of these people used to belong to unions or at least benefited from prevailing wage rates established in collective bargaining agreements. But as the old corporate bureaucracies have flattened into global webs, bargaining leverage has been lost. Indeed, the tacit national bargain is no more.

Despite the growth in the number of new jobs in the United States, union 13 membership has withered. In 1960, 35 percent of all nonagricultural workers in America belonged to a union. But by 1980 that portion had fallen to just under a quarter, and by 1989 to about 17 percent. Excluding government employees, union membership was down to 13.4 percent.[4] This was a smaller proportion even than in the early 1930s, before the National Labor Relations Act created a legally protected right to labor representation. The drop in membership has been accompanied by a growing number of collective bargaining agreements to freeze wages at current levels, reduce wage levels of entering workers, or reduce wages overall. This is an important reason why the long economic recovery that began in 1982 produced a smaller rise in unit labor costs than any of the eight recoveries since World War II—the low rate of unemployment during its course notwithstanding.

Routine production jobs have vanished fastest in traditional unionized indus- 14 tries (autos, steel, and rubber, for example), where average wages have kept up with inflation. This is because the jobs of older workers in such industries are protected by seniority; the youngest workers are the first to be laid off. Faced with a choice of cutting wages or cutting the number of jobs, a majority of union members (secure in the knowledge that there are many who are junior to them who will be laid off first) often have voted for the latter.

Thus the decline in union membership has been most striking among young 15 men entering the work force without a college education. In the early 1950s, more

---

[3]Udayan Gupta, "U.S.-Indian Satellite Link Stands to Cut Software Costs," *Wall Street Journal,* March 6, 1989, p. B2.
[4]*Statistical Abstract of the United States* (Washington, D.C.: U.S. Government Printing Office, 1989), p. 416, table 684.

than 40 percent of this group joined unions; by the late 1980s, less than 20 percent (if public employees are excluded, less than 10 percent).[5] In steelmaking, for example, although many older workers remained employed, almost half of all routine steelmaking jobs in America vanished between 1974 and 1988 (from 480,000 to 260,000). Similarly with automobiles: During the 1980s, the United Auto Workers lost 500,000 members—one-third of their total at the start of the decade. General Motors alone cut 150,000 American production jobs during the 1980s (even as it added employment abroad). Another consequence of the same phenomenon: The gap between the average wages of unionized and nonunionized workers widened dramatically—from 14.6 percent in 1973 to 20.4 percent by the end of the 1980s.[6] The lesson is clear. If you drop out of high school or have no more than a high school diploma, do not expect a good routine production job to be awaiting you.

16   Also vanishing are lower- and middle-level management jobs involving routine production. Between 1981 and 1986, more than 780,000 foremen, supervisors, and section chiefs lost their jobs through plant closings and layoffs.[7] Large numbers of assistant division heads, assistant directors, assistant managers, and vice presidents also found themselves jobless. GM shed more than 40,000 white-collar employees and planned to eliminate another 25,000 by the mid-1990s.[8] As America's core pyramids metamorphosed into global webs, many middle-level routine producers were as obsolete as routine workers on the line.

17   As has been noted, foreign-owned webs are hiring some Americans to do routine production in the United States. Philips, Sony, and Toyota factories are popping up all over—to the self-congratulatory applause of the nation's governors and mayors, who have lured them with promises of tax abatements and new sewers, among other amenities. But as these ebullient politicians will soon discover, the foreign-owned factories are highly automated and will become far more so in years to come. Routine production jobs account for a small fraction of the cost of producing most items in the United States and other advanced nations, and this fraction will continue to decline sharply as computer-integrated robots take over. In 1977, it took routine producers thirty-five hours to assemble an automobile in the United States; it is estimated that by the mid-1990s, Japanese-owned factories in America will be producing finished automobiles using only eight hours of a routine producer's time.[9]

18   The productivity and resulting wages of American workers who run such robotic machinery may be relatively high, but there may not be many such jobs to

[5]Calculations from Current Population Surveys by L. Katz and A. Revenga, "Changes in the Structure of Wages: U.S. and Japan," National Bureau of Economic Research, September 1989.
[6]U.S. Department of Commerce, Bureau of Labor Statistics, "Wages of Unionized and Nonunionized Workers," various issues.
[7]U.S. Department of Labor, Bureau of Labor Statistics, "Reemployment Increases among Displaced Workers," *BLS News,* USDL 86-414, October 14, 1986, table 6.
[8]*Wall Street Journal,* February 16, 1990, p. A5.
[9]Figures from the International Motor Vehicles Program, Massachusetts Institute of Technology, 1989.

go around. A case in point: In the late 1980s, Nippon Steel joined with America's ailing Inland Steel to build a new $400 million cold-rolling mill fifty miles west of Gary, Indiana. The mill was celebrated for its state-of-the-art technology, which cut the time to produce a coil of steel from twelve days to about one hour. In fact, the entire plant could be run by a small team of technicians, which became clear when Inland subsequently closed two of its old cold-rolling mills, laying off hundreds of routine workers. Governors and mayors take note: Your much-ballyhooed foreign factories may end up employing distressingly few of your constituents.

Overall, the decline in routine jobs has hurt men more than women. This is 19 because the routine production jobs held by men in high-volume metal bending manufacturing industries had paid higher wages than the routine production jobs held by women in textiles and data processing. As both sets of jobs have been lost, American women in routine production have gained more equal footing with American men—equally poor footing, that is. This is a major reason why the gender gap between male and female wages began to close during the 1980s.

The second of the three boats, carrying in-person servers, is sinking as well, but 20 somewhat more slowly and unevenly. Most in-person servers are paid at or just slightly above the minimum wage and many work only part-time, with the result that their take-home pay is modest, to say the least. Nor do they typically receive all the benefits (health care, life insurance, disability, and so forth) garnered by routine producers in large manufacturing corporations or by symbolic analysts affiliated with the more affluent threads of global webs.[10] In-person servers are sheltered from the direct effects of global competition and, like everyone else, benefit from access to lower-cost products from around the world. But they are not immune to its indirect effects.

For one thing, in-person servers increasingly compete with former routine 21 production workers, who, no longer able to find well-paying routine production jobs, have few alternatives but to seek in-person service jobs. The Bureau of Labor Statistics estimates that of the 2.8 million manufacturing workers who lost their jobs during the early 1980s, fully one-third were rehired in service jobs paying at least 20 percent less.[11] In-person servers must also compete with high school graduates and dropouts who years before had moved easily into routine production jobs but no longer can. And if demographic predictions about the American work force in the first decades of the twenty-first century are correct (and they are likely to be, since most of the people who will comprise the work force are already identifiable), most new entrants into the job market will be black or Hispanic men, or women—groups that in years past have possessed relatively weak technical skills. This will result in an even larger number of people crowding

[10]The growing portion of the American labor force engaged in in-person services, relative to routine production, thus helps explain why the number of Americans lacking health insurance increased by at least 6 million during the 1980s.

[11]U.S. Department of Labor, Bureau of Labor Statistics, "Reemployment Increases among Disabled Workers," October 14, 1986.

into in-person services. Finally, in-person servers will be competing with growing numbers of immigrants, both legal and illegal, for whom in-person services will comprise the most accessible jobs. (It is estimated that between the mid-1980s and the end of the century, about a quarter of all workers entering the American labor force will be immigrants.[12])

22   Perhaps the fiercest competition that in-person servers face comes from labor-saving machinery (much of it invented, designed, fabricated, or assembled in other nations, of course). Automated tellers, computerized cashiers, automatic car washes, robotized vending machines, self-service gasoline pumps, and all similar gadgets substitute for the human beings that customers once encountered. Even telephone operators are fast disappearing, as electronic sensors and voice simulators become capable of carrying on conversations that are reasonably intelligent and always polite. Retail sales workers—among the largest groups of in-person servers—are similarly imperiled. Through personal computers linked to television screens, tomorrow's consumers will be able to buy furniture, appliances, and all sorts of electronic toys from their living rooms—examining the merchandise from all angles, selecting whatever color, size, special features, and price seem most appealing, and then transmitting the order instantly to warehouses from which the selections will be shipped directly to their homes. So, too, with financial transactions, airline and hotel reservations, rental car agreements, and similar contracts, which will be executed between consumers in their homes and computer banks somewhere else on the globe.[13]

23   Advanced economies like the United States will continue to generate sizable numbers of new in-person service jobs, of course, the automation of older ones notwithstanding. For every bank teller who loses her job to an automated teller, three new jobs open for aerobics instructors. Human beings, it seems, have an almost insatiable desire for personal attention. But the intense competition nevertheless ensures that the wages of in-person servers will remain relatively low. In-person servers—working on their own, or else dispersed widely amid many small establishments, filling all sorts of personal-care niches—cannot readily organize themselves into labor unions or create powerful lobbies to limit the impact of such competition.

24   In two respects, demographics will work in favor of in-person servers, buoying their collective boat slightly. First, as has been noted, the rate of growth of the American work force is slowing. In particular, the number of young workers is shrinking. Between 1985 and 1995, the number of the eighteen- to twenty-four-year-olds will have declined by 17.5 percent. Thus, employers will have more incentive to hire and train in-person servers whom they might previously have avoided. But this demographic relief from the competitive pressures will be only temporary. The cumulative procreative energies of the postwar baby-boomers

[12]Federal Immigration and Naturalization Service, *Statistical Yearbook* (Washington, D.C.: U.S. Government Printing Office, 1986, 1987).
[13]See Claudia H. Deutsch, "The Powerful Push for Self-Service," *New York Times,* April 9, 1989, section 3, p. 1.

(born between 1946 and 1964) will result in a new surge of workers by 2010 or thereabouts.[14] And immigration—both legal and illegal—shows every sign of increasing in years to come.

Next, by the second decade of the twenty-first century, the number of Americans aged sixty-five and over will be rising precipitously, as the babyboomers reach retirement age and live longer. Their life expectancies will lengthen not just because fewer of them will have smoked their way to their graves and more will have eaten better than their parents, but also because they will receive all sorts of expensive drugs and therapies designed to keep them alive—barely. By 2035, twice as many Americans will be elderly as in 1988, and the number of octogenarians is expected to triple. As these decaying baby-boomers ingest all the chemicals and receive all the treatments, they will need a great deal of personal attention. Millions of deteriorating bodies will require nurses, nursing-home operators, hospital administrators, orderlies, home-care providers, hospice aides, and technicians to operate and maintain all the expensive machinery that will monitor and temporarily stave off final disintegration. There might even be a booming market for euthanasia specialists. In-person servers catering to the old and ailing will be in strong demand.[15]

One small problem: the decaying baby-boomers will not have enough money to pay for these services. They will have used up their personal savings years before. Their Social Security payments will, of course, have been used by the government to pay for the previous generation's retirement and to finance much of the budget deficits of the 1980s. Moreover, with relatively fewer young Americans in the population, the supply of housing will likely exceed the demand, with the result that the boomers' major investments—their homes—will be worth less (in inflation-adjusted dollars) when they retire than they planned for. In consequence, the huge cost of caring for the graying boomers will fall on many of the same people who will be paid to care for them. It will be like a great sump pump: In-person servers of the twenty-first century will have an abundance of health-care jobs, but a large portion of their earnings will be devoted to Social Security payments and income taxes, which will in turn be used to pay their salaries. The net result: No real improvement in their standard of living.

The standard of living of in-person servers also depends, indirectly, on the standard of living of the Americans they serve who are engaged in world commerce. To the extent that *these* Americans are richly rewarded by the rest of the world for what they contribute, they will have more money to lavish upon in-person services. Here we find the only form of "trickle-down" economics that has a basis in reality. A waitress in a town whose major factory has just been closed is unlikely to earn a high wage or enjoy much job security; in a swank resort populated by film producers and

---

[14]U.S. Bureau of the Census, Current Population Reports, Series P-23, no. 138, tables 2-1, 4-6. See W. Johnson, A. Packer, et al., *Workforce 2000: Work and Workers for the 21st Century* (Indianapolis: Hudson Institute, 1987).

[15]The Census Bureau estimates that by the year 2000, at least 12 million Americans will work in health services—well over 6 percent of the total work force.

banking moguls, she is apt to do reasonably well. So, too, with nations. In-person servers in Bangladesh may spend their days performing roughly the same tasks as in-person servers in the United States, but have a far lower standard of living for their efforts. The difference comes in the value that their customers add to the world economy.

28   Unlike the boats of routine producers and in-person servers, however, the vessel containing America's symbolic analysts is rising. Worldwide demand for their insights is growing as the ease and speed of communicating them steadily increases. Not every symbolic analyst is rising as quickly or as dramatically as every other, of course; symbolic analysts at the low end are barely holding their own in the world economy. But symbolic analysts at the top are in such great demand worldwide that they have difficulty keeping track of all their earnings. Never before in history has opulence on such a scale been gained by people who have earned it, and done so legally.

29   Among symbolic analysts in the middle range are American scientists and researchers who are busily selling their discoveries to global enterprise webs. They are not limited to American customers. If the strategic brokers in General Motors' headquarters refuse to pay a high price for a new means of making high-strength ceramic engines dreamed up by a team of engineers affiliated with Carnegie Mellon University in Pittsburgh, the strategic brokers of Honda or Mercedes-Benz are likely to be more than willing.

30   So, too, with the insights of America's ubiquitous management consultants, which are being sold for large sums to eager entrepreneurs in Europe and Latin America. Also, the insights of America's energy consultants, sold for even larger sums to Arab sheikhs. American design engineers are providing insights to Olivetti, Mazda, Siemens, and other global webs; American marketers, techniques for learning what worldwide consumers will buy; American advertisers, ploys for ensuring that they actually do. American architects are issuing designs and blueprints for opera houses, art galleries, museums, luxury hotels, and residential complexes in the world's major cities; American commercial property developers, marketing these properties to worldwide investors and purchasers.

31   Americans who specialize in the gentle art of public relations are in demand by corporations, governments, and politicians in virtually every nation. So, too, are American political consultants, some of whom, at this writing, are advising the Hungarian Socialist Party, the remnant of Hungary's ruling Communists, on how to salvage a few parliamentary seats in the nation's first free election in more than forty years. Also at this writing, a team of American agricultural consultants is advising the managers of a Soviet farm collective employing 1,700 Russians eighty miles outside Moscow. As noted, American investment bankers and lawyers specializing in financial circumnavigations are selling their insights to Asians and Europeans who are eager to discover how to make large amounts of money by moving large amounts of money.

32   Developing nations, meanwhile, are hiring American civil engineers to advise on building roads and dams. The present thaw in the Cold War will no doubt expand these opportunities. American engineers from Bechtel (a global firm notable

for having employed both Caspar Weinberger and George Shultz for much larger sums than either earned in the Reagan administration) have begun helping the Soviets design and install a new generation of nuclear reactors. Nations also are hiring American bankers and lawyers to help them renegotiate the terms of their loans with global banks, and Washington lobbyists to help them with Congress, the Treasury, the World Bank, the IMF, and other politically sensitive institutions. In fits of obvious desperation, several nations emerging from communism have even hired American economists to teach them about capitalism.

Almost everyone around the world is buying the skills and insights of Americans 33 who manipulate oral and visual symbols—musicians, sound engineers, film producers, makeup artists, directors, cinematographers, actors and actresses, boxers, scriptwriters, songwriters, and set designers. Among the wealthiest of symbolic analysts are Steven Spielberg, Bill Cosby, Charles Schulz, Eddie Murphy, Sylvester Stallone, Madonna, and other star directors and performers—who are almost as well known on the streets of Dresden and Tokyo as in the Back Bay of Boston. Less well rewarded but no less renowned are the unctuous anchors on Turner Broadcasting's Cable News, who appear daily, via satellite, in places ranging from Vietnam to Nigeria. Vanna White is the world's most-watched game-show hostess. Behind each of these familiar faces is a collection of American problem-solvers, -identifiers, and brokers who train, coach, advise, promote, amplify, direct, groom, represent, and otherwise add value to their talents.[16]

There are also the insights of senior American executives who occupy the 34 world headquarters of global "American" corporations and the national or regional headquarters of global "foreign" corporations. Their insights are duly exported to the rest of the world through the webs of global enterprise. IBM does not export many machines from the United States, for example. Big Blue makes machines all over the globe and services them on the spot. Its prime American exports are symbolic and analytic. From IBM's world headquarters in Armonk, New York, emanate strategic brokerage and related management services bound for the rest of the world. In return, IBM's top executives are generously rewarded.

The most important reason for this expanding world market and increasing global 35 demand for the symbolic and analytic insights of Americans has been the dramatic improvement in worldwide communication and transportation technologies. Designs, instructions, advice, and visual and audio symbols can be communicated more and more rapidly around the globe, with ever greater precision and at ever-lower cost. Madonna's voice can be transported to billions of listeners, with perfect clarity, on digital compact discs. A new invention emanating from engineers in Battelle's laboratory in Columbus, Ohio, can be sent almost anywhere via modem, in a form that will allow others to examine it in three dimensions through enhanced computer graphics. When face-to-face meetings are still

---

[16]In 1989, the entertainment business summoned to the United States $5.5 billion in foreign earnings— making it among the nation's largest export industries, just behind aerospace. U.S. Department of Commerce, International Trade Commission, "Composition of U.S. Exports," various issues.

required—and videoconferencing will not suffice—it is relatively easy for designers, consultants, advisers, artists, and executives to board supersonic jets and, in a matter of hours, meet directly with their worldwide clients, customers, audiences, and employees.

36   With rising demand comes rising compensation. Whether in the form of licensing fees, fees for service, salaries, or shares in final profits, the economic result is much the same. There are also nonpecuniary rewards. One of the best-kept secrets among symbolic analysts is that so many of them enjoy their work. In fact, much of it does not count as work at all, in the traditional sense. The work of routine producers and in-person servers is typically monotonous; it causes muscles to tire or weaken and involves little independence or discretion. The "work" of symbolic analysts, by contrast, often involves puzzles, experiments, games, a significant amount of chatter, and substantial discretion over what to do next. Few routine producers or in-person servers would "work" if they did not need to earn the money. Many symbolic analysts would "work" even if money were no object.

37 At mid-century, when America was a national market dominated by core pyramid-shaped corporations, there were constraints on the earnings of people at the highest rungs. First and most obviously, the market for their services was largely limited to the borders of the nation. In addition, whatever conceptual value they might contribute was small relative to the value gleaned from large scale—and it was dependent on large scale for whatever income it was to summon. Most of the problems to be identified and solved had to do with enhancing the efficiency of production and improving the flow of materials, parts, assembly, and distribution. Inventors searched for the rare breakthrough revealing an entirely new product to be made in high volume; management consultants, executives, and engineers thereafter tried to speed and synchronize its manufacture, to better achieve scale efficiencies; advertisers and marketers sought then to whet the public's appetite for the standard item that emerged. Since white-collar earnings increased with larger scale, there was considerable incentive to expand the firm; indeed, many of America's core corporations grew far larger than scale economies would appear to have justified.

38   By the 1990s, in contrast, the earnings of symbolic analysts were limited neither by the size of the national market nor by the volume of production of the firms with which they were affiliated. The marketplace was worldwide, and conceptual value was high relative to value added from scale efficiencies.

39   There had been another constraint on high earnings, which also gave way by the 1990s. At mid-century, the compensation awarded to top executives and advisers of the largest of America's core corporations could not be grossly out of proportion to that of low-level production workers. It would be unseemly for executives who engaged in highly visible rounds of bargaining with labor unions, and who routinely responded to government requests to moderate prices, to take home wages and benefits wildly in excess of what other Americans earned. Unless white-collar executives restrained themselves, moreover, blue-collar production workers could not be expected to restrain their own demands for higher wages. Unless both groups exercised

restraint, the government could not be expected to forbear from imposing direct controls and regulations.

At the same time, the wages of production workers could not be allowed to 40 sink too low, lest there be insufficient purchasing power in the economy. After all, who would buy all the goods flowing out of American factories if not American workers? This, too, was part of the tacit bargain struck between American managers and their workers.

Recall the oft-repeated corporate platitude of the era about the chief executive's 41 responsibility to carefully weigh and balance the interests of the corporation's disparate stakeholders. Under the stewardship of the corporate statesman, no set of stakeholders—least of all white-collar executives—was to gain a disproportionately large share of the benefits of corporate activity; nor was any stakeholder— especially the average worker—to be left with a share that was disproportionately small. Banal though it was, this idea helped to maintain the legitimacy of the core American corporation in the eyes of most Americans, and to ensure continued economic growth.

But by the 1990s, these informal norms were evaporating, just as (and largely 42 because) the core American corporation was vanishing. The links between top executives and the American production worker were fading: An ever-increasing number of subordinates and contractees were foreign, and a steadily growing number of American routine producers were working for foreign-owned firms. An entire cohort of middle-level managers, who had once been deemed "white collar," had disappeared; and, increasingly, American executives were exporting their insights to global enterprise webs.

As the American corporation itself became a global web almost indistinguish- 43 able from any other, its stakeholders were turning into a large and diffuse group, spread over the world. Such global stakeholders were less visible, and far less noisy, than national stakeholders. And as the American corporation sold its goods and services all over the world, the purchasing power of American workers became far less relevant to its economic survival.

Thus have the inhibitions been removed. The salaries and benefits of America's 44 top executives, and many of their advisers and consultants, have soared to what years before would have been unimaginable heights, even as those of other Americans have declined.

COMPREHENSION

1. To what does the title allude? Why is this allusion significant to the meaning of the title?
2. To whom does Reich refer when he mentions "symbolic analysts"? Regardless of their occupation, what do all symbolic analysts have in common regarding the nature of their work?
3. What has traditionally been the image of and the nature of work among the white-collar workers to whom Reich alludes? Why are they now one of the groups in danger of losing employment opportunities?

RHETORIC

1. Reich uses the central metaphor of the "boat" in describing the state of economics and employment. Why? What connotations are associated with this image in regard to financial security?
2. How does Reich's introduction prepare you for the major themes he addresses in the body of his essay?
3. Examine the section breaks at the start of paragraphs 3, 11, 20, 35, and 37. How does each section relate to the theme of the essay as a whole? What transitional devices does Reich use to bridge one section to the next?
4. Paragraphs 5, 6, 9, and 16 cite specific and detailed examples of the effects of the changing global economy. How does this contribute to conveying Reich's authority regarding the subject he is discussing?
5. Reich describes a dire situation for the American worker. How would you characterize the tone of this description? Is it angry, resigned, impartial, or accusatory? You may use these or any other adjectives as long as you explain your view.
6. Why does Reich open his essay with an epigraph from Adam Smith? What is the relationship of the quotation to the overall theme of the essay? How does the tone of the epigraph contrast with the tone of the title?
7. What is the author's purpose? Is it to inform, to explain, to warn, to enlighten, to offer solutions, or a combination of any of these? Explain your view.

WRITING

1. In a classification essay, describe three areas of academic concentration at your college or university that can help prepare one for a job as a symbolic analyst.
2. In an expository essay, explain whether you believe the discrepancy between high-wage and low-wage workers will increase, decrease, or remain the same. Reference at least one essay from Chapter 1's casebook on class.
3. **Writing an Argument:** In an essay, argue for or against the proposition that as long as one knows which careers command the highest salaries, it is up to the individual to decide whether he or she should pursue a job in those fields.

NETWORKING
Applying Digital and Multimedia Literacies

Participating in a Newsgroup: Join a newsgroup with a special interest in the global economy. Post a general question to its members, asking whether they agree with Reich's analysis of the changing job market. Collect and synthesize the responses.

A Modest Proposal Preventing the Children of Poor People in Ireland from Being a Burden to Their Parents or Country, and for Making Them Beneficial to the Public

Jonathan Swift

Jonathan Swift (1667–1745) is best known as the author of three satires: A Tale of a Tub *(1704),* Gulliver's Travels *(1726), and* A Modest Proposal *(1729). In these satires, Swift pricks the balloon of many of his contemporaries' and our own most cherished prejudices, pomposities, and delusions. He was also a famous churchman, an eloquent spokesman for Irish rights, and a political journalist. The following selection, perhaps the most famous satiric essay in the English language, offers modest advice to a nation suffering from poverty, overpopulation, and political injustice.*

It is a melancholy object to those who walk through this great town or travel in 1 the country, when they see the streets, the roads, and cabin doors, crowded with beggars of the female-sex, followed by three, four, or six children, all in rags and importuning every passenger for an alms. These mothers, instead of being able to work for their honest livelihood, are forced to employ all their time in strolling to beg sustenance for their helpless infants, who, as they grow up, either turn thieves for want of work, or leave their dear native country to fight for the Pretender in Spain, or sell themselves to the Barbadoes.

I think it is agreed by all parties that this prodigious number of children in 2 the arms, or on the backs, or at the heels of their mothers, and frequently of their fathers, is in the present deplorable state of the kingdom a very great additional grievance; and therefore whoever could find out a fair, cheap, and easy method of making these children sound, useful members of the commonwealth would deserve so well of the public as to have his statue set up for a preserver of the nation.

But my intention is very far from being confined to provide only for the children 3 of professed beggars; it is of a much greater extent, and shall take in the whole number of infants at a certain age who are born of parents in effect as little able to support them as those who demand our charity in the streets.

As to my own part, having turned my thoughts for many years upon this 4 important subject, and maturely weighted the several schemes of other projectors, I have always found them grossly mistaken in their computation. It is true, a child just dropped from its dam may be supported by her milk for a solar year, with little other nourishment; at most not above the value of two shillings, which the mother may certainly get, or the value in scraps, by her lawful occupation of begging; and it is exactly at one year old that I propose to provide for them in such a manner as instead of being a charge upon their parents or the parish, or wanting food and raiment for the rest of their lives, they shall on the contrary contribute to the feeding, and partly to the clothing, of many thousands.

5   There is likewise another great advantage in my scheme, that it will prevent those voluntary abortions, and that horrid practice of women murdering their bastard children, alas, too frequent among us, sacrificing the poor innocent babes, I doubt, more to avoid the expense than the shame, which would move tears and pity in the most savage and inhuman breast.

6   The number of souls in this kingdom being usually reckoned one million and a half, of these I calculate there may be about two hundred thousand couples whose wives are breeders; from which number I subtract thirty thousand couples who are able to maintain their own children, although I apprehend there cannot be so many under the present distresses of the kingdom; but this being granted, there will remain an hundred and seventy thousand breeders. I again subtract fifty thousand for those women who miscarry, or whose children die by accident or disease within the year. There only remain an hundred and twenty thousand children of poor parents annually born. The question therefore is, how this number shall be reared and provided for, which, as I have already said, under the present situation of affairs, is utterly impossible by all the methods hitherto proposed. For we can neither employ them in handicraft or agriculture; we neither build houses (I mean in the country) nor cultivate land. They can very seldom pick up a livelihood by stealing till they arrive at six years old, except where they are of towardly parts; although I confess they learn the rudiments much earlier, during which time they can however be looked upon only as probationers, as I have been informed by a principal gentleman in the county of Cavan, who protested to me that he never knew above one or two instances under the age of six, even in a part of the kingdom so renowned for the quickest proficiency in that art.

7   I am assured by our merchants that a boy or girl before twelve years old is no salable commodity; and even when they come to this age they will not yield above three pounds, or three pounds and half a crown at most on the Exchange; which cannot turn to account either to the parents or the kingdom, the charge of nutriment and rags having been at least four times that value.

8   I shall now therefore humbly propose my own thoughts, which I hope will not be liable to the least objection.

9   I have been assured by a very knowing American of my acquaintance in London, that a young healthy child well nursed is at a year old a most delicious, nourishing, and wholesome food, whether stewed, roasted, baked or boiled; and I make no doubt that it will equally serve in a fricassee or a ragout.

I do therefore humbly offer it to public consideration that of the hundred and 10 twenty thousand children, already computed, twenty thousand may be reserved for breed, whereof only one fourth part to be males, which is more than we allow to sheep, black cattle, or swine; and my reason is that these children are seldom the fruits of marriage, a circumstance not much regarded by our savages, therefore one male will be sufficient to serve four females. That the remaining hundred thousand may at a year old be offered in sale to the persons of quality and fortune through the kingdom, always advising the mother to let them suck plentifully in the last month, so as to render them plump and fat for a good table. A child will make two dishes at an entertainment for friends; and when the family dines alone, the fore or hind quarter will make a reasonable dish, and seasoned with a little pepper or salt will be very good boiled on the fourth day, especially in winter.

I have reckoned upon a medium that a child just born will weigh twelve 11 pounds, and in a solar year if tolerably nursed increaseth to twenty-eight pounds.

I grant this food will be somewhat dear, and therefore very proper for land- 12 lords, who, as they have already devoured most of the parents, seem to have the best title to the children.

Infant's flesh will be in season throughout the year, but more plentiful in 13 March, and a little before and after. For we are told by a grave author, an eminent French physician, that fish being a prolific diet, there are more children born in Roman Catholic countries about nine months after Lent than at any other season: therefore, reckoning a year after Lent, the markets will be more glutted than usual, because the number of popish infants is at least three to one in this kingdom; and therefore it will have one other collateral advantage, by lessening the number of Papists among us.

I have already computed the charge of nursing a beggar's child (in which 14 list I reckon all cottagers, laborers, and four fifths of the farmers) to be about two shillings per annum, rags included: and I believe no gentleman would repine to give ten shillings for the carcass of a good fat child, which, as I have said, will make four dishes of excellent nutritive meat, when he hath only some particular friend or his own family to dine with him. Thus the squire will learn to be a good landlord, and grow popular among the tenants; the mother will have eight shillings net profit, and be fit for work till she produces another child.

Those who are more thrifty (as I must confess the times require) may flay 15 the carcass; the skin of which artificially dressed will make admirable gloves for ladies, and summer boots for fine gentlemen.

As to our city of Dublin, shambles may be appointed for this purpose in the 16 most convenient parts of it, and butchers we may be assured will not be wanting; although I rather recommend buying the children alive, and dressing them hot from the knife as we do roasting pigs.

A very worthy person, a true lover of his country, and whose virtues I highly 17 esteem, was lately pleased in discoursing on this matter to offer a refinement upon my scheme. He said that many gentlemen of this kingdom, having of late destroyed their deer, he conceived that the want of venison might be well supplied by the bodies of young lads and maidens, not exceeding fourteen years of age nor under twelve, so great a number of both sexes in every county being now ready to starve for want of work and service; and these to be disposed of by their parents, if alive, or otherwise by their nearest relations. But with due deference to so excellent a friend and so deserving a patriot, I cannot be altogether in his sentiments; for as to the males, my American acquaintance assured me from frequent experience that their flesh was generally tough and lean, like that of our schoolboys, by continual exercise, and their taste disagreeable; and to fatten them would not answer the charge. Then as to the females, it would, I think with humble submission, be a loss to the public, because they soon would become breeders themselves: and besides, it is not improbable that some scrupulous people might be apt to censure such a practice (although indeed very unjustly) as a little bordering upon cruelty; which, I confess, hath always been with me the strongest objection against any project, how well so ever intended.

18   But in order to justify my friend, he confessed that this expedient was put into his head by the famous Psalmanazar, a native of the island Formosa, who came from thence to London above twenty years ago, and in conversation told my friend that in his country when any young person happened to be put to death, the executioner sold the carcass to persons of quality as a prime dainty; and that in his time the body of a plump girl of fifteen, who was crucified for an attempt to poison the emperor, was sold to his Imperial Majesty's prime minister of state, and other great mandarins of the court, in joints from the gibbet, at four hundred crowns. Neither indeed can I deny that if the same use were made of several plump young girls in this town, who without one single groat to their fortunes cannot stir abroad without a chair, and appear at the playhouse and assemblies in foreign fineries which they never will pay for, the kingdom would not be the worse.

19   Some persons of a desponding spirit are in great concern about that vast number of poor people who are aged, diseased, or maimed, and I have been desired to employ my thoughts what course may be taken to ease the nation of so grievous an encumbrance. But I am not in the least pain upon that matter, because it is very well known that they are every day dying and rotting by cold and famine, and filth and vermin, as fast as can be reasonably expected. And as to the younger laborers, they are now in almost as hopeful a condition. They cannot get work, and consequently pine away for want of nourishment, to a degree that if at any time they are accidentally hired to common labor, they have not strength to perform it; and thus the country and themselves are happily delivered from the evils to come.

20   I have too long digressed, and therefore shall return to my subject. I think the advantages by the proposal which I have made are obvious and many, as well as of the highest importance.

For first, as I have already observed, it would greatly lessen the number of 21 Papists, with whom we are yearly overrun, being the principal breeders of the nation as well as our most dangerous enemies; and who stay at home on purpose to deliver the kingdom to the Pretender, hoping to take their advantage by the absence of so many good Protestants, who have chosen rather to leave their country than to stay at home and pay tithes against their conscience to an Episcopal curate.

Secondly, the poorer tenants will have something valuable of their own, which 22 by law may be made liable to distress, and help to pay their landlord's rent, their corn and cattle being already seized and money a thing unknown.

Thirdly, whereas the maintenance of an hundred thousand children, from 23 two years old and upwards, cannot be computed at less than ten shillings a piece per annum, the nation's stock will be thereby increased fifty thousand pounds per annum, besides the profit of a new dish introduced to the tables of all gentlemen of fortune in the kingdom who have any refinement in taste. And the money will circulate among ourselves, the goods being entirely of our own growth and manufacture.

Fourthly, the constant breeders, besides the gain of eight shillings sterling 24 per annum by the sale of their children, will be rid of the charge of maintaining them after the first year.

Fifthly, this food would likewise bring great custom to taverns, where the 25 vintners will certainly be so prudent as to procure the best receipts for dressing it to perfection, and consequently have their houses frequented by all the fine gentlemen, who justly value themselves upon their knowledge in good eating; and a skillful cook, who understands how to oblige his guests, will contrive to make it as expensive as they please.

Sixthly, this would be a great inducement to marriage, which all wise nations 26 have either encouraged by rewards or enforced by laws and penalties. It would increase the care and tenderness of mothers toward their children, when they were sure of a settlement for life to the poor babes, provided in some sort by the public, to their annual profit instead of expense. We should see an honest emulation among the married women, which of them could bring the fattest child to the market. Men would become as fond of their wives during the time of their pregnancy as they are now of their mares in foal, their cows in calf, or sows when they are ready to farrow; nor offer to beat or kick them (as is too frequent a practice) for fear of a miscarriage.

Many other advantages might be enumerated. For instance, the addition of 27 some thousand carcasses in our exportation of barreled beef, the propagation of swine's flesh, and improvement in the art of making good bacon, so much wanted among us by the great destruction of pigs, too frequent at our tables, which are no way comparable in taste or magnificence to a well-grown, fat yearling child, which roasted whole will make a considerable figure at a lord mayor's feast or any other public entertainment. But this and many others I omit, being studious of brevity.

28   Supposing that one thousand families in this city would be constant customers for infants' flesh, besides others who might have it at merry meetings, particularly weddings and christenings, I compute that Dublin would take off annually about twenty thousand carcasses, and the rest of the kingdom (where probably they will be sold somewhat cheaper) the remaining eighty thousand.

29   I can think of no one objection that will possibly be raised against this proposal, unless it should be urged that the number of people will be thereby much lessened in the kingdom. This I freely own, and it was indeed one principal design in offering it to the world. I desire the reader will observe, that I calculate my remedy for this one individual kingdom of Ireland and for no other that ever was, is, or I think ever can be upon earth. Therefore let no man talk to me of other expedients: of taxing our absentees at five shillings a pound: of using neither clothes nor household furniture except what is of our own growth and manufacture: of utterly rejecting the materials and instruments that promote foreign luxury: of curing the expensiveness of pride, vanity, idleness, and gaming in our women: of introducing a vein of parsimony, prudence, and temperance: of learning to love our country, in the want of which we differ even from Laplanders and the inhabitants of Topinamboo: of quitting our animosities and factions, nor acting any longer like the Jews, who were murdering one another at the very moment their city was taken: of being a little cautious not to sell our country and conscience for nothing: of teaching landlords to have at least one degree of mercy toward their tenants: lastly, of putting a spirit of honesty, industry, and skill into our shopkeepers; who, if a resolution could be now taken to buy only our native goods, would immediately unite to cheat and exact upon us in the price, the measure and the goodness, nor could ever yet be brought to make one fair proposal of just dealing, though often and earnestly invited to it.

30   Therefore I repeat, let no man talk to me of these and the like expedients, till he hath at least some glimpse of hope that there will ever be some hearty and sincere attempt to put them in practice.

31   But as to myself, having been wearied out for many years with offering vain, idle, visionary thoughts, and at length utterly despairing of success, I fortunately fell upon this proposal, which, as it is wholly new, so it hath something solid and real, of no expense and little trouble, full in our own power, and whereby we can incur no danger in disobliging England. For this kind of commodity will not bear exportation, the flesh being of too tender a consistence to admit a long continuance in salt, although perhaps I could name a country which would be glad to eat up our whole nation without it.

32   After all, I am not so violently bent upon my own opinion as to reject any offer proposed by wise men, which shall be found equally innocent, cheap, easy, and effectual. But before something of that kind shall be advanced in contradiction to my scheme, and offering a better, I desire the author or authors will be pleased maturely to consider two points. First, as things now stand, how they will be able to find food and raiment for an hundred thousand useless mouths

and backs. And secondly, there being a round million of creatures in human figure throughout this kingdom, whose sole subsistence put into a common stock would leave them in debt two millions of pounds sterling, adding those who are beggars by profession to the bulk of farmers, cottagers, and laborers, with their wives and children who are beggars in effect; I desire those politicians who dislike my overture, and may perhaps be so bold to attempt an answer, that they will first ask the parents of these mortals whether they would not at this day think it a great happiness to have been sold for food at a year old in the manner I prescribe, and thereby have avoided such a perpetual scene of misfortunes as they have since gone through by the oppression of landlords, the impossibility of paying rent without money or trade, the want of common sustenance, with neither house nor clothes to cover them from the inclemencies of the weather, and the most inevitable prospect of entailing the like or greater miseries upon their breed forever.

I profess, in the sincerity of my heart, that I have not the least personal inter- 33 est in endeavoring to promote this necessary work, having no other motive than the public good of my country, by advancing our trade, providing for infants, relieving the poor, and giving some pleasure to the rich. I have no children by which I can propose to get a single penny; the youngest being nine years old, and my wife past childbearing.

COMPREHENSION

1. Who is Swift's audience for this essay? Defend your answer.
2. Describe the persona in this essay. How is the unusual narrative personality (as distinguished from Swift's personality) revealed by the author in degrees? How can we tell that the speaker's opinions are not shared by Swift?
3. What are the major propositions behind Swift's modest proposal? What are the minor propositions?

RHETORIC

1. Explain the importance of the word *modest* in the title. What stylistic devices does this "modesty" contrast with?
2. What is the effect of Swift's persistent reference to people as "breeders," "dams," "carcass," and the like? Why does he define *children* in economic terms? Find other words that contribute to this motif.
3. Analyze the purpose of the relatively long introduction, consisting of paragraphs 1–7. How does Swift establish his ironic-satiric tone in this initial section?
4. What contrasts and discrepancies are at the heart of Swift's ironic statement in paragraphs 9 and 10? Explain both the subtlety and savagery of the satire in paragraph 12.
5. Paragraphs 13–20 develop six advantages of Swift's proposal, while paragraphs 21–26 list them in enumerative manner. Analyze the progression of these propositions. What is the effect of the listing? Why is Swift parodying argumentative techniques?

6. How does the author both sustain and suspend the irony in paragraph 29? How is the strategy repeated in paragraph 32? How does the concluding paragraph cap his satiric commentary on human nature?

WRITING

1. Discuss Swift's social, political, religious, and economic views as they are revealed in the essay.
2. Write a comprehensive critique of America's failure to address the needs of its poor.
3. **Writing an Argument:** Write a modest proposal—on, for example, how to end the drug problem—advancing an absurd proposition through various argumentative techniques.

NETWORKING
Applying Digital and Multimedia Literacies

Navigating Online Criticism: Go online to locate various critical responses to Swift's famous essay. Review at least five entries from online journals, magazines, or blogs that you would determine *credible sources*, analyzing the basic thesis or claim by each writer. Synthesize your findings in a brief essay.

Synthesis: Connections for Critical Thinking

1. Using the essays of Ehrenreich and Reich, compare the effects of work on human relationships.
2. Write a definition essay titled "What Is Work?" Refer to any of the selections in this chapter to substantiate your opinions.
3. Describe the potential effect of the global marketplace as described by Reich and Friedman.
4. Compare the writings of Swift, Ehrenreich, Krugman, and Reich in terms of the options of those on the lowest rungs of the economic system in Western society.
5. Woolf and Swift are considered to be "classic" writers. What makes their essays "classics"?
6. Monitor and record three business news television shows that focus on analysis and commentary. Analyze the discourse of the moderators, hosts, and guests. As an alternative method, review selected business news Web sites, and subject them to the same analysis.

7. To what extent is American society guided by a business ethic? For example, have Americans historically been so preoccupied with wealth that the quest for money has actually become a distinguishing mark of the national character? Or does the merging of business and religion (what social scientists term the Protestant work ethic) reflect a uniquely American trait? Discuss these issues in an analytical and argumentative essay.
8. Compare and contrast the use of irony and satire in the essays by Diaz and Swift.

NETWORKING
Applying Digital and Multimedia Literacies

---

1. Examine your own college's or university's Web site, and review its philosophy regarding the relationship of college studies to the world of work.
2. Locate several Web sites for job seekers—for example, Monster.com, Idealist.org, and Craigslist. Enter the job classification you are interested in, and compare and contrast the number and types of jobs advertised for three cities. Do a similar search and comparison for federal and state government jobs advertised online.

chapter 9

Media and Popular Culture
What Is the Message?

We are surrounded today as never before by images, sounds, and texts—by what Todd Gitlin, who has an essay in this chapter, terms a "media torrent." Radio and television programs, newspapers and Internet sites, MTV and video games, iPods and cell phone gadgetry increasingly mold our place in culture and society. Indeed, the power of media in our waking and subliminal lives might very well condition our understanding (or misunderstanding) of reality. Today, we can download "reality."

Today's media universe, fueled by new technology, is transforming our sense of the world. Consider the ways in which computers permit us to enter the media stream, making us willing, even compulsive, participants in and consumers of popular culture. Video games, streaming advertisements, wraparound music, newsgroups, chat rooms, and more—all provide data and sensation at warp computer speed. Some slow down the torrent: Bloggers (a word that didn't exist until recently) interrogate their lives and the "facts," even holding newspapers and television news channels accountable for information. But if, as Marshall McLuhan declared, the medium is the message, then any medium, whether old or new, has the power to reflect or construct versions of reality.

Perhaps Americans have moved from a print-based culture to an aural/visual one, preferring electronic media for information, distraction, and entertainment. For centuries books were the molders of popular taste and culture. Tocqueville in *Democracy in America* was amazed by the fact that in the rudest pioneer's hut there was a copy of Shakespeare—and probably, we might add, a copy of the best seller of all time, the Bible. Today's typical household might have more media for iPads, MP3 players, and gaming consoles than books in a library. Of course, print media—say, a book on the ways in which major political parties manipulate the media—offer us the opportunity to scrutinize facts and sources in ways that shock jocks on radio, or talk show hosts on television, or participants in chat rooms cannot. The *medium* or *source* from which we receive sounds, images, and text—the place from which we enter the media torrent—determines the version of reality we carry with us. We can even drown in this torrent, as people who have been captured in virtual reality can attest.

The writers in this chapter invite us to enter the media deluge from a variety of places. They ask broad cultural questions about how we conduct our everyday lives and what choices we make. These questions have both local and worldwide implications, because media and their technological helpmates have created a global village permitting the instant transmission of ideas and images, as well as a subtle transfer of culture—typically American—to the remotest parts of the planet. Whether we navigate the torrent intelligently or succumb passively to the images and sounds washing over us, it is clear that the media in this century will have an increasingly significant impact on human experience.

PREVIEWING THE CHAPTER

As you read the essays in this chapter and respond to them in discussion and writing, consider the following questions:

- What is the main media form and issue on which the author focuses?
- What tone or attitude does the author take toward the subject?
- How does the author fit his or her analysis into the context of popular culture? What social, economic, psychological, or political problems or controversies are treated?
- Which areas of expertise does the author bring to bear on the subject?
- What form of rhetoric—narration and description, exposition, argument—does the writer use? If argument, what is the author's claim? What evidence does she or he provide to support this claim?
- Which essays are similar in subject, thesis, style, purpose, or method, and why?
- What have you learned about the media and popular culture from reading these essays?
- Which essays did you find the most compelling or persuasive? The least? Why?

Ghosts in the machine
- let people know about fathers death via social media
- mourning on social media becomes communal and collective   *mass shootings* can't avert
- death is in our daily interactions   eyes from tragedy

Killer Selfie
- selfie caused fatalities = new phenomenon
- fallen down stairs + off bridges
- narcissism

We want Privacy
— internet = no privacy
- "cyber-snooping"
- no agreement over what constitutes private info
- more people disclose the more privacy they desire but continue b/c dont wanna be left out

Classic and Contemporary Images

What Do Gangster Films Reveal about Us?

Using a Critical Perspective   The best gangster films—like *Little Caesar, The Godfather,* and the *Sopranos* series—challenge viewers to form ethical opinions about and interpretations of the tale of crime that unfolds. Even if you haven't seen either the film or TV show depicted here, what do you think is happening in each frame? What details do you focus on? Do the two characters capture the essence of the gangster life, and why? What aspects of film art—framing, the use of close-up or distance shots, the handling of light, shadow, and color—convey an ethical statement? More broadly, in what ways can film art serve as a commentary on American life?

During the 1930s, the first decade of sound films, actors such as Edward G. Robinson, James Cagney, and Paul Muni created the classic portrait of the gangster as a tough-talking, violent outlaw in films such as *Little Caesar* (1930), *The Public Enemy* (1931), and *Scarface* (1932).

HBO's award-winning series *The Sopranos* provided a more nuanced
portrait of the gangster as a member of a corrupt, and corrupting,
organization with shifting loyalties. For example, Tony Soprano, the
character played by James Gandolfini, is a family man
beset by so many problems that he must seek psychiatric help.

✳

Classic and Contemporary Essays
WHY ARE WE FASCINATED BY BAD MEN
IN POPULAR CULTURE?

Both Robert Warshow and Lauren Goodlad examine the portrayal of "bad" men in popular culture, and specifically our fascination with this type in television and film. Warshow in his highly allusive essay argues that the gangster in American film is a type of urban tragic hero. On the other hand, Goodlad, whose essay is also filled with references to other works, argues from a feminist perspective that Don Draper, the protagonist in the wildly popular AMC series *Mad Men,* is an "icon of masculinity-in-crisis." Essentially, both writers suggest that bad, mad men—gangsters, rogues, outlaws, even some businessmen—exert a powerful hold on our imagination because they represent a flawed mythology of American success. These bad men are ill-fated from the start because they are compelled to operate in an unforgiving cultural and economic universe. They are doomed to anxiety and failure because their key point of cultural reference—the American Dream—is intrinsically corrupt. Ultimately both writers urge us to go beyond our fascination with media types of tragic men to examine the ethical dimensions of the world they inhabit.

❁

The Gangster as Tragic Hero

Robert Warshow

Robert Warshow (1917–1955) attended the University of Michigan and worked for the U.S. Army Security Agency from 1942 to 1946. After the war, he served as an editor of Commentary, *writing film criticism for this magazine and also for* Partisan Review. *Before his untimely death from a heart attack, Warshow had written several brilliant essays on film and on popular culture. Writing of Warshow, Lionel Trilling observed, "I believe that certain of his pieces establish themselves in the line of Hazlitt, a tradition in which I would place only one other writer of our time, George Orwell." One of these brilliant essays, focusing on the interrelation of film and society, is "The Gangster as Tragic Hero," which appeared in* The Immediate Experience: Movies, Games, Theatre and Other Aspects of Popular Culture *(1962).*

1 America, as a social and political organization, is committed to a cheerful view of life. It could not be otherwise. The sense of tragedy is a luxury of aristocratic societies, where the fate of the individual is not conceived of as having a direct and legitimate political importance, being determined by a fixed and supra-political—that is,

non-controversial—moral order or fate. Modern equalitarian societies, however, whether democratic or authoritarian in their political forms, always base themselves on the claim that they are making life happier; the avowed function of the modern state, at least in its ultimate terms, is not only to regulate social relations, but also to determine the quality and possibilities of human life in general. Happiness thus becomes the chief political issue—in a sense, the only political issue—and for that reason it can never be treated as an issue at all. If an American or a Russian is unhappy, it implies a certain reprobation of his society, and therefore, by a logic of which we can all recognize the necessity, it becomes an obligation of citizenship to be cheerful; if the authorities find it necessary, the citizen may even be compelled to make a public display of his cheerfulness on important occasions, just as he may be conscripted into the army in time of war.

Naturally, this civic responsibility rests most strongly upon the organs of 2 mass culture. The individual citizen may still be permitted his private unhappiness so long as it does not take on political significance, the extent of this tolerance being determined by how large an area of private life the society can accommodate. But every production of mass culture is a public act and must conform with accepted notions of the public good. Nobody seriously questions the principle that it is the function of mass culture to maintain public morale, and certainly nobody in the mass audience objects to having his morale maintained.[1] At a time when the normal condition of the citizen is a state of anxiety, euphoria spreads over our culture like the broad smile of an idiot. In terms of attitudes towards life, there is very little difference between a "happy" movie like *Good News,* which ignores death and suffering, and a "sad" movie like *A Tree Grows in Brooklyn,* which uses death and suffering as incidents in the service of a higher optimism.

But, whatever its effectiveness as a source of consolation and a means of pres- 3 sure for maintaining "positive" social attitudes, this optimism is fundamentally satisfying to no one, not even to those who would be most disoriented without its support. Even within the area of mass culture, there always exists a current of opposition, seeking to express by whatever means are available to it that sense of desperation and inevitable failure which optimism itself helps to create. Most often, this opposition is confined to rudimentary or semi-literate forms: in mob politics and journalism, for example, or in certain kinds of religious enthusiasm. When it does enter the field of art, it is likely to be disguised or attenuated: in an unspecific form of expression like jazz, in the basically harmless nihilism of the Marx Brothers, in the continually reasserted strain of hopelessness that often seems to be the real meaning of the soap opera. The gangster film is remarkable

---

[1]In her testimony before the House Committee on Un-American Activities, Mrs. Leila Rogers said that the movie *None But the Lonely Heart* was un-American because it was gloomy. Like so much else that was said during the unhappy investigation of Hollywood, this statement was at once stupid and illuminating. One knew immediately what Mrs. Rogers was talking about; she had simply been insensitive enough to carry her philistinism to its conclusion.

in that it fills the need for disguise (though not sufficiently to avoid arousing uneasiness) without requiring any serious distortion. From its beginnings, it has been a consistent and astonishingly complete presentation of the modern sense of tragedy.[2]

4   In its initial character, the gangster film is simply one example of the movies' constant tendency to create fixed dramatic patterns that can be repeated indefinitely with a reasonable expectation of profit. One gangster film follows another as one musical or one Western follows another. But this rigidity is not necessarily opposed to the requirements of art. There have been very successful types of art in the past which developed such specific and detailed conventions as almost to make individual examples of the type interchangeable. This is true, for example, of Elizabethan revenge tragedy and Restoration comedy.

5   For such a type to be successful means that its conventions have imposed themselves upon the general consciousness and become the accepted vehicles of a particular set of attitudes and a particular aesthetic effect. One goes to any individual example of the type with very definite expectations, and originality is to be welcomed only in the degree that it intensifies the expected experience without fundamentally altering it. Moreover, the relationship between the conventions which go to make up such a type and the real experience of its audience or the real facts of whatever situation it pretends to describe is of only secondary importance and does not determine its aesthetic force. It is only in an ultimate sense that the type appeals to its audience's experience of reality; much more immediately, it appeals to previous experience of the type itself: It creates its own field of reference.

6   Thus the importance of the gangster film, and the nature and intensity of its emotional and aesthetic impact, cannot be measured in terms of the place of the gangster himself or the importance of the problem of crime in American life. Those European moviegoers who think there is a gangster on every corner in New York are certainly deceived, but defenders of the "positive" side of American culture are equally deceived if they think it relevant to point out that most Americans have never seen a gangster. What matters is that the experience of the gangster *as an experience of art* is universal to Americans. There is almost nothing we understand better or react to more readily or with quicker intelligence. The Western film, though it seems never to diminish in popularity, is for most of us no more than the folklore of the past, familiar and understandable only because it has been repeated so often. The gangster film comes much closer. In ways that we do not easily or willingly define, the gangster speaks for us, expressing that part of the American psyche which rejects the qualities and the demands of modern life, which rejects "Americanism" itself.

---

[2]Efforts have been made from time to time to bring the gangster film into line with the prevailing optimism and social constructiveness of our culture; *Kiss of Death* is a recent example. These efforts are usually unsuccessful; the reasons for their lack of success are interesting in themselves, but I shall not be able to discuss them here.

The gangster is the man of the city, with the city's language and knowledge,   7
with its queer and dishonest skills and its terrible daring, carrying his life in his
hands like a placard, like a club. For everyone else, there is at least the theoretical
possibility of another world—in that happier American culture which the gangster
denies, the city does not really exist; it is only a more crowded and more brightly
lit country—but for the gangster there is only the city; he must inhabit it in order
to personify it: not the real city, but that dangerous and sad city of the imagination
which is so much more important, which is the modern world. And the gangster—though there are real gangsters—is also, and primarily, a creature of the
imagination. The real city, one might say, produces only criminals; the imaginary
city produces the gangster: He is what we want to be and what we are afraid we
may become.

Thrown into the crowd without background or advantages, with only those   8
ambiguous skills which the rest of us—the real people of the real city—can only
pretend to have, the gangster is required to make his way, to make his life and
impose it on others. Usually, when we come upon him, he has already made his
choice or the choice has already been made for him, it doesn't matter which: We
are not permitted to ask whether at some point he could have chosen to be something else than what he is.

The gangster's activity is actually a form of rational enterprise, involving fairly   9
definite goals and various techniques for achieving them. But this rationality is
usually no more than a vague background; we know, perhaps, that the gangster
sells liquor or that he operates a numbers racket; often we are not given even that
much information. So his activity becomes a kind of pure criminality: He hurts
people. Certainly our response to the gangster film is most consistently and most
universally a response to sadism; we gain the double satisfaction of participating
vicariously in the gangster's sadism and then seeing it turned against the gangster himself.

But on another level the quality of irrational brutality and the quality of   10
rational enterprise become one. Since we do not see the rational and routine
aspects of the gangster's behavior, the practice of brutality—the quality of
unmixed criminality—becomes the totality of his career. At the same time, we
are always conscious that the whole meaning of this career is a drive for success: the typical gangster film presents a steady upward progress followed by
a very precipitate fall. Thus brutality itself becomes at once the means to success and the content of success—a success that is defined in its most general
terms, not as accomplishment or specific gain, but simply as the unlimited
possibility of aggression. (In the same way, film presentations of businessmen
tend to make it appear that they achieve their success by talking on the telephone and holding conferences and that success *is* talking on the telephone
and holding conferences.)

From this point of view, the initial contact between the film and its audi-   11
ence is an agreed conception of human life: that man is a being with the possibilities of success or failure. This principle, too, belongs to the city; one must
emerge from the crowd or else one is nothing. On that basis the necessity of

the action is established, and it progresses, by inalterable paths to the point where the gangster lies dead and the principle has been modified: There is really only one possibility—failure. The final meaning of the city is anonymity and death.

12   In the opening scene of *Scarface,* we are shown a successful man; we know he is successful because he has just given a party of opulent proportions and because he is called Big Louie. Through some monstrous lack of caution, he permits himself to be alone for a few moments. We understand from this immediately that he is about to be killed. No convention of the gangster film is more strongly established than this: It is dangerous to be alone. And yet the very conditions of success make it impossible not to be alone, for success is always the establishment of an *individual* pre-eminence that must be imposed on others, in whom it automatically arouses hatred; the successful man is an outlaw. The gangster's whole life is an effort to assert himself as an individual, to draw himself out of the crowd, and he always dies *because* he is an individual; the final bullet thrusts him back, makes him, after all, a failure. "Mother of God," says the dying Little Caesar, "is this the end of Rico?"—speaking of himself thus in the third person because what has been brought low is not the undifferentiated *man,* but the individual with a name, the gangster, the success; even to himself he is a creature of the imagination. (T. S. Eliot has pointed out that a number of Shakespeare's tragic heroes have this trick of looking at themselves dramatically; their true identity, the thing that is destroyed when they die, is something outside themselves—not a man, but a style of life, a kind of meaning.)

13   At bottom, the gangster is doomed because he is under the obligation to succeed, not because the means he employs are unlawful. In the deeper layers of the modern consciousness, *all* means are unlawful, every attempt to succeed is an act of aggression, leaving one alone and guilty and defenseless among enemies: One is *punished* for success. This is our intolerable dilemma: that failure is a kind of death and success is evil and dangerous, is—ultimately—impossible. The effect of the gangster film is to embody this dilemma in the person of the gangster and resolve it by his death. The dilemma is resolved because it is *his* death, not ours. We are safe; for the moment, we can acquiesce in our failure, we can choose to fail.

COMPREHENSION

1. What are the "organs of mass culture" (paragraph 2)? What properties do they all have in common?
2. Define the term *tragic hero* as Warshow uses it in his title.
3. Compare and contrast Warshow's concepts of the "real city" with those of the "imaginary city" as they relate to modern life and mass culture.

RHETORIC

1. Although the ultimate focus of the essay is on the "gangster," the subject is not referred to until paragraph 4. Why does Warshow need so much exposition before focusing on his main topic?

2. What do terms such as *supra-political* (paragraph 1), *harmless nihilism* (paragraph 3), and *general consciousness* (paragraph 5) suggest about the tone of the essay? What do they imply concerning the target audience for the essay?

3. Study the topic sentence of each paragraph. Are the topic sentences successful in setting up the material that follows? How does this strategy enhance or detract from the coherence of the author's argument?

4. Essayists usually provide their thesis at the beginning of their essays. Where does Warshow provide the thesis in his essay? What is the purpose and effect of placing it where he does?

5. The author explains the nature of the gangster film genre—its function, characters, themes, plots, meanings, and so on—*before* he cites specific films. Is this a rhetorical weakness in the essay, or does it give the essay particular potency? Explain.

6. Does the conclusion summarize the main points of the essay, bolster them, or provide new insights into them? Or does it do a combination of these things? Explain.

7. Study the introductory paragraph and the conclusion. What themes are reiterated or complemented? How do these two paragraphs serve to provide both thematic and structural coherence?

WRITING

1. Select a genre of television show or movie. Analyze its conventions and the degree to which these conventions transgress the implicit values of our society.

2. **Writing an Argument:** Argue for or against the proposition that genre movies are a form of escapism that distorts the individual's concept of the actual society he or she lives in and its citizens.

NETWORKING
Applying Digital and Multimedia Literacies

Analyzing a Film: Select a contemporary gangster movie. Using Warshow's criteria, demonstrate—via reference to its characters, plot, and theme—how your selection reinforces the author's thesis.

✳

Why We Love "Mad Men"

Lauren M. E. Goodlad

Lauren M. E. Goodlad has degrees from Cornell University (BS), New York University (MA), and Columbia University (PhD). She is an associate professor of English at the University of Illinois at Urbana-Champaign, where she teaches Victorian literature and directs the Unit for Criticism and Interpretative Theory. Goodlad has published Victorian Literature and the Victorian State *(2003) and most recently is a co-editor of* Goth: Undead Subculture *(2007). She worked in the 1980s as a cosmetics and fragrance copywriter in New York City. In the following essay, which was published in the* Chronicle of Higher Education *in 2009, Goodlad combines her personal response to* Mad Men *with unique feminist critical inquiry.*

1   Like most women who call themselves feminists, I've spent my life avoiding men like Don Draper, the incorrigible ladies' man at the center of *Mad Men,* a show about a Madison Avenue advertising agency in the early 1960s. I took a pass on the show during its first season, catching up with it on DVD when the mounting enthusiasm of friends and co-workers piqued my curiosity.

2   By the time the season-three premier was promoted this month, my friends (men and women in their 30s and 40s) had taken to posting Madmenized avatars of themselves on their Facebook pages. And I was one of them, styling myself on madmenyourself.com in a chic red dress, gloves, and cat's-eye glasses. What had happened to make these politically progressive adults in the last days of their youth identify with characters from their parents' generation?

3   I have been intrigued by the mysteries of culture before. In the 1990s, I was writing on gothic subculture and the phenomenon of "men who feel and cry"— men like Anne Rice's vampires, Tim Burton's Edward Scissorhands, and Nine Inch Nails' Trent Reznor, all of whom beckoned young men to dramatize emotion in ways that previous generations had scorned as unmasculine. Alongside those men in black were harsher specimens of masculinity in crisis: men like Tyler Durden, the split personality who launches an underground subculture called Fight Club.

4   While superficially different, both kinds of men were desperate to feel, through catharsis or brutal violence. Yet most of these tales focused on men's relationships with one another, like Tyler's two halves, or Lestat and Louis in Rice's *Interview with the Vampire.* They were men searching for their feelings in the company of other men.

5   And now comes Don Draper, icon of masculinity-in-crisis for the 21st century. Don is in pain, yes, and hurting himself, too (for all his spectacular emotional reserve). But he is also different. No tears or blood on that impeccably pressed

Jon Hamm as Don Draper in the AMC series *Mad Men*.

suit. No close ties to other men. What is it that makes this odd blend of Jay Gatsby, American Gigolo, and the Man in the Gray Flannel Suit so captivating a figure for today?

When I asked a sample of folks close to hand what they thought of the show, strangely enough, the first three said virtually the same thing—all references to Don: *"The guy is hot."* (OK, my mother, a veteran of the *Mad Men* era, said "very handsome," not "hot.") To be sure, the show need not be experienced as the story of a "hot" guy in crisis. A close female colleague, indifferent to Don's eros, tunes in mostly for the Peggy Olson narrative. And there is my husband, who enjoys the show for its complexity and period detail, but hates Don Draper for his selfishness and lies. Like Don, my husband is a hard-working professional father of two in his late 30s. Unlike Don . . . well, you could call him the anti-Don.

Although Don Draper is the show's center of gravity, a constellation of intriguing personalities surrounds him. Several of those characters suggest series that might have been: *Mad Women,* in which Joan Holloway and Peggy Olson take different paths in the struggle for integrity in a man's world; *Mad Closet,* the story of Salvatore Romano's slow-motion sexual awakening; *Bad Men,* a close study of Pete Campbell's toxic cocktail of ambition and insecurity; *Race Men,* in which Paul Kinsey strives to be a hero in the civil-rights movement without exposing himself as an insufferable honkie; *Sad Men,* a nighttime soap in which Roger Sterling deludes himself about his impending mortality; and of course *Mod Men,* a show about style.

8   And then there is Don's beautiful wife, Betty, who, though clearly his better half, is not his patsy. A kind of Donna Reed on steroids, she is much, much more than the first woman on television to have a passionate affair with a household appliance. Her vigorous horsemanship, her facility with a shotgun: These are the signs that though raised to follow the grooves, Betty cannot be underestimated. Witness the end of the first season when, opening the phone bill, she learns that Don has been checking up on her with her psychoanalyst. We think she is in the dark about Don's infidelity; but then, as she lies on the couch, we learn that she has known all along. Betty's decision to tell the good doctor wasn't Freud's talking cure but a savvy move on the chess board that is the Draper marriage. She knows that the shrink will tell Don, so that Don will learn, with a minimum of confrontation, that his fooling around isn't fooling anyone.

9   Conventional wisdom says that women are irresistibly attracted to power. And yet, professionally speaking, Don's position is precarious. Less Gordon Gekko in *Wall Street* than Montgomery Clift's character in *A Place in the Sun,* he is vulnerable to corporate management, professional rivals, and the whims of clients. With no family connections to buttress him, Don has nothing to sell but himself. If he is powerful, it's because the particular commodity he has to offer is selling itself: the trick of making selling seem magical in a consumer society. That is why Don's "hotness" is not the garden-variety sort—not the televised equivalent of an Abercrombie & Fitch ad—but the aspect of his character that connects his existential crisis to ours.

10   Don's sexual tensions bespeak his brilliance as an ad man. His genius for spinning fantasies works in boardroom and bedroom alike. Though superficially a "man's man," he does not long for intimacy with other men. Women are his métier; their desire is the complement to the seductive powers his clients pay him to wield. This is not to say that "sex sells"—a crude logic that Don despises. It is to say that in a consumer society, the fine art of selling is a lot like sex.

11   While his milieu is fundamentally misogynistic, Don himself is far less so. At home he is a possessive, philandering husband, but at work he is the least sexist of the lot, respecting the feelings of middle-age women and promoting his talented secretary.

12   If Betty is stuck playing Don's Madonna—the angelic mother he never had— the other women in his life are more like female variations on Don. There is Midge, the independent bohemian who doesn't make breakfast; Bobbie Barrett, the shrewd businesswoman whose frank sexual hunger ignites Don's kinky side; and Rachel, also a businesswoman, but memorable as the one who got away. Her Jewishness stands for a kind of depth that might cut through Don's mad world if only his desire to connect could trump his need to seduce. In one of many grace

notes, Don, in need of a pseudonym, calls himself Tilden Katz—the man Rachel marries after she ends their affair. It is Don imagining himself as an anti-Don.

In the title poem of *Meditations in an Emergency,* a collection by Frank O'Hara 13 that Don reads, the speaker writes, "no one trusts me" because "I am always looking away." As we eventually learn, Don sends this book to the widow of the man whose identity he stole. But Don's past is really window dressing for a more systemic crisis. There are lots of men with Don's issues who aren't orphans and didn't change their names. If there is anyone who trusts Don it is Peggy, a woman whose loyalty he values too much to throw away—perhaps because he knows that she is like him: Her talent for selling will take her places.

For some viewers, the secret of *Mad Men'*s success is the pleasure of watch- 14 ing characters who don't know, as we do, that "change is gonna come." If that's true, we have more reason to be anxious voyeurs than smug ones. We may know more than Don, Roger, and Betty about the dangers of booze and cigarettes—but we still die as they do (and die increasingly of cancer). And while we have made real gains in sexual and racial equality, the price we have paid is the reactionary anger that haunts every aspect of our social being.

The open secret of our time is that we are less secure than were our precursors 15 in the *Mad Men* era. If we know them to be in the grips of a cold war that finally came to an end, we know ourselves to be losing wars of our own making—a boundless "war on terror" and the destruction of our own environment. We do not watch *Mad Men* because we imagine ourselves as free of vice and illusions; we watch it because we know that our lives, too, are one long meditation in an emergency.

In the dwindling prosperity that is capitalism in the 21st century, every one of 16 us knows that we must sell ourselves, make our pitch, compete for our place in the sun. Though Don has a nice house and car, like most of us, he will never join the big leagues. Among us today, he would not be a Wall Street banker or CEO, for he is not cut from that cloth. His golden parachute is the dream of another life in a California that, if it ever existed, exists no more.

"The guy is hot." If we feast our eyes on Don, wanting him and wanting to be 17 like him, it is perhaps because we, too, want to make it look that good. As Frank O'Hara wrote, "It is easy to be beautiful; it is difficult to appear so." Don gratifies the illusion that a life lived as a commodity can somehow be meaningful; that if we close our eyes, the art of selling will be like the best sex we ever had.

COMPREHENSION

1. Why does Goodlad identify herself as a feminist and why would a self-styled feminist defend a character like Don Draper? How does this defense of Don work in Goodlad's feminist interpretation of *Mad Men?* Provide examples from the essay to support your response.

2. According to Goodlad, the main character in *Mad Men,* Don Draper, is an "icon of masculinity-in-crisis" (paragraph 5). What does she mean by this phrase? Where in the essay does she explore this idea?

3. What observations does Goodlad make about American culture in this essay?

RHETORIC

1. Goodlad summarizes various plotlines and introduces primary characters in *Mad Men*. Why does she devote so much space to this overview? What assumptions is she making about her primary audience, who typically would be college teachers and administrators? (Recall that this essay appeared in the *Chronicle of Higher Education.*) What information does she convey that the average viewer might not know or find interesting?

2. What is Goodlad's thesis? Does she state or imply her main idea? Explain.

3. Identify the allusions that Goodlad uses in this essay. What is her purpose in referring to other characters and works, ranging from Anne Rice's vampires to Frank O'Hara? (Who *was* Frank O'Hara?)

4. Goodlad makes a number of assertions regarding the cultural significance of *Mad Men*. What are they, and do they effectively support her thesis? Are these assertions facts or opinions? Explain your viewpoint.

5. Which paragraphs constitute what we might consider to be Goodlad's conclusion? Is this conclusion effective? Why or why not?

WRITING

1. Watch one episode of *Mad Men*, and then write your own critical response to it.

2. **Writing an Argument:** It could be argued that television series like *Mad Men*, *Boardwalk Empire,* and *Breaking Bad* engage in negative stereotyping. Which side of the debate do you take? Write an argumentative essay on this topic. State your claim, offer evidence, and structure the argument carefully in a series of key reasons in support of your claim.

NETWORKING
Applying Digital and Multimedia Literacies

Critically Interpreting a Television Series: Write a feminist interpretation of a television series that you watch regularly or are familiar with.

Synthesis: Classic and Contemporary Questions for Comparison

1. Warshow critiques the function and role of the gangster in popular media, whereas Goodlad focuses on an analysis of one television series in which the life of an ad man is articulated. How do these different focuses determine the thesis of each essay? What are the positive and negative consequences of addressing a broad issue in "The Gangster as Tragic Hero" without using one extended example, as opposed to the detailed analysis of one TV series in "Why We Love 'Mad Men'"?

2. Goodlad writes an admittedly feminist critique of *Mad Men*. How would you categorize Warshow's critical approach? Is he interested in theory? Why or why not?

3. Compare and contrast Warshow's and Goodlad's observations about American culture in their respective essays. In which of these essays do you find these cultural insights to be most convincing, and why?

✺

A Nation of Vidiots

Jeffrey Sachs

Jeffrey Sachs (b. 1954) is an internationally renowned economics advisor, the director of Earth Institute, and joint professor of sustainable development and health policy and management at Columbia University. Sachs was born in Detroit, Michigan. He received his BA (1976), MA (1978), and PhD (1980) from Harvard University, and subsequently taught there for twenty years before moving to Columbia. As an advisor to the World Bank, World Health Organization, United Nations, and other international organizations, Sachs is in the forefront of efforts to promote sustainable development, disease control, and environmental protection. He is the author of hundreds of popular and scholarly articles and many books, including The End of Poverty *(2005),* Common Wealth *(2008), and* The Price of Civilization *(2011). The essay that follows appeared in the online magazine* Project Syndicate *in 2011.*

The past half-century has been the age of electronic mass media. Television has 1 reshaped society in every corner of the world. Now an explosion of new media devices is joining the TV set: DVDs, computers, game boxes, smart phones, and more. A growing body of evidence suggests that this media proliferation has countless ill effects.

The United States led the world into the television age, and the implications 2 can be seen most directly in America's long love affair with what Harlan Ellison memorably called "the glass teat." In 1950, fewer than 8% of American households owned a TV; by 1960, 90% had one. That level of penetration took decades longer to achieve elsewhere, and the poorest countries are still not there.

True to form, Americans became the greatest TV watchers, which is probably 3 still true today, even though the data are somewhat sketchy and incomplete. The best evidence suggests that Americans watch more than five hours per day of television on average—a staggering amount, given that several hours more are spent in front of other video-streaming devices. Other countries log far fewer viewing hours. In Scandinavia, for example, time spent watching TV is roughly half the US average.

The consequences for American society are profound, troubling, and a 4 warning to the world—though it probably comes far too late to be heeded. First, heavy TV viewing brings little pleasure. Many surveys show that it is almost like an addiction, with a short-term benefit leading to long-term unhappiness and remorse. Such viewers say that they would prefer to watch less than they do.

5   Moreover, heavy TV viewing has contributed to social fragmentation. Time that used to be spent together in the community is now spent alone in front of the screen. Robert Putnam, the leading scholar of America's declining sense of community, has found that TV viewing is the central explanation of the decline of "social capital," the trust that binds communities together. Americans simply trust each other less than they did a generation ago. Of course, many other factors are at work, but television-driven social atomization should not be understated.

6   Certainly, heavy TV viewing is bad for one's physical and mental health. Americans lead the world in obesity, with roughly two-thirds of the US population now overweight. Again, many factors underlie this, including a diet of cheap, unhealthy fried foods, but the sedentary time spent in front of the TV is an important influence as well.

7   At the same time, what happens mentally is as important as what happens physically. Television and related media have been the greatest purveyors and conveyors of corporate and political propaganda in society.

8   America's TV ownership is almost entirely in private hands, and owners make much of their money through relentless advertising. Effective advertising campaigns, appealing to unconscious urges—typically related to food, sex, and status—create cravings for products and purchases that have little real value for consumers or society.

9   The same, of course, has happened to politics. American politicians are now brand names, packaged like breakfast cereal. Anybody—and any idea—can be sold with a bright ribbon and a catchy jingle.

10   All roads to power in America lead through TV, and all access to TV depends on big money. This simple logic has put American politics in the hands of the rich as never before.

11   Even war can be rolled out as a new product. The Bush administration promoted the premises of the Iraq war—Saddam Hussein's non-existent weapons of mass destruction—in the familiar colorful, fast-paced, and graphics-heavy style of television advertising. Then the war itself began with the so-called "shock and awe" bombing of Baghdad—a made-for-TV live spectacle aimed at ensuring high ratings for the US-led invasion.

12   Many neuroscientists believe that the mental-health effects of TV viewing might run even deeper than addiction, consumerism, loss of social trust, and political propaganda. Perhaps TV is rewiring heavy viewers' brains and impairing their cognitive capacities. The American Academy of Pediatrics recently warned that TV viewing by young children is dangerous for their brain development, and called on parents to keep children under two away from the TV and similar media.

13   A recent survey in the US by the organization Common Sense Media reveals a paradox, but one that is perfectly understandable. Children in poor American households today not only watch more TV than children in wealthy households, but are also more likely to have a television in their room. When a commodity's consumption falls as income rises, economists call it an "inferior" good.

To be sure, the mass media can be useful as a provider of information, educa- 14
tion, entertainment, and even political awareness. But too much of it is confronting us with dangers that we need to avoid.

At the very least, we can minimize those dangers. Successful approaches 15
around the world include limits on TV advertising, especially to young children;
noncommercial, publicly owned TV networks like the BBC; and free (but limited)
TV time for political campaigns.

Of course, the best defense is our own self-control. We can all leave the TV off 16
more hours per day and spend that time reading, talking with each other, and re-
building the bases of personal health and social trust.

COMPREHENSION

1. Do you find Sachs's article too harsh or extreme? Justify your response with reference
   to the text.
2. List, highlight, or circle the objections Sachs has to television viewing.
3. Does Sachs find any useful value in watching television? Why or why not?

RHETORIC

1. Which paragraphs constitute Sachs's introduction? How does this introduction relate
   to the body of the essay?
2. Where does Sachs present his claim? Why does he place it here?
3. How does Sachs develop his argument? What forms of support does he provide?
4. How does the author's use of colloquial language, starting with his coinage "vidiots,"
   affect the tone of his argument?
5. Where does Sachs incorporate emotional and ethical appeals into his argument? What
   is the effect?

WRITING

1. Analyze in depth one of the many issues raised by Sachs in his essay—for example,
   television viewing and obesity, or cognitive development, or poverty.
2. Write a personal essay on your own television viewing habits.
3. **Writing an Argument:** Agree or disagree with Sachs's assertion that we have become "a nation of vidiots."

NETWORKING
Applying Digital and Multimedia Literacies

Researching an Organization: Sachs is president and co-founder of the *Millennium
Promise Alliance.* Conduct online research on this organization (see Chapters 15
and 16) and evaluate it. Share your findings—including a list of your sources—
and insights in a brief report, written or oral.

❋

My Creature from the Black Lagoon

Stephen King

Stephen King *(b. 1947) was born in Portland, Maine. Raised by his mother, he spent parts of his childhood in Indiana, Connecticut, Massachusetts, and Maine. He graduated from the University of Maine at Orono in 1970 with a degree in English. During his early writing career, he sold several stories to mass market men's magazines and taught English in Hampden, Maine. In 1973, his novel* Carrie *sold enough copies that he could devote his energies to writing full-time. He is the author of about 100 books, most focusing on horror and the occult. A number have been adapted for film and television, including* Carrie, The Dead Zone, The Shining, Christine, Pet Sematary, Stand by Me, *and* The Green Mile. *Besides writing, he belongs to an all-writers rock-and-roll band (with Dave Barry and Amy Tan) and is a major contributor to local and national charities. In the following selection, taken from* Danse Macabre *(1981), King compares and contrasts the responses of adults and children to horror movies.*

1   The first movie I can remember seeing as a kid was *Creature from the Black Lagoon.* It was at the drive-in, and unless it was a second-run job I must have been about seven, because the film, which starred Richard Carlson and Richard Denning, was released in 1954. It was also originally released in 3-D, but I cannot remember wearing the glasses, so perhaps I did see a rerelease.

2   I remember only one scene clearly from the movie, but it left a lasting impression. The hero (Carlson) and the heroine (Julia Adams, who looked absolutely spectacular in a one-piece white bathing suit) are on an expedition somewhere in the Amazon basin. They make their way up a swampy, narrow waterway and into a wide pond that seems an idyllic South American version of the Garden of Eden.

3   But the Creature is lurking—naturally. It's a scaly, batrachian monster that is remarkably like Lovecraft's half-breed, degenerate aberrations—the crazed and blasphemous results of liaisons between gods and human women (it's difficult to get away from Lovecraft). This monster is slowly and patiently barricading the mouth of the stream with sticks and branches, irrevocably sealing the party of anthropologists in.

4   I was barely old enough to read at that time, the discovery of my father's box of weird fiction still years away. I have a vague memory of boyfriends in my mom's life during that period—from 1952 until 1958 or so; enough of a memory to be sure she had a social life, not enough to even guess if she had a sex life. There was Norville, who smoked Luckies and kept three fans going in his two-room apartment during the summer; and there was Milt, who drove a Buick and wore gigantic blue shorts in the summertime; and another fellow, very small, who was, I believe, a cook in a French restaurant. So far as I know, my mother came close to marrying none of them. She'd gone that route once. Also, that was a time when

a woman, once married, became a shadow figure in the process of decision-making and bread-winning. I think my mom, who could be stubborn, intractable, grimly persevering and nearly impossible to discourage, had gotten a taste for captaining her own life. And so she went out with guys, but none of them became permanent fixtures.

It was Milt we were out with that night, he of the Buick and the large blue 5 shorts. He seemed to genuinely like my brother and me, and to genuinely not mind having us along in the back seat from time to time (it may be that when you have reached the calmer waters of your early forties, the idea of necking at the drive-in no longer appeals so strongly . . . even if you have a Buick as large as a cabin cruiser to do it in). By the time the Creature made his appearance, my brother had slithered down onto the floor of the back and had fallen asleep. My mother and Milt were talking, perhaps passing a Kool back and forth. They don't matter, at least not in this context; nothing matters except the big black-and-white images up on the screen, where the unspeakable Thing is walling the handsome hero and the sexy heroine into . . . into . . . the Black Lagoon!

I knew, watching, that the Creature had become *my* Creature; I had bought it. 6 Even to a seven-year-old, it was not a terribly convincing Creature. I did not know then it was good old Ricou Browning, the famed underwater stuntman, in a molded latex suit, but I surely knew it was some guy in some kind of a monster suit . . . just as I knew that, later on that night, he would visit me in the black lagoon of my dreams, looking much more realistic. He might be waiting in the closet when we got back; he might be standing slumped in the blackness of the bathroom at the end of the hall, stinking of algae and swamp rot, all ready for a post-midnight snack of small boy. Seven isn't old, but it is old enough to know that you get what you pay for. You own it, you bought it, it's yours. It is old enough to feel the dowser suddenly come alive, grow heavy, and roll over in your hands, pointing at hidden water.

My reaction to the Creature on that night was perhaps the perfect reaction, 7 the one every writer of horror fiction or director who has worked in the field hopes for when he or she uncaps a pen or a lens: total emotional involvement, pretty much undiluted by any real thinking process—and you understand, don't you, that when it comes to horror movies, the only thought process really necessary to break the mood is for a friend to lean over and whisper, "See the zipper running down his back?"

I think that only people who have worked in the field for some time truly un- 8 derstand how fragile this stuff really is, and what an amazing commitment it imposes on the reader or viewer of intellect and maturity. When Coleridge spoke of "the suspension of disbelief" in his essay on imaginative poetry, I believe he knew that disbelief is not like a balloon, which may be suspended in air with a minimum of effort; it is like a lead weight, which has to be hoisted with a clean and a jerk and held up by main force. Disbelief isn't light; it's heavy. The difference in sales between Arthur Hailey and H. P. Lovecraft may exist because everyone believes in cars, and banks, but it takes a sophisticated and muscular intellectual act to believe, even for a little while, in Nyarlathotep, the Blind Faceless One, the Howler in the Night. And whenever I run into someone who expresses a feeling along the lines of, "I don't read fantasy or go to any of those movies; none of it's real," I feel a kind of sympathy. They simply can't lift the weight of fantasy. The muscles of the imagination have grown too weak.

9   In this sense, kids are the perfect audience for horror. The paradox is this: Children, who are physically quite weak, lift the weight of unbelief with ease. They are the jugglers of the invisible world—a perfectly understandable phenomenon when you consider the perspective they must view things from. Children deftly manipulate the logistics of Santa Claus's entry on Christmas Eve (he can get down small chimneys by making himself small, and if there's no chimney there's the letter slot, and if there's no letter slot there's always the crack under the door), the Easter Bunny, God (big guy, sorta old, white beard, throne), Jesus ("How do you think he turned the water into wine?" I asked my son Joe when he—Joe, not Jesus—was five; Joe's idea was that he had something "kinda like magic Kool-Aid, you get what I mean?"), the devil (big guy, red skin, horse feet, tail with an arrow on the end of it, Snidely Whiplash moustache), Ronald McDonald, the Burger King, the Keebler Elves, Dorothy and Toto, the Lone Ranger and Tonto, a thousand more.

10   Most parents think they understand this openness better than, in many cases, they actually do, and try to keep their children away from anything that smacks too much of horror and terror—"Rated PG (or G in the case of *The Andromeda Strain*), but may be too intense for younger children," the ads for *Jaws* read—believing, I suppose, that to allow their kids to go to a real horror movie would be tantamount to rolling a live hand grenade into a nursery school.

11   But one of the odd Döppler effects that seems to occur during the selective forgetting that is so much a part of "growing up" is the fact that almost *everything* has a scare potential for the child under eight. Children are literally afraid of their own shadows at the right time and place. There is the story of the four-year-old who refused to go to bed at night without a light on in his closet. His parents at last discovered he was frightened of a creature he had heard his father speak of often; this creature, which had grown large and dreadful in the child's imagination, was the "twi-night double-header."

12   Seen in this light, even Disney movies are minefields of terror, and the animated cartoons, which will apparently be released and rereleased even unto the end of the world,[1] are usually the worst offenders. There are adults today, who, when questioned, will tell you that the most frightening thing they saw at the movies as children was Bambi's father shot by the hunter, or Bambi and his mother

---

[1]In one of my favorite Arthur C. Clarke stories, this actually happens. In this vignette, aliens from space land on earth after the Big One has finally gone down. As the story closes, the best brains of this alien culture are trying to figure out the meaning of a film they have found and learned how to play back. The film ends with the words *A Walt Disney Production*. I have moments when I really believe that there would be no better epitaph for the human race, or for a world where the only sentient being absolutely guaranteed of immortality is not Hitler, Charlemagne, Albert Schweitzer, or even Jesus Christ—but is, instead, Richard M. Nixon, whose name is engraved on a plaque placed on the airless surface of the moon.

running before the forest fire. Other Disney memories which are right up there with the batrachian horror inhabiting the Black Lagoon include the marching brooms that have gone totally out of control in *Fantasia* (and for the small child, the real horror inherent in the situation is probably buried in the implied father-son relationship between Mickey Mouse and the old sorcerer; those brooms are making a terrible mess, and when the sorcerer/father gets home, there may be PUNISHMENT. . . . This sequence might well send the child of strict parents into an ecstasy of terror); the night on Bald Mountain from the same film; the witches in *Snow White* and *Sleeping Beauty,* one with her enticingly red poisoned apple (and what small child is not taught early to fear the idea of POISON?), the other with her deadly spinning wheel; this holds all the way up to the relatively innocuous *One Hundred and One Dalmatians* which features the logical granddaughter of those Disney witches from the thirties and forties—the evil Cruella DeVille, with her scrawny, nasty face, her loud voice (grownups sometimes forget how terrified young children are of loud voices, which come from the giants of their world, the adults), and her plan to kill all the dalmatian puppies (read "children," if you're a little person) and turn them into dogskin coats.

Yet it is the parents, of course, who continue to underwrite the Disney pro- 13 cedure of release and rerelease, often discovering goosebumps on their own arms as they rediscover what terrified them as children . . . because what the good horror film (or horror sequence in what may be billed a "comedy" or an "animated cartoon") does above all else is to knock the adult props out from under us and tumble us back down the slide into childhood. And there our own shadow may once again become that of a mean dog, a gaping mouth, or a beckoning dark figure.

Perhaps the supreme realization of this return to childhood comes in David 14 Cronenberg's marvelous horror film *The Brood,* where a disturbed woman is literally producing "children of rage" who go out and murder the members of her family, one by one. About halfway through the film, her father sits dispiritedly on the bed in an upstairs room, drinking and mourning his wife, who has been the first to feel the wrath of the brood. We cut to the bed itself . . . and clawed hands suddenly reach out from beneath it and dig into the carpeting near the doomed father's shoes. And so Cronenberg pushes us down the slide; we are four again, and all of our worst surmises about what might be lurking under the bed have turned out to be true.

The irony of all this is that children are better able to deal with fantasy and 15 terror *on its own terms* than their elders are. You'll note I've italicized the phrase "on its own terms." An adult is able to deal with the cataclysmic terror of something like *The Texas Chainsaw Massacre* because he or she understands that it is all make-believe, and that when the take is done the dead people will simply get up and wash off the stage blood. The child is not so able to make this distinction, and *Chainsaw Massacre* is quite rightly rated R. Little kids do not need this scene, any more than they need the one at the end of *The Fury* where John Cassavetes quite literally blows apart. But the point is, if you put a little kid of six in the front row at a screening of *The Texas Chainsaw Massacre* along with an adult who was temporarily unable to distinguish between make-believe and "real things" (as Danny Torrance, the little boy in *The Shining* puts it)—if, for instance, you had given the adult a hit of Yellow Sunshine LSD about two hours before the movie started—my guess is that the kid would have maybe a week's worth of bad dreams. The adult might spend a year or so in a rubber room, writing home with Crayolas.

16   A certain amount of fantasy and horror in a child's life seems to me a perfectly okay, useful sort of thing. Because of the size of their imaginative capacity, children are able to handle it, and because of their unique position in life, they are able to put such feelings to work. They understand their position very well, too. Even in such a relatively ordered society as our own, they understand that their survival is a matter almost totally out of their hands. Children are "dependents" up until the age of eight or so in every sense of the word; dependent on mother and father (or some reasonable facsimile thereof) not only for food, clothing, and shelter, but dependent on them not to crash the car into a bridge abutment, to meet the school bus on time, to walk them home from Cub Scouts or Brownies, to buy medicines with childproof caps, dependent on them to make sure they don't electrocute themselves while screwing around with the toaster or while trying to play with Barbie's Beauty Salon in the bathtub.

17   Running directly counter to this necessary dependence is the survival directive built into all of us. The child realizes his or her essential lack of control, and I suspect it is this very realization which makes the child uneasy. It is the same sort of free-floating anxiety that many air travelers feel. They are not afraid because they believe air travel to be unsafe; they are afraid because they have surrendered control, and if something goes wrong all they can do is sit there clutching airsick bags or the in-flight magazine. To surrender control runs counter to the survival directive. Conversely, while a thinking, informed person may understand intellectually that travel by car is much more dangerous than flying, he or she is still apt to feel much more comfortable behind the wheel, because she/he has control . . . or at least an illusion of it.

18   This hidden hostility and anxiety toward the airline pilots of their lives may be one explanation why, like the Disney pictures which are released during school vacations in perpetuity, the old fairy tales also seem to go on forever. A parent who would raise his or her hands in horror at the thought of taking his/her child to see *Dracula* or *The Changeling* (with its pervasive imagery of the drowning child) would be unlikely to object to the baby sitter reading "Hansel and Gretel" to the child before bedtime. But consider: The tale of Hansel and Gretel begins with deliberate abandonment (oh yes, the stepmother masterminds that one, but she is the symbolic mother all the same, and the father is a spaghetti-brained nurd who goes along with everything she suggests even though he knows it's wrong— thus we can see her as amoral, him as actively evil in the Biblical and Miltonian sense), it progresses to kidnapping (the witch in the candy house), enslavement, illegal detention, and finally justifiable homicide and cremation. Most mothers and fathers would never take their children to see *Survive*, that quickie Mexican exploitation flick about the rugby players who survived the aftermath of a plane

crash in the Andes by eating their dead teammates, but these same parents find little to object to in "Hansel and Gretel," where the witch is fattening the children up so she can eat them. We give this stuff to the kids almost instinctively, understanding on a deeper level, perhaps, that such fairy stories are the perfect points of crystallization for those fears and hostilities.

Even anxiety-ridden air travelers have their own fairy tales—all those *Airport* movies, which, like "Hansel and Gretel" and all those Disney cartoons, show every sign of going on forever . . . but which should only be viewed on Thanksgivings, since all of them feature a large cast of turkeys. 19

My gut reaction to *Creature from the Black Lagoon* on that long-ago night was a kind of terrible, waking swoon. The nightmare was happening right in front of me; every hideous possibility that human flesh is heir to was being played out on that drive-in screen. 20

Approximately twenty-two years later, I had a chance to see *Creature from the Black Lagoon* again—not on TV, with any kind of dramatic build and mood broken up by adverts for used cars, K-Tel disco anthologies, and Underalls pantyhose, thank God, but intact, uncut . . . and even in 3-D. Guys like me who wear glasses have a hell of a time with 3-D, you know; ask anyone who wears specs how they like those nifty little cardboard glasses they give you when you walk in the door. If 3-D ever comes back in a big way, I'm going to take myself down to the local Pearle Vision Center and invest seventy bucks in a special pair of prescription lenses: one red, one blue. Annoying glasses aside, I should add that I took my son Joe with me—he was then five, about the age I had been myself, that night at the drive-in (and imagine my surprise—my *rueful* surprise—to discover that the movie which had so terrified me on that long-ago night had been rated G by the MPAA . . . just like the Disney pictures). 21

As a result, I had a chance to experience that weird doubling back in time that I believe most parents only experience at the Disney films with their children, or when reading them the Pooh books or perhaps taking them to the Shrine or the Barnum & Bailey circus. A popular record is apt to create a particular "set" in a listener's mind, precisely because of its brief life of six weeks to three months, and "golden oldies" continue to be played because they are the emotional equivalent of freeze-dried coffee. When the Beach Boys come on the radio singing "Help Me, Rhonda," there is always that wonderful second or two when I can re-experience the wonderful, guilty joy of copping my first feel (and if you do the mental subtraction from my present age of thirty-three, you'll see that I was a little backward in that respect). Movies and books do the same thing, although I would argue that the mental set, its depth and texture, tends to be a little richer, a little more complex, when re-experiencing films and a lot more complex when dealing with books. 22

With Joe that day I experienced *Creature from the Black Lagoon* from the other end of the telescope, but this particular theory of set identification still applied; in fact, it prevailed. Time and age and experience have all left their marks on me, just as they have on you; time is not a river, as Einstein theorized—it's a big . . . buffalo herd that runs us down and eventually mashes us into the ground, 23 dead and bleeding, with a hearing-aid plugged into one ear and a colostomy bag instead of a .44 clapped on one leg. Twenty-two years later I knew that the Creature was really good old Ricou Browning, the famed underwater stuntman, in a molded latex suit, and the suspension of disbelief, that mental clean-and-jerk, had become a lot harder to accomplish. But I did it, which may mean nothing, or which may mean (I hope!) that the buffalo haven't got me yet. But when that weight of disbelief was finally up there, the old feelings came flooding in, as they flooded in some five years ago when I took Joe and my daughter Naomi to their first movie, a reissue of *Snow White and the Seven Dwarfs*. There is a scene in that film where, after Snow White has taken a bite from the poisoned apple, the dwarfs take her into the forest, weeping copiously. Half the audience of little kids was also in tears; the lower lips of the other half were trembling. The set identification in that case was strong enough so that I was also surprised into tears. I hated myself for being so blatantly manipulated, but manipulated I was, and there I sat, blubbering into my beard over a bunch of cartoon characters. But it wasn't Disney that manipulated me; I did it myself. It was the kid inside who wept, surprised out of dormancy and into schmaltzy tears . . . but at least awake for awhile.

24   During the final two reels of *Creature from the Black Lagoon,* the weight of disbelief is nicely balanced somewhere above my head, and once again director Jack Arnold places the symbols in front of me and produces the old equation of the fairy tales, each symbol as big and as easy to handle as a child's alphabet block. Watching, the child awakes again and knows that this is what dying is like. Dying is when the Creature from the Black Lagoon dams up the exit. Dying is when the monster gets you.

25   In the end, of course, the hero and heroine, very much alive, not only survive but triumph—as Hansel and Gretel do. As the drive-in floodlights over the screen came on and the projector flashed its GOOD NIGHT, DRIVE SAFELY slide on that big white space (along with the virtuous suggestion that you ATTEND THE CHURCH OF YOUR CHOICE), there was a brief feeling of relief, almost of resurrection. But the feeling that stuck longest was the swooning sensation that good old Richard Carlson and Julia Adams were surely going down for the third time, and the image that remains forever after is of the creature slowly and patiently walling its victims into the Black Lagoon; even now I can see it peering over that growing wall of mud and sticks.

26   Its eyes. Its ancient eyes.

COMPREHENSION

1. Why does King claim that it is harder for an author to successfully bring a horror tale to life than a standard "realistic" one? What special skills does the horror writer need?
2. Why are children the "perfect audience for horror" (paragraph 9)? What exists in the structure of most horror films that makes them suitable for children?
3. King titles his essay "My Creature from the Black Lagoon" rather than using the original title *The Creature from the Black Lagoon*. Why?

4. Why does King think it is ironic that many Disney movies are G-rated while "horror" movies often contain warnings about content for children?
5. In paragraph 23, King remarks that he is pleased that he is still able to get a thrill from watching a horror movie even though he is an adult and understands the artifice behind the monster. Why does he feel this is a positive response? Why does he believe it would be beneficial for most adults to react this way?

RHETORIC

1. In paragraph 9, King attempts to reproduce the sense of what it is like to think like a child. How does he achieve this effect? What is his purpose?
2. How does King structure paragraph 18 to compare and contrast horror movies with "fairy tales"? What is his rhetorical intent?
3. What vocabulary choices does King use in his introduction to set up his conversational style of writing? What relationship does King intend to create between the writer and reader by employing this type of discourse?
4. In paragraphs 4 and 5, King recounts a childhood anecdote. What is the purpose of describing the outing to the drive-in theater with his mother's boyfriend, Milt? How does King structure these two paragraphs so that they culminate rhetorically in a device similar to that employed in horror movies?
5. Although much of King's writing is informal, he does use references to popular culture, literature, and science in his writing. What is the significance and meaning of the following terms and phrases: *batrachian* (paragraph 3), *suspension of disbelief* (paragraph 8), *Döppler effects* (paragraph 11), *twi-night double-header* (paragraph 11), *possibility that human flesh is heir to* (paragraph 20), and *golden oldies* (paragraph 22)?
6. The conclusion is only five words: two sentence fragments. Why did King choose to end his essay this way?
7. King uses irony in his essay for comic effect; for example, in paragraph 25, what is the irony in the "sign-off" at the drive-in movie theater that reads: ATTEND THE CHURCH OF YOUR CHOICE?

WRITING

1. Compare and contrast the benefits or drawbacks, or both, of an adult reading a story to a child versus taking a child to the movies.
2. **Writing an Argument:** In an essay, argue for or against the proposition that horror movies are scarier when viewed at the movie theater than on home video.

NETWORKING
Applying Digital and Multimedia Literacies

Comparing Print and Film: Select a horror or science fiction book you've read that has been adapted for the screen. Compare and contrast the effects of each version. Which was more captivating? More engaging? More horrifying? More believable? Explain your view.

Red, White, and Beer

Dave Barry

Dave Barry *(b. 1947) was born in Armonk, New York. He graduated from Haverford College in 1969 and was a reporter and editor at the* Daily Local News *from 1971 to 1975 and subsequently a columnist for the* Miami Herald. *Besides writing his columns, Barry has written numerous books, all with his unique, amusing point of view. His books include* Stay Fit and Healthy until You're Dead *(1985),* Dave Barry's Greatest Hits *(1988),* Dave Barry Turns 40 *(1990),* Dave Barry's Only Travel Guide You'll Ever Need *(1991), and* Dave Barry's History of the Millennium (So Far) *(2007). Barry won the 1988 Pulitzer Prize for commentary. In the following piece, he comments on the relation between television commercials and patriotism.*

1   Lately I've been feeling very patriotic, especially during commercials. Like, when I see those strongly pro-American Chrysler commercials, the ones where the winner of the Bruce Springsteen Sound-Alike Contest sings about how The Pride Is Back, the ones where Lee Iacocca himself comes striding out and practically challenges the president of Toyota to a knife fight, I get this warm, proud feeling inside, the same kind of feeling I get whenever we hold routine naval maneuvers off the coast of Libya.

2   But if you want to talk about *real* patriotism, of course, you have to talk about beer commercials. I would have to say that Miller is the most patriotic brand of beer. I grant you it tastes like rat saliva, but we are not talking about taste here. What we are talking about, according to the commercials, is that Miller is by God an *American* beer, "born and brewed in the U.S.A.," and the men who drink it are American men, the kind of men who aren't afraid to perspire freely and shake a man's hand. That's mainly what happens in Miller commercials: Burly American men go around, drenched in perspiration, shaking each other's hands in a violent and patriotic fashion.

3   You never find out exactly why these men spend so much time shaking hands. Maybe shaking hands is just their simple straightforward burly masculine American patriotic way of saying to each other: "Floyd, I am truly sorry I drank all that Miller beer last night and went to the bathroom in your glove compartment." Another possible explanation is that, since there are never any women in the part of America where beer commercials are made, the burly men have become lonesome and desperate for any form of physical contact. I have noticed that sometimes, in addition to shaking hands, they hug each other. Maybe very late at night, after the David Letterman show, there are Miller commercials in which the burly men engage in slow dancing. I don't know.

I do know that in one beer commercial, I think this is for Miller—although it ₄ could be for Budweiser, which is also a very patriotic beer—the burly men build a house. You see them all getting together and pushing up a brand-new wall. Me, I worry some about a house built by men drinking beer. In my experience, you run into trouble when you ask a group of beer-drinking men to perform any task more complex than remembering not to light the filter ends of cigarettes.

For example, in my younger days, whenever anybody in my circle of friends ₅ wanted to move, he'd get the rest of us to help, and, as an inducement, he'd buy a couple of cases of beer. This almost always produced unfortunate results, such as the time we were trying to move Dick "The Wretch" Curry from a horrible fourth-floor walk-up apartment in Manhattan's Lower East Side to another horrible fourth-floor walk-up apartment in Manhattan's Lower East Side, and we hit upon the labor-saving concept of, instead of carrying The Wretch's possessions manually down the stairs, simply dropping them out the window, down onto the street, where The Wretch was racing around, gathering up the broken pieces of his life and shrieking at us to stop helping him move, his emotions reaching a fever pitch when his bed, which had been swinging wildly from a rope, entered the apartment two floors below his through what had until seconds earlier been a window.

This is the kind of thinking you get, with beer. So I figure what happens, in ₆ the beer commercial where the burly men are building the house, is they push the wall up so it's vertical, and then, after the camera stops filming them, they just keep pushing, and the wall crashes down on the other side, possibly onto somebody's pickup truck. And then they all shake hands.

But other than that, I'm in favor of the upsurge in retail patriotism, which is ₇ lucky for me because the airwaves are saturated with pro-American commercials. Especially popular are commercials in which the newly restored Statue of Liberty— and by the way, I say Lee Iacocca should get some kind of medal for that, or at least be elected president—appears to be endorsing various products, as if she were Mary Lou Retton or somebody. I saw one commercial strongly suggesting that the Statue of Liberty uses Sure brand underarm deodorant.

I have yet to see a patriotic laxative commercial, but I imagine it's only a mat- ₈ ter of time. They'll show some actors dressed up as hard-working country folk, maybe at a church picnic, smiling at each other and eating pieces of pie. At least one of them will be a black person. The Statue of Liberty will appear in the background. Then you'll hear a country-style singer singing:

Folks 'round here they love this land;
They stand by their beliefs;
An' when they git themselves stopped up;
They want some quick relief.

Well, what do you think? Pretty good commercial concept, huh? ₉

Nah, you're right. They'd never try to pull something like that. They'd put the ₁₀ statue in the *foreground.*

COMPREHENSION

1. What does Barry mean by "retail patriotism" (paragraph 7)? How does the essay's title illustrate this concept?
2. According to Barry, what makes beer commercials, especially those for Miller, patriotic?
3. In Barry's opinion, what do sexism, patriotism, and beer have in common?

RHETORIC

1. Barry doesn't explicitly state his thesis anywhere in the essay. In your own words, what is his implied thesis? Use evidence from the essay to support your view.
2. Barry uses irony and humor very effectively in this piece. Cite some examples of his humor, and analyze how he achieves the desired effect.
3. The writer uses specific brand names in his essay. How does this device help strengthen his argument? Would eliminating them make the essay less persuasive? Why or why not?
4. Barry seems to digress from his point in paragraphs 4–6. Why does he do this? How does this digression serve the purpose of the piece?
5. Does the anecdote Barry uses in paragraph 5 ring true? Why or why not? What purpose does it serve in the essay? Does its plausibility affect the strength of Barry's argument?
6. How does paragraph 10 function as a conclusion? Is it in keeping with the essay's tone and style? Is it an effective device? Justify your response.

WRITING

1. Write an essay titled "Patriotism," using both denotative and connotative definitions of the word.
2. **Writing an Argument:** In an essay, argue for or against the claim that television advertising has had a harmful impact on American and global consumers.

NETWORKING
Applying Digital and Multimedia Literacies

Analyzing TV Commercials: Barry's essay examines how television sells patriotism. Write an essay analyzing how television sells other abstract ideas, such as success, love, freedom, or democracy. Pattern your essay after Barry's, using humor. Also, use specific television commercials you have seen as examples.

❋

Wonder Woman

Gloria Steinem

Gloria Steinem *(b. 1934) was born and raised in Toledo, Ohio; she attended Smith College, receiving a BA in government in 1956. A noted feminist and political activist, Steinem in 1968 helped to found* New York *magazine; in 1971 she cofounded* Ms. *magazine and served as its editor. Whether campaigning for Robert Kennedy, defending raising money for the United Farm Workers, or championing women's reproductive rights, Steinem has been on the cutting edge of American politics and social activism for almost five decades. Her books include* The Thousand Indias *(1957),* Outrageous Acts and Everyday Rebellions *(1983),* Marilyn: Norma Jean *(1986),* Revolution from Within *(1992),* Moving beyond Words *(1994), and* Doing Sixty and Seventy *(2006). In the following essay, Steinem explains why the comic book heroine Wonder Woman (who was on the first cover of* Ms.*) was such a formative influence during her childhood.*

Wonder Woman is the only female super-hero to be published continuously since 1 comic books began—indeed, she is one of the few to have existed at all or to be anything other than part of a male super-hero group—but this may strike many readers as a difference without much distinction. After all, haven't comic books always been a little disreputable? Something that would never have been assigned in school? The answer to those questions is yes, which is exactly why they are important. Comic books have power—including over the child who still lives within each of us—because they are *not* part of the "serious" grown-up world.

I remember hundreds of nights reading comic books under the covers with a 2 flashlight; dozens of car trips while my parents told me I was ruining my eyes and perhaps my mind ("brain-deadeners" was what my mother called them); and countless hours spent hiding in a tree or some other inaccessible spot where I could pore over their pages in sweet freedom. Because my family's traveling meant I didn't go to school regularly until I was about twelve, comic books joined cereal boxes and ketchup labels as the primers that taught me how to read. They were even cheap enough to be the first things I bought on my own—a customer who couldn't see over the countertop but whose dignity was greatly enhanced by making a choice, counting out carefully hoarded coins, and completing a grown-up exchange.

I've always wondered if this seemingly innate drive toward independence in 3 children isn't more than just "a movement toward mastery," as psychologists say. After all, each of us is the result of millennia of environment and heredity, a unique combination that could never happen before—or again. Like a seed that contains a plant, a child is already a unique person; an ancient spirit born into a body too small to express itself, or even cope with the world. I remember feeling the greatest love for my parents whenever they allowed me to express my own will, whether that meant wearing an inappropriate hat for days on end, or eating dessert before I had finished dinner.

4   Perhaps it's our memories of past competence and dreams for the future that create the need for super-heroes in the first place. Leaping skyscrapers in a single bound, seeing through walls, and forcing people to tell the truth by encircling them in a magic lasso—all would be satisfying fantasies at any age, but they may be psychological necessities when we have trouble tying our shoes, escaping a worldview composed mainly of belts and knees, and getting grown-ups to *pay attention.*

5   The problem is that the super-heroes who perform magical feats—indeed, even mortal heroes who are merely competent—are almost always men. A female child is left to believe that, even when her body is as big as her spirit, she will still be helping with minor tasks, appreciating the accomplishments of others, and waiting to be rescued. Of course, pleasure is to be found in all these experiences of helping, appreciating, and being rescued; pleasure that should be open to boys, too. Even in comic books, heroes sometimes work in groups or are called upon to protect their own kind, not just helpless females. But the truth is that a male super-hero is more likely to be vulnerable, if only to create suspense, than a female character is to be powerful or independent. For little girls, the only alternative is suppressing a crucial part of ourselves by transplanting our consciousness into a male character—which usually means a white one, thus penalizing girls of color doubly, and boys of color, too. Otherwise, choices remain limited: in the case of girls, to an "ideal" life of sitting around like a Technicolor clotheshorse, getting into jams with villains, and saying things like, "Oh, Superman! I'll always be grateful to you"; in the case of boys of color, to identifying with villains who may be the only ethnic characters with any power; and in the case of girls of color, to making an impossible choice between parts of their identity. It hardly seems worth learning to tie our shoes.

6   I'm happy to say that I was rescued from this dependent fate at the age of seven or so; rescued (Great Hera!) by a woman. Not only did she have the wisdom of Athena and Aphrodite's power to inspire love, she was also faster than Mercury and stronger than Hercules. In her all-woman home on Paradise Island, a refuge of ancient Amazon culture protected from nosy travelers by magnetic thought-fields that created an area known to the world as the Bermuda Triangle, she had come to her many and amazing powers naturally. Together with her Amazon sisters, she had been trained in them from infancy and perfected them in Greek-style contests of dexterity, strength, and speed. The lesson was that each of us might have unknown powers within us, if we only believed and practiced them. (To me, it always seemed boring that Superman had bullet-proof skin, X-ray vision, and the ability to fly. Where was the contest?) Though definitely white, as were all her Amazon sisters, she was tall and strong, with dark hair and eyes—a relief from the weak, bosomy, blonde heroines of the 1940s.

Of course, this Amazon did need a few fantastic gadgets to help her once she 7
entered a modern world governed by Ares, God of War, not Aphrodite, Goddess
of Love: a magic golden lasso that compelled all within its coils to obey her
command, silver bracelets that repelled bullets, and an invisible plane that carried
her through time as well as space. But she still had to learn how to throw the lasso
with accuracy, be agile enough to deflect bullets from her silver-encased wrists,
and navigate an invisible plane.

Charles Moulton, whose name appeared on each episode as Wonder Woman's 8
writer and creator, had seen straight into my heart and understood the fears of
violence and humiliation hidden there. No longer did I have to pretend to like
the "POW!" and "SPLAT!" of boys' comic books, from Captain Marvel to the Green
Hornet. No longer did I have nightmares after looking at ghoulish images of torture
and murder, bloody scenes made all the more realistic by steel-booted Nazis and
fang-toothed Japanese who were caricatures of World War II enemies then marching in every newsreel. (Eventually, the sadism of boys' comic books was so
extreme that it inspired Congressional hearings, and publishers were asked to limit
the number of severed heads and dripping entrails—a reminder that television
wasn't the first popular medium selling sadism to boys.) Best of all, I could stop
pretending to enjoy the ridicule, bossing-around, and constant endangering of
female characters. In these Amazon adventures, only the villains bought the idea
that "masculine" meant aggression and "feminine" meant submission. Only the
occasional female accomplice said things like "Girls want superior men to boss
them around," and even they were usually converted to the joys of self-respect by
the story's end.

This was an Amazon super-hero who never killed her enemies. Instead, she 9
converted them to a belief in equality and peace, to self-reliance, and respect for
the rights of others. If villains destroyed themselves, it was through their own actions or some unbloody accident. Otherwise, they might be conquered by force,
but it was a force tempered by love and justice.

In short, she was wise, beautiful, brave, and explicitly out to change "a world 10
torn by the hatreds and wars of men."

She was Wonder Woman. 11

Only much later, when I was in my thirties and modern feminism had begun 12
to explain the political roots of women's status—instead of accepting some
"natural" inferiority decreed by biology, God, or Freud—did I realize how hard
Charles Moulton had tried to get an egalitarian worldview into comic book form.
From Wonder Woman's birth myth as Princess Diana of Paradise Island, "that
enlightened land," to her adventures in America disguised as Diana Prince, a
be-spectacled army nurse and intelligence officer (a clear steal from Superman's
Clark Kent), this female super-hero was devoted to democracy, peace, justice, and
"liberty and freedom for all womankind."

One typical story centers on Prudence, a young pioneer in the days of the 13
American frontier, where Wonder Woman has been transported by the invisible
plane that doubles as a time machine. After being rescued from a Perils of Pauline
life, Prudence finally realizes her own worth, and also the worth of all women.

"From now on," she says proudly to Wonder Woman, "I'll rely on myself, not on a man." Another story ends with Wonder Woman explaining her own long-running romance with Captain Steve Trevor, the American pilot whose crash-landing on Paradise Island was Aphrodite's signal that the strongest and wisest of all the Amazons must answer the call of a war-torn world. As Wonder Woman says of this colleague whom she so often rescues: "I can never love a dominant man."

14   The most consistent villain is Ares, God of War, a kind of metavillain who considers women "the natural spoils of war" and insists they stay home as the slaves of men. Otherwise, he fears women will spread their antiwar sentiments, create democracy in the world, and leave him dishonored and unemployed. That's why he keeps trying to trick Queen Hippolyte, Princess Diana's mother, into giving up her powers as Queen of the Amazons, thus allowing him to conquer Paradise Island and destroy the last refuge of ancient feminism. It is in memory of a past time when the Amazons did give in to the soldiers of Ares, and were enslaved by them, that Aphrodite requires each Amazon to wear a pair of cufflike bracelets. If captured and bound by them (as Wonder Woman sometimes is in particularly harrowing episodes), an Amazon loses all her power. Wearing them is a reminder of the fragility of female freedom.

15   In America, however, villains are marked not only by their violence, but by their prejudice and lust for money. Thomas Tighe, woman-hating industrialist, is typical. After being rescued by Wonder Woman from accidental imprisonment in his own bank vault, he refuses to give her the promised reward of a million dollars. Though the money is needed to support Holliday College, the home of the band of college girls who aid Wonder Woman, Tighe insists that its students must first complete impossible tests of strength and daring. Only after Wonder Woman's powers allow them to meet every challenge does Tighe finally admit: "You win, Wonder Woman! . . . I am no longer a woman hater." She replies: "Then you're the real winner, Mr. Tighe! Because when one ceases to hate, he becomes stronger!"

16   Other villains are not so easily converted. Chief among them is Dr. Psycho, perhaps a parody of Sigmund Freud. An "evil genius" who "abhors women," the mad doctor's intentions are summed up in this scene-setting preface to an episode called "Battle for Womanhood": "With weird cunning and dark, forbidden knowledge of the occult, Dr. Psycho prepares to change the independent status of modern American women back to the days of the sultans and slave markets, clanking chains and abject captivity. But sly and subtle Psycho reckons without Wonder Woman!"

17   When I looked into the origins of my proto-feminist super-hero, I discovered that her pseudonymous creator had been a very non-Freudian psychologist named William Moulton Marston. Also a lawyer, businessman, prison reformer, and inventor of the lie-detector test (no doubt the inspiration for Wonder Woman's magic lasso), he had invented Wonder Woman as a heroine for little girls, and also as a conscious alternative to the violence of comic books for boys. In fact, Wonder Woman did attract some boys as readers, but the integrated world of comic book trading revealed her true status: at least three Wonder Woman comic books were

necessary to trade for one of Superman. Among the many male super-heroes, only Superman and Batman were to be as long-lived as Wonder Woman, yet she was still a second-class citizen.

Of course, it's also true that Marston's message wasn't as feminist as it might 18 have been. Instead of portraying the goal of full humanity for women and men, which is what feminism has in mind, he often got stuck in the subject/object, winner/loser paradigm of "masculine" versus "feminine," and came up with female superiority instead. As he wrote: "Women represent love; men represent force. Man's use of force without love brings evil and unhappiness. Wonder Woman proves that women are superior to men because they have love in addition to force." No wonder I was inspired but confused by the isolationism of Paradise Island: Did women have to live separately in order to be happy and courageous? No wonder even boys who could accept equality might have felt less than good about themselves in some of these stories: Were there *any* men who could escape the cultural instruction to be violent?

Wonder Woman herself sometimes got trapped in this either/or choice. As 19 she muses to herself: "Some girls love to have a man stronger than they are to make them do things. Do I like it? I don't know, it's sort of thrilling. But isn't it more fun to make a man obey?" Even female villains weren't capable of being evil on their own. Instead, they were hyperfeminine followers of men's commands. Consider Priscilla Rich, the upper-class antagonist who metamorphoses into the Cheetah, a dangerous she-animal. "Women have been submissive to men," wrote Marston, "and taken men's psychology [force without love] as their own."

In those wartime years, stories could verge on a jingoistic, even racist patrio- 20 tism. Wonder Woman sometimes forgot her initial shock at America's unjust patriarchal system and confined herself to defeating a sinister foreign threat by proving that women could be just as loyal and brave as men in service of their country. Her costume was a version of the Stars and Stripes. Some of her adversaries were suspiciously short, ugly, fat, or ethnic as a symbol of "un-American" status. In spite of her preaching against violence and for democracy, the good guys were often in uniform, and no country but the United States was seen as a bastion of freedom.

But Marston didn't succumb to stereotypes as often as most comic book writ- 21 ers of the 1940s. Though Prudence, his frontier heroine, is threatened by monosyllabic Indians, Prudence's father turns out to be the true villain, who has been cheating the Indians. And the irrepressible Etta Candy, one of Wonder Woman's band of college girls, is surely one of the few fat-girl heroines in comics.

There are other unusual rewards. Queen Hippolyte, for instance, is a rare 22 example of a mother who is good, powerful, and a mentor to her daughter. She founds nations, fights to protect Paradise Island, and is a source of strength to Wonder Woman as she battles the forces of evil and inequality. Mother and daughter stay in touch through a sort of telepathic TV set, and the result is a team of equals who are separated only by experience. In the flashback episode in which Queen Hippolyte succumbs to Hercules, she is even seen as a sexual being. How many girl children grew to adulthood with no such example of a strong, sensual mother—except for these slender stories? How many mothers preferred sons, or believed the patriarchal myth that competition is "natural" between mothers and daughters, or tamed their daughters instead of encouraging their wildness and strength? We are just beginning to realize the sense of anger and loss in girls whose mothers had no power to protect them, or forced them to conform out of fear for their safety, or left them to identify only with their fathers if they had any ambition at all.

23   Finally, there is Wonder Woman's ability to unleash the power of self-respect within the women around her; to help them work together and support each other. This may not seem revolutionary to male readers accustomed to stories that depict men working together, but for females who are usually seen as competing for the favors of men—especially little girls who may just be getting to the age when girlfriends betray each other for the approval of boys—this discovery of sisterhood can be exhilarating indeed. Women get a rare message of independence, of depending on themselves, not even on Wonder Woman. "You saved yourselves," as she says in one of her inevitable morals at story's end. "I only showed you that you could."

24   Whatever the shortcomings of William Marston, his virtues became clear after his death in 1947. Looking back at the post-Marston stories I had missed the first time around—for at twelve or thirteen, I thought I had outgrown Wonder Woman and had abandoned her—I could see how little her later writers understood her spirit. She became sexier-looking and more submissive, violent episodes increased, more of her adversaries were female, and Wonder Woman herself required more help from men in order to triumph. Like so many of her real-life sisters in the postwar era of conservatism and "togetherness" of the 1950s, she had fallen on very hard times.

25   By the 1960s, Wonder Woman had given up her magic lasso, her bullet-deflecting bracelets, her invisible plane, and all her Amazonian powers. Though she still had adventures and even practiced karate, any attractive man could disarm her. She had become a kind of female James Bond, though much more boring because she was denied his sexual freedom. She was Diana Prince, a mortal who walked about in boutique, car-hop clothes and took the advice of a male mastermind named "I Ching."

26   It was in this sad state that I first rediscovered my Amazon super-hero in 1972. *Ms.* magazine had just begun, and we were looking for a cover story for its first regular issue to appear in July. Since Joanne Edgar and other of its founding editors had also been rescued by Wonder Woman in their childhoods, we decided to rescue Wonder Woman in return. Though it wasn't easy to persuade her publishers to let us put her original image on the cover of a new and unknown feminist magazine, or to reprint her 1940s Golden Age episodes inside, we finally succeeded. Wonder Woman appeared on newsstands again in all her original glory, striding through city streets like a colossus, stopping planes and bombs with one hand and rescuing buildings with the other.

27   Clearly, there were many nostalgic grown-ups and heroine-starved readers of all ages. The consensus of response seemed to be that if we had all read more about Wonder Woman and less about Dick and Jane, we might have been a lot better off.

As for her publishers, they, too, were impressed. Under the direction of Dorothy Woolfolk, the first woman editor of Wonder Woman in all her long history, she was returned to her original Amazon status—golden lasso, bracelets, and all.

One day some months after her rebirth, I got a phone call from one of Wonder 28 Woman's tougher male writers. "Okay," he said, "she's got all her Amazon powers back. She talks to the Amazons on Paradise Island. She even has a Black Amazon sister named Nubia. Now will you leave me alone?"

I said we would. 29

In the 1970s, Wonder Woman became the star of a television series. As played by 30 Lynda Carter, she was a little blue of eye and large of breast, but she still retained her Amazon powers, her ability to convert instead of kill, and her appeal for many young female viewers. There were some who refused to leave their TV sets on Wonder Woman night. A few young boys even began to dress up as Wonder Woman on Halloween—a true revolution.

In the 1980s, Wonder Woman's story line was revamped by DC Comics, 31 which reinvented its male super-heroes Superman and Batman at about the same time. Steve Trevor became a veteran of Vietnam; he remained a friend, but was romantically involved with Etta Candy. Wonder Woman acquired a Katharine Hepburn–Spencer Tracy relationship with a street-smart Boston detective named Ed Indelicato, whose tough-guy attitude played off Wonder Woman's idealism. She also gained a friend and surrogate mother in Julia Kapatelis, a leading archaeologist and professor of Greek culture at Harvard University who can understand the ancient Greek that is Wonder Woman's native tongue, and be a model of a smart, caring, single mother for girl readers. Julia's teenage daughter, Vanessa, is the age of many readers and goes through all of their uncertainties, trials, and tribulations, but has the joy of having a powerful older sister in Wonder Woman. There is even Myndi Mayer, a slick Hollywood public relations agent who turns Wonder Woman into America's hero, and is also in constant danger of betraying Diana's idealistic spirit. In other words, there are many of the currents of society today, from single mothers to the worries of teenage daughters and a commercial culture, instead of the simpler plots of America's dangers in World War II.

You will see whether Wonder Woman carries her true Amazon spirit into the 32 present. If not, let her publishers know. She belongs to you.

Since Wonder Woman's beginnings more than a half century ago, however, a 33 strange thing has happened: The Amazon myth has been rethought as archaeological relics have come to light. Though Amazons had been considered figments of the imagination, perhaps the mythological evidence of man's fear of woman, there is a tentative but growing body of evidence to support the theory that some Amazon-like societies did exist. In Europe, graves once thought to contain male skeletons—because they were buried with weapons or were killed by battle wounds—have turned out to hold skeletons of females after all. In the jungles of Brazil, scientists have found caves of what appears to have been an all-female society. The caves are strikingly devoid of the usual phallic design and theme;

they feature, instead, the triangular female symbol, and the only cave that does bear male designs is believed to have been the copulatorium, where Amazons mated with males from surrounding tribes, kept only the female children, and returned male infants to the tribe. Such archaeological finds have turned up not only along the Amazon River in Brazil, but at the foot of the Atlas Mountains in northwestern Africa, and on the European and Asiatic sides of the Black Sea.

34   There is still far more controversy than agreement, but a shared supposition of these myths is this: Imposing patriarchy on the gynocracy of pre-history took many centuries and great cruelty. Rather than give up freedom and worship only male gods, some bands of women resisted. They formed all-woman cultures that survived by capturing men from local tribes, mating with them, and raising their girl children to have great skills of body and mind. These bands became warriors and healers who were sometimes employed for their skills by patriarchal cultures around them. As a backlash culture, they were doomed, but they may also have lasted for centuries.

35   Perhaps that's the appeal of Wonder Woman, Paradise Island, and this comic book message. It's not only a child's need for a lost independence, but an adult's need for a lost balance between women and men, between humans and nature. As the new Wonder Woman says to Vanessa, "Remember your *power*, little sister."

36   However simplified, that is Wonder Woman's message: Remember Our Power.

COMPREHENSION

1. According to Steinem, why are children drawn to comic books and superheroes?
2. Why did Wonder Woman appeal especially to Steinem? What distinctions does she draw between the ways boys and girls view action heroes?
3. The writer traces the development of Wonder Woman from her inception during the 1940s to the 1980s. How did Wonder Woman change over the years? How did she remain true to her creator's (William Marston) conception of her? What does Steinem think about these changes?

RHETORIC

1. What is this essay's persuasive thesis?
2. At whom is this essay aimed—lovers of comic books, or women, or a general audience? On what do you base your conclusion?
3. In part, this is a personal essay. How does Steinem create her persona or self-image? Does the personal element enhance or detract from the analysis? Explain your response.
4. Sort out the complex cause-and-effect relationships in this essay. How does the comparative method reinforce the writer's analysis?
5. What types of evidence does the writer provide? Is it sufficient to convince readers? Where, if anywhere, would more detail be helpful?
6. Steinem divides the essay into five sections. What is her purpose? How successful is she in maintaining the essay's unity by employing this method?
7. What paragraphs form the writer's conclusion? How do they recapitulate and add to the substance of the overall essay?

WRITING

1. Compare and contrast the ways in which females and males approach action heroes. Refer to specific icons like Batman, Spiderman, Ellen Ripley, or Buffy the Vampire Slayer to support your assessment.
2. **Writing an Argument:** Think about the numerous action or superheroes that young children and adolescents encounter today in various media forms. Write an essay in which you contend that exposure to such superheroes either does or does not encourage violent behavior in young people.

NETWORKING
Applying Digital and Multimedia Literacies

Reading Action Heroes in Different Media: Write a personal essay about your favorite action hero or heroine—drawn from comics, television shows, or computer games. Explain why this figure appeals to you and what this appeal reveals about the broader culture. In your exploration, include a discussion of how this particular medium/genre was ideal for this character.

Supersaturation, or, The Media Torrent and Disposable Feeling

Todd Gitlin

Todd Gitlin (b. 1943) was born and grew up in New York City. He received a PhD in sociology from the University of California at Berkeley and was president of Students for a Democratic Society (SDS) in the 1960s. Gitlin is professor of culture, journalism, and sociology at New York University and has held the chair in American civilization at the École des hautes études en sciences sociales *in Paris. Gitlin also lectures at home and abroad on contemporary culture and history. He is the North American editor of the Web site openDemocracy.net. Among his notable books are* Inside Prime Time *(1983),* The Twilight of Common Dreams: Why America Is Wracked by Culture Wars *(1995),* Media Unlimited: How the Torrent of Images and Sounds Overwhelms Our Lives *(2001), and* The Bulldozer and the Big Tent: Blind Republicans *(2008). In the selection from* Media Unlimited *that follows, Gitlin offers an overview of the ways in which the media influence our contemporary lives.*

On my bedroom wall hangs a print of Vermeer's *The Concert,* painted around 1660. A young woman is playing a spinet. A second woman, probably her maid, holds a letter. A cavalier stands between them, his back to us. A landscape is

painted on the raised lid of the spinet, and on the wall hang two paintings, a landscape and *The Procuress,* a work by Baburen, another Dutch artist, depicting a
man and two women in a brothel. As in many seventeenth-century Dutch paintings, the domestic space is decorated by paintings. In wealthy Holland, many
homes, and not only bourgeois ones, featured such renderings of the outer world.
These pictures were pleasing, but more: They were proofs of taste and prosperity,
amusements and news at once.

2   Vermeer froze instants, but instants that spoke of the relative constancy of the
world in which his subjects lived. If he had painted the same room in the same
house an hour, a day, or a month later, the letter in the maid's hand would have
been different, and the woman might have been playing a different selection, but
the paintings on the far wall would likely have been the same. There might have
been other paintings, etchings, and prints elsewhere in the house, but they would
not have changed much from month to month, year to year.

3   In what was then the richest country in the world, "everyone strives to embel-
lish his house with precious pieces, especially the room toward the street," as one
English visitor to Amsterdam wrote in 1640, noting that he had observed paintings in bakeries, butcher's shops, and the workshops of blacksmiths and cob-
blers.[1] Of course, the number of paintings, etchings, and prints in homes varied
considerably. One tailor owned five paintings, for example, while at the high end,
a 1665 inventory of a lavish patrician's house in Amsterdam held two maps and
thirteen paintings in one grand room, twelve paintings in his widow's bedroom,
and seven in the maid's room. Still, compared with today's domestic imagery, the
grandest Dutch inventories of that prosperous era were tiny.[2] Even in the better-
off households depicted by Vermeer, the visual field inhabited by his figures was
relatively scanty and fixed.[3]

4   Today, Vermeer's equivalent, if he were painting domestic scenes, or shooting
a spread for *Vanity Fair,* or directing commercials or movies, would also display
his figures against a background of images; and if his work appeared on-screen,
there is a good chance that he would mix in a soundtrack as well. Most of the images would be portraits of individuals who have never walked in the door—not in
the flesh—and yet are recognized and welcomed, though not like actual persons.
They would rapidly segue into others—either because they had been edited into
a video montage, or because they appear on pages meant to be leafed through.
Today's Vermeer would discover that the private space of the home offers up

[1]Peter Mundy, quoted by Geert Mak, *Amsterdam,* trans. Philipp Blom (Cambridge, Mass.: Harvard
University Press, 2000), p. 109.
[2]Simon Schama, *The Embarrassment of Riches: An Interpretation of Dutch Culture in the Golden Age*
(New York: Knopf, 1987), pp. 313–19. Schama notes that research in the relevant archives is "still in
its early days" (p. 315).
[3]Many bourgeois Dutch houses also featured a camera lucida, a mounted magnifying lens trained on
objects in the vicinity. Because the lens was movable, motion could be simulated—distant objects
being brought nearer and sent farther away. But because the apparatus was mounted in a fixed
location, the range of objects in motion was limited to those actually visible from the window.
(Svetlana Alpers, personal communication, October 8, 1999.)

vastly more impressions of the larger world than was possible in 1660. In seventeenth-century Delft, painters did not knock on the door day and night offering fresh images for sale. Today, though living space has been set apart from working space, as would have been the case only for the wealthier burghers of Vermeer's time, the outside world has entered the home with a vengeance—in the profusion of media.

The flow of images and sounds through the households of the rich world, and 5 the richer parts of the poor world, seems unremarkable today. Only a visitor from an earlier century or an impoverished country could be startled by the fact that life is now played out against a shimmering multitude of images and sounds, emanating from television, videotapes, videodiscs, video games, VCRs, computer screens, digital displays of all sorts, always in flux, chosen partly at will, partly by whim, supplemented by words, numbers, symbols, phrases, fragments, all passing through screens that in a single minute can display more pictures than a prosperous seventeenth-century Dutch household contained over several lifetimes, portraying in one day more individuals than the Dutch burgher would have beheld in the course of years, and in one week more bits of what we have come to call "information" than all the books in all the households in Vermeer's Delft. And this is not yet to speak of our sonic surroundings: the music, voices, and sound effects from radios, CD players, and turntables. Nor is it to speak of newspapers, magazines, newsletters, and books. Most of the faces we shall ever behold, we shall behold in the form of images.

Because they arrive with sound, at home, in the car, the elevator, or the wait- 6 ing room, today's images are capable of attracting our attention during much of the day. We may ignore most of them most of the time, take issue with them or shrug them off (or think we are shrugging them off), but we must do the work of dispelling them—and even then, we know we can usher them into our presence whenever we like. Iconic plenitude is the contemporary condition, and it is taken for granted. To grow up in this culture is to grow into an expectation that images and sounds will be there for us on command, and that the stories they compose will be succeeded by still other stories, all bidding for our attention, all striving to make sense, all, in some sense, *ours*. Raymond Williams, the first analyst to pay attention to the fact that television is not just pictures but flow, and not just flow but drama upon drama, pointed out more than a quarter century ago, long before hundred-channel cable TV and VCRs, that

> we have never as a society acted so much or watched so many others acting. . . .
> [W]hat is really new . . . is that drama . . . is built into the rhythms of everyday life.
> In earlier periods drama was important at a festival, in a season, or as a conscious
> journey to a theater; from honouring Dionysus or Christ to taking in a show.
> What we have now is drama as habitual experience: more in a week, in many
> cases, than most human beings would previously have seen in a lifetime.[4]

[4]"Drama in a Dramatised Society," in Alan O'Connor, ed., *Raymond Williams on Television* (Toronto: Between the Lines, 1989 [1974]), pp. 3–5. *Flow* comes up in Williams's *Television: Technology and Cultural Form* (New York: Schocken, 1975), p. 86 ff.

7   Around the time Vermeer painted *The Concert,* Blaise Pascal, who worried about the seductive power of distraction among the French royalty, wrote that "near the persons of kings there never fail to be a great number of people who see to it that amusement follows business, and who watch all the time of their leisure to supply them with delights and games, so that there is no blank in it."[5] In this one respect, today almost everyone—even the poor—in the rich countries resembles a king, attended by the courtiers of the media offering a divine right of choice.

Measures of Magnitude

8   Statistics begin—but barely—to convey the sheer magnitude of this in-touchness, access, exposure, plenitude, glut, however we want to think of it.

9   In 1999, a television set was on in the average American household more than seven hours a day, a figure that has remained fairly steady since 1983. According to the measurements of the A. C. Nielsen Company, the standard used by advertisers and the television business itself, the average individual watched television about four hours a day, not counting the time when the set was on but the individual in question was not watching. When Americans were asked to keep diaries of how they spend their time, the time spent actually watching dropped to a still striking three hours a day—probably an undercount. In 1995, of those who watched, the percentage who watched "whatever's on," as opposed to any specific program, was 43 percent, up from 29 percent in 1979.[6] Though cross-national comparisons are elusive because of differences in measurement systems, the numbers in other industrialized nations seem to be comparable—France, for example, averaging three and a half hours per person.[7] One survey of forty-three nations showed the United States ranking third in viewing hours, after Japan and Mexico. None of this counts time spent discussing programs, reading about their stars, or thinking about either.[8]

10   Overall, wrote one major researcher in 1990, "watching TV is the dominant leisure activity of Americans, consuming 40 percent of the average person's free time as a primary activity [when people give television their undivided attention]. Television takes up more than half of our free time if you count . . . watching TV while doing something else like eating or reading . . . [or] when you have the set on but you aren't paying attention to it."[9] Sex, race, income, age, and marital status

---

[5]*Pensées,* trans. W. F. Trotter (www.eserver.org/philosophy/pascal-pensees.txt), sec. 2, par. 142.

[6]Robert D. Putnam, *Bowling Alone: The Collapse and Revival of American Community* (New York: Simon and Schuster, 2000), p. 222, citing John P. Robinson and Geoffrey Godbey, *Time for Life: The Surprising Ways Americans Use Their Time,* 2nd ed. (University Park: Pennsylvania State University Press, 1999), pp. 136–53, 340–41, 222.

[7]This April 2001 figure for individuals fifteen and older comes from Mediamat (Mediametrie www.mediametria.fr/television/mediamat_mensuel/2001/avril.html).

[8]Putnam, *Bowling Alone,* p. 480, citing Eurodata TV (*One Television Year in the World: Audience Report,* April 1999).

[9]John P. Robinson, "I Love My TV," *American Demographics,* September 1990, p. 24.

make surprisingly little difference in time spent.[10] Neither, at this writing, has the Internet diminished total media use, even if you don't count the Web as part of the media. While Internet users do watch 28 percent less television, they spend more time than nonusers playing video games and listening to the radio and recorded music—obviously a younger crowd. Long-term users (four or more years) say they go on-line for more than two hours a day, and boys and girls alike spend the bulk of their Internet time entertaining themselves with games, hobbies, and the like.[11] In other words, the Internet redistributes the flow of unlimited media but does not dry it up. When one considers the overlapping and additional hours of exposure to radio, magazines, newspapers, compact discs, movies (available via a range of technologies as well as in theaters), and comic books, as well as the accompanying articles, books, and chats about what's on or was on or is coming up via all these means, it is clear that the media flow into the home—not to mention outside—has swelled into a torrent of immense force and constancy, an accompaniment to life that has become a central experience *of* life.

The place of media in the lives of children is worth special attention—not 11 simply because children are uniquely impressionable but because their experience shapes everyone's future; if we today take a media-soaked environment for granted, surely one reason is that we grew up in it and can no longer see how remarkable it is. Here are some findings from a national survey of media conditions among American children aged two through eighteen. The average American child lives in a household with 2.9 televisions, 1.8 VCRs, 3.1 radios, 2.6 tape players, 2.1 CD players, 1.4 video game players, and 1 computer. Ninety-nine percent of these children live in homes with one or more TVs, 97 percent with a VCR, 97 percent with a radio, 94 percent with a tape player, 90 percent with a CD player, 70 percent with a video game player, 69 percent with a computer. Eighty-eight percent live in homes with two or more TVs, 60 percent in homes with three or more. Of the 99 percent with a TV, 74 percent have cable or satellite service.[12] And so on, and on, and on.

The uniformity of this picture is no less astounding. A great deal about the 12 lives of children depends on their race, sex, and social class, but access to major media does not. For TV, VCR, and radio ownership, rates do not vary significantly among white, black, and Hispanic children, or between girls and boys.

[10]Robert Kubey and Mihaly Csikszentmihalyi, *Television and the Quality of Life: How Viewing Shapes Everyday Experience* (Hillsdale, N.J.: Lawrence Erlbaum Associates, 1990), pp. 71–73.

[11]UCLA Center for Communication Policy, *The UCLA Internet Report: Surveying the Digital Future,* November 2000, pp. 10, 17, 18, 14 (www.ccp.ucla.edu).

[12]Donald F. Roberts, *Kids and Media @ the New Millennium* (Menlo Park, Calif.: Henry J. Kaiser Family Foundation, 1999), p. 9, table 1. There were 3,155 children in the sample, including over-samples of black and Hispanic children, to ensure that results in these minority populations would also be statistically significant. As best as a reader can discern, this was a reliable study, with a margin of error of no more than plus-or-minus five percentage points. Since the results for younger children, ages two to seven, come from parents' reports, they may well be conservative, since parents may be uninformed of the extent of their children's viewing or may be underplaying it in order not to feel ashamed before interviewers.

For television and radio, rates do not vary significantly according to the income of the community.[13]

13   How accessible, then, is the media cavalcade at home? Of children eight to eighteen, 65 percent have a TV in their bedrooms, 86 percent a radio, 81 percent a tape player, 75 percent a CD player. Boys and girls are not significantly different in possessing this bounty, though the relative usages do vary by medium. Researchers also asked children whether the television was "on in their homes even if no one is watching 'most of the time,' 'some of the time,' 'a little of the time,' or 'never.'" Homes in which television is on "most of the time" are termed *constant television households*. By this measure, 42 percent of all American households with children are constant television households. Blacks are more likely than whites or Hispanics to experience TV in their lives: 56 percent of black children live in constant television households (and 69 percent have a TV in their bedrooms, compared to 48 percent of whites). The lower the family education and the median income of the community, the greater the chance that a household is a constant television household.[14]

14   As for time, the average child spent six hours and thirty-two minutes per day exposed to media of all kinds, of which the time spent reading books and magazines—not counting schoolwork—averaged about forty-five minutes. For ages two to seven, the average for total media was four hours and seventeen minutes; for ages eight to thirteen, eight hours and eight minutes, falling to seven hours and thirty-five minutes for ages fourteen to eighteen.[15] Here, race and social class do count. Black children are most exposed, followed by Hispanics, then whites. At all age levels, the amount of exposure to all media varies inversely with class, from six hours and fifty-nine minutes a day for children in households where the median income for the zip code is under $25,000 to six hours and two minutes for children whose zip code median income is over $40,000. The discrepancy for TV exposure is especially pronounced, ranging from three hours and six minutes a day for children whose zip code incomes are under $25,000 to two hours and twenty-nine minutes for children whose zip code incomes are over $40,000.[16] Still,

[13]Ibid., p. 11, tables 3-A, 3-B, 3-C.
[14]Ibid., pp. 13–15, tables 4, 5-A, 5-B, 6. In general, fewer western European or Israeli children than Americans have TVs in their bedrooms, but 70 percent in Great Britain do. Next highest in Europe is 64 percent in Denmark. The lows are 31 percent in Holland and 24 percent in Switzerland. Leen d'Haenens, "Old and New Media: Access and Ownership in the Home," in Sonia Livingstone and Moira Bovill, eds., *Children and Their Changing Media Environment: A European Comparative Study* (London: Lawrence Erlbaum Associates, 2001), p. 57.
[15]Roberts, *Kids and Media*, pp. 21–23, tables 8-C, 8-D.
[16]The same point applies to differences in media use throughout the prosperous world. As the economist Adair Turner writes: "European Internet penetration lags the US by 18 to 24 months. When cars or television sets were first introduced, the lag was more like 15 years. . . . The shortness of the lag also suggests that social concern about a 'digital divide,' whether within or between nations, is largely misplaced. . . . Time lags between different income groups in the penetration of personal computers, Internet connections or mobile phones are much shorter, once again because all these products are cheap. . . . At the global level the same scepticism about a digital divide should prevail. Africa may lag 15 years or so behind US levels of PC and Internet penetration, but it lags more like a century behind in basic literacy and health care." Adair Turner, "Not the e-conomy," *Prospect* (London), April 2001 (www.prospect-magazine.co.uk/highlights/essay_turner_april01).

these differences are not vast. Given everything that divides the rich from the poor, the professional from the working class—differences in physical and mental health, infant mortality, longevity, safety, vulnerability to crime, prospects for stable employment, and so on—the class differences in media access and use are surprisingly slender. So are the differences between American and western European children, the latter averaging six hours a day total, though in Europe only two and a quarter of those hours are spent with TV.[17]

All such statistics are crude, of course. Most of them register the time 15 that people *say* they spend. They are—thankfully—not checked by total surveillance. Moreover, the meaning of *exposure* is hard to assess, since the concept encompasses rapt attention, vague awareness, oblivious coexistence, and all possible shadings in between. As the images glide by and the voices come and go, how can we assess what goes on in people's heads? Still, the figures do convey some sense of the media saturation with which we live—and so far we have counted only what can be counted at home. These numbers don't take into account the billboards, the TVs at bars and on planes, the Muzak in restaurants and shops, the magazines in the doctor's waiting room, the digital displays at the gas pump and over the urinal, the ads, insignias, and logos whizzing by on the sides of buses and taxis, climbing the walls of buildings, making announcements from caps, bags, T-shirts, and sneakers. To vary our experience, we can pay to watch stories about individuals unfold across larger-than-life-size movie screens, or visit theme parks and troop from image to image, display to display. Whenever we like, on foot or in vehicles, we can convert ourselves into movable nodes of communication, thanks to car radios, tape, CD, and game players, cell phones, beepers, Walkmen, and the latest in "personal communication systems"—and even if we ourselves refrain, we find ourselves drawn willy-nilly into the soundscape that others broadcast around us.

Crucially, who we are is how we live our time—or *spend* it, to use the term 16 that registers its intrinsic scarcity. What we believe, or say we believe, is less important. We vote for a way of life with our time. And increasingly, when we are not at work or asleep, we are in the media torrent. (Sometimes at work, we are also there, listening to the radio or checking out sports scores, pin-ups, or headlines on the Internet.) Steadily more inhabitants of the wealthy part of the world have the means, incentives, and opportunities to seek private electronic companionship. The more money we have to spend, the more personal space each household member gets. With personal space comes solitude, but this solitude is instantly crowded with images and soundtracks. To a degree that was unthinkable in the seventeenth century, life experience has become an experience in the presence of media.

---

[17]Johannes W. J. Beentjes et al., "Children's Use of Different Media: For How Long and Why?" in Livingstone and Bovill, eds., *Children and Their Changing Media Environment*, p. 96.

COMPREHENSION

1. What does Gitlin's title mean? How are the concepts of "supersaturation" and "disposable feeling" reflected in the essay?
2. Summarize Gitlin's treatment of Vermeer. Who was Vermeer? How, according to the writer, would Vermeer's art be produced today?
3. List some of the facts and statistics that the writer presents to support his idea that we are caught in a "media torrent."

RHETORIC

1. What is Gitlin's argument? Where does he state his claim most clearly? What appeals to logic, ethics, and emotion does he make? Does he rely on his own opinions? Justify your answer.
2. How does the writer maintain unity between the two parts of this essay? Why, for example, does he open his essay with the story of Vermeer? How does Vermeer serve as a unifying element? What other unifying motifs can you find?
3. What varieties of evidence does the writer provide to bolster his argument? Does he rely on anecdotal or actual evidence? How do you know?
4. The writer employs a range of rhetorical strategies in this essay. Point to places where he uses description, comparison and contrast, classification, definition, and causal analysis.
5. Is the author's style personal, informal, or formal? How does this style explain Gitlin's relationship to his audience and the expectations he holds of his readers?
6. What strategy does the writer use in his conclusion? Is this strategy effective? Why or why not?
7. What do Gitlin's footnotes add to the essay? Why are they important?

WRITING

1. Write an essay in which you explain how one medium—television or the Internet, for example—has affected or changed your life. Make sure that you provide adequate detail or evidence.
2. **Writing an Argument:** Write an essay in which you either agree or disagree with Gitlin's claim that increasingly "we are in a media torrent." Use appeals to logic, ethics, and emotion to advance your claim. Make certain that you have adequate evidence to support your major and minor propositions.

NETWORKING
Applying Digital and Multimedia Literacies

Comparing New and Old Media: Write a comparative essay in which you analyze the similarities and differences between an "old" and a "new" component of the media—actual books and e-books or audio books, or telephones and cell phones, for example. Use visuals to enhance and support your comparisons.

Escape from Wonderland: Disney and the Female Imagination

Deborah Ross

Deborah Ross *is professor of English at Hawai'i Pacific University, where she teaches writing, literature, and humanities. She specializes in popular culture, especially from the perspective of gender. In the following research paper, published in a 2004 issue of* Marvels & Tales: Journal of Fairy-Tale Studies, *Ross analyzes a series of Disney films, all based on children's books and fairy tales; she evaluates the Disney ideology as it affects the imaginative and actual lives of girls.*

In 1989, Disney's little mermaid first asked the musical question, "When's it my 1 turn?" She asked it again in 1996, when her movie was re-released in theaters, and she continues to ask it, frequently, in many of our living rooms. Never has a protagonist had so many turns to demand a turn: Yet, seemingly, she remains unsatisfied. If even the heroine in a Disney "girls' movie" does not enjoy being a girl, how must the girls watching her feel about it?

Behind this gender question lurks a larger political one. If Ariel's feminist 2 rhetoric is undercut by more conservative elements in her movie, so is the environmentalism of *The Lion King,* the multiculturalism of *Pocahontas,* the valuing of difference in *The Hunchback of Notre Dame*—in short, all the quasi-liberal sentiments that focus groups have no doubt caused to grace the surface of the last decade's Disney features. Ideology in Disney is a much vexed question, and I will not attempt here to untangle a knot which began forming for critics when Walt first denied having any politics back in the thirties, and which has only grown in mass and complexity since his death, as his corporation's management style has evolved to cope with a burgeoning staff of artists and technicians, changing public tastes, and changing perceptions of those tastes.

One generalization I do suggest, however, is that Disney the man and the 3 corporation are known for a belief in control. The top-down management style Disney epitomizes—Auschwitz (Giroux 55), or Mouschwitz (Lewis 88), is a frequent analogy—thrives on homogeneity and rigid adherence to rules. These are features often decried in Disney production and product, both by critics of capitalism, such as Benjamin and Adorno,[1] and by far less radical proponents of individualism and open debate, from early Disney biographer Richard Schickel to educator Henry Giroux. Yet imagination, the company's major commodity, does

---

[1]Miriam Hansen discusses Benjamin's and Adorno's objections to Disney in some detail. Jack Zipes's critique of Disney also occurs within a larger argument about the "freezing" of fairy tales into myths to perpetuate bourgeois, patriarchal values (see his Introduction and Chapter 3).

not easily lend itself to a program of control. To encourage imagination in artists, and arouse it in viewers, is to invite unique self-expression rather than homogeneity, and spontaneity rather than predictability. Link imagination to the animated cartoon, an art form with roots in dada, surrealism, and radical politics, and matters could well get out of hand.[2]

4   I believe that this conflict between control and imaginative freedom is visible in the animated features that have come out of the Disney studios, from *Snow White and the Seven Dwarfs* to *Lilo and Stitch*. Of course, ambiguity is rarely viewed now as either a moral or an aesthetic flaw, and the presence of elements that contradict each other may well be preferable to consistent, monologic disapproval of imagination. Neither, however, do conflict and contradiction in themselves necessarily create a space for viewers to question values and exercise judgment. Much depends on how the elements relate to each other, or how an audience is likely to relate them. An audience even partially looking for guides to behavior along with entertainment will have to resolve apparent ambiguities into one suggested course of action. Giroux's attack on Disney rests on the contention that for children, these movies, however apparently bland, do have a didactic effect (18). For them, ambiguity at its best ultimately resolves into a connected but complex world view that embraces difference and spontaneity; at its worst, it can produce confusion and anxiety.

5   I wish to explore the overall impressions these films may give children about the value of their own imaginations, and thus about their own value as unique individuals able to envision, and eventually to enact, change. In particular, to get back to Ariel, I am concerned about what girls may learn about this potentially explosive aspect of their characters that could so easily burst the bounds of traditional femininity. To help answer this question, I have chosen to examine the way various elements of image, story, and dialogue interact to influence the valuation of imagination in three of Disney's girls' movies: *Alice in Wonderland* (1951), *The Little Mermaid* (1989), and *Beauty and the Beast* (1991, re-released 2001).

6   I have chosen these three because, although one might be called "prefeminist" and the other two "post-," all specifically concern young women who fantasize about a life more vivid and exciting than their reality. I will suggest that some of these films' discomfort with female imagination has roots far back in didactic narrative for girls by looking at Charlotte Lennox's 1759 novel, *The Female Quixote,* which concerns the fortunes of a young woman who might be considered the great-grandmother, or prototype, of the Disney heroine. Then, comparing the three Disney movies with their written fairy-tale sources, I will show how much more confusing a many-tongued message can become when it is told in pictures as well as words.

---

[2]Janet Wasko notes that Disney deliberately avoided the more "anarchistic and inventive" styles of animation employed at other studios (115). My own belief, on which my approach to Disney is based, is that where there is animation, anarchy can never be wholly suppressed. For discussion of the roots of animation in surrealism and dada, see Inez Hedges.

Girls have been learning from stories where to draw the line between fantasy and   7
reality probably since the first story was told, but one sees this didactic purpose especially clearly beginning in the seventeenth century, when romances and literary
fairy tales were first written specifically for, about, and even by women. Samuel
Johnson was greatly concerned about the effects of fiction on "the young, the ignorant, and the idle," and Paul Hunter has shown that there was indeed a class of new
readers early in the eighteenth century who were socially displaced and looking to
novels for moral and social guidance as well as entertainment (Hunter 271–72).
From that time till the present, conservative authors have used romances and
novels to teach girls that their dreams are dangerous and of little relevance to their
daily lives. Progressive or feminist authors, on the other hand, have encouraged
young women readers' belief in fantasy to help them visualize what they want,
perhaps as a first step toward going after it. For example, it can be argued (as I have
done elsewhere) that European women's experience with romantic fiction gradually
gained them the right, first, to refuse to cooperate in arranged marriages, and eventually, to choose husbands for themselves.[3]

Charlotte Lennox's *The Female Quixote* illustrates both these conservative   8
and progressive plot patterns, for it both draws upon and criticizes earlier romances, which themselves often both celebrated and punished female imagination and expressiveness.[4] Therefore, like Disney's movies today, which also use
material from the romance and fairy-tale tradition, Lennox's novel can be more
muddling than enlightening to young people seeking instruction on the conduct
of real life. As the title suggests, the premise is that a young girl is at least as likely
to have her head turned by reading romances as Cervantes's knight-errant had
been over a century before. Appropriately, the romances devoured by this quixote,
Arabella, are the largely female-centered French romances of d'Urfé and Scudéry,
which focus more on love than on questing, and in which males are present
mainly either to carry off or rescue heroines. A reader who takes too literally
stories in which women wield such power, albeit of a limited kind, will not adjust
well to woman's lot: being ignored, submitting always to others' convenience, like
Jane Austen in her letters, perpetually waiting to be "fetched" by a male relative
(Austen 9–10). Thus Arabella's reading sets her up to make many ridiculous
mistakes, and ultimately to be humbled, or humiliated, when she learns her own
real unimportance.

The novel shows its author's ambivalence about Arabella's fantasy in several   9
ways. Overtly, she presents it as an adolescent error the heroine must grow out of
in order to find happiness. Yet her very frank satire of the world to which Arabella's
cure forces her to conform leaves readers wondering, along with the heroine,

---

[3]I develop this argument in *The Excellence of Falsehood.* Marina Warner (169, 277–78) and Jack
Zipes (21–23, 28) discuss the seventeenth-century *précieuses'* preoccupation with the issue of
forced marriage.

[4]Warner discusses ambivalence about the old woman or "Mother Goose" figure who narrates fairy
tales throughout the first half of *From the Beast to the Blonde,* and more specifically the power of the
female voice in her discussion of "The Little Mermaid" (394).

whether the world of romance might not be preferable. Romances also receive implicit support from the central "real" narrative's resemblance to romance: beautiful heroine, beloved by the perfect man, whom after trials and separations she marries, presumably to live happily ever after. If the novel presents a romantic story under the guise of realism, then perhaps Arabella is not so quixotic after all.

10   *The Female Quixote* thus presents contradictory impressions about the worthiness of the heroine's desires, the degree to which those desires are ultimately fulfilled or frustrated, and the amount of satisfaction with the outcome the tone directs the reader to feel. Critics of our own time naturally enjoy this ambivalence (the novel has had a comeback of sorts in the last decades and is available in paperback), which particularly lends itself to feminist approaches of the *Madwoman in the Attic,* conformist text–radical subtext variety. Yet the fact that this novel might well make a madwoman out of any young female reader looking for a framework for understanding life should also be part of our critical awareness. Critics may find it a useful model for highlighting similar constellations of ideological paradox in other stories about women's imagination, stories which also leave their audiences struggling to integrate contradictory messages.

11   Disney's female quixotes are at least as sorely beset by ambiguity as Arabella. The heroines' fantasies reveal desires for many things, including novelty, excitement, power, sex, and knowledge. Some of these desires are ridiculed, others respected; some are fulfilled, others surrendered. And the paradoxes in the plots are further complicated by words and images that seem at times to be telling stories of their own.

12 The presence of conservative elements in Disney's *Alice in Wonderland* is not surprising, considering that it was released in 1951, when "Hollywood's dark prince" was still very much alive, fighting unions, castigating the League of Women Voters, and exerting strong control over the studio's output.[5] One would perhaps not expect, though, to find an American movie of the mid-twentieth century so much more stereotypically Victorian than its nineteenth-century British source.

13   Of course, Lewis Carroll's *Alice's Adventures in Wonderland* and *Through the Looking Glass* are not typical of Victorian children's literature. In particular, most girls' stories of this era promoted humility, devotion, punctuality, and tidiness, implying that adventure (as a countess once told Lennox's Arabella) is something a nice girl would be wise to avoid (Lennox 365). The Alice stories, on the other hand, present adventure as positive: Whether wondrous or frightening, it leads the heroine in the direction of personal growth and control over her surroundings. Alice learns how to manage her size, how to talk back to a queen, and, finally, how to wear the crown of adulthood. Carroll celebrates childhood as a brief, fleeting time in which even girls may follow talking rabbits before being overtaken by the "dull reality" (115) of womanhood.

---

[5]I refer here to the title of Marc Eliot's Disney biography. Holly Allen and Michael Denning discuss politics at the Disney studio during the 1940s. For a full discussion of Disney's rather complex politics, see Steven Watts.

The Disney movie begins with the same positive message about girls' fanta- 14 sies. In her opening conversation, Disney's Alice, like Carroll's, expresses the usual quixotic desires: to escape boredom (with lessons), to satisfy curiosity (about the white rabbit), and above all, to exert power. Things would be different "in my world," she notes, though her sister ridicules her ambition. Books, for one thing, would all have pictures—a remark given to Alice by Carroll in a way that almost invites someone to make an Alice movie. The first few minutes of the movie do seem to deliver what Alice wants by introducing such pictorial wonders as singing flowers and surrealistic insects.

Soon, however, the plot darkens, signaled by small but significant cuts and 15 alterations in the original dialogue. Speaking with the Cheshire Cat, who tells her everyone in the neighborhood is mad, Alice speaks Carroll's line, "But I don't want to go among mad people" (63). The cat responds that everyone in Wonderland is mad, but he does not go on to say that Alice too is mad, so that already Disney's Alice is presented as out of her element, the lone sane and rational creature among lunatics.

After the mad tea party, in a section of plot invented for the movie, Disney's 16 Alice has had enough craziness and wants to go home. Overjoyed to find what looks like a path—symbolic of her now acknowledged need for order and direction—she is reduced to helpless tears when it is erased by a fanciful broom creature. She then passively sits down to wait to be rescued, all the while lecturing herself about the importance of reason and patience, and berating herself for the curiosity that once again has led her into trouble. The movie takes a line from early in the story, "She generally gave herself very good advice (though she very seldom followed it)" (23), puts it in the first person, and makes it the center of a self-lacerating musical lament in which Alice abandons for good her fantasy of excitement and power to dwindle into a tiny, forlorn figure in the center of a large, dark frame. In the end of the movie, the defiance and assertiveness of the line, "You're only a pack of cards," are lost, as she utters it while fleeing for her life from the menacing gang of wonders she has created. She is saved, not by facing them down with dawning maturity and confidence, like the "real" Alice, but by waking up.[6]

British reviewers at the time of the movie's release, when the militantly in- 17 nocuous Enid Blyton held sway over English children's imaginations, objected to Disney's "anarchic" alteration of what they saw as a serene and placid children's tale (Allan 137). But Carroll's story is in fact far more tolerant of anarchy, in the sense of irrationality, than the Disney version. The images used to tell the story further support this rationalist message. Despite Disney artist Claude Coats's comment that the staff had "let [them]selves go with some wild designs" (Allan 138), the visuals in fact are rather staid and restrained, mainly literal, representational renderings of the story done in the highly finished, realistic style for which the

---

[6]Donald Britton comments that in the Disney cartoon universe, "children don't become adults; rather, adults kill children" (120).

studio was famous. The fall down the rabbit hole, for example, which marks Alice's entry into the dream state, might have lent itself to surrealistic treatment like that of *Dumbo's* "Pink Elephants on Parade" sequence, but instead it is simply a serial listing in images of the objects Carroll mentions that Alice sees on her way down.

18   Surrealism does appear, briefly, in the visual puns formed by the caterpillar's smoke (as he asks "why [k]not"), and in the wild proliferation of crockery at the tea party, the cups and saucers truly "animated" and seeming to breed like, well, rabbits. Yet the story-line ensures that just as this style reaches its climax, Alice is reaching the limits of her fear of imagination. What might have been delightful Daliesque creatures—telephone-ducks, drum-frogs—function rather to frighten the heroine at a point in the plot when she has rejected all this "nonsense" and is anxious to get home to write a book about it.[7] Writing a story, she has decided, is much safer than living one.

19   Thus all elements combine to entrap the unwary viewer: to entice her to fantasize—even to pay money for the privilege—and then to make her feel, like Alice, guilty and ashamed.

20   Contrasting Alice's defeated whining with Ariel's anthem of independence in *The Little Mermaid,* one is apt to feel girls have come a long way. Here, as Laura Sells and Marina Warner observe, the tale on which the movie is based is ostensibly more conservative than Disney's retelling (Sells 176, 177, 181; Warner 397, 403).[8] Hans Christian Andersen's story is a tragic celebration of feminine self sacrifice. His mermaid fantasizes about becoming human partly because, like Alice, she is curious about a world she has only glimpsed (here, from below rather than from above). But that world interests her mainly because in it dwells a man who resembles a handsome statue she already adores. Her love is partly sexual, of course, since she needs to be human from the waist down to win the hero. But her ultimate desire is spiritual, for only by marrying a human can a mermaid, who normally lives three hundred years and then turns into sea-foam, gain a soul and eternal life.

21   In pursuit of this desire Andersen's mermaid is willing to spend all she has: her voice, her health, and eventually her life. She buys her new legs, from which blood oozes with every agonizing step, by letting the sea witch cut out her tongue. The permanent loss of her voice means playing dumb in more ways than one, as she can only listen demurely as the prince lectures her about her own world, the sea (166).[9] Failing to bring the prince to a proposal, she could save her own life by killing him, but she chooses instead to die. Her many acts of self-torture earn her a slight reprieve as she is turned into a spirit of the air, instead of sea-foam,

[7]Dali had been at the studio in 1946, and Robin Allan believes his influence was still apparent in Alice (137).

[8]See also Wasko 134.

[9]See Warner's discussion on the significance of this silence, and of the blood which in Andersen's tale connects pain with the dawning of female sexuality (387–408).

and given a chance to gain a soul by performing more selfless deeds. Andersen gives her this reward, not for having a dream, but for desiring martyrdom. No real authorial punishment is needed for a female quixote so intent on punishing herself.

Naturally in the Disney version the mutilation and blood would have to go. 22 But much more would have to be altered to make this tragic story look and sound so convincingly like a triumph of adolescent self-will and entitlement, as befit the close of the "me decade." (Warner comments on how often, while she can speak, Ariel utters the verb "want" [403].) For example, instead of making the mermaid love the human world because she loves a human, the movie has Ariel love a human mainly because she is already curious enough about his world to have collected a cave full of human souvenirs (in Andersen's story this collection belongs to a mermaid sister). Like Alice before her initiation, Ariel imagines this other world as in a sense more her own than her actual world. She believes it to be a utopia of free movement: She dreams of legs first for "jumping" and "dancing" and "strolling," and only secondarily for marrying.

There is nothing masochistic about this mermaid's fantasy; nor is she willing 23 to sacrifice herself to fulfill it, though she is willing to gamble. Her voice, for example, is not permanently lost but poured into a shell, ready to be returned to her if she succeeds, and she has every intention of succeeding. Eighties heroine that she is, she means to have it all: voice, soul, legs, and husband.

For the most part, the movie seems to present this female quixote's fantasy 24 positively and reward her with her desire, as the older generation, in the person of her father, learns to abandon prejudice and let teenagers live their own lives. But there are undercurrents here, so to speak, that work against the theme of imaginative freedom. The odd thing about Ariel's quixotism—what makes the audience recognize it *as* quixotism—is that the exotic world of her fantasy is, to us, boring and commonplace. Even a two-year-old viewer knows, as the heroine does not, that forks are not used to comb hair, and that human fathers do indeed "reprimand their daughters," just like old King Triton. Thus we laugh at Ariel's naïve reveries, as Andersen's listeners must have laughed at his mermaid's amazed reaction to birds (150). In the end, it seems ludicrous that Ariel should put so much rebellious energy into becoming the girl next door.

The visual style of the movie makes Andersen's painful story seem oddly 25 encouraging by comparison. Andersen shifts points of view back and forth between the mermaids, who see our world as exotic, and his own audience, who glamorize the unknown world below. He provides lavish descriptions of the shore as well as the sea in order to reawaken his listeners' sense of wonder at their own city lights, sunsets, forests, and hills (151–52). An outsider's desire to live here thus becomes quite understandable. The movie contains no such balance, for beauty and splendor are mainly found "Under the Sea," the title of the dizzying production number in which Sebastian the crab tries to convince Ariel that there's no place like home. Here creatures and objects are surrealistically combined and transformed into an underwater orchestra. Here in abundance are the magical bubbles that have signaled fun with physics in Disney movies from *Snow White* to

Dumbo to *Cinderella.* The world of humans, in contrast, though picturesque, is static and finite. When Ariel takes a bath at Eric's palace,while mundane, gossiping laundresses wash her clothes, one is forced to notice that bubbles here just don't *do* anything. Similarly, Grimsby's pipe, which Ariel mistakes for a musical instrument, produces more soot than smoke—nothing approaching the punning puffs from the caterpillar's hookah in *Alice,* or even the smoky ink that billows about in the sea witch's cave. Clearly, Sebastian is right: It is "better down where it's wetter."

26   The images the movie uses to tell the story thus give its trendy feminism a reverse spin. Whatever Ariel might *say,* or sing, what we see her *do* is flee a world of infinite possibility to settle in the land of the banal. Her fantasy is a sort of anti-fantasy. Yes, she gets her legs, she makes her stand, she marches—but only down the aisle, to marry some guy named Eric.

27 Many fairy tales, and many more movies, end with a wedding, and for this reason they often draw censure from critics, such as Janet Wasko (116) and Elizabeth Bell (114, 155), who would like to see our daughters presented with other options. Without question there ought to be more than one girls' story out there, relentlessly repeated with minor variations. I would also argue, however, that just as in life there are marriages and marriages, so in fiction living happily ever after is not always a euphemism for dying. When the marriage seems to grant the heroine true personal fulfillment and possibilities for further growth, the ending may actually seem like the beginning of a new life. Such is the case with *Beauty and the Beast,* a tale endowed by ancient archetypes with a feminine power that resists the attempts of individual authors, such as Madame Leprince de Beaumont in 1757, to tie its heroine down to mediocrity. With *The Little Mermaid* behind us, we might expect Disney's version to dole out a similarly dull and didactic message, clothed in mock-progressive nineties clichés of gender equality. But in Disney's *Beauty and the Beast,* thanks in part to the screenplay by Linda Woolverton (the first woman writer of a Disney animated feature), imagination flows freely in the words and the images, allowing the tale to work its magic.[10]

28   One problem with the plot that ends in marriage, of course, is its reduction of the heroine to an object of desire, and therefore a heroine actually named Beauty would not, on the face of it, seem like a good role model. In this tale, however, with its roots penetrating beyond the Cupid and Psyche tale from Apuleius's *The Golden Ass* to very old stories about beast bridegrooms (Warner 275; Zipes 24–25), the heroine is more subject than object because her quest for a desirable mate drives the plot. (Apuleius intensifies the female point of view by having the tale narrated by an old woman [Warner 275].) Of course, the whole question of the story's sexual politics hinges on whether the heroine's desire can be consciously controlled, by herself or by others; whether, as is often said in Christian wedding ceremonies, love is an act of will rather than a feeling; whether, therefore, she can make herself love the one she "ought." Conservative versions of

[10]See Bell 114; Murphy 133–34; Warner 313.

Beauty and the Beast do tend to assume such schooling of the will is possible, as Jack Zipes emphasizes (29–40). Nevertheless, an important feature even in such versions is that the beast, though he may be dutifully or even cheerfully endured, cannot become a handsome prince until the heroine actively wants him, truly chooses him for reasons of her own. The young female audience is thus reassured that sex in conjunction with love is pleasant rather than frightening (Bettelheim 306; Warner 312–13); in other words, the beast of one's choice is not a beast at all.

At about the same time Charlotte Lennox was composing *The Female Quixote,* 29 Madame Leprince de Beaumont, with similar concerns about young women's imaginations, was dressing this ancient tale in anti-romance, turning to her own purpose a Scudérian vocabulary of love that, to her readers, would be all too familiar. Beauty feels "esteem" for the Beast because of his "great service" to her, and eventually she comes to feel "tenderness" for him as she wants to care for him and ease his distress (Beaumont 37). Out of this tenderness comes a desire to marry him—including, one supposes, some sexual feeling. The romance code word for active sexual desire—"inclination"—never appears.[11] By telling her young readers that esteem and tenderness are the best basis for marriage, Beaumont warns them not to wait for the handsome, witty lover of their fantasies; in the closing words of the rewarding fairy: "You have preferred virtue before either wit or beauty, and you deserve to find one in whom all these are united" (47). In this way, the author joins the tradition of conservative writers who urge girls to face reality and, to the very limited extent they will be permitted to choose, to choose wisely.[12] Still, while schooling the reader in what she ought to desire, Beaumont cannot avoid conveying the importance of the heroine's will, for until Beauty desires the Beast, a beast he will remain.

The Disney movie reaches past Beaumont to draw upon older strains of the 30 story. For example, here, as in some older versions, including that of Beaumont's immediate predecessor, Madame de Villeneuve (Warner 290–91), it is the Beast rather than Beauty who is supposed to learn self-control. The heroine is therefore permitted—even encouraged—to fantasize to her heart's content. Where Beaumont only noted that Beauty liked to read, Disney enlarges on Belle's taste in books, which turns out to be just like Arabella's: fairy tales and romances about swordfights, magic, a prince in disguise, and above all, a "she" at the center of the action. Nor is she content just to read about "adventure in the great wide somewhere." Given the chance to tour the Beast's library—ordinarily for Belle the greatest of temptations—she chooses instead to explore the forbidden west wing of his castle, as if somehow aware that she will find there the escape from "provincial life" she has been longing and singing for. For all her quixotism, however, Belle, unlike Arabella, is seen as "rather odd" only by her neighbors, not by her audience.

---

[11]See the Map of Tender in Scudéry's *Clelia* (1:42).
[12]See Warner 292–94.

31   Certainly, as several commentators observe, the movie has its share of politically correct modern touches to underscore the heroine's self-determination
(Warner 316–17; Zipes 46). Interestingly, however, each apparent innovation in
fact draws on the French romance tradition that Belle and Arabella revere. Most
notably, the movie makes contemporary-sounding statements about gender stereotypes by introducing a new character as foil to the Beast, the hypermasculine Gaston,
who boasts in a Sigmund Romberg-ish aria, "I'm especially good at expectorating," "I
use antlers in all of my decorating," and "every last inch of me's covered with hair." He
is the real beast, of course, an animal who sneers at the Beast for being so openly in
touch with his feminine side, "the Male Chauvinist Pig [. . .] that would turn the
women of any primetime talkshow audience into beasts themselves" (Jeffords 170).
But Gaston is not really new. He dates back, beyond the Cocteau movie often cited as
his source, to the French romance villain who loves the heroine selfishly, determined
to possess her by force: by winning her in a duel, carrying her off, or scheming to get
her parents to give her to him. Gaston arranges to have Belle's eccentric father locked
in a madhouse unless she agrees to marry him. Then he nearly kills the Beast under
the illusion that the winner gets Belle as prize. The Beast, in contrast, is the romance
hero who fights the villain to win the heroine's freedom, not her hand, which he will
accept only as her gift. In fact, he would rather die than oppress her. By choosing the
Beast over Gaston, Belle helps this ancient story confirm the value of a woman's equal
right to a will of her own.

32   Gaston also helps this movie make another observation mistakenly thought of
as modern: that men and women aren't nearly as different as some men would like
them to be. This idea is found in women's romantic writing from the seventeenth
century on,[13] and it reverberates in Belle's opening song as she wishes for someone
who understands her and shares her interests. Naturally she chooses to marry the
gentleman who gives her the key to his extensive library, not the "positively
primeval" clod who throws her book in the mud with a warning about what happens
to society when women are taught to read. And in the end, when the spell is broken
and the Beast resumes his original shape, he markedly resembles Belle, unruly
bangs and all. By marrying a man who can help her get what she wants, and who
wants the same things, symbolically she is marrying an aspect of herself.[14]

33   The Beast's oddly familiar new face is not the only image in the movie that
makes one feel the heroine's fantasy is a worthy one. Much creativity was
lavished on the look of the castle that provides the atmosphere of old romance.
Although for most of the movie it resembles a Gothic ruin, and Belle comes here
at first as a prisoner, it is really a house of magic in which every object is alive, or
"animated"— most famously the dinnerware that dances and sings "Be Our
Guest." And the enchantment does not quite end with the breaking of the spell,

---

[13]See for example the pastoral lyrics of Aphra Behn.
[14]See Clarissa Pinkola Estes for an interpretation of the Beast as an aspect of the heroine's own
personality (272–73). Warner also discusses how the beast in modern versions of the tale, including
Disney's, functions to help the heroine get in touch with her own inner beast, or sexuality (307–13).

but is rather replaced with a different kind of magic as the castle comes into its original baroque splendor with a seeming infinity of detail, something new around every corner, and always a new corner, for the eye to explore. As Belle waltzes with her Prince around that gorgeous marble hall, the title tune welling up around them, one may see as well as feel that she's getting not just a husband, but more books than she can read in a lifetime, and a home as big and beautiful as her imagination.

Neither age, divorce, nor parenthood has yet made me cynical enough to see the 34 ending of this movie without a sob of satisfaction. But then Disney did begin training me to react in just that way from a very early age (the first movie I ever saw, at the age of five, was *Sleeping Beauty*). Critics have been warning the public for decades about the Disney program to bring about the complete "invasion and control of children's imaginations" (Schickel 18), as well as the silencing of fairy tales' originally female voice (Warner 416–17); no doubt I am a cipher in the company's success. How much more complete the Disney conquest will become for our children and grandchildren, with the constant replay made possible by video and DVD, is definitely cause for concern.

The market forces that drive Disney today are dangerous, to be sure, as is the 35 ideology of the marketplace the movies promote, as Giroux and others warn. Fortunately, however, because the overriding goal is self-promotion—because Disney will absorb and use whatever works, or whatever sells the product—the movies lack the philosophical consistency of propaganda.[15] Thus films like *Beauty and the Beast,* which pays more than lip-service to the liberating potential of fantasy, can sometimes appear.

Nevertheless, the fact that many Disney movies implant seeds of guilt and fear 36 to spring up along with children's developing imaginations is a serious problem. The mixed messages noticeable in *Alice* are present in earlier movies such as *Dumbo* and "The Sorcerer's Apprentice" in *Fantasia.* They continue in more recent examples such as *Hercules* and *The Hunchback of Notre Dame,* in which only evil and terrifying characters wield the transformative power that is, in essence, the animator's art; thus these movies almost identify themselves as products of black magic.[16] Some recent films seem almost to reject the notion of animation altogether, striking the eye most forcibly with stills such as the battlefield in *Mulan,* or the cathedral of Notre Dame—breathtaking, to be sure, but unlike the Beast's castle, completely static. Clearly the reluctance to embrace imagination with both arms is still present among the many and shifting ideas that make up the Disney ethos.

The inconsistencies found in these movies do not lighten either the parent's 37 burden of guiding the young in their adventures with the media, or the critic's task

---

[15]Giroux notes inconsistent values among elements in the films (5, 91). Wasko emphasizes consistent elements that make "classic Disney" a recognizable "brand" (3, 152), but does not explore tensions among the elements she lists as consistent, such as "work ethic" vs. "escape fantasy" (114).

[16]A notable exception is *The Emperor's New Groove,* in which magic transformative potions intended as evil by the villain turn positive and bring about both the narrative and visual climax of the movie.

of understanding the various manifestations of culture. On the contrary, they oblige us to do more than count the number of profane words or violent acts or exposed body parts; and also to do more than catalogue plots, count the numbers of males and females, and quantify relative levels of aggression. Instead, we must watch carefully the interplay of elements within the films and notice how many stories are going on at one time. Watching the faces of our children as they watch, we will often find that imagination, in these movies, is like Alice's garden—just beyond a little locked door, the key to which is tantalizingly, frustratingly out of reach.

WORKS CITED*

Alice in Wonderland. Dir. Clyde Geronimi, Hamilton Luske, and Wilfred Jackson. Walt Disney Company, 1951.

Allan, Robin. "Alice in Disneyland." *Sight and Sound* 54 (Spring 1985): 136–38.

Allen, Holly, and Michael Denning. "The Cartoonists' Front." *South Atlantic Quarterly* 92.1 (1993): 89–117.

Andersen, Hans Christian. "The Little Mermaid." *Hans Christian Andersen: His Classic Fairy Tales.* Trans. Erik Haugaard. Garden City, NY: Doubleday, 1978. 149–70.

Apuleius. *Transformations of Lucius Otherwise Known as the Golden Ass.* Trans. Robert Graves. New York: Noonday, 1998.

Austen, Jane. *Selected Letters.* Oxford: Oxford UP, 1985.

Beaumont, Madame Leprince de. *Beauty and the Beast.* Trans. P. H. Muir. New York: Knopf, 1968.

Beauty and the Beast. Dir. Gary Trousdale and Kirk Wise. Walt Disney Company, 1991.

Behn, Aphra. *The Works of Aphra Behn: Poetry.* Ed. Janet Todd. Columbus: Ohio UP, 1992.

Bell, Elizabeth. "Somatexts at the Disney Shop." Bell, Haas, and Sells 107–24.

Bell, Elizabeth, Lynda Haas, and Laura Sells, eds. *From Mouse to Mermaid: The Politics of Film, Gender, and Culture.* Bloomington: Indiana UP, 1995.

Bettelheim, Bruno. *The Uses of Enchantment.* New York: Vintage, 1977.

Britton, Donald. "The Dark Side of Disneyland." *Mythomania: Fantasies, Fables, and Sheer Lies in Contemporary American Popular Art.* By Bernard Welt. Los Angeles: Art Issues, 1996. 113–26.

Carroll, Lewis. *Alice's Adventures in Wonderland and Through the Looking-Glass.* New York: New American Library, 1960.

Cinderella. Dir. Hamilton Luske and Wilfred Jackson. Walt Disney Company, 1950.

Dumbo. Dir. Ben Sharpsteen. Walt Disney Company, 1941.

Eliot, Marc. *Walt Disney: Hollywood's Dark Prince.* New York: Birch Lane, 1993.

The Emperor's New Groove. Dir. Mark Dindal. Walt Disney Company, 2000.

Estes, Clarissa Pinkola. *Women Who Run with the Wolves.* New York: Ballantine, 1992.

*As noted in the Networking question that follows, this Works Cited section does not follow the latest MLA style. The spacing has also been condensed.

Fantasia. Dir. Ford Beebe and Bill Roberts. Walt Disney Company, 1942.

Gilbert, Sandra, and Susan Gubar. *The Madwoman in the Attic.* New Haven: Yale UP, 1979.

Giroux, Henry. *The Mouse That Roared: Disney and the End of Innocence.* Lanham, MD: Rowman, 1999.

Hansen, Miriam. "Of Mice and Ducks: Benjamin and Adorno on Disney." *South Atlantic Quarterly* 92.1 (1993): 27–61.

Hedges, Inez. *Languages of Revolt: Dada and Surrealist Literature and Film.* Durham: Duke UP, 1983.

Hercules. Dir. Ron Clements and John Musker. Walt Disney Company, 1997.

The Hunchback of Notre Dame. Dir. Gary Trousdale and Kirk Wise. Walt Disney Company, 1996.

Hunter, J. Paul. "'The Young, the Ignorant, and the Idle': Some Notes on Readers and the Beginnings of the English Novel." *Anticipations of the Enlightenment in England, France, and Germany.* Ed. Alan Charles Kors and Paul J. Korshin. Philadelphia: U of Pennsylvania P, 1987. 259–82.

Jeffords, Susan. "The Curse of Masculinity." Bell, Haas, and Sells 161–72.

Johnson, Samuel. *The Rambler.* Ed. W. J. Bate and Albrecht B. Strauss. New Haven: Yale UP, 1969.

Lennox, Charlotte. *The Female Quixote,* 1759. Boston: Pandora, 1986.

Lewis, Jon. "Disney after Disney." *Disney Discourse: Producing the Magic Kingdom.* Ed. Eric Smoodin. New York: Routledge, 1994.

Lilo and Stitch. Dir. Dean DeBlois and Chris Sanders (III). Walt Disney Company, 2002.

The Lion King. Dir. Rob Minkoff and Roger Allers. Walt Disney Company, 1994.

The Little Mermaid. Dir. John Musker and Ron Clements. Walt Disney Company, 1989.

Mulan. Dir. Tony Bancroft and Barry Cook. Walt Disney Company, 1998.

Murphy, Patrick D. "'The Whole Wide World Was Scrubbed Clean': The Androcentric Animation of Denatured Disney." Bell, Haas, and Sells 125–36.

Pocahontas. Dir. Mike Gabriel and Eric Goldberg. Walt Disney Company, 1995.

Ross, Deborah. *The Excellence of Falsehood.* Lexington: UP of Kentucky, 1991.

Schickel, Richard. *The Disney Version.* New York: Simon, 1968.

Scudéry, Madeleine de. *Clelia.* Trans. John Davies. London: Herringman, 1678.

Sells, Laura. "'Where Do the Mermaids Stand?' Voice and Body in *The Little Mermaid.*" Bell, Haas, and Sells 175–92.

The Sleeping Beauty. Dir. Clyde Geronimi. Walt Disney Company, 1959.

Snow White and the Seven Dwarfs. Dir. David Hand. Walt Disney Company, 1938.

Warner, Marina. *From the Beast to the Blonde: On Fairy Tales and Their Tellers.* New York: Noonday, 1994.

Wasko, Janet. *Understanding Disney.* Cambridge, UK: Polity, 2001.

Watts, Steven. "Walt Disney: Art and Politics in the American Century." *Journal of American History* 82.1 (June 1995): 84–110.

Zipes, Jack. *Fairy Tale as Myth/Myth as Fairy Tale.* Lexington: UP of Kentucky, 1994.

COMPREHENSION

1. How does Ross define the ideology inherent in Disney's films for girls?
2. Summarize the content of the three films that Ross discusses. What similarities and differences does Ross see among them?
3. According to the writer, what is a "female quixote"? Where does she treat this concept directly and indirectly?

RHETORIC

1. This essay appeared in a specialized scholarly journal. What "scholarly" elements appear in the paper? How does Ross adjust her style to this specialized audience? What strategies does she use to make the essay accessible to a wider audience?
2. Where does Ross state her claim most clearly? Analyze the varieties of evidence that she uses to support her claim and the minor propositions.
3. How does the writer organize her essay? What are the main divisions, and how do they cohere?
4. Why does Ross cite other scholars and writers? How does this strategy affect the power of her argument?
5. Ross elaborates a definition of the Disney "program" or ideology. What rhetorical strategies does she use to create this extended definition?
6. How effective do you find the concluding paragraph? Justify your response.

WRITING

1. Select one Disney movie and write an analysis of its "program"—its ethical message or ideology.
2. In an expository essay, explain why children's stories or fairy tales have such a hold on young people's imaginations.
3. **Writing an Argument:** Write a persuasive essay on the benefits of children's literature and film—even the films that Walt Disney produced. Present at least three extended examples to support your claim.

NETWORKING
Applying Digital and Multimedia Literacies

Updating Citations to Reflect Current MLA Style: Since this essay was published, the MLA has made some changes to their guidelines for documenting sources; one change includes noting the medium of each source. Refer to Chapter 15 to help update Ross's Works Cited page; beyond this book's coverage, consult the MLA's Web site, or the seventh edition of the *MLA Handbook,* published in 2009.

Synthesis: Connections for Critical Thinking

1. Examine the role of the media in society and the responsibilities or duties to humanity of individuals associated with the media. Use at least three essays from this chapter to illustrate or support your thesis.
2. Define *popular culture,* using the essays of Barry, Sachs, Ross, and Steinem as reference points, along with any additional essays that you consider relevant.
3. Use the essays of Warshow, Goodlad, Ross, and Gitlin to explore the connections of media representations to American cultural experience. What strategies do these writers use? Are their goals similar?
4. Use the essays of Sachs and Barry to explore the importance of both the causes and effects of the media promoting particular lifestyles to the public.
5. Goodlad explores the cultural significance of *Mad Men,* and Barry presents beer commercials as communicating the traditional "patriotic symbols" of America. Do these authors have similar or differing points of view regarding the issues they address? Refer specifically to selections in each essay to support your view.
6. After reading the essays of Warshow, Sachs, and King, research the issue of the difference between popular entertainment and art. On the basis of your research, discuss whether there are legitimate criteria that distinguish the two forms. Apply these criteria to gangster films, rap music, and horror films.

NETWORKING
Applying Digital and Multimedia Literacies

Select several images of real "gangsters" or other "bad" men from magazines, or print out online images of them. Compare and contrast them with advertisements depicting gangsters from contemporary crime movies such as *The Departed* or *Pulp Fiction*. What are the similarities and differences in the subjects' dress, demeanor, facial expression, and so on? What can you conclude from your comparisons?

chapter *10*

Literature and the Arts
Why Do They Matter?

Imagine a world without fiction, poetry, or drama, without music, art, or other fine arts. We are so accustomed to taking the arts in their totality for granted that it is hard for us to conceive of contemporary culture without them. Our fondness for stories or paintings or any other creative form might help us understand our culture or might even move us to action. Yet the value of various artistic forms doesn't derive exclusively from their ability to tell us something about life. The arts can also take us into an imaginative realm offering perhaps more intense experiences than anything we encounter in the "real" world.

Think of literature and the arts as an exercise in imaginative freedom. You are free to select the books you read, the music that appeals to you, the exhibitions and concerts you attend, and the entertainment software with which you interact. Some of your decisions might be serious and consequential to your education. Other decisions, perhaps to watch a few soap operas on a rainy afternoon or to buy the latest potboiler, are less important. The way you view the arts—whether as a way to learn something about the temper of civilization or as a temporary escape from conventional reality—is entirely a matter of taste. Regardless of your purpose or intent, you approach literature and the arts initially for the sheer exhilaration and pleasure they provide. Art, as Plato observed, is a dream for awakened minds.

The arts awaken you to the power and intensity of the creative spirit. At the same time, you make judgments and evaluations of the nature of your creative encounter. When you assert that you like this painting or dislike that poem, you are assessing the work and the value of the artistic experience. Clearly, you develop taste and become more equipped to discern the more subtle elements of art the more you are exposed to it. Perhaps you prefer to keep your experience of literature and the other arts a pleasurable pastime or an escape from reality. Or you may wish to participate in them as a creative writer, musician, painter, or photographer. Ultimately, you may come to view literature and the arts as a transformational experience, a voyage of discovery in which you encounter diverse peoples and cultures, learn to see the world in creative terms, and begin to perceive your own creative potential in a new light.

PREVIEWING THE CHAPTER

As you read the essays in this chapter and respond to them in discussion and writing, consider the following questions:

- According to the author, what is the value of the art or literary form under discussion?
- What function does literature or art serve?
- Is the writer's perspective subjective or objective, and why?
- How does the author define his or her subject—whether it is poetry, fiction, art, or photography?
- Is the writer's experience of literature or art similar to or different from your own?
- In what ways do gender and race influence the writer's perspective on the subject?
- What is the main idea that the author wants to present about literature or the arts? Do you agree or disagree with this key concept?
- What have you learned about the importance of literature and the arts from reading these essays?

Classic and Contemporary Images
HOW DO WE EVALUATE A WORK OF ART?

Using a Critical Perspective Although "greatness" in art and literature might be in the mind of the beholder, it could be argued that you need certain standards of excellence or judgment to determine the quality of any work. The artist's or writer's control of the medium, the projection of a unique vision, the evidence of a superlative style—all enter into the evaluation process. As you consider these sculptures by Auguste Rodin and Jeff Koons, try to evaluate their relative worth. Which work reflects greater artistic control? What makes the sculpture appealing, and why? Which work strikes you as "new" or original, or modern? Explain your response and criteria for evaluation.

Auguste Rodin (1840–1917), a French sculptor famous for his bronze and marble figures, is thought by some critics to be one of the greatest portraitists in the history of sculpture. Yet he was also criticized in his time for the excessive realism and sensuousness of his figures. *Walking Man* hints at some of the objections contemporary critics lodged against Rodin's work.

Jeff Koons (b. 1955) is an American artist who, like Rodin, has had his admirers and detractors. Koons studied at the Art Institute of Chicago and elsewhere before becoming a commodities trader in New York City, which helped fund the materials for his art. *Rabbit* reflects Koons's fondness for popular culture and the way in which he takes consumer goods and repositions them as art objects.

✳

Classic and Contemporary Essays
WHAT IS THE VALUE OF LITERATURE?

Although Eudora Welty was born at the beginning of the 20th century in a small Mississippi town and Sherman Alexie half a century later on a tribal reservation in the state of Washington, half a continent away, these writers share a reverence for the importance of literature in their childhood. Of course, there are understandable differences in the types of literature that formed their young minds. Welty, you will discover, grew up in a loving, middle-class household where virtually every room contained books—a treasury of English and European novels, classic fairy tales, and famous works of literature in the Western tradition. Alexie, on the other hand, from a family that was "middle-class by reservation standards" but in actuality poor, had a father who was addicted to alcohol but also to pulp fiction—westerns, detective stories, spy thrillers, comic books featuring action heroes. And despite their disparate backgrounds, lives, and reading tastes, Welty and Alexie grew up to be writers. They might represent different regional, ethnic, and cultural backgrounds, and they speak as a woman and man of different forms of knowledge and experience, but both attest to the value of literature. As they recount their childhood, Welty and Alexie struggle to establish an identity that will last a lifetime. They succeed in convincing us that whether one child reads Dickens and the other Superman comic books, their ideas and insights into the world derive from the active reading of texts.

❊

One Writer's Beginnings
Eudora Welty

Eudora Welty *(1909–2001), a celebrated American writer, was born and died in Jackson, Mississippi. Raised in a close-knit bookish family, Welty attended the Mississippi State College for Women for two years and then the University of Wisconsin (BA, 1929). In the 1930s she returned to Mississippi and worked for the Works Progress Administration as a reporter and photographer, traveling the state and recording the lives of its citizens during the Depression years. She also began a career as a short-story writer and novelist. Welty's superb short fiction collections include* A Curtain of Green *(1941),* The Wide Net *(1943), and* Collected Stories *(1980), which received an American Book Award. She received the Pulitzer Prize for her novel* The Optimist's Daughter *(1972). The recipient of the President's Medal of Freedom and numerous other major awards, Welty spent virtually her entire life writing about the South but in ways that transcend her region, radiating outward to embrace universal truths. In the selection that* *follows, one of three lectures delivered at Harvard University in 1983 and published in her memoir* One Writer's Beginnings *(1984), Welty speaks of the value of literature and the arts in her life.*

I learned from the age of two or three that any room in our house, at any time of 1 day, was there to read in, or to be read to. My mother read to me. She'd read to me in the big bedroom in the mornings, when we were in her rocker together, which ticked in rhythm as we rocked, as though we had a cricket accompanying the story. She'd read to me in the diningroom on winter afternoons in front of the coal fire, with our cuckoo clock ending the story with "Cuckoo," and at night when I'd got in my own bed. I must have given her no peace. Sometimes she read to me in the kitchen while she sat churning, and the churning sobbed along with *any* story. It was my ambition to have her read to me while *I* churned; once she granted my wish, but she read off my story before I brought her butter. She was an expressive reader. When she was reading "Puss in Boots," for instance, it was impossible not to know that she distrusted *all* cats.

It had been startling and disappointing to me to find out that story books had 2 been written by *people,* that books were not natural wonders, coming up of themselves like grass. Yet regardless of where they came from, I cannot remember a time when I was not in love with them—with the books themselves, cover and binding and the paper they were printed on, with their smell and their weight and with their possession in my arms, captured and carried off to myself. Still illiterate, I was ready for them, committed to all the reading I could give them.

Neither of my parents had come from homes that could afford to buy many 3 books, but though it must have been something of a strain on his salary, as the youngest officer in a young insurance company, my father was all the while carefully selecting and ordering away for what he and Mother thought we children should grow up with. They bought first for the future.

Besides the bookcase in the livingroom, which was always called "the library," 4 there were the encyclopedia tables and dictionary stand under windows in our diningroom. Here to help us grow up arguing around the diningroom table were the Unabridged Webster, the Columbia Encyclopedia, Compton's Pictured Encyclopedia, the Lincoln Library of Information, and later the Book of Knowledge. And the year we moved into our new house, there was room to celebrate it with the new 1925 edition of the Britannica, which my father, his face always deliberately turned toward the future, was of course disposed to think better than any previous edition.

In "the library," inside the mission-style bookcase with its three diamond-latticed 5 glass doors, with my father's Morris chair and the glass-shaded lamp on its table beside it, were books I could soon begin on—and I did, reading them all alike and as they came, straight down their rows, top shelf to bottom. There was the set of Stoddard's Lectures, in all its late nineteenth-century vocabulary and vignettes of peasant life and quaint beliefs and customs, with matching halftone illustrations: Vesuvius erupting, Venice by moonlight, gypsies glimpsed by their campfires. I didn't know then the clue they were to my father's longing to see the rest of the world. I read straight through his other love-from-afar: the Victrola Book of the

Opera, with opera after opera in synopsis, with portraits in costume of Melba, Caruso, Galli-Curci, and Geraldine Farrar, some of whose voices we could listen to on our Red Seal records.

6   My mother read secondarily for information; she sank as a hedonist into novels. She read Dickens in the spirit in which she would have eloped with him. The novels of her girlhood that had stayed on in her imagination, besides those of Dickens and Scott and Robert Louis Stevenson, were *Jane Eyre, Trilby, The Woman in White, Green Mansions, King Solomon's Mines.* Marie Corelli's name would crop up but I understood she had gone out of favor with my mother, who had only kept *Ardath* out of loyalty. In time she absorbed herself in Galsworthy, Edith Wharton, above all in Thomas Mann of the *Joseph* volumes.

7   *St. Elmo* was not in our house; I saw it often in other houses. This wildly popular Southern novel is where all the Edna Earles in our population started coming from. They're all named for the heroine, who succeeded in bringing a dissolute, sinning roué and atheist of a lover (St. Elmo) to his knees. My mother was able to forgo it. But she remembered the classic advice given to rose growers on how to water their bushes long enough: "Take a chair and *St. Elmo.*"

8   To both my parents I owe my early acquaintance with a beloved Mark Twain. There was a full set of Mark Twain and a short set of Ring Lardner in our bookcase, and those were the volumes that in time united us all, parents and children.

9   Reading everything that stood before me was how I came upon a worn old book without a back that had belonged to my father as a child. It was called *Sanford and Morton.* Is there anyone left who recognizes it, I wonder? It is the famous moral tale written by Thomas Day in the 1780s, but of him no mention is made on the title page of *this* book; here it is *Sanford and Merton in Words of One Syllable* by Mary Godolphin. Here are the rich boy and the poor boy and Mr. Barlow, their teacher and interlocutor, in long discourses alternating with dramatic scenes— danger and rescue allotted to the rich and the poor respectively. It may have only words of one syllable, but one of them is "quoth." It ends with not one but two morals, both engraved on rings: "Do what you ought, come what may," and "If we would be great, we must first learn to be good."

10   This book was lacking its front cover, the back held on by strips of pasted paper, now turned golden, in several layers, and the pages stained, flecked, and tattered around the edges; its garish illustrations had come unattached but were preserved, laid in. I had the feeling even in my heedless childhood that this was the only book my father as a little boy had of his own. He had held onto it, and might have gone to sleep on its coverless face: He had lost his mother when he was seven. My father had never made any mention to his own children of the book, but he had brought it along with him from Ohio to our house and shelved it in our bookcase.

11   My mother had brought from West Virginia that set of Dickens; those books looked sad, too—they had been through fire and water before I was born, she told me, and there they were, lined up—as I later realized, waiting for *me.*

12   I was presented, from as early as I can remember, with books of my own, which appeared on my birthday and Christmas morning. Indeed, my parents could not give me books enough. They must have sacrificed to give me on my sixth or

seventh birthday—it was after I became a reader for myself—the ten-volume set of Our Wonder World. These were beautifully made, heavy books I would lie down with on the floor in front of the diningroom hearth, and more often than the rest volume 5, *Every Child's Story Book,* was under my eyes. There were the fairy tales—Grimm, Andersen, the English, the French, "Ali Baba and the Forty Thieves"; and there was Aesop and Reynard the Fox; there were the myths and legends, Robin Hood, King Arthur, and St. George and the Dragon, even the history of Joan of Arc; a whack of *Pilgrim's Progress* and a long piece of *Gulliver.* They all carried their classic illustrations. I located myself in these pages and could go straight to the stories and pictures I loved; very often "The Yellow Dwarf" was first choice, with Walter Crane's Yellow Dwarf in full color making his terrifying appearance flanked by turkeys. Now that volume is as worn and backless and hanging apart as my father's poor *Sanford and Merton.* The precious page with Edward Lear's "Jumblies" on it has been in danger of slipping out for all these years. One measure of my love for Our Wonder World was that for a long time I wondered if I would go through fire and water for it as my mother had done for Charles Dickens; and the only comfort was to think I could ask my mother to do it for me.

I believe I'm the only child I know of who grew up with this treasure in the 13 house. I used to ask others, "Did you have Our Wonder World?" I'd have to tell them The Book of Knowledge could not hold a candle to it.

I live in gratitude to my parents for initiating me—and as early as I begged for 14 it, without keeping me waiting—into knowledge of the word, into reading and spelling, by way of the alphabet. They taught it to me at home in time for me to begin to read before starting to school. I believe the alphabet is no longer considered an essential piece of equipment for traveling through life. In my day it was the keystone to knowledge. You learned the alphabet as you learned to count to ten, as you learned "Now I lay me" and the Lord's Prayer and your father's and mother's name and address and telephone number, all in case you were lost.

My love for the alphabet, which endures, grew out of reciting it but, before that, 15 out of seeing the letters on the page. In my own story books, before I could read them for myself, I fell in love with various winding, enchanting-looking initials drawn by Walter Crane at the heads of fairy tales. In "Once upon a time," an "O" had a rabbit running it as a treadmill, his feet upon flowers. When the day came, years later, for me to see the Book of Kells, all the wizardry of letter, initial, and word swept over me a thousand times over, and the illumination, the gold, seemed a part of the word's beauty and holiness that had been there from the start.

· · ·

Learning stamps you with its moments. Childhood's learning is made up of moments. It isn't steady. It's a pulse. 16

In a children's art class, we sat in a ring on kindergarten chairs and drew 17 three daffodils that had just been picked out of the yard; and while I was drawing, my sharpened pencil and the cup of the yellow daffodil gave off whiffs just alike. That the pencil doing the drawing should give off the same smell as the flower it drew seemed a part of the art lesson—as shouldn't it be? Children, like animals, use all their senses to discover the world. Then artists come along and discover it the same way, all over again. Here and there, it's the same world. Or now and then we'll hear from an artist who's never lost it.

18   In my sensory education I include my physical awareness of the *word*. Of a certain word, that is; the connection it has with what it stands for. At around age six, perhaps, I was standing by myself in our front yard waiting for supper, just at that hour in a late summer day when the sun is already below the horizon and the risen full moon in the visible sky stops being chalky and begins to take on light. There comes the moment, and I saw it then, when the moon goes from flat to round. For the first time it met my eyes as a globe. The word "moon" came into my mouth as though fed to me out of a silver spoon. Held in my mouth the moon became a word. It had the roundness of a Concord grape Grandpa took off his vine and gave me to suck out of its skin and swallow whole, in Ohio.

19   This love did not prevent me from living for years in foolish error about the moon. The new moon just appearing in the west was the rising moon to me. The new should be rising. And in early childhood the sun and moon, those opposite reigning powers, I just as easily assumed rose in east and west respectively in their opposite sides of the sky, and like partners in a reel they advanced, sun from the east, moon from the west, crossed over (when I wasn't looking) and went down on the other side. My father couldn't have known I believed that when, bending behind me and guiding my shoulder, he positioned me at our telescope in the front yard and, with careful adjustment of the focus, brought the moon close to me.

20   The night sky over my childhood Jackson was velvety black. I could see the full constellations in it and call their names; when I could read, I knew their myths. Though I was always waked for eclipses, and indeed carried to the window as an infant in arms and shown Halley's Comet in my sleep, and though I'd been taught at our diningroom table about the solar system and knew the earth revolved around the sun, and our moon around us, I never found out the moon didn't come up in the west until I was a writer and Herschel Brickell, the literary critic, told me after I misplaced it in a story. He said valuable words to me about my new profession: "Always be sure you get your moon in the right part of the sky."

. . .

21   My mother always sang to her children. Her voice came out just a little bit in the minor key. "Wee Willie Winkie's" song was wonderfully sad when she sang the lullabies.

22   "Oh, but now there's a record. She could have her own record to listen to," my father would have said. For there came a Victrola record of "Bobby Shafftoe" and "Rock-a-Bye Baby," all of Mother's lullabies, which could be played to take her place. Soon I was able to play her my own lullabies all day long.

23   Our Victrola stood in the diningroom. I was allowed to climb onto the seat of a diningroom chair to wind it, start the record turning, and set the needle playing. In a second I'd jumped to the floor, to spin or march around the table as the music called for—now there were all the other records I could play too. I skinned back onto the chair just in time to lift the needle at the end, stop the record and turn it over, then change the needle. That brass receptacle with a hole in the lid gave off a metallic smell like human sweat, from all the hot needles that were fed it. Winding

up, dancing, being cocked to start and stop the record, was of course all in one the act of *listening*—to "Overture to *Daughter of the Regiment*," "Selections from *The Fortune Teller*," "Kiss Me Again," "Gypsy Dance from *Carmen*," "Stars and Stripes Forever," "When the Midnight Choo-Choo Leaves for Alabam," or whatever came next. Movement must be at the very heart of listening.

Ever since I was first read to, then started reading to myself, there has never 24 been a line read that I didn't *hear*. As my eyes followed the sentence, a voice was saying it silently to me. It isn't my mother's voice, or the voice of any person I can identify, certainly not my own. It is human, but inward, and it is inwardly that I listen to it. It is to me the voice of the story or the poem itself. The cadence, whatever it is that asks you to believe, the feeling that resides in the printed word, reaches me through the reader-voice. I have supposed, but never found out, that this is the case with all readers—to read as listeners—and with all writers, to write as listeners. It may be part of the desire to write. The sound of what falls on the page begins the process of testing it for truth, for me. Whether I am right to trust so far I don't know. By now I don't know whether I could do either one, reading or writing, without the other.

My own words, when I am at work on a story, I hear too as they go, in the same 25 voice that I hear when I read in books. When I write and the sound of it comes back to my ears, then I act to make my changes. I have always trusted this voice.

COMPREHENSION

1. What is the significance of the essay's title? Does Welty write about one continuous "beginning" or a series of beginnings? Explain.
2. What does Welty mean when she says that her mother was a "hedonist" (paragraph 6)? Does Welty also become a hedonist? Why or why not?
3. Explain the nature of Welty's "sensory" education.

RHETORIC

1. Welty alludes to dozens of works of literature. What does she assume about her audience's knowledge of these works? Can you appreciate the essay even if you are not familiar with most of this literature? Justify your response.
2. What is Welty's thesis, and how does she develop it?
3. What determines the order in which Welty organizes her essay, which she divides into three parts?
4. Welty includes several descriptive passages in this essay. Where are these passages, and what do they contribute to the overall meaning of the selection?
5. How do the last two paragraphs of the essay echo the first two paragraphs?

WRITING

1. Write a description of a scene or series of events from your childhood in which you were reading (or being read to), engaged in an art project, or listening to music. In your essay, explain the impact of this memory or activity on your current life.

2. Write an essay explaining the importance of providing children with sensory stimuli involving reading, artwork, and music.

3. **Writing an Argument:** Argue for or against the proposition that children today read less than those of previous generations—and suffer the consequences.

NETWORKING
Applying Digital and Multimedia Literacies

Can e-Readers Save Reading? It's looking likely that children will soon be reading most texts—from textbooks to novels to comics—electronically. How might an electronic format make reading *more* engaging for today's kids? How might this new form enhance, rather than detract from, reading as a sensory experience?

✳

Superman and Me

Sherman Alexie

Sherman Alexie *(b. 1966) grew up and still lives on the Spokane Indian Reservation in Wellpinit, Washington. A Spokane/Coeur d'Alene tribal member, Alexie contended with a life-threatening illness when he was young, but managed to attend Gonzaga University before transferring to Washington State University (BA, 1991). Alexie writes and creates in many modes, and is also a performer. As many of the titles of his works suggest, the Native American experience informs his short stories, novels, poetry, songs, and films. Alexie's fiction includes* Reservation Blues *(1995),* Ten Little Indians: Stories *(2003), and* Flight, A Novel *(2007); his poetry has been collected in* First Indian on the Moon *(1993),* The Man Who Loves Salmon *(1998), and other volumes. In the following essay, Alexie attests to the importance of literature—all kinds of literature—in his life.*

1   I learned to read with a Superman comic book. Simple enough, I suppose. I cannot recall which particular Superman comic book I read, nor can I remember which villain he fought in that issue. I cannot remember the plot, nor the means by which I obtained the comic book. What I can remember is this: I was 3 years old, a Spokane Indian boy living with his family on the Spokane Indian Reservation in eastern Washington state. We were poor by most standards, but one of my parents usually managed to find some minimum-wage job or another, which made us middle-class by reservation standards. I had a brother and three sisters. We lived on a combination of irregular paychecks, hope, fear, and government surplus food.

2   My father, who is one of the few Indians who went to Catholic school on purpose, was an avid reader of westerns, spy thrillers, murder mysteries, gangster epics, basketball player biographies, and anything else he could find. He bought

his books by the pound at Dutch's Pawn Shop, Goodwill, Salvation Army, and Value Village. When he had extra money, he bought new novels at supermarkets, convenience stores, and hospital gift shops. Our house was filled with books. They were stacked in crazy piles in the bathroom, bedrooms, and living room. In a fit of unemployment-inspired creative energy, my father built a set of bookshelves and soon filled them with a random assortment of books about the Kennedy assassination, Watergate, the Vietnam War, and the entire 23-book series of the Apache westerns. My father loved books, and since I loved my father with an aching devotion, I decided to love books as well.

I can remember picking up my father's books before I could read. The words 3 themselves were mostly foreign, but I still remember the exact moment when I first understood, with a sudden clarity, the purpose of a paragraph. I didn't have the vocabulary to say "paragraph," but I realized that a paragraph was a fence that held words. The words inside a paragraph worked together for a common purpose. They had some specific reason for being inside the same fence. This knowledge delighted me. I began to think of everything in terms of paragraphs. Our reservation was a small paragraph within the United States. My family's house was a paragraph, distinct from the other paragraphs of the LeBrets to the north, the Fords to our south, and the Tribal School to the west. Inside our house, each family member existed as a separate paragraph but still had genetics and common experiences to link us. Now, using this logic, I can see my changed family as an essay of seven paragraphs: mother, father, older brother, the deceased sister, my younger twin sisters, and our adopted little brother.

At the same time I was seeing the world in paragraphs, I also picked up that 4 Superman comic book. Each panel, complete with picture, dialogue, and narrative was a three-dimensional paragraph. In one panel, Superman breaks through a door. His suit is red, blue, and yellow. The brown door shatters into many pieces. I look at the narrative above the picture. I cannot read the words, but I assume it tells me that "Superman is breaking down the door." Aloud, I pretend to read the words and say, "Superman is breaking down the door." Words, dialogue, also float out of Superman's mouth. Because he is breaking down the door, I assume he says, "I am breaking down the door." Once again, I pretend to read the words and say aloud, "I am breaking down the door." In this way, I learned to read.

This might be an interesting story all by itself. A little Indian boy teaches 5 himself to read at an early age and advances quickly. He reads "Grapes of Wrath" in kindergarten when other children are struggling through "Dick and Jane." If he'd been anything but an Indian boy living on the reservation, he might have been called a prodigy. But he is an Indian boy living on the reservation and is simply an oddity. He grows into a man who often speaks of his childhood in the third person, as if it will somehow dull the pain and make him sound more modest about his talents.

A smart Indian is a dangerous person, widely feared and ridiculed by Indians and 6 non-Indians alike. I fought with my classmates on a daily basis. They wanted me to stay quiet when the non-Indian teacher asked for answers, for volunteers, for help. We were Indian children who were expected to be stupid. Most lived up to those expectations inside the classroom but subverted them on the outside. They struggled with basic reading in school but could remember how to sing a few dozen powwow songs. They were monosyllabic in front of their non-Indian teachers but could tell complicated stories and jokes at the dinner table. They submissively ducked their heads when confronted by a non-Indian adult but would slug it out with the Indian bully who was 10 years older. As Indian children, we were expected to fail in the non-Indian world. Those who failed were ceremonially accepted by other Indians and appropriately pitied by non-Indians.

7   I refused to fail. I was smart. I was arrogant. I was lucky. I read books late into the night, until I could barely keep my eyes open. I read books at recess, then during lunch, and in the few minutes left after I had finished my classroom assignments. I read books in the car when my family traveled to powwows or basketball games. In shopping malls, I ran to the bookstores and read bits and pieces of as many books as I could. I read the books my father brought home from the pawnshops and secondhand. I read the books I borrowed from the library. I read the backs of cereal boxes. I read the newspaper. I read the bulletins posted on the walls of the school, the clinic, the tribal offices, the post office. I read junk mail. I read auto-repair manuals. I read magazines. I read anything that had words and paragraphs. I read with equal parts joy and desperation. I loved those books, but I also knew that love had only one purpose. I was trying to save my life.

8   Despite all the books I read, I am still surprised I became a writer. I was going to be a pediatrician. These days, I write novels, short stories, and poems. I visit schools and teach creative writing to Indian kids. In all my years in the reservation school system, I was never taught how to write poetry, short stories, or novels. I was certainly never taught that Indians wrote poetry, short stories, and novels. Writing was something beyond Indians. I cannot recall a single time that a guest teacher visited the reservation. There must have been visiting teachers. Who were they? Where are they now? Do they exist? I visit the schools as often as possible. The Indian kids crowd the classroom. Many are writing their own poems, short stories, and novels. They have read my books. They have read many other books. They look at me with bright eyes and arrogant wonder. They are trying to save their lives. Then there are the sullen and already defeated Indian kids who sit in the back rows and ignore me with theatrical precision. The pages of their notebooks are empty. They carry neither pencil nor pen. They stare out the window. They refuse and resist. "Books," I say to them. "Books," I say. I throw my weight against their locked doors. The door holds. I am smart. I am arrogant. I am lucky. I am trying to save our lives.

COMPREHENSION

1. Do you find it paradoxical that Alexie learned to read with a Superman comic book? Why or why not? What does Alexie learn from reading the Superman comic?
2. What connections do you see between Alexie and his father?
3. What does Alexie mean when he writes, "A smart Indian is a dangerous person . . . " (paragraph 6)?

RHETORIC

1. Does Alexie state or imply his thesis? State his thesis in your own words.
2. What is Alexie's purpose in writing this essay?
3. Why does Alexie divide his essay into two parts? Do you find this organizational scheme effective? Why or why not?
4. Explain the importance of comparison and contrast in this essay.
5. Alexie's concluding paragraph is quite long. Does it serve as an effective ending? Why or why not?

WRITING

1. Write a personal essay about the types of popular literature that you liked to read as a child.
2. **Writing an Argument:** Do you agree or disagree with Alexie's claim that a literate person—especially a member of any group that has experienced discrimination—is necessarily a dangerous individual? Write an argumentative essay in response to this question.

NETWORKING
Applying Digital and Multimedia Literacies

Comparing Reading and Viewing Habits: Write a comparative essay in which you discuss the reading and viewing habits of your parents and your own tastes. Which media do each of you prefer for popular entertainment, and which do you prefer to get the news? Do you tend to *learn* more from watching a program, reading a print text, or reading an online hyperlinked text? Explore why.

Synthesis: Classic and Contemporary Essays for Comparison

1. Summarize and critique these two writers' agendas, explaining where their ideas overlap and where they diverge.
2. According to both writers, reading in childhood is important. How do Welty and Alexie support this claim? What types of evidence do they present?
3. Compare and contrast the style of each essay. Which essay seems more accessible to you, and why?
4. Imagine what Alexie might say about Welty's essay. What would he see in it that might inform his own writing?

NETWORKING
Applying Digital and Multimedia Literacies

Go online and find out more about these two writers. Focus on Welty's life in Jackson, Mississippi, and Alexie's life on the Spokane Indian Reservation. Then write a brief essay summarizing the importance of place in their writing.

Moving Along

John Updike

John Updike (1932–2009), a major American novelist, short-story writer, poet, and critic, was born in Shillington, Pennsylvania. He graduated from Harvard University (AB, 1954) and attended the Ruskin School of Drawing and Fine Art at Oxford University. Associated for decades with the New Yorker, where his short fiction, poetry, reviews, and criticism frequently appeared, Updike carved for himself a rare reputation as a master of several literary genres. He published more than 40 books during his career. Focusing in his fiction on suburban middle-class life, Updike received two Pulitzer prizes and many other major awards, including a National Book Award for his novel The Centaur (1963). His fiction includes the much-admired "Rabbit" quintet, five novels that track one central character, first introduced in Rabbit, Run (1960), through the passages in his life. Updike's poetry collections include The Carpentered Hen and Other Tame Creatures (1958) and Americana: And Other Poems (2001). Updike included the following essay in Just Looking (1981), a collection of his art criticism.

1   In dreams, one is frequently travelling, and the more hallucinatory moments of our waking life, many of them, are spent in cars, trains, and airplanes. For millennia, Man has walked or run to where he wanted to go; the first naked ape who had the mad idea of mounting a horse (or was it a *Camelops?*) launched a series of subtle internal dislocations of which jet lag is a vivid modern form. When men come to fly through space at near the speed of light, they will return to earth a century later but only a few years older. Now, driving (say) from Boston to Pittsburgh in a day, we arrive feeling greatly aged by the engine's innumerable explosive heartbeats, by the monotony of the highway surface and the constant windy press of unnatural speed. Beside the highway, a clamorous parasitic life signals for attention and halt; localities where generations have lived, bred, labored, and died are flung through the windshield and out through the rearview mirror. Men on the move brutalize themselves and render the world they arrow through phantasmal.

2   Our two artists, separated by two centuries, capture well the eeriness of travel. In the Punjab Hills painting, Baz Bahadur, prince of Malwa, has eloped with the lovely Rupmati; in order to keep him faithful to her, the legend goes, she takes him riding by moonlight. The moon appears to exist not only in the sky but behind a grove of trees. Deer almost blend into the mauve-gray hills. A little citadel basks in starlight on a hilltop. In this soft night, nothing is brighter than the scarlet pasterns of the horses. Baz Bahadur's steed bears on his hide a paler version of the starry sky, and in his violet genitals carries a hint of this nocturnal ride's sexual undercurrent. To judge from the delicacy of their gestures and glances, the riders are being borne along as smoothly as on a merry-go-round. Though these lovers and their panoply are formalized to static perfection, if we cover them, a surprising depth appears in the top third of the painting, and carries the eye away.

Artist unknown, *Baz Bahadur and Rupmati Riding by Moonlight,* c. 1780. Pahari miniature in Kangra style, 8¾ × 6¼". The British Museum, Department of Oriental Antiquities, London.

The riders in Roy de Forest's contemporary painting move through a forest as 3 crowded, garish, and menacing as the neon-lit main drag of a city. A throng of sinister bystanders, one built of brick and another with eyes that are paste gems, witness the passage of this *Canoe of Fate,* which with the coarseness of its stitching and the bulk of its passengers would make slow headway even on a less crowded canvas. Beyond the mountains, heavenly medallions and balloons of stippled color pre-empt space. Only the gesture of the black brave, echoing that of George Washington in another fabulous American crossing, gives a sense of direction and promises to open a path. Two exotic birds, a slavering wolf, and what may be a fair captive (gazing backward toward settlements where other red-haired bluefaces mourn her) freight the canoe with a suggestion of allegory, of myths to which we have lost the key. The personnel of the aboriginal New World, at any rate, are here deep-dyed but not extinguished by the glitter and jazz of an urban-feeling wilderness.

In both representations, the movement is from right to left, like that of writing 4 in the Semitic languages, like the motion of a mother when she instinctively shifts

Roy de Forest, *Canoe of Fate*, 1974. Polymer on canvas, 66¾ × 90¼". Philadelphia Museum of Art, The Adele Haas Turner and Beatrice Pastorius Turner Fund.

her baby to her left arm, to hold it closer to her heart. It feels natural, this direction, and slightly uphill. We gaze at these dreamlike tapestries of travel confident that no progress will be made—we will awaken in our beds.

COMPREHENSION

1. According to Updike, why does the idea of travel have such a hold on the collective imagination? What is the relationship of the travel motif to art?
2. Describe the two paintings that Updike analyzes in this essay. What other famous painting does he allude to in paragraph 3?
3. Why does Updike emphasize the "eeriness" of the two paintings? What is he saying about the human psyche?

RHETORIC

1. How does Updike design his introductory paragraph? What is his purpose?
2. What is Updike's thesis? Does he state or imply it? Explain.
3. Identify specific passages that highlight Updike's descriptive style. What types of figurative language does he employ?

4. Explain Updike's comparative method. What do the reproductions of the two paintings contribute to the overall comparative effect? Would this brief essay be as effective without these images? Why or why not?
5. Why is Updike's concluding paragraph relatively brief when compared with the preceding paragraphs? Is this end paragraph effective? Justify your response.

WRITING

1. Consider the two paintings that Updike reproduces, and write your own comparative essay based on them.
2. **Writing an Argument:** Argue for or against the proposition that when viewing a work of art, it is not necessary to relate it—as Updike does—to human behavior.

NETWORKING
Applying Digital and Multimedia Literacies

Analyzing Themes in Fine Art: Select two paintings that reflect what you consider to be a common theme, and write a comparative essay about them. Provide images of these paintings in your essay. Recommended sites for viewing paintings include the Metropolitan Museum of Art, the Art Institute of Chicago, the Louvre, the New Mexico Museum of Art, the Tate, and Online Museum Resources on Asian Art.

Understanding Comics

Scott McCloud

Scott McCloud *(b. 1960) is an award-winning cartoonist and leading theorist on comic art. He was born in Boston, Massachusetts and raised in the nearby town of Lexington. McCloud decided in his junior year in high school that he wanted to be a comic artist; he received a Bachelor of Fine Arts from Syracuse University (1982), majoring in illustration. He created the science fiction superhero series* Zot! *in 1984, a comics odyssey tracing the adventures of two teenagers existing in parallel worlds. McCloud also composes for mainstream comics including DC Comics'* Superman *series. He is equally well known as a theorist of the genre, the "Aristotle of comics." In* Understanding Comics *(1993),* Reinventing Comics *(2000), and* Making Comics *(2006), McCloud offers a far-ranging account of the history, vocabulary, and methods of the medium. On his Web site McCloud is an active promoter of new comics technology, the rights of comic artists to royalties, and the importance of comics in popular culture. In this excerpt from* Understanding Comics, *McCloud establishes the uniqueness of comics as an art form.*

COMPREHENSION

1. What does McCloud mean by "the curse of being judged by the standards of the old"? What new standards does he propose?
2. Underline, circle, or highlight the "categories" that McCloud presents.
3. How does McCloud explain the world of comics as an art form?

RHETORIC

1. Explain the sequence of words and images that McCloud creates in order to establish a definition of comic art.
2. How does the author create an argument about comics? What is his claim?
3. Identify the forms of support presented by McCloud to sustain his argument.
4. How does McCloud use classification as a method to organize his sequence of words and images?
5. How does the author create a narrative voice or persona? Do you find this personal voice to be engaging? Why or why not?

WRITING

1. Write an essay entitled "Comics and Culture."
2. Select a comic or graphic novel and analyze the ways in which it conforms to the prescriptions laid down by McCloud.
3. **Writing an Argument:** Argue for or against the proposition that comics are a legitimate form of art.

NETWORKING
Applying Digital and Multimedia Literacies

Purpose, Audience, and Design in a Professional Web Site: Go to the artist's official Web site *(http://www.ScottMcCloud.com)*. Review the contents, sample the links, find out more about the artist, and in discussion or writing, consider how the design and layout of the site serves its contents' purpose. In your response, be sure to address what this purpose is and who McCloud would probably identify as the site's intended audience.

✵

Finding Neverland

David Gates

David Gates *(b. 1947) is an American journalist and fiction writer. Gates attended Bard College and the University of Connecticut in the mid-1960s, subsequently working as a cab driver and in other capacities while refining his literary craft. His first novel,* Jernigan *(1991), was nominated for a Pulitzer Prize. Both his second novel,* Preston Falls *(1998), and the collection* The Wonders of the Invisible World: Stories *(1999), were finalists for the National Book Critics Circle Award. Gates is a senior editor and writer at* Newsweek, *covering books, music, and the arts. He also teaches in the graduate writing programs at Bennington College and New School University. In this essay from the July 13, 2009, issue of* Newsweek, *Gates surveys the life, death, and career of music legend Michael Jackson.*

True, for a while he was the king of pop—a term apparently originated by his   1
friend Elizabeth Taylor—and he's the last we're ever likely to have. Before Michael Jackson came Frank Sinatra, Elvis Presley, and the Beatles; after him has come absolutely no one, however brilliant or however popular, who couldn't be ignored by vast segments of an ever-more-fragmented audience. Not Kurt Cobain, not Puffy, not Mariah Carey, not Céline Dion, not Beyoncé, not Radiohead—not even Madonna, his closest competitor. When the news of his death broke, the traffic on Twitter caused the site to crash, even though he hadn't had a hit song for years. But starting long before and continuing long after he lorded over the world of entertainment in the 1980s—his 1982 *Thriller* remains the bestselling album of all time—Jackson was the Prince of Artifice. As the prepubescent frontboy of the Jackson 5, he sang in a cherubic mezzo-soprano of sexual longing he could not yet have fully felt. As a young man, however accomplished and even impassioned his singing was, he never had the sexual credibility of a James Brown or a Wilson Pickett, in part because of his still-high-pitched voice, in part because he seemed never to fully inhabit himself—whoever that self was. In middle age, he consciously took on the role of Peter Pan, with his Neverland Ranch and its amusement-park rides, with his lost-boy "friends" and with what he seemed to believe was an ageless, androgynous physical appearance—let's hope he believed it—thanks to straightened hair and plastic surgery. (No one—least of all Jackson himself—would have wanted to see the Dorian Gray portrait in his attic.) He did his best to construct an alternate reality on top of what must have been an initially miserable life: Imagine *Gypsy* with—as Jackson claimed in interviews—a physically abusive

David Gates, "Finding Neverland." From *Newsweek*, July 13, 2009. © 2009 Newsweek, Inc. All rights reserved. Used by permission and protected by the Copyright Laws of the United States. The printing, copying, redistribution, or retransmission of the Material without express written permission is prohibited.

father in place of Mama Rose, set among Jehovah's Witnesses. Which was the more imaginative creation: his music or his persona?

2   In retrospect, so much of what Jackson achieved seems baldly symbolic. This was the black kid from Gary, Ind., who ended up marrying Elvis's daughter, setting up Neverland in place of Graceland, and buying the Beatles' song catalog—bold acts of appropriation and mastery, if not outright aggression. (Of course, Elvis and the Beatles had come out of obscurity, too, but that was a long, long time ago, in a galaxy far away.) He made trademarks of the very emblems of his remoteness: his moonwalk dance and his jeweled glove—*noli me tangere,* and vice versa. He morphed relentlessly from the most adorable of kiddie performers (his 1972 movie-soundtrack hit, "Ben," was a love song to a pet rat) to the most sinister of superstars: not by adopting a campy persona, like those of his older contemporaries Alice Cooper or Ozzy Osbourne, but in real life, dodging accusations of child molestation, one of which led to a trial and acquittal in 2005. (One shrink concluded at the time that he was not a pedophile, but merely a case of arrested development.) The 2002 episode in which he briefly dangled his son Prince Michael II (a.k.a. Blanket) over a balcony in Berlin, above horrified, fascinated

fans, seemed like a ritualized attempt to dispose of his own younger self. And eventually his several facial surgeries, a skin ailment, serious weight loss, and God knows what else made him look like both a vampire and a mummy—Peter Pan's undead evil twins. That is, like the skeletal, pale-faced zombies he danced with in Jon Landis's 14-minute "Thriller" video. When you watch it today, it appears to be a whole stage full of Michael Jacksons, the real one now the least familiar-looking, the most unreal of all.

But whatever strictly personal traumas Jackson may have reenacted and 3 transcended—and then re-reenacted—he performed his dance of death as a central figure in America's long racial horror show. He was, quintessentially, one of those "pure products of America," who, as William Carlos Williams wrote in 1923, "go crazy." To take the uplifting view, enunciated after his death by the likes of the Rev. Al Sharpton, he was a transracial icon, a black person whom white Americans took to their hearts and whose blackness came to seem incidental. In this he resembles such figures as Nat (King) Cole, Sammy Davis Jr., Sidney Poitier, Harry Belafonte, Sam Cooke, Jimi Hendrix, Arthur Ashe, Michael Jordan, Oprah Winfrey, Tiger Woods, and, inevitably, Barack Obama. As a singer-dancer, he clearly belongs not just in the tradition of Jackie Wilson, James Brown, and the Temptations—who seem to have been among his immediate inspirations—but also in the tradition of such dancing entertainers as Fred Astaire and Gene Kelly, who, in turn, drew from such black performers as Bill (Bojangles) Robinson. In the 1978 film version of *The Wiz*, Jackson even seemed to appropriate and reinvent Ray Bolger's role as the Scarecrow in *The Wizard of Oz*. And as a messianic global superstar, he resembles no one so much as his father-in-law, Elvis Presley (who died long before Jackson married his daughter), a transracial figure from the other side of the color line. When Presley's first records were played on the radio in Memphis, DJs made a point of noting that he graduated from the city's all-white Humes High School, lest listeners mistake him for black. Given the ubiquity of television, nobody mistook the wispy-voiced young Michael Jackson for white, but it seemed, superficially, not to matter.

Yet Jackson, always the artificer, surely knew that part of his own appeal to 4 white audiences—who contributed substantially to the $50 million to $75 million a year he earned in his prime—lay initially in his precocious cuteness, and when he was a grown man, in his apparent lack of adult sexuality. He was energetic, charismatic, and supremely gifted, but sexually unassertive—unlike swaggeringly heterosexual black male performers from Big Joe Turner ("Shake, Rattle, and Roll") to Jay-Z ("Big Pimpin'"). He neutered himself racially, too: his hair went from kinky to straight, his lips from full to thin, his nose from broad to pinched, his skin from dark to a ghastly pallor. You can't miss the connection between these forms of neutering if you know the history of white America's atavistic dread of black male sexuality; the 1955 murder of 14-year-old Emmett Till, for supposedly flirting with a white woman, is just one *locus classicus*. That happened only three years before Jackson was born; when he was 13, he was singing "Ben." No wonder Jackson chose—with whatever degree of calculation—to remake himself as an American Dream of innocence and belovedness.

5   No wonder, either, that the artifice eventually turned scary, and the face of the icon came to look more and more corpselike. Readers of Toni Morrison's latest novel, *A Mercy*, might recall the passage in which an African woman tells about her first sight of white slavers: "There we see men we believe are ill or dead. We soon learn they are neither. Their skin is confusing." That's the middle-aged Michael Jackson to a T. Jackson arguably looked his "blackest" on the original cover of 1979's *Off the Wall*; by *Thriller*, the transformation had begun. *Off the Wall* was his declaration of manhood: It came out the year he turned 21, and you could make the case that it was his greatest purely musical moment. Why did he feel so deeply uncomfortable with himself? The hopeless task of sculpting and bleaching yourself into a simulacrum of a white man suggests a profound loathing of blackness. If Michael Jackson couldn't be denounced as a race traitor, who could? Somehow, though, black America overlooked it, and continued to buy his records, perhaps because some African-Americans, with their hair relaxers and skin-lightening creams, understood why Jackson was remaking himself, even if they couldn't condone it.

6   As with Ernest Hemingway—another case of deeply confused identity and (who knew?) androgynous sexuality—we need to look past the deliberate creation of an image and a persona to appreciate the artistry. A more masterly entertainer never took the stage. In 1988, the *New York Times* dance critic Anna Kisselgoff called him "a virtuoso . . . who uses movement for its own sake. Yes, Michael Jackson is an avant-garde dancer, and his dances could be called abstract. Like Merce Cunningham, he shows us that movement has a value of its own." Better yet, Astaire himself once called Jackson to offer his compliments. As a singer, Jackson was too much of a chameleon—from the tenderness of "I'll Be There" to the rawness of "The Way You Make Me Feel" to the silken sorrow of "She's Out of My Life"—to stamp every song with his distinct personality, as Sinatra did, or Ray Charles, or Hank Williams. But these are demigods—Jackson was merely a giant. (And how'd you like *their* dancing?) As a musical conceptualizer, probably only James Brown has had a comparable influence: Jackson and his visionary producer, Quincy Jones, fused disco, soul, and pop in a manner that can still be heard every hour of every day on every top-40 radio station—only not as well. Tommy Mottola, former head of Sony Music, called Jackson "the corner-stone to the entire music business." The best recordings by Jackson and Jones—"Don't Stop 'Til You Get Enough," "Billie Jean"—belong identifiably to their time, as do Sinatra's 1950s recordings with the arranger Nelson Riddle. Yet like Sinatra's "I've Got the World on a String" or "In the Wee Small Hours of the Morning," they're so perfect of their kind that they'll never sound dated.

7   The night before he died, Jackson was rehearsing at the Staples Center in Los Angeles for an epic comeback—a series of 50 concerts, beginning in July, at London's O2 Arena. If that sounds impossibly grandiose, consider that all 50 shows had already sold out. People around him had been wondering if he was really up to it, and the opening had already been put off by a week. He was 50 years old, after all: long in the tooth for a *puer aeternus*—eight years older than Elvis when he left the building, and a quarter century past his peak. Jackson had had

health problems for years. Drug problems, too, apparently: In 2007, according to the Associated Press, an L.A. pharmacy sued him, claiming he owed $100,000 for two years' worth of prescription meds. And money problems: In 2008, the ranch nearly went into foreclosure—he defaulted on a $24.5 million debt—and even the $50 million he stood to realize from his potentially grueling London concerts might not have helped that much. And of course, just problems: His very existence—as a son, as a black man—was problematic. In his last days, did the prospect of a comeback, of remythologizing himself one more time, excite him as much as it excited his fans? Did his magical moments in performance have an incandescent density that outweighed what must often have been burdensome hours and days? Ask him sometime, if you see him. Whatever his life felt like from inside, from outside it was manifestly a work of genius, whether you want to call it a triumph or a freak show—those are just words. We'd never seen anyone like this before, either in his artistic inventiveness or his equally artistic self-invention, and we won't forget him—until the big Neverland swallows us all.

COMPREHENSION

1. Summarize Gates's perception of Michael Jackson. How do you interpret the title? Why does Gates call Jackson an "artificer"? What does Gates mean by Jackson's "androgynous sexuality"?
2. Gates alludes to many stars from the world of music, dance, literature, and the arts. Which celebrities can you identify? What is Gates's purpose in listing so many of them?
3. What, in Gates's opinion, is Michael Jackson's legacy?

RHETORIC

1. Does this essay have an explicitly stated thesis? If so, where is it? If the thesis is implied, paraphrase it.
2. The first paragraph of this essay is quite long. What is Gates's strategy and purpose here? Does this lengthy opening paragraph weaken or strengthen the body of the essay? Explain.
3. Identify and comment on Gates's use of figurative language in this essay. How does figurative language—and Gates's overall style—influence the essay's tone?
4. What comparative points does Gates make about Jackson and other artists? How does the comparative method serve to organize the essay?
5. Explain the effect of the last paragraph, which resembles the introductory paragraph in length. Do you think this resemblance was intentional? Why or why not?

WRITING

1. Write your own evaluation of Michael Jackson or another celebrity musician who died within the last 10 years (such as Amy Winehouse or Whitney Houston), explaining why you think this artist's achievement is important.

2. Write a comparative essay in which you discuss two artists from the world of music, film, or television.

3. **Writing an Argument:** Argue for or against the proposition that the media make too much of the deaths of prominent celebrities.

NETWORKING
Applying Digital and Multimedia Literacies

Creating a Photo Biography: Strengthen your position in question 1 under Writing by adding a photo biography of Michael Jackson (or another musician-celebrity whose career you've chosen to evaluate). This biography should consist of 12 to 15 images that help tell the story of the celebrity's career; use succinct but compelling captions to supply narration that informs your evaluation.

The Dark Art of Description

Patricia Hampl

Patricia Hampl (b. 1946) is an American writer, poet, memoirist, and educator. Hampl was born in St. Paul, Minnesota. She earned a BA from the University of Minnesota in 1968 and an MFA at the University of Iowa in 1970. After stints as an editor and freelance writer between 1973 and 1978, Hampl joined the faculty at the University of Minnesota in Minneapolis where she is currently the English Regents Professor. A recipient of prestigious Guggenheim and MacArthur fellowships, Hampl is best known as a superb memoirist. Her first autobiography, A Romantic Education *(1981), is an introspective account of Hampl's Czech heritage. A second memoir,* Virgin Time: In Search of the Contemplative Life *(1992), explores her Roman Catholic upbringing. Hampl's critically acclaimed* The Florist's Daughter *(2007) is an emotionally charged account of her mother's death. Hampl lectures widely and is on the permanent faculty at the Prague Summer Program. This essay was originally the keynote address at the Bedell NonfictioNow conference on November 1, 2007.*

1   I was coming down the last lap of my most recent book, a memoir about my mother and father, and I was painfully aware of just how specific every bit of writing is, full of choices and chances, not theoretical at all, not the business of sweeping statements or smart ideas about "form" or "genre" or anything remotely theoretical. Just subject-verb-object and the hope of meaning.

2   Two nights away from the finish of my book, I was working late. I looked away from the computer screen for a moment and there was my dog staring at me intently. She was on the verge of speech. I could see it. *Come to bed.* Her eyes said

this clearly. It was almost 2 a.m. and for the past four hours I'd been changing commas to dashes and then back again to commas with the obsessive focus only a fanatic can sustain.

You've become a crazy person again, I said right out loud. The dog padded   3
away.

The great short story writer J.F. Powers was once stopped by a colleague in   4
the corridor at their university. The man asked him how things were going. Powers allowed that it had been a tough day—"I spent the morning trying to decide whether to have my character call his friend *pal* or *chum*," he said.

That's where I often find myself—thinking how important the choice of *pal* or   5
chum is, how whatever truth writing lays claim to resides in a passion for just such quite mad distinctions. This monomania is what a friend of mine calls the 600-pound gorilla of a book. Once the 600-pound gorilla gets hold of you, you're his (or hers). "Those last weeks of finishing a book are a world in themselves," she said. "I think that gorilla is the reason most of us write—it's a real high, but it's also a subconscious agreement not to be available or even normal for as long as it takes."

But as soon as you—or I, anyway—break away from the gorilla's embrace of a   6
particular book, those big, rangy theoretical questions begin to make their approach again. Maybe this is especially true of memoir, the odd enterprise of "writing a life" that has captivated our literary life for the last two decades or so. We tend to think of the novel as the classic narrative form—ever evolving, but familiar, its stately provenance long the preserve of academic interest and the center of trade publishing. Whereas the memoir seems new or somehow "modern," a rather suspect literary upstart. And therefore a form that invites interrogation.

But strictly speaking, autobiography is a genre far older than the novel and is   7
hard-wired into Western literary history. Perhaps from that first injunction of the oracle at Delphi—*Know thyself*—Western culture has been devoted to the exploration of individual consciousness and the unspooling of individual life.

That commandment to *know thyself* was central to antiquity. Plato uttered a   8
version of it; Cicero used it in a tract on the development of social concord. It was such a pillar of cultural, even spiritual value that in the early Christian period Clement of Alexandria felt compelled to claim that the saying had been borrowed by the Greeks from scripture, thus binding the two developing spiritualities— pagan and monotheistic—together in a seamless endeavor.

Closer to modernity, Goethe is supposed to have said with a shudder, "Know   9
thyself? If I knew myself, I'd run away." And Andre Gide probably expressed this revulsion best: "Know thyself! A maxim as pernicious as it is ugly. Whoever observes himself arrests his own development. A caterpillar who wanted to know itself well would never become a butterfly."

But the strongest indictment of the form I have ever encountered came from   10
a student in Indiana who had been conscripted by his Freshman Comp teacher to attend a reading I gave some years ago. He sprawled in his chair with his baseball cap on backwards, his eloquent body language making it clear he was far, far away. Can't win them all, I decided, and carried on, my eye straying back to him like a tongue drawn to the absence of a just-pulled tooth.

11   During the Q&A I fielded the decorous questions the students posed. And then, suddenly, apparently in response to something I'd said, my anti-hero sat bolt-upright and was waving his hand urgently, his face alight with interest. Ah—a convert. I called on him, smiling.

12   "I get it," he said. "Nothin's ever happened to you—and you write books about it."

13   He was right, of course. And in pronouncing this acute literary critical remark, he touched on the most peculiar aspect of the rise of the memoir in our times— namely, that fundamentally it isn't about having a more interesting life than someone else. True, there is a strand of autobiographical writing that relies on the documenta- tion of extraordinary circumstances, lives lived in extremity, often at great peril. But such memoirs have always been part of literary history. What characterizes the rise of memoir in recent times is precisely the opposite condition—not a gripping "narrative arc," but the quality of voice, the story of perception rather than action.

14   The self is not the subject of memoir, in this kind of book, but its instrument. And the work of the self is not to "narrate" but to describe. There is something fundamentally photographic about memoir, photographic rather than cinematic. Not a story, but a series of tableaus we are given to consider. No memoirist is surprised by the absences and blanks in action, for another unavoidable quality of autobiography as I am thinking of it—as lyrical quest literature—is that it is as much about reticence as it is about revelation.

15   It is often remarked that the advent of the movies and the ever faster pace of modern life have conspired to make description a less essential part of prose narrative in our own times. We don't need to be told what things look like—we are inundated with images, pictures, moving or static. In this view, we need the op- posite of the photographic quality so beloved of nineteenth-century descriptive writing in which the landscape is rolled out, sentence after sentence, the interior of a room and the interior of the character's mind meticulously presented.

16   We require writing, instead, that subsumes description, leaps right over it to frame episode and to create the much sought-after "narrative arc." The motto— even the mantra—of this narrative model is of course the commandment of intro- ductory fiction writing workshops: *Show, don't tell.*

17   But as recent memoir writing shows, descriptive writing abounds. And it proves, finally, not to be about the object described. Or not only. Description in memoir is where the consciousness of the writer and the material of the story are established in harmony, where the self is lost in the material, in a sense. In fiction of the show-don't-tell variety narrative scenes that "show" and dutifully do not "tell" are advanced by volleys of dialogue in which the author's presence is suc- cessfully obscured by the dramatic action of the dialogue of his characters. But in description we hear and feel the absorption of the author in the material. We sense the presence of the creator of the scene.

18   This personal absorption is what we mean by "style." It is strange that we would choose so oddly surfacey a word—style—for this most soulful aspect of writing. We could, perhaps more exactly, call this relation between consciousness and its subject "integrity." What else is the articulation of perception?

Style is a word usually claimed by fashion and the most passing aesthetic 19 values. But maybe that's as it should be because style in writing is terribly perishable. It can rot—that is what we mean when we recognize writing to be "precious," for example. But at its best and most essential, style is the register between a writer's consciousness and the material he is committed to wrestling to the page. It is the real authority of a writer, more substantial than plot, less ego-dependent than voice.

In 1951, Alfred Kazin published his memoir of his boyhood in Brooklyn, *A* 20 *Walker in the City,* the book that establishes modern American memoir. The critic Leslie Fiedler admired the book but was also frustrated by it. It "perversely refuses to be a novel," he said with some annoyance, as if Kazin's book, deeply dependent on descriptive writing, were refusing to behave. And it was. It was refusing to obey the commandment to "Show, Don't Tell."

When you read "The Block and Beyond," a much-anthologized chapter from 21 Kazin's memoir, it is impossible to discuss the main characters and certainly not its plot or even its narrative structure. It is a rhapsodic evocation of a place and time. And once read, it is impossible to forget, as indelible and inevitable as a poem.

What Kazin was able to do—what every memoirist can attempt—in liberating 22 himself from the demands of show-don't-tell narrative was to enter into reflection, into speculation, into interpretation, and to use the fragment, the image, the vignette, rather than narratively linked scenes to form his world and his book. He was able to show *and* tell. To write a story and write an essay—all in the same tale, braided and twined together. The root of this double power lies in description.

I was one of those enthralled teenage readers of long nineteenth-century Eng- 23 lish novels. I toiled my way through dense descriptions of gloomy heaths and bogs to get to the airy volleys of dialogue that lofted back and forth down the page to give me what I wanted—would Jane and Mr. Rochester . . . or would they not? Would Dorothea Brooke awaken—would Mr. Lydgate? I didn't relish the descriptive passages. I endured them. Just as Jane and Dorothea endured their parched lives, as if these endless descriptive passages were the desert to be crossed before the paradise of dialogue and the love story could be entered.

Yet all this description was, after all, the *world* of the book—not simply be- 24 cause it gave the book "a sense of place" as the old literary cliche puts it. It wasn't a "sense of place" I cared about in these passages, but the meeting place of perception with story—the place where someone *claimed* the story, where I could glimpse the individual consciousness, the creator of the scene. The person pulling the wires and making Jane and Dorothea move. I was looking, I suppose, for a sign of intimacy with the invisible author. That "dear reader" moment so familiar in nineteenth-century novels—think of Thackeray pausing to have a chat with the reader—with you!—about how to live on nothing a year. Think of George Eliot breaking off to describe the furnishings of Dorothea's ardent mind.

Henry James is probably the crown prince of nineteenth-century describers, a 25 *flâneur* of the sentence, a lounge lizard of the paragraph, taking his own sweet time to unfurl an observation, smoking the cheroot of his thought in the contemplative after-dinner puffery of a man who knows how to draw out the pleasure of his rare tobacco. Or—because James himself never hesitates to pile up opposing figures of speech until he has sliced his thought to the refracted transparency he adores—maybe I'll just switch metaphors and say that James sits mildly at his torture apparatus, turning the crank in meticulously calibrated movements as the reader lies helplessly strained upon the rack of his ever-expanding sentences, the exquisite pain of the lengthening description almost breaking the bones of attention. In short (as James often says after gassing on for a nice fat paragraph or two on the quality of a Venetian sunset or the knowing lift of a European eyebrow glimpsed across a table by an artless American ingénue), in short, he loves to carry on.

26   Carrying on, I was discovering, is what it is to describe. A lot. At length. To trust description above plot, past character development, and even theme. To understand that to describe is both humbler and more essential than to think of compositional imponderables such as "voice" or to strain toward superstructures like "narrative arc." To trust that the act of description will *find* voice and out of its streaming attention will take hold of narration.

27   By the time I was considering all of this, I had passed from being a reader and had become that more desperate literary type—a writer trying to figure out how to do it myself. I had no idea how to "sustain a narrative" and didn't even understand at the time (the late 1970s) that I was writing something called "a memoir." Yet when I read *Speak, Memory* by Vladimir Nabokov and later read his command—*Caress the detail, the divine detail*—I knew I had found the motto I could live by, the one that prevailed over "Show, Don't Tell."

28   Perhaps only someone as thoroughly divested of his paradise as Nabokov had been of his boyhood Russia and his family, his native language and all his beloved associations and privileged expectations, could enshrine the detail, the fragment, as the divinity of his literary religion, could trust the truths to be found in the DNA of detail, attentively rendered in ardent description. The dutiful observation that is the yeoman's work of description finally ascended, Nabokov demonstrated, to the transcendent reality of literature, to metaphor itself.

29   Nabokov was asked in an interview if his characters ever "took over." He replied icily that *his* characters were his galley slaves.

30   Yet when it was a matter of locating the godhead of literary endeavor, even a writer as unabashedly imperious as Nabokov did not point to himself and his intentions but to the lowly detail. *Caress the detail, the divine detail.* Next to grand conceptions like plot, which is the legitimate government of most stories, or character, which is the crowned sovereign, the detail looks like a ragged peasant with a half-baked idea of revolution and a crazy, sure glint in its eye. But here, according to Nabokov, resides divinity.

31   Henry James put his faith in something at least as insubstantial. "If one was to undertake to . . . report with truth on the human scene," he wrote, "it could but be because notes had been from the cradle the ineluctable consequence of one's greatest inward energy . . . to take them was as natural as to look, to think, to feel, to recognize, to remember." He considered his habit the basis of literature and called it "the rich principle of the Note."

Such "notes" are of course details, observations. Description. In attending 32 to these details, in the act of description, the more dynamic aspects of narrative have a chance to reveal themselves—not as "action" or "conflict" or any of the theoretical and technical terms we persist in thinking of as the sources of form. Rather, description gives the authorial mind a place to be in relation with the reality of the world.

It was surely this desire for the world—that is for the world's memoir, which 33 is history—that drew me to memoir, that seemingly personal form. And it was to description I tended, not to narrative, not to story. Maybe the root of the desire to write is always lost—properly lost—in the non-literary earth of our real lives. And craft, as we think of it, is just the jargon we give to that darker, earthier medium.

I know it was my mother who was the storyteller in our house. I was her audi- 34 ence. Her dear reader, in a way. I dimly—and sometimes bitterly—understood that nothing much was happening in our modest Midwestern lives, yet I clung to the drama with which she infused every vignette, every encounter at the grocery store.

And when I sought to make sense of the world that kept slipping away to the 35 past, to loss and forgetfulness, when I protested inwardly at that disappearance, it was to description I instinctively turned. Coming from a background in poetry and therefore being a literalist, it didn't occur to me to copy other prose writers. If I wanted to learn to write descriptively, I needed—what else?—pictures.

I took myself off to the Minneapolis Institute of Arts and plunked myself 36 down in front of a Bonnard. I wrote the painting. Described it. I went home and looked at a teacup on my table—I wrote that too. Still life descriptions that ran on for several pages. I wrote and wrote, describing my way through art galleries and the inadvertent still lives of my house and my memory, my grandmother's garden, her Sunday dinners.

To my growing astonishment, these long descriptive passages, sometimes 37 running two, three pages or longer, had a way of sheering off into narrative after all. The teacup I was describing had been given to me by my mother. And once I thought of the fact that she had bought these cups, made in Czechoslovakia, as a bride just before the Second World War, I was writing about that war, about my mother and her later disappointments which somehow were—and were not—part of this fragile cup. Description—which had seemed like background in novels, static and inert as a butterfly pinned to the page of my notebook, proved to be a dynamic engine that stoked voice and even more propelled the occasional narrative arc. Description, written from the personal voice of my own perception, proved even to be the link with the world's story, with history itself. Here was my mother's teacup, made in Czechoslovakia before the War, and here, therefore, was not only my mother's heartbreak but Europe's. The detail was surely divine, offering up miracle after miracle of connections out of the faithful consideration of the fragments before me.

We sense this historical power at the heart of autobiographical writing in the 38 testaments from the Holocaust, from the Gulag, from every marginal and abused life that has found the courage to speak its truth which is often its horror, to preserve its demonic details—and in so doing has seen them become divine. Nadezhda Mandelstam, Anne Frank, Primo Levi—to name only a very few. In time we will, surely, see such documents from Guantanamo and the unknown places of extreme rendition.

39   The history of whole countries, of an entire era and even lost populations depends sometimes on a little girl faithfully keeping her diary. The great contract of literature consists in this: you tell me your story and somehow I get my story. If we are looking for another reason to explain the strangely powerful grip of the first-person voice on contemporary writing perhaps we need look no farther than the power of Anne Frank's equation—that to write one's life enables the world to preserve its history.

40   But what of lives lived in the flyover? Lives that don't have that powerful, if terrible, historical resonance of radical suffering. Ordinary lives, in a word. Alfred Kazin's life—or yours. And certainly mine in middling Minnesota in the middle of the twentieth century. Why bother to describe it? Because of course, all details are divine, not just Nabokov's. In fact, perhaps the poorer the supposed value, the more the detail requires description to assure its divinity.

41   Which brings me to—if not a story, at least a fragment, a vignette. Early in my teaching life, I went (foolishly) through a killer snowstorm in Minneapolis to get to my University office because I had student conferences scheduled. By the time I arrived, the University had closed and the campus was empty, whipped by white shrouds of blizzard snow, the wind whistling down the Mall. I sat in my office in the empty building, cursing my ruinous work ethic, wondering if the buses would keep running so I could get home.

42   Then a rap on my office door. I opened it and there, like an extra out of *Doctor Zhivago,* stood my 11 a.m. appointment, a quiet sophomore named Tommy.

43   He looked anxious. He was really glad I was there, he said, because he had a big problem with the assignment. I had asked the students to write short autobiographies. "I just can't write anything about my life," he said miserably, his head down, his overshoes puddling on the floor.

44   I waited for the disclosure. What would it be—child abuse, incest, what murder or mayhem could this boy not divulge? What had brought him trooping through the blizzard to get help with his life story? How would I get him to Student Counseling?

45   "See, I come from Fridley," he said, naming one of the nowhere-suburbs sprawling drearily beyond the freeway north of Minneapolis.

46   I stared at him. I didn't, for a moment, comprehend that this was the dark disclosure, this the occasion of his misery: being from Fridley meant, surely, that he had nothing worth writing about.

47   There it was again—nothin' had ever happened to him and I was asking him to write about it.

48   "I have good news for you, Tommy," I said. "The field's wide open—nobody has told what it's like to grow up in Fridley yet. It's all yours."

49   All he needed to do was sit down and describe. And because the detail is divine, if you caress it into life, you find the world you have lost or ignored, the

world ruined or devalued. The world you alone can bring into being, bit by broken bit. And so you create your own integrity, which is to say your voice, your style.

COMPREHENSION

1. Summarize what the author means by "the dark art of description." Highlight key passages that illuminate her definition.
2. According to Hampl, what is the uniqueness and value of memoir?
3. What distinctions does Hampl draw between the novel and memoir? Which writers does she use most prominently to establish this comparison?

RHETORIC

1. What rhetorical function does Hampl's opening anecdote serve in the overall context of the essay? How does her concluding anecdote reinforce her meaning?
2. What is Hampl's purpose in alluding to so many writers? Do you find this catalogue of writers to be useful in framing her thesis? Justify your response by referring to passages in the text.
3. Hampl wrote this piece as a keynote address at a literary conference. What assumptions does she make about the values and interests of her audience? How does she demonstrate special authority in dealing with her subject?
4. How does Hampl employ definition and the comparative method as rhetorical strategies?
5. What types of figurative language appear in the essay? How do similes, metaphors, and other varieties affect the tone of the piece?

WRITING

1. Compose a brief memoir about a place where you grew up. Use the "dark art of description" to evoke this place.
2. Select one writer's quotation from Hampl's text and respond to it in an essay of reflection.
3. **Writing an Argument:** Hampl asserts that "ordinary lives" are worthy of memoir. Agree or disagree with her claim in an argumentative essay.

NETWORKING
Applying Digital and Multimedia Literacies

Memoirs across Media: Hampl alludes to the Holocaust, the Gulag, Guantanamo, and "the historical power at the heart of autobiographical writing" (paragraph 38). Conduct online research into the writers she mentions in the context of this paragraph. Then expand your research to include examples of video autobiographies or documentaries. Consider what hearing or seeing a person's story contributes to its historical power. Conversely, what are some advantages of using only written words? Prepare a research paper using these examples to explain the power of memoir to capture the horrors of contemporary history.

Regarding the Torture of Others

Susan Sontag

Susan Sontag *(1933–2004), one of the most influential critics of her generation, was born in New York City and grew up in Tucson, Arizona, and Los Angeles. After graduating from high school at the age of 15, she started studies at the University of California at Berkeley; subsequently, she received degrees from the University of Chicago and Harvard University. As an art critic as well as a political and cultural commentator, Sontag brought intellectual rigor to her subjects. The main body of her work in prose consists of two collections of essays,* Against Interpretation *(1966) and* Where the Stress Falls *(2001), as well as* Trip to Hanoi *(1968),* Illness as Metaphor *(1978), and* AIDS and Its Metaphors *(1988). In addition, Sontag wrote fiction, including* Volcano Lover *(1992) and* In America: A Novel *(2001), and several films and plays. In this essay, published in the* New York Times Magazine *in 2004, Sontag offers a meditation on the photographs of torture taken by American troops at Abu Ghraib prison in Baghdad.*

I.

1   For a long time—at least six decades—photographs have laid down the tracks of how important conflicts are judged and remembered. The Western memory museum is now mostly a visual one. Photographs have an insuperable power to determine what we recall of events, and it now seems probable that the defining association of people everywhere with the war that the United States launched pre-emptively in Iraq last year will be photographs of the torture of Iraqi prisoners by Americans in the most infamous of Saddam Hussein's prisons, Abu Ghraib.

An Iraqi detainee at Abu Ghraib: The horror of what is shown in the photographs cannot be separated from the horror that the photographs were taken.

The Bush administration and its defenders have chiefly sought to limit a public- 2 relations disaster—the dissemination of the photographs—rather than deal with the complex crimes of leadership and of policy revealed by the pictures. There was, first of all, the displacement of the reality onto the photographs themselves. The administration's initial response was to say that the president was shocked and disgusted by the photographs—as if the fault or horror lay in the images, not in what they depict. There was also the avoidance of the word "torture." The prisoners had possibly been the objects of "abuse," eventually of "humiliation"—that was the most to be admitted. "My impression is that what has been charged thus far is abuse, which I believe technically is different from torture," Secretary of Defense Donald Rumsfeld said at a press conference. "And therefore I'm not going to address the 'torture' word."

Words alter, words add, words subtract. It was the strenuous avoidance of the 3 word "genocide" while some 800,000 Tutsis in Rwanda were being slaughtered, over a few weeks' time, by their Hutu neighbors 10 years ago that indicated the American government had no intention of doing anything. To refuse to call what took place in Abu Ghraib—and what has taken place elsewhere in Iraq and in Afghanistan and at Guantánamo Bay—by its true name, torture, is as outrageous as the refusal to call the Rwandan genocide a genocide. Here is one of the definitions of torture contained in a convention to which the United States is a signatory: *"any act by which severe pain or suffering, whether physical or mental, is intentionally inflicted on a person for such purposes as obtaining from him or a third person information or a confession."* (The definition comes from the 1984 Convention Against Torture and Other Cruel, Inhuman or Degrading Treatment or Punishment. Similar definitions have existed for some time in customary law and in treaties, starting with Article 3—common to the four Geneva conventions of 1949—and many recent human rights conventions.) The 1984 convention declares, *"No exceptional circumstances whatsoever, whether a state of war or a threat of war, internal political instability or any other public emergency may be invoked as a justification of torture."* And all covenants on torture specify that it includes treatment intended to humiliate the victim, like leaving prisoners naked in cells and corridors.

Whatever actions this administration undertakes to limit the damage of the 4 widening revelations of the torture of prisoners in Abu Ghraib and elsewhere— trials, courts-martial, dishonorable discharges, resignation of senior military figures and responsible administration officials and substantial compensation to the victims—it is probable that the "torture" word will continue to be banned. To acknowledge that Americans torture their prisoners would contradict everything this administration has invited the public to believe about the virtue of American intentions and America's right, flowing from that virtue, to undertake unilateral action on the world stage.

Even when the president was finally compelled, as the damage to America's 5 reputation everywhere in the world widened and deepened, to use the "sorry" word, the focus of regret still seemed the damage to America's claim to moral superiority. Yes, President Bush said in Washington on May 6, standing alongside

King Abdullah II of Jordan, he was "sorry for the humiliation suffered by the Iraqi prisoners and the humiliation suffered by their families." But, he went on, he was "equally sorry that people seeing these pictures didn't understand the true nature and heart of America."

6   To have the American effort in Iraq summed up by these images must seem, to those who saw some justification in a war that did overthrow one of the monster tyrants of modern times, "unfair." A war, an occupation, is inevitably a huge tapestry of actions. What makes some actions representative and others not? The issue is not whether the torture was done by individuals (i.e., "not by everybody")—but whether it was systematic. Authorized. Condoned. All acts are done by individuals. The issue is not whether a majority or a minority of Americans performs such acts but whether the nature of the policies prosecuted by this administration and the hierarchies deployed to carry them out makes such acts likely.

II.

7 Considered in this light, the photographs are us. That is, they are representative of the fundamental corruptions of any foreign occupation together with the Bush adminstration's distinctive policies. The Belgians in the Congo, the French in Algeria, practiced torture and sexual humiliation on despised recalcitrant natives. Add to this generic corruption the mystifying, near-total unpreparedness of the American rulers of Iraq to deal with the complex realities of the country after its "liberation." And add to that the overarching, distinctive doctrines of the Bush administration, namely that the United States has embarked on an endless war and that those detained in this war are, if the president so decides, "unlawful combatants"—a policy enunciated by Donald Rumsfeld for Taliban and Qaeda prisoners as early as January 2002—and thus, as Rumsfeld said, "technically" they "do not have any rights under the Geneva Convention," and you have a perfect recipe for the cruelties and crimes committed against the thousands incarcerated without charges or access to lawyers in American-run prisons that have been set up since the attacks of Sept. 11, 2001.

8   So, then, is the real issue not the photographs themselves but what the photographs reveal to have happened to "suspects" in American custody? No: the horror of what is shown in the photographs cannot be separated from the horror that the photographs were taken—with the perpetrators posing, gloating, over their helpless captives. German soldiers in the Second World War took photographs of the atrocities they were committing in Poland and Russia, but snapshots in which the executioners placed themselves among their victims are exceedingly rare, as may be seen in a book just published, "Photographing the Holocaust," by Janina Struk. If there is something comparable to what these pictures show it would be some of the photographs of black victims of lynching taken between the 1880's and 1930's, which show Americans grinning beneath the naked mutilated body of a black man or woman hanging behind them from a tree. The lynching photographs were souvenirs of a collective action whose participants felt perfectly justified in what they had done. So are the pictures from Abu Ghraib.

The lynching pictures were in the nature of photographs as trophies—taken 9
by a photographer in order to be collected, stored in albums, displayed. The pictures taken by American soldiers in Abu Ghraib, however, reflect a shift in the use made of pictures—less objects to be saved than messages to be disseminated, circulated. A digital camera is a common possession among soldiers. Where once photographing war was the province of photojournalists, now the soldiers themselves are all photographers—recording their war, their fun, their observations of what they find picturesque, their atrocities—and swapping images among themselves and e-mailing them around the globe.

There is more and more recording of what people do, by themselves. At least 10
or especially in America, Andy Warhol's ideal of filming real events in real time—life isn't edited, why should its record be edited?—has become a norm for countless Webcasts, in which people record their day, each in his or her own reality show. Here I am—waking and yawning and stretching, brushing my teeth, making breakfast, getting the kids off to school. People record all aspects of their lives, store them in computer files and send the files around. Family life goes with the recording of family life—even when, or especially when, the family is in the throes of crisis and disgrace. Surely the dedicated, incessant home-videoing of one another, in conversation and monologue, over many years was the most astonishing material in "Capturing the Friedmans," the recent documentary by Andrew Jarecki about a Long Island family embroiled in pedophilia charges.

An erotic life is, for more and more people, that which can be captured in 11
digital photographs and on video. And perhaps the torture is more attractive, as something to record, when it has a sexual component. It is surely revealing, as more Abu Ghraib photographs enter public view, that torture photographs are interleaved with pornographic images of American soldiers having sex with one

Most of the pictures, like this one of a young woman with a naked man on a leash, seem to depict part of a larger confluence of torture and pornography.

another. In fact, most of the torture photographs have a sexual theme, as in those showing the coercing of prisoners to perform, or simulate, sexual acts among themselves. One exception, already canonical, is the photograph of the man made to stand on a box, hooded and sprouting wires, reportedly told he would be electrocuted if he fell off. Yet pictures of prisoners bound in painful positions, or made to stand with outstretched arms, are infrequent. That they count as torture cannot be doubted. You have only to look at the terror on the victim's face, although such "stress" fell within the Pentagon's limits of the acceptable. But most of the pictures seem part of a larger confluence of torture and pornography: A young woman leading a naked man around on a leash is classic dominatrix imagery. And you wonder how much of the sexual tortures inflicted on the inmates of Abu Ghraib was inspired by the vast repertory of pornographic imagery available on the Internet—and which ordinary people, by sending out Webcasts of themselves, try to emulate.

III.

12 To live is to be photographed, to have a record of one's life, and therefore to go on with one's life oblivious, or claiming to be oblivious, to the camera's nonstop attentions. But to live is also to pose. To act is to share in the community of actions recorded as images. The expression of satisfaction at the acts of torture being inflicted on helpless, trussed, naked victims is only part of the story. There is the deep satisfaction of being photographed, to which one is now more inclined to respond not with a stiff, direct gaze (as in former times) but with glee. The events are in part designed to be photographed. The grin is a grin for the camera. There would be something missing if, after stacking the naked men, you couldn't take a picture of them.

13   Looking at these photographs, you ask yourself, How can someone grin at the sufferings and humiliation of another human being? Set guard dogs at the genitals and legs of cowering naked prisoners? Force shackled, hooded prisoners to masturbate or simulate oral sex with one another? And you feel naïve for asking, since the answer is, self-evidently, People do these things to other people. Rape and pain inflicted on the genitals are among the most common forms of torture. Not just in Nazi concentration camps and in Abu Ghraib when it was run by Saddam Hussein. Americans, too, have done and do them when they are told, or made to feel, that those over whom they have absolute power deserve to be humiliated, tormented. They do them when they are led to believe that the people they are torturing belong to an inferior race or religion. For the meaning of these pictures is not just that these acts were performed, but that their perpetrators apparently had no sense that there was anything wrong in what the pictures show.

14   Even more appalling, since the pictures were meant to be circulated and seen by many people: it was all fun. And this idea of fun is, alas, more and more—contrary to what President Bush is telling the world—part of "the true nature and heart of America." It is hard to measure the increasing acceptance of brutality in American life, but its evidence is everywhere, starting with the video games of killing that

are a principal entertainment of boys—can the video game "Interrogating the Terrorists" really be far behind?—and on to the violence that has become endemic in the group rites of youth on an exuberant kick. Violent crime is down, yet the easy delight taken in violence seems to have grown. From the harsh torments inflicted on incoming students in many American suburban high schools—depicted in Richard Linklater's 1993 film, "Dazed and Confused"—to the hazing rituals of physical brutality and sexual humiliation in college fraternities and on sports teams, America has become a country in which the fantasies and the practice of violence are seen as good entertainment, fun.

What formerly was segregated as pornography, as the exercise of extreme 15 sadomasochistic longings—as in Pier Paolo Pasolini's last, near-unwatchable film, "Salò" (1975), depicting orgies of torture in the Fascist redoubt in northern Italy at the end of the Mussolini era—is now being normalized, by some, as high-spirited play or venting. To "stack naked men" is like a college fraternity prank, said a caller to Rush Limbaugh and the many millions of Americans who listen to his radio show. Had the caller, one wonders, seen the photographs? No matter. The observation—or is it the fantasy?—was on the mark. What may still be capable of shocking some Americans was Limbaugh's response: "Exactly!" he exclaimed. "Exactly my point. This is no different than what happens at the Skull and Bones initiation, and we're going to ruin people's lives over it, and we're going to hamper our military effort, and then we are going to really hammer them because they had a good time." "They" are the American soldiers, the torturers. And Limbaugh went on: "You know, these people are being fired at every day. I'm talking about people having a good time, these people. You ever heard of emotional release?"

Shock and awe were what our military promised the Iraqis. And shock and 16 the awful are what these photographs announce to the world that the Americans have delivered: a pattern of criminal behavior in open contempt of international

What formerly was segregated as pornography, as the exercise of extreme sadomasochistic longings, is being normalized, by some, as high-spirited play or venting.

humanitarian conventions. Soldiers now pose, thumbs up, before the atrocities they commit, and send off the pictures to their buddies. Secrets of private life that, formerly, you would have given nearly anything to conceal, you now clamor to be invited on a television show to reveal. What is illustrated by these photographs is as much the culture of shamelessness as the reigning admiration for unapologetic brutality.

IV.

17   The notion that apologies or professions of "disgust" by the president and the secretary of defense are a sufficient response is an insult to one's historical and moral sense. The torture of prisoners is not an aberration. It is a direct conse-quence of the with-us-or-against-us doctrines of world struggle with which the Bush administration has sought to change, change radically, the international stance of the United States and to recast many domestic institutions and pre-rogatives. The Bush administration has committed the country to a pseudo-religious doctrine of war, endless war—for "the war on terror" is nothing less than that. Endless war is taken to justify endless incarcerations. Those held in the extralegal American penal empire are "detainees"; "prisoners," a newly obsolete word, might suggest that they have the rights accorded by interna-tional law and the laws of all civilized countries. This endless "global war on terrorism"—into which both the quite justified invasion of Afghanistan and the unwinnable folly in Iraq have been folded by Pentagon decree—inevitably leads to the demonizing and dehumanizing of anyone declared by the Bush administration to be a possible terrorist: a definition that is not up for debate and is, in fact, usually made in secret.

18   The charges against most of the people detained in the prisons in Iraq and Afghanistan being nonexistent—the Red Cross reports that 70 to 90 percent of those being held seem to have committed no crime other than simply being in the wrong place at the wrong time, caught up in some sweep of "suspects"—the prin-cipal justification for holding them is "interrogation." Interrogation about what? About anything. Whatever the detainee might know. If interrogation is the point of detaining prisoners indefinitely, then physical coercion, humiliation and torture become inevitable.

19   Remember: We are not talking about that rarest of cases, the "ticking time bomb" situation, which is sometimes used as a limiting case that justi-fies torture of prisoners who have knowledge of an imminent attack. This is general or nonspecific information gathering, authorized by American mili-tary and civilian administrators to learn more of a shadowy empire of evildo-ers about whom Americans know virtually nothing, in countries about which they are singularly ignorant: In principle, any information at all might be use-ful. An interrogation that produced no information (whatever information might consist of) would count as a failure. All the more justification for pre-paring prisoners to talk. Softening them up, stressing them out—these are the euphemisms for the bestial practices in American prisons where suspected

terrorists are being held. Unfortunately, as Staff Sgt. Ivan (Chip) Frederick noted in his diary, a prisoner can get too stressed out and die. The picture of a man in a body bag with ice on his chest may well be of the man Frederick was describing.

The pictures will not go away. That is the nature of the digital world in which   20 we live. Indeed, it seems they were necessary to get our leaders to acknowledge that they had a problem on their hands. After all, the conclusions of reports compiled by the International Committee of the Red Cross, and other reports by journalists and protests by humanitarian organizations about the atrocious punishments inflicted on "detainees" and "suspected terrorists" in prisons run by the American military, first in Afghanistan and later in Iraq, have been circulating for more than a year. It seems doubtful that such reports were read by President Bush or Vice President Dick Cheney or Condoleezza Rice or Rumsfeld. Apparently it took the photographs to get their attention, when it became clear they could not be suppressed; it was the photographs that made all this "real" to Bush and his associates. Up to then, there had been only words, which are easier to cover up in our age of infinite digital self-reproduction and self-dissemination, and so much easier to forget.

So now the pictures will continue to "assault" us—as many Americans are   21 bound to feel. Will people get used to them? Some Americans are already saying they have seen enough. Not, however, the rest of the world. Endless war: endless stream of photographs. Will editors now debate whether showing more of them, or showing them uncropped (which, with some of the best-known images, like that of a hooded man on a box, gives a different and in some instances more appalling view), would be in "bad taste" or too implicitly political? By "political," read: critical of the Bush administration's imperial project. For there can be no doubt that the photographs damage, as Rumsfeld testified, "the reputation of the honorable men and women of the armed forces who are courageously and responsibly and professionally defending our freedom across the globe." This damage—to our reputation, our image, our success as the lone superpower—is what the Bush administration principally deplores. How the protection of "our freedom"—the freedom of 5 percent of humanity—came to require having American soldiers "across the globe" is hardly debated by our elected officials.

Already the backlash has begun. Americans are being warned against indulg-   22 ing in an orgy of self-condemnation. The continuing publication of the pictures is being taken by many Americans as suggesting that we do not have the right to defend ourselves: After all, they (the terrorists) started it. They—Osama bin Laden? Saddam Hussein? what's the difference?—attacked us first. Senator James Inhofe of Oklahoma, a Republican member of the Senate Armed Services Committee, before which Secretary Rumsfeld testified, avowed that he was sure he was not the only member of the committee "more outraged by the outrage" over the photographs than by what the photographs show. "These prisoners," Senator Inhofe explained, "you know they're not there for traffic violations. If they're in Cellblock 1-A or 1-B, these prisoners, they're murderers, they're terrorists,

In this photograph, Specialist Charles Graner Jr., who identified men in another Abu Ghraib photo, poses over handcuffed detainees lying on the floor.

they're insurgents. Many of them probably have American blood on their hands, and here we're so concerned about the treatment of those individuals." It's the fault of "the media" which are provoking, and will continue to provoke, further violence against Americans around the world. More Americans will die. Because of these photos.

23   There is an answer to this charge, of course. Americans are dying not because of the photographs but because of what the photographs reveal to be happening, happening with the complicity of a chain of command—so Maj. Gen. Antonio Taguba implied, and Pfc. Lynndie England said, and (among others) Senator Lindsey Graham of South Carolina, a Republican, suggested, after he saw the Pentagon's full range of images on May 12. "Some of it has an elaborate nature to it that makes me very suspicious of whether or not others were directing or encouraging," Senator Graham said. Senator Bill Nelson, a Florida Democrat, said that viewing an uncropped version of one photo showing a stack of naked men in a hallway—a version that revealed how many other soldiers were at the scene, some not even paying attention—contradicted the Pentagon's assertion that only rogue soldiers were involved. "Somewhere along the line," Senator Nelson said of the torturers, "they were either told or winked at." An attorney for Specialist Charles Graner Jr., who is in the picture, has had his client identify the men in the uncropped version; according to the *Wall Street Journal*, Graner said that four of the men were military intelligence and one a civilian contractor working with military intelligence.

V.

24 But the distinction between photograph and reality—as between spin and policy—can easily evaporate. And that is what the administration wishes to happen. "There are a lot more photographs and videos that exist," Rumsfeld

acknowledged in his testimony. "If these are released to the public, obviously, it's going to make matters worse." Worse for the administration and its programs, presumably, not for those who are the actual—and potential?—victims of torture.

The media may self-censor but, as Rumsfeld acknowledged, it's hard to 25 censor soldiers overseas, who don't write letters home, as in the old days, that can be opened by military censors who ink out unacceptable lines. Today's soldiers instead function like tourists, as Rumsfeld put it, "running around with digital cameras and taking these unbelievable photographs and then passing them off, against the law, to the media, to our surprise." The administration's effort to withhold pictures is proceeding along several fronts. Currently, the argument is taking a legalistic turn: now the photographs are classified as evidence in future criminal cases, whose outcome may be prejudiced if they are made public. The Republican chairman of the Senate Armed Services Committee, John Warner of Virginia, after the May 12 slide show of image after image of sexual humiliation and violence against Iraqi prisoners, said he felt "very strongly" that the newer photos "should not be made public. I feel that it could possibly endanger the men and women of the armed forces as they are serving and at great risk."

But the real push to limit the accessibility of the photographs will come 26 from the continuing effort to protect the administration and cover up our misrule in Iraq—to identify "outrage" over the photographs with a campaign to undermine American military might and the purposes it currently serves. Just as it was regarded by many as an implicit criticism of the war to show on television photographs of American soldiers who have been killed in the course of the invasion and occupation of Iraq, it will increasingly be thought unpatriotic to disseminate the new photographs and further tarnish the image of America.

After all, we're at war. Endless war. And war is hell, more so than any of the 27 people who got us into this rotten war seem to have expected. In our digital hall of mirrors, the pictures aren't going to go away. Yes, it seems that one picture is worth a thousand words. And even if our leaders choose not to look at them, there will be thousands more snapshots and videos. Unstoppable.

COMPREHENSION

1. Summarize Sontag's harsh condemnation of the Bush administration's prosecution of the Iraq war.
2. Sontag writes that the photographs coming out of Abu Ghraib "are us" (paragraph 7). What does she mean? Would you agree or disagree with the implications of her statement? Why?
3. Explain what Sontag finds to be uniquely powerful about photography as an art form.

RHETORIC

1. Sontag structures her essay around the dual subjects of photography and the American involvement in Iraq. Explain what her purpose is and how she links these two subjects.
2. What is Sontag's claim and in what place(s) does she state it? Where does she make logical, ethical, and emotional appeals? Are you persuaded by her argument? Why or why not?
3. Sontag includes six illustrations in the essay similar to the four we have included here. What is her objective? Does she mention additional photographs? How do the photographs enhance the message?
4. Sontag divides her essay into five numbered sections. How does each section serve to advance her argument?
5. How does Sontag's use of connotation and definition—of *torture, enemy combatants, the erotic life,* and so forth—serve her purpose?
6. What conclusions does Sontag draw "regarding the torture of others"?

WRITING

1. Sontag alludes to the popular radio commentator Rush Limbaugh. Find out more about this personality, and in an expository essay explain why Limbaugh would disagree with Sontag's argument.
2. **Writing an Argument:** Conduct your own research on Abu Ghraib, and then stake out an argumentative position on it. Develop logical, ethical, and emotional appeals to support your position.

NETWORKING
Applying Digital and Multimedia Literacies

Using Visuals and Hyperlinks to Enhance a Definition Essay: Write your own extended definition of torture, linking it to a specific situation like Abu Ghraib. Add visuals and hyperlinks to support your definition.

Saving the Life That Is Your Own: The Importance of Models in the Artist's Life

Alice Walker

Alice Walker (b. 1941) was born in Eatonton, Georgia, and now lives in San Francisco and Mendocino County, California. She attended Spelman College and graduated from Sarah Lawrence College. A celebrated and prolific novelist, short-story writer, poet, and essayist, she has also been active in the civil rights movement. Walker often draws on both her personal experience and historical records to reflect on the African American experience. Her books include The Color Purple *(1976), which won the American Book Award and the Pulitzer prize;* You Can't Keep a Good Woman Down *(1981);* Living in the World: Selected Essays, 1973–1987 *(1987);* The Temple of My Familiar *(1989);* By the Light of My Father's Smile *(1999);* The Way Forward Is with a Broken Heart *(2001) and* Devil's My Enemy *(2008). The following essay, from* In Search of Our Mothers' Gardens *(1983), offers a highly personalized and perceptive analysis of the importance of influence on both art and life.*

There is a letter Vincent van Gogh wrote to Emile Bernard that is very meaning- 1 ful to me. A year before he wrote the letter, van Gogh had had a fight with his domineering friend Gauguin, left his company, and cut off, in desperation and anguish, his own ear. The letter was written in Saint-Remy, in the South of France, from a mental institution to which van Gogh had voluntarily committed himself.

I imagine van Gogh sitting at a rough desk too small for him, looking out 2 at the lovely Southern light, and occasionally glancing critically next to him at his own paintings of the landscape he loved so much. The date of the letter is December 1889. Van Gogh wrote:

> However hateful painting may be, and however cumbersome in the times we are living in, if anyone who has chosen this handicraft pursues it zealously, he is a man of duty, sound and faithful.
>
> Society makes our existence wretchedly difficult at times, hence our impotence and the imperfection of our work.
>
> ... I myself am suffering under an absolute lack of models.
>
> But on the other hand, there are beautiful spots here. I have just done five size 30 canvasses, olive trees. And the reason I am staying on here is that my health is improving a great deal.
>
> What I am doing is hard, dry, but that is because I am trying to gather new strength by doing some rough work, and I'm afraid abstractions would make me soft.

3   Six months later, van Gogh—whose health was "improving a great deal"—
committed suicide. He had sold one painting during his lifetime. Three times was
his work noticed in the press. But these are just details.

4   The real Vincent van Gogh is the man who has "just done five size 30 canvasses,
olive trees." To me, in context, one of the most moving and revealing descriptions of
how a real artist thinks. And the knowledge that when he spoke of "suffering under
an absolute lack of models" he spoke of that lack in terms of both the intensity of his
commitment and the quality and singularity of his work, which was frequently ridiculed in his day.

5   The absence of models, in literature as in life, to say nothing of painting, is an
occupational hazard for the artist, simply because models in art, in behavior, in
growth of spirit and intellects—even if rejected—enrich and enlarge one's view of
existence. Deadlier still, to the artist who lacks models, is the curse of ridicule,
the bringing to bear on an artist's best work, especially his or her most original,
most strikingly deviant, only a fund of ignorance and the presumption that, as an
artist's critic, one's judgment is free of the restrictions imposed by prejudice, and
is well informed, indeed, about all the art in the world that really matters.

6   What is always needed in the appreciation of art, or life, is the larger perspective. Connections made, or at least attempted, where none existed before,
the straining to encompass in one's glance at the varied world the common
thread, the unifying theme through immense diversity, a fearlessness of
growth, of search, of looking, that enlarges the private and the public world.
And yet, in our particular society, it is the narrowed and narrowing view of life
that often wins.

7   Recently, I read at a college and was asked by one of the audience what I considered the major difference between the literature written by black and by white
Americans. I had not spent a lot of time considering this question, since it is not
the difference between them that interests me, but, rather, the way black writers
and white writers seem to me to be writing one immense story—the same story,
for the most part—with different parts of this immense story coming from a multitude of different perspectives. Until this is generally recognized, literature will
always be broken into bits, black and white, and there will always be questions,
wanting neat answers, such as this.

8   Still, I answered that I thought, for the most part, white American writers
tended to end their books and their characters' lives as if there were no better
existence for which to struggle. The gloom of defeat is thick.

9   By comparison, black writers seem always involved in a moral and/or physical struggle, the result of which is expected to be some kind of larger freedom.
Perhaps this is because our literary tradition is based on the slave narratives,
where escape for the body and freedom for the soul went together, or perhaps this
is because black people have never felt themselves guilty of global, cosmic sins.

10   This comparison does not hold up in every case, of course, and perhaps
does not really hold up at all. I am not a gatherer of statistics, only a curious
reader, and this has been my impression from reading many books by black and
white writers.

There are, however, two books by American women that illustrate what I am 11
talking about: *The Awakening,* by Kate Chopin, and *Their Eyes Were Watching God,*
by Zora Neale Hurston.

The plight of Mme Pontellier is quite similar to that of Janie Crawford. 12
Each woman is married to a dull, society-conscious husband and living in a
dull, propriety-conscious community. Each woman desires a life of her own and
a man who loves her and makes her feel alive. Each woman finds such a man.

Mme Pontellier, overcome by the strictures of society and the existence of 13
her children (along with the cowardice of her lover), kills herself rather than
defy the one and abandon the other. Janie Crawford, on the other hand, refuses
to allow society to dictate behavior to her, enjoys the love of a much younger,
freedom-loving man, and lives to tell others of her experience.

When I mentioned these two books to my audience, I was not surprised to 14
learn that only one person, a young black poet in the first row, had ever heard of
Their Eyes Were Watching God (*The Awakening* they had fortunately read in their
"Women in Literature" class), primarily because it was written by a black woman,
whose experience—in love and life—was apparently assumed to be unimportant
to the students (and the teachers) of a predominantly white school.

Certainly, as a student, I was not directed toward this book, which would have 15
urged me more toward freedom and experience than toward comfort and security, but was directed instead toward a plethora of books by mainly white male
writers who thought most women worthless if they didn't enjoy bullfighting or
hadn't volunteered for the trenches in World War I.

Loving both these books, knowing each to be indispensable to my own 16
growth, my own life, I choose the model, the example, of Janie Crawford. And yet
this book, as necessary to me and to other women as air and water, is again out of
print. But I have distilled as much as I could of its wisdom in this poem about its
heroine, Janie Crawford:

> I love the way Janie Crawford
> left her husbands
> the one who wanted to change her
> into a mule
> and the other who tried to interest her
> in being a queen.
> A woman, unless she submits,
> is neither a mule
> nor a queen
> though like a mule she may suffer
> and like a queen pace the floor.

It has been said that someone asked Toni Morrison why she writes the kind 17
of books she writes, and that she replied: Because they are the kind of books I
want to read.

This remains my favorite reply to that kind of question. As if anyone reading 18
the magnificent, mysterious *Sula* or the grim, poetic *The Bluest Eye* would require more of a reason for their existence than for the brooding, haunting

Wuthering Heights, for example, or the melancholy, triumphant *Jane Eyre.* (I am not speaking here of the most famous short line of that book, "Reader, I married him," as the triumph, but, rather, of the triumph of Jane Eyre's control over her own sense of morality and her own stout will, which are but reflections of her creator's, Charlotte Brontë, who no doubt wished to write the sort of books *she* wished to read.)

19   Flannery O'Connor has written that more and more the serious novelist will write, not what other people want, and certainly not what other people expect, but whatever interests her or him. And that the direction taken, therefore, will be away from sociology, away from the "writing of explanation," of statistics, and further into mystery, into poetry, and into prophecy. I believe this is true, *fortunately true;* especially for "Third World Writers"; Morrison, Marquez, Ahmadi, Camara Laye make good examples. And not only do I believe it is true for serious writers in general, but I believe, as firmly as did O'Connor, that this is our only hope—in a culture so in love with flash, with trendiness, with superficiality, as ours—of acquiring a sense of essence, of timelessness, and of vision. Therefore, to write the books one wants to read is both to point in the direction of vision and, at the same time, to follow it.

20   When Toni Morrison said she writes the kind of books she wants to read, she was acknowledging the fact that in a society in which "accepted literature" is so often sexist and racist and otherwise irrelevant or offensive to so many lives, she must do the work of two. She must be her own model as well as the artist attending, creating, learning from, realizing the model, which is to say, herself.

21   (It should be remembered that, as a black person, one cannot completely identify with a Jane Eyre, or with her creator, no matter how much one admires them. And certainly, if one allows history to impinge on one's reading pleasure, one must cringe at the thought of how Heathcliff, in the New World far from Wuthering Heights, amassed his Cathy-dazzling fortune.) I have often been asked why, in my own life and work, I have felt such a desperate need to know and assimilate the experiences of earlier black women writers, most of them unheard of by you and by me, until quite recently; why I felt a need to study them and to teach them.

22   I don't recall the exact moment I set out to explore the works of black women, mainly those in the past, and certainly, in the beginning, I had no desire to teach them. Teaching being for me, at that time, less rewarding than stargazing on a frigid night. My discovery of them—most of them out of print, abandoned, discredited, maligned, nearly lost—came about, as many things of value do, almost by accident. As it turned out—and this should not have surprised me—I found I was in need of something that only one of them could provide.

23   Mindful that throughout my four years at a prestigious black and then a prestigious white college I had heard not one word about early black women writers, one of my first tasks was simply to determine whether they had existed. After this, I could breathe easier, with more assurance about the profession I myself had chosen.

But the incident that started my search began several years ago: I sat down at 24 my desk one day, in a room of my own, with key and lock, and began preparations for a story about voodoo, a subject that had always fascinated me. Many of the elements of this story I had gathered from a story my mother several times told me. She had gone, during the Depression, into town to apply for some government surplus food at the local commissary, and had been turned down, in a particularly humiliating way, by the white woman in charge.

My mother always told this story with a most curious expression on her face. 25 She automatically raised her head higher than ever—it was always high—and there was a look of righteousness, a kind of holy *heat* coming from her eyes. She said she had lived to see this same white woman grow old and senile and so badly crippled she had to get about on *two* sticks.

To her, this was clearly the working of God, who, as in the old spiritual, "... may 26 not come when you want him, but he's right on time!" To me, hearing the story for about the fiftieth time, something else was discernible: the possibilities of the story, for fiction.

What, I asked myself, would have happened if, after the crippled old lady died, 27 it was discovered that someone, my mother perhaps (who would have been mortified at the thought, Christian that she is), had voodooed her?

Then, my thoughts sweeping me away into the world of hexes and conjurings 28 of centuries past, I wondered how a larger story could be created out of my mother's story; one that would be true to the magnitude of her humiliation and grief, and to the white woman's lack of sensitivity and compassion.

My third quandary was: How could I find out all I needed to know in order to 29 write a story that used *authentic* black witchcraft?

Which brings me back, almost, to the day I became really interested in black 30 women writers. I say "almost" because one other thing, from my childhood, made the choice of black magic a logical and irresistible one for my story. Aside from my mother's several stories about root doctors she had heard of or known, there was the story I had often heard about my "crazy" Walker aunt.

Many years ago, when my aunt was a meek and obedient girl growing up in a 31 strict, conventionally religious house in the rural South, she had suddenly thrown off her meekness and had run away from home, escorted by a rogue of a man permanently attached elsewhere.

When she was returned home by her father, she was declared quite mad. In the 32 backwoods South at the turn of the century, "madness" of this sort was cured not by psychiatry but by powders and by spells. (One can see Scott Joplin's *Treemonisha* to understand the role voodoo played among black people of that period.) My aunt's madness was treated by the community conjurer, who promised, and delivered, the desired results. His treatment was a bag of white powder, bought for fifty cents, and sprinkled on the ground around her house, with some of it sewed, I believe, into the bodice of her nightgown.

So when I sat down to write my story about voodoo, my crazy Walker aunt 33 was definitely on my mind.

34   But she had experienced her temporary craziness so long ago that her story had all the excitement of a might-have-been. I needed, instead of family memories, some hard facts about the *craft* of voodoo, as practiced by Southern blacks in the nineteenth century. (It never once, fortunately, occurred to me that voodoo was not worthy of the interest I had in it, or was too ridiculous to study seriously.)

35   I began reading all I could find on the subject of "The Negro and His Folk-ways and Superstitions." There were Botkin and Puckett and others, all white, most racist. How was I to believe anything they wrote, since at least one of them, Puckett, was capable of wondering, in his book, if "The Negro" had a large enough brain?

36   Well, I thought, where are the *black* collectors of folklore? Where is the *black* anthropologist? Where is the *black* person who took the time to travel the back roads of the South and collect the information I need: how to cure heat trouble, treat dropsy, hex somebody to death, lock bowels, cause joints to swell, eyes to fall out, and so on. Where was this black person?

37   And that is when I first saw, in a *footnote* to the white voices of authority, the name Zora Neale Hurston.

38   Folklorist, novelist, anthropologist, serious student of voodoo, also all-around black woman, with guts enough to take a slide rule and measure random black heads in Harlem; not to prove their inferiority, but to prove that whatever their size, shape, or present condition of servitude, those heads contained all the intelligence anyone could use to get through this world.

39   Zora Hurston, who went to Barnard to learn how to study what she really wanted to learn: the ways of her own people, and what ancient rituals, customs, and beliefs had made them unique.

40   Zora, of the sandy-colored hair and the daredevil eyes, a girl who escaped poverty and parental neglect by hard work and a sharp eye for the main chance.

41   Zora, who left the South only to return to look at it again. Who went to root doctors from Florida to Louisiana and said, "Here I am. I want to learn your trade."

42   Zora, who had collected all the black folklore I could ever use.

43   *That Zora.*

44   And having found *that Zora* (like a golden key to a storehouse of varied treasure), I was hooked.

45   What I had discovered, of course, was a model. A model, who, as it happened, provided more than voodoo for my story, more than one of the greatest novels America had produced—though, being America, it did not realize this. She had provided, as if she knew someday I would come along wandering in the wilderness, a nearly complete record of her life. And though her life sprouted an occasional wart, I am eternally grateful for that life, warts and all.

46   It is not irrelevant, nor is it bragging (except perhaps to gloat a little on the happy relatedness of Zora, my mother and me), to mention here that the story I

wrote, called "The Revenge of Hannah Kemhuff," based on my mother's experiences during the Depression, and on Zora Hurston's folklore collection of the 1920s, and on my own response to both out of a contemporary existence, was immediately published and was later selected, by a reputable collector of short stories, as one of the *Best Short Stories of 1974.*

I mention it because this story might never have been written, because 47 the very bases of its structure, authentic black folklore, viewed from a black perspective, might have been lost.

Had it been lost, my mother's story would have had no historical underpinning, 48 none I could trust, anyway. I would not have written the story, which I enjoyed writing as much as I've enjoyed writing anything in my life, had I not known that Zora had already done a thorough job of preparing the ground over which I was then moving.

In that story I gathered up the historical and psychological threads of the life 49 my ancestors lived, and in the writing of it I felt joy and strength and my own continuity. I had that wonderful feeling writers get sometimes, not very often, of being *with* a great many people, ancient spirits, all very happy to see me consulting and acknowledging them, and eager to let me know, through the joy of their presence, that, indeed, I am not alone.

To take Toni Morrison's statement further, if that is possible, in my own 50 work I write not only what I want to read—understanding fully and indelibly that if I don't do it no one else is so vitally interested, or capable of doing it to my satisfaction—I write all the things *I should have been able to read.* Consulting, as belatedly discovered models, those writers—most of whom, not surprisingly, are women—who understood that their experience as ordinary human beings was also valuable, and in danger of being misrepresented, distorted, or lost:

Zora Hurston—novelist, essayist, anthropologist, autobiographer;

Jean Toomer—novelist, poet, philosopher, visionary, a man who cared what women felt;

Colette—whose crinkly hair enhances her French, part-black face; novelist, playwright, dancer, essayist, newspaperwoman, lover of women, men, small dogs; fortunate not to have been born in America;

Anaïs Nin—recorder of everything, no matter how minute;

Tillie Olson—a writer of such generosity and honesty, she literally saves lives;

Virginia Woolf—who has saved so many of us.

It is, in the end, the saving of lives that we writers are about. Whether we are 51 "minority" writers or "majority." It is simply in our power to do this.

We do it because we care. We care that Vincent van Gogh mutilated his ear. 52 We care that behind a pile of manure in the yard he destroyed his life. We care that Scott Joplin's music *lives!* We care because we know this: *The life we save is our own.*

COMPREHENSION

1. Explain the significance of Walker's title. How does it serve her purpose and guide readers to her thesis? What is her thesis?
2. According to the author, what is the importance of models in art? What is the relationship of models to life? List the models in Walker's life. Which of them stand out?
3. Paraphrase Walker's remarks on the relationship between black American and white American writing.

RHETORIC

1. Walker uses many allusions in this essay. Identify as many as you can. What is the allusion in the title? Comment on the general effectiveness of her allusions.
2. Is the author's style and choice of diction suitable to her subject matter and to her audience? Why or why not?
3. Why does the author personalize her treatment of the topic? What does she gain? Is there anything lost?
4. Walker employs several unique structuring devices in this essay. Cite at least three, and analyze their utility.
5. Explain Walker's use of examples to reinforce her generalizations and to organize the essay.
6. Which paragraphs constitute Walker's conclusion? What is their effect?

WRITING

1. Write an essay expanding the meaning of Walker's remark "What is always needed in the appreciation of art, or life, is the larger perspective" (paragraph 6).
2. If you were planning on a career as a writer, artist, actor, or musician, who would your models be, and why?
3. **Writing an Argument:** Argue for or against Walker's proposition that the absence of models in art and life is an "occupational hazard" (paragraph 5).

NETWORKING
Applying Digital and Multimedia Literacies

Keeping an "Importance of Models" Blog: Consider the importance of models in your life as a student (and as whatever else you are becoming or hope to become: a dancer, a basketball player, a social worker, a business executive, a nurse). Start and maintain a blog where you devote entries to individuals whom you've either studied from afar or studied with, who inform and influence your intellectual, artistic, athletic, professional, and/or personal growth. In each entry, describe this person and explain, with examples, what he or she has done or said that inspires you; record what you've learned and are continuing to learn from this person.

Synthesis: Connections for Critical Thinking

1. Write an essay comparing and contrasting literature and any other art form. What merits does each form have? Are there any limitations in either form? Which do you find more satisfying? Which form is more accessible? Use at least three essays in this chapter to illustrate or support your thesis.
2. Write an essay exploring the importance of role models in art and literature. Refer to the essays by Walker, Welty, Hampl, and McCloud to address the issue.
3. Analyze the illustrations that appear in the essays by Updike, McCloud, and Sontag. What is the purpose of these illustrations? What do the images contribute to the text?
4. Welty, Alexie, Walker, and other writers in this chapter provide extended examples of art and artists. How do they develop these examples? What strategies do they use? Are their goals similar or not? Explain your response.
5. Use the essays by Welty, Updike, and Hampl to explore the question of excellence in the arts. Answer this question: How do you know the work of art is good?
6. Examine the role of the artist in society and the artist's purpose in or duty to society. How would the writers in this chapter address this issue?

NETWORKING
Applying Digital and Multimedia Literacies

After visiting several news Web sites, write an essay in which you explain the importance of photography and photojournalism. Connect your findings to the ideas presented by Sontag in her essay.

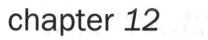

chapter *12*

Health and Medicine

What Are the Challenges?

Today, medicine and the health sciences are recasting our lives and the world we know. From stem-cell research, to the abortion debate, to the AIDS epidemic, we are dealing with enormous medical challenges and controversies. At the same time, commonplace conditions ranging from starvation to the common cold continue to defy solutions. There are surely medical breakthroughs—new drugs, therapies, technologies, and delivery systems—that offer some cause for optimism. However, we must acknowledge the ongoing reality of illness, both physical and psychological, and the serious imbalance in individuals' access to health care.

It could be argued that medical science presents an unequal playing field to Americans and people worldwide, for health care clearly is a privilege rather than a right. For millions of people in the United States and billions around the world, health care is rudimentary or nonexistent. College students, of course, are among the privileged. They typically enjoy health insurance, access to campus clinics or affiliated hospitals, counseling and psychiatric intervention, and an entire network of other health care support systems. Health care at an American college or university is a model that we would wish for any culture, society, or nation.

Medicine and health care are also subjects for civic discourse, cultural argument, and political debate. Disputes over medicine—abortion, cloning, drug addiction, and more— are also part of everyday life. The subject was an integral part of the most recent U.S. presidential election and assuredly will resurface in future election cycles. And, of course, the media (as we discussed in an earlier chapter) exploit our fascination with health and medicine. Television shows feature extreme surgical makeovers and contests among oversized people competing to lose the most weight. Magazines and television promote potentially dangerous body images. On the Internet, people suffering from anorexia and other dietary disorders can find solace and support.

The writers in this chapter contend with some of the most pressing issues confronting medical science today. Some of the writers are physicians. Some authors personalize their subject; others offer objective analysis or compelling arguments. All raise moral and ethical issues as they deal with ways in which medicine is shaping our personalities and our lives.

PREVIEWING THE CHAPTER

As you read the essays in this chapter and respond to them in discussion and writing, consider the following questions:

- What is the writer's subject? What perspective on medicine or health does she or he take?
- What is the writer's purpose: to explain, narrate, argue, or persuade?
- Do you find the writer's tone to be subjective or objective? Does the author have a personal motive in addressing the topic in the way he or she does?
- What moral, ethical, or religious issues does the writer raise in connection with medicine or health science?
- What logical, emotional, and ethical appeals does the author make to his or her audience?
- Which level of specialized knowledge—history, science, medicine, or some other area—does the author bring to bear on the subject? What level of authority does she or he bring to the topic?
- What cultural, economic, or political problems does the author connect to the medical topic under consideration?
- Do you agree or disagree with the author's thesis or claim, and why?
- Which essays appear similar in subject, thesis, or perspective?
- Which essays did you find most compelling or convincing, and why?
- Which ones changed your opinion or altered your thinking on the subject?

Classic and Contemporary Images
WHAT DOES MEDICAL RESEARCH TELL US?

Using a Critical Perspective   The medical universe has changed radically since 1632, when Rembrandt painted *The Anatomy Lesson of Professor Nicolaes Tulp*. Flash forward to 2004 and move from Holland to New York City, where photographer Gary Bramnick captured the release of conjoined twins after successful surgery. As you consider these visual texts, answer these questions: What is the main purpose of the artist or the photographer? What elements in each image contribute to the overall effect? How is the human subject portrayed, and which scene evokes the strongest emotional reaction? How does the much earlier scene relate to the contemporary one?

Rembrandt van Rijn (1606–1669) was the most gifted painter, draftsman, and etcher of Holland's Golden Age. *The Anatomy Lesson* (1632) is a group portrait of the Amsterdam surgeon's guild, whose members, led by Dr. Nicolaes Tulp, were unsurpassed in the surgical techniques of the period.

Clarence and Carl Aguirre, formerly conjoined twins who were separated by surgery, are followed by their mother Arlene Aguirre, center left, and grandmother Evelyn, center right, as they leave Children's Hospital at Montefiore in New York, flanked by the doctors who performed the surgery, Dr. James T. Goodrich, left, and Dr. David A. Staffenberg. Nurses loaded the boys into separate ambulances, which took off with a police escort for Blythedale Children's Hospital in Valhalla, where they and their mother lived between operations at Montefiore.

✳

Classic and Contemporary Essays
CAN WE AVOID EPIDEMICS?

We would like to think that the 21st century will avoid a plague like the one that swept through Asia and Europe during the 14th century. Yet the AIDS epidemic proves to be intractable and growing in sub-Saharan Africa, Asia, Russia, and the Indian subcontinent, while outbreaks of new potential epidemics like Ebola and SARS pose serious challenges for medical researchers and dangers for humankind. Plagues seem to be as old and persistent as civilization itself. Looking back to the 14th century, the noted historian Barbara Tuchman tells the story of the Black Death—the bubonic plague—that devastated Europe, resulting in the extinction of perhaps one-third of the population. With a historian's eye for narrative and detail, she describes the symptoms associated with plague, the process by which it spread inexorably from one nation to the next, and the religious, political, and cultural impact of the disease on the continent. Like Tuchman, Jill Lepore is a historian with wide-ranging research interests in American culture and civilization. However, Lepore in her essay deals with the 20th century while implying that we are facing new epidemics or plague years. Both writers trace the origins of emerging plagues and their consequences. Lepore also makes a pointed argument about the failure of the American health care system and the media to deal rationally with diseases that might or might not be of epidemic proportions. As you read these two essays, consider the rhetorical strategies that Tuchman and Lepore employ to render their respective vision of epidemics in vivid and compelling ways.

❀

"This Is the End of the World":
The Black Death

Barbara Tuchman

Barbara Tuchman (1912–1989) was born in New York City and graduated from Radcliffe College. A self-taught historian, she worked as a writer for the Nation *magazine and during World War II served as an editor at the U.S. Office of War Information. Her book* The Guns of August *(1960), a narrative history of the outbreak of World War I, won the Pulitzer prize. She won it again for her book* Stilwell and the American Experience in China: 1911–45 *(1971). Her other books include such best-sellers as* A Distant Mirror: The Calamitous 14th Century *(1978) and* The First Salute *(1989). In her later years, she was a lecturer at Harvard University and at the U.S. Naval War College. In this selection, excerpted from* A Distant Mirror, *Tuchman explains in her vivid narrative style the effects of the bubonic plague on Western Europe.*

In October 1347, two months after the fall of Calais, Genoese trading ships put into the harbor of Messina in Sicily with dead and dying men at the oars. The ships had come from the Black Sea port of Caffa (now Feodosiya) in the Crimea, where the Genoese maintained a trading post. The diseased sailors showed strange black swellings about the size of an egg or an apple in the armpits and groin. The swellings oozed blood and pus and were followed by spreading boils and black blotches on the skin from internal bleeding. The sick suffered severe pain and died quickly within five days of the first symptoms. As the disease spread, other symptoms of continuous fever and spitting of blood appeared instead of the swellings or buboes. These victims coughed and sweated heavily and died even more quickly, within three days or less, sometimes in 24 hours. In both types everything that issued from the body—breath, sweat, blood from the buboes and lungs, bloody urine, and blood-blackened excrement—smelled foul. Depression and despair accompanied the physical symptoms, and before the end "death is seen seated on the face."

The disease was bubonic plague, present in two forms: one that infected the bloodstream, causing the buboes and internal bleeding, and was spread by contact; and a second, more virulent pneumonic type that infected the lungs and was spread by respiratory infection. The presence of both at once caused the high mortality and speed of contagion. So lethal was the disease that cases were known of persons going to bed well and dying before they woke, of doctors catching the illness at a bedside and dying before the patient. So rapidly did it spread from one to another that to a French physician, Simon de Covino, it seemed as if one sick person "could infect the whole world." The malignity of the pestilence appeared more terrible because its victims knew no prevention and no remedy.

The physical suffering of the disease and its aspect of evil mystery were expressed in a strange Welsh lament which saw "death coming into our midst like black smoke, a plague which cuts off the young, a rootless phantom which has no mercy for fair countenance. Woe is me of the shilling in the armpit! It is seething, terrible . . . a head that gives pain and causes a loud cry . . . a painful angry knob. . . . Great is its seething like a burning cinder . . . a grievous thing of ashy color." Its eruption is ugly like the "seeds of black peas, broken fragments of brittle sea-coal . . . the early ornaments of black death, cinders of the peelings of the cockle weed, a mixed multitude, a black plague like halfpence, like berries. . . . "

Rumors of a terrible plague supposedly arising in China and spreading through Tartary (Central Asia) to India and Persia, Mesopotamia, Syria, Egypt, and all of Asia Minor had reached Europe in 1346. They told of a death toll so devastating that all of India was said to be depopulated, whole territories covered by dead bodies, other areas with no one left alive. As added up by Pope Clement VI at Avignon, the total of reported dead reached 23,840,000. In the absence of a concept of contagion, no serious alarm was felt in Europe until the trading ships brought their black burden of pestilence into Messina while other infected ships from the Levant carried it to Genoa and Venice.

By January 1348 it penetrated France via Marseille, and North Africa via Tunis. Shipborne along coasts and navigable rivers, it spread westward from Marseille through the ports of Languedoc to Spain and northward up the Rhône to Avignon, where it arrived in March. It reached Narbonne, Montpellier, Carcassonne, and Toulouse between February and May, and at the same time in Italy spread to Rome and Florence and their hinterlands. Between June and August it reached Bordeaux, Lyon, and Paris, spread to Burgundy and Normandy, and crossed the Channel from Normandy into southern England. From Italy during the same summer it crossed the Alps into Switzerland and reached eastward to Hungary.

6   In a given area the plague accomplished its kill within four to six months and then faded, except in the larger cities, where, rooting into the close-quartered population, it abated during the winter, only to reappear in spring and rage for another six months.

7   In 1349 it resumed in Paris, spread to Picardy, Flanders, and the Low Countries, and from England to Scotland and Ireland as well as to Norway, where a ghost ship with a cargo of wool and a dead crew drifted offshore until it ran aground near Bergen. From there the plague passed into Sweden, Denmark, Prussia, Iceland, and as far as Greenland. Leaving a strange pocket of immunity in Bohemia, and Russia unattacked until 1351, it had passed from most of Europe by mid-1350. Although the mortality rate was erratic, ranging from one fifth in some places to nine tenths or almost total elimination in others, the overall estimate of modern demographers has settled—for the area extending from India to Iceland—around the same figure expressed in Froissart's casual words: "a third of the world died." His estimate, the common one at the time, was not an inspired guess but a borrowing of St. John's figure for mortality from plague in Revelation, the favorite guide to human affairs of the Middle Ages.

8   A third of Europe would have meant about 20 million deaths. No one knows in truth how many died. Contemporary reports were an awed impression, not an accurate count. In crowded Avignon, it was said, 400 died daily; 7,000 houses emptied by death were shut up; a single graveyard received 11,000 corpses in six weeks; half the city's inhabitants reportedly died, including 9 cardinals or one third of the total, and 70 lesser prelates. Watching the endlessly passing death carts, chroniclers let normal exaggeration take wings and put the Avignon death toll at 62,000 and even at 120,000, although the city's total population was probably less than 50,000.

9   When graveyards filled up, bodies at Avignon were thrown into the Rhône until mass burial pits were dug for dumping the corpses. In London in such pits corpses piled up in layers until they overflowed. Everywhere reports speak of the sick dying too fast for the living to bury. Corpses were dragged out of homes and left in front of doorways. Morning light revealed new piles of bodies. In Florence the dead were gathered up by the Compagnia della Misericordia—founded in 1244 to care for the sick—whose members wore red robes and hoods masking the face except for the eyes. When their efforts failed, the dead lay putrid in the streets for days at a time. When no coffins were to be had, the bodies were laid on boards, two or three at once, to be carried to graveyards or common pits. Families dumped their own relatives into the pits, or buried them so hastily and thinly "that dogs dragged them forth and devoured their bodies."

Burial of the plague victims. From Annales de Gilles de Muisit.

Amid accumulating death and fear of contagion, people died without last rites 10 and were buried without prayers, a prospect that terrified the last hours of the stricken. A bishop in England gave permission to laymen to make confession to each other as was done by the Apostles, "or if no man is present then even to a woman," and if no priest could be found to administer extreme unction, "then faith must suffice." Clement VI found it necessary to grant remissions of sin to all who died of the plague because so many were unattended by priests. "And no bells tolled," wrote a chronicler of Siena, "and nobody wept no matter what his loss because almost everyone expected death. . . . And people said and believed, 'This is the end of the world.'"

In Paris, where the plague lasted through 1349, the reported death rate was 11 800 a day, in Pisa 500, in Vienna 500 to 600. The total dead in Paris numbered 50,000 or half the population. Florence, weakened by the famine of 1347, lost three to four fifths of its citizens, Venice two thirds, Hamburg and Bremen, though smaller in size, about the same proportion. Cities, as centers of transportation, were more likely to be affected than villages, although once a village was infected, its death rate was equally high. At Givry, a prosperous village in Burgundy of 1,200 to 1,500 people, the parish register records 615 deaths in the space of four-teen weeks, compared to an average of thirty deaths a year in the previous de-cade. In three villages of Cambridgeshire, manorial records show a death rate of 47 percent, 57 percent, and in one case 70 percent. When the last survivors, too few to carry on, moved away, a deserted village sank back into the wilderness and disappeared from the map altogether, leaving only a grass-covered ghostly outline to show where mortals once had lived.

12   In enclosed places such as monasteries and prisons, the infection of one person usually meant that of all, as happened in the Franciscan convents of Carcassonne and Marseille, where every inmate without exception died. Of the 140 Dominicans at Montpellier only seven survived. Petrarch's brother Gherardo, member of a Carthusian monastery, buried the prior and 34 fellow monks one by one, sometimes three a day, until he was left alone with his dog and fled to look for a place that would take him in. Watching every comrade die, men in such places could not but wonder whether the strange peril that filled the air had not been sent to exterminate the human race. In Kilkenny, Ireland, Brother John Clyn of the Friars Minor, another monk left alone among dead men, kept a record of what had happened lest "things which should be remembered perish with time and vanish from the memory of those who come after us." Sensing "the whole world, as it were, placed within the grasp of the Evil One," and waiting for death to visit him too, he wrote, "I leave parchment to continue this work, if perchance any man survive and any of the race of Adam escape this pestilence and carry on the work which I have begun." Brother John, as noted by another hand, died of the pestilence, but he foiled oblivion.

13   The largest cities of Europe, with populations of about 100,000, were Paris and Florence, Venice and Genoa. At the next level, more than 50,000 were Ghent and Bruges in Flanders, Milan, Bologna, Rome, Naples, and Palermo, and Cologne. London hovered below 50,000, the only city in England except York with more than 10,000. At the level of 20,000 to 50,000 were Bordeaux, Toulouse, Montpellier, Marseille, and Lyon in France, Barcelona, Seville, and Toledo in Spain, Siena, Pisa, and other secondary cities in Italy, and the Hanseatic trading cities of the Empire. The plague raged through them all, killing anywhere from one third to two thirds of their inhabitants. Italy, with a total population of 10 to 11 million, probably suffered the heaviest toll. Following the Florentine bankruptcies, the crop failures and workers' riots of 1346–47, the revolt of Cola di Rienzi that plunged Rome into anarchy, the plague came as the peak of successive calamities. As if the world were indeed in the grasp of the Evil One, its first appearance on the European mainland in January 1348 coincided with a fearsome earthquake that carved a path of wreckage from Naples up to Venice. Houses collapsed, church towers toppled, villages were crushed, and the destruction reached as far as Germany and Greece. Emotional response, dulled by horrors, underwent a kind of atrophy epitomized by the chronicler who wrote, "And in these days was burying without sorrowe and wedding without friendschippe."

14   In Siena, where more than half the inhabitants died of the plague, work was abandoned on the great cathedral, planned to be the largest in the world, and never resumed, owing to loss of workers and master masons and "the melancholy and grief" of the survivors. The cathedral's truncated transept still stands in permanent witness to the sweep of death's scythe. Angolo di Tura, a chronicler of Siena, recorded the fear of contagion that froze every other instinct. "Father abandoned child, wife husband, one brother another," he wrote, "for this plague seemed to strike through the breath and sight. And so they died. And no one

could be found to bury the dead for money or friendship. . . . And I, Angolo di Tura, called the Fat, buried my five children with my own hands, and so did many others likewise."

There were many to echo his account of inhumanity and few to balance it, for 15 the plague was not the kind of calamity that inspired mutual help. Its loathsomeness and deadliness did not herd people together in mutual distress, but only prompted their desire to escape each other. "Magistrates and notaries refused to come and make the wills of the dying," reported a Franciscan friar of Piazza in Sicily; what was worse, "even the priests did not come to hear their confessions." A clerk of the Archbishop of Canterbury reported the same of English priests who "turned away from the care of their benefices from fear of death." Cases of parents deserting children and children their parents were reported across Europe from Scotland to Russia. The calamity chilled the hearts of men, wrote Boccaccio in his famous account of the plague in Florence that serves as introduction to the *Decameron.* "One man shunned another . . . kinsfolk held aloof, brother was forsaken by brother, oftentimes husband by wife; nay, what is more, and scarcely to be believed, fathers and mothers were found to abandon their own children to their fate, untended, unvisited as if they had been strangers." Exaggeration and literary pessimism were common in the 14th century, but the Pope's physician, Guy de Chauliac, was a sober, careful observer who reported the same phenomenon: "A father did not visit his son, nor the son his father. Charity was dead."

Yet not entirely. In Paris, according to the chronicler Jean de Venette, the 16 nuns of the Hôtel Dieu or municipal hospital, "having no fear of death, tended the sick with all sweetness and humility." New nuns repeatedly took the places of those who died, until the majority "many times renewed by death now rest in peace with Christ as we may piously believe."

When the plague entered northern France in July 1348, it settled first in Normandy 17 and, checked by winter, gave Picardy a deceptive interim until the next summer. Either in mourning or warning, black flags were flown from church towers of the worst-stricken villages of Normandy. "And in that time," wrote a monk of the abbey of Fourcarment, "the mortality was so great among the people of Normandy that those of Picardy mocked them." The same unneighborly reaction was reported of the Scots, separated by a winter's immunity from the English. Delighted to hear of the disease that was scourging the "southrons," they gathered forces for an invasion, "laughing at their enemies." Before they could move, the savage mortality fell upon them too, scattering some in death and the rest in panic to spread the infection as they fled.

In Picardy in the summer of 1349 the pestilence penetrated the castle of 18 Coucy to kill Enguerrand's mother, Catherine, and her new husband. Whether her nine-year-old son escaped by chance or was perhaps living elsewhere with one of his guardians is unrecorded. In nearby Amiens, tannery workers, responding quickly to losses in the labor force, combined to bargain for higher wages. In another place villagers were seen dancing to drums and trumpets, and on being asked the reason, answered that, seeing their neighbors die day by day while their village remained immune, they believed they could keep the plague from entering "by the jollity that is in us. That is why we dance." Further north in Tournai on the border of Flanders, Gilles de Muisit, Abbot of St. Martin's, kept one of the epidemic's most vivid accounts. The passing bells rang all day and all night, he recorded, because sextons were anxious to obtain their fees while they could. Filled with the sound of mourning, the city became oppressed by fear, so that the authorities forbade the tolling of bells and the wearing of black and restricted funeral services to two mourners. The silencing of funeral bells and of criers' announcements of deaths was ordained by most cities. Siena imposed a fine on the wearing of mourning clothes by all except widows.

19   Flight was the chief recourse of those who could afford it or arrange it. The rich fled to their country places like Boccaccio's young patricians of Florence, who settled in a pastoral palace "removed on every side from the roads" with "wells of cool water and vaults of rare wines." The urban poor died in their burrows, "and only the stench of their bodies informed neighbors of their death." That the poor were more heavily afflicted than the rich was clearly remarked at the time, in the north as in the south. A Scottish chronicler, John of Fordun, stated flatly that the pest "attacked especially the meaner sort and common people— seldom the magnates." Simon de Covino of Montpellier made the same observation. He ascribed it to the misery and want and hard lives that made the poor more susceptible, which was half the truth. Close contact and lack of sanitation was the unrecognized other half. It was noticed too that the young died in greater proportion than the old. Simon de Covino compared the disappearance of youth to the withering of flowers in the fields.

20   In the countryside peasants dropped dead on the roads, in the fields, in their houses. Survivors in growing helplessness fell into apathy, leaving ripe wheat uncut and livestock untended. Oxen and asses, sheep and goats, pigs and chickens ran wild and they too, according to local reports, succumbed to the pest. English sheep, bearers of the precious wool, died throughout the country. The chronicler Henry Knighton, canon of Leicester Abbey, reported 5,000 dead in one field alone, "their bodies so corrupted by the plague that neither beast nor bird would touch them," and spreading an appalling stench. In the Austrian Alps wolves came down to prey upon sheep and then, "as if alarmed by some invisible warning, turned and fled back into the wilderness." In remote Dalmatia bolder wolves descended upon a plague-stricken city and attacked human survivors. For want of herdsmen, cattle strayed from place to place and died in hedgerows and ditches. Dogs and cats fell like the rest.

21   The dearth of labor held a fearful prospect because the 14th century lived close to the annual harvest both for food and for next year's seed. "So few servants and laborers were left," wrote Knighton, "that no one knew where to turn for help." The sense of a vanishing future created a kind of dementia of despair. A Bavarian chronicler of Neuberg on the Danube recorded that "Men and women . . . wandered around as if mad" and let their cattle stray "because no one had any inclination to concern themselves about the future." Fields went uncultivated, spring seed unsown. Second growth with nature's awful energy

crept back over cleared land, dikes crumbled, salt water reinvaded and soured the lowlands. With so few hands remaining to restore the work of centuries, people felt, in Walsingham's words, that "the world could never again regain its former prosperity."

Though the death rate was higher among the anonymous poor, the known 22 and the great died too. King Alfonso XI of Castile was the only reigning monarch killed by the pest, but his neighbor King Pedro of Aragon lost his wife, Queen Leonora, his daughter Marie, and a niece in the space of six months. John Cantacuzene, Emperor of Byzantium, lost his son. In France the lame Queen Jeanne and her daughter-in-law Bonne de Luxemburg, wife of the Dauphin, both died in 1349 in the same phase that took the life of Enguerrand's mother. Jeanne, Queen of Navarre, daughter of Louis X, was another victim. Edward III's second daughter, Joanna, who was on her way to marry Pedro, the heir of Castile, died in Bordeaux. Women appear to have been more vulnerable than men, perhaps because, being more housebound, they were more exposed to fleas. Boccaccio's mistress Fiammetta, illegitimate daughter of the King of Naples, died, as did Laura, the beloved—whether real or fictional—of Petrarch. Reaching out to us in the future, Petrarch cried, "Oh happy posterity who will not experience such abysmal woe and will look upon our testimony as a fable."

In Florence Giovanni Villani, the great historian of his time, died at 68 in 23 the midst of an unfinished sentence: "*. . . e dure questo pistolenza fino a . . .* (in the midst of this pestilence there came to an end . . .)." Siena's master painters, the brothers Ambrogio and Pietro Lorenzetti, whose names never appear after 1348, presumably perished in the plague, as did Andrea Pisano, architect and sculptor of Florence. William of Ockham and the English mystic Richard Rolle of Hampole both disappear from mention after 1349. Francisco Datini, merchant of Prato, lost both his parents and two siblings. Curious sweeps of mortality afflicted certain bodies of merchants in London. All eight wardens of the Company of Cutters, all six wardens of the Hatters, and four wardens of the Goldsmiths died before July 1350. Sir John Pulteney, master draper and four times Mayor of London, was a victim, likewise Sir John Montgomery, Governor of Calais.

Among the clergy and doctors the mortality was naturally high because of the 24 nature of their professions. Out of 24 physicians in Venice, 20 were said to have lost their lives in the plague, although according to another account, some were believed to have fled or to have shut themselves up in their houses. At Montpellier, site of the leading medieval medical school, the physician Simon de Covino reported that, despite the great number of doctors, "hardly one of them escaped." In Avignon, Guy de Chauliac confessed that he performed his medical visits only because he dared not stay away for fear of infamy, but "I was in continual fear." He claimed to have contracted the disease but to have cured himself by his own treatment; if so, he was one of the few who recovered.

Clerical mortality varied with rank. Although the one-third toll of cardinals 25 reflects the same proportion as the whole, this was probably due to their concentration in Avignon. In England, in strange and almost sinister procession, the

Archbishop of Canterbury, John Stratford, died in August 1348, his appointed successor died in May 1349, and the next appointee three months later, all three within a year. Despite such weird vagaries, prelates in general managed to sustain a higher survival rate than the lesser clergy. Among bishops the deaths have been estimated at about one in twenty. The loss of priests, even if many avoided their fearful duty of attending the dying, was about the same as among the population as a whole.

26   Government officials, whose loss contributed to the general chaos, found, on the whole, no special shelter. In Siena four of the nine members of the governing oligarchy died, in France one third of the royal notaries, in Bristol 15 out of the 52 members of the Town Council or almost one third. Tax-collecting obviously suffered, with the result that Philip VI was unable to collect more than a fraction of the subsidy granted him by the Estates in the winter of 1347–48.

27   Lawlessness and debauchery accompanied the plague as they had during the great plague of Athens of 430 B.C., when according to Thucydides, men grew bold in the indulgence of pleasure: "For seeing how the rich died in a moment and those who had nothing immediately inherited their property, they reflected that life and riches were alike transitory and they resolved to enjoy themselves while they could." Human behavior is timeless. When St. John had his vision of plague in Revelation, he knew from some experience or race memory that those who survived "repented not of the work of their hands. . . . Neither repented they of their murders, nor of their sorceries, nor of their fornication, nor of their thefts."

COMPREHENSION

1. The title of this essay suggests a religious theme. Why did intellectuals and religious leaders associate the bubonic plague with biblical prophecy?
2. Does this essay have a thesis, or does it merely record in detail a period in European history? If it does have a thesis, is it implied or expressed directly? Explain your answer.
3. Does Tuchman suggest that Europe was "fated" to endure the tragic consequences of the plague owing to a higher power, or does she attribute the disaster to a confluence of history and chance? Explain your answer.

RHETORIC

1. Tuchman begins her essay by describing in detail the physical symptoms of the plague. What strategy lies behind this rhetorical decision?
2. Tuchman has a reputation as a historian whose goal was to bring "history to life." What methods does she use to realize this goal? Is she successful? Why or why not? What does the illustration on page 599 contribute?
3. Contemporary authors and filmmakers often select morbid themes for their sensational value or for financial gain, or both. For example, there is a plethora of "true-crime" stories, "re-creations" of natural disasters, and profiles of aberrant and

murderous personalities such as Jeffrey Dahmer, Ted Bundy, and the "Hillside Strangler." Is this Tuchman's purpose? Explain why or why not.

4. Note the particular parts of speech Tuchman uses to begin paragraphs 5–7, 9, 11, 12, 14, 16–18, 20, 22, and 23. All begin with either conjunctions or prepositions. How do these grammatical devices help maintain the flow of Tuchman's narrative?

5. Tuchman makes references to a vast number of historical figures and specific locations in 14th-century Europe. What is her assumption about the educational level of her intended audience? About the specialization of her readership? Is it necessary to know something about the people and places she cites to appreciate the essay? Or is Tuchman writing a book of general interest, with the implicit supposition that different readers will extract their own level of appreciation from her narrative? Explain.

6. Tuchman uses direct quotations from the observers and chroniclers of the times. Examine the use of such sources in paragraphs 10, 13, 15–20, and 23, among others. How does Tuchman weave their observations into her own narrative so that the essay maintains unity and coherence? How does her use of these citations affect the strength of her writing?

WRITING

1. Write a 300-word summary of Tuchman's essay.

2. For a research project, study Tuchman's philosophy regarding how history should be reported. Apply your research to her treatment of the Black Death.

3. **Writing an Argument:** Argue for or against the proposition that an epidemic as severe as the one that Tuchman describes could not possibly occur in the 21st century.

NETWORKING
Applying Digital and Multimedia Literacies

Using Visuals to Make Logical Appeals: In your response to question 3 under Writing, include at least one visual that supports your argument with hard data. If you use an existing chart or graph, be sure to document your source; and if you create a visual from data, be sure to cite the source that the data came from.

It's Spreading

Jill Lepore

Jill Lepore (b. 1966) is a prize-winning historian who teaches at Harvard University. She was born in Worcester, Massachusetts, and received degrees from Tufts University (BA, 1987), the University of Michigan (MA, 1990), and Yale University (1995)

before embarking on her academic career. Among her several books are King Philip's
War and the Origins of American Identity *(1998) and* New York Burning: Liberty
and Slavery in an Eighteenth Century City *(2005). Lepore is also a staff writer at the*
New Yorker, *in which the following essay on American epidemics appeared in 2009.*

1   On December 14, 1929, during a holiday shopping season darkened by the greatest stock-market crash in American history, Simon S. Martin bought a parrot for
his wife, Lillian, at a pet shop on North Eutaw Street, in Baltimore. It was not, as it
happened, a well parrot. Hoping to surprise his wife, Martin seems to have asked
his daughter, Edith, and her husband, Lee Kalmey, the owner of an auto repair
shop, to take care of the bird and bring it over to his house in Annapolis in ten
days' time. By Christmas Eve, the parrot must have shown signs of illness: puffy
eyes, a drooping head, and feathers as ruffled as if it had flown through a squall.
Come Yuletide, the Martins had a dead parrot on their hands.

2   The pet-shop owner, who may have been wise to the fact that Simon Martin
was secretary of the Annapolis Chamber of Commerce, at first offered a replacement, although by New Year's, when Lillian Martin and Edith and Lee Kalmey fell
dangerously ill, he was backpedalling, denying that he had ever sold Martin a
bird. Meanwhile, the Kalmeys were getting sicker and sicker, showing symptoms
of both pneumonia and typhoid.

3   On January 6th, a local doctor examined the patients. He had just read a
newspaper article about something called parrot fever: It had shown up in Argentina
months earlier, when an actor playing a sailor had caught it from his stage parrot.
The disease, also called psittacosis, had since spread through South America and
Europe. No one seemed to know much about it except that it was deadly. The
doctor sent a telegram to the U.S. Public Health Service, in Washington: "Can you
place supply parrot fever serum our disposal immediately." Unfortunately, there
was no serum, or any known treatment. The mayor alerted the governor. Within
forty-eight hours, epidemiologists from the Baltimore City Health Department,
the Maryland Department of Health, the United States Navy and Army, and the
Public Health Service, including a team of men from the Hygienic Laboratory in
Washington, arrived on the scene. Someone called the newspaper.

4   "'Parrot' Disease Baffles Experts" the Washington *Post* reported in an issue
that went to press the night of January 8th, thrilling readers with a medical mystery that would capture the nation's attention with the prospect of a parrot-fever
pandemic. Reports, cabled and wired and radioed across land and sea, were
printed in the daily paper or broadcast, within minutes, on the radio: tallies, theo-
ries, postmortems, more to fear. Before it was over, an admiral in the U.S. Navy
ordered sailors at sea to cast their pet parrots into the ocean. One city health com-
missioner urged everyone who owned a parrot to wring its neck. People abandoned their pet parrots on the streets. Every sneeze seemed a symptom. As the
story grew, it took on certain familiar—and, as it turned out, durable—features,
features that borrow as much from pulp fiction as from public health: super scientists fight super bugs in race to defeat foreign menace invading American homes,
beneath the very Christmas tree.

Epidemics follow patterns because diseases follow patterns. Viruses spread; they ₅ reproduce; they die. Epidemiologists study patterns in order to combat infection. Stories about epidemics follow patterns, too. Stories aren't often deadly but they can be virulent: spreading fast, weakening resistance, wreaking havoc. During the recent swine-flu panic, Joe Biden warned Americans not to ride the subway or fly on an airplane, and pharmacies ran out of surgical masks. Why was it so hard to tell, as the story was breaking, if a flu outbreak of pandemic proportions was under way? The world is a far better place for the work epidemiologists do. Maybe, though, we could do with a few more narratologists.

The stories about epidemics that are told in the American press—their plots ₆ and tropes—date to the nineteen-twenties, when modern research science, science journalism, and science fiction were born. The germ theory of disease dates to the mid-eighteen-hundreds. Pasteur developed a rabies vaccine in 1885, launching a global battle against infectious illness. By the nineteen-twenties, scientists had developed a vaccine for diphtheria; other vaccines, like the one for polio, would take decades, but hopes ran high. In *The Conquest of Disease* (1927), Thurman B. Rice, a professor of sanitary science, predicted the eradication of sickness itself.

Meanwhile, ordinary people learned to blame germs, not God, for catastrophes ₇ like the pandemic of 1918, when at least fifty million people, including nearly seven hundred thousand Americans, died of influenza. Germ theory, which secularized infectious disease, had a side effect: It sacralized epidemiology. The nineteen-twenties witnessed the inauguration of what the historian of medicine Nancy Tomes has called the "epidemic exposé," the hair-raising account of a disease that threatens to destroy the human race. The genre's master was a bacteriologist turned journalist named Paul de Kruif. He had taught at the University of Michigan and worked for the U.S. Sanitary Corps, studying the gangrene bacillus. After the war, he turned to writing. In 1925, his collaboration with Sinclair Lewis led to the publication of *Arrowsmith,* a novel about a young doctor fighting bubonic plague—an early medical thriller, for which de Kruif received twenty-five percent of the royalties. In 1926, de Kruif turned to nonfiction, publishing *Microbe Hunters,* a book of profiles of scientists, starting with Leeuwenhoek, who can see tiny things the rest of us can't, things that are trying to kill us.

Microbe Hunters, which inspired a generation of young readers to pursue ₈ careers in science, appeared a month before the first issue of Hugo Gernsback's *Amazing Stories,* the first magazine of what is now called science fiction. Many of its stories concern the work of laboratory scientists; the issue of July, 1929, included "The Purple Death," the story of a young doctor who keeps a copy of *Microbe Hunters* on his desk.

The coming plague was Paul de Kruif's bread and butter. Three months be- ₉ fore Simon Martin bought his wife a parrot for Christmas, de Kruif issued a warning in the lead article of *Ladies' Home Journal:* "In American milk today there lurks a terrible, wasting fever, that may keep you in bed for a couple of weeks, that may fasten itself on you for one, or for two, or even for seven years—that might culminate by killing you." What was this dread malady? Undulant fever. "At least

50,000 people are sick with it at this very moment," their ailment virtually un-known to "their baffled doctors." De Kruif's article, titled "Before You Drink a Glass of Milk," scared a lot of people and sold a lot of magazines. Boasting of its success, the editor of *Ladies' Home Journal* explained, "Nobody had ever heard of undulant fever before."

10   The experts who descended on Annapolis in early January, 1930, weren't half as baffled as the Washington *Post* made them out to be, but the reading public must have been at least twice as confused. Was parrot fever really something to worry about? Reading the newspaper, it was hard to say. "Not Contagious in Man," the *Times* announced. "Highly contagious," the Washington *Post* said. Who knew? Nobody had ever heard of it before. It lurked in American homes. It came from afar. It was invisible. It might kill you. It made a very good story. In the late hours of January 8th, editors at the Los Angeles *Times* decided to put it on the front page: "Two Women and Man in Annapolis Believed to Have 'Parrot Fever.'"

11   The next day, in Toledo, Mrs. Percy Q. Williams, whose husband had just returned from Cuba with two parrots, died in Mercy Hospital; in Baltimore, Mrs. Louise Schaeffer succumbed to what had at first appeared to be pneumonia. (Women, many of them widows, constituted the majority of the outbreak's victims. There were suggestions that lonely old women had got the disease by feeding their parrots mouth to mouth. Some called the disease "old maid's pneumonia.") Those deaths would normally have been unremarkable: two older women fading away in the cold of winter. Not this week. On learning that Schaeffer "had been in contact with a parrot several days before she became ill," physicians suspected parrot fever and ordered an autopsy, whereupon the Surgeon General, Dr. Hugh Smith Cumming (a eugenicist best known to history for launching the Tuskegee syphilis experiment, that same year), warned Americans to stay away from re-cently imported parrots. He insisted that he "did not fear an epidemic," but that, of course, only got people talking about one. Although the results of Schaeffer's au-topsy were not yet available, "Baltimore Woman Dies" made it onto the front page of the Chicago *Daily Tribune* on January 11th and "Parrot Fever Kills 2 in this Country" appeared on page 3 of the *Times*. That paper also reported on efforts to trace deadly Argentine parrots that had come to the United States through what were called, as if they were criminals, "two suspected New York dealers."

12   Some people were worried about more than parrots. On January 11th, after several clerks in the poultry department of a Toledo store started coughing, the city's Health Department launched an investigation into "incipient cases" of psittacosis. Two days later, in a story that appeared on the front page of William Randolph Hearst's San Francisco *Examiner*, the Associated Press announced that the country's scientists had declared war: "The disease-fighting armament of the nation today was directed against a new and mysterious enemy." The microbe hunters had taken out their microscopes.

13   In the years following the First World War, a great many American scientists were looking for sources to fund their vital research. The nation's scientific organizations

hired publicity firms. In 1926, a coalition of scientists launched a campaign to raise "A National Fund for the Support of Research in Pure Science." Half the battle, though, had to do with winning over the public, and de Kruif's work made clear that stories were powerful ammunition. Before the First World War, journalists didn't generally report on science, and they certainly didn't profile scientists. After the war, scientists tried writing for newspapers and magazines, attempting to explain the value of their work, but, year by year, the number of scientists writing for a popular audience fell while the number of journalists specializing in science writing rose. Perhaps the era's most effective pro-science publicity machine was the Science Service, a wire service founded in 1920 and edited by a chemist named Edwin E. Slosson. Its purpose was to promote scientific research by feeding stories to newspapers. The service, Slosson said, would not "indulge in propaganda unless it be propaganda to urge the value of research and the usefulness of science." Financed by the newspaper publisher E. W. Scripps, and later by the American Association for the Advancement of Science and the National Research Council, the Science Service reached a fifth of the American reading public by the mid-nineteen-thirties.

What a microbe hunter needed to do to get funding was to hunt and kill a 14 microbe, preferably a lethal one that nobody had ever heard of before. On January 6, 1930, when that family doctor sent his telegram to the U.S. Public Health Service, the message was sent on to the Hygienic Laboratory, where Dr. Charles Armstrong, a forty-five-year-old pathologist, was charged with heading the investigation. Armstrong wanted to contain the outbreak, urgently; he also wanted to develop a serum, to save the lives of people already infected. Doing so would require experiments; those experiments required infected parrots and infected people. To gather subjects, Armstrong needed to spread the word about psittacosis. What Armstrong needed was a parrot-fever panic.

As Armstrong arrived in Annapolis, a team of public-health officials was sent 15 to that North Eutaw Street pet shop in Baltimore—where four employees were now sick—to track down the purchasers of all the recently imported parrots. Not all those parrots had stayed in town. Mrs. Hugh Lett bought a parrot in Baltimore on December 18th; the bird died on New Year's Eve; Mrs. Lett took sick on January 7th, by which time she was in Cambridge. Armstrong wired messages to public-health officials across the country, asking them to be on the lookout for psittacosis. In city after city, parrot dealers handed over to investigators sick parrots and lists of the people who had bought parrots for Christmas. Dead birds, some of which were exhumed, were shipped to Washington. Cases of suspected psittacosis cropped up in Providence and Chicago, New Haven and Los Angeles. The home of an Ohio family was quarantined after yet another Christmas parrot died. Inevitably, there were cases merely "simulating psittacosis," like the parents of fifteen-year-old Lillian Muller, of the Bronx, who had bought their daughter a parrot, imported from Argentina, at a pet shop in Harlem. The *Times* offered reassurance: "The Mullers' parrot has been eating regularly and has exhibited no signs of drooping." (One constabulary note: The A.P. reported from North

Adams, Massachusetts, on January 13th, "A parrot in a local family, whose name was not given out, recently died." Polly?)

16   By January 15th, the *Times* reported fifty cases nationwide, including eleven in New York City, and seven deaths, including one in Queens and one in Yonkers. Doctors insisted, in vain, that "there was no occasion for general alarm," and "stressed the fact that in none of the cases reported so far in New York has the diagnosis been definitely established as psittacosis." Later that day—after the *Times* went to press with the death count—authorities revealed that blood tests on the New York dead had all come out negative. The *Times,* whose coverage of parrot fever was, all things considered, a model of restraint and clarity, made a point of announcing those negative tests. Elsewhere, though, autopsies and blood cultures that came out negative for psittacosis didn't make it into the papers. By now, Lillian Martin and Edith and Lee Kalmey were fast improving; this was not widely reported, either. People who got better simply fell out of the news.

17 The nationwide sweep for psittacosis soon supplied Armstrong with enough samples—parrots, healthy, sick, and dead; the blood from infected humans; and even the scrapings from Lillian Martin's birdcage—to begin his work, which he conducted in two basement rooms in the Hygienic Laboratory, aided by his technician, Henry (Shorty) Anderson. "Those parrots were sure mean bastards," Armstrong said. Armstrong and Anderson wore rubber gloves, put trays filled with cresol in the doorways, and covered the birds' cages with disinfectant-soaked curtains. They were not, however, especially fastidious. "The only thing hygienic about the Hygienic Laboratory was its name," one researcher there said. Armstrong explained, "If we'd got too careful, we'd have spent all our time being careful and how could we have found out anything about it?"

18   This was yet another hallmark of the swashbuckling microbe hunter, who lacked the fussiness of the housewife. "Germ" became a household word in the nineteen-teens. By the twenties, Americans, and especially housewives, lived in fear of germs. Not only did newspapers and magazines run almost daily stories about newly discovered germs like undulant fever but their pages were filled with advertisements for hygiene products, like Listerine (first sold over the counter in 1914 and, in many ways, the granddaddy of Purell), Lysol (marketed, in 1918, as an anti-flu measure), Kotex ("feminine hygiene," the first menstrual pad, introduced in 1920, a postwar conversion of a surgical dressing developed by Kimberly-Clark), Cellophane (1923), and Kleenex (1924; another Kimberly-Clark product, sold as a towel for removing makeup until a consumer survey revealed that people were using it to blow their noses). Perhaps because kitchens and laboratories have much in common, journalists like de Kruif strove to underscore the manliness of the microbe hunter. Armstrong, de Kruif wrote, "was definitely not the kind of man who would even own a parrot, let alone kiss it."

19   Armstrong and Anderson and other government scientists worked night and day. On January 13th, the Chicago *Daily Tribune* reported a landmark success: "Parrot Fever Germ Isolated."

The parrot-fever story made the malady out to be virulent, mysterious, and exotic, 20 despite these facts: The disease was not baffling; it had been identified in the nineteenth century; it was known to infect members of the Psittacidae family, which includes parrots, parakeets, macaws, and cockatoos; in the nineteen-thirties, the only birds likely to be contagious were those brought to the United States during the last months of 1929; it is possible to catch the disease only from an infected bird (people can't spread it); it infected then, and continues to infect today, between one and two hundred Americans every year. There was a danger, to be sure. Psittacosis is now easily treated with antibiotics like doxycycline, but that wasn't the case in 1930, when one in five people infected with the disease died. Nevertheless, the only people who had much to worry about were people who had been in quite close contact with certain tropical birds very recently imported from South America.

Psittacosis incited, if briefly, a sizable panic among people who, by any rea- 21 sonable measure, had nothing to fear. That was dangerous. Even as the story unfolded, what to make of parrot fever and just how much responsibility the press or the scientific community bore for the panic proved matters of dispute. But what happened next seems nearly as dangerous as the panic itself: People suddenly started insisting that parrot fever didn't exist.

"U.S. Alarm Over Parrot Disease Not Warranted," the Chicago *Daily Tribune* 22 declared, on January 15th. Less than two weeks into the story, parrot fever looked, suddenly, silly. Parrot fever became a national joke. A Washington correspondent for the *Times* filed a story about a parrot owned by Secretary of State Henry Stimson. The parrot, named the Old Soak, had been locked in the basement of the Pan-American Building, "not because he has psittacosis" but because he had a habit of swearing. The *Wall Street Journal* ran this joke: What did the janitor say when the professor at the Polytechnic Institute asked him why he was cleaning the lab with carbolic acid? "'So none of de Poly students gets dis new parrot fever.'" Even the straight stories weren't taken seriously. "A parrot foundling made its appearance early yesterday morning when a green bird with a chipped beak was discovered in the vestibule of John Schreyer's home, 25–27 Humphreys Street, East Elmhurst, Queens," the *Times* reported, whereupon jailbirds at Sing Sing offered asylum for all unwanted parrots; the warden said, "The inmates here think this talk about parrot fever is nonsense."

A pro-parrot lobby formed. On January 17th, six of the country's leading 23 importers of winged pets, including the Odenwald Bird Company, the Imperial Pet Shop, and the Dahle Bird Company of Philadelphia, gathered at the Hotel Commodore in New York, where they founded the Bird Dealers' Association of America. Prussia and Bavaria, suffering from their own outbreaks, had already instituted parrot embargoes. The bird business was in a bad way. The Bird Dealers fought back by claiming that the disease did not exist, had never existed in human beings, "and that the scare over 'parrot fever' had been chiefly brought about by the active imagination of a Baltimore newspaper man."

Exaggeration breeds exaggeration. The counter-story spread as wildly as the 24 story had. And the Bird Dealers had a point about the imagination of newspapermen.

The first American doctor to believe he had seen psittacosis had read about it in the newspaper. The Martins' doctor probably read Hearst's Baltimore *American.* Every Sunday, Hearst produced for his papers a supplement called the *American Weekly.* Edited by Morrill Goddard, the *American Weekly* was something between *Parade* and the *National Enquirer.* Goddard knew how to sell a plague and knew, too, that selling plagues was good for his advertising accounts with hygiene-product manufacturers. In March, 1930, Goddard was interviewed by the staff of the J. Walter Thompson Company, one of the nation's most influential advertising agencies. "There is a lot of interest now in parrot fever," the interviewer observed, asking, "How far will the research on parrot fever have to go before you print something about it?" Goddard took umbrage at the suggestion that he had not already covered parrot fever—that he had not, in fact, *scooped* parrot fever. "We were the first newspaper to present it to the American public," he claimed, not quite accurately, "to warn them that parrots might be deadly in the home." As to how he had come by the story, Goddard explained that he spent his evenings reading obscure scientific journals, where he read about the outbreak in Buenos Aires:

> I sent down to our man there and he sent me a wretched story without details and I cabled him and he sent me a second story with further details and pictures and that story was printed about four or five weeks before the first case developed in New York. It gave all the details of what is known as "psittacosis." Now, it is a matter of dispute whether it is a germ or a virus but it is a matter of no consequence as far as making a feature out of it.

25   Goddard had no real interest in the science. He wanted to run a story about a danger lurking in American homes: "The fact that the parrot in the cage at your house may put you in the cemetery is enough for me."

26 On January 16th, just over one week after the Washington *Post* printed its first parrot-fever piece, the *Times* ran a story radioed in by a correspondent in Austria: A Viennese scientist believed that Americans were suffering from "mass suggestion." Dr. Julius Bauer said, "Psittacosis has been known to science since 1892. Now for some reason it has assumed in the public mind the dimensions of a plague." The next day, the Science Service, reporting on an article in the *Journal of the American Medical Association,* reminded Americans that "the possibility of unusual disorders must be ever present in the medical mind." Who knew what might infect us next? Parrot fever ought to serve as proof that "it is no longer possible for any person or any nation to live in isolation." The world, in short, was a dangerous place.

27   Or was it just a gullible one? "Every winter, America has to have a new malady, and this year it is Parrot Fever," a columnist for the *Post* wrote. "People are getting all worked up over this new 'parrot-fever,'" a writer for *Life* scoffed, "but Lord! it's been endemic at the Capitol since Polly was an egg." E. B. White figured that the country was suffering from nothing so much as a bad case of the heebie-jeebies, brought on by extended exposure to newspapers that were

forever issuing warnings about sharks infesting the beaches of New Jersey, anthrax spores contaminating unsterilized shaving brushes, and noxious gases escaping from iceboxes in the middle of the night. In an issue that went to press on January 20th, the *New Yorker's* Talk of the Town included a piece by White calling parrot fever merely "the latest and most amusing example of the national hypochondria":

> There have been hundreds of national menaces, keeping us all on tenterhooks, keeping the populace feeling the national pulse and applying the national stethoscope. Psittacosis is one of the best, because one of the most picturesque. What will probably happen will be that some reporter will invent a disease traceable to something that happens to everybody: "Otis heart" from riding in elevators, maybe, or "corn-flakes itch" from eating breakfast food, and we'll all die of autosuggestion.

That hasn't happened quite yet, but we still can't tell whether we are all about 28 to die or whether we are being sold a bill of goods. This condition is chronic.

On January 22, 1930, the *Post* reported that Lillian Martin and Edith and Lee 29 Kalmey had recovered. Herbert Hoover prepared to sign an executive order banning the importation of parrots. The story seemed more or less wrapped up. But then, terribly, scientists starting dying. On January 23rd, Dr. Daniel S. Hatfield, the chief of the bureau of communicable diseases of the Baltimore City Health Department, succumbed to psittacosis. Hatfield's colleague Dr. William Stokes died on February 10th. Shorty Anderson died on February 8th. That same day, Charles Armstrong was admitted to the U.S. Naval Hospital with a fever of 104 degrees.

The director of the Hygienic Laboratory, George McCoy, insisted on taking 30 over Armstrong's work himself. He took blood from a patient who had recovered from psittacosis and injected it into Armstrong's veins. Armstrong improved, and eventually recovered. Afterward, he wrote up his report, according to which there had been a total of a hundred and sixty-nine cases of psittacosis nationwide, and thirty-three fatalities. In his report, Armstrong credited the press, without which, he believed, "this outbreak would largely have escaped detection." Armstrong's work earned him a place in de Kruif's 1932 sequel to *Microbe Hunters,* a book titled *Men Against Death.*

In February and early March of 1930, while Armstrong was still recovering, 31 nine other people at the Hygienic Laboratory became sick. Psittacosis seemed to have contaminated the whole building. On March 15th, McCoy ordered the building evacuated. Alone, he walked down the stairs to Armstrong's basement laboratory. He killed, with chloroform, every parrot, mouse, pigeon, guinea pig, rat, and monkey that had been used in the psittacosis experiments. "He murdered and murdered and made a slick and clean job of it," de Kruif wrote. He burned the bodies in the building's incinerator. He sealed all the windows. The fumigation squad arrived at 2 P.M. and began spraying the building with cyanide. Sparrows flying fifty feet over the building froze, mid-flight, and fell to earth. The next day, the headline in the *Post* read, "Parrot Fever Panic Seizes Laboratory." Two months later, on May 26, 1930, Congress rewarded the Hygienic Laboratory by expanding it and granting it a new name: the National Institute of Health.

COMPREHENSION

1. Summarize the parrot fever epidemic that Lepore recounts. According to Lepore, what significance does this episode have for people today?
2. In paragraph 5, Lepore states, "Epidemics follow patterns because diseases follow patterns." What does she mean? What additional information in the essay supports this observation?
3. What does Lepore think about disease and epidemic "experts"? What is her opinion of media representatives who report on epidemics? Refer to the text to support your answer.

RHETORIC

1. How clearly does the essay's title express Lepore's thesis in this essay? How does she use the opening event in relation to her thesis? What sorts of materials does she use to develop her thesis?
2. Is Lepore's account objective or subjective? Explain your answer.
3. What primary organizational strategy does Lepore use to structure this essay? What other strategies are evident?
4. What transitional devices does Lepore use as she moves from section to section?
5. Explain the purpose of Lepore's concluding paragraph. What point is she trying to make?

WRITING

1. Select a current epidemic or pandemic, and write your own account of this disease.
2. Examine the proper role of the media in warning the public about epidemics.
3. **Writing an Argument:** Argue for or against the proposition that we are overly concerned about epidemics today.

NETWORKING
Applying Digital and Multimedia Literacies

Conducting a Multimedia Research Project: Respond to question 1 under Writing with a research project that incorporates multiple media to inform your audience about a current epidemic or pandemic. Consider approaching this as a documentary that includes visuals like graphs, maps, and photographs—or as a hyperlinked paper that includes links to interviews, newscasts, and so on. You could also do an oral presentation that incorporates audio, video, and even a print handout. Don't choose your project's components at random; figure out what genres and media would best suit your purpose: to educate your audience about this disease.

Synthesis: Classic and Contemporary Questions for Comparison

1. Discuss Tuchman's and Lepore's essays in terms of style, method, and tone. What level of language do they employ? What forms of authority do they bring to bear on their subject? What rhetorical strategies do they use? How does the fact that both writers are historians affect their approach to the subject? Does one argue and the other explain or do they both make similar assertions?
2. Compare Tuchman's view of the bubonic plague of the 14th century with Lepore's presentation of the parrot fever epidemic.
3. In groups of three or four, conduct research on epidemics throughout history not mentioned by either Tuchman or Lepore. How do these epidemics serve to reinforce the assertions that the two writers make?

Topic of Cancer

Christopher Hitchens

Christopher Hitchens (1949–2011) was a controversial author, essayist, journalist, and public intellectual. He was born in Portsmouth, England, and received an undergraduate degree from Balliol College, Oxford in 1970. For decades, Hitchens was a columnist and literary critic in England and the United States. (He moved to the United States in 1970 and became a U.S. citizen in 2007.) Hitchens wrote for the Atlantic, Free Inquiry, Nation, Salon, Slate, *and* Vanity Fair, *among other publications. His articulate and combative debating style also made him a regular on talk shows. For years a stalwart defender of left-wing causes, Hitchens revised his thinking after the West's "tepid" response to the 1989 fatwa issued by Ayatollah Khomeini calling for the death of the writer's friend, Salman Rushdie. Renouncing socialism, Hitchens became a champion of the values of the Enlightenment. He also riled people by professing a "new atheism." His bestseller* God Is Not Great *(2007), followed by a memoir,* Hitch-22 *(2010), kept Hitchens in the limelight up to the time of his death from pneumonia brought on by esophageal cancer. In this harrowing essay on his medical condition, published in* Vanity Fair *in 2010, Hitchens enters into debate with a new adversary.*

I have more than once in my time woken up feeling like death. But nothing pre-   1
pared me for the early morning last June when I came to consciousness feeling as if I were actually shackled to my own corpse. The whole cave of my chest and thorax seemed to have been hollowed out and then refilled with slow-drying cement. I could faintly hear myself breathe but could not manage to inflate my lungs. My heart was beating either much too much or much too little. Any movement, however slight, required forethought and planning. It took strenuous effort

for me to cross the room of my New York hotel and summon the emergency services. They arrived with great dispatch and behaved with immense courtesy and professionalism. I had the time to wonder why they needed so many boots and helmets and so much heavy backup equipment, but now that I view the scene in retrospect I see it as a very gentle and firm deportation, taking me from the country of the well across the stark frontier that marks off the land of malady. Within a few hours, having had to do quite a lot of emergency work on my heart and my lungs, the physicians at this sad border post had shown me a few other postcards from the interior and told me that my immediate next stop would have to be with an oncologist. Some kind of shadow was throwing itself across the negatives.

2   The previous evening, I had been launching my latest book at a successful event in New Haven. The night of the terrible morning, I was supposed to go on *The Daily Show* with Jon Stewart and then appear at a sold-out event at the 92nd Street Y, on the Upper East Side, in conversation with Salman Rushdie. My very short-lived campaign of denial took this form: I would not cancel these appearances or let down my friends or miss the chance of selling a stack of books. I managed to pull off both gigs without anyone noticing anything amiss, though I did vomit two times, with an extraordinary combination of accuracy, neatness, violence, and profusion, just before each show. This is what citizens of the sick country do while they are still hopelessly clinging to their old domicile.

3   The new land is quite welcoming in its way. Everybody smiles encouragingly and there appears to be absolutely no racism. A generally egalitarian spirit prevails, and those who run the place have obviously got where they are on merit and hard work. As against that, the humor is a touch feeble and repetitive, there seems to be almost no talk of sex, and the cuisine is the worst of any destination I have ever visited. The country has a language of its own, a lingua franca that manages to be both dull and difficult and that contains names like ondansetron, for anti-nausea medication, as well as some unsettling gestures that require a bit of getting used to. For example, an official met for the first time may abruptly sink his fingers into your neck. That's how I discovered that my cancer had spread to my lymph nodes, and that one of these deformed beauties, located on my right clavicle, or collarbone, was big enough to be seen and felt. It's not at all good when your cancer is palpable from the outside. Especially when, as at this stage, they didn't even know where the primary source was. Carcinoma works cunningly from the inside out. Detection and treatment often work more slowly and gropingly, from the outside in. Many needles were sunk into my clavicle area, *Tissue is the issue* being a hot slogan in the local Tumorville tongue, and I was told the biopsy results might take a week.

4   Working back from the cancer-ridden squamous cells that these first results disclosed, it took rather longer than that to discover the disagreeable truth. The word *metastasized* was the one in the report that first caught my eye, and ear. The alien had colonized a bit of my lung as well as quite a bit of my lymph node. And its original base of operations was located, had been located for quite some time, in my esophagus. My father had died, and very swiftly, too, of cancer of the esophagus. He was 79. I am 61. In whatever kind of a race life may be, I have very abruptly become a finalist.

The notorious stage theory of Elisabeth Kübler-Ross, whereby one pro- 5
gresses from denial to rage through bargaining to depression and the eventual
bliss of acceptance, hasn't so far had much application in my case. In one way, I
suppose, I have been in denial for some time, knowingly burning the candle at
both ends and finding that it often gives a lovely light. But for precisely that reason, I can't see myself smiting my brow with shock or hear myself whining about
how it's all so unfair: I have been taunting the Reaper into taking a free scythe in
my direction and have now succumbed to something so predictable and banal
that it bores even me. Rage would be beside the point for the same reason. Instead, I am badly oppressed by a gnawing sense of waste. I had real plans for my
next decade and felt I'd worked hard enough to earn it. Will I really not live to see
my children married? To watch the World Trade Center rise again? To read if not
indeed write the obituaries of elderly villains like Henry Kissinger and Joseph
Ratzinger? But I understand this sort of non-thinking for what it is: sentimentality
and self-pity. Of course my book hit the best-seller list on the day that I received
the grimmest of news bulletins, and for that matter the last flight I took as a
healthy-feeling person (to a fine, big audience at the Chicago Book Fair) was the
one that made me a million-miler on United Airlines, with a lifetime of free up-
grades to look forward to. But irony is my business and I just can't see any ironies
here: would it be less poignant to get cancer on the day that my memoirs were
remaindered as a box-office turkey, or that I was bounced from a coach-class
flight and left on the tarmac? To the dumb question Why me? the cosmos barely
bothers to return the reply: Why not?

The bargaining stage, though. Maybe there's a loophole here. The oncology 6
bargain is that, in return for at least the chance of a few more useful years, you
agree to submit to chemotherapy and then, if you are lucky with that, to radiation
or even surgery. So here's the wager: you stick around for a bit, but in return we
are going to need some things from you. These things may include your taste
buds, your ability to concentrate, your ability to digest, and the hair on your head.
This certainly appears to be a reasonable trade. Unfortunately, it also involves
confronting one of the most appealing clichés in our language. You've heard it all
right. People don't have cancer: they are reported to be battling cancer. No well-
wisher omits the combative image: You can beat this. It's even in obituaries for
cancer losers, as if one might reasonably say of someone that they died after a
long and brave struggle with mortality. You don't hear it about long-term sufferers
from heart disease or kidney failure.

Myself, I love the imagery of struggle. I sometimes wish I were suffering in a 7
good cause, or risking my life for the good of others, instead of just being a gravely
endangered patient. Allow me to inform you, though, that when you sit in a room
with a set of other finalists, and kindly people bring a huge transparent bag of
poison and plug it into your arm, and you either read or don't read a book while
the venom sack gradually empties itself into your system, the image of the ardent
soldier or revolutionary is the very last one that will occur to you. You feel
swamped with passivity and impotence: dissolving in powerlessness like a sugar
lump in water.

8   It's quite something, this chemo-poison. It has caused me to lose about 14 pounds, though without making me feel any lighter. It has cleared up a vicious rash on my shins that no doctor could ever name, let alone cure. (Some venom, to get rid of those furious red dots without a struggle.) Let it please be this mean and ruthless with the alien and its spreading dead-zone colonies. But as against that, the death-dealing stuff and life-preserving stuff have also made me strangely neuter. I was fairly reconciled to the loss of my hair, which began to come out in the shower in the first two weeks of treatment, and which I saved in a plastic bag so that it could help fill a floating dam in the Gulf of Mexico. But I wasn't quite prepared for the way that my razorblade would suddenly go slipping pointlessly down my face, meeting no stubble. Or for the way that my newly smooth upper lip would begin to look as if it had undergone electrolysis, causing me to look a bit too much like somebody's maiden auntie. (The chest hair that was once the toast of two continents hasn't yet wilted, but so much of it was shaved off for various hospital incisions that it's a rather patchy affair.) I feel upsettingly de-natured. If Penelope Cruz were one of my nurses, I wouldn't even notice. In the war against Thanatos, if we must term it a war, the immediate loss of Eros is a huge initial sacrifice.

9   These are my first raw reactions to being stricken. I am quietly resolved to resist bodily as best I can, even if only passively, and to seek the most advanced advice. My heart and blood pressure and many other registers are now strong again: indeed, it occurs to me that if I didn't have such a stout constitution I might have led a much healthier life thus far. Against me is the blind, emotionless alien, cheered on by some who have long wished me ill. But on the side of my continued life is a group of brilliant and selfless physicians plus an astonishing number of prayer groups. On both of these I hope to write next time if, as my father invariably said, I am spared.

COMPREHENSION

1. Summarize Hitchens's understanding of his condition. How does he confront his diagnosis?
2. What sense of himself does Hitchens present to his audience?
3. Explain in your own words the concept of the "new land" that Hitchens develops in his essay.

RHETORIC

1. Explain the voice and mood that Hitchens creates in the essay. How do these elements reinforce the thesis?
2. What is Hitchens's purpose in relying heavily on figurative language to compose his essay? What varieties of figurative language can you identify? What is the overall stylistic effect?
3. How does Hitchens use a pattern of cause and effect to organize elements in this essay? Where does he use process analysis?
4. Does Hitchens present an argument in this selection? Why or why not?
5. Where does the writer employ irony to illuminate his topic?

WRITING

1. Reflect on a time when you or someone you know confronted bad medical news.
2. Write an analytical essay in which you examine and evaluate the varieties of figurative language that make the selection by Hitchens so memorable.
3. **Writing an Argument:** Hitchens was an atheist who famously stated that if he ever returned to religion, it was the chemo talking. Argue for or against the proposition that someone who doesn't believe in God can face death with dignity.

NETWORKING
Applying Digital and Multimedia Literacies

Locate and review at least four online videos and/or podcasts of Hitchens's many speeches, debates, and interviews. How would you describe and define Hitchens's views? What about the tone he uses to express them? Do you find him more convincing in writing, or when you can hear and see him speak?

The Masked Marvel's Last Toehold

Richard Selzer

Richard Selzer (b. 1928) is a surgeon who started writing for several hours each night after he had already established a successful medical career. He was born in Troy, New York, and received degrees from Union College (BS, 1948) and Albany Medical College (MD, 1953). For more than two decades Selzer was on the faculty of the Yale School of Medicine. His first collection, Mortal Essays: Notes on the Art of Surgery *(1974), established Selzer as an essayist specializing in the world of medicine and surgery. Selzer employs an elegant prose style in describing the painful and often tragic world of medical procedures and patients. His essays have been collected in several books, among them* Confessions of a Knife *(1979),* Letters to a Young Doctor *(1982),* Taking the World in for Repairs *(1997), and* The Exact Location of the Soul *(2001). Selzer has also written for numerous magazines and has compiled a book of stories,* Imagine a Woman *(1997). The following essay demonstrates Selzer's experience as a surgeon as well as his ability to describe the world of medicine in poetic and haunting terms.*

Morning rounds.

On the fifth floor of the hospital, in the west wing, I know that a man is sitting up 1 in his bed, waiting for me. Elihu Koontz is seventy-five, and he is diabetic. It is two weeks since I amputated his left leg just below the knee. I walk down the corridor, but I do not go straight into his room. Instead, I pause in the doorway. He is not yet aware of my presence, but gazes down at the place in the bed where his leg used to be, and where now there is the collapsed leg of his pajamas. He is totally absorbed, like an athlete appraising the details of his body. What is he thinking, I wonder. Is he dreaming the outline of his toes? Does he see there his foot's incandescent ghost? Could he be angry? Feel that I have taken from him something for which he yearns now with all his heart? Has he forgotten so soon the pain? It was a pain so great as to set him apart from all other men, in a red-hot place where he had no kith or kin. What of those black gorilla toes and the soupy mess that was his heel? I watch him from the doorway. It is a kind of spying, I know.

2   Save for a white fringe open at the front, Elihu Koontz is bald. The hair has grown too long and is wilted. He wears it as one would wear a day-old laurel wreath. He is naked to the waist, so that I can see his breasts. They are the breasts of Buddha, inverted triangles from which the nipples swing, dark as garnets.

3   I have seen enough. I step into the room, and he sees that I am there.

4   "How did the night go, Elihu?"

5   He looks at me for a long moment. "Shut the door," he says.

6   I do, and move to the side of the bed. He takes my left hand in both of his, gazes at it, turns it over, then back, fondling, at last holding it up to his cheek. I do not withdraw from this loving. After a while he relinquishes my hand, and looks up at me.

7   "How is the pain?" I ask.

8   He does not answer, but continues to look at me in silence. I know at once that he has made a decision.

9   "Ever hear of The Masked Marvel?" He says this in a low voice, almost a whisper.

10   "What?"

11   "The Masked Marvel," he says. "You never heard of him?"

12   "No."

13   He clucks his tongue. He is exasperated.

14   All at once there is a recollection. It is dim, distant, but coming near.

15   "Do you mean the wrestler?"

16   Eagerly, he nods, and the breasts bob. How gnomish he looks, oval as the huge helpless egg of some outlandish lizard. He has very long arms, which, now and then, he unfurls to reach for things—a carafe of water, a get-well card. He gazes up at me, urging. He *wants* me to remember.

17   "Well . . . yes," I say. I am straining backward in time. "I saw him wrestle in Toronto long ago."

18   "Ha!" He smiles. "You saw *me.*" And his index finger, held rigid and upright, bounces in the air.

19   The man has said something shocking, unacceptable. It must be challenged.

20   "You?" I am trying to smile.

21   Again that jab of the finger. "You saw *me.*"

22   "No," I say. But even then, something about Elihu Koontz, those prolonged arms, the shape of his head, the sudden agility with which he leans from his bed

to get a large brown envelope from his nightstand, something is forcing me toward a memory. He rummages through his papers, old newspaper clippings, photographs, and I remember . . .

It is almost forty years ago. I am ten years old. I have been sent to Toronto to 23 spend the summer with relatives. Uncle Max has bought two tickets to the wrestling match. He is taking me that night.

"He isn't allowed," says Aunt Sarah to me. Uncle Max has angina.   24

"He gets too excited," she says.   25

"I wish you wouldn't go, Max," she says.   26

"You mind your own business," he says.   27

And we go. Out into the warm Canadian evening. I am not only abroad, I am 28 abroad in the *evening!* I have never been taken out in the evening. I am terribly excited. The trolleys, the lights, the horns. It is a bazaar. At the Maple Leaf Gardens, we sit high and near the center. The vast arena is dark except for the brilliance of the ring at the bottom.

It begins.   29

The wrestlers circle. They grapple. They are all haunch and paunch. I am 30 shocked by their ugliness, but I do not show it. Uncle Max is exhilarated. He leans forward, his eyes unblinking, on his face a look of enormous happiness. One after the other, a pair of wrestlers enter the ring. The two men join, twist, jerk, tug, bend, yank, and throw. Then they leave and are replaced by another pair. At last it is the main event. "The Angel vs. The Masked Marvel."

On the cover of the program notes, there is a picture of The Angel hanging from 31 the limb of a tree, a noose of thick rope around his neck. The Angel hangs just so for an hour every day, it is explained, to strengthen his neck. The Masked Marvel's trademark is a black stocking cap with holes for the eyes and mouth. He is never seen without it, states the program. No one knows who The Masked Marvel really is!

"Good," says Uncle Max. "Now you'll see something." He is fidgeting, waiting 32 for them to appear. They come down separate aisles, climb into the ring from opposite sides. I have never seen anything like them. It is The Angel's neck that first captures the eye. The shaved nape rises in twin columns to puff into the white hood of a sloped and bosselated skull that is too small. As though, strangled by the sinews of that neck, the skull had long since withered and shrunk. The thing about The Angel is the absence of any mystery in his body. It is simply *there.* A monosyllabic announcement. A grunt. One looks and knows everything at once, the fat thighs, the gigantic buttocks, the great spine from which hang knotted ropes and pale aprons of beef. And that prehistoric head. He is all of a single hideous piece, The Angel is. No detachables.

The Masked Marvel seems dwarfish. His fingers dangle kneeward. His short 33 legs are slightly bowed as if under the weight of the cask they are forced to heft about. He has breasts that swing when he moves! I have never seen such breasts on a man before.

There is a sudden ungraceful movement, and they close upon one another. The 34 Angel stoops and hugs The Marvel about the waist, locking his hands behind The

Marvel's back. Now he straightens and lifts The Marvel as though he were uprooting a tree. Thus he holds him, then stoops again, thrusts one hand through The Marvel's crotch, and with the other grabs him by the neck. He rears and . . . The Marvel is aloft! For a long moment, The Angel stands as though deciding where to make the toss. Then throws. Was that board or bone that splintered there? Again and again, The Angel hurls himself upon the body of The Masked Marvel.

35   Now The Angel rises over the fallen Marvel, picks up one foot in both of his hands, and twists the toes downward. It is far beyond the tensile strength of mere ligament, mere cartilage. The Masked Marvel does not hide his agony, but pounds and slaps the floor with his hand, now and then reaching up toward The Angel in an attitude of supplication. I have never seen such suffering. And all the while his black mask rolls from side to side, the mouth pulled to a tight slit through which issues an endless hiss that I can hear from where I sit. All at once, I hear a shouting close by.

36   "Break it off! Tear off a leg and throw it up here!"

37   It is Uncle Max. Even in the darkness I can see that he is gray. A band of sweat stands upon his upper lip. He is on his feet now, panting, one fist pressed at his chest, the other raised warlike toward the ring. For the first time I begin to think that something terrible might happen here. Aunt Sarah was right.

38   "Sit down, Uncle Max," I say. "Take a pill, please."

39   He reaches for the pillbox, gropes, and swallows without taking his gaze from the wrestlers. I wait for him to sit down.

40   "That's not fair," I say, "twisting his toes like that."

41   "It's the toehold," he explains.

42   "But it's not *fair*," I say again. The whole of the evil is laid open for me to perceive. I am trembling.

43   And now The Angel does something unspeakable. Holding the foot of The Marvel at full twist with one hand, he bends and grasps the mask where it clings to the back of The Marvel's head. And he pulls. He is going to strip it off! Lay bare an ultimate carnal mystery! Suddenly it is beyond mere physical violence. Now I am on my feet, shouting into the Maple Leaf Gardens.

44   "Watch out," I scream. "Stop him. Please, somebody, stop him."

45   Next to me, Uncle Max is chuckling.

46   Yet The Masked Marvel hears me, I know it. And rallies from his bed of pain. Thrusting with his free heel, he strikes The Angel at the back of the knee. The Angel falls. The Masked Marvel is on top of him pinning his shoulders to the mat. One! Two! Three! And it is over. Uncle Max is strangely still. I am gasping for breath. All this I remember as I stand at the bedside of Elihu Koontz.

47 Once again, I am in the operating room. It is two years since I amputated the left leg of Elihu Koontz. Now it is his right leg which is gangrenous. I have already scrubbed. I stand to one side wearing my gown and gloves. And . . . *I am masked.* Upon the table lies Elihu Koontz, pinned in a fierce white light. Spinal anesthesia has been administered. One of his arms is taped to a board placed at a right angle to his body. Into this arm, a needle has been placed. Fluid drips here from a bottle

overhead. With his other hand, Elihu Koontz beats feebly at the side of the operating table. His head rolls from side to side. His mouth is pulled into weeping. It seems to me that I have never seen such misery.

An orderly stands at the foot of the table, holding Elihu Koontz's leg aloft by 48 the toes so that the intern can scrub the limb with antiseptic solutions. The intern paints the foot, ankle, leg, and thigh, both front and back, three times. From a corner of the room where I wait, I look down as from an amphitheater. Then I think of Uncle Max yelling, "Tear off a leg. Throw it up here." And I think that forty years later I am making the catch.

"It's not fair," I say aloud. But no one hears me. I step forward to break The 49 Masked Marvel's last toehold.

COMPREHENSION

1. Who is (was) the Masked Marvel? What is Selzer's relation to this man? What are his personal feelings?
2. Is this essay strictly about an amputation? Why or why not?
3. Explain your understanding of the last bit of dialogue in this essay.

RHETORIC

1. Consider the importance of Selzer's title. What does it reveal about Selzer's purpose and thesis?
2. What aspects of narrative and descriptive technique stand out in this essay?
3. What stylistic shifts can you detect in this essay? For example, where does the writer use figurative language, and where does he use technical language? What is the effect?
4. Why does Selzer divide his essay into sections? How does each section function? Is this strategy effective? Justify your response.
5. Explain the atmosphere that Selzer evokes and the final tone of the piece.

WRITING

1. Analyze Selzer's essay as an example of effective narrative and descriptive technique.
2. Select a well-known athlete, and examine the ironies of a seemingly superbly conditioned individual whose career is compromised by injury, drug abuse, aging, or disease.
3. **Writing an Argument:** Argue for or against the proposition that a doctor should not let feelings interfere with his or her treatment of a patient.

NETWORKING
Applying Digital and Multimedia Literacies

Using Images to Enhance a Descriptive/Narrative Essay: Supplement Selzer's essay with images in a meaningful way that contributes to this story's use of narrative and description.

❉

Between a Woman and Her Doctor

Martha Mendoza

Martha Mendoza *(b. 1969) was born and raised in Los Angeles and attended college at the University of California at Santa Cruz (BA, 1988). Based in San Jose, Mendoza is a national investigative reporter for the Associated Press. Her work has appeared in the* Los Angeles Times, Houston Chronicle, Newsday, *and elsewhere. Mendoza is also the co-author of* The Bridge at No Gun Ri: A Hidden Nightmare from the Korean War *(2001). In 2000, she won a Pulitzer Prize for investigative reporting. In this essay, which appeared in* Ms. *magazine in 2004, Mendoza tells of her abortion while at the same time exploring broader medical, social, and legal issues.*

1   I could see my baby's amazing and perfect spine, a precise, pebbled curl of vertebrae. His little round skull. The curve of his nose. I could even see his small leg floating slowly through my uterus.

2   My doctor came in a moment later, slid the ultrasound sensor around my growing, round belly and put her hand on my shoulder. "It's not alive," she said.

3   She turned her back to me and started taking notes. I looked at the wall, breathing deeply, trying not to cry.

4   I can make it through this, I thought. I can handle this.

5   I didn't know I was about to become a pariah.

6   I was 19 weeks pregnant, strong, fit and happy, imagining our fourth child, the newest member of our family. He would have dark hair and bright eyes. He'd be intelligent and strong—really strong, judging by his early kicks.

7   And now this. Not alive?

8   I didn't realize that pressures well beyond my uterus, beyond the too-bright, too-loud, too-small ultrasound room, extending all the way to boardrooms of hospitals, administrative sessions at medical schools and committee hearings in Congress, were going to deepen and expand my sorrow and pain.

9   On November 6, 2003, President Bush signed what he called a "partial birth abortion ban," prohibiting doctors from committing an "overt act" designed to kill a partially delivered fetus. The law, which faces vigorous challenges, is the most significant change to the nation's abortion laws since the U.S. Supreme Court ruled abortion legal in *Roe v. Wade* in 1973. One of the unintended consequences of this new law is that it put people in my position, with a fetus that is already dead, in a technical limbo.

10   Legally, a doctor can still surgically take a dead body out of a pregnant woman. But in reality, the years of angry debate that led to the law's passage, restrictive

state laws and the violence targeting physicians have reduced the number of hospitals and doctors willing to do dilations and evacuations (D&Es) and dilations and extractions (intact D&Es), which involve removing a larger fetus, sometimes in pieces, from the womb.

At the same time, fewer medical schools are training doctors to do these 11 procedures. After all, why spend time training for a surgery that's likely to be made illegal?

At this point, 74 percent of obstetrics and gynecology residency programs do 12 *not* train all residents in abortion procedures, according to reproductive health researchers at the National Abortion Federation. Those that do usually teach only the first trimester abortion procedures such as dilation and curettage—D&C, the 15-minute uterine scraping. Fewer than 7 percent of obstetricians are trained to do D&Es, the procedure used on fetuses from about 13 to 19 weeks. Almost all the doctors doing them are over 50 years old.

"Finding a doctor who will do a D&E is getting very tough," says Ron Fitzsim- 13 mons, executive director of the National Coalition of Abortion Providers.

My doctor turned around and faced me. She told me that because dilation and evacu- 14 ation is rarely offered in my community, I could opt instead to chemically induce labor over several days and then deliver the little body at my local maternity ward.

"It's up to you," she said. 15

I'd been through labor and delivery three times before, with great joy as well 16 as pain, and the notion of going through that profound experience only to deliver a dead fetus (whose skin was already starting to slough off, whose skull might be collapsing) was horrifying.

I also did some research, spoke with friends who were obstetricians and 17 gynecologists, and quickly learned this: Study after study shows D&Es are *safer* than labor and delivery. Women who had D&Es were far less likely to have bleeding requiring transfusion, infection requiring intravenous antibiotics, organ injuries requiring additional surgery or cervical laceration requiring repair and hospital readmission. A review of 300 second-trimester abortions published in 2002 in the *American Journal of Obstetrics & Gynecology* found that 29 percent of women who went through labor and delivery had complications, compared with just 4 percent of those who had D&Es.

The American Medical Association said D&Es, compared to labor and 18 delivery, "may minimize trauma to the woman's uterus, cervix and other vital organs."

There was this fact, too: The intact D&E surgery makes less use of "grasp- 19 ing instruments," which could damage the body of the fetus. If the body were intact, doctors might be able to more easily figure out why my baby died in the womb.

I'm a healthy person. I run, swim and bike. I'm 37 years old and optimistic. 20 Good things happen to me. I didn't want to rule out having more kids, but I did want to know what went wrong before I tried again.

21   We told our doctor we had chosen a dilation and evacuation.

22   "I can't do these myself," said my doctor. "I trained at a Catholic hospital."

23   My doctor recommended a specialist in a neighboring county, but when I called for an appointment, they said they couldn't see me for almost a week.

24   I could feel my baby's dead body inside of mine. This baby had thrilled me with kicks and flutters, those first soft tickles of life bringing a smile to my face and my hand to my rounding belly. Now this baby floated, limp and heavy, from one side to the other, as I rolled in my bed. And within a day, I started to bleed. My body, with or without a doctor's help, was starting to expel the fetus. Technically, I was threatening a spontaneous abortion, the least safe of the available options.

25   I did what any pregnant patient would do. I called my doctor. And she advised me to wait.

26   I lay in my bed, not sleeping day or night, trying not to lose this little baby's body that my own womb was working to expel. Wait, I told myself. Just hold on. Let a doctor take this out. I was scared. Was it going to fall out of my body when I rose, in the middle of the night, to check on my toddler? Would it come apart on its own and double me over, knock me to the floor, as I stood at the stove scrambling eggs for my boys?

27   On my fourth morning, with the bleeding and cramping increasing, I couldn't wait any more. I called my doctor and was told that since I wasn't hemorrhaging, I should not come in. Her partner, on call, pedantically explained that women can safely lose a lot of blood, even during a routine period.

28   I began calling labor and delivery units at the top five medical centers in my area. I told them I had been 19 weeks along. The baby is dead. I'm bleeding, I said. I'm scheduled for a D&E in a few days. If I come in right now, what could you do for me, I asked.

29   Don't come in, they told me again and again. "Go to your emergency room if you are hemorrhaging to avoid bleeding to death. No one here can do a D&E today, and unless you're really in active labor you're safer to wait."

30   More than 66,000 women each year in the U.S. undergo an abortion at some point between 13 and 20 weeks, according to the Centers for Disease Control and Prevention. The CDC doesn't specify the physical circumstances of the women or their fetuses. Other CDC data shows that 4,000 women miscarry in their second trimester. Again, the data doesn't clarify whether those 4,000 women have to go through surgery.

31   Here's what is clear: Most of those women face increasingly limited access to care. One survey showed that half of the women who got abortions after 15 weeks of gestation said they were delayed because of problems in affording, finding or getting to abortion services. No surprise there; abortion is not readily available in 86 percent of the counties in the U.S.

32   Although there are some new, early diagnostic tests available, the most common prenatal screening for neural tube defects or Down syndrome is done around the 16th week of pregnancy. When problems are found—sometimes

life-threatening problems—pregnant women face the same limited options that I did.

At last I found one university teaching hospital that, at least over the telephone, was willing to take me. 33

"We do have one doctor who can do a D&E," they said. "Come in to our emergency room if you want." 34

But when I arrived at the university's emergency room, the source of the tension was clear. After examining me and confirming I was bleeding but not hemorrhaging, the attending obstetrician, obviously pregnant herself, defensively explained that only one of their dozens of obstetricians and gynecologists still does D&Es, and he was simply not available. Not today. Not tomorrow. Not the next day. No, I couldn't have his name. She walked away from me and called my doctor. 35

"You can't just dump these patients on us," she shouted into the phone, her high-pitched voice floating through the heavy curtains surrounding my bed. "You should be dealing with this yourself." 36

Shivering on the narrow, white exam table, I wondered what I had done wrong. Then I pulled back on my loose maternity pants and stumbled into the sunny parking lot, blinking back tears in the dazzling spring day, trying to understand the directions they sent me out with: Find a hotel within a few blocks from a hospital. Rest, monitor the bleeding. Don't go home—the 45-minute drive might be too far. 37

The next few days were a blur of lumpy motel beds, telephone calls to doctors, cramps. The pre-examination for my D&E finally arrived. First, the hospital required me to sign a legal form consenting to terminate the pregnancy. Then they explained I could, at no cost, have the remains incinerated by the hospital pathology department as medical waste, or for a fee have them taken to a funeral home for burial or cremation. 38

They inserted sticks of seaweed into my cervix and told me to go home for the night. A few hours later—when the contractions were regular, strong and frequent—I knew we needed to get to the hospital. 39

"The patient appeared to be in active labor," say my charts, "and I explained this to the patient and offered her pain medication for vaginal delivery." 40

According to the charts, I was "adamant" in demanding a D&E. I remember that I definitely wanted the surgical procedure that was the safest option. One hour later, just as an anesthesiologist was slipping me into unconsciousness, I had the D&E and a little body, my little boy, slipped out. Around his neck, three times and very tight, was the umbilical cord, source of his life, cause of his death. 41

This past spring, as the wildflowers started blooming around the simple cross we built for this baby, the Justice Department began trying to enforce the Bush administration's ban and federal courts in three different cities heard arguments regarding the new law. Doctors explained that D&Es are the safest 42 procedure in many cases, and that the law is particularly cruel to mothers like me whose babies were already dead. In hopes of bolstering their case, prosecutors sent federal subpoenas to various medical centers, asking for records of D&Es. There's an attorney somewhere, someday, who may poke through the files of my loss.

43   I didn't watch the trial because I had another appointment to keep—another ultrasound. Lying on the crisp white paper, watching the monitor, I saw new life, the incredible spine, tiny fingers waving slowly across my uterus, a perfect thigh. Best of all, there it was, a strong, four-chamber heart, beating steady and solid. A soft quiver, baby rolling, rippled across my belly.

44   "Everything looks wonderful," said my doctor. "This baby is doing great."

COMPREHENSION

1. Explain the nature and extent of Mendoza's "sorrow and pain" (paragraph 8).
2. What is "D&E"? What is Mendoza's understanding of the procedure, and how does she react to it?
3. What elements of government policy does Mendoza discuss, and why?

RHETORIC

1. Mendoza's title might contain more than one level of meaning. Would you agree or disagree? Explain.
2. Why does Mendoza begin with personal narrative and then switch to exposition? How does she sustain this back-and-forth movement between narration and exposition?
3. Do you think that Mendoza develops an argument in this essay or attempts to persuade readers to adopt a certain position regarding abortion? Or is she merely investigating, as a journalist, a procedure that she and many other women experience? Elaborate on your response.
4. Mendoza's essay appeared in a feminist magazine. Why would the article and the position that Mendoza stakes out appeal to *Ms.* readers?
5. What elements of investigative reporting do you find in this essay?
6. What is your response to the conclusion? What is Mendoza's purpose in using an emotional appeal at this end point in the essay?

WRITING

1. Investigate "partial birth abortion," and write an essay analyzing the process.
2. Write a personal essay recounting an illness or painful medical procedure that you or someone close to you experienced.
3. **Writing an Argument:** Argue for or against the proposition that abortion should be strictly a matter "between a woman and her doctor."

| **NETWORKING** | |
| *Applying Digital and Multimedia Literacies* | |

Evaluating Web Sites about Abortion: Visit the listed sites about abortion and write a paragraph-long evaluation of each.

In your assessment, note (1) what organization sponsors this Web site, (2) what that organization's agenda or purpose is, (3) what position the site/organization takes on abortion, (4) what they hope visitors will come away with from the site, and (5) how various features on the site—its design, use of visuals, use of interactive features, and so on—contribute to its goals.

- Planned Parenthood
- Abortionfacts.com
- database of information and articles in the *New York Times*
- Friends in Adoption
- East Side Gynecology
- Balanced Politics
- Whole World in His Hands
- StandUpGirl
- Feminists for Life
- NARAL
- About.com
- AdoptionTV.com

Naked

Atul Gawande

Atul Gawande (b. 1965) is a prize-winning author, journalist, physician, and advocate for national and global health causes. He was born in Brooklyn, New York, to Indian immigrant parents who were doctors. Gawande grew up in Athens, Ohio. He received his BA from Stanford University in 1987, and attended Balliol College, Oxford as a Rhodes Scholar. Gawande received his medical degree from Harvard Medical School in 1994. Today he is an endocrine surgeon and associate director of the Center for Surgery and Public Health at Brigham and Women's Hospital in Boston. He is also an associate professor at the Harvard School of Public Health and associate professor of surgery at Harvard Medical School. Active in Democratic politics, Gawande served in the Clinton administration as one of the directors of the Clinton Health Care Task Force. Gawande has been a staff writer for the New Yorker *since 1998, contributing articles on medicine and public health.*

He writes for other magazines as well, including the online publication Slate. *Among his books are* Complications: A Surgeon's Notes on an Imperfect Science *(2002) and* The Checklist Manifesto: How to Get Things Right *(2009). In "Naked," which appeared in the August 18, 2005 issue of the* New England Journal of Medicine, *Gawande offers global insights into delicate procedures.*

1 There is an exquisite and fascinating scene in *Kandahar*, a movie set in Afghanistan under the Taliban regime, in which a male physician is asked to examine a female patient. They are separated by an opaque screen. Behind it, the woman is covered from head to toe by her burka. The two do not talk directly to each other. The patient's young son serves as the go-between. She has a stomachache, he says.

2 "Does she throw up her food?" the doctor asks.

3 "Do you throw up your food?" the boy asks.

4 "No," the woman says, perfectly audibly, but the doctor waits as if he has not heard.

5 "No," the boy tells him.

6 For the exam, the doctor has cut a two-inch circle in the screen. "Tell her to come closer," he says. The boy does. She brings her mouth to the opening, and through it he looks inside. "Have her bring her eye to the hole," he says. And so the exam goes. Such, apparently, can be the demands of decency.

7 When I started my surgical practice two years ago, I was not at all clear about what my own etiquette of examination should be. Expectations are murky; we have no clear standards in the United States; and the topic can be fraught with hazards. Physical examination is deeply intimate, and the way a doctor deals with the naked body—particularly when the doctor is male and the patient female—inevitably raises questions of propriety and trust.

8 No one anywhere seems to have discovered the ideal approach. A surgical colleague who practices in Iraq told me about the customs of physical examination there. He said he feels no hesitation about examining female patients completely when necessary, but because a doctor and a patient of opposite sex cannot be alone together without eyebrows being raised, a family member will always accompany them for the exam. Women do not remove their clothes or change into a gown for the exam, and only a small portion of the body is uncovered at any one time. A nurse, he said, is rarely asked to chaperone: if the doctor is female, it is not necessary, and if male, the family is there to ensure that nothing unseemly occurs.

9 In Caracas, according to a Venezuelan doctor I met, female patients virtually always have a chaperone for a breast or pelvic exam, whether the physician is male or female. "That way there are no mixed messages," the doctor said. The chaperone, however, must be a medical professional. So the family is sent out of the examination room, and a nurse brought in. If a chaperone is unavailable or has refused to participate, the exam is not done.

10 A Ukrainian internist told me that she has not heard of doctors in Kiev using a chaperone. If a family member is present, he or she will be asked to leave. Both patient and doctor wear their uniforms—the patient a white examining gown, the doctor a white coat. Last names are always used. There is no effort at informality

to muddy the occasion. This practice, she believes, is enough to solidify trust and preclude misinterpretation of the conduct of care.

A doctor, it appears, has a range of options.   11

In 2003, I set up my clinic hours, and soon people arrived to see me. I was, I   12
realized, for the first time genuinely alone with patients. No attending physician in
the room or getting ready to come in; no bustle of emergency room personnel on
the other side of a curtain. Just a patient and me. We'd sit down. We'd talk. I'd ask
about whatever had occasioned the visit, about past medical problems, medica-
tions, the family and social history. Then the time would come to have a look.

There were, I will admit, some awkward moments. I had an instinctive aversion   13
to examination gowns. At our clinic they are made of either thin, ill-fitting cloth or
thin, ill-fitting paper. They seem designed to leave patients exposed and cold. I decided to examine my patients while they were in their street clothes. If a patient with
gallstones wore a shirt she could untuck for the abdominal exam, this worked fine.
But then I'd encounter a patient in stockings and a dress, and the next thing I knew,
I had her dress bunched up around her head, her tights around her knees, and both
of us wondering what the hell was going on. An exam for a breast lump one could
manage, in theory: the woman could unhook her brassiere and lift or unbutton her
shirt. But in practice, it just seemed weird. Even checking pulses could be a problem.
Pant legs could not be pushed up high enough. Try pulling them down over shoes,
however, and . . . forget it. I finally began to have patients change into the damn
gowns. (I haven't, however, asked men to do so nearly as often as women.)

As for having a chaperone present with female patients, I hadn't settled on a   14
firm policy. I found that I always asked a medical assistant to come in for pelvic
exams and generally didn't for breast exams. I was completely inconsistent about
rectal exams.

I surveyed my colleagues about what they do and received a variety of answers.   15
Many said they bring in a chaperone for all pelvic and rectal exams—"anything
below the waist"—but only rarely for breast exams. Others have a chaperone for
breast and pelvic exams but not for rectal exams. Some did not have a chaperone
at all. Indeed, an obstetrician-gynecologist estimated that about half the male
physicians in his department do not routinely use a chaperone. He himself detests
the word "chaperone" because it implies that mistrust is warranted, but he offers
to bring in an "assistant" for pelvic and breast exams. Few of his patients, however,
find the presence of the assistant necessary after the first exam, he said. If the
patient prefers to have her sister, boyfriend, or mother stay for the exam, he does
not object—but he is under no illusion that a family chaperone offers protection
against an accusation of misconduct. Instead, he relies on his reading of a patient
to determine whether bringing in a nurse-witness would be wise.

One of our residents, who was trained partly in London, said he found the   16
selectivity here strange. "In Britain, I would never examine a woman's abdomen
without a nurse present. But in the emergency room here, when I asked to have a
nurse come in when I needed to do a rectal exam or check groin nodes on a
woman, they thought I was crazy. 'Just go in there and do it!' they said." In
England, he said, "if you need to do a breast or rectal exam or even check femoral

pulses, especially on a young woman, you would be either foolish or stupid to do it without a chaperone. It doesn't take much—just one patient complaining, 'I came in with a foot pain and the doctor started diving around my groin,' and you could be suspended for a sexual-harassment investigation."

17   Britain's standards are stringent: the General Medical Council, the Royal College of Physicians, and the Royal College of Obstetricians and Gynaecologists specify that a chaperone must be offered to all patients who undergo an "intimate exam" (i.e., involving the breasts, genitalia, or rectum), irrespective of the sex of the patient or of the doctor.[1,2] A chaperone must be present when a male physician performs an intimate exam of a female patient. The chaperone should be a female member of the medical team, and her name should be recorded in the notes. If the patient refuses a chaperone and the examination is not urgent, it should be deferred until it can be performed by a female physician.

18   In the United States, we have no such guidelines. As a result, our patients have little idea of what to expect from us. To be sure, some minimal standards have been established. The Federation of State Medical Boards has spelled out that touching a patient's breasts or genitals for a purpose other than medical care is a disciplinable offense. So are oral contact with a patient, encouraging a patient to masturbate in one's presence, and providing services in exchange for sexual favors. Sexual impropriety which involves no touching but is no less proscribed includes asking a patient for a date, criticizing a patient's sexual orientation, making sexual comments about the patient's body or clothing, and initiating discussion of one's own sexual experiences or fantasies.[3] I can't say anyone taught me these boundaries in medical school, but I would like to think that no one needed to.

19   The difficulty for those of us who do not behave badly is that medical exams remain inherently ambiguous. Any patient can be led to wonder: Did the doctor really need to touch me there? Even when doctors simply inquire about patients' sexual history, can anyone be certain of the intent? The fact that all medical professionals have blushed or found their thoughts straying during a patient visit reveals the potential for impropriety in any encounter.

20   The tone of an office visit can turn on a single word, a joke, a comment about a tattoo in an unexpected place. One surgeon told me of a young patient who expressed concern about a lump in her "boob." But when he used the same word in response, she became extremely uncomfortable and later made a complaint. Another woman I know left her gynecologist after he made an off-hand, probably inadvertent, but admiring comment about her tan lines during a pelvic exam.

21   The examination itself—the how and where of the touching—is, of course, the most potentially dicey territory. If a patient even begins to doubt the propriety of what a doctor is doing, something is not right. So what then should our customs be?

[1]Intimate examinations. London: General Medical Council Standards Committee, December 2001.
[2]Gynaecological examinations: guidelines for specialist practice. London: Royal College of Obstetricians and Gynaecologists, July 2002.
[3]Ad Hoc Committee on Physician Impairment. Report on sexual boundary issues. Dallas: Federation of State Medical Boards of the United States, April,1996.

There are many reasons to consider setting tighter, more uniform profes- 22
sional standards. One is to protect patients from harm. About 4 percent of the
disciplinary orders that state medical boards issue against physicians are for
sex-related offenses. One of every 200 physicians is disciplined for sexual misconduct with patients sometime during his or her career.[4] Some of these cases
involve such outrageous acts as having intercourse with patients during pelvic
exams. The vast majority of cases involved male physicians and female patients,
and virtually all occurred without a chaperone present.[5] About one third of
cases studied in one state involved actual sexual intercourse with patients; two
thirds involved sexual impropriety or inappropriate touching short of sexual
contact. Another goal might be to reduce false accusations arising from misinterpretation.

Nonetheless, eliminating misconduct and accusations would be the wrong 23
aim to guide medical care. The trouble is not that such acts are rare (though the
statistics suggest they are), nor that total prevention—zero tolerance—is impossible. It is that, at some point, the measures required to achieve total prevention
will approach the Taliban-esque and harm care of patients.

Embracing more explicit standards for medical encounters, however, 24
might actually improve relationships with patients and that does stand as a
worthy goal. The new informality of medicine—with white coats disappearing,
and patient and doctor sometimes on a first-name basis—has blurred boundaries
that once guided us. If physicians are unsure about what is appropriate
behavior for themselves, is it any surprise that patients are, too? Or that misinterpretation can occur? We have jettisoned our old customs but have not bothered to replace them.

My father, a urologist, has thought carefully about how to avert such uncer- 25
tainties. From the start, he felt the fragility of his standing as an outsider, an
Indian immigrant practicing in a rural Ohio town. In the absence of guidelines
to reassure patients that what he does as a urologist is routine, he has made pains-
taking efforts to avoid question.

The process begins before the exam. He always arrives in a tie and white 26
coat. He is courtly. Although he often knows patients socially and doesn't hesitate
to speak with them about personal matters (the subjects can range from impotence to sexual affairs), he keeps his language strictly medical. If a female patient
must put on a gown, he steps out while she undresses. He makes a point of
explaining what he is going to do during the examination and why. If the patient
lies down and needs further unzipping or unbuttoning, he is careful not to help.
He wears gloves even for abdominal examinations. If the patient is female or
under 18 years of age, then he brings in a nurse as a chaperone, whether the
exam is "intimate" or not.

[4]Dehlendorf CE, Wolfe SM. Physicians disciplined for sex-related offenses. JAMA 1998; 279:1883-8.
[5]Enbom JA, Thomas CD. Evaluation of sexual misconduct complaints: the Oregon Board of Medical
Examiners, 1991 to 1995. Am J Obstet Gynecol 1997;176:1340-8.

27   His approach has succeeded. I grew up knowing many of his patients, and they trust him completely. I find, however, that some of his practices do not seem quite right for me. My patients are as likely to have problems above the waist as below, and having a chaperone present for a routine abdominal exam or a check of groin pulses feels to me absurd. I don't don gloves for nongenital exams. Nonetheless, I have tried to emulate the spirit of my father's visits—the decorum in language and attire, the respect for modesty, the precision of examination. As I think further about his example, it has also led me to make some changes: I now uniformly use an assistant not just for pelvic exams but also for rectal exams of female patients and as patients desire, for breast exams as well. For the comfort and reassurance of patients, these seem to be reasonable customs, even expectations, for more of us to accept.

28   A professor once told my medical school class that patients can tell when you've seen a thousand naked patients and when you haven't. I now know that's true. But I have also come to recognize that no patient has seen a thousand doctors. They therefore have little idea, coming to a doctor's office, of what is "normal" and what is not. This we can change.

COMPREHENSION

1. Circle, underline, or highlight the different approaches that physicians around the world take to the examination of their patients.
2. Summarize Gawande's findings about the role of "chaperones" during breast and pelvic examinations
3. What is Gawande's own approach to conducting patient examinations? Where did he learn this procedure? What are its characteristics?

RHETORIC

1. What is Gawande's thesis? Does any single sentence state the main idea? Explain.
2. How do the title and introductory anecdote serve to establish the tone of the essay? Do you find a uniform tone in this piece or does the author vary it? Justify your response by referring to specific passages.
3. A professional journal places formal and stylistic demands on a writer. Where do you find these requirements or expectations operating in the essay?
4. Why does Gawande personalize the essay? What is the effect?
5. Identify the author's use of process analysis, classification, comparison and contrast, and causal analysis. Is he successful in mixing so many rhetorical patterns in one essay? Why or why not?

WRITING

1. Imagine that you are a physician. Describe the process you would use to examine a patient.
2. Compose a textual analysis of the various rhetorical strategies that Gawande relies on to develop his essay. Evaluate his relative success.
3. **Writing an Argument:** Argue for or against the proposition that the United States should have a uniform code of conduct and standards for conducting physical examinations.

NETWORKING
Applying Digital and Multimedia Literacies

Hyperlinking a Summary: Download the code of conduct for physicians conducting examinations in Great Britain. Provide a hyperlinked précis of your findings, providing readers with links that help clarify or expand on your summary.

❋

The Terrifying Normalcy of AIDS

Stephen Jay Gould

Stephen Jay Gould *(1941–2002), an acclaimed contemporary science writer, taught biology, geology, and the history of science at Harvard University, where he was Alexander Agassiz Professor of Zoology. Born in New York City, he was educated at Antioch College (BA, 1963) and Columbia University (PhD, 1967). He wrote a monthly column, "This View of Life," for* Natural History *magazine and was the author of* Ever Since Darwin *(1977),* Ontogeny and Phylogeny *(1977),* The Panda's Thumb *(1980),* Wonderful Life *(1989),* Bully for Brontosaurus *(1991),* The Structure of Evolutionary Theory *(2002), and other books. In this 1987 essay, Gould explains in clear, precise language why AIDS is a "natural phenomenon" and warns against viewing it in moral terms.*

Disney's Epcot Center in Orlando, Fla., is a technological tour de force and a conceptual desert. In this permanent World's Fair, American industrial giants have built their versions of an unblemished future. These masterful entertainments convey but one message, brilliantly packaged and relentlessly expressed: Progress through technology is the solution to all human problems. G.E. proclaims from Horizons: "If we can dream it, we can do it." A.T.&T. speaks from on high within its giant golf ball: We are now "unbounded by space and time." United Technologies bubbles from the depths of Living Seas: "With the help of modern technology, we feel there's really no limit to what can be accomplished." 1

Yet several of these exhibits at the Experimental Prototype Community of Tomorrow, all predating last year's space disaster, belie their stated message from within by using the launch of the shuttle as a visual metaphor for technological triumph. The *Challenger* disaster may represent a general malaise, but it remains an incident. The AIDS pandemic, an issue that may rank with nuclear weaponry as the greatest danger of our era, provides a more striking proof that mind and technology are not omnipotent and that we have not canceled our bond to nature. 2

In 1984, John Platt, a biophysicist who taught at the University of Chicago for many years, wrote a short paper for private circulation. At a time when most of us 3 were either ignoring AIDS, or viewing it as a contained and peculiar affliction of homosexual men, Platt recognized that the limited data on the origin of AIDS and its spread in America suggested a more frightening prospect: We are all susceptible to AIDS, and the disease has been spreading in a simple exponential manner.

4   Exponential growth is a geometric increase. Remember the old kiddy problem: If you place a penny on square one of a checkerboard and double the number of coins on each subsequent square—2, 4, 8, 16, 32 . . .—how big is the stack by the sixty-fourth square? The answer: about as high as the universe is wide. Nothing in the external environment inhibits this increase, thus giving to exponential processes their relentless character. In the real, noninfinite world, of course, some limit will eventually arise, and the process slows down, reaches a steady state, or destroys the entire system: The stack of pennies falls over, the bacterial cells exhaust their supply of nutrients.

5   Platt noticed that data for the initial spread of AIDS fell right on an exponential curve. He then followed the simplest possible procedure of extrapolating the curve unabated into the 1990's. Most of us were incredulous, accusing Platt of the mathematical gamesmanship that scientists call "curve fitting." After all, aren't exponential models unrealistic? Surely we are not all susceptible to AIDS. Is it not spread only by odd practices to odd people? Will it not, therefore, quickly run its short course within a confined group?

6   Well, hello 1987—worldwide data still match Platt's extrapolated curve. This will not, of course, go on forever. AIDS has probably already saturated the African areas where it probably originated, and where the sex ratio of afflicted people is 1-to-1, male-female. But AIDS still has far to spread, and may be moving exponentially, through the rest of the world. We have learned enough about the cause of AIDS to slow its spread, if we can make rapid and fundamental changes in our handling of that most powerful part of human biology—our own sexuality. But medicine, as yet, has nothing to offer as a cure and precious little even for palliation.

7   This exponential spread of AIDS not only illuminates its, and our, biology, but also underscores the tragedy of our moralistic misperception. Exponential processes have a definite time and place of origin, an initial point of "inoculation"—in this case, Africa. We didn't notice the spread at first. In a population of billions, we pay little attention when one increases to two, or eight to sixteen, but when one million becomes two million, we panic, even though the *rate* of doubling has not increased.

8   The infection has to start somewhere, and its initial locus may be little more than an accident of circumstance. For a while, it remains confined to those in close contact with the primary source, but only by accident of proximity, not by intrinsic susceptibility. Eventually, given the power and lability of human sexuality, it spreads outside the initial group and into the general population. And now AIDS has begun its march through our own heterosexual community.

9   What a tragedy that our moral stupidity caused us to lose precious time, the greatest enemy in fighting an exponential spread, by down-playing the danger because we thought that AIDS was a disease of three irregular groups of

minorities: minorities of life style (needle users), of sexual preference (homosexuals) and of color (Haitians). If AIDS had first been imported from Africa into a Park Avenue apartment, we would not have dithered as the exponential march began.

The message of Orlando—the inevitability of technological solutions—is 10 wrong, and we need to understand why.

Our species has not won its independence from nature, and we cannot do all 11 that we can dream. Or at least we cannot do it at the rate required to avoid tragedy, for we are not unbounded from time. Viral diseases are preventable in principle, and I suspect that an AIDS vaccine will one day be produced. But how will this discovery avail us if it takes until the millennium, and by then AIDS has fully run its exponential course and saturated our population, killing a substantial percentage of the human race? A fight against an exponential enemy is primarily a race against time.

We must also grasp the perspective of ecology and evolutionary biology 12 and recognize, once we reinsert ourselves properly into nature, that AIDS represents the ordinary workings of biology, not an irrational or diabolical plague with a moral meaning. Disease, including epidemic spread, is a natural phenomenon, part of human history from the beginning. An entire subdiscipline of my profession, paleopathology, studies the evidence of ancient diseases preserved in the fossil remains of organisms. Human history has been marked by episodic plagues. More native peoples died of imported disease than ever fell before the gun during the era of colonial expansion. Our memories are short, and we have had a respite, really, only since the influenza pandemic at the end of World War I, but AIDS must be viewed as a virulent expression of an ordinary natural phenomenon.

I do not say this to foster either comfort or complacency. The evolutionary 13 perspective is correct, but utterly inappropriate for our human scale. Yes, AIDS is a natural phenomenon, one of a recurring class of pandemic diseases. Yes, AIDS may run through the entire population, and may carry off a quarter or more of us. Yes, it may make no *biological* difference to Homo sapiens in the long run: There will still be plenty of us left and we can start again. Evolution cares as little for its agents—organisms struggling for reproductive success—as physics cares for individual atoms of hydrogen in the sun. But we care. These atoms are our neighbors, our lovers, our children and ourselves. AIDS is both a natural phenomenon and, potentially, the greatest natural tragedy in human history.

The cardboard message of Epcot fosters the wrong attitudes: We must both re- 14 insert ourselves into nature and view AIDS as a natural phenomenon in order to fight properly. If we stand above nature and if technology is all-powerful, then AIDS is a horrifying anomaly that must be trying to tell us something. If so, we can adopt one of two attitudes, each potentially fatal. We can either become complacent, because we believe the message of Epcot and assume that medicine will soon generate a cure, or we can panic in confusion and seek a scapegoat for something so irregular that it must have been visited upon us to teach us a moral lesson.

15   But AIDS is not irregular. It is part of nature. So are we. This should galvanize us and give us hope, not prompt the worst of all responses: a kind of "new-age" negativism that equates natural with what we must accept and cannot, or even should not, change. When we view AIDS as natural, and when we recognize both the exponential property of its spread and the accidental character of its point of entry into America, we can break through our destructive tendencies to blame others and to free ourselves of concern.

16   If AIDS is natural, then there is no message in its spread. But by all that science has learned and all that rationality proclaims, AIDS works by a *mechanism*— and we can discover it. Victory is not ordained by any principle of progress, or any slogan of technology, so we shall have to fight like hell, and be watchful. There is no message, but there is a mechanism.

COMPREHENSION

1. What does Gould mean when he defines AIDS as a "natural phenomenon" (paragraph 12)? How does the title support this definition?
2. What does Gould mean by "our moral stupidity" in paragraph 9?
3. What connection does Gould make between our reaction to the AIDS crisis and our alienation from nature?

RHETORIC

1. What is Gould's main idea? Where in the essay is it stated?
2. What is the purpose of paragraphs 1 and 2? How do they contribute to Gould's argument? How do they help establish the tone of the essay? What is the tone? What is the importance of Epcot Center to Gould's thesis?
3. Gould uses scientific terminology in his essay. Define the words *exponential* (paragraph 3) and *pandemic* and *phenomenon* (paragraph 13). Is this essay intended for a specialized audience? Justify your response.
4. Trace the progression of ideas in paragraphs 2–5. What transitions does Gould employ?
5. Does Gould use rhetorical strategies besides argument in his essay? Cite evidence of this varied rhetorical approach.
6. Explain the final sentence in Gould's conclusion. What is its relation to the paragraph as a whole?

WRITING

1. Gould states that we must "reinsert ourselves into nature" (paragraph 14). What does he mean by this? How would this affect the way in which we deal with disease and death in our society? Explore this issue in a brief essay.
2. Write an extended definition of HIV/AIDS, attempting to avoid moralizing about the subject. Conduct research if necessary.
3. **Writing an Argument:** Write an essay in which you expand on Gould's belief that our moral stupidity has not only hindered society's recognition of the AIDS threat but continues to impede AIDS research and treatment.

NETWORKING
Applying Digital and Multimedia Literacies

Creating an Informational Web Page: After completing question 2 under Writing, write and design a single Web page that defines and provides important at-a-glance information about HIV/AIDS. Its purpose should be to inform the public by providing facts and dispelling harmful myths; it should *not* make an argument. Incorporate one image and provide a few select hyperlinks.

The Globalization of Eating Disorders

Susan Bordo

Susan Bordo (b. 1947) was born in Newark, New Jersey, and was educated at Carleton University (BA, 1972) and the State University of New York at Stony Brook (PhD, 1982). She is the Singletary Chair in the Humanities and a professor of English and women's studies at the University of Kentucky. A feminist philosopher and interdisciplinary scholar who focuses on Western culture's attitudes toward gender and the body, Bordo has written The Flight to Objectivity: Essays on Cartesianism and Culture *(1987),* Unbearable Weight: Feminism, Western Culture, and the Body *(1993, 2004),* Twilight Zones: The Hidden Life of Cultural Images from Plato to O.J. *(1997), and* The Male Body: A New Look at Men in Public and in Private *(1999). In this selection, Bordo offers an overview of a new kind of epidemic, fueled by Western media images, that is affecting cultures around the world.*

The young girl stands in front of the mirror. Never fat to begin with, she's been on 1 a no-fat diet for a couple of weeks and has reached her goal weight: 115 lb., at 5′4″—exactly what she should weigh, according to her doctor's chart. But in her eyes she still looks dumpy. She can't shake her mind free of the "Lady Marmelade" video from Moulin Rouge. Christina Aguilera, Pink, L'il Kim, and Mya, each one perfect in her own way: every curve smooth and sleek, lean-sexy, nothing to spare. Self-hatred and shame start to burn in the girl, and envy tears at her stomach, enough to make her sick. She'll never look like them, no matter how much weight she loses. Look at that stomach of hers, see how it sticks out? Those thighs—they actually jiggle. Her butt is monstrous. She's fat, gross, a dough girl.

As you read the imaginary scenario above, whom did you picture standing in 2 front of the mirror? If your images of girls with eating and body image problems have been shaped by *People* magazine and Lifetime movies, she's probably white, North American, and economically secure. A child whose parents have never had to worry about putting food on the family table. A girl with money to spare for fashion magazines and trendy clothing, probably college-bound. If you're familiar with the classic psychological literature on eating disorders, you may also have read that she's an extreme "perfectionist" with a hyper-demanding mother, and that she suffers from "body-image distortion syndrome" and other severe perceptual and cognitive problems that "normal" girls don't share. You probably don't picture her as Black, Asian, or Latina.

3   Read the description again, but this time imagine twenty-something Tenisha Williamson standing in front of the mirror. Tenisha is black, suffers from anorexia, and feels like a traitor to her race. "From an African-American standpoint," she writes, "we as a people are encouraged to embrace our big, voluptuous bodies. This makes me feel terrible because I don't want a big, voluptuous body! I don't ever want to be fat—ever, and I don't ever want to gain weight. I would rather die from starvation than gain a single pound."[1] Tenisha is no longer an anomaly. Eating and body image problems are now not only crossing racial and class lines, but gender lines. They have also become a global phenomenon.

4   Fiji is a striking example. Because of their remote location, the Fiji islands did not have access to television until 1995, when a single station was introduced. It broadcasts programs from the United States, Great Britain, and Australia. Until that time, Fiji had no reported cases of eating disorders, and a study conducted by anthropologist Anne Becker showed that most Fijian girls and women, no matter how large, were comfortable with their bodies. In 1998, just three years after the station began broadcasting, 11 percent of girls reported vomiting to control weight, and 62 percent of the girls surveyed reported dieting during the previous months.[2]

5   Becker was surprised by the change; she had thought that Fijian cultural traditions, which celebrate eating and favor voluptuous bodies, would "withstand" the influence of media images. Becker hadn't yet understood that we live in an empire of images, and that there are no protective borders.

6   In Central Africa, for example, traditional cultures still celebrate voluptuous women. In some regions, brides are sent to fattening farms, to be plumped and massaged into shape for their wedding night. In a country plagued by AIDS, the skinny body has meant—as it used to among Italian, Jewish, and Black Americans—poverty, sickness, death. "An African girl must have hips," says dress designer Frank Osodi, "We have hips. We have bums. We like flesh in Africa." For years, Nigeria sent its local version of beautiful to the Miss World Competition. The contestants did very poorly. Then a savvy entrepreneur went against local ideals and entered Agbani Darego, a light-skinned, hyper-skinny beauty. (He got his inspiration from M-Net, the South African network seen across Africa on satellite television, which broadcasts mostly American movies and television shows.) Agbani Darego won the Miss World Pageant, the first Black African to do so. Now, Nigerian teenagers fast and exercise, trying to become "lepa"—a popular slang phrase for the thin "it" girls that are all the rage. Said one: "People have realized that slim is beautiful."[3]

[1]From the Colours of Ana website (http://coloursofana.com//ss8.asp).
[2]Reported in Nancy Snyderman, *The Girl in the Mirror* (New York: Hyperion, 2002), p. 84.
[3]Norimistsu Onishi, "Globalization of Beauty Makes Slimness Trendy," *The New York Times,* Oct. 3, 2002.

How can mere images be so powerful? For one thing, they are never "just 7 pictures," as the fashion magazines continually maintain (disingenuously) in their own defense. They speak to young people not just about how to be beautiful but also about how to become what the dominant culture admires, values, rewards. They tell them how to be cool, "get it together," overcome their shame. To girls who have been abused they may offer a fantasy of control and invulnerability, immunity from pain and hurt. For racial and ethnic groups whose bodies have been deemed "foreign," earthy, and primitive, and considered unattractive by Anglo-Saxon norms, they may cast the lure of being accepted as "normal" by the dominant culture.

In today's world, it is through images—much more than parents, teachers, or 8 clergy—that we are taught how to be. And it is images, too, that teach us how to see, that educate our vision in what's a defect and what is normal, that give us the models against which our own bodies and the bodies of others are measured. Perceptual pedagogy: "How to Interpret Your Body 101." It's become a global requirement.

I was intrigued, for example, when my articles on eating disorders began to be 9 translated, over the past few years, into Japanese and Chinese. Among the members of audiences at my talks, Asian women had been among the most insistent that eating and body image weren't problems for their people, and indeed, my initial research showed that eating disorders were virtually unknown in Asia. But when, this year, a Korean translation of *Unbearable Weight* was published, I felt I needed to revisit the situation. I discovered multiple reports on dramatic increases in eating disorders in China, South Korea, and Japan. "As many Asian countries become Westernized and infused with the Western aesthetic of a tall, thin, lean body, a virtual tsunami of eating disorders has swamped Asian countries," writes Eunice Park in *Asian Week* magazine. Older people can still remember when it was very different. In China, for example, where revolutionary ideals once condemned any focus on appearance and there have been several disastrous famines, "little fatty" was a term of endearment for children. Now, with fast food on every corner, childhood obesity is on the rise, and the cultural meaning of fat and thin has changed. "When I was young," says Li Xiaojing, who manages a fitness center in Beijing, "people admired and were even jealous of fat people since they thought they had a better life. . . . But now, most of us see a fat person and think 'He looks awful.'"[4]

Clearly, body insecurity can be exported, imported, and marketed—just like 10 any other profitable commodity. In this respect, what's happened with men and boys is illustrative. Ten years ago men tended, if anything, to see themselves as better looking than they (perhaps) actually were. And then (as I chronicle in detail in my book *The Male Body*) the menswear manufacturers, the diet industries, and the plastic surgeons "discovered" the male body. And now, young guys are looking in their mirrors, finding themselves soft and ill defined, no matter how muscular they are. Now they are developing the eating and body image disorders that we once thought only girls had. Now they are abusing steroids, measuring their own muscularity against the oiled and perfected images of professional

[4]Reported in Elizabeth Rosenthal, "Beijing Journal: China's Chic Waistline: Convex to Concave," *The New York Times,* Dec. 9, 1999.

athletes, body-builders, and *Men's Health* models. Now the industries in body-enhancement—cosmetic surgeons, manufacturers of anti-aging creams, spas and salons—are making huge bucks off men, too.

11   What is to be done? I have no easy answers. But I do know that we need to acknowledge, finally and decisively, that we are dealing here with a cultural problem. If eating disorders were biochemical, as some claim, how can we account for their gradual "spread" across race, gender, and nationality? And with mass media culture increasingly providing the dominant "public education" in our children's lives—and those of children around the globe—how can we blame families? Families matter, of course, and so do racial and ethnic traditions. But families exist in cultural time and space—and so do racial groups. In the empire of images, no one lives in a bubble of self-generated "dysfunction" or permanent immunity. The sooner we recognize that—and start paying attention to the culture around us and what it is teaching our children—the sooner we can begin developing some strategies for change.

COMPREHENSION

1. How does Bordo define the "body-image distortion syndrome" (paragraph 2)?
2. Why have body image and weight problems become a global phenomenon? What is the main cause of this phenomenon?
3. How, according to the author, should we deal with the globalization of eating disorders?

RHETORIC

1. How does the author establish herself as an authority on her subject? Do you think that she succeeds? Why or why not?
2. What is the writer's claim? Where does she place it, and why?
3. Bordo begins with an imaginary situation. Does this strategy enhance or detract from the validity of her argument? Justify your response.
4. The writer uses several rhetorical strategies to advance her argument. Identify places where she employs description, illustration, comparison and contrast, and causal analysis.
5. The writer has been praised for her readable or accessible style. Do you think that this essay is well written and thought provoking? Explain.
6. How does Bordo develop this selection as a problem-solution essay? Where does the solution appear, and how effective is its placement within the essay?

WRITING

1. Write a causal essay analyzing young Americans' fascination with body image and the consequences of this preoccupation.
2. Why are women in the United States and around the world more susceptible to eating disorders than men? Answer this question in an analytical essay.
3. **Writing an Argument:** Write an essay titled "Body Images, Eating Disorders, and Cultural Imperialism." In this essay, argue for or against the proposition that American media are exporting potentially unhealthy images of the human body.

NETWORKING
Applying Digital and Multimedia Literacies

Critiquing a Web Site about Eating Disorders: Choose one of the following Web sites and write a careful critique of both its purpose and its effectiveness at achieving that purpose.

Depending on the site you choose and your opinions, your critique might be favorable, mixed, or denunciatory. Whatever your position, it should be carefully illustrated with examples from the Web site, and your points of agreement or contention should be supported by other sources.

- Eating Disorder Research Center
- Women's Health
- Remuda Ranch
- Face the Issue
- Something Fishy
- Family Doctor
- Healthy Place
- ProAnaBlog
- National Eating Disorders Association

Synthesis: Connections for Critical Thinking

1. Research the current status of public health in the United States and what is being done to prevent major outbreaks of disease. Refer to at least three essays in this chapter to support your findings and thesis.
2. Compare approaches to women's health issues as discussed by several writers in this chapter, notably Gawande, Mendoza, and Bordo.
3. Compare and contrast the strategies that Gawande, Hitchens, and Bordo use to develop their arguments.
4. Referring to any three essays in this chapter, analyze some of the major moral, ethical, and religious issues raised by current medical research.
5. Compare and contrast the treatment of death in the essays by Tuchman, Lepore, and Selzer.
6. Compare and contrast the essays by Gawande and Bordo.
7. Research the subject of AIDS, and connect your findings to the essays by Tuchman and Gould.
8. Working with three other class members, develop a PowerPoint presentation informing your college about a health issue of campus concern.

NETWORKING
Applying Digital and Multimedia Literacies

1. Compare and contrast two Web sites devoted to some aspect of medicine and health—for example, stem-cell research, abortion, funeral practices, cosmetic surgery, or dieting.
2. Explore the World Health Organization Web site (*www.who.int/en*), and summarize what you find about global pandemics.

chapter *13*

Nature and the Environment

How Do We Relate to the Natural World?

We are at a point in the history of civilization where consciousness of our fragile relationship with nature and the environment is high. Even as you spend an hour reading a few of the essays in this chapter, it is estimated that we are losing 3,000 acres of rain forest around the world and four species of plants or animals. From pollution, to the population explosion, to the depletion of the ozone layer, to global climate change, we seem to be confronted with ecological catastrophe. Nevertheless, as Rachel Carson reminds us, we have "an obligation to endure," to survive potential natural catastrophes by understanding and managing our relationship with the natural world.

Ecology, or the study of nature and the environment, as many of the essayists in this chapter attest, involves us in the conservation of the earth. It moves us to suppress our rapacious destruction of the planet. Clearly, the biological stability of the planet is increasingly precarious. More plants, insects, birds, and animals became extinct in the 20th century than in any era since the Cretaceous catastrophe more than 65 million years ago that led to the extinction of the dinosaurs. Within this ecological context, writers like Carson become our literary conscience, reminding us of how easily natural processes can break down unless we insist on a degree of ecological economy.

Of course, any modification of human behavior in an effort to conserve nature is a complex matter. To save the spotted owl in the Pacific Northwest, we must sacrifice the jobs of people in the timber industry. To reduce pollution, we must forsake gas and oil for alternate energy sources that are costly to develop. To reduce the waste stream, we must shift from a consumption to a conservation ethos. The ecological debate is complicated, but it is clear that the preservation of the myriad life cycles on earth is crucial, for we, too, could become an endangered species.

The language of nature is as enigmatic as the sounds of dolphins and whales communicating with their respective species. Writers like Barry Lopez and Rachel Carson and the vision expressed in the letter of Chief Seattle help us decipher the language of our environment. These writers encourage us to converse with nature, learn from it, and even revere it. All of us are guests on this planet; the natural world is our host. If we do not protect the earth, how can we guarantee the survival of civilization?

PREVIEWING THE CHAPTER

As you read the essays in this chapter and respond to them in discussion and writing, consider the following questions:

- According to the author, what should our relationship to the natural world be?
- What claims or arguments does the author make about the importance of nature? Do you agree or disagree with these claims and arguments?
- What specific ecological problem does the author investigate?
- How does the author think that nature influences human behavior?
- What cultural factors are involved in our approach to the environment?
- Is the writer optimistic, pessimistic, or neutral in the assessment of our ability to conserve nature?
- Do you find that the author is too idealistic or sentimental in the depiction of nature? Why?
- Based on the author's essay, how does he or she qualify as a nature writer?
- How have you been challenged or changed by the essays in this chapter?

Classic and Contemporary Images
ARE WE DESTROYING OUR NATURAL WORLD?

Using a Critical Perspective   Imagine yourself to be part of each of the scenes depicted in these two illustrations. How do you feel, and why? Now examine the purpose of each image. What details do the artists emphasize to convey their feelings about our relationship to the natural world? What images does each artist create to capture your attention and direct your viewing and thinking toward a specific, dominant impression?

The painters of the Hudson River School such as John Frederick Kensett (1816–1872) celebrated American landscapes in their art, painting breathtaking scenes in meticulous detail. In *Along the Hudson* (1852), the beauty of the river is unspoiled.

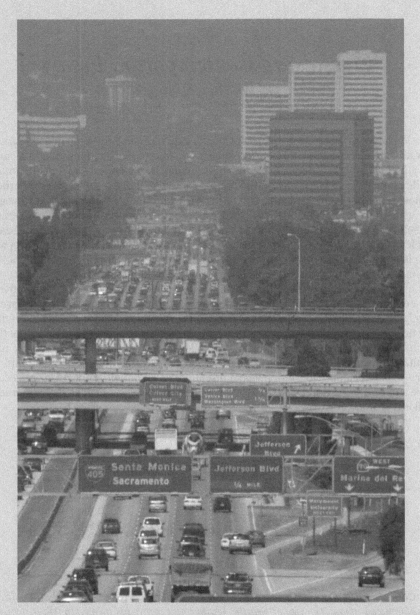

Vehicles travel on the 405 Freeway where it intersects with the 10 West Freeway in Los Angeles. California could take the lead in the international effort to reduce global warming after the state's Air Resources Board gave approval to a package of regulations that would cut vehicle emissions by as much as 25 percent.

Classic and Contemporary Essays
DO WE OWN NATURE?

The simple yet passionate reflections of Chief Seattle regarding the destruction of a world-view are complemented by the more scholarly and learned meditations, nearly a century and a half later, of the esteemed naturalist and writer Barry Lopez. Chief Seattle mourns the death of a way of life, a way of thinking, and a way of being as he accepts that the cultural world of his people is doomed to disappear with the encroachment of "civilization." The white man exploits nature, uses nature, and perhaps most radically of all, perceives himself as apart from nature. This is in profound contrast to the ways of Chief Seattle's people, who saw themselves as in harmony with nature or, more specifically, as inseparable from it—as inseparable perhaps as from a part of their own bodies. Chief Seattle's address is simple. And so perhaps is his message, although one should not confuse simplicity with lack of profundity. Barry Lopez has a similar message. Writing from the perspective of a 21st-century naturalist and teacher, Lopez speaks of "a sense of responsibility toward children." He urges adults to both teach and learn from children about the wonders of nature and how the natural world can inform us about our human condition. With a personal touch, Lopez recounts key encounters with children and nature, finding evidence of that union with nature that Chief Seattle spoke of so eloquently. Although Chief Seattle and Barry Lopez speak in different levels of discourse and from different perspectives, they share an awe of nature and a desire to inform their respective audiences of the sacredness of all life.

Letter to President Pierce, 1855

Chief Seattle

Chief Seattle (1786–1866) was the leader of the Dewamish and other Pacific Northwest tribes. The city of Seattle, Washington, bears his name. In 1854, Chief Seattle reluctantly agreed to sell tribal lands to the U.S. government and move to the government-established reservations. The authenticity of the following speech has been challenged by many scholars. However, most specialists agree that it contains the substance and perspective of Chief Seattle's attitude toward nature and the white race.

1   We know that the white man does not understand our ways. One portion of the land is the same to him as the next, for he is a stranger who comes in the night and takes from the land whatever he needs. The earth is not his brother, but his enemy, and

when he has conquered it, he moves on. He leaves his fathers' graves, and his children's birthright is forgotten. The sight of your cities pains the eyes of the red man. But perhaps it is because the red man is a savage and does not understand.

There is no quiet place in the white man's cities. No place to hear the leaves 2 of spring or the rustle of insect's wings. But perhaps because I am a savage and do not understand, the clatter only seems to insult the ears. The Indian prefers the soft sound of the wind darting over the face of the pond, the smell of the wind itself cleansed by a mid-day rain, or scented with the piñon pine. The air is precious to the red man. For all things share the same breath—the beasts, the trees, the man. Like a man dying for many days, he is numb to the stench.

What is man without the beasts? If all the beasts were gone, men would die from 3 great loneliness of spirit, for whatever happens to the beasts also happens to man. All things are connected. Whatever befalls the earth befalls the sons of the earth.

It matters little where we pass the rest of our days; they are not many. A few 4 more hours, a few more winters, and none of the children of the great tribes that once lived on this earth, or that roamed in small bands in the woods, will be left to mourn the graves of a people once as powerful and hopeful as yours.

The whites, too, shall pass—perhaps sooner than other tribes. Continue to 5 contaminate your bed, and you will one night suffocate in your own waste. When the buffalo are all slaughtered, the wild horses all tamed, the secret corners of the forest heavy with the scent of many men, and the view of the ripe hills blotted by talking wires, where is the thicket? Gone. Where is the eagle? Gone. And what is it to say goodbye to the swift and the hunt, the end of living and the beginning of survival? We might understand if we knew what it was that the white man dreams, what he describes to his children on the long winter nights, what visions he burns into their minds, so they will wish for tomorrow. But we are savages. The white man's dreams are hidden from us.

COMPREHENSION

1. What does Chief Seattle suggest is the major difference between the white man's relationship with nature and that of the red man?
2. Chief Seattle claims that perhaps the red man would understand the white man better if he understood better the "dreams" and "visions" of the white man. What does Chief Seattle suggest by these terms?
3. Chief Seattle refers to Native Americans as "savages." Why?

RHETORIC

1. The author uses a number of sensory details in describing both nature and the white man's crimes against nature. How does the eliciting of sensations help determine the relationship between writer, text, and reader?
2. The letter is written simply, with simply constructed paragraphs and sentences. What does this style suggest about the writer's voice?

3. There is a noted absence of transitional expressions in the writing, that is, such linking words as *in addition, furthermore, nevertheless,* and *moreover.* How does this absence contribute to the directness of the writing?

4. The author uses the convention of the series, as in the following examples: "For all things share the same breath—the beasts, the trees, the man" (paragraph 2) and "When the buffalo are all slaughtered, the wild horses all tamed, the secret corners of the forest heavy with the scent of many men, and the view of the ripe hills blotted by talking wires" (paragraph 5). What is the rhetorical effect of this device?

5. Note the opening and closing sentences of the letter. How do they frame the letter? What do they suggest about one of its major themes?

6. Some scholars dispute the authenticity of the letter, attributing it to a white man who was attempting to articulate the essence of Chief Seattle's oratory in an effort to champion Native American causes. What elements of the letter resemble the rhetorical elements of a speech?

WRITING

1. Write a 250-word summary in which you compare and contrast the major differences between the white man's and the red man's perception of and relationship to nature as conceived by Chief Seattle.

2. For a research project, trace the use of the word *savage* as it has been used to describe Native Americans.

3. **Writing an Argument:** Argue for or against the view that the charge by Chief Seattle that the white man is contemptuous of nature is still valid today. Use at least three points to support your thesis.

NETWORKING
Applying Digital and Multimedia Literacies

Writing a Radio PSA: Public service announcements, or PSAs, which you've likely heard on your campus radio station or NPR, are advertisements designed to raise awareness about issues, not sell products or services. Draft a PSA that informs or educates the public about an environmental issue.

Children in the Woods

Barry Lopez

Barry Lopez (b. 1945) was born in New York City but grew up in southern California's San Fernando Valley, which at the time was still largely rural. He attended the University of Notre Dame (BA, 1966) and the University of Oregon (MA, 1968), and he pursued additional graduate work before starting a career as a full-time writer. Lopez's early essays in such periodicals as National Geographic, Wilderness, Science, *and* Harper's *established him as an authoritative voice in the environmental movement. His first major nonfiction work,* Of Wolves and Men *(1978), brought him national acclaim, an American Book Award nomination, and the John Burroughs medal for nature writing. His venture into fiction with* River Notes: The Dance of Herons *(1979) and* Winter Count *(1980) were also well received. Among Lopez's other books are* Arctic Dreams: Imagination and Desire in a Northern Landscape *(1986),* Crossing Open Ground *(1988),* The Rediscovery of North America *(1991),* Crow and Weasel *(1999), the autobiography* About This Life *(1999), and a short-story collection,* Resistance *(2004). Lopez sees himself as a storyteller, someone who has the responsibility to create an atmosphere in which the wisdom of the work can reveal itself and, as he has written, "make the reader feel part of something." In this essay from his collection* Crossing Open Ground, *Lopez sets himself and other children in the natural world in order to discover their own part of something.*

When I was a child growing up in the San Fernando Valley in California, a trip into   1
Los Angeles was special. The sensation of movement from a rural area into an urban one was sharp. On one of these charged occasions, walking down a sidewalk with my mother, I stopped suddenly, caught by a pattern of sunlight trapped in a spiraling imperfection in a windowpane. A stranger, an elderly woman in a cloth coat and a dark hat, spoke out spontaneously, saying how remarkable it is that children notice these things.

I have never forgotten the texture of this incident. Whenever I recall it I am   2
moved not so much by any sense of my young self but by a sense of responsibility toward children, knowing how acutely I was affected in that moment by that woman's words. The effect, for all I know, has lasted a lifetime.

Now, years later, I live in a rain forest in western Oregon, on the banks of a   3
mountain river in relatively undisturbed country, surrounded by 150-foot-tall Douglas firs, delicate deer-head orchids, and clearings where wild berries grow. White-footed mice and mule deer, mink and coyote move through here. My wife and I do not have children, but children we know, or children whose parents we are close to, are often here. They always want to go into the woods. And I wonder what to tell them.

In the beginning, years ago, I think I said too much. I spoke with an encyclo-   4
pedic knowledge of the names of plants or the names of birds passing through in season. Gradually I came to say less. After a while the only words I spoke, beyond answering a question or calling attention quickly to the slight difference between a sprig of red cedar and a sprig of incense cedar, were to elucidate single objects.

I remember once finding a fragment of a raccoon's jaw in an alder thicket. I   5
sat down alongside the two children with me and encouraged them to find out who this was—with only the three teeth still intact in a piece of the animal's maxilla to guide them. The teeth told by their shape and placement what this animal ate. By a kind of visual extrapolation its size became clear. There were other clues, immediately present, which told, with what I could add of climate and terrain, how

this animal lived, how its broken jaw came to be lying here. Raccoon, they surmised. And tiny tooth marks along the bone's broken edge told of a mouse's hunger for calcium.

6   We set the jaw back and went on.

7   If I had known more about raccoons, finer points of osteology, we might have guessed more: say, whether it was male or female. But what we deduced was all we needed. Hours later, the maxilla, lost behind us in the detritus of the forest floor, continued to effervesce. It was tied faintly to all else we spoke of that afternoon.

8   In speaking with children who might one day take a permanent interest in natural history—as writers, as scientists, as filmmakers, as anthropologists—I have sensed that an extrapolation from a single fragment of the whole is the most invigorating experience I can share with them. I think children know that nearly anyone can learn the names of things; the impression made on them at this level is fleeting. What takes a lifetime to learn, they comprehend, is the existence and substance of myriad relationships: It is these relationships, not the things themselves, that ultimately hold the human imagination.

9   The brightest children, it has often struck me, are fascinated by metaphor—with what is shown in the set of relationships bearing on the raccoon, for example, to lie quite beyond the raccoon. In the end, you are trying to make clear to them that everything found at the edge of one's senses—the high note of the winter wren, the thick perfume of propolis that drifts downwind from spring willows, the brightness of wood chips scattered by beaver—that all this fits together. The indestructibility of these associations conveys a sense of permanence that nurtures the heart, that cripples one of the most insidious of human anxieties, the one that says, you do not belong here, you are unnecessary.

10   Whenever I walk with a child, I think how much I have seen disappear in my own life. What will there be for this person when he is my age? If he senses something ineffable in the landscape, will I know enough to encourage it?—to somehow show him that, yes, when people talk about violent death, spiritual exhilaration, compassion, futility, final causes, they are drawing on forty thousand years of human meditation on *this*—as we embrace Douglas firs, or stand by a river across whose undulating back we skip stones, or dig out a camas bulb, biting down into a taste so much wilder than last night's potatoes.

11   The most moving look I ever saw from a child in the woods was on a mud bar by the footprints of a heron. We were on our knees, making handprints beside the footprints. You could feel the creek vibrating in the silt and sand. The sun beat down heavily on our hair. Our shoes were soaking wet. The look said: I did not know until now that I needed someone much older to confirm this, the feeling I have of life here. I can now grow older, knowing it need never be lost.

12   The quickest door to open in the woods for a child is the one that leads to the smallest room, by knowing the name each thing is called. The door that leads to the cathedral is marked by a hesitancy to speak at all, rather to encourage by example a sharpness of the senses. If one speaks it should only be to say, as well as one can, how wonderfully all this fits together, to indicate what a long, fierce peace can derive from this knowledge.

COMPREHENSION

1. What is Lopez's primary purpose in this essay? How does the title relate to the purpose?
2. Does Lopez assume his audience has the same value position as he does? Why or why not?
3. What, ultimately, does Lopez want children to learn about the natural world? How does he teach them?

RHETORIC

1. Does Lopez state his thesis or imply it? Justify your response.
2. Why does Lopez use a personal tone or voice at the start of this essay? How does his opening paragraph connect to the body of the essay?
3. Cite instances where Lopez moves from vivid description to response and reflection.
4. Where does Lopez employ the comparative method, and toward what objective?
5. What extended metaphor does Lopez establish in the final paragraph? Is this an appropriate and effective metaphor to end the essay? Why or why not?

WRITING

1. Write a narrative and descriptive essay in which you recount a childhood experience that taught you something about the natural world.
2. How would you speak to children if you were taking them on a nature walk? Write a reflective essay addressing this question.
3. **Writing an Argument:** Argue for or against the proposition that you can learn profound truths about yourself and the world by immersing yourself in nature.

NETWORKING
Applying Digital and Multimedia Literacies

Promoting the Natural World from the Virtual One: Create a blog or the home page of a Web site, the purpose of which is to get visitors excited about a natural space—a nearby national park, a reservoir, the Everglades—or an environmental issue—an endangered species, the effects of global climate change, ways to be more "green" around campus, and so on. Think of creative ways to use text, visuals, videos, sound, and even music to appeal to your readers.

Synthesis: Classic and Contemporary Questions for Comparison

1. Chief Seattle and Barry Lopez ponder the destruction of nature as a physical and spiritual presence. In what ways are their stakes in this destruction the same? In what ways are they different? Does either writer have the power to effect a transformation in our attitude toward nature? Explain.

2. It has often been said that intellectual knowledge changes one's relationship with the
   world environment. In what ways has Lopez's "book learning" and erudition made him
   a different person from Chief Seattle? Base your response on the style and tone of
   each author.
3. Chief Seattle is literally the leader and spokesperson of a defeated nation. How does
   he preserve his dignity in the face of being conquered? How does he indicate to the
   white man that his "victory" is temporary? Lopez, on the other hand, is a successful
   member of his society: esteemed naturalist, award-winning writer, popular lecturer.
   What is his relationship to society and to America? Explain by referring to the text.

Why I Hunt

Rick Bass

Rick Bass *(b. 1958) was born in Fort Worth, Texas, and grew up in the Texas hill
country where his grandfather taught him how to hunt. His collection of essays,* The
Deer Pasture *(1985), recounts his Texas years, the ethos of hunting, and the allure
of the outdoors. Bass studied at Utah State University (BS, 1979) and worked as
an oil and gas geologist in Mississippi for eight years. His time working in the oil
fields of the deep South is documented in* Oil Notes *(1979). Bass has written more
than a dozen works of nonfiction and fiction, many of them reflecting environmental
issues and people's search for balance in the natural world. An environmental advocate
and land conservationist, Bass lives in the remote Yaak Valley on the Montana–
Canada border, a region depicted in books such as* Winter: Notes from Montana
(1991), Brown Dog of the Yaak: Essays on Art and Activism *(1999), and* The
Roadless Yaak: Reflections and Observations about One of Our Last Great Wild
Places *(2002). His most recent book of fiction is* Why I Came West *(2008). Bass
wrote this vivid and provocative essay on the allure of the hunt for* Sierra *magazine
in 2001.*

1 I was a hunter before I came far up into northwest Montana, but not to the degree
I am now. It astounds me sometimes to step back particularly at the end of
autumn, the end of the hunting season, and take both mental and physical inventory
of all that was hunted and all that was gathered from this life in the mountains.
The woodshed groaning tight, full of firewood. The fruits and herbs and vegetables from the garden, canned or dried or frozen; the wild mushrooms, huckleber-
ries, thimbleberries, and strawberries. And most precious of all, the flesh of the
wild things that share with us these mountains and the plains to the east—the
elk, the whitetail and mule deer; the ducks and geese, grouse and pheasant and
Hungarian partridge and dove and chukar and wild turkey; the trout and whitefish.
Each year the cumulative bounty seems unbelievable. What heaven is this into
which we've fallen?

How my wife and I got to this valley—the Yaak—15 years ago is a mystery, a ₂ move that I've only recently come to accept as having been inevitable. We got in the truck one day feeling strangely restless in Mississippi, and we drove. What did I know? Only that I missed the West's terrain of space. Young and healthy, and not coincidentally new-in-love, we hit that huge and rugged landscape in full stride. We drove north until we ran out of country—until the road ended, and we reached Canada's thick blue woods—and then we turned west and traveled until we ran almost out of mountains: the backside of the Rockies, to the wet, west-slope rainforest.

We came over a little mountain pass—it was August and winter was already ₃ fast approaching—and looked down on the soft hills, the dense purples of the spruce and fir forests, the ivory crests of the ice-capped peaks, and the slender ribbons of gray thread rising from the chimneys of the few cabins nudged close to the winding river below, and we fell in love with the Yaak Valley and the hard-logged Kootenai National Forest—the way people in movies fall with each other, star and starlet, as if a trap door has been pulled out from beneath them: tumbling through the air, arms windmilling furiously, and suddenly no other world but each other, no other world but this one and eyes for no one, or no place, else.

Right from the beginning, I could see that there was extraordinary bounty in ₄ this low-elevation forest, resting as it does in a magical seam between the Pacific Northwest and the northern Rockies. Some landscapes these days have been reduced to nothing but dandelions and fire ants, knapweed and thistle, where the only remaining wildlife are sparrows, squirrels, and starlings. In the blessed Yaak, however, not a single mammal has gone extinct since the end of the Ice Age. This forest sustains more types of hunters—carnivores—than any valley in North America. It is a predator's showcase, home not just to wolves and grizzlies, but wolverines, lynx, bobcat, marten, fisher, black bear, mountain lion, golden eagle, bald eagle, coyote, fox, weasel. In the Yaak, everything is in motion, either seeking its quarry, or seeking to avoid becoming quarry.

The people who have chosen to live in this remote valley—few phones, very ₅ little electricity, and long, dark winters—possess a hardness and a dreaminess both. They—we—can live a life of deprivation, and yet are willing to enter the comfort of daydreams and imagination. There is something mysterious happening here between the landscape and the people, a thing that stimulates our imagination, and causes many of us to set off deep into the woods in search of the unknown, and sustenance—not just metaphorical or spiritual sustenance, but the real thing.

Only about 5 percent of the nation and 15 to 20 percent of Montanans are ₆ hunters. But in this one valley, almost everyone is a hunter. It is not the peer pressure of the local culture that recruits us into hunting, nor even necessarily the economic boon of a few hundred pounds of meat in a cash-poor society. Rather, it is the terrain itself, and one's gradual integration into it, that summons the hunter. Nearly everyone who has lived here for any length of time has ended up—sometimes almost against one's conscious wishes—becoming a hunter. This wild and powerful landscape sculpts us like clay. I don't find such sculpting an affront to the human spirit, but instead, wonderful testimony to our pliability, our ability to adapt to a place.

7　I myself love to hunt the deer, the elk, and the grouse—to follow them into the mouth of the forest, to disappear in their pursuit—to get lost following their snowy tracks up one mountain and down the next. One sets out after one's quarry with senses fully engaged, wildly alert; entranced, nearly hypnotized. The tiniest of factors can possess the largest significance—the crack of a twig, the shift of a breeze, a single stray hair caught on a piece of bark, a fresh-bent blade of grass.

8　　　Each year during such pursuits, I am struck more and more by the conceit that people in a hunter-gatherer culture might have richer imaginations than those who dwell more fully in an agricultural or even post-agricultural environment. What else is the hunt but a stirring of the imagination, with the quarry, or goal, or treasure lying just around the corner or over the next rise? A hunter's imagination has no choice but to become deeply engaged, for it is never the hunter who is in control, but always the hunted, in that the prey directs the predator's movements.

9　　　The hunted shapes the hunter; the pursuit and evasion of predator and prey are but shadows of the same desire. The thrush wants to remain a thrush. The goshawk wants to consume the thrush and in doing so, partly become the thrush—to take its flesh into its flesh. They weave through the tangled branches of the forest, zigging and zagging, the goshawk right on the thrush's tail, like a shadow. Or perhaps it is the thrush that is the shadow thrown by the light of the goshawk's fiery desire.

10　　　Either way, the escape maneuvers of the thrush help carve and shape and direct the muscles of the goshawk. Even when you are walking through the woods seeing nothing but trees, you can feel the unseen passage of pursuits that might have occurred earlier that morning, precisely where you are standing—pursuits that will doubtless, after you are gone, sweep right back across that same spot again and again.

As does the goshawk, so too do human hunters imagine where their prey might 11 be, or where it might go. They follow tracks hinting at not only distance and direction traveled, but also pace and gait and the general state of mind of the animal that is evading them. They plead to the mountain to deliver to them a deer, an elk. They imagine and hope that they are moving toward their goal of obtaining game.

When you plant a row of corn, there is not so much unknown. You can be 12 fairly sure that, if the rains come, the corn is going to sprout. The corn is not seeking to elude you. But when you step into the woods, looking for a deer—well, there's nothing in your mind, or in your blood, or in the world, but imagination.

Most Americans neither hunt nor gather nor even grow their own food, nor 13 make, with their own hands, any of their other necessities. In this post-agricultural society, too often we confuse anticipation with imagination. When we wander down the aisle of the supermarket searching for a chunk of frozen chicken, or cruise into Dillard's department store looking for a sweater, we can be fairly confident that grayish wad of chicken or that sweater is going to be there, thanks to the vigor and efficiency of a supply-and-demand marketplace. The imagination never quite hits second gear. Does the imagination atrophy, from such chronic inactivity? I suspect that it does.

All I know is that hunting—beyond being a thing I like to do—helps keep my 14 imagination vital. I would hope never to be so blind as to offer it as prescription; I offer it only as testimony to my love of the landscape where I live—a place that is still, against all odds, its own place, quite unlike any other. I don't think I would be able to sustain myself as a dreamer in this strange landscape if I did not take off three months each year to wander the mountains in search of game; to hunt, stretching and exercising not just my imagination, but my spirit. And to wander the mountains, too, in all the other seasons. And to be nourished by the river of spirit that flows, shifting and winding, between me and the land.

COMPREHENSION

1. Why did Bass and his wife fall in love with the Yaak Valley? What does this fondness for wild places tell us about his character and interests?
2. Explain the relationship between the people residing in the Yaak Valley and their fondness for hunting.
3. Does Bass apologize for his fondness for hunting? Explain your response.

RHETORIC

1. Bass wrote this essay for the official magazine of the Sierra Club, of which he is an active member. Why would an organization whose goal is the preservation of wilderness and wildlife agree to publish an article expressing love for hunting? How does Bass anticipate objections to his argument?
2. What is Bass's claim and where does he state it? Does he rely on logical, ethical, or emotional appeal—or a combination—to advance his argument, and why?

3. What causal connection does Bass establish between landscape and human behavior? Where does he use comparison and contrast to distinguish this place and its people from other places and other Americans?
4. Cite examples of Bass's descriptive skills. How does description enhance the appeal of the writer's argument?
5. What is the dominant impression that Bass creates of the Yaak Valley region?
6. Evaluate Bass's conclusion. How does it serve as a writer's justification for hunting?

WRITING

1. Select a natural landscape that you know well and, including description as one rhetorical strategy, explain how this site affects the behavior of people and their ethical values.
2. **Writing an Argument:** What is the difference between killing the game that you consume and buying meat in a grocery store or supermarket? Is one act more ethical than the other? Compose an argumentative essay dealing with this issue.

NETWORKING
Applying Digital and Multimedia Literacies

Interpreting an Organization's Web Site: Go online and locate the Web site for the Sierra Club. Summarize the organization's goals, and then evaluate whether Bass's essay conforms to these objectives.

Parkinson's Alley

Joy Horowitz

Joy Horowitz, *a freelance journalist, was born in Cleveland, Ohio. She graduated from Harvard University in 1975 and worked as a copy girl, sports writer, and investigative reporter for the old* Los Angeles Herald-Examiner. *Subsequently she was a feature writer for the* Los Angeles Times *before attending Yale Law School, where she received a master's in Study of Law in 1982. Her writing has appeared in the* New York Times, *the* New Yorker, Los Angeles *magazine, and other national publications. Horowitz is the author of* Tessie and Pearlie: A Granddaughter's Story *(1996) and* Parts Per Million: The Poisoning of Beverly Hills High School *(2007). In this article, published in* Sierra *magazine in 2012, Horowitz investigates the impact of pesticides on some of the residents of California's Central Valley.*

Bruce McDermott tosses me the keys to his pickup, and I hoist his chrome   1
walker into the truck's bed. "You need to see this," he tells me as he angles his
torso and braced leg into the cab, then slams the door.

It's a rainy fall day in the Central Valley town of Visalia, California, and   2
McDermott wants to show me some of the houses of people here who've been
diagnosed with Parkinson's disease, the incurable neurodegenerative affliction
that, coupled with a recent car crash, has left him unable to drive. I've never been
at the wheel of such a behemoth truck before—or one with shotgun shells in the
door well, for that matter—but I know better than to argue. McDermott was once
the city's chief of police; when he makes suggestions, people tend to say, "Yes, sir."

A big, friendly bear of a man who likes to joke that his doctor calls him "fat   3
boy," McDermott wears khaki shorts, sandals, and a crisply pressed polo shirt.
Diagnosed with early-onset Parkinson's, he was forced to retire from the police
force in 1997, at age 46, after he tried to place his right hand on the Bible to swear
in a new officer but his arm shook so uncontrollably that people thought he was
waving hello.

As we near his boyhood home on Border Links Drive, McDermott points to   4
the house next door, where his godfather, a prominent attorney, died three years
ago from complications of Parkinson's. Nearby, he shows me a field where crop
dusters once landed their planes and routinely dumped their tanks. In a half-mile
stretch, McDermott points to four homes where residents have been diagnosed
with the disease.

Some neurologists dub the 300-mile-long string of Central Valley farm towns   5
between Bakersfield and Sacramento "Parkinson's Alley," and recently released
statistics back them up. A study published last year by researchers at the University of California, Los Angeles, found that Central Valley residents under age 60
who lived near fields where the pesticides paraquat and maneb had been used
between 1974 and 1999 had a Parkinson's rate nearly five times higher than other
residents in the region.

I steer McDermott's truck into the driveway of his friend Margaret Haworth,   6
a former tennis player and expert skier. Like McDermott, Haworth suffers from
early-onset Parkinson's; she was diagnosed 16 years ago, at age 49.

Our visit is a surprise, but Haworth welcomes McDermott as if he's family. As   7
he slowly makes his way up her front steps, she says of his walker, "I see you got
a new hot rod."

Haworth tells us her mother was also afflicted by Parkinson's but never spoke   8
of it. McDermott nods; it's a familiar story. "A lot of people in the valley won't tell
you they have Parkinson's disease if they do," he say. "I know doctors who would
lose their license if their insurance carriers knew they had it."

Research into the link between pesticides and Parkinson's in the Central Valley   9
dates back to 2000, when UCLA epidemiologist Beate Ritz began comparing mortality records with pesticide-application reports. She discovered that California
counties reporting the highest pesticide use also had the highest rates for
Parkinson's-related deaths. Examining agricultural records from 1989 to 1994,
Ritz found that when insecticides were applied to more than a third of a county's

acreage, the risk of its residents' dying from Parkinson's disease increased 2.5-fold. She also found studies that revealed that as many as 40 percent of the area's Parkinson's cases are never mentioned on death certificates, possibly because many migrant workers fail to report the disease, or move on before symptoms arise.

10   Ritz and her research team found that Central Valley residents who consumed private well water and lived within 500 feet of farmland with documented long-term pesticide use were almost twice as likely to get Parkinson's disease. Their 2009 report, produced under the auspices of the federally funded Parkinson's Environment and Genes Study, was the first to quantify residents' exposure to such chemicals by comparing land-use maps with state-mandated pesticide-application records. "We're seeing effects not just on people in their homes but also on farms and in workplaces," Ritz told me in Los Angeles before I traveled 200 miles north to meet with McDermott.

11   Visalia, a 160-year-old gold rush town, has grown by more than a third to about 120,000 people in the past decade. It's in the heart of the Central Valley— the vast farm belt west of the Sierra Nevada where about 7 percent of the nation's crops are grown, producing $20 billion in annual revenues. Growers here use about 115 million pounds of pesticides every year.

12   Some of those pesticides are finding their way into residential water supplies in accumulations that surpass government safety standards, according to a number of studies—including tests of private-well samples gathered exclusively for this article. More than 1 million people in the region have tap water that isn't safe to drink because of nitrate contamination from manure, fertilizers, and leaking septic tanks, according to a collaborative report by the Pacific Institute, Visalia's Community Water Center, the Clean Water Fund, and California Rural Legal Assistance Foundation. Most of those residents are from low-income and Spanish-speaking households.

13   More than half of Central Valley communities rely on water stored underground for their drinking supply, the Community Water Center reports. Recent groundwater sampling found that the water in 75 percent of the private domestic wells in Tulare County, of which Visalia is the seat, contains unsafe levels of nitrates.

14   "We pay twice for water each month," says Susana DeAnda, the center's co-executive director. "Once for contaminated well water and once for bottled water."

15   Nitrates can also be a sign of pesticide contamination, but testing for pesticides in drinking water is expensive and not mandated. Some testing is done, however, and last year the State Water Resources Control Board released the results of a domestic-well-water survey in Tulare County; pesticides turned up in 13 of 19 wells sampled.

16   By the time I park McDermott's truck in his driveway, the rain has stopped. Gripping his walker, he shuffles back inside his home. The walk leaves him breathless. A lifelong Republican who favors Fox News, McDermott says he had long assumed that, in America, if something was wrong, it would be fixed. Now he's not so sure.

17   "It's an ugly thing when you look at it and think maybe something could be done to prevent this," he says. "I'm convinced it's exposure to the environment. Something's going on here."

Currently, no federal or state water quality standards regulate domestic well wa- 18
ter in California, even though private wells are the primary source of drinking
water for 1.6 million people in the state and more than 43 million, or 15 percent of
the population, nationwide. The federal Safe Drinking Water Act covers public
water supplies, but Congress never extended the law to include private wells,
which can be more susceptible to contamination because they tend to draw from
shallower aquifers and often are close to farms that use pesticides.

The federal Clean Water Act largely exempts normal agricultural activities from 19
regulation. California's Safe Drinking Water Act monitors water coming out of the
tap but doesn't regulate the source. Although statutes are in place mandating the
state to monitor and regulate agricultural pollution in drinking water, the program
has yet to be implemented, according to Community Water Center cofounder
Laurel Firestone. In California, the state Department of Pesticide Regulation
conducts an annual survey of some domestic wells. Last year, for example, state
regulators tested 136 wells and found pesticides in 103 of them. But the agency
keeps the location of its testing confidential, citing concerns about terrorism.

"Nobody is testing domestic wells in any systematic way," says Robert J. 20
Gilliom, a hydrologist and the head of pesticide studies for the U.S. Geological
Survey's water quality assessment program.

Since Ritz's UCLA research was based on historical data, I wanted to know 21
what pesticides are in the water now. But no one could tell me. So, I ordered
some water-testing kits and set out to answer two simple questions: What
pesticides are present in Central Valley well water and are any of them implicated
for Parkinson's disease? The lab results revealed a potentially harmful mix of herbicides in tap water from 6 of the 10 private wells I tested. (See "Testing for
Pesticides," below.)

Of course, not everyone wants to know what's in his or her water. When I 22
arrived at a walnut farm in Visalia to take water samples, I asked the grower—
whose hand shook from Parkinson's—what pesticides he used on his property.
He said, "Whatever the gestapo lets us use."

"I'm dying to know, but I also am afraid to find out," the widow of a Parkinson's 23
victim told me when I asked if I could test her drinking water. Her husband had
worked for a program that advises farmers on how to use pesticides, and the couple
had lived on a citrus ranch for more than 40 years. He sometimes came home "up to
his elbows in the stuff." She told me I could take water samples on the ranch, but
only if I didn't reveal her identity.

Off a country road outside Hanford, about 20 miles west of Visalia, I dropped 24
by the home of Peggy and Jim Greaser to take a water sample from their kitchen
sink. Their living room window has a view of the cornfield next door. Both Peggy
and Jim, a former Sears technician, complained that the "drift" from crop dusters
often burns their eyes and has ruined the paint job on their car.

Jim, now a part-time DJ known as Jim Dee on K6RGZ, suffers from Parkinson's 25
disease. He drives a motorized cart from his front door to a nearby shack that
houses his radio studio. Leather straps hang from shelves crammed with tape decks
and vinyl records, so he has something to grasp.

26   "You start losing your walking ability," he said. "I've fallen so many times I've lost track."

27   Parkinson's, one of the most intractable of all neurological diseases, afflicts 500,000 to 1.5 million people in the United States. It's caused when nerve cells die in the area of the brain that produces dopamine, a neurotransmitter that's essential to everything from moving muscles to feeling pleasure. As dopamine levels decrease, messages that control motor function are blocked.

28   Although symptoms have been mentioned in texts dating back to biblical times, the disease was officially "discovered" in 1817, when British physician James Parkinson first described the "shaking palsy." But it wasn't until the mid-1980s that scientists stumbled on a link between pesticide exposure and Parkinson's disease, thanks to a bizarre outbreak among heroin addicts and an astute young San Francisco Bay Area neurologist named J. William Langston.

29   Langston, now scientific director at the Parkinson's Institute in Sunnyvale, California, had been asked to examine a cluster of young patients who looked like living statues; they could neither move nor speak and appeared to be in the advanced stages of Parkinson's disease. He learned that all of them had injected a new form of synthetic heroin. Alarmed, he called a press conference to alert the public to his "frozen addicts" and warn of bad drugs on the streets. When he prescribed levodopa, which is used to treat Parkinson's, the addicts, whose faces were so stiffened that they drooled uncontrollably, soon found that their symptoms abated.

30   The illicit drug they'd taken contained a compound known as MPTP, which has a similar chemical structure to that of paraquat—one of the most widely used herbicides in the world. Paraquat is of particular concern to Parkinson's researchers because of its synergistic effect, particularly when used with the fungicide maneb.

31   Taking their cues from Langston's earlier work, Ritz and her team discovered that long-term exposures to paraquat and maneb caused an eight-fold increase in the development of Parkinson's for people under age 60. Paraquat was banned by the European Union in 2007 but is still widely used in the United States; about 75,000 pounds of it are applied annually to alfalfa, grapes, and other crops in Tulare County. The EPA banned maneb for use on corn, grapes, and apples in 2005 but continues to allow its use on almonds, which are abundant in the Central Valley.

32   Another chemical of particular concern to Parkinson's researchers is the fungicide ziram. When the EPA proposed prohibiting ziram use on 35 crops in 2003, a plant pathologist with the U.S. Department of Agriculture insisted that the pesticide had a "clean bill of health" and said workers could protect themselves by wearing "long pants and long sleeves." But cell studies by the UCLA researchers and others have shown that ziram kills certain brain cells whose absence leads to Parkinson's, and the UCLA team found that people exposed to the fungicide for 25 years or longer have a three-times-greater chance of developing the disease.

33   In 2008, California regulators placed ziram on their risk-assessment "priority" list. Four years later, no one's followed up.

"We have no estimated date for the assessment," Lea Brooks, communica- 34
tions director with California's Department of Pesticide Regulation, told me. "Our
work schedule is behind due to furloughs, retirements, and a hiring freeze. It's on
the priority list for a risk assessment, but there is no timeline."

Once a month for the past 10 years, neurologist Jeff Bronstein has left his hillside 35
home in Los Angeles at four A.M. to drive more than 150 miles north to the Central
Valley, where he meets with Parkinson's patients before they take their daily medi-
cations, which mask symptoms. As part of the UCLA Parkinson's research team,
Bronstein, a professor of neurology and molecular toxicology at the university's
David Geffen School of Medicine and director of its Movement Disorders Program,
needs to make sure that patients enrolled in the Parkinson's Environment and
Genes Study have been correctly diagnosed (since it's easy to mistake other neuro-
logical symptoms for those of Parkinson's disease) and to chart their progress.

Over the years, Bronstein has met with farmworkers, corporate executives, 36
police officers, college professors, and, of course, pesticide applicators. Although
he lacks irrefutable evidence, he is convinced that pesticides are the culprit behind
his patients' affliction.

"It's worth it," he told me of his five- to seven-hour round-trip commutes. 37
During one of them, he spoke to me on his car phone as a crop duster roared
overhead. "How many years did it take to prove smoking causes lung cancer?
That's where we are with pesticides. The onus is on us to prove this stuff is bad.
And what's really goofy is that what's considered an 'acceptable' level is completely arbitrary. They come up with numbers based on acute toxicity. But it's
years and years of low-level exposure that matter, not acute toxicity. You need to
look at chronic exposure before any meaningful discussion can take place."

In 2007 the U.S. Department of Agriculture partnered with the EPA to begin 38
testing for pesticides at extremely low concentration levels in domestic well water.
In 2009, the agencies took samples from 278 domestic, school, and farm wells in
16 states and detected pesticides in 152, or 45 percent, of them. "In the future,
we'll see more and more pesticides in groundwater," said hydrologist Terry
Councell, who runs the USDA's water monitoring program. "A lot of these pesticides
haven't even hit the water table yet."

One morning I meet over coffee with Donna DeVries, former president of the Cen- 39
tral Valley Parkinson's Disease Support Group. DeVries, a 57-year-old dental office
manager, tells me she spends the first Friday of every month at the local Methodist
church, with the Visalia-based support group, which ranks second in the United
States in fundraising. She spent years caring for her father and father-in-law, both of
whom died after battling the disease.

"All of our doctors have told us, 'Move. Get out of the valley. It's not a healthy 40
place to be,'" she says. As she speaks, she sits on her right hand to control its
shaking. She suspects she has Parkinson's too. "My doctor told me not to worry
about it, but how can I not?"

Several dozen people attend the support group's Friday-morning meeting, 41
and the conversation ranges from sharing medication tips to dealing with the

inevitable depression that accompanies the disease. "I told my wife, 'Put the guns in the safe,' " says a man in his 40s who has driven several hours to be here.

42   Not everyone is keen on such frank talk, though. Bruce McDermott, for one, swore off the group after he sat through a downer of a discussion about morticians. He likes to think of Visalia as a "roll-up-your-sleeves kind of town" where people who share his disease can live a normal life, and where he and others can change the future for the better by verifying—and publicizing—a link between pesticides and Parkinson's.

43   "If I can help one person," McDermott says, "I feel good."

TESTING FOR PESTICIDES

I don't profess to be a trained water quality researcher, but I wanted to know whether private water wells in California's farm belt are contaminated with pesticides. And since few public records of such tests exist, I decided to do it myself—with the help of a government scientist.

I took water samples from 10 wells, following procedures provided by an EPA-approved laboratory that specializes in analyzing chemicals in the parts-per-trillion range, an exacting and expensive testing process. My source inside the lab, which is connected to a government agency, offered to test the samples as long as I collected them myself and agreed not to identify the lab or the agency.

Using 10 specially equipped boxes, each containing ice packs to refrigerate the water for overnight delivery to the lab, I gathered my samples from garden hoses and kitchen sinks in the Central Valley. The toxicity tests revealed pesticide traces in 6 of 10 samples from private water wells. Five of the wells—in Visalia, Dinuba, and Orosi—contained three or more herbicides. A sample of tap water drawn from an Orosi home contained residues of five weed killers.

Four of the 10 samples came from households where a resident had been diagnosed with Parkinson's disease; 3 of those 4 showed signs of pesticide contamination.

Not surprisingly, half of the samples showed traces of the herbicides bromacil, diuron, and simazine—known groundwater contaminants in the area, according to California's Department of Pesticide Regulation. Despite the widespread presence of these weed killers in groundwater, there are no federal or state drinking water standards for bromacil or diuron in California.

The tests also detected metabolites, or breakdown products, of the weed killer atrazine, which was banned by the European Union in 2003 but is still one of the most widely used herbicides in the United States and one of the nation's most common herbicidal contaminants in groundwater. (Pesticide metabolites form when sunlight, high temperature, or microbial activity breaks down a parent chemical.) Two of the water samples contained atrazine metabolites at levels 20 times higher than what the EPA says is safe for atrazine in drinking water.

Atrazine's metabolites are a reliable sign of atrazine contamination and, according to the EPA, are nearly as toxic as the parent chemical. In 2007, researchers at the Centers for Disease Control and Prevention warned that by failing to include all of its metabolites in exposure assessments, public agencies are systematically underestimating Americans' exposure to atrazine.

COMPREHENSION

1. According to Horowitz, what is the impact of pesticides on people in Visalia, California?
2. Who are the people that Horowitz interviews and profiles? What are they like? What do they share in common? How do they differ in personalities and attitudes?
3. What would Horowitz have us learn from the lives of the people she portrays in her essay?

RHETORIC

1. How does Horowitz design her introductory section? Which rhetorical strategies does she blend in order to create a picture of people and landscape in Visalia and the Central Valley?
2. Horowitz is an investigative reporter. What stylistic and formal attributes of investigative reporting do you find in this essay? Should an investigative reporter be objective or subjective? Explain.
3. What is Horowitz's claim and how does she support it? What appeals to reason, emotion, and ethics does she make and where do they appear?
4. How many sections comprise this essay? What is the focus of each section? How do these sections interrelate and serve to advance the writer's argument?
5. Explain the relevance of the subsection "Testing for Pesticides" to the essay.

WRITING

1. Write a brief personal essay on your feelings about the water supply in your home town. Explain whether or not you drink tap water, and why.
2. Write a comparative essay linking Horowitz's article with the piece by Rachel Carson in this chapter.
3. **Writing an Argument:** Agree or disagree with the proposition that most tap water in the United States does not cause debilitating diseases, that our national water supply is safe.

NETWORKING
Applying Digital and Multimedia Literacies

Researching in a Group: Collaborating with other students, conduct online research into the relatively new method of oil extraction known as "fracking." Summarize the results of your research and offer a conclusion on whether you think that fracking is safe for the environment and especially for an area's water supply. If group members disagree, put forth several supported opinions.

✵

The Environmental Issue from Hell

Bill McKibben

Bill McKibben *(b. 1960) was born in Palo Alto, California. After receiving a BA from Harvard University (1982), McKibben became a staff writer for the* New Yorker. *McKibben's chief concern is the impact of humans on the environment and the ways in which consumerism affects the global ecosystem. A prominent writer for the environmental movement, he has published several books, among them* The End of Nature *(1989),* The Age of Missing Information *(1992),* Long Distance: A Year of Living Strenuously *(2000),* Enough: Staying Human in an Engineered Age *(2003), and* The Bill McKibben Reader: Pieces from an Active Life *(2009). In the essay that follows, which was published in* These Times *in 2001, McKibben argues for a new approach to global warming.*

1   When global warming first emerged as a potential crisis in the late 1980s, one academic analyst called it "the public policy problem from hell." The years since have only proven him more astute: Fifteen years into our understanding of climate change, we have yet to figure out how we're going to tackle it. And environmentalists are just as clueless as anyone else: Do we need to work on lifestyle or on lobbying, on photovoltaics or on politics? And is there a difference? How well we handle global warming will determine what kind of century we inhabit—and indeed what kind of planet we leave behind. The issue cuts close to home and also floats off easily into the abstract. So far it has been the ultimate "can't get there from here" problem, but the time has come to draw a road map—one that may help us deal with the handful of other issues on the list of real, world-shattering problems.

2   Typically, when you're mounting a campaign, you look for self-interest, you scare people by saying what will happen to us if we don't do something: All the birds will die, the canyon will disappear beneath a reservoir, we will choke to death on smog. But in the case of global warming, that doesn't exactly do the trick, at least in the time frame we're discussing. In temperate latitudes, climate change will creep up on us. Severe storms already have grown more frequent and more damaging. The progression of seasons is less steady. Some agriculture is less reliable. But face it: Our economy is so enormous that it takes those changes in stride. Economists who work on this stuff talk about how it will shave a percentage or two off the GNP over the next few decades. And most of us live lives so divorced from the natural world that we hardly notice the changes anyway. Hotter? Turn up the air-conditioning. Stormier? Well, an enormous percentage of Americans commute from remote-controlled garage to office parking garage—it may have been some time since they got good and wet in a rainstorm. By the time the magnitude of the change is truly in our faces, it will be too late to do much

about it: There's such a lag time to increased levels of carbon dioxide in the atmosphere that we need to be making the switch to solar and wind and hydrogen power right now to prevent disaster decades away. Yesterday, in fact.

So maybe we should think of global warming in a different way—as the great 3 moral crisis of our time, the equivalent of the civil rights movement of the 1960s.

Why a moral question? In the first place, no one's ever figured out a more 4 effective way to screw the marginalized and poor of this planet than climate change. Having taken their dignity, their resources, and their freedom under a variety of other schemes, we now are taking the very physical stability on which their already difficult lives depend.

Our economy can absorb these changes for a while, but consider Bangladesh 5 for a moment. In 1998 the sea level in the Bay of Bengal was higher than normal, just the sort of thing we can expect to become more frequent and severe. The waters sweeping down the Ganges and the Brahmaputra rivers from the Himalayas could not drain easily into the ocean—they backed up across the country, forcing most of its inhabitants to spend three months in thigh-deep water. The fall rice crop didn't get planted. We've seen this same kind of disaster over the past few years in Mozambique and Honduras and Venezuela and other places.

And global warming is a moral crisis, too, if you place any value on the rest of 6 creation. Coral reef researchers indicate that these spectacularly intricate ecosystems are also spectacularly vulnerable. Rising water temperatures are likely to bleach them to extinction by mid-century. In the Arctic, polar bears are 20 percent scrawnier than they were a decade ago: As pack ice melts, so does the opportunity for hunting seals. All in all, the 21st century seems poised to see extinctions at a rate not observed since the last big asteroid slammed into the planet. But this time the asteroid is us.

It's a moral question, finally, if you think we owe any debt to the future. No 7 one ever has figured out a more thoroughgoing way to strip-mine the present and degrade what comes after—all the people who will ever be related to you. Ever. No generation yet to come will ever forget us—we are the ones present at the moment when the temperature starts to spike, and so far we have not reacted. If it had been done to us, we would loathe the generation that did it, precisely as we will one day be loathed.

But trying to launch a moral campaign is no easy task. In most moral crises, 8 there is a villain—some person or class or institution that must be overcome. Once the villain is identified, the battle can commence. But you can't really get angry at carbon dioxide, and the people responsible for its production are, well, us. So perhaps we need some symbols to get us started, some places to sharpen the debate and rally ourselves to action. There are plenty to choose from: our taste for ever bigger houses and the heating and cooling bills that come with them, our penchant for jumping on airplanes at the drop of a hat. But if you wanted one glaring example of our lack of balance, you could do worse than point the finger at sport utility vehicles.

SUVs are more than mere symbols. They are a major part of the problem—we 9 emit so much more carbon dioxide now than we did a decade ago in part because our fleet of cars and trucks actually has gotten steadily less fuel efficient for the past 10 years. If you switched today from the average American car to a big SUV, and drove it for just one year, the difference in carbon dioxide that you produced would be the equivalent of opening your refrigerator door and then forgetting to close it for six years. SUVs essentially are machines for burning fossil fuel that just happen to also move you and your stuff around.

10   But what makes them such a perfect symbol is the brute fact that they are simply unnecessary. Go to the parking lot of the nearest suburban supermarket and look around: The only conclusion you can draw is that to reach the grocery, people must drive through three or four raging rivers and up the side of a canyon. These are semi-military machines, armored trucks on a slight diet. While they do not keep their occupants appreciably safer, they do wreck whatever they plow into, making them the perfect metaphor for a heedless, supersized society.

11   That's why we need a much broader politics than the Washington lobbying that's occupied the big environmental groups for the past decade. We need to take all the brilliant and energetic strategies of local grassroots groups fighting dumps and cleaning up rivers and apply those tactics in the national and international arenas. That's why some pastors are starting to talk with their congregations about what cars to buy, and why some college seniors are passing around petitions pledging to stay away from the Ford Explorers and Excursions, and why some auto dealers have begun to notice informational picketers outside their showrooms on Saturday mornings urging customers to think about gas mileage when they look at cars.

12   The point is not that such actions by themselves—any individual actions—will make any real dent in the levels of carbon dioxide pouring into our atmosphere. Even if you got 10 percent of Americans really committed to changing their energy use, their solar homes wouldn't make much of a difference in our national totals. But 10 percent would be enough to change the politics around the issue, enough to pressure politicians to pass laws that would cause us all to shift our habits. And so we need to begin to take an issue that is now the province of technicians and turn it into a political issue, just as bus boycotts began to make public the issue of race, forcing the system to respond. That response is likely to be ugly—there are huge companies with a lot to lose, and many people so tied in to their current ways of life that advocating change smacks of subversion. But this has to become a political issue—and fast. The only way that may happen, short of a hideous drought or monster flood, is if it becomes a personal issue first.

COMPREHENSION

1. According to McKibben, what are the causes of global warming?
2. What instances of ecological disaster does the writer say will occur if we do not change our habits?
3. Why is a new approach to the problem of global warming needed? What approach does McKibben suggest?

RHETORIC

1. How does McKibben's title capture the tone of the essay? What is his purpose in writing the essay? Does he see his readers as hostile or sympathetic to his position? How do you know?
2. How does McKibben develop his introduction? Why does he pose questions? Where does he state his claim?
3. Does McKibben make his argument through appeals to reason, emotion, ethics—or a combination of these elements? Justify your response.
4. How does the writer contend with possible objections to his position on global warming?
5. Explain the pattern of cause and effect that McKibben uses to structure his essay.
6. What varieties of evidence does the writer present to support his claim? What extended illustration does he provide? How effective is it, and why?
7. In the concluding paragraph, McKibben issues a call to action. How does the body of the essay prepare the reader for this persuasive appeal?

WRITING

1. Write an essay in which you explain your own sense of the causes and effects of global warming.
2. Research your state's policy toward global warming. Present your findings in a summary essay.
3. **Writing an Argument:** McKibben argues that SUVs are a primary cause of wastefulness and global warming and that both moral persuasion and political activism are required to change consumers' habits. Do you agree or disagree with his assertions? Write an argumentative essay responding to this issue.

NETWORKING
Applying Digital and Multimedia Literacies

Delivering an Oral Presentation: Reshape your response to any of the three assignments under Writing to function as an oral presentation; incorporate visual aids (digital or hard copy) and one carefully designed and written handout for your listeners.

The Obligation to Endure

Rachel Carson

Rachel Carson (1907–1964) was a seminal figure in the environmental movement. Born in Pennsylvania, she awakened public consciousness to environmental issues through her writing. Her style was both literary and scientific as she described

nature's riches in such books as The Sea around Us *(1951) and* The Edge of the
Sea *(1954). Her last book,* Silent Spring *(1962), aroused controversy and concern
with its indictment of insecticides. In the following excerpt from that important book,
Carson provides compelling evidence of the damage caused by indiscriminate use of
insecticides and the danger of disturbing the earth's delicate balance.*

1   The history of life on earth has been a history of interaction between living things
and their surroundings. To a large extent, the physical form and the habits of the
earth's vegetation and its animal life have been molded by the environment.
Considering the whole span of earthly time, the opposite effect, in which life actually modifies its surroundings, has been relatively slight. Only within the moment
of time represented by the present century has one species—man—acquired
significant power to alter the nature of his world.

2   During the past quarter century this power has not only increased to one of
disturbing magnitude but it has changed in character. The most alarming of all
man's assaults upon the environment is the contamination of air, earth, rivers, and
sea with dangerous and even lethal materials. This pollution is for the most part
irrecoverable; the chain of evil it initiates not only in the world that must support
life but in living tissues is for the most part irreversible. In this now universal
contamination of the environment, chemicals are the sinister and little-recognized
partners of radiation in changing the very nature of the world—the very nature of
its life. Strontium 90, released through nuclear explosions into the air, comes to
earth in rain or drifts down as fallout, lodges in soil, enters into the grass or corn
or wheat grown there, and in time takes up its abode in the bones of a human
being, there to remain until his death. Similarly, chemicals sprayed on croplands
or forests or gardens lie long in soil, entering into living organisms, passing from
one to another in a chain of poisoning and death. Or they pass mysteriously by
underground streams until they emerge and, through the alchemy of air and
sunlight, combine into new forms that kill vegetation, sicken cattle, and work
unknown harm on those who drink from once pure wells. As Albert Schweitzer
has said, "Man can hardly even recognize the devils of his own creation."

3   It took hundreds of millions of years to produce the life that now inhabits the
earth—eons of time in which that developing and evolving and diversifying life
reached a state of adjustment and balance with its surroundings. The environment, rigorously shaping and directing the life it supported, contained elements
that were hostile as well as supporting. Certain rocks gave out dangerous radiation; even within the light of the sun, from which all life draws its energy, there
were shortwave radiations with power to injure. Given time—time not in years but
in millennia—life adjusts, and a balance has been reached. For time is the essential ingredient; but in the modern world there is no time.

4   The rapidity of change and the speed with which new situations are created
follow the impetuous and heedless pace of man rather than the deliberate pace of nature. Radiation is no longer merely the background radiation of rocks, the bombard-
ment of cosmic rays, the ultraviolet of the sun that have existed before there was any
life on earth; radiation is now the unnatural creation of man's tampering with the

atom. The chemicals to which life is asked to make its adjustment are no longer merely the calcium and silica and copper and all the rest of the minerals washed out of the rocks and carried in rivers to the sea; they are the synthetic creations of man's inventive mind, brewed in his laboratories, and having no counterparts in nature.

To adjust to these chemicals would require time on the scale that is nature's; 5 it would require not merely the years of a man's life but the life of generations. And even this, were it by some miracle possible, would be futile, for the new chemicals come from our laboratories in an endless stream; almost five hundred annually find their way into actual use in the United States alone. The figure is staggering and its implications are not easily grasped—500 new chemicals to which the bodies of men and animals are required somehow to adapt each year, chemicals totally outside the limits of biologic experience.

Among them are many that are used in man's war against nature. Since the 6 mid-1940s over 200 basic chemicals have been created for use in killing insects, weeds, rodents, and other organisms described in the modern vernacular as "pests"; and they are sold under several thousand different brand names.

These sprays, dusts, and aerosols are now applied almost universally to farms, 7 gardens, forests, and homes—nonselective chemicals that have the power to kill every insect, the "good" and the "bad," to still the song of birds and the leaping of fish in the streams, to coat the leaves with a deadly film, and to linger on in soil— all this though the intended target may be only a few weeds or insects. Can anyone believe it is possible to lay down such a barrage of poisons on the surface of the earth without making it unfit for all life? They should not be called "insecticides," but "biocides."

The whole process of spraying seems caught up in an endless spiral. Since 8 DDT was released for civilian use, a process of escalation has been going on in which ever more toxic materials must be found. This has happened because insects, in a triumphant vindication of Darwin's principle of the survival of the fittest, have evolved super races immune to the particular insecticide used, hence a deadlier one has always to be developed—and then a deadlier one than that. It has happened also because, for reasons to be described later, destructive insects often undergo a "flareback," or resurgence, after spraying in numbers greater than before. Thus the chemical war is never won, and all life is caught in its violent crossfire.

Along with the possibility of the extinction of mankind by nuclear war, the 9 central problem of our age has therefore become the contamination of man's total environment with such substances of incredible potential for harm—substances that accumulate in the tissues of plants and animals and even penetrate the germ cells to shatter or alter the very material of heredity upon which the shape of the future depends.

Some would-be architects of our future look toward a time when it will be pos- 10 sible to alter the human germ plasm by design. But we may easily be doing so now by inadvertence, for many chemicals, like radiation, bring about gene mutations. It is ironic to think that man might determine his own future by something so seemingly trivial as the choice of an insect spray.

11   All this has been risked—for what? Future historians may well be amazed by our distorted sense of proportion. How could intelligent beings seek to control a few unwanted species by a method that contaminated the entire environment and brought the threat of disease and death even to their own kind? Yet this is precisely what we have done. We have done it, moreover, for reasons that collapse the moment we examine them. We are told that the enormous and expanding use of pesticides is necessary to maintain farm production. Yet is our real problem not one of *overproduction?* Our farms, despite measures to remove acreages from production and to pay farmers *not* to produce, have yielded such a staggering excess of crops that the American taxpayer in 1962 is paying out more than one billion dollars a year as the total carrying cost of the surplus-food storage program. And is the situation helped when one branch of the Agriculture Department tries to reduce production while another states, as it did in 1958, "It is believed generally that reduction of crop acreages under provisions of the Soil Bank will stimulate interest in use of chemicals to obtain maximum production on the land retained in crops."

12   All this is not to say there is no insect problem and no need of control. I am saying, rather, that control must be geared to realities, not to mythical situations, and that the methods employed must be such that they do not destroy us along with the insects.

13   The problem whose attempted solution has brought such a train of disaster in its wake is an accompaniment of our modern way of life. Long before the age of man, insects inhabited the earth—a group of extraordinarily varied and adaptable beings. Over the course of time since man's advent, a small percentage of the more than half a million species of insects have come into conflict with human welfare in two principal ways: as competitors for the food supply and as carriers of human disease.

14   Disease-carrying insects become important where human beings are crowded together, especially under conditions where sanitation is poor, as in times of natural disaster or war or in situations of extreme poverty and deprivation. Then control of some sort becomes necessary. It is a sobering fact, however, as we shall presently see, that the method of massive chemical control has had only limited success, and also threatens to worsen the very conditions it is intended to curb.

15   Under primitive agricultural conditions the farmer had few insect problems. These arose with the intensification of agriculture—the devotion of immense acreages to a single crop. Such a system set the stage for explosive increases in specific insect populations. Single-crop farming does not take advantage of the principles by which nature works; it is agriculture as an engineer might conceive it to be. Nature has introduced great variety into the landscape, but man has displayed a passion for simplifying it. Thus he undoes the built-in checks and balances by which nature holds the species within bounds. One important natural check is a limit on the amount of suitable habitat for each species. Obviously then, an insect that lives on wheat can build up its population to much higher levels on a farm devoted to wheat than on one in which wheat is intermingled with other crops to which the insect is not adapted.

The same thing happens in other situations. A generation or more ago, the 16
towns of large areas of the United States lined their streets with the noble elm
tree. Now the beauty they hopefully created is threatened with complete destruction as disease sweeps through the elms, carried by a beetle that would have only
limited chance to build up large populations and to spread from tree to tree if the
elms were only occasional trees in a richly diversified planting.

Another factor in the modern insect problem is one that must be viewed against 17
a background of geologic and human history: the spreading of thousands of different
kinds of organisms from their native homes to invade new territories. This worldwide
migration has been studied and graphically described by the British ecologist Charles
Elton in his recent book *The Ecology of Invasions.* During the Cretaceous Period,
some hundred million years ago, flooding seas cut many land bridges between continents and living things found themselves confined in what Elton calls "colossal separate nature reserves." There, isolated from others of their kind, they developed many
new species. When some of the land masses were joined again, about 15 million years
ago, these species began to move out into new territories—a movement that is not
only still in progress but is now receiving considerable assistance from man.

The importation of plants is the primary agent in the modern spread of 18
species, for animals have almost invariably gone along with the plants, quarantine
being a comparatively recent and not completely effective innovation. The United
States Office of Plant Introduction alone has introduced almost 200,000 species
and varieties of plants from all over the world. Nearly half of the 180 or so major
insect enemies of plants in the United States are accidental imports from abroad,
and most of them have come as hitchhikers on plants.

In new territory, out of reach of the restraining hand of the natural enemies 19
that kept down its numbers in its native land, an invading plant or animal is able to
become enormously abundant. Thus it is no accident that our most troublesome
insects are introduced species.

These invasions, both the naturally occurring and those dependent on human 20
assistance, are likely to continue indefinitely. Quarantine and massive chemical
campaigns are only extremely expensive ways of buying time. We are faced, according to Dr. Elton, "with a life-and-death need not just to find new technological means
of suppressing this plant or that animal"; instead we need the basic knowledge of
animal populations and their relations to their surroundings that will "promote an
even balance and damp down the explosive power of outbreaks and new invasions."

Much of the necessary knowledge is now available but we do not use it. We 21
train ecologists in our universities and even employ them in our governmental
agencies but we seldom take their advice. We allow the chemical death rain to fall
as though there were no alternative, whereas in fact there are many, and our inge-
nuity could soon discover many more if given opportunity.

Have we fallen into a mesmerized state that makes us accept as inevitable that 22
which is inferior or detrimental, as though having lost the will or the vision to
demand that which is good? Such thinking, in the words of the ecologist Paul
Shepard, "idealizes life with only its head out of water, inches above the limits of
toleration of the corruption of its own environment. . . . Why should we tolerate a

diet of weak poisons, a home in insipid surroundings, a circle of acquaintances who are not quite our enemies, the noise of motors with just enough relief to prevent insanity? Who would want to live in a world which is just not quite fatal?"

23　　　Yet such a world is pressed upon us. The crusade to create a chemically sterile, insect-free world seems to have engendered a fanatic zeal on the part of many specialists and most of the so-called control agencies. On every hand there is evidence that those engaged in spraying operations exercise a ruthless power. "The regulatory entomologists . . . function as prosecutor, judge and jury, tax assessor and collector and sheriff to enforce their own orders," said Connecticut entomologist Neely Turner. The most flagrant abuses go unchecked in both state and federal agencies.

24　　　It is not my contention that chemical insecticides must never be used. I do contend that we have put poisonous and biologically potent chemicals indiscriminately into the hands of persons largely or wholly ignorant of their potentials for harm. We have subjected enormous numbers of people to contact with these poisons, without their consent and often without their knowledge. If the Bill of Rights contains no guarantee that a citizen shall be secure against lethal poisons distributed either by private individuals or by public officials, it is surely only because our forefathers, despite their considerable wisdom and foresight, could conceive of no such problem.

25　　　I contend, furthermore, that we have allowed these chemicals to be used with little or no advance investigation of their effect on soil, water, wildlife, and man himself. Future generations are unlikely to condone our lack of prudent concern for the integrity of the natural world that supports all life.

26　　　There is still very limited awareness of the nature of the threat. This is an era of specialists, each of whom sees his own problem and is unaware of or intolerant of the larger frame into which it fits. It is also an era dominated by industry, in which the right to make a dollar at whatever cost is seldom challenged. When the public protests, confronted with some obvious evidence of damaging results of pesticide applications, it is fed little tranquilizing pills of half truth. We urgently need an end to these false assurances, to the sugar coating of unpalatable facts. It is the public that is being asked to assume the risks that the insect controllers calculate. The public must decide whether it wishes to continue on the present road, and it can do so only when in full possession of the facts. In the words of Jean Rostand, "The obligation to endure gives us the right to know."

COMPREHENSION

1. What does Carson mean by "the obligation to endure"?
2. What reasons does the author cite for the overpopulation of insects?
3. What remedies does Carson propose?

RHETORIC

1. What tone does Carson use in her essay? Does she seem to be a subjective or an objective writer? Give specific support for your response.

2. How does the use of words such as *dangerous, evil, irrevocable,* and *sinister* help shape the reader's reaction to the piece? What emotional and ethical appeals do such words indicate?
3. Examine the ordering of ideas in paragraph 4, and consider how such an order serves to reinforce Carson's argument.
4. Paragraph 9 consists of only one (long) sentence. What is its function in the essay's scheme?
5. Examine Carson's use of expert testimony. How does it help strengthen her thesis?
6. How effectively does the essay's conclusion help tie up Carson's points? What is the writer's intent in this final paragraph? How does she accomplish this aim?

WRITING

1. Write an essay in which you suggest solutions to the problems brought up in Carson's piece. You may want to suggest measures that the average citizen can take to eliminate the casual use of insecticides to control the insect population.
2. Write a biographical research paper on Carson that focuses on her involvement with nature and environmental issues.
3. **Writing an Argument:** Write an essay titled "Insects Are Not the Problem; Humanity Is." In this essay, argue that it is humanity's greed that has caused such an imbalance in nature as to threaten the planet's survival.

NETWORKING
Applying Digital and Multimedia Literacies

Composing an Interactive Argument Essay: Create question 1 or 3 under Writing as an electronic document, one that readers can interact with by clicking on links that take them to other essays and articles that both support *and* refute your position. Post the essay on a blog and enable comments so your classmates can actively engage with your topic. Respond to at least two comments, being sure to keep dialogue civil and arguments well supported. Make your Works Cited page interactive as well, documenting all sources and linking to any that are available online.

The Greenest Campuses: An Idiosyncratic Guide

Noel Perrin

Noel Perrin *(1927–2004) was born in New York City and worked as an editor before starting a career as a college instructor at the University of North Carolina and then Dartmouth College, where he taught beginning in 1959. He was awarded two*

Guggenheim Fellowships, contributed to numerous periodicals, and authored more than 10 books. His subject matter ranges from the scholarly, such as Dr. Bowdler's Legacy *(1969) and* Giving Up the Gun: Japan's Reversion to the Sword, 1543–1879 *(1979), to his experiences as a part-time farmer. Among the latter are* First Person Rural *(1978),* Second Person Rural *(1980),* Third Person Rural *(1983),* Last Person Rural *(1991), and* A Child's Delight *(1998). His concerns about the environment made him a popular speaker on ecological issues. In the following essay, first published in the* Chronicle of Higher Education *in April 2001, Perrin creates his own "best" college guide by ranking institutions of higher learning according to their environmental awareness.*

1   About 1,100 American colleges and universities run at least a token environmental-studies program, and many hundreds of those programs offer well-designed and useful courses. But only a drastically smaller number practice even a portion of what they teach. The one exception is recycling. Nearly every institution that has so much as one lonely environmental-studies course also does a little halfhearted recycling. Paper and glass, usually.

2   There are some glorious exceptions to those rather churlish observations, I'm glad to say. How many? Nobody knows. No one has yet done the necessary research (though the National Wildlife Federation's Campus Ecology program is planning a survey).

3   Certainly *U.S. News & World Report* hasn't. Look at the rankings in their annual college issue. The magazine uses a complex formula something like this: Institution's reputation, 25 percent, student-retention rate, 20 percent; faculty resources, 20 percent; and so on, down to alumni giving, 5 percent. The lead criterion may help explain why Harvard, Yale, and Princeton Universities so frequently do a little dance at the top of the list.

4   But *U.S. News* has nothing at all to say about the degree to which a college or university attempts to behave sustainably—that is, to manage its campus and activities in ways that promote the long-term health of the planet. The magazine is equally mum about which of the institutions it is ranking can serve as models to society in a threatened world.

5   And, of course, the world is threatened. When the Royal Society in London and the National Academy of Sciences in Washington issued their first-ever joint statement, it ended like this: "The future of our planet is in the balance. Sustainable development can be achieved, but only if irreversible degradation of the environment can be halted in time. The next 30 years may be crucial." They said that in 1992. If all those top scientists are right, we have a little more than 20 years left in which to make major changes in how we live.

6   All this affects colleges. I have one environmentalist friend who loves to point out to the deans and trustees she meets that if we don't make such changes, and if the irreversible degradation of earth does occur, Harvard's huge endowment and Yale's lofty reputation will count for nothing.

7   But though *U.S. News* has nothing to say, fortunately there is a fairly good grapevine in the green world. I have spent considerable time in the past two

years using it like an organic cell phone. By that means I have come up with a short, idiosyncratic list of green colleges, consisting of six that are a healthy green, two that are greener still, and three that I believe are the greenest in the United States.

Which approved surveying techniques have I used? None at all. Some of my 8
evidence is anecdotal, and some of my conclusions are affected by my personal beliefs, such as that electric and hybrid cars are not just a good idea, but instruments of salvation.

Obviously I did not examine, even casually, all 1,100 institutions. I'm sure I 9
have missed some outstanding performers. I hope I have missed a great many.

Now, here are the 11, starting with **Brown University.**   10

It is generally harder for a large urban university to move toward sustainable 11
behavior than it is for a small-town college with maybe a thousand students. But it's not impossible. Both Brown, in the heart of Providence, R.I., and Yale University (by no means an environmental leader in other respects), in the heart of New Haven, Conn., have found a country way of dealing with food waste. Pigs. Both rely on pigs.

For the past 10 years, Brown has been shipping nearly all of its food waste to 12
a Rhode Island piggery. Actually, not shipping it—just leaving it out at dawn each morning. The farmer comes to the campus and gets it. Not since Ralph Waldo Emerson took food scraps out to the family pig have these creatures enjoyed such a high intellectual connection.

But there is a big difference in scale. Where Emerson might have one pail of 13
slops now and then, Brown generates 700 tons of edible garbage each year. Haulage fee: $0. Tipping fee: $0. (That's the cost of dumping the garbage into huge cookers, where it is heated for the pigs.) Annual savings to Brown: about $50,000. Addition to the American food supply: many tons of ham and bacon each year.

Of course, Brown does far more than feed a balanced diet to a lot of pigs. 14
That's just the most exotic (for an urban institution) of its green actions. "Brown is Green" became the official motto of the university in August 1990. It was accurate then, and it remains accurate now.

Yale is the only other urban institution I'm aware of that supports a pig 15
population. Much of the credit goes to Cyril May, the university's environmental coordinator, just as much of the credit at Brown goes to its environmental coordinator, Kurt Teichert.

May has managed to locate two Connecticut piggeries. The one to which he 16
sends garbage presents problems. The farmer has demanded—and received—a collection fee. And he has developed an antagonistic relationship with some of Yale's food-service people. (There are a lot of them: The campus has 16 dining facilities.) May is working on an arrangement with the second piggery. But if it falls through, he says, "I may go back on semibended knee to the other."

Yale does not make the list as a green college, for reasons you will learn later 17
in this essay. But it might in a few more years

Carleton College is an interesting example of an institution turning green 18
almost overnight. No pig slops here; the dining halls are catered by Marriott. But change is coming fast.

19   In the summer of 1999, Carleton appointed its first-ever environmental coordinator, a brand-new graduate named Rachel Smit. The one-year appointment was an experiment, with a cobbled-together salary and the humble title of "fifth-year intern." The experiment worked beyond anyone's expectation.

20   Smit began publishing an environmental newsletter called *The Green Bean* and organized a small committee of undergraduates to explore the feasibility of composting the college's food waste, an effort that will soon begin. A surprised Marriott has already found itself serving organic dinners on Earth Day.

21   Better yet, the college set up an environmental-advisory committee of three administrators, three faculty members, and three students to review all campus projects from a green perspective. Naturally, many of those projects will be buildings, and to evaluate them, Carleton is using the *Minnesota Sustainable Design Guide,* itself cowritten by Richard Strong, director of facilities.

22   The position of fifth-year intern is now a permanent one-year position, and its salary is a regular part of the budget.

23   What's next? If Carleton gets a grant it has applied for, there will be a massive increase in environmental-studies courses and faculty seminars and, says the dean of budgets, "a whole range of green campus projects under the rubric of 'participatory learning.'"

24   And if Carleton doesn't get the grant? Same plans, slower pace.

25   Twenty years ago, **Dartmouth College** would have been a contender for the title of greenest college in America, had such a title existed. It's still fairly green. It has a large and distinguished group of faculty members who teach environmental studies, good recycling, an organic farm that was used last summer in six courses, years of experience with solar panels, and a fair number of midlevel administrators (including three in the purchasing office) who are ardent believers in sustainability.

26   But the college has lost ground. Most troubling is its new $50-million library, which has an actual anti-environmental twist: A portion of the roof requires steam from the power plant to melt snow off of it. The architect, Robert Venturi, may be famous, but he's no environmentalist.

27   Dartmouth is a striking example of what I shall modestly call Perrin's Law: No college or university can move far toward sustainability without the active support of at least two senior administrators. Dartmouth has no such committed senior administrators at all. It used to. James Hornig, a former dean of sciences, and Frank Smallwood, a former provost, were instrumental in creating the environmental-studies program, back in 1970. They are now emeriti. The current senior administrators are not in the least hostile to sustainability, they just give a very low priority to the college's practicing what it preaches.

28   **Emory University** is probably further into the use of nonpolluting and low-polluting motor vehicles than any other college in the country. According to Eric Gaither, senior associate vice president for business affairs, 60 percent of Emory's fleet is powered by alternative fuels. The facilities-management office has 40 electric carts, which maintenance workers use for getting around campus. The community-service office (security and parking) has its own

electric carts and an electric patrol vehicle. There are five electric shuttle buses and 14 compressed–natural-gas buses on order, plus one natural-gas bus in service.

Bill Chace, Emory's president, has a battery-charging station for electric cars 29 in his garage, and until recently an electric car to charge. Georgia Power, which lent the car, has recalled it, but Chace hopes to get it back. Meanwhile, he rides his bike to work most of the time.

How has Emory made such giant strides? "It's easy to do," says Gaither, 30 "when your president wants you to."

If Carleton is a model of how a small college turns green, the **University of** 31 **Michigan at Ann Arbor** is a model of how a big university does. Carleton is changing pretty much as an entity, while Michigan is more like the Electoral College—50 separate entities. The School of Natural Resources casts its 6 votes for sustainability, the English department casts its 12 for humanistic studies, the recycling coordinator casts her 1, the electric-vehicle program casts its 2, and so on. An institution of Michigan's size changes in bits and pieces.

Some of the bits show true leadership. For example, the university is within 32 weeks of buying a modest amount of green power. It makes about half of its own electricity (at its heating plant) and buys the other half. Five percent of that other half soon will come from renewable sources: hydro (water power) and biomass (so-called fuel crops, which are grown specifically to be burned for power).

The supporters of sustainability at Michigan would like to see the university 33 adopt a version of what is known as the Kyoto Protocol. The agreement, which the United States so far has refused to sign, requires that by 2012 each nation reduce its emission of greenhouse gases to 7 percent below its 1990 figure. Michigan's version of the protocol, at present a pipe dream, would require the university to do what the government won't—accept that reduction as a goal.

The immediate goal of "sustainabilists" at Ann Arbor is the creation of a 34 universitywide environmental coordinator, who would work either in the president's or the provost's office.

Giants are slow, but they are also strong.   35

Tulane University has the usual programs, among green institutions, in recy- 36 cling, composting, and energy efficiency. But what sets it apart is the Tulane Environmental Law Clinic, which is staffed by third-year law students. The director is a faculty member, and there are three law "fellows," all lawyers, who work with the students. The clinic does legal work for environmental organizations across Louisiana and "most likely has had a greater environmental impact than all our other efforts combined," says Elizabeth Davey, Tulane's first-ever environmental coordinator.

At least two campuses of the **University of California** (Berkeley is not among 37 them) have taken a first and even a second step toward sustainable behavior. First step: symbolic action, like installing a few solar panels, to produce clean energy and to help educate students. With luck, one of those little solar arrays might produce as much as a 20th of a percent of the electricity the university uses. It's a start.

The two campuses are Davis and Santa Cruz, and I think Davis nudges 38 ahead of Santa Cruz. That is primarily because Davis the city and Davis the university have done something almost miraculous. They have brought car culture at least partially under control, greatly reducing air pollution as a result.

39   The city has a population of about 58,000, which includes 24,000 students. According to reliable estimates, there are something over 50,000 bikes in town or on the campus, all but a few hundred owned by their riders. Most of the bikes are used regularly on the city's 45 miles of bike paths (closed to cars) and the 47 miles of bike lanes (cars permitted in the other lanes). The university maintains an additional 14 miles of bike paths on its large campus.

40   What happens on rainy days? "A surprising number continue to bike," says David Takemoto-Weerts, coordinator of Davis's bicycle program.

41   If every American college in a suitable climate were to behave like Davis, we could close a medium-sized oil refinery. Maybe we could even get rid of one coal-fired power plant, and thus seriously improve air quality.

42   The **University of New Hampshire** is trying to jump straight from symbolic gestures, like installing a handful of solar panels, to the hardest task of all for an institution trying to become green—establishing a completely new mind-set among students, administrators, and faculty and staff members. It may well succeed.

43   Campuses that have managed to change attitudes are rare. Prescott College, in Prescott, Ariz., and Sterling College, in Craftsbury Common, Vt., are rumored to have done so, and there may be two or three others. They're not on my list—because they're so small, because their students tend to be bright green even before they arrive, and because I have limited space.

44   New Hampshire has several token green projects, including a tiny solar array, able to produce one kilowatt at noon on a good day. And last April it inaugurated the Yellow Bike Cooperative. It is much smaller than anything that happens at Davis, where a bike rack might be a hundred yards long. But it's also more original and more communitarian. Anyone in Durham—student, burger flipper, associate dean—can join the Yellow Bike program by paying a $5 fee.

45   What you get right away is a key that unlocks all 50 bikes owned by the cooperative. (They are repaired and painted by student volunteers.) Want to cross campus? Just go to the nearest bike rack, unlock a Yellow, and pedal off. The goal, says Julie Newman, of the Office of Sustainability Programs, is "to greatly decrease one-person car trips on campus."

46   But the main thrust at New Hampshire is consciousness-raising. When the subject of composting food waste came up, the university held a seminar for its food workers.

47   New Hampshire's striking vigor is partly the result of a special endowment—about $12.8 million—exclusively for the sustainability office. Tom Kelly, the director, refuses to equate sustainability with greenness. Being green, in the sense of avoiding pollution and promoting reuse, is just one aspect of living sustainably, which involves "the balancing of economic viability with ecological health and human well-being," he says.

Oberlin College is an exception to Perrin's Law. The college has gotten 48 deeply into environmental behavior without the active support of two or, indeed, any senior administrators. As at Dartmouth, the top people are not hostile; they just have other priorities.

Apparently, until this year, Oberlin's environmental-studies program was 49 housed in a dreary cellar. Now it's in the $8.2-million Adam Joseph Lewis Environmental Studies Center, which is one of the most environmentally benign college buildings in the world. The money for it was raised as a result of a deal that the department chairman, David Orr, made with the administration: He could raise money for his own program, provided that he approached only people and foundations that had never shown the faintest interest in Oberlin.

It's too soon for a full report on the building. It is loaded with solar panels— 50 690 of them, covering the roof (for a diagram of the building, see www.oberlin. edu/newserv/esc/escabout.html). In about a year, data will be available on how much energy the panels have saved and whether, as Orr hopes, the center will not only make all its own power, but even export some.

Northland College, in Wisconsin, also goes way beyond tokenism. Its 51 McLean Environmental Living and Learning Center, a two-year-old residence hall for 114 students, is topped by a 120-foot wind tower that, with a good breeze coming off Lake Superior, can generate 20 kilowatts of electricity. The building also includes three arrays of solar panels. They are only token-size, generating a total of 3.2 kilowatts at most. But one array does heat most of the water for one wing of McLean, while the other three form a test project.

One test array is fixed in place—it can't be aimed. Another is like that sun- 52 flower in Blake's poem—it countest the steps of the sun. Put more prosaically, it tracks the sun across the sky each day. The third array does that and can also be tilted to get the best angle for each season of the year.

Inside the dorm is a pair of composting toilets—an experiment, to see if stu- 53 dents will use them. Because no one is forced to try the new ones if they don't want to—plenty of conventional toilets are close by—it means something when James Miller, vice president and dean of student development and enrollment, reports, "Students almost always choose the composting bathrooms."

From the start, the college's goal has been to have McLean operate so effi- 54 ciently that it consumes 40 percent less outside energy than would a conventional dormitory of the same dimensions. The building didn't reach that goal in its first year; energy use dropped only 34.2 percent. But anyone dealing with a new system knows to expect bugs at the beginning. There were some at Northland, including the wind generator's being down for three months. (As I write, it's turning busily.) Dean Miller is confident that the building will meet or exceed the college's energy-efficiency goal.

There is no room here to talk about the octagonal classroom structure made 55 of bales of straw, built largely by students. Or about the fact that Northland's grounds are pesticide- and herbicide-free.

If Oberlin is a flagrant exception to Perrin's Law, **Middlebury College** is a 56 strong confirmation. Middlebury is unique, as far as I know, in having not only senior administrators who strongly back environmentalism, but one senior administrator right inside the program. What Michigan wants, Middlebury has.

57   Nan Jenks-Jay, director of environmental affairs, reports directly to the provost. She is responsible for both the teaching side and the living-sustainably side of environmentalism. Under her are an environmental coordinator, Amy Self, and an academic-program coordinator, Janet Wiseman.

58   The program has powerful backers, including the president, John M. McCardell Jr.; the provost and executive vice president, Ronald D. Liebowitz; and the executive vice president for facilities planning, David W. Ginevan. But everyone I talked with at Middlebury, except for the occasional student who didn't want to trouble his mind with things like returnable bottles—to say nothing of acid rain—seemed at least somewhat committed to sustainable living.

59   Middlebury has what I think is the oldest environmental-studies program in the country; it began back in 1965. It has the best composting program I've ever seen. And, like Northland, it is pesticide- and herbicide-free.

60 Let me end as I began, with Harvard, Yale, and Princeton. And with *U.S. News*'s consistently ranking them in the top five, accompanied from time to time by the California Institute of Technology, Stanford University, and the Massachusetts Institute of Technology.

61   What if *U.S. News* did a green ranking? What if it based the listings on one of the few bits of hard data that can be widely compared: the percentage of waste that a college recycles?

62   Harvard would come out okay, though hardly at the top. The university recycled 24 percent of its waste last year, thanks in considerable part to the presence of Rob Gogan, the waste manager. He hopes to achieve 28 percent this year. That's feeble compared with Brown's 35 percent, and downright puny against Middlebury's 64 percent.

63   But compared with Yale and Princeton, it's magnificent. Most of the information I could get from Princeton is sadly dated. It comes from the 1995 report of the Princeton Environmental Reform Committee, whose primary recommendation was that the university hire a full-time waste manager. The university has not yet done so. And if any administrators on the campus know the current recycling percentage, they're not telling.

64   And Yale—poor Yale! It does have a figure. Among the performances of the 20 or so other colleges and universities whose percentages I'm aware of, only Carnegie Mellon's is worse. Yale: 19 percent. Carnegie Mellon: 11 percent.

65   What should universities—and society—be shooting for? How can you ask? One-hundred-percent retrieval of everything retrievable, of course.

COMPREHENSION

1. Why does Perrin call his essay an "idiosyncratic guide" when environmentalism has become a major issue in most municipalities, regions, and countries?
2. Is Perrin's purpose to inform, argue, or both? Does he have a clear-cut thesis, or does he leave it up to the reader to infer the thesis? Explain.

3. What information is Perrin's informal guide providing that is not offered in more conventional college rankings? Is he suggesting that parents and students consider "green rankings" in choosing which college to apply to? Explain.

RHETORIC

1. What purpose might Perrin have for choosing to create a "green guide" for colleges when there are so many other institutions or items he could have selected for review, such as corporations, towns, cities, automobiles, and numerous household products? What makes colleges and universities a particularly apt target?
2. Usually, Ivy League colleges are at the top of college guide lists as most desirable. Where do they rank on Perrin's list? What ironic statement is Perrin making by providing their rankings on the "green scale"? What is he implying about American values, particularly as they pertain to education?
3. Colleges and universities often pride themselves on the renown of their faculties. Who are the people Perrin cites as models of academic worth? Why has he chosen them?
4. What is the ironic purpose behind the author mentioning "Perrin's Law" (paragraph 27)? Is it a true "law," like the law of gravity? What body of knowledge is the author satirizing by invoking such a law?
5. Perrin is not didactic, since he does not recommend that other colleges adopt the environmental measures his model colleges have chosen. Would more direct advocacy on his part have strengthened his argument or weakened it, or not have had any effect? Explain.
6. In Perrin's conclusion, he changes his purpose from providing a purely informational assessment to offering a strong reprimand and recommendation. Why does he wait until the concluding paragraph to do so?

WRITING

1. Describe an environmentally friendly practice conducted at your college or university. Is it truly helpful for the environment, or is it largely symbolic?
2. Compare and contrast the academically oriented courses and programs offered at your school with what your institution actually does in the way of helping the environment. Discuss which of the two priorities is more prominent, and why.
3. **Writing an Argument:** Argue for or against the proposition that a magazine such as *U.S. News & World Report* should include environmental awareness and practice in its formula for assessing the rankings of colleges.

NETWORKING
Applying Digital and Multimedia Literacies

Creating a Facebook Group for a Cause: With several of your classmates, create a Facebook group that calls for action or raises awareness about an environmental issue or natural space that is relevant to your campus or local community. Consider carefully what you'll call the group (names are important!), and in a mission statement, articulate what you hope to accomplish by organizing it.

❋

The Last Americans: Environmental Collapse and the End of Civilization

Jared Diamond

Jared Diamond (b. 1937), who was born in Boston, is a physiologist, ecologist, and prolific writer who has published hundreds of popular and scientific articles. He has a BA from Harvard University (1958) and a PhD from Cambridge University (1961). Currently a professor of geography at UCLA and formerly professor of physiology at UCLA's School of Medicine, Diamond has conducted research in ecology and evolutionary biology in New Guinea and other southwest Pacific islands. As a field researcher and director of the World Wildlife Fund, Diamond helped to establish New Guinea's national park system. He received the Pulitzer Prize for Guns, Germs, and Steel: The Fates of Human Societies *(1997). Another well-received book of Diamonds's is* Collapse: How Societies Choose to Fail or Succeed *(2004). In the following essay, which appeared in the June 2003 issue of* Harper's, *Diamond examines the environmental crises and failures of previous societies and civilizations, and how we might be able to learn lessons from these lost worlds.*

I met a traveler from an antique land
Who said: Two vast and trunkless legs of stone
Stand in the desert. . . . Near them, on the sand,
Half sunk, a shattered visage lies, whose frown,
And wrinkled lip, and sneer of cold command,
Tell that its sculptor well those passions read
Which yet survive, stamped on these lifeless things,
The hand that mocked them, and the heart that fed:
And on the pedestal these words appear:
"My name is Ozymandias, king of kings:
Look on my works, ye Mighty, and despair!"
Nothing beside remains. Round the decay
Of that colossal wreck, boundless and bare
The lone and level sands stretch far away.

— *"Ozymandias," Percy Bysshe Shelley*

1   One of the disturbing facts of history is that so many civilizations collapse. Few people, however, least of all our politicians, realize that a primary cause of the collapse of those societies has been the destruction of the environmental resources on which they depended. Fewer still appreciate that many of those civilizations share a sharp curve of decline. Indeed, a society's demise may begin only a decade or two after it reaches its peak population, wealth, and power.

2   Recent archaeological discoveries have revealed similar courses of collapse in such otherwise dissimilar ancient societies as the Maya in the Yucatán, the

Anasazi in the American Southwest, the Cahokia mound builders outside St. Louis, the Greenland Norse, the statue builders of Easter Island, ancient Mesopotamia in the Fertile Crescent, Great Zimbabwe in Africa, and Angkor Wat in Cambodia. These civilizations, and many others, succumbed to various combinations of environmental degradation and climate change, aggression from enemies taking advantage of their resulting weakness, and declining trade with neighbors who faced their own environmental problems. Because peak population, wealth, resource consumption, and waste production are accompanied by peak environmental impact—approaching the limit at which impact outstrips resources—we can now understand why declines of societies tend to follow swiftly on their peaks.

These combinations of undermining factors were compounded by cultural 3 attitudes preventing those in power from perceiving or resolving the crisis. That's a familiar problem today. Some of us are inclined to dismiss the importance of a healthy environment, or at least to suggest that it's just one of many problems facing us—an "issue." That dismissal is based on three dangerous misconceptions.

Foremost among these misconceptions is that we must balance the environ- 4 ment against human needs. That reasoning is exactly upside-down. Human needs and a healthy environment are not opposing claims that must be balanced; instead, they are inexorably linked by chains of cause and effect. We need a healthy environment because we need clean water, clean air, wood, and food from the ocean, plus soil and sunlight to grow crops. We need functioning natural ecosystems, with their native species of earthworms, bees, plants, and microbes, to generate and aerate our soils, pollinate our crops, decompose our wastes, and produce our oxygen. We need to prevent toxic substances from accumulating in our water and air and soil. We need to prevent weeds, germs, and other pest species from becoming established in places where they aren't native and where they cause economic damage. Our strongest arguments for a healthy environment are selfish: We want it for ourselves, not for threatened species like snail darters, spotted owls, and Furbish louseworts.

Another popular misconception is that we can trust in technology to solve our 5 problems. Whatever environmental problem you name, you can also name some hoped-for technological solution under discussion. Some of us have faith that we shall solve our dependence on fossil fuels by developing new technologies for hydrogen engines, wind energy, or solar energy. Some of us have faith that we shall solve our food problems with new or soon-to-be-developed genetically modified crops. Some of us have faith that new technologies will succeed in cleaning up the toxic materials in our air, water, soil, and foods without the horrendous cleanup expenses that we now incur.

6   Those with such faith assume that the new technologies will ultimately succeed, but in fact some of them may succeed and others may not. They assume that the new technologies will succeed quickly enough to make a big difference soon, but all of these major technological changes will actually take five to thirty years to develop and implement—if they catch on at all. Most of all, those with faith assume that new technology won't cause any new problems. In fact, technology merely constitutes increased power, which produces changes that can be either for the better or for the worse. All of our current environmental problems are unanticipated harmful consequences of our existing technology. There is no basis for believing that technology will miraculously stop causing new and unanticipated problems while it is solving the problems that it previously produced.

7   The final misconception holds that environmentalists are fear-mongering, overreacting extremists whose predictions of impending disaster have been proved wrong before and will be proved wrong again. Behold, say the optimists: Water still flows from our faucets, the grass is still green, and the supermarkets are full of food. We are more prosperous than ever before, and that's the final proof that our system works.

8   Well, for a few billion of the world's people who are causing us increasing trouble, there isn't any clean water, there is less and less green grass, and there are no supermarkets full of food. To appreciate what the environmental problems of those billions of people mean for us Americans, compare the following two lists of countries. First ask some ivory-tower academic ecologist who knows a lot about the environment but never reads a newspaper and has no interest in politics to list the overseas countries facing some of the worst problems of environmental stress, overpopulation, or both. The ecologist would answer, "That's a no-brainer, it's obvious. Your list of environmentally stressed or overpopulated countries should surely include Afghanistan, Bangladesh, Burundi, Haiti, Indonesia, Iraq, Nepal, Pakistan, the Philippines, Rwanda, the Solomon Islands, and Somalia, plus others." Then ask a First World politician who knows nothing, and cares less, about the environment and population problems to list the world's worst trouble spots: countries where state government has already been overwhelmed and has collapsed, or is now at risk of collapsing, or has been wracked by recent civil wars; and countries that, as a result of their problems, are also creating problems for us rich First World countries, which may be deluged by illegal immigrants, or have to provide foreign aid to those countries, or may decide to provide them with military assistance to deal with rebellions and terrorists, or may even (God forbid) have to send in our own troops. The politician would answer, "That's a no-brainer, it's obvious. Your list of political trouble spots should surely include Afghanistan, Bangladesh,

Burundi, Haiti, Indonesia, Iraq, Nepal, Pakistan, the Philippines, Rwanda, the Solomon Islands, and Somalia, plus others."

The connection between the two lists is transparent. Today, just as in the   9 past, countries that are environmentally stressed, overpopulated or both are at risk of becoming politically stressed, and of seeing their governments collapse. When people are desperate and undernourished, they blame their government, which they see as responsible for failing to solve their problems. They try to emigrate at any cost. They start civil wars. They kill one another. They figure that they have nothing to lose, so they become terrorists, or they support or tolerate terrorism. The results are genocides such as the ones that already have exploded in Burundi, Indonesia, and Rwanda; civil wars, as in Afghanistan, Indonesia, Nepal, the Philippines, and the Solomon Islands; calls for the dispatch of First World troops, as to Afghanistan, Indonesia, Iraq, the Philippines, Rwanda, the Solomon Islands, and Somalia; the collapse of central government, as has already happened in Somalia; and overwhelming poverty, as in all of the countries on these lists.

But what about the United States? Some might argue that the environ-   10 mental collapse of ancient societies is relevant to the modern decline of weak, far-off, overpopulated Rwanda and environmentally devastated Somalia, but isn't it ridiculous to suggest any possible relevance to the fate of our own society? After all, we might reason, those ancients didn't enjoy the wonders of modern environment-friendly technologies. Those ancients had the misfortune to suffer from the effects of climate change. They behaved stupidly and ruined their own environment by doing obviously dumb things, like cutting down their forests, watching their topsoil erode, and building cities in dry areas likely to run short of water. They had foolish leaders who didn't have books and so couldn't learn from history, and who embroiled them in destabilizing wars and didn't pay attention to problems at home. They were overwhelmed by desperate immigrants, as one society after another collapsed, sending floods of economic refugees to tax the resources of the societies that weren't collapsing. In all those respects, we modern Americans are fundamentally different from those primitive ancients, and there is nothing that we could learn from them.

11   Or so the argument goes. It's an argument so ingrained both in our subconscious and in public discourse that it has assumed the status of objective reality. We think we are different. In fact, of course, all of those powerful societies of the past thought that they too were unique, right up to the moment of their collapse. It's sobering to consider the swift decline of the ancient Maya, who 1,200 years ago were themselves the most advanced society in the Western Hemisphere, and who, like us now, were then at the apex of their own power and numbers. Two excellent recent books, David Webster's *The Fall of the Ancient Maya* and Richardson Gill's *The Great Maya Droughts,* help bring the trajectory of Maya civilization back to life for us. Their studies illustrate how even sophisticated societies like that of the Maya (and ours) can be undermined by details of rainfall, farming methods, and motives of leaders.

12 By now, millions of modern Americans have visited Maya ruins. To do so, one need only take a direct flight from the United States to the Yucatán capital of Mérida, jump into a rental car or minibus, and drive an hour on a paved highway. Most Maya ruins, with their great temples and monuments, lie surrounded by jungles (seasonal tropical forests), far from current human settlement. They are "pure" archaeological sites. That is, their locations became depopulated, so they were not covered up by later buildings as were so many other ancient cities, like the Aztec capital of Tenochtitlán—now buried under modern Mexico City—and Rome.

13   One of the reasons few people live there now is that the Maya homeland poses serious environmental challenges to would-be farmers. Although it has a somewhat unpredictable rainy season from May to October, it also has a dry season from January through April. Indeed, if one focuses on the dry months, one could describe the Yucatán as a "seasonal desert."

14   Complicating things, from a farmer's perspective, is that the part of the Yucatán with the most rain, the south, is also the part at the highest elevation above the water table. Most of the Yucatán consists of karst—a porous, spongelike, limestone terrain—and so rain runs straight into the ground, leaving little or no surface water. The Maya in the lower-elevation regions of the north were able to reach the water table by way of deep sinkholes called cenotes, and the Maya in low coastal areas without sinkholes could reach it by digging wells up to 75 feet deep. Most Maya, however, lived in the south. How did they deal with their resulting water problem?

Technology provided an answer. The Maya plugged up leaks on karst prom- 15
ontories by plastering the bottoms of depressions to create reservoirs, which collected rain and stored it for use in the dry season. The reservoirs at the Maya city
of Tikal, for example, held enough water to meet the needs of about 10,000 people
for eighteen months. If a drought lasted longer than that, though, the inhabitants
of Tikal were in deep trouble.

Maya farmers grew mostly corn, which constituted the astonishingly high 16
proportion of about 70 percent of their diet, as deduced from isotope analyses
of ancient Maya skeletons. They grew corn by means of a modified version of
swidden slash-and-burn agriculture, in which forest is cleared, crops are
grown in the resulting clearing for a few years until the soil is exhausted, and
then the field is abandoned for fifteen to twenty years until regrowth of wild
vegetation restores the soil's fertility. Because most of the land under a swidden
agricultural system is fallow at any given time, it can support only modest
population densities. Thus, it was a surprise for archaeologists to discover that
ancient Maya population densities, judging from numbers of stone foundations
of farmhouses, were often far higher than what unmodified swidden agriculture could support: often 250 to 750 people per square mile. The Maya probably achieved those high populations by such means as shortening the fallow
period and tilling the soil to restore soil fertility, or omitting the fallow period
entirely and growing crops every year, or, in especially moist areas, growing
two crops per year.

Socially stratified societies, ours included, consist of farmers who produce 17
food, plus nonfarmers such as bureaucrats and soldiers who do not produce
food and are in effect parasites on farmers. The farmers must grow enough food
to meet not only their own needs but also those of everybody else. The number
of nonproducing consumers who can be supported depends on the society's

agricultural productivity. In the United States today, with its highly efficient agriculture, farmers make up only 2 percent of our population, and each farmer can feed, on the average, 129 other people. Ancient Egyptian agriculture was efficient enough for an Egyptian peasant to produce five times the food required for himself and his family. But a Maya peasant could produce only twice the needs of himself and his family.

18   Fully 80 percent of Maya society consisted of peasants. Their inability to support many nonfarmers resulted from several limitations of their agriculture. It produced little protein, because corn has much lower protein content than wheat, and because the few edible domestic animals kept by the Maya (turkeys, ducks, and dogs) included no large animals like our cows and sheep. There was little use of terracing or irrigation to increase production. In the Maya area's humid climate, stored corn would rot or become infested after a year, so the Maya couldn't get through a longer drought by eating surplus corn accumulated in good years. And unlike Old World peoples with their horses, oxen, donkeys, and camels, the Maya had no animal-powered transport. Indeed, the Maya lacked not only pack animals and animal-drawn plows but also metal tools, wheels, and boats with sails. All of those great Maya temples were built by stone and wooden tools and human muscle power alone, and all overland transport went on the backs of human porters.

19   Those limitations on food supply and food transport may in part explain why Maya society remained politically organized in small kingdoms that were perpetually at war with one another and that never became unified into large empires like the Aztec empire of the Valley of Mexico (fed by highly productive agriculture) or the Inca empire of the Andes (fed by diverse crops carried on llamas). Maya armies were small and unable to mount lengthy campaigns over long distances. The typical Maya kingdom held a population of only up to 50,000 people, within a radius of two or three days' walk from the king's palace. From the top of the temple of some Maya kingdoms, one could see the tops of the temples of other kingdoms.

20   Presiding over the temple was the king himself, who functioned both as head priest and as political leader. It was his responsibility to pray to the gods, to perform astronomical and calendrical rituals, to ensure the timely arrival of the rains on which agriculture depended, and thereby to bring prosperity. The king claimed to have the supernatural power to deliver those good things because of his asserted family relationship to the gods. Of course, that exposed him to the risk that his subjects would become disillusioned if he couldn't fulfill his boast of being able to deliver rains and prosperity

21 Those are the basic outlines of Classic Maya society, which for all its limitations lasted more than 500 years. Indeed, the Maya themselves believed that it had lasted for much longer. Their remarkable Long Count calendar had its starting date (analogous to January 1, A.D. 1 of our calendar) backdated into the remote preliterate past, at August 11, 3114 B.C. The first physical evidence of civilization within the Maya area, in the form of villagers and pottery, appeared around 1400 B.C., substantial buildings around 500 B.C., and writing around 400 B.C.

The so-called Classic period of Maya history arose around A.D. 250, when evidence for the first kings and dynasties emerged. From then, the Maya population increased almost exponentially, to reach peak numbers in the eighth century A.D. The largest monuments were erected toward the end of that century. All the indicators of a complex society declined throughout the ninth century, until the last date on any monument was A.D. 909. This decline of Maya population and architecture constitutes what is known as the Classic Maya collapse.

What happened? Let's consider in more detail a city whose ruins now lie in 22 western Honduras at the world-famous site of Copán. The most fertile ground in the Copán area consists of five pockets of flat land along a river valley with a total area of only one square mile; the largest of those five pockets, known as the Copán pocket, has an area of half a square mile. Much of the land around Copán consists of steep hills with poor soil. Today, corn yields from valley-bottom fields are two or three times those of fields on hill slopes, which suffer rapid erosion and lose most of their productivity within a decade of farming.

To judge by the number of house sites, population growth in the Copán valley 23 rose steeply from the fifth century up to a peak estimated at around 27,000 people between A.D. 750 and 900. Construction of royal monuments glorifying kings became especially massive from A.D. 650 onward. After A.D. 700, nobles other than kings got into the act and began erecting their own palaces, increasing the burden that the king and his own court already imposed on the peasants. The last big buildings at Copán were put up around A.D. 800; the last date on an incomplete altar possibly bearing a king's name is A.D. 822.

Archaeological surveys of different types of habitats in the Copán valley show 24 that they were occupied in a regular sequence. The first area farmed was the large Copán pocket of bottomland, followed by occupation of the other four bottomland pockets. During that time the human population was growing, but the hills remained uninhabited. Hence that increased population must have been accommodated by intensifying production in the bottomland pockets: probably some combination of shorter fallow periods and double-cropping. By A.D. 500, people had started to settle the hill slopes, but those sites were occupied only briefly. The percentage of Copán's total population that was in the hills, rather than in the valleys, peaked in the year 575 and then declined, as the population again became concentrated in the pockets.

What caused that pullback of population from the hills? From excavation of 25 building foundations on the valley floor we know that they became covered with sediment during the eighth century, meaning that the hill slopes were becoming eroded and probably also leached of nutrients. The acidic hill soils being carried down into the valley would have reduced agricultural yields. The reason for that erosion of the hillsides is clear: the forests that formerly covered them and protected their soil were being cut down. Dated pollen samples show that the pine forests originally covering the hilltops were eventually all cleared, to be burned for fuel. Besides causing sediment accumulation in the valleys and depriving valley inhabitants of wood supplies, that deforestation may have begun to cause a "man-made drought" in the valley bottom, because forests play a major role in water cycling, such that massive deforestation tends to result in lowered rainfall.

26   Hundreds of skeletons recovered from Copán archaeological sites have been studied for signs of disease and poor nutrition, such as porous bones and stress lines in the teeth. Those skeletal signs show that the health of Copán's inhabitants deteriorated from A.D. 650 to 850, among both the elite and commoners, though the health of commoners was worse.

27   Recall that Copán's population was growing rapidly while the hills were being occupied. The subsequent abandonment of all of those hill fields meant that the burden of feeding the extra population formerly dependent on the hills now fell increasingly on the valley floor, and that more and more people were competing for the food grown on that one square mile of bottomland. That would have led to fighting among the farmers themselves for the best land, or for any land, just as in modern Rwanda. Because the king was failing to deliver on his promises of rain and prosperity, he would have been the scapegoat for this agricultural failure, which explains why the last that we hear of any king is A.D. 822, and why the royal palace was burned around A.D. 850.

28   Datable pieces of obsidian, the sharp rock from which the Maya made their stone tools, suggest that Copán's total population decreased more gradually than did its signs of kings and nobles. The estimated population in the year A.D. 950 was still around 15,000, or 55 percent of the peak population of 27,000. That population continued to dwindle, until there are few signs of anyone in the Copán valley after around A.D. 1235. The reappearance of pollen from forest trees thereafter provides independent evidence that the valley became virtually empty of people.

29   The Maya history that I have just related, and Copán's history in particular, illustrate why we talk about "the Maya collapse." But the story grows more complicated, for at least five reasons. There was not only that enormous Classic collapse but also at least two smaller pre-Classic collapses, around A.D. 150 and 600, as well as some post-Classic collapses. The Classic collapse was obviously not complete, because hundreds of thousands of Maya survived, in areas with stable water supplies, to meet and fight the Spaniards. The collapse of population (as gauged by numbers of house sites and of obsidian tools) was in some cases much slower than the decline in numbers of Long Count dates. Many apparent collapses of cities were nothing more than "power cycling"; i.e., particular cities becoming more powerful at the expense of neighboring cities, then declining or getting conquered by neighbors, without changes in the whole population. Finally, cities in different parts of the Maya area rose and fell on different trajectories.

30   Some archaeologists focus on these complications and don't want to recognize a Classic Maya collapse at all. But this overlooks the obvious fact that cries out for explanation: the disappearance of between 90 and 99 percent of the Maya population after A.D. 800, and of the institution of the kingship, Long

Count calendars, and other complex political and cultural institutions. Before we can understand those disappearances, however, we need first to understand the roles of warfare and of drought.

Archaeologists for a long time believed the ancient Maya to be gentle and 31 peaceful people. We now know that Maya warfare was intense, chronic, and unresolvable, because limitations of food supply and transportation made it impossible for any Maya principality to unite the whole region in an empire. The archaeological record shows that wars became more intense and frequent toward the time of the Classic collapse. That evidence comes from discoveries of several types since the Second World War: archaeological excavations of massive fortifications surrounding many Maya sites; vivid depictions of warfare and captives on stone monuments and on the famous painted murals discovered in 1946 at Bonampak; and the decipherment of Maya writing, much of which proved to consist of royal inscriptions boasting of conquests. Maya kings fought to capture and torture one another; an unfortunate loser was a Copán king with the to us unforgettable name of King 18 Rabbit.

Maya warfare involved well-documented types of violence: wars among 32 separate kingdoms; attempts of cities within a kingdom to secede by revolting against the capital; and civil wars resulting from frequent violent attempts by would-be kings to usurp the throne. All of these events were described or depicted on monuments, because they involved kings and nobles. Not considered worthy of description, but probably even more frequent, were fights between commoners over land, as overpopulation became excessive and land became scarce.

The other phenomenon important to understanding all of these collapses is 33 the repeated occurrence of droughts, as inferred by climatologists from evidence of lake evaporation preserved in lake sediments, and as summarized by Gill in *The Great Maya Droughts*. The rise of Maya civilization may have been facilitated by a rainy period beginning around 250 B.C., until a temporary drought after A.D. 125 was associated with a pre-Classic collapse at some sites. That collapse was followed by the resumption of rainy conditions and the buildup of Classic Maya cities, briefly interrupted by another drought around 600 corresponding to a decline at Tikal and some other sites. Finally, around A.D. 750 there began the worst drought in the past 7,000 years, peaking around the year A.D. 800, and suspiciously associated with the Classic collapse.

The area most affected by the Classic collapse was the southern high- 34 lands, probably for the two reasons already mentioned: It was the area with the densest population, and it also had the most severe water problems because it lay too high above the water table for cenotes or wells to provide water. The southern highlands lost more than 99 percent of its population in the course of the Classic collapse. When Cortés and his Spanish army marched in 1524 and 1525 through an area formerly inhabited by millions of Maya, he nearly starved because he encountered so few villagers from whom to acquire corn. The Spaniards passed within only a few miles of the abandoned ruins of the great Classic cities of Tikal and Palenque, but still they heard or saw nothing of them.

35 We can identify increasingly familiar strands in the Classic Maya collapse. One consisted of population growth outstripping available resources: the dilemma foreseen by Thomas Malthus in 1798. As Webster succinctly puts it in *The Fall of the Ancient Maya,* "Too many farmers grew too many crops on too much of the landscape." While population was increasing, the area of usable farmland paradoxically was decreasing from the effects of deforestation and hillside erosion.

36   The next strand consisted of increased fighting as more and more people fought over fewer resources. Maya warfare, already endemic, peaked just before the collapse. That is not surprising when one reflects that at least 5 million people, most of them farmers, were crammed into an area smaller than the state of Colorado. That's a high population by the standards of ancient farming societies, even if it wouldn't strike modern Manhattan-dwellers as crowded.

37   Bringing matters to a head was a drought that, although not the first one the Maya had been through, was the most severe. At the time of previous droughts, there were still uninhabited parts of the Maya landscape, and people in a drought area or dust bowl could save themselves by moving to another site. By the time of the Classic collapse, however, there was no useful unoccupied land in the vicinity on which to begin anew, and the whole population could not be accommodated in the few areas that continued to have reliable water supplies.

38   The final strand is political. Why did the kings and nobles not recognize and solve these problems? A major reason was that their attention was evidently focused on the short-term concerns of enriching themselves, waging wars, erecting monuments, competing with one another, and extracting enough food from the

peasants to support all those activities. Like most leaders throughout human history, the Maya kings and nobles did not have the leisure to focus on long-term problems, insofar as they perceived them.

What about those same strands today? The United States is also at the peak of 39 its power, and it is also suffering from many environmental problems. Most of us have become aware of more crowding and stress. Most of us living in large American cities are encountering increased commuting delays, because the number of people and hence of cars is increasing faster than the number of freeway lanes. I know plenty of people who in the abstract doubt that the world has a population problem, but almost all of those same people complain to me about crowding, space issues, and traffic experienced in their personal lives.

Many parts of the United States face locally severe problems of water re- 40 striction (especially southern California, Arizona, the Everglades, and, increasingly, the Northeast); forest fires resulting from logging and forest-management practices throughout the intermontane West; and losses of farmlands to salinization, drought, and climate change in the northern Great Plains. Many of us frequently experience problems of air quality, and some of us also experience problems of water quality and taste. We are losing economically valuable natural resources. We have already lost American chestnut trees, the Grand Banks cod fishery, and the Monterey sardine fishery; we are in the process of losing swordfish and tuna and Chesapeake Bay oysters and elm trees; and we are losing topsoil.

The list goes on: All of us are experiencing personal consequences of our 41 national dependence on imported energy, which affects us not only through higher gas prices but also through the current contraction of the national economy, itself the partial result of political problems associated with our oil dependence. We are saddled with expensive toxic cleanups at many locations, most notoriously near Montana mines, on the Hudson River, and in the Chesapeake Bay. We also face expensive eradication problems resulting from hundreds of introduced pest species—including zebra mussels, Mediterranean fruit flies, Asian longhorn beetles, water hyacinth, and spotted knapweed—that now affect our agriculture, forests, waterways, and pastures.

These particular environmental problems, and many others, are enor- 42 mously expensive in terms of resources lost, cleanup and restoration costs, and the cost of finding substitutes for lost resources: a billion dollars here, 10 billion there, in dozens and dozens of cases. Some of the problems, especially those of air quality and toxic substances, also exact health costs that are large, whether measured in dollars or in lost years or in quality of life. The cost of our home-grown environmental problems adds up to a large fraction of our gross national product, even without mentioning the costs that we incur from environmental problems overseas, such as the military operations that they inspire. Even the mildest of bad scenarios for our future include a gradual economic decline, as happened to the Roman and British empires. Actually, in case you didn't notice it, our economic decline is already well under way. Just check the numbers for our national debt, yearly government budget deficit, unemployment statistics, and the value of your investment and pension funds.

43 The environmental problems of the United States are still modest compared with those of the rest of the world. But the problems of environmentally devastated, overpopulated, distant countries are now our problems as well. We are accustomed to thinking of globalization in terms of us rich, advanced First Worlders sending our good things, such as the Internet and Coca-Cola, to those poor backward Third Worlders. Globalization, however, means nothing more than improved worldwide communication and transportation, which can convey many things in either direction; it is not restricted to good things carried only from the First to the Third World. They in the Third World can now, intentionally or unintentionally, send us their bad things: terrorists; diseases such as AIDS, SARS, cholera, and West Nile fever, carried inadvertently by passengers on transcontinental airplanes; unstoppable numbers of immigrants, both legal and illegal, arriving by boat, truck, train, plane, and on foot; and other consequences of their Third World problems. We in the United States are no longer the isolated Fortress America to which some of us aspired in the 1930s; instead, we are tightly and irreversibly connected to overseas countries. The United States is the world's leading importer, and it is also the world's leading exporter. Our own society opted long ago to become interlocked with the rest of the world.

That's why political stability anywhere in the world now affects us, our trade 44 routes, and our overseas markets and suppliers. We are so dependent on the rest of the world that if a decade ago you had asked a politician to name the countries most geopolitically irrelevant to U.S. interests because of their being so remote, poor, and weak, the list would have begun with Afghanistan and Somalia, yet these countries were subsequently considered important enough to warrant our dispatching U.S. troops. The Maya were "globalized" only within the Yucatán: the southern Yucatán Maya affected the northern Yucatán Maya and may have had some effects on the Valley of Mexico, but they had no contact with Somalia. That's because Maya transportation was slow, short-distance, on foot or else in canoes, and had low cargo capacity. Our transport today is much more rapid and has much higher cargo capacity. The Maya lived in a globalized Yucatán; we live in a globalized world.

If all of this reasoning seems straightforward when expressed so bluntly, one has 45 to wonder: Why don't those in power today get the message? Why didn't the leaders of the Maya, Anasazi, and those other societies also recognize and solve their problems? What were the Maya thinking while they watched loggers clearing the last pine forests on the hills above Copán? Here, the past really is a useful guide to the present. It turns out that there are at least a dozen reasons why past societies failed to *anticipate* some problems before they developed, or failed to *perceive* problems that had already developed, or failed even to try to solve problems that they did perceive. All of those dozen reasons still can be seen operating today. Let me mention just three of them.

First, it's difficult to recognize a slow trend in some quantity that fluctuates widely 46 up and down anyway, such as seasonal temperature, annual rainfall, or economic indicators. That's surely why the Maya didn't recognize the oncoming drought until it was too late, given that rainfall in the Yucatán varies several-fold from year to year. Natural fluctuations also explain why it's only within the last few years that all climatologists have become convinced of the reality of climate change, and why our president still isn't convinced but thinks that we need more research to test for it.

Second, when a problem *is* recognized, those in power may not attempt to 47 solve it because of a clash between their short-term interests and the interests of the rest of us. Pumping that oil, cutting down those trees, and catching those fish may benefit the elite by bringing them money or prestige and yet be bad for society as a whole (including the children of the elite) in the long run. Maya kings were consumed by immediate concerns for their prestige (requiring more and bigger temples) and their success in the next war (requiring more followers), rather than for the happiness of commoners or of the next generation. Those people with the greatest power to make decisions in our own society today regularly make money from activities that may be bad for society as a whole and for their own children; those decision-makers include Enron executives, many land developers, and advocates of tax cuts for the rich.

Finally, it's difficult for us to acknowledge the wisdom of policies that clash 48 with strongly held values. For example, a belief in individual freedom and a distrust of big government are deeply ingrained in Americans, and they make sense under some circumstances and up to a certain point. But they also make it hard for us to accept big government's legitimate role in ensuring that each individual's freedom to maximize the value of his or her land holdings doesn't decrease the value of the collective land of all Americans.

49 Not all societies make fatal mistakes. There are parts of the world where societies have unfolded for thousands of years without any collapse, such as Java, Tonga, and (until 1945) Japan. Today, Germany and Japan are successfully managing their forests, which are even expanding in area rather than shrinking. The Alaskan salmon fishery and the Australian lobster fishery are being managed sustainably. The Dominican Republic, hardly a rich country, nevertheless has set aside a comprehensive system of protected areas encompassing most of the country's natural habitats.

50   Is there any secret to explain why some societies acquire good environmental sense while others don't? Naturally, part of the answer depends on accidents of individual leaders' wisdom (or lack thereof). But part also depends upon whether a society is organized so as to minimize built-in clashes of interest between its decision-making elites and its masses. Given how our society is organized, the executives of Enron, Tyco, and Adelphi correctly calculated that their own interests would be best promoted by looting the company coffers, and that they would probably get away with most of their loot. A good example of a society that minimizes such clashes of interest is the Netherlands, whose citizens have perhaps the world's highest level of environmental awareness and of membership in environmental organizations. I never understood why, until on a recent trip to the Netherlands I posed the question to three of my Dutch friends while driving through their countryside.

51   Just look around you, they said. All of this farmland that you see lies below sea level. One fifth of the total area of the Netherlands is below sea level, as much as 22 feet below, because it used to be shallow bays, and we reclaimed it from the sea by surrounding the bays with dikes and then gradually pumping out the water. We call these reclaimed lands "polders." We began draining our polders nearly a thousand years ago. Today, we still have to keep pumping out the water that gradually seeps in. That's what our windmills used to be for, to drive the pumps to pump out the polders. Now we use steam, diesel, and electric pumps instead. In each polder there are lines of them, starting with those farthest from the sea, pumping the water in sequence until the last pump finally deposits it into a river or the ocean. And all of us, rich or poor, live down in the polders. It's not the case that rich people live safely up on top of the dikes while poor people live in the polder bottoms below sea level. If the dikes and pumps fail, we'll all drown together.

52   Throughout human history, all peoples have been connected to some other peoples, living together in virtual polders. For the ancient Maya, their polder consisted of most of the Yucatán and neighboring areas. When the Classic Maya cities collapsed in the southern Yucatán, refugees may have

reached the northern Yucatán, but probably not the Valley of Mexico, and certainly not Florida. Today, our whole world has become one polder, such that events in even Afghanistan and Somalia affect Americans. We do indeed differ from the Maya, but not in ways we might like: We have a much larger population, we have more potent destructive technology, and we face the risk of a worldwide rather than a local decline. Fortunately, we also differ from the Maya in that we know their fate, and they did not. Perhaps we can learn.

COMPREHENSION

1. Explain the significance of Shelley's poem "Ozymandias" for Diamond's essay.
2. What are the "three dangerous misconceptions" (paragraph 3) about the environment that Diamond discusses?
3. List all the civilizations that Diamond mentions in this essay. Which civilization does he emphasize? According to Diamond, why did previous civilizations fail, and how do these collapses provide guides to the state of contemporary American civilization?

RHETORIC

1. State Diamond's argument or major proposition. Where does his claim appear most clearly? What minor propositions does he develop? How does he deal with opposing viewpoints?
2. What types of evidence does the writer provide to support his claim?
3. Why does Diamond divide his essay into so many sections? What relationships do you detect between and among these sections?
4. Where does Diamond use comparison and contrast and causal analysis to organize parts of his essay?
5. How does classification operate as a rhetorical element in this article?
6. Assess the relative effectiveness of Diamond's conclusion. How does the ending serve as a coda for the entire essay?

WRITING

1. Write an essay focusing on a local environmental problem. Analyze the ways in which this environmental problem affects the lives of nearby residents.
2. Select one civilization that Diamond mentions. Conduct research on this civilization, and then write a report on the environmental factors that led to the decline of that society.
3. **Writing an Argument:** Write a persuasive essay in which you warn readers about three environmental dangers confronting the United States today.

NETWORKING
Applying Digital and Multimedia Literacies

Analyzing the Use of Images: How do the illustrations in this essay interact with Diamond's written text? What is their rhetorical purpose, and how do they influence the text's tone?

Synthesis: Connections for Critical Thinking

1. Using support from the works of Lopez, Carson, Chief Seattle, and others, write a causal-analysis essay tracing our relationship to the land. To what extent have history, greed, and fear helped shape our attitude? Can this attitude be changed? How?

2. Consider the empathy and sensitivity Lopez has toward animals. How do his attitude and perceptions coincide with the views expressed by Bass and Chief Seattle concerning the natural world?

3. Write a letter to the op-ed page of a newspaper objecting to a governmental ruling harmful to the environment. State the nature of the policy, its possible dangers, and your reasons for opposing it. Use support from Horowitz, McKibben, Diamond, and any other writers in this chapter. Extra reading or research may be necessary.

4. Consider why we fear nature. Why do we consider it an enemy, an alien, something to be destroyed? How would Bass, Lopez, and Chief Seattle respond to this question? Do you agree or disagree with them?

5. Both Lopez and Diamond use narration and description to explore our relationship to the land. How do they approach their subject in terms of language, attitude, and style?

6. Choose an author in this chapter whose essay, in your opinion, romanticizes nature. Compare his or her attitude with that of a writer with a more pragmatic approach to the subject. Compare the two views, and specify the elements in their writing that contribute to the overall strength of their arguments.

7. Perrin uses enumeration and illustration to structure his essay. What are some of the strengths and weaknesses of employing traditional and orderly means of presenting one's thoughts?

8. Write an essay titled "Nature's Revenge" in which you examine the consequences of environmental abuse. Consider the short- as well as the long-term effects on the quality of life. Use support from any three writers in this chapter to defend your opinion.

9. Write specifically about our relationship to other living creatures on our planet. Is it one of exploitation, cooperation, or tyranny? How does this relationship influence how we treat each other? Explore the answers to these questions in an essay. Use the works of Lopez, Bass, and Chief Seattle to support your thesis.

NETWORKING
Applying Digital and Multimedia Literacies

Join an online newsgroup devoted to addressing a specific environmental issue—for example, atomic waste, overdevelopment, or environmental regulations and deregulations. Follow the conversation of the newsgroup for one month. Write an essay describing what the chief concerns of the newsgroup members are, how they address issues regarding the environment, and what specific actions they recommend or take over the course of your membership.

Chapter 14

Science and Technology
What Can Science Teach Us?

Contrary to popular assumptions, contemporary science and technology are not dry subjects but rather are bodies of specialized knowledge concerned with the great how and why questions of our time. In fact, we are currently in the midst of a whole series of scientific revolutions that will radically transform our lives in the 21st century. The essential problem for humankind is to make sense of all this revolutionary scientific and technological knowledge, invest it with value, use it ethically, and make it serve our cultural and global needs.

As you will see in the essays in this chapter, human beings are always the ultimate subject of scientific investigation. Science and mathematics attempt to understand the physical, biological, and chemical events that shape our lives. Whenever we switch on a light or turn on a computer, take an aspirin or start the car, we see that science and technology have intervened effectively in our lives. Often the specialized knowledge of science forces us to make painful decisions, and the misuse of science can have disastrous results.

The technology that arises from science affects everyday decisions as well as the larger culture. Nowhere is the impact of science more apparent than in the field of biotechnology. As Dinesh D'Souza observes in his essay on the biotech revolution, science is intended to serve us, to help us with our common dilemmas. At the same time, biotechnology reminds us that despite advances, we are still mortals confronting ethical dilemmas. Even as knowledge flows from research laboratories, these mortal paradoxes tend to perplex and goad us as we seek scientific solutions to the complex problems of our era.

Science and technology as specialized bodies of knowledge can send contradictory messages because science and technology are socially constructed and reflect the contours of culture. How we manage the revolution in science—how we harness nuclear power or battle the ravages of AIDS—will determine the health of civilization in our century.

PREVIEWING THE CHAPTER

As you read the essays in this chapter and respond to them in discussion and writing, consider the following questions:

- Does the author take a personal or an objective approach to the subject? What is the effect?
- What area of scientific or technological inquiry does the writer focus on?
- What scientific conflicts arise in the course of the essay?
- Is the writer a specialist, a layperson, a journalist, or a commentator? How does the background of the writer affect the tone of the essay?
- What assumptions does the author make about his or her audience? How much specialized knowledge must you bring to the essay?
- How do social issues enter into the author's presentation?
- What gender issues are raised by the author?
- How have your perceptions of the author's topic been changed or enhanced? What new knowledge have you gained? Does the writer contradict any of your assumptions or beliefs?
- Is the writer optimistic or pessimistic about the state of technology or science? How do you know?

Classic and Contemporary Images
WHERE IS SCIENCE TAKING US?

Using a Critical Perspective Make a series of observations about each of these images. Where does your eye rest in each one? How many objects and details do you see? What reasonable inferences can you draw about the relationship of the artist who created the 15th-century image to the culture and historical period? What purpose did the scientists who created and control the Hubble Space Telescope have? What purposes do the 15th-century artist and 20th-century scientist have in common? Argue for or against the proposition that art can actually capture the advances in science, technology, and humanity that we have experienced over time.

During the Renaissance in Europe, scientists such as Nicolaus Copernicus
(1473–1543) and Galileo Galilei (1564–1642) revolutionized the way
Europeans viewed the universe and their place in it by proving that
the earth and the planets revolve around the sun, thus changing forever
the worldview exemplified by the 15th-century Flemish
depiction of the movements of the sun and moon shown here.

Galileo's primitive telescope was a distant forerunner of the powerful
Hubble Space Telescope, launched in 1990, which is able to take
photographs of extremely distant stars and other phenomena,
such as the gaseous pillars shown here, as it orbits the earth.

❉

Classic and Contemporary Essays
HOW HAS NATURE EVOLVED?

Evolution seems to be more highly and hotly debated each year, insinuating itself into educational, political, scientific, and religious debates. Unfortunately, extreme positions on evolution tend to obscure what is valuable about the concept. The idea or theory of evolution is rooted in scientific creativity and the scientific method. Scientists are observers and collectors of information, and they use facts to build an explanation of the natural world and our place in it. Darwin looked carefully at nature and the physical world, as the following reading on natural selection illustrates. In his autobiography, Darwin observed that he "collected facts on a wholesale scale" before arriving at his theory of natural selection, and this inductive approach, at the heart of *On the Origin of Species* (1859), typifies his method of inquiry. But does evolutionary theory explain all the facts—all of humankind's problems? Does evolution mark the progress of human civilization, or are dimensions needed to explain our relationship to the world and the world's events? Verlyn Klinkenborg, who writes editorials and vignettes on science and nature for the *New York Times*, touches on these questions in an essay he composed celebrating the bicentennial of Darwin's birth. But Klinkenborg broadens his inquiry to touch on the scientific ideas of Mendel, the structure of DNA, and the broader issue of "our failure to come to terms with science and the teaching of science." Darwin's great idea, as Klinkenborg suggests, helps to explain our struggle for existence and meaning in the modern world.

❉

Natural Selection

Charles Darwin

Charles Darwin *(1809–1882) was born in England and studied medicine at Edinburgh. He also studied for the ministry at Cambridge but soon turned his interest to natural history. Through his friendship with a well-known botanist, he was given the opportunity to take a five-year cruise around the world (1831–1836) aboard the H.M.S.* Beagle, *serving as a naturalist. This started Darwin on a career of accumulating and assimilating data that resulted in the formulation of his concept of evolution. He spent the remainder of his life carefully and methodically working over the information from his copious notes. He first published his findings in 1858 and a year later published his influential* On the Origin of Species. *This seminal work was supplemented and elaborated on in many later books, including* The Descent of Man *(1871). The following selection demonstrates the methodical and meticulous method Darwin used in developing his concepts.*

In order to make it clear how, as I believe, natural selection acts, I must beg permis- 1
sion to give one or two imaginary illustrations. Let us take the case of a wolf, which
preys on various animals, securing some by craft, some by strength, and some by
fleetness; and let us suppose that the fleetest prey, a deer for instance, had from any
change in the country increased in numbers, or that other prey had decreased in
numbers, during that season of the year when the wolf is hardest pressed for food.
I can under such circumstances see no reason to doubt that the swiftest and slim-
mest wolves would have the best chance of surviving, and so be preserved or
selected, provided always that they retained strength to master their prey at this or at
some other period of the year, when they might be compelled to prey on other animals. I can see no more reason to doubt this, than that man can improve the fleetness of his greyhounds by careful and methodical selection, or by that unconscious
selection which results from each man trying to keep the best dogs without any
thought of modifying the breed.

Even without any change in the proportional numbers of the animals on 2
which our wolf preyed, a cub might be born with an innate tendency to pursue
certain kinds of prey. Nor can this be thought very improbable; for we often
observe great differences in the natural tendencies of our domestic animals;
one cat, for instance, taking to catch rats, another mice; one cat, according
to Mr. St. John, bringing home winged game, another hares or rabbits, and
another hunting on marshy ground and almost nightly catching woodcocks or
snipes. The tendency to catch rats rather than mice is known to be inherited.
Now, if any slight innate change of habit or of structure benefited an individual
wolf, it would have the best chance of surviving and of leaving offspring. Some
of its young would probably inherit the same habits or structure, and by the
repetition of this process, a new variety might be formed which would either
supplant or coexist with the parent-form of wolf. Or, again, the wolves inhabiting
a mountainous district, and those frequenting the lowlands, would naturally be
forced to hunt different prey; and from the continued preservation of the individuals best fitted for the two sites, two varieties might slowly be formed. These
varieties would cross and blend where they met; but to this subject of inter-
crossing we shall soon have to return. I may add, that, according to Mr. Pierce,
there are two varieties of the wolf inhabiting the Catskill Mountains in the
United States, one with a light greyhound-like form, which pursues deer, and
the other more bulky, with shorter legs, which more frequently attacks the
shepherd's flocks.

Let us now take a more complex case. Certain plants excrete a sweet juice, 3
apparently for the sake of eliminating something injurious from their sap; this is
effected by glands at the base of the stipules in some Leguminosae, and at the
back of the leaf of the common laurel. This juice, though small in quantity, is
greedily sought by insects. Let us now suppose a little sweet juice or nectar to be
excreted by the inner bases of the petals of a flower. In this case insects in seeking
the nectar would get dusted with pollen, and would certainly often transport the
pollen from one flower to the stigma of another flower. The flowers of two distinct
individuals of the same species would thus get crossed; and the act of crossing,

we have good reason to believe (as will hereafter be more fully alluded to), would produce very vigorous seedlings, which consequently would have the best chance of flourishing and surviving. Some of these seedlings would probably inherit the nectar-excreting power. Those individual flowers which had the largest glands or nectaries, and which excreted most nectar, would be oftenest visited by insects, and would be oftenest crossed; and so in the long-run would gain the upper hand. Those flowers, also, which had their stamens and pistils placed, in relation to the size and habits of the particular insects which visited them, so as to favor in any degree the transportal of their pollen from flower to flower, would likewise be favored or selected. We might have taken the case of insects visiting flowers for the sake of collecting pollen instead of nectar; and as pollen is formed for the sole object of fertilization, its destruction appears a simple loss to the plant; yet if a little pollen were carried, at first occasionally and then habitually, by the pollen-devouring insects from flower to flower, and a cross thus effected, although nine-tenths of the pollen were destroyed, it might still be a great gain to the plant; and those individuals which produced more and more pollen, and had larger and larger anthers, would be selected.

4   When our plant, by this process of the continued preservation or natural selection of more and more attractive flowers, had been rendered highly attractive to insects, they would, unintentionally on their part, regularly carry pollen from flower to flower; and that they can most effectually do this, I could easily show by many striking instances. I will give only one—not as a very striking case, but as likewise illustrating one step in the separation of the sexes of plants, presently to be alluded to. Some holly-trees bear only male flowers, which have four stamens producing rather a small quantity of pollen, and a rudimentary pistil; other holly-trees bear only female flowers; these have a full-sized pistil, and four stamens with shriveled anthers, in which not a grain of pollen can be detected. Having found a female tree exactly sixty yards from a male tree, I put the stigmas of twenty flowers, taken from different branches, under the microscope, and on all, without exception, there were pollen-grains, and on some a profusion of pollen. As the wind had set for several days from the female to the male tree, the pollen could not thus have been carried. The weather had been cold and boisterous, and therefore not favorable to bees; nevertheless every female flower which I examined had been effectually fertilized by the bees, accidentally dusted with pollen, having flown from tree to tree in search of nectar. But to return to our imaginary case: As soon as the plant had been rendered so highly attractive to insects that pollen was regularly carried from flower to flower, another process might commence. No naturalist doubts the advantage of what has been called the "physiological division of labor"; hence we may believe that it would be advantageous to a plant to produce stamens alone in one flower or on one whole plant, and pistils alone in another flower or on another plant. In plants under culture and placed under new conditions of life, sometimes the male organs and sometimes the female organs become more or less impotent; now if we suppose this to occur in ever so slight a degree under nature, then as pollen is already carried regularly from flower to flower, and as a more complete

separation of the sexes of our plant would be advantageous on the principle of the division of labor, individuals with this tendency more and more increased, would be continually favored or selected, until at last a complete separation of the sexes would be effected.

Let us now turn to the nectar-feeding insects in our imaginary case: We may 5 suppose the plant of which we have been slowly increasing the nectar by continued selection, to be a common plant; and that certain insects depended in main part on its nectar for food. I could give many facts, showing how anxious bees are to save time; for instance, their habit of cutting holes and sucking the nectar at the bases of certain flowers, which they can, with a very little more trouble, enter by the mouth. Bearing such facts in mind, I can see no reason to doubt that an accidental deviation in the size and form of the body, or in the curvature and length of the proboscis, etc., far too slight to be appreciated by us, might profit a bee or other insect, so that an individual so characterized would be able to obtain its food more quickly, and so have a better chance of living and leaving descendants. Its descendants would probably inherit a tendency to a similar slight deviation of structure. The tubes of the corollas of the common red and incarnate clovers (Trifolium pratense and incarnatum) do not on a hasty glance appear to differ in length; yet the hive-bee can easily suck the nectar out of the incarnate clover, but not out of the common red clover, which is visited by humble-bees alone; so that the whole fields of the red clover offer in vain an abundant supply of precious nectar to the hive-bee. Thus it might be a great advantage to the hive-bee to have a slightly longer or differently constructed proboscis. On the other hand, I have found by experiment that the fertility of clover greatly depends on bees visiting and moving parts of the corolla, so as to push the pollen on to the stigmatic surface. Hence, again, if humble-bees were to become rare in any country, it might be a great advantage to the red clover to have a shorter or more deeply divided tube to its corolla, so that the hive-bee could visit its flowers. Thus I can understand how a flower and a bee might slowly become, either simultaneously or one after the other, modified and adapted in the most perfect manner to each other, by the continued preservation of individuals presenting mutual and slightly favorable deviations of structure.

I am well aware that this doctrine of natural selection, exemplified in the 6 above imaginary instances, is open to the same objections which were at first urged against Sir Charles Lyell's noble views on "the modern changes of the earth, as illustrative of geology"; but we now very seldom hear the action, for instance, of the coast-waves, called a trifling and insignificant cause, when applied to the excavation of gigantic valleys or to the formation of the longest lines of inland cliffs. Natural selection can act only by the preservation and accumulation of infinitesimally small inherited modifications, each profitable to the preserved being; and as modern geology has almost banished such views as the excavation of a great valley by a single diluvial wave, so will natural selection, if it be a true principle, banish the belief of the continued creation of new organic beings, or of any great and sudden modification in their structure.

COMPREHENSION

1. What does Darwin mean by the term *natural selection?*
2. What is Darwin attempting to refute by his concept of natural selection? Where in the essay is this refutation articulated?
3. Explain what Darwin means by the "physiological division of labor" (paragraph 4).
4. Define the following terms: *innate* (paragraph 2), *stamens* and *pistils* (paragraph 3), *rudimentary* (paragraph 4), *incarnate* (paragraph 5), and *doctrine* (paragraph 6).

RHETORIC

1. In the introduction, Darwin makes an analogy between the needs of humans and those of nature. What is this analogy, and why is it important in devising his argument?
2. What is the tone of the essay? Consider such phrases as "beg permission" (paragraph 1) and "Let us now" (paragraph 3).
3. Darwin uses two "imaginary illustrations" in an attempt to prove his point. What are they, and why are these hypothetical illustrations more effective than real-life ones for his purpose?
4. Darwin tends to use extremely long sentences when he wishes to illustrate a process. For example, the sentence in paragraph 3 that begins "We might have taken" is 101 words long. Deconstruct this sentence by paying special attention to its punctuation, its logical succession of clauses, and its effect on the reader of describing so many processes within its boundaries. What is the relationship between its rhetorical style and purpose?
5. Who is the implied audience for the essay? Cite specific aspects of the rhetoric that led you to your conclusion.
6. What gives Darwin his authority? Specifically, how is his authority linked to the specialized vocabulary of the essay and to the way Darwin uses language to articulate natural processes?
7. Darwin uses the argumentative technique of disarming potential critics in the final paragraph. What is the rhetorical function of this device? Does it strengthen or weaken his argument? Explain your view.

WRITING

1. Write a précis of the essay, focusing on the major points Darwin is trying to assert in his theory of natural selection.
2. **Writing an Argument:** In an essay, argue for or against the proposition that in order to agree with or refute Darwin's ideas of natural selection, one would have to have at least as much experience in observing nature as Darwin obviously had.
3. **Writing an Argument:** Argue for or against the view that Darwin's theory can have disastrous consequences for the human species if applied to politics, sociology, or economics.

NETWORKING
Applying Digital and Multimedia Literacies

Exploring a Museum's Online Exhibit: Locate online and visit the American Museum of Natural History's Web site and virtual exhibit about Charles Darwin, including an informational video. Which aspect of this exhibit do you find the most interesting, and why? How many types of media does the site make use of? What are your thoughts on the site's navigability? What about its design? How do all of these aspects contribute to its purpose?

Darwin at 200: The Ongoing Force of His Unconventional Idea

Verlyn Klinkenborg

Verlyn Klinkenborg (b. 1952) was born in Colorado and raised on an Iowa farm until he was 14, at which time his family moved to the San Francisco Bay Area. Klinkenborg studied at Pomona College (BA, 1974) and Princeton University (PhD, 1982); he has taught at Princeton, Pomona, Harvard University, Fordham University, Bard College, and elsewhere. His books include Making Hay *(1986),* The Last Fine Time *(1991),* The Rural Life *(2003), and* Timothy: Or, Notes on an Abject Reptile *(2006). Klinkenborg, who now lives on a farm in upstate New York, joined the editorial board of the* New York Times *in 1997, and his essays on rural life are a regular feature of the newspaper's editorial page. In this essay, published in the* Times *in 2009, Klinkenborg celebrates the bicentennial of Charles Darwin.*

I can't help wondering what Charles Darwin would think if he could survey the 1 state of his intellectual achievement today, 200 years after his birth and 150 years after the publication of *On the Origin of Species*, the book that changed everything. His central idea—evolution by means of natural selection—was in some sense the product of his time, as Darwin well knew. He was the grandson of Erasmus Darwin, who grasped that there was something wrong with the conventional notion of fixed species. And his theory was hastened into print and into joint presentation by the independent discoveries of Alfred Russel Wallace half a world away.

Verlyn Klinkenborg, "Darwin at 200: The Ongoing Force of His Unconventional Idea." From *The New York Times*, February 12, 2009. © 2009 The New York Times. All rights reserved. Used by permission and protected by the Copyright Laws of the United States. The printing, copying, redistribution, or retransmission of the Material without express written permission is prohibited.

2   But Darwin's theory was the product of years of patient observation. We love to believe in science by epiphany, but the work of real scientists is to rigorously test their epiphanies after they have been boiled down to working hypotheses. Most of Darwin's life was devoted to gathering evidence for just such tests. He writes with an air of incompleteness because he was aware that it would take the work of many scientists to confirm his theory in detail.

3   I doubt that much in the subsequent history of Darwin's idea would have surprised him. The most important discoveries—Mendel's genetics and the structure of DNA—would almost certainly have gratified him because they reveal the physical basis for the variation underlying evolution. It would have gratified him to see his ideas so thoroughly tested and to see so many of them confirmed. He could hardly have expected to be right so often.

4   Perhaps one day we will not call evolution "Darwinism." After all, we do not call classical mechanics "Newtonism." But that raises the question of whether a biological Einstein is possible, someone who demonstrates that Darwin's theory is a limited case. What Darwin proposed was not a set of immutable mathematical formulas. It was a theory of biological history that was itself set in history. That the details have changed does not invalidate his accomplishment. If anything, it enhances it. His writings were not intended to be scriptural. They were meant to be tested.

5   As for the other fate of so-called Darwinism—the reductionist controversy fostered by religious conservatives—well, Darwin knew plenty about that, too. The cultural opposition to evolution was then, as now, scientifically irrelevant. Perhaps the persistence of opposition to evolution is a reminder that culture is not biological, or else we might have evolved past such a gnashing of sensibilities. In a way, our peculiarly American failure to come to terms with Darwin's theory and what it's become since 1859 is a sign of something broader: our failure to come to terms with science and the teaching of science.

6   Darwin does not fit our image of a scientist. From the 21st century, he seems at first to bear a closer resemblance to an amateur naturalist like Gilbert White in the 18th century. But that is an illusion. Darwin's funding was private, his habit was retiring and he lacked the kind of institutional support that we associate with science because it did not exist. But Darwin's extensive scientific correspondence makes it clear that he was not the least bit reclusive intellectually and that he understood the character of science as it was practiced in his day as well as anyone.

7   We expect these days that a boy or girl obsessed with beetles may eventually find a home in a university or a laboratory or a museum. But Darwin's life was his museum, and he was its curator. In June 1833, still early in the five-year voyage of the *Beagle*, he wrote about rounding Cape Horn: "It is a grand spectacle to see all nature thus raging; but Heaven knows every one in the *Beagle* has seen enough in this one summer to last them their natural lives." (In this same letter, he celebrates the parliamentary attack on slavery in England.)

8   The rest of Darwin's life did in fact revolve around that voyage. As you sift through the notes and letters and publications that stemmed from his years on the *Beagle*, you begin to understand how careful, how inquisitive and how various

his mind was. The voyage of the *Beagle*—and of a young naturalist who was 22 at its outset—is still one of the most compelling stories in science.

Darwin recedes, but his idea does not. It is absorbed, with adaptations, into 9 the foundation of the biological sciences. In a very real sense, it is the cornerstone of what we know about life on earth. Darwin's version of that great idea was very much of its time, and yet the whole weight of his time was set against it. From one perspective, Darwin looks completely conventional—white, male, well born, leisured, patrician. But from another, he turned the fortune of his circumstances into the most unconventional idea of all: the one that showed humans their true ancestry in nature.

COMPREHENSION

1. According to Klinkenborg, why was Darwin's idea "unconventional"?
2. How does Darwin's theory reflect the scientific method?
3. What is Klinkenborg's opinion concerning "Darwinism" and "so-called Darwinism"? Would he be happy to see both terms disappear? Why or why not?

RHETORIC

1. Does Klinkenborg establish a claim in this essay, or does he simply want to celebrate the bicentennial of Darwin's birth? Justify your answer.
2. How does Klinkenborg use exemplification as a compositional strategy? What examples does he provide, and why?
3. Klinkenborg alludes to Erasmus Darwin, Alfred Russel Wallace, Mendel, Newton, and Gilbert White. Who were they, and what is the writer's purpose in referring to them?
4. Explain the way that definition serves to structure parts of this essay.
5. Do you find Klinkenborg's conclusion effective? Why or why not?

WRITING

1. Compose your own brief celebration of Charles Darwin.
2. Write an extended definition of evolutionary theory.
3. **Writing an Argument:** Argue for or against the proposition that "Darwinism" is no longer a useful term to describe evolutionary theory.

NETWORKING
Applying Digital and Multimedia Literacies

Creating a Hyperlinked Extended Definition: Format question 2 under Writing as an electronic text, using hyperlinks to clarify and expand on your definition of evolutionary theory.

Synthesis: Classic and Contemporary
Questions for Comparison

1. How do Darwin and Klinkenborg approach the subject of evolution? Do they have the
   same or different priorities, and why? Are they writing for the same audience? Use
   examples from both selections to support your response.
2. Analyze the language used in the two essays. What is similar or different about the
   style and diction of the two pieces? How does each use details? Is one essay more
   accessible to the modern reader? Why or why not?
3. How do both essays treat the scientific method? Is one selection more "scientific" in its
   approach than the other? Explain your response.

❋

Planets in the Sky with Diamonds

Diane Ackerman

Diane Ackerman (b. 1948) *is an American naturalist, essayist, poet, and children's
book author. She was born in Waukegan, Illinois, where she lived for eight years
before the family moved to Allentown, Pennsylvania. Ackerman attended Pennsylvania
State University where she earned her BA. She received MA, MFA, and PhD degrees
from Cornell University. She is best known for* A Natural History of the Senses
(1990), which inspired a Nova *miniseries; and her memoir,* The Zookeeper's Wife:
A War Story *(2007), among more than a dozen nonfiction works. Ackerman has
taught at several universities including Cornell and Columbia. In this essay from the
October 2, 2011, issue of the* New York Times, *Ackerman scans the universe for
signs of life.*

1 Goldilocks is alive in the constellation Vela. Her real name is HD 85512b, which
may not roll off the tongue, but it's sheer poetry to the ears of sky watchers like
me, who long for signs of an Earth-like planet that might harbor life.

2 This newly discovered planet orbits its sun in what's called the "Goldilocks,"
or habitable zone, at the right distance for liquid water to sparkle on the surface
and life to bloom in the shallows. Life as we know it, anyway, with wings and
dreams, if the planet has a rocky surface—and isn't too hot or too cold—as well as
a tent of clouds for shade.

3 That's a lot of ifs, which is why other candidates have been scarce. This is our
best hope, though she's 36 light-years away, beyond the reach of our spacecrafts
or clear view of present telescopes, but well within the imagination. Her temperatures may range from 85 to 120 degrees, which conjures up images of equatorial
Africa, or much of the hot, muggy United States this past July.

The past month has been a marvel in the planetary world. In addition to HD 4 85512b, astronomers spotted a planet that may be fashioned entirely of diamond, a brilliant diadem set in the black velvet of space. For all we know, it has baguette moons in tow. And a few weeks later, planet hunters confirmed the discovery of Kepler-16b, a planet that circles two suns in the constellation Cygnus.

In the *Star Wars* saga, Luke Skywalker hailed from such a world, Tatooine, 5 where he paused from work on his uncle's moisture farm to enjoy a smoldery suns-set. Until now a stable planet orbiting twin suns was science fiction, strictly hints and hunches. Wouldn't the quarreling gravity of two suns shear the planet apart, swallow it whole, or hurtle it off into space? Apparently not. Such solar systems, with winking suns that eclipse one another every few weeks, may be common throughout the universe. That's the best thing about discovery, how it widens the mind's eye, refines the scope of our inquiries.

However, we won't be glimpsing these worlds anytime soon, I'm afraid. If we 6 want to explore in fine detail, we'll need better eyes in the sky and faster robotic spaceships. I'm for both. Despite all the problems that beset us, we're on the threshold of a new era of exploration and discovery. Scientists are asking thrilling questions, like: what existed before the universe? How did we get from the Big Bang to the whole shebang? Can we design spaceships that fly faster than the speed of light? Do other planetarians haunt the wilderness of space, or are we alone? I hope we'll continue sending scouts around our solar system, and use the planets as stepping stones to the stars.

This is not a new goal, but one of humanity's oldest yearnings. Every society 7 has been tantalized by the great loom of the sky with its flowing quilt of stars. The Egyptian pyramids may have been arranged like the belt stars of Orion, pointing to Sirius, so that the pharaoh's soul would be launched into the heavens where he'd shimmer as a star. To the San people in the Kalahari, the Milky Way is the "backbone of night."

In the 20th century, we sent robot emissaries to explore the solar system and 8 voyage deep into space. With the cupped ears of radio telescopes, we began listening for voices from other worlds. We rode fierce winds to the Moon and looked back in wonder, amazed to see Earth whole. Viewed from space, Earth had no visible fences, military zones or national borders. But it did have the thinnest rind—an atmosphere embracing the sky, weather systems and all of human history. That image from an Apollo mission changed everything.

We're explorers by design, right down to our cells, and we thrive on quests. 9 Stars flare like distant campfires overhead, and we wonder if they're home to other worlds like our own. Or made of diamond. I'm hoping NASA will continue to find the boosters it needs, because our compass points to the stars.

COMPREHENSION

1. Does Ackerman support space exploration? Why or why not?
2. Why does Ackerman refer to *Star Wars*, ancient Egypt, and the San people of the Kalahari?

3. Why does Ackerman write in her concluding paragraph, "I'm hoping NASA will continue to find the boosters it needs"? What is the context here?

RHETORIC

1. Explain the allusion in Ackerman's title. How does this reference relate to the content of the essay?
2. How do the journalistic requirements of an op-ed newspaper piece dictate the style, organization, and content of Ackerman's essay?
3. What is the writer's tone? Is she objective or subjective? Explain.
4. What is Ackerman's claim? Where does she make appeals to reason and emotion?
5. Ackerman is the author of several books of poetry. What poetic elements do you find in this essay?

WRITING

1. Write an essay on the impact of science fiction films like *Star Wars* on the ways we think about the universe.
2. Ackerman's dissertation advisor at Cornell was the noted writer Carl Sagan, who has an essay in this chapter. Read Sagan's essay, and then write a comparative essay linking his piece to the article by Ackerman.
3. **Writing an Argument:** Do you think that life exists elsewhere in the universe? Respond in an argumentative essay.

NETWORKING
Applying Digital and Multimedia Literacies

Starting with an Author Web Site: Go to Ackerman's Web site. Explore the links that she provides, which will take you to interviews, talks, reviews, and other informational sites. Then compose a brief critical biography of the author.

※

Nutcracker.com

David Sedaris

David Sedaris *(b. 1957), who was born in Johnson City, New York, and grew up in Raleigh, North Carolina, is a well-known humorist, essayist, diarist, short-story writer, and radio commentator. After graduating from the Art Institute of Chicago in 1987, Sedaris held several temporary jobs, ranging from a cleaner of apartments to an elf in SantaLand at Macy's. His stint on National Public Radio's* Morning

Edition *established Sedaris as a popular if quirky humorist and led to his first collection of essays,* Barrel Fever *(2000).* Termed by Entertainment Weekly *"a crackpot in the best sense of the word," Sedaris has also written* Naked *(1997),* Me Talk Pretty One Day *(2000),* Dress Your Family in Corduroy and Denim *(2004),* When You're Engulfed in Flames *(2008), and other works. In this essay, Sedaris humorously explains why he is a technophobe.*

It was my father's dream that one day the people of the world would be connected 1 to one another through a network of blocky, refrigerator-size computers, much like those he was helping develop at IBM. He envisioned families of the future gathered around their mammoth terminals, ordering groceries and paying their taxes from the comfort of their own homes. A person could compose music, design a doghouse, and . . . something more, something even better. "A person could . . . he could . . . "

When predicting this utopia, he would eventually reach a point where words 2 failed him. His eyes would widen and sparkle at the thought of this indescribable something more. "I mean, my God," he'd say, "just think about it."

My sisters and I preferred not to. I didn't know about them, but I was hoping 3 the people of the world might be united by something more interesting, like drugs or an armed struggle against the undead. Unfortunately, my father's team won, so computers it is. My only regret is that this had to happen during my lifetime.

Somewhere in the back of my mind is a dim memory of standing in some line 4 holding a perforated card. I remember the cheap, slightly clinical feeling it gave me, and recall thinking that the computer would never advance much further than this. Call me naive, but I seem to have underestimated the universal desire to sit in a hard plastic chair and stare at a screen until your eyes cross. My father saw it coming, but this was a future that took me completely by surprise. There were no computers in my high school, and the first two times I attempted college, people were still counting on their fingers and removing their shoes when the numbers got above ten. I wasn't really aware of computers until the mid-1980s. For some reason, I seemed to know quite a few graphic designers whose homes and offices pleasantly stank of Spray Mount. Their floors were always collaged with stray bits of paper, and trapped flies waved for help from the gummy killing fields of their tabletops. I had always counted on these friends to loan me the adhesive of my choice, but then, seemingly overnight, their Scotch tape and rubber cement were gone, replaced with odorless computers and spongy mouse pads. They had nothing left that I wanted to borrow, and so I dropped them and fell in with a group of typesetters who ultimately betrayed me as well.

Thanks to my complete lack of office skills, I found it fairly easy to avoid 5 direct contact with the new technology. The indirect contact was disturbing enough. I was still living in Chicago when I began to receive creepy Christmas newsletters designed to look like tabloids and annual reports. Word processors made writing fun. They did not, however, make reading fun, a point made painfully evident by such publications as *The Herald Family Tribune* and *Wassup with the Wexlers!*

6   Friends who had previously expressed no interest in torture began sending
letters composed to resemble Chinese take out menus and the Dead Sea Scrolls.
Everybody had a font, and I was told that I should get one, too. The authors of
these letters shared an enthusiasm with the sort of people who now arrived at dinner parties hoisting expensive new video cameras and suggesting that, after dessert, we all sit down and replay the evening on TV. We, the regular people of the
world, now had access to the means of production, but still I failed to see what all
the fuss was about. A dopey letter is still a dopey letter, no matter how you dress
it up; and there's a reason regular people don't appear on TV: We're boring.

7   By the early 1990s I was living in New York and working for a housecleaning
company. My job taught me that regardless of their purported virtues, computers
are a pain in the ass to keep clean. The pebbled surface is a magnet for grease and
dirt, and you can pretty much forget about reaming out the gaps in the keyboard.
More than once I accidentally pushed a button and recoiled in terror as the blank
screen came to life with exotic tropical fish or swarms of flying toasters. Equally
distressing was the way people used the slanted roofs of their terminals to display
framed photographs and great populations of plush and plastic creatures, which
would fall behind the desk the moment I began cleaning the screen. There was
never any place to plug in the vacuum, as every outlet was occupied by some member of the computer family. Cords ran wild, and everyone seemed to own one of
those ominous foot-long power strips with the blinking red light that sends the
message YOU MUST LEAVE US ALONE. I was more than happy to comply, and the com
plaints came rolling in.

8   Due to my general aversion to machines and a few pronounced episodes of
screaming, I was labeled a technophobe, a term that ranks fairly low on my scale
of fightin' words. The word *phobic* has its place when properly used, but lately it's
been declawed by the pompous insistence that most animosity is based upon fear
rather than loathing. No credit is given for distinguishing between these two very
different emotions. I fear snakes. I hate computers. My hatred is entrenched, and
I nourish it daily. I'm comfortable with it, and no community outreach program
will change my mind.

9   I hate computers for getting their own section in the *New York Times* and for
lengthening commercials with the mention of a Web site address. Who really
wants to find out more about Procter & Gamble? Just buy the toothpaste or laun-
dry detergent, and get on with it. I hate them for creating the word *org* and I hate
them for e-mail, which isn't real mail but a variation of the pointless notes people
used to pass in class. I hate computers for replacing the card catalog in the New
York Public Library and I hate the way they've invaded the movies. I'm not talking
about their contribution to the world of special effects. I have nothing against a
well-defined mutant or full-scale alien invasion—that's *good* technology. I'm talking about their actual presence *in* any given movie. They've become like horses in
a western—they may not be the main focus, but everybody seems to have one.
Each tiresome new thriller includes a scene in which the hero, trapped by some
version of the enemy, runs for his desk in a desperate race against time. Music
swells and droplets of sweat rain down onto the keyboard as he sits at his laptop,

frantically pawing for answers. It might be different if he were flagging down a passing car or trying to phone for help, but typing, in and of itself, is not an inherently dramatic activity.

I hate computers for any number of reasons, but I despise them most for what 10 they've done to my friend the typewriter. In a democratic country you'd think there would be room for both of them, but computers won't rest until I'm making my ribbons from torn shirts and brewing Wite-Out in my bathtub. Their goal is to place the IBM Selectric II beside the feather quill and chisel in the museum of antiquated writing implements. They're power hungry, and someone needs to stop them.

When told I'm like the guy still pining for his eight-track tapes, I say, "You 11 have eight-tracks? Where?" In reality I know nothing about them, yet I feel it's important to express some solidarity with others who have had the rug pulled out from beneath them. I don't care if it can count words or rearrange paragraphs at the push of a button, I don't want a computer. Unlike the faint scurry raised by fingers against a plastic computer keyboard, the smack and clatter of a typewriter suggests that you're actually building something. At the end of a miserable day, instead of grieving my virtual nothing, I can always look at my loaded wastepaper basket and tell myself that if I failed, at least I took a few trees down with me.

When forced to leave my house for an extended period of time, I take my 12 typewriter with me, and together we endure the wretchedness of passing through the X-ray scanner. The laptops roll merrily down the belt, while I'm instructed to stand aside and open my bag. To me it seems like a normal enough thing to be carrying, but the typewriter's declining popularity arouses suspicion and I wind up eliciting the sort of reaction one might expect when traveling with a cannon.

"It's a typewriter," I say. "You use it to write angry letters to airport authorities." 13

The keys are then slapped and pounded, and I'm forced to explain that if you 14 want the words to appear, you first have to plug it in and insert a sheet of paper.

The goons shake their heads and tell me I really should be using a computer. 15 That's their job, to stand around in an ill-fitting uniform and tell you how you should lead your life. I'm told the exact same thing later in the evening when the bellhop knocks on my hotel door. The people whose televisions I can hear have complained about my typing, and he has come to make me stop. To hear him talk, you'd think I'd been playing the kettledrum. In the great scheme of things, the typewriter is not nearly as loud as he makes it out to be, but there's no use arguing with him. "You know," he says, "you really should be using a computer."

You have to wonder where you've gone wrong when twice a day you're 16 offered writing advice from men in funny hats. The harder I'm pressured to use a computer, the harder I resist. One by one, all of my friends have deserted me and fled to the dark side. "How can I write you if you don't have an e-mail address?" they ask. They talk of their B-trees and Disk Doctors and then have the nerve to complain when I discuss bowel obstructions at the dinner table.

Who needs them? I think. I figured I'd always have my family and was devas- 17 tated when my sister Amy brought home a candy-colored laptop. "I only use it for e-mail," she said. Coming from her, these words made me physically ill. "It's fun," she said. "People send you things. Look at this." She pushed a button, and there, on the screen, was a naked man lying facedown on a carpet. His hair was graying and his hands were cuffed behind his doughy back. A woman entered the room. You couldn't see her face, just her legs and feet, which were big and mean-looking, forced into sharp-toed shoes with high, pencil-thin heels. The man on the carpet shifted position, and when his testicles came into view, the woman reacted as if she had seen an old balding mouse, one that she had been trying to kill for a long time. She stomped on the man's testicles with the toes of her shoes and then she turned around and stomped on them with the heels. She kicked them mercilessly and, just when I thought she'd finished, she got her second wind and started all over again.

18   I'd never realized that a computer could act so much like a TV set. No one had ever told me that the picture could be so clear, that the cries of pain could be heard so distinctly. This, I thought, was what my father had been envisioning all those years ago when words had failed him, not necessarily this scene, but something equally capable of provoking such wonder.

19   "Again?" Amy pushed a button and, our faces bathed in the glow of the screen, we watched the future a second time.

COMPREHENSION

1. What distinguishes the author from his father and his sister Amy?
2. Why does Sedaris hate computers? Does he actually enjoy being a "technophobe"? How do you know?
3. What sort of writer is Sedaris? Why doesn't he want to use computers to help him in the writing process?

RHETORIC

1. How do you interpret the title? How does the title prepare us for the tone of this selection?
2. Sedaris employs a personal voice in this essay. What does the "I" point of view contribute to the selection?
3. What comic strategies does the author develop? What details stand out? Does comedy serve to support or undercut his claim?
4. How does Sedaris argue his case? Does he actually have a case, or a cause, or is his purpose simply to amuse the reader? How do you know?
5. What principle of classification appears in the essay, and how does this rhetorical strategy serve the author's purpose?
6. How does the writer use comparison and contrast, narration, and description to develop the essay?
7. Explain the impact and significance of the concluding scene. How does the tone alter here? What is the final effect? What is the writer's parting message to his readers?

WRITING

1. In a personal essay employing narration and description as well as analysis, describe the impact of computers on your family life. Use a comic approach to the subject.
2. Write an analysis of the elements of humor that appear in Sedaris's essay. Why is comedy an appropriate strategy for dealing with the subject of computer technology?
3. **Writing an Argument:** Write an essay about why you love or hate computers. Use ironic humor to undercut your argument—to convince readers that your opinions are actually the opposite of what you proclaim.

NETWORKING
Applying Digital and Multimedia Literacies

Using Technology (and Humor) to Critique Technology: Make your response to question 3 under Writing even more humorous by employing specific aspects of technology just as you are declaring your dislike for or frustration with them. For instance, you might create a blog that complains about bloggers, or bemoan the lack of focus in hyperlinked texts in an essay that is rife with linkage. Have a little fun with this one.

How Computers Change the Way We Think

Sherry Turkle

Sherry Turkle (b. 1948), born and raised in New York City, attended Harvard University where she received her BA (1970), MA (1973), and PhD (1976). A professor in the Program in Science, Technology, and Society at the Massachusetts Institute of Technology, Turkle observes: "I study the sociology of sciences of mind, a study of the interactions among technical, literary, and popular discourses about the self as they develop in specific social contexts." The results of Turkle's research appear in Psychoanalytic Politics: Freud's French Revolution *(1992),* The Second Self: Computers and the Human Spirit *(1984),* Life on the Screen: Identity in the Age of the Internet *(1995) and* Simulation and Its Discontents *(2009). "My work on computation," Turkle states, "begins with the premise that we live in a nascent computer culture that will exert an analogous influence on the way we think"—an idea she explores in the following essay, which appeared in a 2004 issue of the* Chronicle of Higher Education.

1   The tools we use to think change the ways in which we think. The invention of written language brought about a radical shift in how we process, organize, store, and transmit representations of the world. Although writing remains our primary information technology, today when we think about the impact of technology on our habits of mind, we think primarily of the computer.

2   My first encounters with how computers change the way we think came soon after I joined the faculty at the Massachusetts Institute of Technology in the late 1970s, at the end of the era of the slide rule and the beginning of the era of the personal computer. At a lunch for new faculty members, several senior professors in engineering complained that the transition from slide rules to calculators had affected their students' ability to deal with issues of scale. When students used slide rules, they had to insert decimal points themselves. The professors insisted that that required students to maintain a mental sense of scale, whereas those who relied on calculators made frequent errors in orders of magnitude. Additionally, the students with calculators had lost their ability to do "back of the envelope" calculations, and with that, an intuitive feel for the material.

3   That same semester, I taught a course in the history of psychology. There, I experienced the impact of computational objects on students' ideas about their emotional lives. My class had read Freud's essay on slips of the tongue, with its famous first example: The chairman of a parliamentary session opens a meeting by declaring it closed. The students discussed how Freud interpreted such errors as revealing a person's mixed emotions. A computer-science major disagreed with Freud's approach. The mind, she argued, is a computer. And in a computational dictionary—like we have in the human mind—"closed" and "open" are designated by the same symbol, separated by a sign for opposition. "Closed" equals "minus open." To substitute "closed" for "open" does not require the notion of ambivalence or conflict.

4   "When the chairman made that substitution," she declared, "a bit was dropped; a minus sign was lost. There was a power surge. No problem."

5   The young woman turned a Freudian slip into an information-processing error. An explanation in terms of meaning had become an explanation in terms of mechanism.

6   Such encounters turned me to the study of both the instrumental and the subjective sides of the nascent computer culture. As an ethnographer and psychologist, I began to study not only what the computer was doing for us, but what it was doing to us, including how it was changing the way we see ourselves, our sense of human identity.

7   In the 1980s, I surveyed the psychological effects of computational objects in everyday life—largely the unintended side effects of people's tendency to project thoughts and feelings onto their machines. In the 20 years since, computational objects have become more explicitly designed to have emotional and cognitive effects. And those "effects by design" will become even stronger in the decade to come. Machines are being designed to serve explicitly as companions, pets, and tutors. And they are introduced in school settings for the youngest children.

Today, starting in elementary school, students use e-mail, word processing, 8
computer simulations, virtual communities, and PowerPoint software. In the
process, they are absorbing more than the content of what appears on their
screens. They are learning new ways to think about what it means to know and
understand.

What follows is a short and certainly not comprehensive list of areas where 9
I see information technology encouraging changes in thinking. There can be
no simple way of cataloging whether any particular change is good or bad.
That is contested terrain. At every step we have to ask, as educators and citizens, whether current technology is leading us in directions that serve our
human purposes. Such questions are not technical; they are social, moral, and
political. For me, addressing that subjective side of computation is one of the
more significant challenges for the next decade of information technology in
higher education. Technology does not determine change, but it encourages
us to take certain directions. If we make those directions clear, we can more
easily exert human choice.

Thinking about privacy. Today's college students are habituated to a world 10
of online blogging, instant messaging, and Web browsing that leaves electronic
traces. Yet they have had little experience with the right to privacy. Unlike past
generations of Americans, who grew up with the notion that the privacy of their
mail was sacrosanct, our children are accustomed to electronic surveillance as
part of their daily lives.

I have colleagues who feel that the increased incursions on privacy have put 11
the topic more in the news, and that this is a positive change. But middle-school
and high-school students tend to be willing to provide personal information online
with no safeguards, and college students seem uninterested in violations of privacy and in increased governmental and commercial surveillance. Professors find
that students do not understand that in a democracy, privacy is a right, not merely
a privilege. In 10 years, ideas about the relationship of privacy and government
will require even more active pedagogy. (One might also hope that increased education about the kinds of silent surveillance that technology makes possible may
inspire more active political engagement with the issue.)

Avatars or a self? Chat rooms, role-playing games, and other technological 12
venues offer us many different contexts for presenting ourselves online. Those
possibilities are particularly important for adolescents because they offer what
Erik Erikson described as a moratorium, a time out or safe space for the personal
experimentation that is so crucial for adolescent development. Our dangerous
world—with crime, terrorism, drugs, and AIDS—offers little in the way of safe
spaces. Online worlds can provide valuable spaces for identity play.

But some people who gain fluency in expressing multiple aspects of self may 13
find it harder to develop authentic selves. Some children who write narratives for
their screen avatars may grow up with too little experience of how to share their
real feelings with other people. For those who are lonely yet afraid of intimacy,
information technology has made it possible to have the illusion of companionship without the demands of friendship.

14   **From powerful ideas to PowerPoint.** In the 1970s and early 1980s, some educators wanted to make programming part of the regular curriculum for K 13 education. They argued that because information technology carries ideas, it might as well carry the most powerful ideas that computer science has to offer. It is ironic that in most elementary schools today, the ideas being carried by information technology are not ideas from computer science like procedural thinking, but more likely to be those embedded in productivity tools like PowerPoint presentation software.

15   PowerPoint does more than provide a way of transmitting content. It carries its own way of thinking, its own aesthetic—which not surprisingly shows up in the aesthetic of college freshmen. In that aesthetic, presentation becomes its own powerful idea.

16   To be sure, the software cannot be blamed for lower intellectual standards. Misuse of the former is as much a symptom as a cause of the latter. Indeed, the culture in which our children are raised is increasingly a culture of presentation, a corporate culture in which appearance is often more important than reality. In contemporary political discourse, the bar has also been lowered. Use of rhetorical devices at the expense of cogent argument regularly goes without notice. But it is precisely because standards of intellectual rigor outside the educational sphere have fallen that educators must attend to how we use, and when we introduce, software that has been designed to simplify the organization and processing of information.

17   In *The Cognitive Style of PowerPoint* (Graphics Press, 2003), Edward R. Tufts suggests that PowerPoint equates bulleting with clear thinking. It does not teach students to begin a discussion or construct a narrative. It encourages presentation, not conversation. Of course, in the hands of a master teacher, a PowerPoint presentation with few words and powerful images can serve as the jumping-off point for a brilliant lecture. But in the hands of elementary-school students, often introduced to PowerPoint in the third grade, and often infatuated with its swooshing sounds, animated icons, and flashing text, a slide show is more likely to close down debate than open it up.

18   Developed to serve the needs of the corporate boardroom, the software is designed to convey absolute authority. Teachers used to tell students that clear exposition depended on clear outlining, but presentation software has fetishized the outline at the expense of the content.

19   Narrative, the exposition of content, takes time. PowerPoint, like so much in the computer culture, speeds up the pace

20   **Word processing vs. thinking.** The catalog for the Vermont Country Store advertises a manual typewriter, which the advertising copy says "moves at a pace that allows time to compose your thoughts." As many of us know, it is possible to manipulate text on a computer screen and see how it looks faster than we can think about what the words mean.

21   Word processing has its own complex psychology. From a pedagogical point of view, it can make dedicated students into better writers because it allows them to revise text, rearrange paragraphs, and experiment with the tone and shape of

an essay. Few professional writers would part with their computers; some claim that they simply cannot think without their hands on the keyboard. Yet the ability to quickly fill the page, to see it before you can think it, can make bad writers even worse.

A seventh grader once told me that the typewriter she found in her mother's 22 attic is "cool because you have to type each letter by itself. You have to know what you are doing in advance or it comes out a mess." The idea of thinking ahead has become exotic.

Taking things at interface value. We expect software to be easy to use, 23 and we assume that we don't have to know how a computer works. In the early 1980s, most computer users who spoke of transparency meant that, as with any other machine, you could "open the hood" and poke around. But only a few years later, Macintosh users began to use the term when they talked about seeing their documents and programs represented by attractive and easy-to-interpret icons. They were referring to an ability to make things work without needing to go below the screen surface. Paradoxically, it was the screen's opacity that permitted that kind of transparency. Today, when people say that something is transparent, they mean that they can see how to make it work, not that they know how it works. In other words, transparency means epistemic opacity.

The people who built or bought the first generation of personal computers 24 understood them down to the bits and bytes. The next generation of operating systems were more complex, but they still invited that old-time reductive understanding. Contemporary information technology encourages different habits of mind. Today's college students are already used to taking things at (inter) face value; their successors in 2014 will be even less accustomed to probing below the surface.

Simulation and its discontents. Some thinkers argue that the new opacity 25 is empowering, enabling anyone to use the most sophisticated technological tools and to experiment with simulation in complex and creative ways. But it is also true that our tools carry the message that they are beyond our understanding. It is possible that in daily life, epistemic opacity can lead to passivity.

I first became aware of that possibility in the early 1990s, when the first gen- 26 eration of complex simulation games were introduced and immediately became popular for home as well as school use. SimLife teaches the principles of evolution by getting children involved in the development of complex ecosystems; in that sense it is an extraordinary learning tool. During one session in which I played SimLife with Tim, a 13-year-old, the screen before us flashed a message: "Your orgot is being eaten up." "What's an orgot?" I asked. Tim didn't know. "I just ignore that," he said confidently. "You don't need to know that kind of stuff to play."

For me, that story serves as a cautionary tale. Computer simulations enable 27 their users to think about complex phenomena as dynamic, evolving systems. But they also accustom us to manipulating systems whose core assumptions we may not understand and that may not be true.

We live in a culture of simulation. Our games, our economic and political sys- 28 tems, and the ways architects design buildings, chemists envisage molecules, and surgeons perform operations all use simulation technology. In 10 years the degree to which simulations are embedded in every area of life will have increased exponentially. We need to develop a new form of media literacy: readership for the culture of simulation.

29   We come to written text with habits of readership based on centuries of civilization. At the very least, we have learned to begin with the journalist's traditional questions: who, what, when, where, why, and how. Who wrote these words, what is their message, why were they written, and how are they situated in time and place, politically and socially? A central project for higher education during the next 10 years should be creating programs in information-technology literacy, with the goal of teaching students to interrogate simulations in much the same spirit, challenging their built-in assumptions.

30   Despite the ever-increasing complexity of software, most computer environments put users in worlds based on constrained choices. In other words, immersion in programmed worlds puts us in reassuring environments where the rules are clear. For example, when you play a video game, you often go through a series of frightening situations that you escape by mastering the rules—you experience life as a reassuring dichotomy of scary and safe. Children grow up in a culture of video games, action films, fantasy epics, and computer programs that all rely on that familiar scenario of almost losing but then regaining total mastery: There is danger. It is mastered. A still-more-powerful monster appears. It is subdued. Scary. Safe.

31   Yet in the real world, we have never had a greater need to work our way out of binary assumptions. In the decade ahead, we need to rebuild the culture around information technology. In that new sociotechnical culture, assumptions about the nature of mastery would be less absolute. The new culture would make it easier, not more difficult, to consider life in shades of gray, to see moral dilemmas in terms other than a battle between Good and Evil. For never has our world been more complex, hybridized, and global. Never have we so needed to have many contradictory thoughts and feelings at the same time. Our tools must help us accomplish that, not fight against us.

32   Information technology is identity technology. Embedding it in a culture that supports democracy, freedom of expression, tolerance, diversity, and complexity of opinion is one of the next decade's greatest challenges. We cannot afford to fail.

33   When I first began studying the computer culture, a small breed of highly trained technologists thought of themselves as "computer people." That is no longer the case. If we take the computer as a carrier of a way of knowing, a way of seeing the world and our place in it, we are all computer people now.

COMPREHENSION

1. According to Turkle, in what ways do computers change the ways we think?
2. What does Turkle mean by "the instrumental and subjective sides of nascent computer culture" (paragraph 6)? What examples of these two sides does she offer?
3. What are some of the challenges facing the "sociotechnical culture" Turkle says we are entering?

RHETORIC

1. Turkle published this essay in a weekly newspaper designed for people in higher education. What stylistic elements suggest that she gears her writing to this specialized audience? How does she make the article accessible to a broader, secondary audience?
2. What is Turkle's thesis, and where does she state it?
3. How does Turkle use classification to advance her thesis and organize the essay? Where does she employ process and causal analysis?
4. What comparative points does the writer draw between actual and virtual reality?
5. Turkle's paragraphs are relatively brief, some no more than two or three sentences. Why does she employ this method? Does this strategy ruin the coherence of the essay or weaken the emphasis on certain ideas? Why or why not?
6. In the final analysis, does Turkle prove the point made in the final paragraph, that "we are all computer people now"?

WRITING

1. Using Turkle's essay as a model, write a classification essay on the ways that computers are changing the way we think.
2. Select one area where information technology is changing our processes and habits of thought, and write an essay explaining this phenomenon.
3. **Writing an Argument:** Do you agree or disagree with Turkle's assertion that information technology can foster democracy? Write a persuasive essay that articulates your position on the issue.

NETWORKING
Applying Digital and Multimedia Literacies

Using Images to Strengthen a Classification Essay: Enhance question 1 under Writing by incorporating four or five images that help illustrate the classifications you put forth in the essay. Take care to use images purposefully, not merely for decoration.

Can We Know the Universe? Reflections on a Grain of Salt

Carl Sagan

__Carl Edward Sagan__ (1931–1996) received BA, BS, MA, and PhD degrees from the University of Chicago. Probably the most popular scientist in America in the 1970s and 1980s, he was the host of several television series on science and wrote a number *of best-selling books on science, including* The Dragons of Eden *(1977) and* Broca's Brain *(1979). The former earned him a Pulitzer Prize for general nonfiction in 1978. He also contributed hundreds of papers to scientific journals. Besides writing, Sagan served as a full-time professor at Cornell University and a visiting professor at dozens of other institutions of higher learning in the United States and abroad. He was also an activist for many philanthropic causes and served as an advisor to groups such as the Council for a Livable World Education Fund, the Children's Health Fund, and the American Committee on U.S.–Soviet Relations. Despite controversies surrounding the speculative nature of his work, Carl Sagan was one of modern science's most popular spokespersons. Sagan's philosophy may be summed up in a statement he made in a* Time *interview: "We make our world significant by the courage of our questions and by the depth of our answers."*

Nothing is rich but the inexhaustible wealth of nature. She shows us only surfaces, but she is a million fathoms deep.

—Ralph Waldo Emerson

1   Science is a way of thinking much more than it is a body of knowledge. Its goal is to find out how the world works, to seek what regularities there may be, to penetrate to the connections of things—from subnuclear particles, which may be the constituents of all matter, to living organisms, the human social community, and thence to the cosmos as a whole. Our intuition is by no means an infallible guide. Our perceptions may be distorted by training and prejudice or merely because of the limitations of our sense organs, which, of course, perceive directly but a small fraction of the phenomena of the world. Even so straightforward a question as whether in the absence of friction a pound of lead falls faster than a gram of fluff was answered incorrectly by Aristotle and almost everyone else before the time of Galileo. Science is based on experiment, on a willingness to challenge old dogma, on an openness to see the universe as it really is. Accordingly, science sometimes requires courage—at the very least the courage to question the conventional wisdom.

2   Beyond this the main trick of science is to *really* think of something: the shape of clouds and their occasional sharp bottom edges at the same altitude everywhere in the sky; the formation of a dewdrop on a leaf; the origin of a name or a word—Shakespeare, say, or "philanthropic"; the reason for human social customs—the incest taboo, for example; how it is that a lens in sunlight can make paper burn; how a "walking stick" got to look so much like a twig; why the Moon seems to follow us as we walk; what prevents us from digging a hole down to the center of the Earth; what the definition is of "down" on a spherical Earth; how it is possible for the body to convert yesterday's lunch into today's muscle and sinew; or how far is up—does the universe go on forever, or if it does not, is there any meaning to the question of what lies on the other side? Some of these questions are pretty easy. Others, especially the last, are mysteries to which no one even today knows the answer. They are natural questions to ask. Every culture has posed such questions in one way or another. Almost always the proposed answers

are in the nature of "Just So Stories," attempted explanations divorced from experiment, or even from careful comparative observations.

But the scientific cast of mind examines the world critically as if many alter- 3 native worlds might exist, as if other things might be here which are not. Then we are forced to ask why what we see is present and not something else. Why are the Sun and the Moon and the planets spheres? Why not pyramids, or cubes, or dodecahedra? Why not irregular, jumbly shapes? Why so symmetrical worlds? If you spend any time spinning hypotheses, checking to see whether they make sense, whether they conform to what else we know, thinking of tests you can pose to substantiate or deflate your hypotheses, you will find yourself doing science. And as you come to practice this habit of thought more and more you will get better and better at it. To penetrate into the heart of the thing—even a little thing, a blade of grass, as Walt Whitman said—is to experience a kind of exhilaration that, it may be, only human beings of all the beings on this planet can feel. We are an intelligent species and the use of our intelligence quite properly gives us pleasure. In this respect the brain is like a muscle. When we think well, we feel good. Understanding is a kind of ecstasy.

But to what extent can we *really* know the universe around us? Sometimes 4 this question is posed by people who hope the answer will be in the negative, who are fearful of a universe in which everything might one day be known. And sometimes we hear pronouncements from scientists who confidently state that everything worth knowing will soon be known—or even is already known—and who paint pictures of a Dionysian or Polynesian age in which the zest for intellectual discovery has withered, to be replaced by a kind of subdued languor, the lotus eaters drinking fermented coconut milk or some other mild hallucinogen. In addition to maligning both the Polynesians, who were intrepid explorers (and whose brief respite in paradise is now sadly ending), as well as the inducements to intellectual discovery provided by some hallucinogens, this contention turns out to be trivially mistaken.

Let us approach a much more modest question: not whether we can know the 5 universe or the Milky Way Galaxy or a star or a world. Can we know, ultimately and in detail, a grain of salt? Consider one microgram of table salt, a speck just barely large enough for someone with keen eyesight to make out without a microscope. In that grain of salt there are about 10^{16} sodium and chlorine atoms. This is a 1 followed by 16 zeros, 10 million billion atoms. If we wish to know a grain of salt, we must know at least the three-dimensional positions of each of these atoms. (In fact, there is much more to be known—for example, the nature of the forces between the atoms—but we are making only a modest calculation.) Now, is this number more or less than the number of things which the brain can know?

How much *can* the brain know? There are perhaps 10^{11} neurons in the 6 brain, the circuit elements and switches that are responsible in their electrical and chemical activity for the functioning of our minds. A typical brain neuron has perhaps a thousand little wires, called dendrites, which connect it with its fellows. If, as seems likely, every bit of information in the brain corresponds to one of these connections, the total number of things knowable by the brain is no more than 10^{14}, one hundred trillion. But this number is only one percent of the number of atoms in our speck of salt.

7   So in this sense the universe is intractable, astonishingly immune to any human attempt at full knowledge. We cannot on this level understand a grain of salt, much less the universe.

8   But let us look a little more deeply at our microgram of salt. Salt happens to be a crystal in which, except for defects in the structure of the crystal lattice, the position of every sodium and chlorine atom is predetermined. If we could shrink ourselves into this crystalline world, we would see rank upon rank of atoms in an ordered array, a regularly alternating structure—sodium, chlorine, sodium, chlorine, specifying the sheet of atoms we are standing on and all the sheets above us and below us. An absolutely pure crystal of salt could have the position of every atom specified by something like 10 bits of information.[1] This would not strain the information-carrying capacity of the brain.

9   If the universe had natural laws that governed its behavior to the same degree of regularity that determines a crystal of salt, then, of course, the universe would be knowable. Even if there were many such laws, each of considerable complexity, human beings might have the capability to understand them all. Even if such knowledge exceeded the information-carrying capacity of the brain, we might store the additional information outside our bodies—in books, for example, or in computer memories—and still, in some sense, know the universe.

10   Human beings are, understandably, highly motivated to find regularities, natural laws. The search for rules, the only possible way to understand such a vast and complex universe, is called science. The universe forces those who live in it to understand it. Those creatures who find everyday experience a muddled jumble of events with no predictability, no regularity, are in grave peril. The universe belongs to those who, at least to some degree, have figured it out.

11   It is an astonishing fact that there *are* laws of nature, rules that summarize conveniently—not just qualitatively but quantitatively—how the world works. We might imagine a universe in which there are no such laws, in which the 10^{80} elementary particles that make up a universe like our own behave with utter and uncompromising abandon. To understand such a universe we would need a brain at least as massive as the universe. It seems unlikely that such a universe could have life and intelligence, because beings and brains require some degree of internal stability and order. But even if in a much more random universe there were such beings with an intelligence much greater than our own, there could not be much knowledge, passion or joy.

12   Fortunately for us, we live in a universe that has at least important parts that are knowable. Our common-sense experience and our evolutionary history have prepared us to understand something of the workaday world. When we go into

[1]Chlorine is a deadly poison gas employed on European battlefields in World War I. Sodium is a corrosive metal which burns upon contact with water. Together they make a placid and unpoisonous material, table salt. Why each of these substances has the properties it does is a subject called chemistry, which requires more than 10 bits of information to understand.

other realms, however, common sense and ordinary intuition turn out to be highly unreliable guides. It is stunning that as we go close to the speed of light our mass increases indefinitely, we shrink toward zero thickness in the direction of motion, and time for us comes as near to stopping as we would like. Many people think that this is silly, and every week or two I get a letter from someone who complains to me about it. But it is a virtually certain consequence not just of experiment but also of Albert Einstein's brilliant analysis of space and time called the Special Theory of Relativity. It does not matter that these effects seem unreasonable to us. We are not in the habit of traveling close to the speed of light. The testimony of our common sense is suspect at high velocities.

Or consider an isolated molecule composed of two atoms shaped something 13 like a dumbbell—a molecule of salt, it might be. Such a molecule rotates about an axis through the line connecting the two atoms. But in the world of quantum mechanics, the realm of the very small, not all orientations of our dumbbell molecule are possible. It might be that the molecule could be oriented in a horizontal position, say, or in a vertical position, but not at many angles in between. Some rotational positions are forbidden. Forbidden by what? By the laws of nature. The universe is built in such a way as to limit, or quantize, rotation. We do not experience this directly in everyday life; we would find it startling as well as awkward in sitting-up exercises, to find arms outstretched from the sides or pointed up to the skies permitted but many intermediate positions forbidden. We do not live in the world of the small, on the scale of 10^{-13} centimeters, in the realm where there are twelve zeros between the decimal place and the one. Our common-sense intuitions do not count. What does count is experiment—in this case observations from the far infrared spectra of molecules. They show molecular rotation to be quantized.

The idea that the world places restrictions on what humans might do is frus- 14 trating. Why *shouldn't* we be able to have intermediate rotational positions? Why *can't* we travel faster than the speed of light? But so far as we can tell, this is the way the universe is constructed. Such prohibitions not only press us toward a little humility; they also make the world more knowable. Every restriction corresponds to a law of nature, a regularization of the universe. The more restrictions there are on what matter and energy can do, the more knowledge human beings can attain. Whether in some sense the universe is ultimately knowable depends not only on how many natural laws there are that encompass widely divergent phenomena, but also on whether we have the openness and the intellectual capacity to understand such laws. Our formulations of the regularities of nature are surely dependent on how the brain is built, but also, and to a significant degree, on how the universe is built.

For myself, I like a universe that includes much that is unknown and, at the 15 same time, much that is knowable. A universe in which everything is known would be static and dull, as boring as the heaven of some weak-minded theologians. A universe that is unknowable is no fit place for a thinking being. The ideal universe for us is one very much like the universe we inhabit. And I would guess that this is not really much of a coincidence.

COMPREHENSION

1. What is the thesis of the essay? In what paragraph is this thesis most clearly expressed?
2. Why does Sagan say, in paragraph 12, that in many circumstances, "common sense and ordinary intuition turn out to be highly unreliable guides"?
3. Why does Sagan say, in his conclusion, that "the ideal universe for us is one very much like the universe we inhabit"?

RHETORIC

1. What is the function of the epigram by Emerson? How does it relate to the essay proper?
2. Many of the paragraphs in the essay begin with coordinating conjunctions (a structure frowned on by many high school English teachers). What is Sagan's rhetorical purpose in using them as connecting devices?
3. What specific clues are there in the essay that Sagan's tone is one of excitement and celebration regarding science?
4. Sagan refers often to what he calls "a law of nature." Where and how in the essay does he explain, describe, or define this term?
5. The essay begins abruptly with an explanation of the concept of science. What purpose is served by diving into the subject so dramatically?
6. What is the intended effect of combining the terms *universe* and *grain of salt* in the title and subtitle? How does the author exploit this juxtaposition in his essay?
7. Examine the italicized words in the essay. Why has Sagan chosen to italicize these words? Explain.

WRITING

1. Write a personal essay in which you describe how you felt when you suddenly understood a particular topic in school that had previously eluded you.
2. For a research paper, select one of the items Sagan enumerates in paragraph 2, such as "the formation of a dewdrop on a leaf," the origin of the name *Shakespeare* or the word *philanthropic,* "the incest taboo," or "how a 'walking stick' got to look so much like a twig." Write an expository essay on your topic.
3. **Writing an Argument:** Argue for or against the proposition that scientific knowledge takes the mystery out of life.

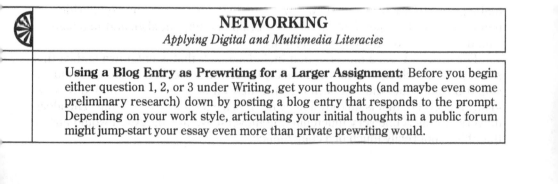

NETWORKING
Applying Digital and Multimedia Literacies

Using a Blog Entry as Prewriting for a Larger Assignment: Before you begin either question 1, 2, or 3 under Writing, get your thoughts (and maybe even some preliminary research) down by posting a blog entry that responds to the prompt. Depending on your work style, articulating your initial thoughts in a public forum might jump-start your essay even more than private prewriting would.

Staying Human

Dinesh D'Souza

Dinesh D'Souza, a leading conservative thinker, was born in Bombay, India, and came to the United States for his high school education. He graduated from Dartmouth College (BA, 1983) and subsequently wrote for several magazines, notably the National Review, *before becoming a policy analyst for the Reagan administration. His books include* Illiberal Education: The Politics of Race and Sex on Campus *(1991),* The End of Racism: Principles for a Multicultural Society *(1995),* The Virtue of Prosperity: Finding Values in an Age of Techno-Affluence *(2001),* What's So Great about America *(2002),* What's So Great about Christianity *(2007), and* The Enemy at Home: The Cultural Left and Its Responsibility for 9/11 *(2007). D'Souza has been a visiting scholar at the Hoover Institution and a research scholar at the American Enterprise Institute. In the following essay, written for the* National Review *in 2001, D'Souza offers a wide-ranging assessment of our emerging "techno-utopia."*

We are as gods, and we might as well get good at it.
　　　　　　　　　　　　　　—Kevin Kelly, author and techno-utopian

The most important technological advance of recent times is not the Internet, but 1 rather the biotech revolution—which promises to give us unprecedented power to transform human nature. How should we use that power? A group of cutting-edge scientists, entrepreneurs, and intellectuals has a bold answer. This group—I call them the techno-utopians—argues that science will soon give us the means to straighten the crooked timber of humanity, and even to remake our species into something "post-human."

One of the leading techno-utopians is Lee Silver, who teaches molecular biol- 2 ogy at Princeton University. Silver reports that biotechnology is moving beyond cloning to offer us a momentous possibility: designer children. He envisions that, in the not too distant future, couples who want to have a child will review a long list of traits on a computer screen, put together combinations of "virtual children," decide on the one they want, click on the appropriate selection, and thus—in effect—design their own offspring. "Parents are going to be able to give their children . . . genes that increase athletic ability, genes that increase musical talents . . . and ultimately genes that affect cognitive abilities."

But even this, the techno-utopians say, is a relatively small step: People living 3 today can determine the genetic destiny of all future generations. Some writers, including physicist Stephen Hawking, have suggested that genetic engineering could be used to reduce human aggression, thus solving the crime problem and making war less likely. James Watson, co-discoverer of the structure of DNA, argues that if biological interventions could be used to "cure what I feel is a very serious disease—that is, stupidity—it would be a great thing for people." Silver himself forecasts a general elevation of intellectual, athletic, temperamental, and artistic abilities so that we can over time create "a special group of mental beings" who will "trace their ancestry back to Homo sapiens," but who will be "as different from humans as humans are from the primitive worms with tiny brains that first crawled along the earth's surface."

4   These ideas might seem implausible, but they are taken very seriously by some of the best minds in the scientific community. The confidence of the techno-utopians is based on stunning advances that have made cloning and genetic engineering feasible. In theoretical terms, biotechnology crossed a major threshold with James Watson and Francis Crick's 1953 discovery of the structure of DNA, but practical applications were slow in coming. In 1997, an obscure animal-husbandry laboratory in Scotland cloned a sheep named Dolly; today, the knowledge and the means of cloning human beings already exist, and the only question is whether we are going to do it. And why stop there? As the scientific journal *Nature* editorialized shortly after the emergence of Dolly, "The growing power of molecular genetics confronts us with future prospects of being able to change the nature of our species."

5   In 1999, neurobiologist Joe Tsien boosted the intelligence of mice by inserting extra copies of a gene that enhances memory and learning; these mouse genes are virtually identical to those found in human beings. Gene therapy has already been successfully carried out in people, and now that the Human Genome Project has made possible a comprehensive understanding of the human genetic code, scientists will possess a new kind of power: the power to design our children, and even to redesign humanity itself.

The Hitler Scenario

6 The fact that these things are possible does not, of course, mean that they should be done. As one might expect, cloning and genetic engineering are attracting criticism. The techno-utopians have not yet made their products and services available to consumers; but one can reasonably expect that a society that is anxious about eating genetically modified tomatoes is going to be vastly more anxious about a scheme to engineer our offspring and our species.

7   A recent book communicating that sense of outrage is Jeremy Rifkin's *The Biotech Century*. Rifkin alleges that we are heading for a nightmarish future "where babies are genetically designed and customized in the womb, and where people are identified, stereotyped and discriminated against on the basis of their genotype." How can living beings be considered sacred, Rifkin asks, if they are treated as nothing more than "bundles of genetic information"? Biotechnology, he charges, is launching us into a new age of eugenics. In Rifkin's view, the Nazi idea of the superman is very much alive, but now in a different form: the illusion of the "perfect child."

Although Rifkin has a propensity for inflammatory rhetoric, he is raising 8
some important concerns: The new technology is unprecedented, so we should
be very cautious in developing it. It poses grave risks to human health. Cloning
and genetic engineering are unnatural; human beings have no right to do this to
nature and to ourselves.

These criticisms meet with derision on the part of the techno-utopians. Every 9
time a major new technology is developed, they say, there are people who forecast
the apocalypse. The techno-utopians point out that the new technology will deliver
amazing medical benefits, including cures for genetic diseases. How can it be
ethical, they ask, to withhold these technologies from people who need and want
them?

Lee Silver, the biologist, is annoyed at critics such as Rifkin who keep raising 10
the specter of Hitler and eugenics. "It is individuals and couples, not governments, who will seize control of these new technologies," Silver writes. The premise of the techno-utopians is that if the market produces a result, it is good. In this
view, what is wrong with the old eugenics is not that it sought to eliminate defec-
tive types and produce a superior kind of being, but that it sought to do so in a
coercive and collectivist way. The new advocates of biotechnology speak approv-
ingly of what they term "free-market eugenics."

The champions of biotechnology concede that cloning and genetic engineer- 11
ing should not be permitted in human beings until they are safe. But "safe," they
say, does not mean "error-free"; it means safe compared with existing forms of
reproduction. And they are confident that the new forms of reproduction will soon
be as safe as giving birth the natural way.

The techno-utopians are also not very concerned that the availability of 12
enhancement technologies will create two classes in society, the genetically advan-
taged and the genetically disadvantaged. They correctly point to the fact that two
such classes exist now, even in the absence of new therapies. Physicist Freeman
Dyson says that genetic enhancement might be costly at first, but won't remain
permanently expensive: "Most of our socially important technologies, such as
telephones, automobiles, television, and computers, began as expensive toys for
the rich and afterwards became cheap enough for ordinary people."

Dyson is right that time will make genetic enhancements more widely avail- 13
able, just as cars and TV sets are now. But the poor family still drives a secondhand Plymouth while the rich family can afford a new Porsche. This may not be
highly significant when it comes to cars, because both groups can still get around
fairly well. What about when it comes to genetic advantages conferred at birth?
Democratic societies can live with inequalities conferred by the lottery of nature,
but can they countenance the deliberate introduction of biological alterations that
give some citizens a better chance to succeed than others?

The techno-utopians have not, to my knowledge, addressed this concern. 14
They emphasize instead that it is well established in law, and widely recognized in
society, that parents have a right to determine what is best for their children.
"There are already plenty of ways in which we design our children," remarks
biologist Gregory Stock. "One of them is called piano lessons. Another is called

private school." Stock's point is that engineering their children's genes is simply one more way in which parents can make their children better people.

15   Some people might find it weird and unnatural to fix their child in the same way they fix their car—but, say the techno-utopians, this is purely a function of habit. We're not used to genetic engineering, so it seems "unnatural" to us. But think about how unnatural driving a car seemed for people who previously got around on horses and in carriages. "The smallpox virus was part of the natural order," Silver wryly observes, "until it was forced into extinction by human intervention." Diseases and death are natural; life-saving surgery is unnatural.

Not Sacred after All?

16 Nor are the techno-utopians worried about diminishing the sanctity of human life because, they say, it isn't intrinsically sacred. "This is not an ethical argument but a religious one," says Silver. "There is no logic to it." Biologist David Baltimore, a Nobel laureate, argues that "statements about morally and ethically unacceptable practices" have no place in the biotechnology debate "because those are subjective grounds and therefore provide no basis for discussion." Silver and Baltimore's shared assumption is that the moralists are talking about values while they, the hard scientists, are dealing in facts.

17   In this view, the subjective preferences of those who seek to mystify human life do not square with the truths about human biology taught by science. The cells of human beings, Silver points out, are not different in their chemical makeup from the cells of horses and bacteria. If there is such a thing as human dignity, Silver argues, it derives exclusively from consciousness, from our ability to perceive and apprehend our environment. "The human mind," Silver writes, "is much more than the genes that brought it into existence." Somehow the electrochemical reactions in our brain produce consciousness, and it is this consciousness, Silver contends, that is the source of man's autonomy and power. While genes fully control the activity of all life forms, Silver writes that in human beings "master and slave have switched positions." Consciousness enables man to complete his dominance over nature by prevailing over his human nature. Silver concludes that, in a bold assertion of will, we can defeat the program of our genes, we can take over the reins of evolution, we can choose the genetic code we want for our children, and we can collectively determine the future of our species.

18   This triumphant note is echoed by many techno-utopians. Biotech, writes journalist Ronald Bailey, "will liberate future generations from today's limitations and offer them a much wider scope of freedom." Physicist Gregory Benford is even more enthusiastic: "It is as though prodigious, bountiful Nature for billions of years has tossed off variations on its themes like a careless, prolific Picasso. Now Nature finds that one of its casual creations has come back with a piercing, searching vision, and its own pictures to paint."

19   These are ringing statements. But do they make sense? Clearly there are many problems with Silver's definition of human dignity as based in consciousness. Animals are conscious; do they deserve the same dignity as human beings?

Moreover, are human beings entitled to dignity only when they are conscious? Do we lose our right to be respected, and become legitimate subjects for discarding medical experiments, when we fall asleep, or into a coma? Surely Silver would disavow these conclusions. They do, however, flow directly from his definition, which is, in fact, just as heavily freighted with values as are the statements of his opponents.

There is, behind the proclamations of scientific neutrality, an ideology that 20 needs to be spelled out, a techno-Nietzschean doctrine that proclaims: We are molecules, but molecules that know how to rebel. Our values do not derive from nature or nature's God; rather, they arise from the arbitrary force of our wills. And now our wills can make the most momentous choice ever exercised on behalf of our species: the choice to reject our human nature. Why should we remain subject to the constraints of our mortality and destiny? Wealth and technology have given us the keys to unlimited, indeed godlike, power: the dawn of the post-human era.

What is one to make of all this? In many respects, we should celebrate the 21 advent of technologies that enable us to alleviate suffering and extend life. I have no problem with genetic therapy to cure disease; I am even willing to endorse therapy that not only cures illness in patients but also prevents it from being transmitted to the next generation. Under certain circumstances, I can see the benefits of cloning. The cloning of animals can provide organs for transplant as well as animals with medicinal properties ("drugstores on the hoof"). Even human cloning seems defensible when it offers the prospect of a biological child to married couples who might not otherwise be able to have one.

Creating the Perfect Child

But there is a seduction contained in these exercises in humanitarianism: They 22 urge us to keep going, to take the next step. And when we take that step, when we start designing our children, when we start remaking human beings, I think we will have crossed a perilous frontier. Even cloning does not cross this frontier, because it merely replicates an existing genetic palate. It is unconvincing to argue, as some techno-utopians do, that giving a child a heightened genetic capacity for music or athletics or intelligence is no different from giving a child piano, swimming, or math lessons. In fact, there is a big difference. It is one thing to take a person's given nature and given capacity, and seek to develop it, and quite another to shape that person's nature in accordance with one's will.

There is no reason to object to people's attempting brain implants and 23 somatic gene enhancements on themselves. Perhaps, in some cases, these will do some good; others may end up doing injury. But at least these people have, through their free choices, done it to themselves. The problem arises when people seek to use enhancement technologies to shape the destiny of others, and especially their children.

But, argues Lee Silver, we have the right to terminate pregnancy and control 24 our children's lives in every other way; why shouldn't parents be permitted to alter their child's genetic constitution? In the single instance of gene therapy to cure disease, I'd agree   because, In this one limited case, we can trust the parents to make a decision that there is every rational reason to believe their offspring would decide in the identical manner, were they in a position to make the choice. No child would say, "I can't believe my parents did that to me. I would have chosen to have Parkinson's disease."

25   But I would contend that in no other case do people have the right to bend the genetic constitution of their children—or anyone else—to their will. But they might, in good conscience, be tempted to do so; and this temptation must be resisted. Indeed, it must be outlawed—because what the techno-utopians want does, in fact, represent a fundamental attack on the value of human life, and the core principle of America.

Rescuing Humanity and the American Idea

26 The scientific-capitalist project at the heart of the American experiment was an attempted "conquest of nature." Never did the early philosophers of science, like Francis Bacon, or the American Founders conceive that this enterprise would eventually seek to conquer human nature. Their goal was to take human nature as a given, as something less elevated than the angels, and thus requiring a government characterized by separation of offices, checks and balances, limited power. At the same time, the Founders saw human nature as more elevated than that of other animals. They held that human beings have claims to dignity and rights that do not extend to animals: Human beings cannot be killed for sport or rightfully governed without their consent.

27   The principles of the Founders were extremely far-reaching. They called into question the legitimacy of every existing government, because at the time of the American founding, no government in the world was entirely based on the consent of the governed. The ideals of the Founders even called into question their own practices, such as slavery. It took the genius of Abraham Lincoln, and the tragedy of the Civil War, to compel the enforcement of the central principle of the Declaration of Independence: that we each have an inalienable right to life, liberty, and the pursuit of happiness, and that these rights shall not be abridged without our consent.

28   The attempt to enhance and redesign other human beings represents a flagrant denial of this principle that is the basis of our dignity and rights. Indeed, it is a restoration of the principle underlying slavery, and the argument between the defenders and critics of genetic enhancement is identical in principle, and very nearly in form, to the argument between Stephen Douglas and Abraham Lincoln on the issue of human enslavement.

29   In that tempestuous exchange, which laid the groundwork for the Civil War, Douglas argued for the pro-choice position. He wanted to let each new territory decide for itself whether it wanted slavery. He wanted the American people to agree to disagree on the issue. He advocated for each community a very high value: the right to self-determination.

Lincoln challenged him on the grounds that choice cannot be exercised with- 30 out reference to the content of the choice. How can it make sense to permit people to choose to enslave another human being? How can self-determination be invoked to deny others the same? A free people can disagree on many things, but it cannot disagree on the distinction between freedom and despotism. Lincoln summarized Douglas's argument as follows: "If any one man choose to enslave another, no third man shall be allowed to object."

Lincoln's argument was based on a simple premise: "As I would not be a 31 slave, so I would not be a master." Lincoln rejects in principle the subordination implied in the master-slave relationship. Those who want freedom for themselves, he insists, must also show themselves willing to extend it to others. At its deepest level, Lincoln's argument is that the legitimacy of popular consent is itself dependent on a doctrine of natural rights that arises out of a specific understanding of human nature and human dignity. "Slavery," he said, "is founded in the selfishness of man's nature-opposition to it, in his love of justice. These principles are in eternal antagonism; and when brought into collision so fiercely . . . convulsions must ceaselessly follow." What Lincoln is saying is that self-interest by itself is too base a foundation for the new experiment called America. Selfishness is part of our nature, but it is not the best part of our nature. It should be subordinated to a nobler ideal. Lincoln seeks to dedicate America to a higher proposition: the proposition that all men are created equal. It is the denial of this truth, Lincoln warns, that will bring on the cataclysm.

Let me restate Lincoln's position for our current context. We speak of "our 32 children," but they are not really ours; we do not own them. At most, we own ourselves. It is true that *Roe v. Wade* gives us the right to kill our unborn in the womb. The right to abortion has been defended, both by its advocates and by the Supreme Court, as the right of a woman to control her own body. This is not the same as saying the woman has ownership of the fetus, that the fetus is the woman's property. The Supreme Court has said that as long as the fetus is occupying her womb, she can treat it as an unwelcome intruder, and get rid of it. (Even here, technology is changing the shape of the debate by moving up the period when the fetus can survive outside the womb.) But once a woman decides to carry the pregnancy to term, she has already exercised her choice. She has chosen to give birth to the child, which is in the process of becoming an independent human being with its own dignity and rights.

No Place for Parental Tyranny

As parents, we have been entrusted with our children, and it is our privilege and 33 responsibility to raise them as best we can. Undoubtedly we will infuse them with our values and expectations, but even so, the good parent will respect the child's right to follow his own path. There is something perversely restrictive about parents who apply relentless pressure on their children to conform to their will—to follow the same professional paths that they did, or to become the "first doctor in the family." These efforts, however well intentioned, are a betrayal of the true meaning of parenthood. Indeed, American culture encourages a certain measure of adolescent rebellion against parental expectations, precisely so that young people making the transition to independence can "find themselves" and discover their own identity.

34   Consequently, parents have no right to treat their children as chattels; but this is precisely the enterprise that is being championed by the techno-utopians. Some of these people profess to be libertarians, but they are in fact totalitarians. They speak about freedom and choice, although what they advocate is despotism and human bondage. The power they seek to exercise is not over "nature" but over other human beings.

35   Parents who try to design their children are in some ways more tyrannical than slaveowners, who merely sought to steal the labor of their slaves. Undoubtedly some will protest that they only wish the best for their children, that they are only doing this for their own good. But the slaveowners made similar arguments, saying that they ruled the Negroes in the Negroes' own interest. The argument was as self-serving then as it is now. What makes us think that in designing our children it will be their objective good—rather than our desires and preferences—that will predominate?

36   The argument against slavery is that you may not tyrannize over the life and freedom of another person for any reason whatsoever. Even that individual's consent cannot overturn "inalienable" rights: One does not have the right to sell oneself into slavery. This is the clear meaning of the American proposition. The object of the American Revolution that is now spreading throughout the world has always been the affirmation, not the repudiation, of human nature. The Founders envisioned technology and capitalism as providing the framework and the tools for human beings to live richer, fuller lives. They would have scorned, as we should, the preposterous view that we are the servants of our technology. They would have strenuously opposed, as we should, the effort on the part of the techno-utopians to design their offspring; to alter, improve, and perfect human nature; or to relinquish our humanity in pursuit of some post-human ideal.

37   Mary Shelley's 1818 novel *Frankenstein* describes a monster that is the laboratory creation of a doctor who refuses to accept the natural limits of humanity. He wants to appropriate to himself the traditional prerogatives of the deity, such as control over human mortality. He even talks about making "a new species" with "me as its creator and source." In his rhetoric, Frankenstein sounds very much like today's techno-utopians. And, contrary to what most people think, the real monster in the novel isn't the lumbering, tragic creature; it is the doctor who creates him. This is the prophetic message of Shelley's work: In seeking to become gods, we are going to make monsters of ourselves.

COMPREHENSION

1. What is the meaning of D'Souza's title? According to the writer, what are the dangers we face in our effort to "stay human"? What must we do to retain our essential humanity?

2. What aspects of the biotech revolution does the author treat? What is his opinion of each?
3. What does the writer mean by the "Hitler Scenario" and the "American Idea"?

RHETORIC

1. What is D'Souza's purpose? What is his tone? Does he seem reasonable or unnecessarily argumentative? Objective or biased? How do you know? For what type of audience does he seem to be writing?
2. D'Souza begins his essay by introducing the ideas of such "leading techno-utopians" as Lee Silver, Stephen Hawking, James Watson and Francis Crick, and Joe Tsien. It this an effective opening strategy? Why or why not?
3. Explain the author's claim. What minor propositions does he provide? Where does he advance logical, ethical, and emotional appeals? Cite instances in which he employs refutation to advance his argument. What faults does he find with the techno-utopians?
4. Consider the essay's section headings. How do they serve to focus the content of each section? What characterizes the progression of ideas from section to section? How does the author's decision to divide the essay into sections help him to construct his argument?
5. Does D'Souza reveal any of his own biases in this essay? Explain.
6. In the concluding paragraph, D'Souza alludes to Mary Shelley's novel *Frankenstein*. Does this allusion flow naturally from the introduction and body? Why or why not?

WRITING

1. Write a 300-word summary of this essay, transcribing all of the main aspects of D'Souza's argument.
2. Write your own survey of the biotech revolution. Refer to some of the topics and ideas mentioned by D'Souza in his essay.
3. **Writing an Argument:** Select one aspect of the biotech revolution—for instance, cloning or stem-cell research—and write an argumentative essay supporting or opposing developments in the field.

NETWORKING
Applying Digital and Multimedia Literacies

Debating the Ethics behind Cloning: Work in groups of three to prepare for and engage in a debate about some aspect of cloning or stem-cell research. Two of you will be debaters, each doing research to inform your assigned position: one for and one against a proposed development. Come to the debate with notes and solid arguments and counterarguments prepared. The third person will serve as the moderator, who will come prepared with questions and possible follow-up questions, as well as with a one- or two-page informative, unbiased introduction to the issues. He or she will open the debate by reading this document. If possible, record the debate, and review it later. Discuss each of your strengths and weaknesses as public speakers/ debaters, providing constructive criticism and praise.

✳

Anybody Out There?

Oliver Sacks

Oliver Sacks *(b. 1933), a well-known neurologist, was born in London and immigrated to the United States in 1960. He was educated at Queens College, Oxford, where he received a BA (1954) and subsequent degrees in chemistry and medicine. Sacks has practiced and taught medicine, surgery, and neurology at several institutions, including Albert Einstein College of Medicine, Bronx Psychiatric Hospital, and New York University Medical Center. An award-winning physician and science writer, Sacks has written numerous books, including* Awakenings *(1973), which was made into a film starring Robin Williams and Robert De Niro;* The Man Who Mistook His Wife for a Hat, and Other Clinical Tales *(1985);* An Anthropologist on Mars *(1995);* Uncle Tungsten: Memories of a Chemical Boyhood *(2001);* Vintage Sacks *(2004), and* Musicophilia: Tales of Music and the Brain *(2007). In this essay, published in* Natural History *in 2002, Sacks speculates about the existence of life-forms in the universe.*

1   One of the first books I read as a boy was H. G. Wells's 1901 fable, *The First Men in the Moon.* The two men, Cavor and Bedford, land in a crater, apparently barren and lifeless, just before the lunar dawn; then, as the sun rises, they realize there is an atmosphere. They spot small pools and eddies of water, and then little round objects scattered on the ground. One of them, as it is warmed by the sun, bursts open and reveals a sliver of green. ("'A seed,' said Cavor . . . And then . . . very softly, 'Life!'") They light a piece of paper and throw it onto the surface of the Moon. It glows and sends up a thread of smoke, indicating that the atmosphere, though thin, is rich in oxygen and will support life as they know it.

2   Here, then, was how Wells conceived the prerequisites of life: water, sunlight (a source of energy), and oxygen. "A Lunar Morning," the eighth chapter in his book, was my first introduction to astrobiology.

3   It was apparent, even in Wells's day, that most of the planets in our solar system were not possible homes for life. The only reasonable surrogate for the Earth was Mars, which was known to be a solid planet of reasonable size, in stable orbit, not too distant from the sun, and so, it was thought, having a range of surface temperatures compatible with the presence of liquid water.

4   But free oxygen gas—how could that occur in a planet's atmosphere? What would keep it from being mopped up by ferrous iron and other oxygen-hungry chemicals on the surface unless, somehow, it was continuously pumped out in huge quantities, enough to oxidize all the surface minerals and keep the atmosphere charged as well?

5   It was the blue-green algae, or cyanobacteria, that infused the Earth's atmosphere with oxygen, a process that took between a billion and two billion years. The fossil

record shows that cyanobacteria go back three and a half billion years. Yet, amazingly, some of them still thrive today in odd corners of the world, forming strange, cushion-shaped colonies called stromatolites. It is an extraordinary experience to go to Shark Bay in western Australia, where stromatolites flourish in the hypersaline waters, to watch them slowly bubbling oxygen, and to reflect that, three billion years ago, this was how the Earth was transformed. The cyanobacteria invented photosynthesis: by capturing the energy of the sun, they were able to combine carbon dioxide (massively present in the Earth's early atmosphere) with water to create complex molecules—sugars, carbohydrates—which the bacteria could then store and tap for energy as needed. This process generated free oxygen as a byproduct—a waste product that was to determine the future course of evolution.

Although free oxygen in a planet's atmosphere would be an infallible marker 6 of life, and one that, if present, should be readily detected in the spectra of extrasolar planets, it is not a prerequisite for life. Planets, after all, get started without free oxygen, and may remain without it all their lives. Anaerobic organisms swarmed before oxygen was available, perfectly at home in the atmosphere of the early Earth, converting nitrogen to ammonia, sulfur to hydrogen sulfide, carbon dioxide to formaldehyde, and so forth. (From formaldehyde and ammonia the bacteria could make every organic compound they needed.)

There may be planets in our solar system and elsewhere that lack an atmo- 7 sphere of oxygen but are nonetheless teeming with anaerobes. And such anaerobes need not live on the surface of the planet; they could occur well below the surface, in boiling vents and sulfurous hot pots, as they do on Earth today, to say nothing of subterranean oceans and lakes. (There is thought to be such a subsurface ocean on Jupiter's moon Europa, locked beneath a shell of ice several miles thick, and its exploration is one of the astrobiological priorities of this century. Curiously, Wells, in *The First Men in the Moon,* imagines life originating in a central sea in the middle of the Moon and then spreading outward to its inhospitable periphery.)

It is not clear whether life has to "advance"—whether evolution must take place— 8 if there is a satisfactory status quo. Brachiopods—lampshells—for instance, have remained virtually unchanged since they first appeared in the Cambrian Period, more than 500 million years ago. But there does seem to be a drive for organisms to become more highly organized and more efficient in retaining energy, at least when environmental conditions are changing rapidly, as they were before the Cambrian. The evidence indicates that the first primitive anaerobes on Earth were prokaryotes: small, simple cells—just cytoplasm, usually bounded by a cell wall, but with little if any internal structure.

By degrees, however—and the process took place with glacial slowness— 9 prokaryotes became more complex, acquiring internal structure, nuclei, mitochondria, and so on. The microbiologist Lynn Margulis of the University of Massachusetts, Amherst, has convincingly suggested that these complex so-called eukaryotes arose when prokaryotes began incorporating other prokaryotes within their own cells. The incorporated organisms at first became symbiotic and later came to function as essential organelles of their hosts, enabling the resultant organisms to use what was originally a noxious poison: oxygen.

10 Primitive as they are, prokaryotes are still highly sophisticated organisms with formidable genetic and metabolic machinery. Even the simplest ones manufacture more than five hundred proteins, and their DNA includes at least half a million base pairs. Hence it is certain that still more primitive life forms must have preceded the prokaryotes.

11 Perhaps, as the physicist Freeman Dyson of the Institute for Advanced Study in Princeton has suggested, there were "pro-genotes" capable of metabolizing, growing, and dividing but lacking any genetic mechanism for precise replication. And before them there must have been millions of years of purely chemical, pre-biotic evolution—the synthesis, over eons, of formaldehyde and cyanide, of amino acids and peptides, of proteins and self-replicating molecules. Perhaps that chemistry took place in the minute vesicles, or globules, that develop when fluids at very different temperatures meet, as may well have happened around the boiling midocean vents of the Archaean sea.

12 Life as we know it is not imaginable without proteins, and proteins are built from peptides, and ultimately from amino acids. It is easy to imagine that amino acids were abundant in the early Earth, either formed as a result of lightning discharges or brought to the planet by comets and meteors.

13 The real problem is to get from amino acids and other simple compounds to peptides, nucleotides, proteins, and so on. It is unlikely that such delicate chemical syntheses would occur in "some warm little pond," as Darwin imagined, or on the surface of a primordial sea. Instead, they would probably require unusual conditions of heat and concentration, as well as the presence of special catalysts and energy-rich compounds to make them proceed. The biochemist Christian de Duve of Rockefeller University suggests that complex organic sulfur compounds played a crucial role in providing chemical energy, and that these compounds may have formed spontaneously early in Earth's history, perhaps in the hot, acidic, sulfurous depths of the seafloor vents (where, it is increasingly believed, life probably originated). De Duve imagines this purely chemical world as the precursor of an "RNA world," believed by many to represent the first form of self-replicating life. He thinks that the movement from one to the other was both inevitable and fast.

14 The two preeminent evolutionary changes in the early history of life on Earth—from prokaryote to eukaryote, from anaerobe to aerobe—took the better part of two billion years. And there then had to pass another 1,200 or 1,300 million years before life rose above the microscopic forms, and the first "higher," multicellular organisms appeared. So if the Earth's history is anything to go by, we should not expect to find any higher life on a planet that is still young. Even if extraterrestrial life has appeared, and all goes well, it could take billions of years for evolutionary processes to move it along to the multicellular stage.

15 Moreover, all those "stages" of evolution—including the evolution of intelligent, conscious beings from the first multicellular forms—may have happened against daunting odds. Stephen Jay Gould spoke of life as "a glorious accident";

Richard Dawkins of Oxford University likens evolution to "climbing Mount Improbable." And life, once started, is subject to vicissitudes of all kinds: from meteors and volcanic eruptions to global overheating and cooling; from dead ends in evolution to mysterious mass extinctions; and finally (if things get that far) the fateful proclivities of a species like ourselves.

We know there are microfossils in some of the Earth's most ancient rocks, 16 rocks more than three and a half billion years old. So life must have appeared within 100 or 200 million years after the Earth had cooled off sufficiently for water to become liquid. That astonishingly rapid transformation makes one think that life may develop readily, perhaps inevitably, as soon as the right physical and chemical conditions appear.

But can one argue from a single example? Can one speak confidently of 17 "earthlike" planets, or is the Earth physically, chemically, and geologically unique? And even if there are other "habitable" planets, what are the chances that life, with its thousands of physical and chemical coincidences and contingencies, will emerge? Life may be a one-off event.

Opinion here varies as widely as it can. The French biochemist Jacques 18 Monod regarded life as a fantastically improbable accident, unlikely to have arisen anywhere else in the universe. In his book *Chance and Necessity,* he writes, "The universe was not pregnant with life." De Duve takes issue with this, and sees the origin of life as determined by a large number of steps, most of which must have had a "high likelihood of taking place under the prevailing conditions." Indeed, de Duve believes that there is not merely unicellular life throughout the universe but complex, intelligent life, too, on trillions of planets. How are we to align ourselves between these utterly opposite but theoretically defensible positions?

What we need, what we must have, is hard evidence of life on another planet 19 or heavenly body. Mars is the obvious candidate: It was wet and warm there once, with lakes and hydrothermal vents and perhaps deposits of clay and iron ore. It is especially in such places that we should look, suggests Malcolm Walter, an expert on fossil bacteria that date from the Earth's earliest epochs. If the evidence shows that life once existed on Mars, we will then need to know, crucially, whether it originated there or was transported (as would have been readily possible) from the young, teeming, volcanic Earth. If we can determine that life originated independently on Mars (if Mars, for instance, once harbored DNA nucleotides different from our own), we will have made an incredible discovery—one that will alter our view of the universe and enable us to perceive it, in the words of the physicist Paul Davies, as a "biofriendly" one. It would help us to gauge the probability of finding life elsewhere instead of bombinating in a vacuum of data, caught between the poles of inevitability and uniqueness.

In just the past twenty years life has been discovered in previously unex- 20 pected places on our own planet, such as the life-rich black smokers of the ocean depths, where organisms thrive in conditions biologists would once have dismissed as utterly deadly. Life is much tougher, much more resilient, than we once thought. It now seems to me quite possible that microorganisms or their remains will be found on Mars and perhaps on some of the satellites of Jupiter and Saturn.

21   It seems far less likely, many orders of magnitude less likely, that we will find any evidence of higher-order, intelligent life forms, at least in our own solar system. But who knows? Given the vastness and age of the universe at large, the innumerable stars and planets it must contain, and our radical uncertainties about life's origin and evolution, the possibility cannot be ruled out. And though the rate of evolutionary and geochemical processes is incredibly slow, that of technological progress is incredibly fast. Who is to say (if humanity survives) what we may not be capable of, or discover, in the next thousand years?

22   For myself, since I cannot wait, I turn to science fiction on occasion—and, not least, back to my favorite Wells. Although it was written a hundred years ago, "A Lunar Morning" has the freshness of a new dawn, and it remains for me, as when I first read it, the most poetic evocation of how it may be when, finally, we encounter alien life.

COMPREHENSION

1. What is Sacks's answer to the question he poses in the title?
2. Explain the connection between the writer's boyhood reading and his interest in life elsewhere in the universe.
3. List and define some of the scientific evidence and scientific principles Sacks mentions in his essay.

RHETORIC

1. Why does Sacks begin with an anecdote about his boyhood? How might this strategy appeal to readers of *Natural History,* where the essay first appeared?
2. In what ways does Sacks demonstrate his expertise and authority as a scientist in this essay? What tone does he take in presenting this information?
3. What is Sacks's thesis? What types of evidence does he offer to support his main idea?
4. Identify the main sections in this essay and the transitions Sacks uses to link them.
5. Where does Sacks use definition, comparison and contrast, process analysis, and causal analysis? Does he mix patterns successfully? Why or why not?
6. Examine the conclusion. Why does Sacks ask questions, and why does he end on a provisional note?

WRITING

1. In an expository essay, examine the popularity of science fiction in literature and/or film. How does science fiction present the notion of life in the universe? Be certain to develop examples to support your thesis.
2. Conduct research on H. G. Wells, and then write an evaluative paper in which you highlight the ways in which he predicted the future.
3. **Writing an Argument:** Do you think that extraterrestrial life exists? Answer this question in an argumentative essay.

NETWORKING
Applying Digital and Multimedia Literacies

Creating an Online Literature Review: For question 1, 2, or 3 under Writing, compile a review of the literature you would use to research this topic and help write an essay about it. For each source, provide a Works Cited entry and a paragraph-long summary of the source and how it relates to your topic; for online sources, also provide a direct link to the source. If you work with question 1, be sure to include the science fiction novels you would like to discuss.

Synthesis: Connections for Critical Thinking

1. Using the essay of D'Souza, discuss the need for strict ethics among scientists in regard to their concern over the well-being of the general populace.
2. Imagine a conversation between Sedaris and Turkle. What would they say to each other?
3. Compare the process of natural selection as advanced by Darwin with the concept of evolution as defined by Sacks and Klinkenborg.
4. Rent the DVD version of the television series *Cosmos,* which was based on a novel by Carl Sagan. Compare the ideas set forth in the film with those in Sagan's essay "Can We Know the Universe? Reflections on a Grain of Salt."
5. Compare and contrast the expository methods Darwin uses to explain the process of natural selection and the narrative technique Sedaris uses to describe his technophobia.
6. Using Ackerman's and Sacks's essays, explore how science can be either a friend or a foe of humankind.

NETWORKING
Applying Digital and Multimedia Literacies

---

1. Search the Web for two sites: one promoting the idea of evolution, the other promoting the idea of creationism. Compare and contrast the approach of each site as well as responses by the visitors to each site.
2. Have your class create a private blog with user names that do not divulge the gender of the participants. Discuss the pros and cons of computers as described by Sedaris. Have a host tally the nature of the responses, reveal the gender of the students who participated, and discuss any differences between the responses of the male and female students.

Glossary

Abstract/concrete   patterns of language reflect an author's word choice. Abstract words (for example, *wisdom, power,* and *beauty*) refer to general ideas, qualities, or conditions. Concrete words name material objects and items associated with the five senses—words like *rock, pizza,* and *basketball.* Both abstract and concrete language are useful in communicating ideas. Generally, you should not be too abstract in writing. It is best to employ concrete words, naming things that can be seen, touched, smelled, heard, or tasted in order to support generalizations, topic sentences, or more abstract ideas.

Acronym   is a word formed from the first or first few letters of several words, as in OPEC (Organization of Petroleum Exporting Countries).

Action   in narrative writing is the sequence of happenings or events. This movement of events may occupy just a few minutes or extend over a period of years or centuries.

Alliteration   is the repetition of initial consonant sounds in words placed closely next to each other, as in "what a *t*ale of *t*error now their *t*urbulency *t*ells." Prose that is highly rhythmical or "poetic" often makes use of this method.

Allusion   is a literary, biographical, or historical reference, whether real or imaginary. It is a "figure of speech" (a fresh, useful comparison) employed to illuminate an idea. A writer's prose style can be made richer through this economical method of evoking an idea or emotion, as in E. M. Forster's biblical allusion in this sentence: "Property produces men of weight, and it was a man of weight who failed to get into the Kingdom of Heaven."

Analogy   is a form of comparison that uses a clear illustration to explain a difficult idea or function. It is unlike a formal comparison in that its subjects of comparison are from different categories or areas. For example, an analogy likening "division of labor" to the activity of bees in a hive makes the first concept more concrete by showing it to the reader through the figurative comparison with the bees. Analogy in exposition can involve a few sentences, a paragraph or set of paragraphs, or an entire essay. Analogies can also be used in argumentation to heighten an appeal to emotion, but they cannot actually *prove* anything.

Analysis   is a method of exposition in which a subject is broken up into its parts to explain their nature, function, proportion, or relationship. Analysis thus explores connections and processes within the context of a given subject. (See *causal analysis* and *process analysis.*)

Anecdote   is a brief, engaging account of some happening, often historical, biographical, or personal. As a technique in writing, anecdote is especially effective in creating interesting essay introductions and also in illuminating abstract concepts in the body of the essay.

Antecedent   in grammar refers to the word, phrase, or clause to which a pronoun refers. In writing, antecedent also refers to any happening or thing that is prior to another or to anything that logically precedes a subject.

Antithesis   is the balancing of one idea or term against another for emphasis.

Antonym   is a word whose meaning is opposite to that of another word.

Aphorism   is a short, pointed statement expressing a general truism or an idea in an original or imaginative way. Marshall McLuhan's statement that "the medium is the message" is a well-known contemporary aphorism.

Archaic   language is vocabulary or usage that belongs to an earlier period and is old-fashioned today. The word *thee* for *you* is an archaism still in use in certain situations.

Archetypes   are special images or symbols that, according to Carl Jung, appeal to the total racial or cultural understanding of a people. Such images or symbols as the mother archetype, the cowboy in American film, a sacred mountain, or spring as a time of renewal tend to trigger the "collective unconscious" of the human race.

Argumentation   is a formal variety of writing that offers reasons for or against something. Its goal is to persuade or convince the reader through logical reasoning and carefully controlled emotional appeal. Argumentation as a formal mode of writing contains many properties that distinguish it from exposition. (See *assumption, deduction, evidence, induction, logic, persuasion, proposition,* and *refutation.*)

Assonance   is defined generally as likeness or rough similarity of sound. Its specific definition is a partial rhyme in which the stressed vowel sounds are alike but the consonant sounds are unlike, as in *late* and *make.* Although more common to poetry, assonance can also be detected in highly rhythmic prose.

Assumption   in argumentation is anything taken for granted or presumed to be accepted by the audience and therefore unstated. Assumptions in argumentative writing can be dangerous because the audience might not always accept the idea implicit in them. (See *begging the question.*)

Audience   is that readership toward which an author directs his or her essay. In composing essays, writers must acknowledge the nature of their expected readers—whether specialized or general, minimally educated or highly educated, sympathetic or unsympathetic toward the writer's opinions, and so forth. Failure to focus on the writer's true audience can lead to confusion in language and usage, presentation of inappropriate content, and failure to appeal to the expected reader.

Balance   in sentence structure refers to the assignment of equal treatment in the arrangement of coordinate ideas. It is often used to heighten a contrast of ideas.

Begging the question   is an error or a fallacy in reasoning and argumentation in which the writer assumes as a truth something for which evidence or proof is actually needed.

Causal analysis   is a form of writing that examines causes and effects of events or conditions as they relate to a specific subject. Writers can investigate the causes of a particular effect or the effects of a particular cause or combine both methods. Basically, however, causal analysis looks for connections between things and reasons behind them.

Characterization is the creation of people involved in the action. It is used especially in narrative or descriptive writing. Authors use techniques of dialogue, description, reportage, and observation in attempting to present vivid and distinctive characters.

Chronology or chronological order is the arrangement of events in the order in which they happened. Chronological order can be used in such diverse narrative situations as history, biography, scientific process, and personal account. Essays that are ordered by chronology move from one step or point to the next in time.

Cinematic technique in narration, description, and occasionally exposition is the conscious application of film art to the development of the contemporary essay. Modern writers often are aware of such film techniques as montage (the process of cutting and arranging film so that short scenes are presented in rapid succession), zoom (intense enlargement of subject), and various forms of juxtaposition, and use these methods to enhance the quality of their essays.

Classification is a form of exposition in which the writer divides a subject into categories and then groups elements in each of those categories according to their relationships with one another. Thus a writer using classification takes a topic, divides it into several major groups, and then often subdivides those groups, moving always from larger categories to smaller ones.

Cliché is an expression that once was fresh and original but that has lost much of its vitality through overuse. Because expressions like "as quick as a wink" and "blew her stack" are trite or common today, they should be avoided in writing.

Climactic ordering is the arrangement of a paragraph or essay so that the most important items are saved for last. The effect is to build slowly through a sequence of events or ideas to the most critical part of the composition.

Coherence is a quality in effective writing that results from the careful ordering of each sentence in a paragraph and each paragraph in the essay. If an essay is coherent, each part will grow naturally and logically from those parts that come before it. Following careful chronological, logical, spatial, or sequential order is the most natural way to achieve coherence in writing. The main devices used in achieving coherence are transitions, which help connect one thought with another.

Colloquial language is conversational language used in certain types of informal and narrative writing but rarely in essays, business writing, or research writing. Expressions like "cool," "pal," or "I can dig it" often have a place in conversational settings. However, they should be used sparingly in essay writing for special effects.

Comparison/contrast as an essay pattern treats similarities and differences between two subjects. Any useful comparison involves two items from the same class. Moreover, there must be a clear reason for the comparison or contrast. Finally, there must be a balanced treatment of the various comparative or contrasting points between the two subjects.

Conclusions are the endings of essays. Without a conclusion, an essay would be incomplete, leaving the reader with the feeling that something important has been left out. There are numerous strategies for conclusions available to writers: summarizing main points in the essay, restating the main idea, using an effective quotation, offering the reader the climax to a series of events, returning to the beginning and echoing it, offering a solution to a problem, emphasizing the topic's significance, or setting a new frame of reference by generalizing from the main thesis. A conclusion should end the essay in a clear, convincing, emphatic way.

Concrete (See *abstract/concrete*.)

Conflict in narrative writing is the clash or opposition of events, characters, or ideas that makes the resolution of action necessary.

Connotation/denotation are terms specifying the way a word has meaning. Connotation refers to the "shades of meaning" that a word might have because of various emotional associations it calls up for writers and readers alike. Words like *patriotism*, *pig*, and *rose* have strong connotative overtones to them. Denotation refers to the "dictionary" definition of a word—its exact meaning. Good writers understand the connotative and denotative value of words and control the shades of meaning that many words possess.

Context is the situation surrounding a word, group of words, or sentence. Often the elements coming before or after a certain confusing or difficult construction will provide insight into the meaning or importance of that item.

Coordination in sentence structure refers to the grammatical arrangement of parts of the same order or equality in rank.

Declarative sentences make a statement or assertion.

Deduction is a form of logic that begins with a generally stated truth or principle and then offers details, examples, and reasoning to support the generalization. In other words, deduction is based on reasoning from a known principle to an unknown principle, from the general to the specific, or from a premise to a logical conclusion. (See *syllogism*.)

Definition in exposition is the extension of a word's meaning through a paragraph or an entire essay. As an extended method of explaining a word, this type of definition relies on other rhetorical methods, including detail, illustration, comparison and contrast, and anecdote.

Denotation (See *connotation/denotation*.)

Description in the prose essay is a variety of writing that uses details of sight, sound, color, smell, taste, and touch to create a word picture and to explain or illustrate an idea.

Development refers to the way a paragraph or an essay elaborates or builds upon a topic or theme. Typical development proceeds either from general illustrations to specific ones or from one generalization to another. (See *horizontal/vertical*.)

Dialogue is the reproduction of speech or conversation between two or more persons in writing. Dialogue can add concreteness and vividness to an essay and can also help reveal character. A writer who reproduces dialogue in an essay must use it for a purpose and not simply as a decorative device.

Diction is the manner of expression in words, choice of words, or wording. Writers must choose vocabulary carefully and precisely to communicate a message and also to address an intended audience effectively; this is good diction.

Digression is a temporary departure from the main subject in writing. Any digression in the essay must serve a purpose or be intended for a specific effect.

Discourse (forms of) relates conventionally to the main categories of writing—narration, description, exposition, and argumentation. In practice, these forms of discourse often blend or overlap. Essayists seek the ideal fusion of forms of discourse in the treatment of their subject.

Division is that aspect of classification in which the writer divides some large subject into categories. Division helps writers split large and potentially complicated subjects into parts for orderly presentation and discussion.

Dominant impression in description is the main impression or effect that writers attempt to create for their subject. It arises from an author's focus on a single subject and from the feelings the writer brings to that subject.

Editorializing is to express personal opinions about the subject of the essay. An editorial tone can have a useful effect in writing, but at other times an author might want to reduce editorializing in favor of a better balanced or more objective tone.

Effect is a term used in causal analysis to describe the outcome or expected result of a chain of happenings.

Emphasis indicates the placement of the most important ideas in key positions in the essay. As a major principle, emphasis relates to phrases, sentences, and paragraphs— the construction of the entire essay. Emphasis can be achieved by repetition, subordination, careful positioning of thesis and topic sentences, climactic ordering, comparison and contrast, and a variety of other methods.

Episodic relates to that variety of narrative writing that develops through a series of incidents or events.

Essay is the name given to a short prose work on a limited topic. Essays take many forms, ranging from personal narratives to critical or argumentative treatments of a subject. Normally, an essay will convey the writer's personal ideas about the subject.

Etymology is the origin and development of a word—tracing a word back as far as possible.

Evidence is material offered to support an argument or a proposition. Typical forms of evidence are facts, details, and expert testimony.

Example is a method of exposition in which the writer offers illustrations in order to explain a generalization or a whole thesis. (See *illustration.*)

Exclamatory sentences in writing express surprise or strong emotion.

Expert testimony as employed in argumentative essays and in expository essays is the use of statements by authorities to support a writer's position or idea. This method often requires careful quotation and acknowledgment of sources.

Exposition is a major form of discourse that informs or explains. Exposition is the form of expression required in much college writing, for it provides facts and information, clarifies ideas, and establishes meaning. The primary methods of exposition are *illustration, comparison and contrast, analogy, definition, classification, causal analysis,* and *process analysis* (see entries).

Extended metaphor is a figurative comparison that is used to structure a significant part of the composition or the whole essay. (See *figurative language* and *metaphor.*)

Fable is a form of narrative containing a moral that normally appears clearly at the end.

Fallacy in argumentation is an error in logic or in the reasoning process. Fallacies occur because of vague development of ideas, lack of awareness on the part of writers of the requirements of logical reasoning, or faulty assumptions about the proposition.

Figurative language as opposed to literal language is a special approach to writing that departs from what is typically a concrete, straightforward style. It is the use of vivid, imaginative statements to illuminate or illustrate an idea. Figurative language adds freshness, meaning, and originality to a writer's style. Major figures of speech include *allusion, hyperbole, metaphor, personification,* and *simile* (see entries).

Flashback   is a narrative technique in which the writer begins at some point in the action and then moves into the past in order to provide crucial information about characters and events.

Foreshadow   is a technique that indicates beforehand what is to occur at a later point in the essay.

Frame   in narration and description is the use of a key object or pattern—typically at the start and end of the essay—that serves as a border or structure for the substance of the composition.

General/specific words   are the basis of writing, although it is wise in college composition to keep vocabulary as specific as possible. General words refer to broad categories and groups, whereas specific words capture with force and clarity the nature of the term. General words refer to large classes, concepts, groups, and emotions; specific words are more particular in providing meanings. The distinction between general and specific language is always a matter of degree.

Generalization   is a broad idea or statement. All generalizations require particulars and illustrations to support them.

Genre   is a type or form of literature—for example, short fiction, novel, poetry, or drama.

Grammatical structure   is a systematic description of language as it relates to the grammatical nature of a sentence.

Horizontal/vertical   paragraph and essay development refers to the basic way a writer moves either from one generalization to another in a carefully related series of generalizations (horizontal) or from a generalization to a series of specific supporting examples (vertical).

Hortatory style   is a variety of writing designed to encourage, give advice, or urge to good deeds.

Hyperbole   is a form of figurative language that uses exaggeration to overstate a position.

Hypothesis   is an unproven theory or proposition that is tentatively accepted to explain certain facts. A working hypothesis provides the basis for further investigation or argumentation.

Hypothetical examples   are illustrations in the form of assumptions that are based on the hypothesis. As such, they are conditional rather than absolute or certain facts.

Identification   as a method of exposition refers to focusing on the main subject of the essay. It involves the clear location of the subject within the context or situation of the composition.

Idiomatic language   is the language or dialect of a people, region, or class—the individual nature of a language.

Ignoring the question   in argumentation is a fallacy that involves the avoidance of the main issue by developing an entirely different one.

Illustration   is the use of one or more examples to support an idea. Illustration permits the writer to support a generalization through particulars or specifics.

Imagery is clear, vivid description that appeals to the sense of sight, smell, touch, sound, or taste. Much imagery exists for its own sake, adding descriptive flavor to an essay. However, imagery (especially when it involves a larger pattern) can also add meaning to an essay.

Induction is a method of logic consisting of the presentation of a series of facts, pieces of information, or instances in order to formulate or build a likely generalization. The key is to provide prior examples before reaching a logical conclusion. Consequently, as a pattern of organization in essay writing, the inductive method requires the careful presentation of relevant data and information before the conclusion is reached at the end of the paper.

Inference involves arriving at a decision or opinion by reasoning from known facts or evidence.

Interrogative sentences are sentences that ask or pose a question.

Introduction is the beginning or opening of an essay. The introduction should alert the reader to the subject by identifying it, set the limits of the essay, and indicate what the thesis (or main idea) will be. Moreover, it should arouse the reader's interest in the subject. Among the devices available in the creation of good introductions are making a simple statement of thesis; giving a clear, vivid description of an important setting; posing a question or series of questions; referring to a relevant historical event; telling an anecdote; using comparison and contrast to frame the subject; using several examples to reinforce the statement of the subject; and presenting a personal attitude about a controversial issue.

Irony is the use of language to suggest the opposite of what is stated. Writers use irony to reveal unpleasant or troublesome realities that exist in life or to poke fun at human weaknesses and foolish attitudes. In an essay there may be verbal irony, in which the result of a sequence of ideas or events is the opposite of what normally would be expected. A key to the identification of irony in an essay is our ability to detect where the author is stating the opposite of what he or she actually believes.

Issue is the main question upon which an entire argument rests. It is the idea that the writer attempts to prove.

Jargon is special words associated with a specific area of knowledge or a particular profession. Writers who employ jargon either assume that readers know specialized terms or take care to define terms for the benefit of the audience.

Juxtaposition as a technique in writing or essay organization is the placing of elements—either similar or contrasting—close together, positioning them side by side in order to illuminate the subject.

Levels of language refer to the kinds of language used in speaking and writing. Basically, there are three main levels of language—formal, informal, and colloquial. Formal English, used in writing or speech, is the type of English employed to address special groups and professional people. Informal English is the sort of writing found in newspapers, magazines, books, and essays. It is popular English for an educated audience but still more formal than colloquial (conversational) English. Colloquial English is spoken (and occasionally written) English used in conversations with friends, employees, and peer group members; it is characterized by the use of slang, idioms, ordinary language, and loose sentence structure.

Linear order in paragraph development means the clear line of movement from one point to another.

Listing is a simple technique of illustration in which facts or examples are used to support a topic or generalization.

Logic as applied to essay writing is correct reasoning based on induction or deduction. The logical basis of an essay must offer reasonable criteria or principles of thought, present these principles in an orderly manner, avoid faults in reasoning, and result in a complete and satisfactory outcome in the reasoning process.

Metaphor is a type of figurative language in which an item from one category is compared briefly and imaginatively with an item from another category. Writers use such implied comparisons to assign meaning in a fresh, vivid, and concrete way.

Metonymy is a figure of language in which a thing is not designated by its own name but by another associated with or suggested by it, as in "The Supreme Court has decided" (meaning the judges of the Supreme Court have decided).

Mood is the creation of atmosphere in descriptive writing.

Motif in an essay is any series of components that can be detected as a pattern. For example, a particular detail, idea, or image can be elaborated upon or designed to form a pattern or motif in the essay.

Myth in literature is a traditional story or series of events explaining some basic phenomenon of nature; the origin of humanity; or the customs, institutions, and religious rites of a people. Myth often relates to the exploits of gods, goddesses, and heroes.

Narration as a form of essay writing is the presentation of a story in order to illustrate an idea.

Non sequitur in argumentation is a conclusion or inference that does not follow from the premises or evidence on which it is based. The non sequitur thus is a type of logical fallacy.

Objective/subjective writing refers to the attitude that writers take toward their subject. When writers are objective, they try not to report their personal feelings about the subject; they attempt to be detached, impersonal, and unbiased. Conversely, subjective writing reveals an author's personal attitudes and emotions. For many varieties of college writing, such as business or laboratory reports, term papers, and literary analyses, it is best to be as objective as possible. But for many personal essays in composition courses, the subjective touch is fine. In the hands of skilled writers, the objective and subjective tones often blend.

Onomatopoeia is the formation of a word by imitating the natural sound associated with the object or action, as in *buzz* or *click*.

Order is the arrangement of information or materials in an essay. The most common ordering techniques are *chronological order* (time in sequence), *spatial order* (the arrangement of descriptive details), *process order* (a step-by-step approach to an activity), *deductive order* (a thesis followed by information to support it), and *inductive order* (evidence and examples first, followed by the thesis in the form of a conclusion). Some rhetorical patterns, such as comparison and contrast, classification, and argumentation, require other ordering methods. Writers should select those ordering principles that permit them to present materials clearly.

Overstatement is an extravagant or exaggerated claim or statement.

Paradox   is a statement that seems to be contradictory but actually contains an element of truth.

Paragraph   is a unit in an essay that serves to present and examine one aspect of a topic. Composed normally of a group of sentences (one-sentence paragraphs can be used for emphasis or special effect), the paragraph elaborates an idea within the larger framework of the essay and the thesis unifying it.

Parallelism   is a variety of sentence structure in which there is balance or coordination in the presentation of elements. "I came, I saw, I conquered" is a standard example of parallelism, presenting both pronouns and verbs in a coordinated manner. Parallelism can appear in a sentence, a group of sentences, or an entire paragraph.

Paraphrase   as a literary method is the process of rewording the thought or meaning expressed in something that has been said or written before.

Parenthetical   refers to giving qualifying information or explanation. This information normally is marked off or placed within parentheses.

Parody   is ridiculing the language or style of another writer or composer. In parody, a serious subject tends to be treated in a nonsensical manner.

Periphrasis   is the use of many words where one or a few would do; it is a roundabout way of speaking or writing.

Persona   is the role or characterization that writers occasionally create for themselves in a personal narrative.

Personification   is giving an object, a thing, or an idea lifelike or human characteristics, as in the common reference to a car as "she." Like all forms of figurative language, personification adds freshness to description and makes ideas vivid by setting up striking comparisons.

Persuasion   is the form of discourse, related to argumentation, that attempts to move a person to action or to influence an audience toward a particular belief.

Point of view   is the angle from which a writer tells a story. Many personal and informal essays take the *first-person* (or "I") point of view, which is natural and fitting for essays in which the author wants to speak in a familiar way to the reader. On the other hand, the *third-person* point of view ("he," "she," "it," "they") distances the reader somewhat from the writer. The third-person point of view is useful in essays in which the writers are not talking exclusively about themselves, but about other people, ideas, and events.

Post hoc, ergo propter hoc   in logic is the fallacy of thinking that a happening that follows another must be its result. It arises from a confusion about the logical causal relationship.

Process analysis   is a pattern of writing that explains in a step-by-step way how something is done, how it is put together, how it works, or how it occurs. The subject can be a mechanical device, a product, an idea, a natural phenomenon, or a historical sequence. However, in all varieties of process analysis, the writer traces all important steps, from beginning to end.

Progression   is the forward movement or succession of acts, events, or ideas presented in an essay.

Proportion   refers to the relative emphasis and length given to an event, an idea, a time, or a topic within the whole essay. Basically, in terms of proportion, the writer gives more emphasis to a major element than to a minor one.

Proposition is the main point of an argumentative essay—the statement to be defended, proved, or upheld. It is like a *thesis* (see entry) except that it presents an idea that is debatable or can be disputed. The *major proposition* is the main argumentative point; *minor propositions* are the reasons given to support or prove the issue.

Purpose is what the writer wants to accomplish in an essay. Writers having a clear purpose will know the proper style, language, tone, and materials to utilize in designing an effective essay.

Refutation in argumentation is a method by which writers recognize and deal effectively with the arguments of their opponents. Their own argument will be stronger if they refute—prove false or wrong—all opposing arguments.

Repetition is a simple method of achieving emphasis by repeating a word, a phrase, or an idea.

Rhetoric is the art of using words effectively in speaking or writing. It is also the art of literary composition, particularly in prose, including both figures of speech and such strategies as *comparison and contrast, definition,* and *analysis.*

Rhetorical question is a question asked only to emphasize a point, introduce a topic, or provoke thought, but not to elicit an answer.

Rhythm in prose writing is a regular recurrence of elements or features in sentences, creating a patterned emphasis, balance, or contrast.

Sarcasm is a sneering or taunting attitude in writing, designed to hurt by evaluating or criticizing. Basically, sarcasm is a heavy-handed form of *irony* (see entry). Writers should try to avoid sarcastic writing and to use more acceptable varieties of irony and satire to criticize their subject.

Satire is the humorous or critical treatment of a subject in order to expose the subject's vices, follies, stupidities, and so forth. The intention of such satire is to reform by exposing the subject to comedy or ridicule.

Sensory language is language that appeals to any of the five senses—sight, sound, touch, taste, or smell.

Sentimentality in prose writing is the excessive display of emotion, whether intended or unintended. Because sentimentality can distort the true nature of a situation or an idea, writers should use it cautiously, or not at all.

Series as a technique in prose is the presentation of several items, often concrete details or similar parts of grammar such as verbs or adjectives, in rapid sequence.

Setting in narrative and descriptive writing is the time, place, environment, background, or surroundings established by an author.

Simile is a figurative comparison using *like* or *as.*

Slang is a kind of language that uses racy or colorful expressions associated more often with speech than with writing. It is colloquial English and should be used in essay writing only to reproduce dialogue or to create a special effect.

Spatial order in descriptive writing is the careful arrangement of details or materials in space—for example, from left to right, top to bottom, or near to far.

Specific words (See *general/specific words.*)

Statistics are facts or data of a numerical kind, assembled and tabulated to present significant information about a given subject. As a technique of illustration, statistics can be useful in analysis and argumentation.

Style is the specific or characteristic manner of expression, execution, construction, or design of an author. As a manner or mode of expression in language, it is the unique way each writer handles ideas. There are numerous stylistic categories—such as literary, formal, argumentative, and satiric—but ultimately, no two writers have the same style.

Subjective (See *objective/subjective.*)

Subordination in sentence structure is the placing of a relatively less important idea in an inferior grammatical position to the main idea. It is the designation of a minor clause that is dependent upon a major clause.

Syllogism is an argument or form of reasoning in which two statements or premises are made and a logical conclusion is drawn from them. As such, it is a form of deductive logic—reasoning from the general to the particular. The *major premise* presents a quality of class ("All writers are mortal"). The *minor premise* states that a particular subject is a member of that class ("Ernest Hemingway was a writer"). The conclusion states that the qualities of the class and the member of the class are the same ("Hemingway was mortal").

Symbol is something—normally a concrete image—that exists in itself but also stands for something else or has greater meaning. As a variety of figurative language, the symbol can be a strong feature in an essay, operating to add depth of meaning and even to unify the composition.

Synonym is a word that means roughly the same as another word. In practice, few words are exactly alike in meaning. Careful writers use synonyms to vary word choice without ever moving too far from the shade of meaning intended.

Theme is the central idea in an essay; it is also termed the *thesis.* Everything in an essay should support the theme in one way or another.

Thesis is the main idea in an essay. The *thesis sentence,* appearing early in the essay (normally somewhere in the first paragraph) serves to convey the main idea to the reader in a clear and emphatic manner.

Tone is the writer's attitude toward his or her subject or material. An essay writer's tone may be objective, subjective, comic, ironic, nostalgic, critical, or a reflection of numerous other attitudes. Tone is the voice that writers give to an essay.

Topic sentence is the main idea that a paragraph develops. Not all paragraphs contain topic sentences; often the topic is implied.

Transition is the linking of ideas in sentences, paragraphs, and larger segments of an essay in order to achieve *coherence* (see entry). Among the most common techniques to achieve smooth transitions are (1) repeating a key word or phrase, (2) using a pronoun to refer to a key word or phrase, (3) relying on traditional connectives such as *thus, however, moreover, for example, therefore, finally,* or *in conclusion,* (4) using parallel structure (see *parallelism*), and (5) creating a sentence or paragraph that serves as a bridge from one part of an essay to another. Transition is best achieved when a writer presents ideas and details carefully and in logical order.

Understatement is a method of making a weaker statement than is warranted by truth, accuracy, or importance.

Unity is a feature in an essay whereby all material relates to a central concept and contributes to the meaning of the whole. To achieve a unified effect in an essay, the writer must design an effective introduction and conclusion, maintain consistent tone or point of view, develop middle paragraphs in a coherent manner, and above all stick to the subject, never permitting unimportant or irrelevant elements to enter.

Usage is the way in which a word, phrase, or sentence is used to express a particular idea; it is the customary manner of using a given language in speaking or writing.

Vertical (See *horizontal/vertical.*)

Voice is the way you express your ideas to the reader, the tone you take in addressing your audience. Voice reflects your attitude toward both your subject and your readers. (See *tone.*)

Credits

Photo

Page 9: © Kazuhiro Ishizu/Hiroshima Peace Memorial Museum; **p. 10:** © Sawami Katagiri/Hiroshima Peace Memorial Museum; **p. 42:** © Joe Rosenthal/AP Photo; **p. 43:** © AP Photo/Thomas E. Franklin/The Record (Bergen Co. NJ); **p. 47:** © Marilyn Humphries/The Image Works; **p. 66:** Library of Congress; **p. 67:** Courtesy of Heather Vogel Frederick; **p. 85:** © Lars A. Niki; **p. 86:** © Mike Theiler/Reuters/Corbis; **p. 138:** Goya y Lucientes, Francisco de (1746–1828), *The Third of May, 1808*. Painted in 1814. Oil on canvas, 266 × 345 cm. Museo del Prado, Madrid, Spain. Photo © Erich Lessing/Art Resource, NY; **p. 139:** © Eddie Adams/AP Photo; **p. 147:** © Kimberly White/Corbis; **p. 148:** © Getty Images; **p. 182:** © Oberlin College Archives, Oberlin, Ohio; **p. 183:** © Tom Stewart/Corbis/Stock Market; **p. 230:** © Museum of Fine Art, Ghent, Belgium/The Bridgeman Art Library; **p. 231:** © Elise Amendola/AP Photo; **p. 273:** © Xinhua/Landov; **p. 280:** National Park Service: Statue of Liberty National Monument; **p. 281:** © Reforma Archivo/AP Photo; **p. 324:** © The Granger Collection, New York; **p. 325:** © Chris Fitzgerald/CandidatePhotos/The Image Works; **p. 374:** © Detroit Institute of Arts, USA/Gift of Edsel B. Ford/The Bridgeman Art Library; © 2010 Banco de Mexico Diego Rivera Frida Kahlo Museums Trust, Mexico, D.F./Artists Rights Society (ARS); **p. 375:** © Digital Vision/PunchStock; **p. 428:** © Photofest; **p. 429:** © HBO/The Kobal Collection; **p. 437:** © AMC/Courtesy: Everett Collection; **p. 488:** © Musee Rodin/Bridgeman Art collection; **p. 489:** Rabbit, 1986, Stainless Steel, 41" × 19" × 11 7/8" © Jeff Koons; **p. 501:** © The Trustees of the British Museum; **p. 502:** Roy De Forest, *Canoe of Fate*, 1974. Polymer on canvas. 1975–83–1. Philadelphia Museum of Art: Purchased with the Adele Haas Turner and Beatrice Pastorius Turner Memorial Fund, 1975. Courtesy of The Philadelphia Museum of Art and the Allan Frumkin Gallery; **p. 512:** © Redferns/Getty Images; **p. 524, p. 527, p. 529, p. 532:** © AP Photo; **p. 546:** With kind permission of the University of Edinburgh/The Bridgeman Art Library; **p. 547:** © Gillian Darley/EDIFICE; **p. 571:** © Angela Wyant/Getty Images; **p. 573:** © Gene Blevins/LA Daily News/Corbis; **p. 594:** © Corbis; **p. 595:** © Gary Bramnick/AP Photo; **p. 599:** © Bibliotheque Royal, Brussels/The Bridgeman Art Library; **p. 646:** Kensett, John Frederick (1816–1872), *Along the Hudson*. 1852. Photo © Smithsonian American Art Museum, Washington, DC/Art Resource, NY; **p. 647:** © Damian Dovarganes/AP Photo; **p. 656:** © image100/PunchStock; **p. 704:** © Musee Condee, Chantilly, France/The Bridgeman Art Library; **p. 705:** © Corbis RF; **p. 795:** Cover of *American Cinema of the 1990s: Themes and Variations*, Edited by Chris Holmlund. © 2008 by Rutgers, the State University. Reprinted by permission of Rutgers University Press; **p. 800 & p. 806:** "Donnie Brasco" © 1997 Mandalay Entertainment. All Rights Reserved. Courtesy of Columbia Pictures; **p. 807:** © Mandalay Ent/Baltimore Pics/The Kobal Collection; **p. 809:** © The Everett Collection.

Color Insert Photos

Page 1: © Mark J. Terrill/AP Photo; **p. 2:** Courtesy of The Advertising Archives; **p. 3 (bottom):** © AMC/Photofest; **p. 3 (top):** Courtesy of Photofest; **p. 4:** © AP Photo; **p. 5 (bottom):** © Tim Graham/Getty Images; **p. 5 (top):** © Kaveh Kazemi/Getty Images; **p. 8:** © Inwin Thompson/The Dallas Morning News/AP Photo.

Text and Illustrations

Ackerman, Diane. "Planets in the Sky with Diamonds." From *New York Times*, October 2, 2011. Copyright © 2011 The New York Times. All rights reserved. Used by permission and protected by the Copyright Laws of the United States. The printing, copying, redistribution, or retransmission of the Material without express written permission is prohibited.

Adler, Mortimer J. "How To Mark a Book." From *The Saturday Review of Literature*, July 6, 1941. Reprinted by permission of the author.

Alexie, Sherman. "Superman and Me." From *Los Angeles Times*, April 19, 1998. Copyright © 1998 by Sherman Alexie. All rights reserved. Reprinted by permission.

Armstrong, Karen. "What's God Got to Do with It?" From *The New Statesman*, April 10, 2006. Copyright © 2006. All rights reserved. Reprinted by permission of The New Statesman.

Baldwin, James. "Stranger in the Village." From *Notes of a Native Son*. Copyright © 1955, renewed 1983, by James Baldwin. Reprinted by permission of Beacon Press, Boston.

Barry, Dave. "Red, White, and Beer." From *Dave Barry's Greatest Hits* by Dave Barry. Copyright © 1988 by Dave Barry. Reprinted by permission of the author.

Bass, Rick. "Why I Hunt." First appeared in *Sierra*, July 2001. Copyright © 2001 by Rick Bass. Reprinted by permission of the author.

Bazelon, Emily. "The Next Kind of Integration." From *New York Times Magazine*, July 20, 2008. Copyright © 2008 The New York Times. All rights reserved. Used by permission and protected by the Copyright Laws of the United States. The printing, copying, redistribution, or retransmission of the Material without express written permission is prohibited.

Berger, John. "Hiroshima." From *The Sense of Sight*. Copyright © 1985 by John Berger. Reprinted by permission of Pantheon Books, a division of Random House, Inc. and the author. Any third party use of this material, outside of this publication, is prohibited. Interested parties must apply directly to Random House, Inc. for permission.

Bloom, Paul. "The Pleasures of Imagination." From *The Chronicle Review*, May 30, 2010. Copyright © 2010 by Paul Bloom. Reprinted by permission of the author.

Bordo, Susan. "The Globalization of Eating Disorders." Copyright © Susan Bordo, Otis A. Singletary Professor of the Humanities, University of Kentucky. Reprinted by permission of the author.

Carr, Nicholas. "Does the Internet Make You Smarter or Dumber?" From *Wall Street Journal*, June 5, 2010. Copyright © 2010 Dow Jones & Company, Inc, all rights reserved worldwide. Reprinted by permission of Wall Street Journal.

Carson, Clayborne. "Two Cheers for *Brown v. Board of Education*." From *Journal of American History*, June 2004: pp. 26–31. Copyright © Organization of American Historians. Reprinted by permission.

Carson, Rachel. "The Obligation to Endure." From *Silent Spring*. Copyright © 1962 by Rachel L. Carson, renewed 1990 by Roger Christie. Reprinted by permission of Houghton Mifflin Harcourt Publishing Company, Pollinger, Limited and the Estate of

Rachel Carson, and Frances Collin, Trustee. All rights reserved. All copying, including electronic, or re-distribution of this text, is expressly forbidden.

Catton, Bruce. "Grant and Lee: A Study in Contrasts." From *The American Story*, edited by Earl Schenck Miers. Reprinted by permission of William Catton.

Chua, Amy. "The Right Road to America?" From *The Washington Post*, December 16, 2007. Copyright © 2007. Reprinted by permission of the author.

Clarke, Kevin. "Tweet Like an Egyptian." From *U.S. Catholic,* April 2011. Copyright © 2011 U.S. Catholic. Reproduced by permission of U.S. Catholic. For subscription information contact: 205 West Monroe, Chicago, IL 60606; call 1-800-328-6515; or visit http://www.uscatholic.org/.

Coles, Robert. "I Listen to My Parents and I Wonder What They Believe." Originally published in *Redbook* Magazine, February 1980. Reprinted by permission of the author.

Danticat, Edwidge. "Turning the Page on Disaster." From *Good Housekeeping*, January 2011, Vol. 52, Issue No. 1. Copyright © 2011. Reprinted by permission of the Hearst Corporation.

Diamond, Jared. "The Last Americans: Environmental Collapse and the End of Civilization." Copyright © 2003 by Harper's Magazine. All rights reserved. Reproduced from the June issue by special permission. Illustrations by Stan Fellows. Copyright © Stan Fellows. Reprinted by permission of the illustrator, c/o Joanie Bernstein, art rep.

Diaz, Junot. "The Money: Starting Out." From *The New Yorker*, June 13–20, 2011. Copyright © 2011. Reprinted by permission of Condé Nast Publications, Inc.

Didion, Joan. "In Sable and Dark Glasses." From *Vogue*, October 2011. Copyright © 2011. Reprinted by permission of Janklow & Nesbit Associates for the author.

Dillard, Annie. "An American Childhood." Excerpt from AN AMERICAN CHILDHOOD by ANNIE DILLARD, pp. 11–17. Copyright © 1987 by Annie Dillard. Reprinted by permission of HarperCollins Publishers and Lippincott Massie McQuilkin.

D'Souza, Dinesh. "Staying Human." From *National Review*, January 22, 2001. Reprinted by permission of the author.

Dyson, Esther. "Cyberspace: If You Don't Love It, Leave It." From *The New York Times*, July 16, 1995. Copyright © 1995 by Esther Dyson. Reprinted by permission.

Ehrenreich, Barbara. Excerpt from "Scrubbing in Maine." From *Nickel and Dimed: On (Not) Getting By in America* by Barbara Ehrenreich. Copyright © 2001 by Barbara Ehrenreich. Reprinted by arrangement with Henry Holt and Company, LLC.

Elbow, Peter. "Freewriting." From *Writing Without Teachers*, 2 ed., pp. 3–7. Copyright © 1973, 1998 by Oxford University Press, Inc. Reprinted by permission of Oxford University Press.

Ferguson, Niall. "America's Oh Sh*t Moment." From *Newsweek*, November 14, 2011. Copyright © 2011 by Niall Ferguson. Reprinted by permission of The Wylie Agency LLC.

Freeland, Chrystia. "The Rich are Different from You and Me." From *Atlantic Monthly*, July/August 2011. Copyright © 2011. All rights reserved. Reprinted by permission of *The Atlantic*.

Friedman, Thomas L. Excerpt from "Globalization the Super-Story." From LONGITUDES AND ATTITUDES by Thomas L. Friedman. Copyright © 2002 by Thomas L. Friedman. Reprinted by permission of Farrar, Straus and Giroux, LLC and International Creative Management, Inc.

Gates, David. "Finding Neverland." From *Newsweek*, July 13, 2009. Copyright © 2009 by David Gates. Reprinted by permission of the author.

Gates, Jr., Henry Louis. "Delusions of Grandeur." Originally published in *Sports Illustrated*, August 19, 1991. Copyright © 1991 by Henry Louis Gates Jr. Reprinted by permission of the author.

Gates, Jr., Henry Louis. "Forty Acres and a Gap in Wealth." From *The New York Times*,
    November 18, 2007. Copyright © 2007 The New York Times. All rights reserved.
    Used by permission and protected by the Copyright Laws of the United States. The
    printing, copying, redistribution, or retransmission of the Material without express
    written permission is prohibited.
Gawande, Atul. "Naked." First appeared in the *New England Journal of Medicine*, Vol. 353,
    Issue No. 7. Copyright © 2005. Reprinted by Massachusetts Medical Society.
Gelernter, David. "Unplugged: The Myth of Computers in the Classroom." From *The New
    Republic*. Copyright © 1994 by David Gelernter. Reprinted by permission of *The New
    Republic*.
Gitlin, Todd. "Supersaturation, or, The Media Torrent and Disposable Feeling." From
    Media Unlimited: How the Torrent of Images and Sounds Overwhelms Our Lives by
    Todd Gitlin. Copyright © 2001 by Todd Gitlin. Reprinted by arrangement with Henry
    Holt and Company, LLC.
Goodlad, Lauren M.E. "Why We Love 'Mad Men.'" From *The Chronicle of Higher
    Education*, August 31, 2009. Reprinted by permission of the author.
Gould, Stephen. "The Terrifying Normalcy of AIDS." Originally appeared in *The New York
    Times Magazine*, April 19, 1987. Reprinted by permission of the author.
Hampl, Patricia. "The Dark Art of Description." From *Iowa Review*, Spring 2008. Copyright ©
    2008. Reprinted by permission of Marly Rusoff & Associates, Inc. on behalf of the author.
Hitchens, Christopher. "Topic of Cancer." From *Vanity Fair*, Vol. 52, Issue 9. Copyright ©
    2010. Reprinted by permission of Condé Nast Publications, Inc.
Hoagland, Edward. "1776 and All That." From *The Nation*, July 22, 2002. Reprinted by
    permission of The Nation. For subscription information, call 1-800-333-8536. Portions
    of each week's Nation magazine can be accessed at http://www.thenation.com.
Hood, Ann Hood. "Street Scenes." From *The American Scholar*, Volume 80, No. 2, Spring
    2011. Copyright © 2011 by the author. Reprinted by permission.
Horowitz, Joy. "Parkinson's Alley." From *Sierra*, Jan/Feb 2012. Copyright © 2012 by Joy
    Horowitz. Reprinted by permission of the author.
Hughes, Langston. "Salvation." From *The Big Sea* by Langston Hughes. Copyright © 1940
    by Langston Hughes and renewed 1968 by Arna Bontemps and George Houston Bass.
    Reprinted by permission of Hill and Wang, a division of Farrar, Straus and Giroux, LLC.
Ivins, Molly. "Is Texas America?" From *The Nation*, November 17, 2003. Copyright ©
    2003 Estate of Molly Ivins. Reprinted by permission of Pom, Inc.
Jacoby, Susan. "When Bright Girls Decide that Math is 'a Waste of Time.'" Originally
    appeared in *The New York Times* (1983). Copyright © 1983 by Susan Jacoby.
    Reprinted by permission of Georges Borchardt, Inc. on behalf of the author.
Kincaid, Jamaica. "The Estrangement." Originally appeared in *AARP, The Magazine*,
    May/June 2008. Copyright © 2008 by Jamaica Kincaid, used by permission of The
    Wylie Agency LLC.
King, Jr., Martin Luther. "I Have a Dream." Copyright © 1963 Dr. Martin Luther King Jr;
    copyright renewed 1991 Coretta Scott King. Reprinted by arrangement with The
    Heirs to the Estate of Martin Luther King Jr., c/o Writers House as agent for the
    proprietor New York, NY.
King, Stephen. "My Creature from the Black Lagoon." Originally appeared in *Playboy*,
    1982. © Stephen King. All rights reserved. Reprinted by permission.
Klinkenborg, Verlyn. "Darwin at 200: The Ongoing Force of His Unconventional Idea."
    From *New York Times*, February 12, 2009. Copyright © 2009 The New York Times.
    All rights reserved. Used by permission and protected by the Copyright Laws of the

United States. The printing, copying, redistribution, or retransmission of the Material without express written permission is prohibited.

Krugman, Paul. "The Death of Horatio Alger." From *The Nation*, January 5, 2004. Reprinted by permission of The Nation. For subscription information, call 1-800-333-8536. Portions of each week's Nation magazine can be accessed at http://www.thenation.com.

Krugman, Paul. "We Are the 99.9%." From *The New York Times*, November 24, 2011. Copyright © 2011 The New York Times. All rights reserved. Used by permission and protected by the Copyright Laws of the United States. The printing, copying, redistribution, or retransmission of the Material without express written permission is prohibited.

Lakoff, Robin Tolmach. "From Ancient Greece to Iraq, the Power of Words in Wartime." From *The New York Times*, May 18, 2004. © 2004 The New York Times. All rights reserved. Used by permission and protected by the Copyright Laws of the United States. The printing, copying, redistribution, or retransmission of the Material without express written permission is prohibited.

Lepore, Jill. "It's Spreading." From *The New Yorker*, first published June 1, 2009. Copyright © 2009 by Jill Lepore. Reprinted by permission of William Morris Endcavor on behalf of the author.

Lopez, Barry. "Children in the Woods." From *Crossing Open Ground*. Copyright by Barry Holstun Lopez. Reprinted by permission of SLL/Sterling Lord Literistic, Inc.

Madrigal, Alexis. "Take the Data Out of Dating." From *Atlantic Monthly*, December 2010. Copyright © 2010. All rights reserved. Reprinted by permission of *The Atlantic*.

Manjoo, Farhad. "Do I *Really* Have to Join Twitter?" From *Slate*, April 10, 2009. Copyright © 2009 The Slate Group. All rights reserved. Used by permission and protected by the Copyright Laws of the United States. The printing, copying, redistribution, or retransmission of the Material without express written permission is prohibited.

Martin, Steve. "Writing Is Easy!" From *The New Yorker*, June 24, 1996. Copyright © 1996 by Steve Martin for The New Yorker. Reprinted by permission of International Creative Management, Inc.

McCloud, Scott. "Understanding Comics." From *Understanding Comics*. Copyright © 1993 by Scott McCloud. Reprinted by permission of HarperCollins Publishers.

McKibben, Bill. "The Environmental Issue from Hell." From *In These Times*, April 30, 2001. Reprinted with permission from *In These Times* magazine, www.inthesetimes.com.

Mendoza, Martha. "Between a Woman and Her Doctor." From *Ms.* Magazine, Summer 2004. Copyright © 2004. Reprinted by permission of Ms. Magazine.

Mernissi, Fatema. "Digital Scheherazades in the Arab World." From *Current History* magazine (March 2006). Copyright © 2012 Current History, Inc. Reprinted with permission from *Current History* magazine.

Miller, Lisa. "Our Mutual Joy: The Religious Case for Gay Marriage." From *Newsweek*, December 15, 2008. Copyright © 2008 Newsweek, Inc. All rights reserved. Used by permission and protected by the Copyright Laws of the United States. The printing, copying, redistribution, or retransmission of the Material without express written permission is prohibited.

Mukherjee, Bharati. "American Dreamer." Originally published by *Mother Jones*, January/February 1997. Copyright © 1997 by Bharati Mukherjee. Reprinted by permission of the author.

Muñoz , Manuel. "Leave Your Name at the Border." From *The New York Times*, August 1, 2007. Copyright © 2007 The New York Times. All rights reserved. Used by permission and protected by the Copyright Laws of the United States. The printing, copying, redistribution, or retransmission of the Material without express written permission is prohibited.

Murray, Donald M. "The Maker's Eye: Revising Your Own Manuscripts" by Donald Murray from *The Writer*, 1973. Copyright © 1973 by Donald M. Murray. Reprinted by permission of the Rosenberg Group.

National Campaign to Prevent Teen and Unplanned Pregnancy. Screenshot from the National Campaign to Prevent Teen and Unplanned Pregnancy website. Copyright © 2012. The National Campaign to Prevent Teen and Unplanned Pregnancy. Reprinted with permission.

New York Times. "The Words They Used." From *The New York Times*, September 4, 2008. Copyright © 2008 The New York Times. All rights reserved. Used by permission and protected by the Copyright Laws of the United States. The printing, copying, redistribution, or retransmission of the Material without express written permission is prohibited.

Ortiz Cofer, Judith. "The Myth of the Latin Woman: I Just Met a Girl Named María." From *The Latin Deli: Prose and Poetry*. Copyright © 1993 by Judith Ortiz Cofer. Reprinted by permission of the University of Georgia Press.

Orwell, George. "Politics and the English Language." From his volume *Shooting an Elephant and Other Essays* and *Politics and the English Language*. Copyright © 1946 by George Orwell and Sonia Brownell Orwell and renewed 1974 by Sonia Orwell. Reprinted by permission of Houghton Mifflin Harcourt Publishing Company and Bill Hamilton as the Literary Executor of the Estate of the Late Sonia Brownwell Orwell. All rights reserved.

Packer, George. "The Broken Contract: Inequality and American Decline." From *Foreign Affairs*, November/December 2011. Copyright © 2011 by the Council on Foreign Relations, Inc., www.ForeignAffairs.com. Reprinted by permission of FOREIGN AFFAIRS.

Perrin, Noel. "The Greenest Campuses: An Idiosyncratic Guide." Originally appeared in *Chronicle of Higher Education*, April 6, 2001. Copyright © 2001 by Noel Perrin. Reprinted by permission of the author.

Priestley, J.B. "Wrong Ism." From *Essays of Five Decades*. Copyright © 1968. Reprinted by permission of United Agents on behalf of The Estate of J.B. Priestley.

Quindlen, Anna. "Sex Ed." From *Living Out Loud* by Anna Quindlen. Copyright © 1987 by Anna Quindlen. Used by permission of Ballantine Books, a division of Random House, Inc., and International Creative Management, Inc. Any third party use of this material, outside of this publication, is prohibited. Interested parties must apply directly to Random House, Inc. for permission.

Reed, Ishmael. "America: The Multinational Society." From *Writin' Is Fightin': Forty-Three Years of Boxing on Paper* by Ishmael Reed. Copyright © Ishmael Reed. Reprinted by permission of Lowenstein Associates.

Reich, Robert. "Why the Rich Are Getting Richer and the Poor, Poorer." From *The Work of Nations* by Robert B. Reich. Copyright © 1991 by Robert B. Reich. Reprinted by permission of Alfred A. Knopf, a division of Random House, Inc.

Rodriguez, Richard. "Family Values." Originally appeared in *The Los Angeles Times* (1992). Copyright © 1992 by Richard Rodriguez. Reprinted by permission of Georges Borchardt, Inc. on behalf of the author.

Rodriguez, Richard. "The Lonely, Good Company of Books." From *Hunger of Memory: The Education of Richard Rodriguez* by Richard Rodriguez. Copyright © 1982 by Richard Rodriguez. Reprinted by permission of David R. Godine, Publisher, Inc.

Rose, Mike. "What College Can Mean to the Other America." From *The Chronicle of Higher Education*, September 11, 2011. Copyright © 2011 by Mike Rose. Reprinted by permission of the author.

Ross, Deborah. "Escape from Wonderland: Disney and the Female Imagination." From *Marvels & Tales: Journal of Fairy-Tale Studies*, Vol. 18, No. 1 (2004), pp. 53–66. Reprinted by permission of Wayne State University.

Rushdie, Salman. "Not about Islam?" From *Step Across This Line* by Salman Rushdie. Copyright © 2002 by Salman Rushdie. Reprinted by permission of Random House, Inc. Any third party use of this material, outside of this publication, is prohibited. Interested parties must apply directly to Random House, Inc. for permission.

Sachs, Jeffrey. "A Nation of Vidiots." From Project Syndicate, October 28, 2011. Copyright © 2011. Reprinted by permission of the author.

Sacks, Oliver. "Anybody Out There?" Originally published in *Natural History* Magazine, November 2002. Copyright © 2002 by Oliver Sacks. Reprinted by permission of The Wylie Agency LLC.

Sagan, Carl. "Can We Know the Universe?: Reflections on a Grain of Salt." From *Broca's Brain: Reflections on the Romance of Science*. Copyright © 1979 Carl Sagan. Reprinted by permission of Democritus Properties, LLC. This material may not be further circulated without consent of Democritus Properties, LLC. All rights reserved.

Satrapi, Marjane. "The Veil." From PERSEPOLIS: THE STORY OF A CHILDHOOD by Marjane Satrapi, translated by Mattias Ripa & Blake Ferris, translation copyright © 2003 by L'Association, Paris, France. Reprinted by permission of Pantheon Books, a division of Random House, Inc. Any third party use of this material, outside of this publication, is prohibited. Interested parties must apply directly to Random House, Inc. for permission.

Schlesinger Jr., Arthur M. "The Cult of Ethnicity, Good and Bad." From *Time*, July 8, 1991. Copyright © 1991 by Arthur M. Schlesinger Jr. Reprinted with permission of The Wylie Agency, LLC.

Sedaris, David. "Nutcracker.com." From ME TALK PRETTY ONE DAY by David Sedaris. Copyright © 2000 by David Sedaris. Reprinted by permission of Little, Brown and Company and Don Congdon Associates, Inc. All rights reserved.

Selzer, Richard. "The Maked Marvel's Last Toehold." From CONFESSIONS OF A KNIFE by Richard Selzer. Copyright © 1987, 2001 by Richard Selzer. Reprinted by permission of Georges Borchardt, Inc. on behalf of the author.

Sen, Amartya. "A World Not Neatly Divided." From *The New York Times*, November 23, 2001. Copyright © 2001 The New York Times Co. Reprinted with permission.

Silko, Leslie Marmon. "Yellow Woman and a Beauty of the Spirit" from YELLOW WOMAN AND A BEAUTY OF THE SPIRIT by Leslie Marmon Silko. Copyright © 1996 Leslie Marmon Silko. Reprinted with the permission of Simon & Schuster, Inc and The Wylie Agency LLC.

Sontag, Susan. "Regarding the Torture of Others." From AT THE SAME TIME: ESSAYS AND SPEECHES by Susan Sontag, edited by Paolo Dilonardo and Anne Jump. Copyright © 1997 by The Estate of Susan Sontag. Reprinted by permission of Farrar, Straus and Giroux, LLC and The Wylie Agency LLC.

Staples, Brent. "Just Walk on By." First appeared in *Literary Cavalcade* February 1998, Vol 50, Issue 5. © 1998 by Brent Staples. Reprinted by permission of the author.

Steinem, Gloria. "Wonder Woman." Copyright © Gloria Steinem. Reprinted by permission of the author.

Sullivan, Andrew. "Why Gay Marriage Is Good for America." From *Newsweek*, July 25, 2011. Copyright © 2011 Newsweek, Inc. All rights reserved. Used by permission and protected by the Copyright Laws of the United States. The printing, copying, redistribution, or retransmission of the Material without express written permission is prohibited.

Tan, Amy. "Mother Tongue." Copyright © 1990 by Amy Tan. First appeared in *The Threepenny Review*. Reprinted by permission of the author and the Sandra Dijkstra Literary Agency.

Tannen, Deborah. "Sex, Lies and Conversation: Why Is It So Hard for Men and Women to Talk to Each Other?" From *The Washington Post,* June 24, 1990. Copyright © by Deborah Tannen. Permission granted by International Creative Management, Inc.

Thompson, Clive. "I'm So Totally, Digitally, Close to You." First published in *New York Times Magazine*, September 7, 2008. Copyright © 2008. Reprinted by permission of Featurewell.com and the author.

Tuchman, Barbara. "'This Is the End of the World': The Black Death." From *A Distant Mirror* by Barbara W. Tuchman. Text copyright © 1978 by Barbara W. Tuchman. Reprinted by permission of Alfred A. Knopf, a division of Random House, Inc. Any third party use of this material, outside of this publication, is prohibited. Interested parties must apply directly to Random House, Inc. for permission.

Turkle, Sherry. "How Computers Change the Way We Think." Originally appeared in *Chronicle of Higher Education*, January 30, 2004. Copyright © 2004 by Sherry Turkle. Reprinted by permission of the author.

Updike, John. "Moving Along." From JUST LOOKING by John Updike. Copyright © 1989 by John Updike. Reprinted by permission of Alfred A. Knopf, a division of Random House, Inc. and Penguin UK. Any third party use of this material, outside of this publication, is prohibited. Interested parties must apply directly to Random House, Inc. for permission.

Walker, Alice. "Saving the Life That Is Your Own: The Importance of Models in the Artist's Life." From *In Search of Our Mothers' Gardens: Womanist Prose*. Copyright 1976 by Alice Walker. Reprinted by permission of Houghton Mifflin Harcourt Publishing, the David Higham Agency, and The Wendy Weil Agency. All right reserved.

Warshow, Robert. "The Gangster as Tragic Hero." From *The Immediate Experience* by Robert Warshow. Copyright © 1962 by Robert Warshow. Reprinted by permission of the Estate of Robert Warshow.

Welty, Eudora. "One Writer's Beginnings" from ONE WRITER'S BEGINNINGS by Eudora Welty, pp. 5–12, Cambridge, Mass.: Harvard University Press. Copyright © 1983, 1984 by Eudora Welty. Reprinted by permission Harvard University Press and Russell & Volkening, as agents for the author's estate.

"Western Civilization's Killer Apps." From *Newsweek*, November 14, 2011. Reprinted by permission.

White, E.B. "Once More to the Lake." From *One Man's Meat*, by E.B. White. Text copyright © 1941 by E.B. White. Copyright renewed. Reprinted by permission of Tilbury House, Publishers, Gardiner, Maine and International Creative Management, Inc.

Woolf, Virginia. "Profession for Women." From *The Death of the Moth and Other Essays* by Virginia Woolf. Copyright 1942 by Houghton Mifflin Harcourt Publishing Company and renewed 1970 by Marjorie T. Parsons, Executrix.

Index

abortion, 624–629
Ackerman, Diane, "Planets in the Sky with Diamonds," 714–716
active reading, 4, 5, 27–29
Adams, Eddie, 39, 139
ad hominem arguments, 158
Adler, Mortimer, "How to Mark a Book," 16–21
ad populum arguments, 158–159
advertisements
    citing as research source, 789
    television commercials, 452–454
affirmative action, 201–211
Aguirre twins, 595
AIDS, 635–639
Alexie, Sherman, "Superman and Me," 490, 496–499
"The Allegory of the Cave" (Plato), 544, 583–587
Along the Hudson (Kensett), 646
alternating method, 78
"America: The Multinational Society" (Reed), 282, 286–290
"An American Childhood" (Dillard), 241–247
American Dream, 326–334
"American Dreamer" (Mukherjee), 355–361
"America's 'Oh Sh*t' Moment" (Ferguson), 291–296
analogies, weak or false, 160
The Anatomy Lesson (Rembrant), 594
angels, 546–547
annotating
    example of, 27–29
    explained, 25–26
    value of, 29
anthologies, citing, 777, 781–782

"Anybody Out There?" (Sacks), 742–747
appeals, in argumentation, 144–148
argumentation
    appeals in, 144–148
    described, 82–83, 136
    in images, 138–139
    impact on life, 150–151
    justification test, 140
    language of, 137–140
    as purpose guide, 65, 68
    purpose of, 144
    reading and analyzing, 140–143
    writing guidelines, 151
    writing process, 151–162
    written vs. oral, 136–137
argumentative perspective, 152
argumentative synthesis
    case study essays, 163–178
    description and guidelines, 36–37, 160–162
argumentum ad hominem, 158
argumentum ad populum, 158–159
Aristotle, 136, 141–142, 145, 147
Armstrong, Karen, "What's God Got to Do with It?", 565–569
art
    citing as research source, 789
    comics as, 503–510
    evaluating, 486–489, 500–503, 524–534
    influence on, 535–543
assertions, 137
attention, in reading, 3
audience analysis
    in argumentation, 153
    in critical reading, 6, 40
    in invention (prewriting), 65, 68
    in process analysis, 76
audio streams or recordings, citing, 787, 788

author names, citing, 776–777, 780–781
authors, illustrations of, 66–67

backing, 137, 142, 157
"bad" men, in popular culture, 430–440
Baker, Sheridan, 71
Baldwin, James, "Stranger in the Village," 361–370
bandwagon approach, 159
Barry, Dave, "Red, White, and Beer," 452–454
Bass, Rick, "Why I Hunt," 654–658
Bazelon, Emily, "The Next Kind of Integration," 201–211
begging the question, 159
Berger, John, "Hiroshima," 7–14
Berrera, Geeta, 80–81
"Between a Woman and Her Doctor" (Mendoza), 624–629
biases, 4, 6
bibliographies
    working bibliography, 764–766
    Works Cited list, 774, 780–790
binocular rivalry, 30
biotechnology, 702
Bird, Caroline, "College Is a Waste of Time and Money," 82–83
block method, 78
blogs, citing, 786
Bloom, Paul, "The Pleasures of Imagination," 577–582
body paragraphs
    development of, 72–73
    example of, 85–87
    rhetorical approaches, 73–83

books
   citing as research source,
      775-776, 782-783
   research example, 795-796
Bordo, Susan, "The Globalization
   of Eating Disorders,"
   639-643
brainstorming, 68-70, 754
broadcasts, citing, 785
broad generalizations, 159
"The Broken Contract" (Packer),
   53-62
Brown v. Board of Education,
   219-227
Brueghel the Younger, Pieter,
   Rustic Wedding, 230
business. See economics

cancer, 615-619
"Can We Know the Universe?
   Reflections on a Grain of
   Salt" (Sagan), 727-732
Carr, Nicholas, "Does the
   Internet Make You Smarter
   or Dumber?", 21-25
Carson, Clayborne, "Two Cheers
   for Brown v. Board of
   Education," 219-227
Carson, Rachel, "The Obligation
   to Endure," 644, 669-675
case studies, creating and using,
   75, 763
Catton, Bruce, "Grant and Lee:
   A Study in Contrasts,"
   351-355
causal analysis, 78-80
causal relationships, false, 160
charts, 40, 764
"Children in the Woods" (Lopez),
   648, 650-654
Chua, Amy, "The Right Road to
   America?", 335-339
citation. See source
   documentation
citizenship, 322
civilization
   American, 291-300
   generalizations and,
      318-321
   universal, 278
civil rights, 324-325, 330-334
Civil War figures, 351-355
claims
   critical reading of, 6
   defined, 137
   evidence supporting, 36-37,
      155-157

grounds for, 137, 142-143,
      154-155
   qualifying, 142
   stating and clarifying,
      152-153
   types of, 141
   understanding, 141-142
Clarke, Kevin, "Tweet Like an
   Egyptian," 166-167
classification, 81-82
classroom handouts, citing, 778
closing statements, 83-84, 87
Cofer, Judith Ortiz, "The Myth of
   the Latin Woman: I Just
   Met a Girl Named Maria,"
   305-309
Coles, Robert, "I Listen to My
   Parents and I Wonder What
   They Believe," 544, 560-565
college campuses, green,
   675-683
"College Is a Waste of Time and
   Money" (Bird), 82-83
comics, as art, 503-510
communication
   language in, 89-93, 99-104
   between men and women,
      117-122
   political oppression and,
      123-133
comparison and contrast, 75,
      77-78
computers. See technology
conclusion, 83-84, 87, 137
consequences, claims about, 141
conservation. See nature and
   environment
content, as message, 29
copyright laws. See plagiarism,
   avoiding
Coventry Cathedral, 547
craft, writing as, 65
Crane, Stephen, Red Badge of
   Courage, 39
critical consciousness, 3
critical reading
   annotating, 25-29
   of argumentation, 140-143
   goal of, 29-30
   guidelines for, 6
   interactive aspect of, 29-31
   strategies for, 3-4
   for synthesis, 37
   of visual texts, 40
critical thinking
   as reading strategy, 3,
      37-38, 40

for research projects, 750
critical writing. See writing and
   writing skills
critiquing, 35, 161
"The Cult of Ethnicity"
   (Schlesinger), 27-29, 33-34,
   69-70, 84
cultural identity, 278, 355-361
cultural selectivity, 30
culture
   ethnic stereotyping,
      305-309
   generalizations and,
      318-321
   Native American, 310-317
   universal definition of,
      286-290
"Cyberspace: If You Don't Love
   It, Leave It" (Dyson),
   346-351

Danticat, Edwidge, "Turning the
   Page on Disaster," 94-99
"The Dark Art of Description"
   (Hampl), 516-523
Darwin, Charles, "Natural
   Selection," 706-711
"Darwin at 200: The Ongoing
   Force of His
   Unconventional Idea"
   (Klinkenborg), 706,
   711-714
databases, as research source,
   760-762
data organization, for research
   projects, 753, 766-771
"The Death of Horatio Alger"
   (Krugman), 387-391
"Declaration of Independence"
   (Jefferson), 322, 326-330
deduction, 137, 144-145, 146
definition, 80-81
"Delusions of Grandeur" (Gates),
   376, 381-384
Democracy in America
   (Tocqueville), 426
description, 65, 68, 73-74
development strategies. See also
   argumentation
   argumentation, 65, 68,
      82-83
   causal analysis, 78-80
   classification, 81-82
   comparison and contrast,
      75, 77-78
   definition, 80-81
   description, 65, 68, 73-74

illustration, 75–76
narration, 65, 68, 74–75
process analysis, 75, 76–77
Diamond, Jared, "The Last Americans: Environmental Collapse and the End of Civilization," 684–700
Diaz, Junot, "The Money: Starting Out," 384–387
Didion, Joan, 750
"In Sable and Dark Glasses," 248–252
"Digital Scheherazades in the Arab World" (Mernissi), 267–277
digital technologies, 30–31
Dillard, Annie, 64–65
"An American Childhood," 241–247
"The Disasters of War" (Goya), 39, 138
discipline-specific standards, 161
disconnected ideas, 160
discrimination, 376–384
doctors. See medicine and health sciences
documentation. See source documentation
"Does the Internet Make You Smarter or Dumber?" (Carr), 21–25
"Do I Really Have to Join Twitter?" (Manjoo), 163–164
domain extensions, 755–756
Douglass, Frederick, "Learning to Read and Write," 180, 184–189
drafting. See also development strategies; revising
in argumentative synthesis, 162
body paragraphs, 72–83, 85–87
end paragraphs, 83–84, 87
introductory paragraphs, 72, 84
research projects, 771
thesis development, 71–72
D'Souza, Dinesh, "Staying Human," 702, 733–741
Dyson, Esther, "Cyberspace: If You Don't Love It, Leave It," 346–351

eating disorders, 639–643
e-books and e-readers, 30–31
ecology. See nature and environment
economics
inequality, 387–391, 404–416
satire on, 417–424
work, 372, 395–403
editorial comments, 88–89
editorial writing, 151. See also argumentation
education
affirmative action in, 201–211
attitudes toward, 180
changes in, 182–183
literacy, 184–194
math and science gender gap, 215–219
policy initiatives for poor, 194–197
school segregation, 219–227
sex education, 198–200
technology in classroom, 212–215
value of, 184
Ehrenreich, Barbara, "Nickel and Dimed," 395–403
Elbow, Peter, 35–36, 69
"Freewriting," 105–108
Eliot, George, 72
Ellis Island, 280
e-mail, citing, 790
e-mail conferences, 763
emotional appeals, 146–147, 158–159
end paragraphs, 83–84, 87
English Prose Style (Read), 73
environment. See nature and environment
"The Environmental Issue from Hell" (McKibben), 666–669
epidemics, 596–615
Epstein, Jacob, 547
equal opportunity, 376–384
"Escape from Wonderland: Disney and the Female Imagination" (Ross), 471–484
Esfandiary, F. M., "The Mystical West Puzzles the Practical East," 145
essays
student examples, 84
writing process, 64

"The Estrangement" (Kincaid), 263–266
ethical appeals, 147–148
ethics
children and, 560–565
as personal philosophy, 544
ethnic stereotyping, 305–309
ethos, 147
evaluation of sources. See source evaluation
evidence
in body paragraphs, 73
defined, 137
reasoning from, 142–143
supporting claims, 36–37, 155–157
in visual texts, 40
evolution, 706–714
examples, for illustration, 75
expert information, 763
explanatory synthesis, 36
exposition, 65, 68
extended definition, 80
extraterrestrial life, 714–716, 742–747

facts, 75, 137
Fairey, Shepard, Hope, 325
fallacies, 140, 158–160
false analogies, 160
false cause-and-effect relationships, 160
families
childhood memories, 232–252
homosexuality and, 257–263
identity and, 228–229
mother relationship, 263–266
"Family Values" (Rodriguez), 257–263
feminism, 436–440, 455–463
Ferguson, Niall, "America's 'Oh Sh*t' Moment," 291–296
The Field of Vision (Morris), 88
field resources, 156, 763
final manuscripts, 773
"Finding Neverland" (Gates), 511–516
forgetting, as reading problem, 29
formal writing assignments, 29
Forms theory, 583–587
"Forty Acres and a Gap in Wealth" (Gates), 47–51
Franklin, Thomas E., 43

freedom, 326–334
Freeland, Chrystia, "The Rich Are Different from You and Me," 51–53
freeways, 647
freewriting, 68–70
"Freewriting" (Elbow), 105–108
Freud, Sigmund, 229, 372
Friedman, Thomas L., "Globalization: The Super-Story," 391–394
"From Ancient Greece to Iraq, the Power of Words in Wartime" (Lakoff), 14–16
full-circle pattern, 83

Gandolfini, James, 429
"The Gangster as Tragic Hero" (Warshow), 430–435
gangster films, 428–435
Gates, David, "Finding Neverland," 511–516
Gates, Henry Louis, Jr.
"Delusions of Grandeur," 376, 381–384
"Forty Acres and a Gap in Wealth," 47–51
Gawande, Atul, "Naked," 629–635
gay marriage, 231, 252–256, 569–576
Gelernter, David, "Unplugged: The Myth of Computers in the Classroom," 212–215
gender discrimination, 376–381
gender gap, in education, 215–219
gender roles
in Arab world, 267–277
identity and, 228–229
in popular culture, 471–484
general academic standards, 161
generalizations, 142, 159
general reference sources, 759–760, 783
"The Gettysburg Address" (Lincoln), 148–150
Gitlin, Todd, "Supersaturation, or, The Media Torrent and Disposable Feeling," 426, 463–470
glittering generalizations, 159
"Globalization: The Super-Story" (Friedman), 391–394
"The Globalization of Eating Disorders" (Bordo), 639–643
global warming, 666–669

goals. See purpose
Godridge, Hillary, 231
Godridge, Julie, 231
good and evil, 546–547
Goodlad, Lauren M. E., "Why We Love 'Mad Men'", 430, 436–440
Goodrich, James T., 595
Gould, Stephen Jay, "The Terrifying Normalcy of AIDS," 635–639
government, 322–323
government publications, citing, 789
Goya, Francisco, "The Disasters of War," 39, 138
"Grant and Lee: A Study in Contrasts" (Catton), 351–355
graphics, 134
graphs, 40, 764
"The Greenest Campuses: An Idiosyncratic Guide" (Perrin), 675–683
grounds (reasons), 137, 142–143, 154–155. See also evidence

Hampl, Patricia, "The Dark Art of Description," 516–523
hasty generalizations, 159
Havel, Václav, 278
headnotes, 6
health. See medicine and health sciences
Hemingway, Ernest, 65
highlighting, 25–26
"Hiroshima" (Berger), 7–14
history
Civil War figures, 351–355
learning from, 278, 322–323
Hitchens, Christopher, "Topic of Cancer," 615–619
Hoagland, Edward, "1776 and All That: America after September 11," 296–300
homosexuality, 257–263
Hood, Ann, "Street Scenes," 232, 238–241
Hope (Fairey), 325
Horowitz, Joy, "Parkinson's Alley," 658–665
"How Computers Change the Way We Think" (Turkle), 721–727
"How to Mark a Book" (Adler), 16–21
Hubble Space Telescope, 705

Hughes, Langston, "Salvation," 4, 548–551
hunting, 654–658
hyperlinks, 35, 763
hypothesis, formation, 751, 752, 753, 754

identity
cultural, 278, 355–361
individual, 228–229
literate, 2
national and global, 282–290
racial, 361–370
"I Have a Dream" (King), 146, 322, 326, 330–334
"I Listen to My Parents and I Wonder What They Believe" (Coles), 544, 560–565
illustration, as development strategy, 75–76
images. See visual media; specific subjects
imagination, 577–582
immigrants, 280–281, 335–339, 384–387
"I'm So Totally, Digitally, Close to You" (Thompson), 168–177
indexes, as research source, 760–762
induction, 137, 145–146
inference, 137
information presentation, 30
"In Sable and Dark Glasses" (Didion), 248–252
insecticides, 669–675
intellectual property, 767
interactive aspect, of reading and writing, 29–31
interdisciplinary concerns, 751
Internet regulation, 346–351. See also Web sites
interviews, 156, 763, 779, 785, 790
in-text citation, 773–780
An Introduction to Reasoning (Toulmin), 140–141
introductory paragraphs, 72, 84
invention (prewriting)
for argumentation, 152, 158
process of, 65–71
in research projects, 750, 754
in writing process, 64
Iranian revolution, 551–560
Islamic terrorism, 587–591

issue identification, in argument, 151–152

"Is Texas America?" (Ivins), 340–346

"It's Spreading" (Lepore), 596, 605–615

Ivins, Molly, "Is Texas America?", 340–346

Iwo Jima, 42

Jackson, Michael, 511–516

Jacobson, Jennifer, 67

Jacoby, Susan, "When Bright Girls Decide That Math Is 'a Waste of Time'", 215–219

Jefferson, Thomas, "Declaration of Independence," 322, 326–330

justification, 140

"Just Walk on By: Black Men and Public Space" (Staples), 300–304

Kensett, John Frederick, *Along the Hudson,* 646

keyword searches, 757–759

Kincaid, Jamaica, "The Estrangement," 263–266

King, Martin Luther, Jr., "I Have a Dream," 146, 322, 326, 330–334

King, Stephen, "My Creature from the Black Lagoon," 444–451

Klinkenborg, Verlyn, "Darwin at 200: The Ongoing Force of His Unconventional Idea," 706, 711–714

Koons, Jeff, *Rabbit,* 489

Krugman, Paul
  "The Death of Horatio Alger," 387–391
  "We Are the 99.9 Percent," 44–47

Kurtz, Jane, 67

Lakoff, Robin Tomach, "From Ancient Greece to Iraq, the Power of Words in Wartime," 14–16

"The Last Americans: Environmental Collapse and the End of Civilization" (Diamond), 684–700

"Learning to Read and Write" (Douglass), 180, 184–189

"Leave Your Name at the Border" (Muñoz), 89–93

lectures, citing, 779

legal cases, citing, 778, 790

Lepore, Jill, "It's Spreading," 596, 605–615

letters, citing, 790

"Letter to President Pierce" (Chief Seattle), 648–650

Lewis, C. S., 544

lexical definition, 80

library resources, 156, 755, 757–760

Lincoln, Abraham, "The Gettysburg Address," 148–150

listservs, 763, 786

literacy
  in 21st century, 2, 65
  and value of education, 184–194

literate identity, 2

literature
  citing as research source, 778
  description in, 516–523
  evaluating, 486
  value of, 490–499

live performances, citing, 779, 788

logic. *See* reason and reasoning

logical appeals, 144–146

logical fallacies, 159–160

"The Lonely, Good Company of Books" (Rodriguez), 180, 184, 189–194

Lopez, Barry, "Children in the Woods," 648, 650–654

Los Angeles, California, 647

machines, vs. workers, 374–375

"Mad Men," 436–440

Madrigal, Alexis, "Take the Data out of Dating," 165–166

main points, 6

major propositions, 137

"The Maker's Eye: Revising Your Own Manuscripts" (Murray), 89, 109–113

Manjoo, Farhad, "Do I *Really* Have to Join Twitter?", 163–164

manuscripts, final, 773

marking text, 16–21

marriage, 230–231, 252–256, 569–576

Martin, Steve, "Writing Is Easy," 114–117

"The Masked Marvel's Last Toehold" (Selzer), 619–623

math gender gap, 215–219

McCloud, Scott, "Understanding Comics," 503–510

McKibben, Bill, "The Environmental Issue from Hell," 666–669

McLuhan, Marshall, 426

meaning
  claims about, 141
  construction of, 4
  interactive aspect of, 29–31

media and popular culture
  "bad" men in, 430–440
  electronic media, 426, 441–443
  feminism in, 455–463
  gender issues, 471–484
  horror movies, 444–451
  influence of, 463–470
  television commercials, 452–454

medicine and health sciences
  abortion, 624–629
  AIDS, 635–639
  cancer, 615–619
  challenges in, 592
  eating disorders, 639–643
  epidemics, 596–615
  patient exams, 629–635
  surgery, 619–623

Mendoza, Martha, "Between a Woman and Her Doctor," 624–629

Mernissi, Fatema, "Digital Scheherazades in the Arab World," 267–277

message-making, 29–31

Miller, Lisa, "Our Mutual Joy: The Religious Case for Gay Marriage," 569–576

minor propositions, 137

MLA Bibliography, 761

MLA Handbook for Writers of Research Papers, 764

MLA (Modern Language Association) style
  parenthetical documentation, 775–780
  student project example, 805–825
  Works Cited list, 780–790

"A Modest Proposal" (Swift),
372, 417–424
"The Money: Starting Out"
(Diaz), 384–387
Moore, James, 69–70
Morris, Wright, *The Field of
Vision,* 88
"Mother Tongue" (Tan), 99–104
"Moving Along" (Updike),
500–503
Mukherjee, Bharati, "American
Dreamer," 355–361
multimedia texts, 30–31
multitasking, 21–25
Muñoz, Manuel, "Leave Your
Name at the Border," 89–93
Murray, Donald M., 36
"The Maker's Eye:
Revising Your Own
Manuscripts," 89,
109–113
"My Creature from the Black
Lagoon" (King), 444–451
"The Mystical West Puzzles the
Practical East"
(Esfandiary), 145
"The Myth of the Latin Woman:
I Just Met a Girl Named
Maria" (Cofer), 305–309

"Naked" (Gawande), 629–635
name calling, 158
narration, 65, 68, 74–75
National Campaign to Prevent
Teen and Unplanned
Pregnancy Web site, 41
nationalism, 282–285
"A Nation of Vidiots" (Sachs),
441–443
"Natural Selection" (Darwin),
706–711
nature and environment
destruction of, 646–647
global warming, 666–669
green college campuses,
675–683
hunting, 654–668
insecticides, 669–675
lessons from lost worlds,
684–700
pesticides, 658–665
relationship to, 644,
648–654
newsgroups, 763, 786
newspapers, citing, 776, 784–785
"The Next Kind of Integration"
(Bazelon), 201–211

"Nickel and Dimed"
(Ehrenreich), 395–403
nonprint sources, 762,
763–764, 790
non sequitur, 160
"Not about Islam?" (Rushdie),
587–591
note taking, 26, 37, 162, 768
"Nutcracker.com" (Sedaris),
716–721

Obama, Barack, 148, 325
Oberlin College, 182
objective, for research
projects, 752
"The Obligation to Endure"
(Carson), 644, 669–675
observations, 763
"Once More to the Lake"
(White), 232–238
online outlining, 71
online research
citing, 780, 783–784
conducting, 156,
755–757, 763
online texts, evaluating, 37–38
opinions, 137, 155
opposing viewpoints, 157–158
organization, in critical
reading, 6
Orwell, George, "Politics and the
English Language," 123–133
"Our Mutual Joy: The Religious
Case for Gay Marriage"
(Miller), 569–576
outlines, 70–71, 770–771
oversimplification, 159

Packer, George, "The Broken
Contract," 53–62
paintings, 39
paragraphs
body, 72–83, 85–87
end, 83–84, 87
introductory, 72, 84
unity and coherence of, 73
paraphrasing, 3, 31–32,
769–770, 771
parenthetical documentation,
773–780
"Parkinson's Alley" (Horowitz),
658–665
perception, 30
periodicals
citing as research source,
776, 784, 785
research example, 798–799

Perrin, Noel, "The Greenest
Campuses: An Idiosyncratic
Guide," 675–683
personal experience, 75, 156
persuasion, 136
pesticides, 658–665
Peter, Laurence J., *The Peter
Prescription,* 76–77
Phaedrus (Plato), 30
philosophy
ethics and religion as, 544
imagination, 577–582
theory of Forms, 583–587
photographs, 39
Pirsig, Robert M., *Zen and the
Art of Motorcycle
Maintenance,* 146
plagiarism, avoiding, 34–35,
767, 771
plagues, 596–615
"Planets in the Sky with
Diamonds" (Ackerman),
714–716
Plato, 486
"The Allegory of the Cave,"
544, 583–587
Phaedrus, 30
plays, citing, 778
"The Pleasures of Imagination"
(Bloom), 577–582
poems, citing, 778
policy claims, 141
politics, 282–285, 322–323
"Politics and the English
Language" (Orwell),
123–133
popular culture. *See* media and
popular culture
post hoc, ergo propter hoc
fallacy, 160
Pound, Ezra, 5
prejudices, 4, 6
premises, 137
prereading activities, 5
prewriting. *See* invention
(prewriting)
Priestley, J. B., "Wrong Ism,"
282–285
primary research, 751
print sources, 755, 759–762
problem-solving, 751
process analysis, 75, 76–77
"Professions for Women"
(Woolf), 376–381
proofreading, 88
propositions, 137
psychological selectivity, 30

publication information, 6
Pueblo culture, 310–317
purpose
    in comparison and
        contrast, 78
    critical reading of, 6, 30
    in invention (prewriting),
        65, 68
    in synthesis, 37
    of visual texts, 40

qualifiers, 142
questioning text, 3, 26
Quindlen, Anna, "Sex Ed,"
    198–200
quotations, 33–34, 75, 84,
    770, 771

Rabbit (Koons), 489
racial issues
    discrimination, 381–384
    racial identity, 361–370
    school segregation,
        219–227
    stereotyping, 300–304
Read, Herbert, *English Prose
    Style,* 73
reading and reading skills
    active reading, 4, 6, 27–29
    critical reading, 3–4, 6,
        25–31, 37, 40,
        140–143
    prereading, 5
    value of, 3, 4, 94–99
    visual texts, 39–43
reason and reasoning
    appeals to, 144–146
    causal analysis, 78–80
    errors in, 159–160
    from evidence, 142–143
rebuttal, 140
"Red, White, and Beer" (Barry),
    452–454
The Red Badge of Courage
    (Crane), 39
Reed, Ismael, "America: The
    Multinational Society," 282,
    286–290
reference books, 759–760, 783
refinement, 88
refutation, 140, 158
"Regarding the Torture of
    Others" (Sontag), 524–534
Reich, Robert, "Why the Rich
    Are Getting Richer and the
    Poor, Poorer," 372,
    404–416

religion
    cross-cultural perspective,
        565–569
    faith from childhood,
        551–560
    gay marriage and, 569–576
    Islamic terrorism, 587–591
    as personal philosophy, 544
Rembrant van Rijn, *The Anatomy
    Lesson,* 594
research projects
    defined, 750
    defining objective (phase 1),
        752, 753–754
    documentation
        requirements, 773–774
    gathering and organizing
        data (phase 3), 753,
        766–771
    invention (prewriting), 750
    locating sources (phase 2),
        752–753, 754–766,
        791–792
    online or electronic
        versions, 763
    preconceptions versus
        practice, 750–752
    reassessing topic, 766
    revising, 771–772
    student example, 805–825
    visuals in, 763
    writing and submitting
        (phase 4), 753,
        771–773
research sources
    documenting, 34, 764–766,
        767, 771, 773–780, 774,
        780–790
    evaluating, 37–38, 757, 762,
        767, 792–795
    field resources, 156, 763
    general references,
        759–760
    indexes and databases,
        760–762
    library resources, 156, 755,
        757–760
    locating, 752–753, 754–766,
        791–792
    nonprint, 762, 763–764
    online, 156, 755–757, 763
    primary, 751
    secondary, 751, 755
    in synthesis, 37
    working with, 795–801
reviews, citing, 785
revising, rewriting

argumentative synthesis, 162
    essay on, 109–113
    research projects,
        771–772
    student example, 801–804
    in writing process, 87–89
rhetorical approaches
    purpose and, 65, 68
    types of, 73–83
"The Rich Are Different from
    You and Me" (Freeland),
    51–53
"The Right Road to America?"
    (Chua), 335–339
Rivera, Diego, 374
Robinson, Edward G., 428
Rodin, Auguste, *Walking
    Man,* 488
Rodriguez, Richard
    "Family Values," 257–263
    "The Lonely, Good
        Company of Books,"
        180, 184, 189–194
Rogerian argument, 147–148
Rogers, Carl, 147
Rose, Mike, "What College Can
    Mean to the Other
    America," 194–197
Rosenthal, Joe, 42
Ross, Deborah, "Escape from
    Wonderland: Disney and the
    Female Imagination,"
    471–484
rough drafts, 169, 187
Rushdie, Salman, "Not about
    Islam?", 587–591
Rustic Wedding (Brueghel the
    Younger), 230

Sachs, Jeffrey, "A Nation of
    Vidiots," 441–443
Sacks, Oliver, "Anybody Out
    There?", 742–747
Sagan, Carl, "Can We Know the
    Universe? Reflections
    on a Grain of Salt,"
    727–732
"Salvation" (Hughes), 4,
    548–551
Santayana, 322
satire, 340–346, 417–424
Satrapi, Marjane, "The Veil," 548,
    551–560
"Saving the Life That Is Your
    Own: The Importance of
    Models in the Artist's Life"
    (Walker), 535–543

Schlesinger, Arthur M., Jr., "The
    Cult of Ethnicity," 27–29,
    00 01, 09 70, 04
scholarly journals
    citing as research source,
        783–784
    research example, 797–798
school segregation, 219–227
science
    extraterrestrial life, 714–716,
        742–747
    gender gap, 215–219
    laboratory settings,
        182–183
    modern revolutions in,
        702–705
    Sagan's philosophy,
        727–732
searches. See keyword searches;
    research sources
Seattle (Chief of Dewamish),
    "Letter to President
    Pierce," 648–650
secondary research, 751, 755
Sedaris, Davis, "Nutcracker.
    com," 716–721
selectivity, 30
Selzer, Richard, "The Masked
    Marvel's Last Toehold,"
    619–623
Sen, Amartya, "A World Not
    Neatly Divided," 318–321
September 2001 terrorist attack,
    43, 296–300, 391–394
serial works, citing, 782
"1776 and All That: America after
    September 11" (Hoagland),
    296–300
"Sex, Lies and Conversation"
    (Tannen), 117–122
"Sex Ed" (Quindlen), 198–200
sex education, 198–200
Sexton, Patricia Cayo, Spanish
    Harlem, 74
Shin, John, 78
signal phrases, 770
Silko, Leslie Marmon, "Yellow
    Woman and a Beauty of the
    Spirit," 310–317
slavery, 324
social inequality, 44–63
social justice, 322–323
social networking, 163–178
software, citing, 786–787
solar system, 704
song lyrics, citing, 778

Sontag, Susan, "Regarding the
    Torture of Others,"
    524–534
The Sopranos series, 429
sound recordings or audio
    streams, citing, 787
source documentation
    in avoiding plagiarism, 34,
        767, 771
    materials that require, 773
    parenthetical citation,
        773–780
    working bibliography,
        764–766
    Works Cited list, 774,
        780–790
source evaluation
    online sources, 37–38, 757
    print sources, 762
    student example, 792–795
    value to project, 767
source types and locations. See
    research sources
Spanish Harlem (Sexton), 74
specificity, in research
    projects, 754
speeches, citing, 779
St. Michael, 547
Staffenberg, David A., 595
Staples, Brent, "Just Walk on By:
    Black Men and Public
    Space," 300–304
"Staying Human" (D'Souza), 702,
    733–741
Steinem, Gloria, "Wonder
    Woman," 455–463
stereotyping, 159, 300–309
stipulative definition, 80
"Stranger in the Village"
    (Baldwin), 361–370
"Street Scenes" (Hood), 232,
    238–241
subject directories, online, 755
subject indexing, 757
subordinate points, 6
Sullivan, Andrew, "Why Gay
    Marriage Is Good for
    Straight America," 252–256
summarizing, 26, 29, 32–33, 37,
    768–769, 771
"Superman and Me" (Alexie),
    490, 496–499
"Supersaturation, or, The Media
    Torrent and Disposable
    Feeling" (Gitlin), 426,
    463–470

surgery, 619–623
surveys, 763
Swift, Jonathan, "A Modest
    Proposal," 372, 417–424
syllogism, 145
synthesis
    case study essays, 163–178
    description and guidelines,
        35–37, 160–162

tables, 40
"Take the Data out of Dating"
    (Madrigal), 165–166
Tan, Amy, "Mother Tongue,"
    99–104
Tannen, Deborah, "Sex, Lies and
    Conversation," 117–122
Taylor, Jamie, 70, 84–87
technology
    in classroom, 212–215
    computer culture, 721–727
    e-books and e-readers,
        30–31
    electronic media, 426
    impact on workers, 374–375
    in modern literacy, 2
    technophobia, 716–721
    techno utopia, 700 741
technophobia, 716–721
teenage pregnancy, 41, 198–200
telescoping technique, 751
"The Terrifying Normalcy of
    AIDS" (Gould), 635–639
Texas, 340–346
"The Obligation to Endure"
    (Carson), 644
thesis
    claim as statement of, 153
    critical reading of, 6, 40
    defined, 137
    development of, 71–72
    restating in conclusion, 84
    of visual texts, 40
"'This Is the End of the World':
    The Black Death"
    (Tuchman), 596–605
Thompson, Clive, 'I'm So Totally,
    Digitally, Close to You,"
    168–177
title, significance of, 6
Tocqueville, Alexis de, Democracy
    in America, 426
Tolstoy, Leo, 228
tone, 68, 72, 147, 154
"Topic of Cancer" (Hitchens),
    615–619

torture, images of, 524–534
Toulmin, Stephen
    *An Introduction to
        Reasoning,* 140
    claim model, 141, 142
    The Uses of Argument, 140
transfer, 158
translations, citing, 782
truth, in deductive argument, 145
Tuchman, Barbara, "'This Is the
    End of the World': The
    Black Death," 596–605
Turkle, Sherry, "How Computers
    Change the Way We
    Think," 721–727
"Turning the Page on Disaster"
    (Danticat), 94–99
"Tweet Like an Egyptian"
    (Clarke), 166–167
twins, conjoined, 595
"Two Cheers for *Brown v. Board
    of Education*" (Carson),
    219–227

UCLA Library Web site, 38
underlining, 25–26
"Understanding Comics"
    (McCloud), 503–510
University of Maine, 183
"Unplugged: The Myth of
    Computers in the
    Classroom" (Gelernter),
    212–215
Updike, John, 87
    "Moving Along," 500–503
The Uses of Argument (Toulmin),
    140–141

validity, in deductive
    argument, 145
value claims, 141
"The Veil" (Satrapi), 548, 551–560
video recordings, citing, 787
viewpoints, opposing, 157–158
visual media
    citing as research source,
        779, 788
    reading and analyzing,
        39–43
    research example, 800–801
    in research project, 763

voice (tone), 68, 72, 147, 154
Voltaire, 65

Walker, Alice, "Saving the Life
    That Is Your Own: The
    Importance of Models in
    the Artist's Life," 535–543
Walking Man (Rodin), 488
war, 7–16, 39, 138–139
warrants
    in argumentation, 157
    defined, 137, 140
    understanding, 142
Warshow, Robert, "The Gangster
    as Tragic Hero," 430–435
"We Are the 99.9 Percent"
    (Krugman), 44–47
Web 2.0, 30
Web sites. *See also* Internet
    regulation
    citing as research source,
        786, 789
    evaluating, 37–38, 757
    multitasking and, 21–24
    research example, 799–800
    as research source,
        755–757
Welty, Eudora, "One Writer's
    Beginnings," 490–496
Wharton, Edith, 66
"What College Can Mean to the
    Other America" (Rose),
    194–197
"What's God Got to Do with It?"
    (Armstrong), 565–569
"When Bright Girls Decide That
    Math Is 'a Waste of Time'"
    (Jacoby), 215–219
White, E. B., 87
    "Once More to the Lake,"
        232–238
"Why Gay Marriage Is Good for
    Straight America"
    (Sullivan), 252–256
"Why I Hunt" (Bass), 654–658
"Why the Rich Are Getting
    Richer and the Poor,
    Poorer" (Reich), 372,
    404–416
"Why We Love 'Mad Men'"
    (Goodlad), 430, 436–440

"Wonder Woman" (Steinem),
    455–463
Woolf, Virginia, 82
    "Professions for Women,"
        376–381
work, 372, 395–403
workers, vs. machines, 374–375
Works Cited list
    guidelines, 774
    MLA style, 780–790
    working bibliography,
        764–766
"A World Not Neatly Divided"
    (Sen), 318–321
World Trade Center attack
    (2001), 43, 296–300,
    391–394
writing and writing skills. *See
    also* argumentation;
    research projects
    drafting, 71–87
    formal writing
        assignments, 29
    forms of, 65
    illustration of, 66–67
    interactive aspect of, 29–31
    invention (prewriting), 64,
        65–71, 152, 158,
        750, 754
    paraphrasing, 3, 31–32,
        769–770, 771
    process overview, 64–65
    quoting, 33–34, 75, 84,
        770, 771
    revising, 87–89, 109–113,
        162, 771–772, 801–804
    summarizing, 26, 29, 32–33,
        37, 768–769, 771
    synthesis, 35–37, 160–162
    value of, 3
"Writing Is Easy" (Martin),
    114–117
"Wrong Ism" (Priestley),
    282–285

"Yellow Woman and a Beauty of
    the Spirit" (Silko), 310–317

*Zen and the Art of Motorcycle
    Maintenance* (Pirsig), 146